WHO'S WHO

AND

WHAT'S WHAT

IN

SHAKESPEARE

WHO'S WHO

AND

WHAT'S WHAT

IN

SHAKESPEARE

GIVING

*References by Topics to Notable Passages and
Significant Expressions; Brief Histories
of the Plays; Geographical Names
and Historical Incidents;
Mention of all Characters
and Sketches of
Important Ones*

TOGETHER WITH EXPLANATIONS OF ALLUSIONS
AND OBSCURE AND OBSOLETE WORDS AND PHRASES

BY

EVANGELINE M. O'CONNOR

WITH A FOREWORD
BY ALICE SACHS

AVENEL BOOKS
NEW YORK

Originally published in 1887 as *Topical Index to the Booklover's Edition of Shakespeare.*

Special material copyright © MCMLXXVIII by
Crown Publishers, Inc.
All rights reserved.
This edition is published by Avenel Books,
Distributed by Crown Publishers, Inc.

a b c d e f g h

AVENEL 1978 PRINTING

Library of Congress Cataloging in Publication Data
O'Connor, Evangeline Maria Johnson.
Who's who and what's what in Shakespeare.

Reprint of the 1887 ed. published by University
Society, New York under title: Topical index to the
Booklover's edition of Shakespeare; with new introd.
Includes index.
1. Shakespeare, William 1564-1616—Dictionaries,
indexes, etc. I. Title.
PR2892.O44   822.3'3   78-17348
ISBN 0-517-25923-0

FOREWORD.

No writer in the English language—indeed no writer in any language—has continued, century after century, to influence literature, language, and imagery as much as Shakespeare. Even if there is someone somewhere in the civilized world who has not seen or read several of his plays, that person undoubtedly quotes him regularly without realizing it, so pervasive has been his influence on the very language we use to express the ordinary truths of everyday life. And to many the names of Romeo and Juliet, of Hamlet and of Brutus, are more familiar than the names of their Congressional representatives, and possibly even their mayors and governors.

Yet, strangely, this work, originally published in 1887 and now again made available to the public for the first time in many years, remains a uniquely comprehensive Shakespearean reference work. There are books on Shakespeare's politics, his imagery, his legal maxims, his treatment of love and marriage, his stagecraft and various other aspects of his multifaceted genius, as well as a concordance in four volumes. Yet this volume is outstanding in that it combines the attributes of a concordance—an alphabetical list of all of the important words in Shakespeare, with an indication of the passages in which they occur—with an index according to subject matter, outlines of Shakespeare's plays, historical backgrounds and dates, sketches of the principal dramatis personae and brief excerpts from reputable critics. Moreover, it can be consulted with equal ease by erudite Shakespearean scholars, beginning students and that vast lay population which simply delights in the works of the Bard and wishes occasionally to check sources or allusions.

All in all, this is an indispensable manual for anyone who wishes to enhance his understanding and appreciation of the greatest and most timeless of playwrights.

ALICE SACHS
May, 1978

PREFACE
TO THE ORIGINAL EDITION

It has been my intention to refer, in the following pages, to every passage of any importance under the word that best expresses its subject, whether that word is in the text or not, and in cases of doubt as to what word a passage would be looked for under, I have entered it under two or more. But, that significant expressions may be found readily, I have also indexed under their most prominent word all that seemed to me to be such. To have indexed all expressions under their principal words, would have been to defeat the aim of this book by overloading it and wearying the student with references to a mass of unimportant allusions. Here the question of judgment necessarily comes in, and I may have omitted some references that a better editor would deem as significant as many that are included. I trust, however, that references to passages of importance under each topic will not be found wanting.

In order to make the book a convenient manual, and include information that a Shakespearean student needs but would otherwise only find scattered through a great number of books, I have given short, outline histories of the plays, and sketches of the principal characters, with brief extracts from the ablest critics. In the case of historical characters and events, I have given dates and statements of the facts as found in history. The explanations of allusions, of unusual words and phrases, and of words used in obsolete or peculiar senses, will be valuable, I believe, to the younger class of readers. Under some general heads — as "Bible," "Diseases," "Law," "Omens," and "Proverbs" — I have grouped together references that will enable students to consult as a whole Shakespeare's expressions and allusions to the sciences of law and medicine, to the Bible, and to the folk-lore of his time as expressed in proverbs and popular superstitions. Under "Order and Dates of the Plays," and "Sources," I have repeated information that is given in the various histories of the plays, so as to place it in convenient form for comparison.

It may at first sight seem unnecessary to add another to the multitude of books on Shakespeare's works, and aids to the study of them. But I think it will be found that no other of the same character—none that is properly an index, as distinguished from a concordance—has been published. One prepared by Francis Twiss, in two volumes (London, 1805), involved a vast amount of labor, but was rendered almost useless by over-condensation. It was essentially a concordance, as its full title shows : "A Complete Verbal Index to the Plays of Shakspere ; adapted to all editions. Comprehending every substantive, adjective, verb, participle, and adverb used by Shakspere." With the exception of about two hundred copies, the entire impression was destroyed by fire, and the book is now so rare that a copy has been sold for over seven pounds. Samuel Ayscough's Index (London, 1790) was made for a special edition of the plays. Though long since out of print, it is not very rare ; but this also is simply a concordance. Mrs. Cowden Clarke's elaborate and exhaustive concordance (London, 1846) is well known ; but it is rather costly, and though admirable for all that it professes to be, is not an index to anything but words. Davenport Adams's concordance (London, 1885) is less bulky than Mrs. Clarke's, but still clings closely to the purely verbal plan. Other books give quotations by topics—notably John Bartlett's excellent "Shakspeare Phrase-Book" (Boston, 1882)—and some editions of the works give histories and sketches of the plays; but the combination of information here presented is new, and I have aimed to include those points which the reader would most desire to have in compact and convenient form for reference.

E. M. O'C.

For excerpts from the works described above, see the following page.

FACSIMILES.

From Samuel Ayscough's "Index to the Remarkable Passages and Words Made Use of by Shakspeare."

			A.	S.	P.	C.	L.
Medicine. The miserable have no other medicine but only hope	*Meas. for Meas.*		3	1	87	1	26
— To apply a moral medicine to a mortifying mischief	*Much Ado About Noth.*		1	3	124	2	46
— I have seen a medicin that's able to breathe life into a stone, quicken a rock, and make you dance canary with sprightly power and motion	*All's Well*		2	1	283	2	37
— Camillo,—preserver of my father, now of me! the medicin of our house	*Winter's Tale*		4	3	355	1	54
— Meet we the medicin of the sickly weal	*Macbeth*		5	2	38	1	20
— That great medicine hath with his tinct gilded thee	*Antony and Cleop.*		1	5	773	1	2
— Work on, my medicine, work! thus credulous fools are caught	*Othello*		4	1	1067	2	20

From Francis Twiss's "Index to the Plays of Shakspeare."

Medicine(s). M. W. iii. 3. M. M. ii. 2. iii. 1. M. A. i. 3. v. 1. M. N. D. iii. 2. A. L. ii. 7. A. W. i. 3. ii. 1. v. 3. J. v. 1. H. 4. S. P. iii. 1. iv. 4.

T. C. v. 11. A. C. i. 5. Cy. v. 5. L. iv. 7. R. J. ii. 3. H. v. 2. O. iv. 1. Medicine(v). Cy. iv. 2. O. iii. 3.

From Mary Cowden Clarke's "Complete Concordance to Shakspere."

MEDICINE—obey this medicine.... *Merry Wives.* iii. 3
yet a kind of medicine in itself... *Meas. for Meas.* ii. 2
have no other medicine, but only hope — iii. 1
a moral medicine to a mortifying.... *Much Ado.* i. 3
would give preceptial medicine to rage — v. 1
out loathed medicine! hated potion. *Mid. N. Dr.* iii. 2
patiently receive my medicine....*As you Like it.* ii. 7
else Paris, and the medicine.........*All's Well.* i. 3
I have seen a medicine that's able to.. — ii. 1
the tinct and multiplying medicine.. — v. 3
the medicine of our house!....... *Winter's Tale.* iv. 3
let's make us medicines of our great....*Macbeth.* iv. 3
meet we the medicine of the sickly.... — v. 2
that present medicine must be... ....*King John.* v. 1
medicines to make me love him.....1 *Henry IV.* ii. 2

MEDICINE—I have drunk medicines; Poins!
1 *Henry IV.* ii. 2
good advice, and little medicine....2 *Henry IV.* iii. 1
preserving life in medicine potable.. — iv. 4
medicine for my aching bones!.*Troil. and Cress.* v. 11
that great medicine hath with his.*An. and Cleo.* i. 5
great griefs, I see, medicine the less..*Cymbeline.* iv. 2
by medicine life may be prolonged... — v. 5
hang thy medicine on my lips............*Lear.* iv. 7
[*Knt.*] if not, I'll ne'er trust medicine..... — v. 3
residence, and medicine power..*Romeo and Jul.* ii. 3
no medicine in the world can do thee...*Hamlet.* v. 2
and medicines bought of mountebanks...*Othello.* i. 3
shall ever medicine thee to that sweet... — iii. 3
work on, my medicine, work!........... — iv. 1

From W. H. Davenport Adams's "Concordance to the Plays of Shakespeare."

Medicine. The miserable have no other medicine But only hope. *Mea. for Mea. III.* 1.——If the rascal have not given me medicines to make me love him, I'll be hanged. 1 *Hen. IV. II.* 2.——To apply a moral medicine to a mortifying mischief. *Much Ado Ab. Noth. I.* 3.——I have seen a medicine that's able to breathe life into a stone, quicken a rock, and make you dance canary with sprightly power and motion! *All's Well, II.* 1.——Camillo, Preserver of my Father, now of me! The medicine of our house. *Wint. Tale, IV.* 3.——Meet we the medicine of the sickly weal? *Macb. V.* 2.——That great medicine hath With his tinct gilded thee. *Ant. and Cleo. I.* 5.——Work on, My medicine, work! thus credulous fools are caught. *Oth. IV.* 1.

WHO'S WHO

AND

WHAT'S WHAT

IN

SHAKESPEARE

Aaron, a Moor, a character in *Titus Andronicus*, introduced in *i., 1* or *2*, as a prisoner. He is a lover of Tamora, Queen of the Goths. In *ii. 1*, he declares his designs against Rome and the emperor; in *ii. 3*, hides gold; discloses his plans, *iv. 2;* kills the nurse, *iv. 2;* exchanges his child, *iv. 2;* avows his deeds, *v. 1;* his sentence, *v. 3*. He is a hideous and unnatural character, cursing the day in which he has not done "some notorious ill."

Abbess. See ÆMILIA.

Abbey, an, scene of a part of the *Comedy of Errors*, *Act v.*

Abbeys. See SWINSTEAD and WESTMINSTER.

Abbot of Westminster. See WESTMINSTER, ABBOT OF.

Abbots, robbery of, for expenses of war, *King John, iii. 3.*

Abdication, of a sovereign, *Richard II., iv. 1.*

Abel, *Richard II., i. 1; I. Henry VI., i. 3.*

Abergavenny, George Neville, Lord, a character in *Henry VIII.*, introduced in *i. 1.* He was suspected of taking part in Suffolk's conspiracy in the reign of Henry VII., but afterwards became a favourite with the king, as he was also with Henry VIII.

Abhorrence. See HATRED.

Abhorson, an executioner introduced in *Measure for Measure, iv. 2,* who speaks of his occupation as a mystery.

Abjects (menials), *Richard III., i. 1.*

Able (to be responsible for), *Lear, iv. 6.*

Abode, abodement (to bode, an evil omen), *III. Henry VI., iv. 7; v. 6.*

Abraham. See under BIBLE.

Abraham, Montague's servant in *Romeo and Juliet*, appears in *i. 1.*

Abram (flaxen or auburn?), *Coriolanus, ii. 3; Romeo and Juliet, ii. 1.*

Absence, doted on, *Merchant of Venice, i. 2;* of lovers, *Othello, iii. 4;* effect of, *Antony and Cleopatra, i. 4;* love in, *Sonnets xcvii., xcviii.*

Absey-book (A B C book), *King John, i. 1.*

Absolute (decided), *Measure for Measure, iii. 1.*

Absolute (perfect), *Pericles, iv.,* prologue.

Absolution, death without, *Hamlet, i. 5.*

Absyrtus. See MEDEA.

Aby (atone for), *Midsummer-Night's Dream, iii. 2.*

Academe, at the court of Navarre, *Love's Labour's Lost, i. 1.*

Accidents, guilty, *A Winter's Tale, iv. 3;* have hurt my brother, *Hamlet, v. 2;* moving, *Othello, i. 3.*

Accited (summoned), *Titus Andronicus, i. 1.*

Accommodated, definition of, *II. Henry IV., iii. 2;* ridiculing the cant use of the word.

Account, the final, with Heaven, *King John, iv. 2; Richard II., i. 1; Hamlet, i. 5; iii. 3.*

Accusations. See CRIME.

Acheron, a river of hell, *Midsummer-Night's Dream, iii. 2; Titus Andronicus, iv. 3; Macbeth, iii. 5..*

Achievement, never answers to expectation, *Troilus and Cressida, i. 3.*

Achilles, a general of the Greeks, character in *Troilus and Cressida,* introduced in the first scene. In the third, his pride is described by Ulysses, who plans to humble it by sending Ajax to fight with Hector; his quarrel with Agamemnon, *ii. 3.* In *iii. 3,* Ulysses once more plots against his vanity. In *v. 9,* he slays Hector.

"Shakspere has allowed the Homeric Achilles, who purchased lasting fame with a short life, to degenerate into a vain, morbidly proud, and effeminate mocker."—GERVINUS.

Allusions to Achilles: his spear, *II. Henry VI., v. 1;* in a painting, *Lucrece, l. 1424.*

Achitophel. See BIBLE.

Aconitum, strong poison, *II. Henry IV., iv. 4.*

Acquaintance, cut in adversity, *Twelfth Night, v. 1.*

Actæon (a hunter changed into a stag by Diana), *Merry Wives of Windsor, ii. 1; iii. 2; Twelfth Night, i. 1; Titus Andronicus, ii. 3.*

Acting, advice on, *Hamlet, iii. 2;* representations of, *Love's*

Labour's Lost, v. 2, the Nine Worthies; *Midsummer-Night's Dream,* Pyramus and Thisbe; *Hamlet,* the murder of Gonzago.

Action, prompt, *Macbeth, i. 7,* "If 'twere done," etc.; *III. Henry VI., v. 4,* "Wise men ne'er," etc.; *Troilus and Cressida, iii 3.* See also PROMPTNESS.

Actions, criticism of, *Henry VIII., i. 2;* checks in the highest, *Troilus and Cressida, i. 3;* evil and good, *Julius Cæsar, iii. 2.*

Action-taking (suing at law instead of fighting), *Lear, ii. 2.*

Actium, battle of (31 B. c.), *Antony and Cleopatra, iii. 8–10; iv. 7, 8, 10–12.*

Activity, enjoyment in, *Troilus and Cressida, i. 2; Macbeth, ii. 3; Cymbeline, iv. 4.*

Actor(s), a strutting, *Troilus and Cressida, i. 3;* best in the world, *Hamlet, ii. 2;* better to have a bad epitaph than their ill report,—feigned passion of an, *Hamlet, ii. 2;* abstracts and brief chronicles of the time, *Hamlet, ii. 2;* advice to, *Hamlet, iii. 1;* an imperfect, *Sonnet xxiii.;* the author's dissatisfaction with the profession of, expressed, *Sonnets, cx., cxi.*

Adallas, King of Thrace, *Antony and Cleopatra, iii. 6.*

Adam, penalty of, *As You Like It, ii. 1;* first that bore arms, *Hamlet, v. 1.* See BIBLE.

Adam, an officer, apparently, spoken of in *Comedy of Errors, iv. 3.*

Adam, called, *Much Ado about Nothing, i. 1;* Adam Bell, an outlaw, famous for his archery.

Adam, the faithful old servant in *As You Like It,* introduced in *i. 1,* who follows the fortunes of Orlando. In *ii. 3,* he offers his savings to his young master; in *ii. 6,* he is famishing in the forest; in *ii. 7,* he is brought in before the duke and fed.

Adamant (magnet), *Midsummer-Night's Dream, ii. 1.*

Adder, the, in a bright day, *Julius Cæsar, ii. 1;* deafness of the, *Sonnet cxii.*

Addition (titles), *All's Well that Ends Well, ii. 3; Troilus and Cressida, ii. 3; Lear, ii.; Hamlet, i. 4; Othello, iv. 1,* and elsewhere; (attributes), boasts of their, *Troilus and Cressida, i. 2.*

Adhere (fit), *Macbeth, i. 7.*

Adieus. See PARTING.

Admiration (wonder), *Lear, i. 4; Hamlet, iii. 2;* and in various places.

Adonis, story of, in *Venus and Adonis.* His death, *l. 1030;* flower of, *l. 1168.* See ANEMONE. Allusions to Adonis: *Taming*

*of the Shrew, Induction, 2 ; Sonnet liii.; The Passionate Pilgrim,
iv., vi., ix., xi.*

Adonis's gardens, *I. Henry VI., i. 5* or *6.* These were "nothing
but portable earthen pots, with some lettuce or fennel growing in
them. On his yearly festival, every woman carried one of them in
honour of Adonis, because Venus had once laid him in a lettuce-bed.
The next day they were thrown away."

Adoption, of children, *All's Well that Ends Well, i. 3.*

Adrian, a lord, character in *The Tempest,* introduced in *ii. 1.*

Adriana, wife of Antipholus of Ephesus, in the *Comedy of Errors,* introduced in *ii. 1;* made shrewish by jealousy.

Adriano de Armado, Don. See ARMADO.

Adriatic Seas, rough as, *Taming of the Shrew, i. 2.*

Advanced (lifted), *Twelfth Night, ii. 5,* and elsewhere.

Adventures, tales of, *Othello, i. 3.*

Adversity, patience at the, of others, *Comedy of Errors, ii. 1;*
uses of, are sweet, *As You Like It, ii. 1;* compensations of, *All's
Well that Ends Well, iv. 3 ; Richard III., iv. 4; Cymbeline, iv. 2;*
false friends in, *Henry VIII., ii. 1,* "Where you are liberal," etc.;
*Troilus and Cressida, iii. 3 ; Timon of Athens, i. 1, 2 ; ii. 2 ; iii. 6;
iv. 2; Hamlet, iii. 2; Lear, ii. 4;* fallen suddenly on greatness, *Henry
VIII., iii. 2;* winnows men, *Troilus and Cressida, i. 3;* the noble
in, *Coriolanus, iv. 1;* melancholy in, *Timon of Athens, iv. 3.*

Adversity (one adverse or contrary), *Troilus and Cressida, v. 1.*

Advertisement (admonition), *Much Ado about Nothing, v. 1;
All's Well that Ends Well, iv. 3 ; 1. Henry IV., iv. 1;* (intelligence),
I. Henry IV., iii. 2, end.

Advertising and holy (attentive and faithful), *Measure for
Measure, v. 1.*

Advice, concerning friends and conversation, *All's Well that
Ends Well, i. 1; Hamlet, i. 3;* to the wretched, *Comedy of Errors,
ii. 1;* like water in a sieve, *Much Ado about Nothing, v. 1;* to the
wilful, and from the dying, *Richard II., ii. 1;* has an effect contrary
to that intended, *The Lover's Complaint, l. 160.*

Advice (deliberation), *Titus Andronicus, ii. 1,* "She will fill our
engines with," etc.

Ædiles, *Coriolanus, iii. 1.* They had care of the public buildings, streets, processions, etc.

Ægeon, a merchant of Syracuse, father of the twin Antipholuses,
in the *Comedy of Errors.*

Ægle, *Midsummer-Night's Dream, ii. 1.*

Æmilia, mother of the twin Antipholuses, in the *Comedy of Errors*, introduced in *v. 1*, as abbess at a convent in Ephesus, which she had entered after losing her sons, whom, with her husband, she finds in the same scene.

Æmilius, a noble Roman, unimportant character in *Titus Andronicus*, introduced in *iv. 4.*

Æneas, one of the Trojan commanders, and leader of those that escaped after the siege, a character in *Troilus and Cressida*, introduced in *i. 1.* In *i. 3*, he brings Hector's challenge; in *v. 6*, he is said to have been taken by Ajax, but he appears again in *v. 10*, leading the Trojans. Allusions to Æneas : *The Tempest, ii. 1; II. Henry VI., v. 2 ; Titus Andronicus, iii. 2 ; Julius Cæsar, i. 2 ; Hamlet, ii. 2 ; Antony and Cleopatra, iv. 12* or *14 ; Cymbeline, iii. 4.*

Æolus, *II. Henry VI., iii. 2.* The god of the winds.

Aery (brood), *Richard III., i. 3.*

Æsculapius, *Merry Wives of Windsor, ii. 3.* The god of physicians.

Æson, *Merchant of Venice, v. 1.* The father of Jason, restored by Medea to youth.

Æsop, *III. Henry VI., v. 5.* The fabulist is said to have been humpbacked, and Richard is called so on account of his deformity.

Affectation in language, *Love's Labour's Lost, v. 2;* "Taffeta phrases," etc., *Hamlet, v. 2.* Osric's is travestied by Hamlet in the same scene ; called affection, *Love's Labour's Lost, v. 2.*

Affectioned (affected), *Twelfth Night, ii. 3.*

Affections, human, *The Tempest, v. 2 ;* wrestle with, *As You Like It, i. 3 ;* intention of, *A Winter's Tale, i. 2.* See LOVE.

Affects (affections), not mastered by might, *Love's Labour's Lost, i. 1.*

Affied (affianced), *Taming of the Shrew, iv. 4.*

Affined (of the same sort), *Troilus and Cressida, i. 3 ;* (under obligation), *Othello, i. 1 ; ii. 3.*

Affliction, cannot subdue the mind, *A Winter's Tale, iv. 4 ;* sweet, *A Winter's Tale, v. 3 ;* religion in, *II. Henry VI., ii. 1 ;* enamoured, *Romeo and Juliet, iii. 3 ;* a test of men, *Troilus and Cressida, i. 3 ; Coriolanus, iv. 1 ;* patience in, *Othello, iv. 2.* See SORROW.

Affy (have faith), *Titus Andronicus, i. 1.*

Africa, *II. Henry IV., v. 3 ; Coriolanus, i. 8.*

Agamemnon, brother of Menelaus, and general-in-chief of the Greeks at the siege of Troy ; character in *Troilus and Cressida*, introduced in *i. 3.* In the same scene, Ulysses describes to him how he is mimicked by Patroclus, who puts on his "topless deputation" (deputed power in which he has no superior), to amuse Achilles; allusions to him, *II. Henry IV., ii. 4; Henry V., iii. 6; III. Henry VI., ii. 2.*

Agate, *Much Ado about Nothing, iii. 1; II. Henry IV., i. 2.* A small person, so called in allusion to the little figures cut in agate, for rings, etc.

Age, a degenerate, *Julius Cæsar, i. 3;* one poor retiring minute in an, *Lucrece, l. 962;* pattern of the worn-out, *Lucrece, l. 1350;* peace proclaims olives of endless, *Sonnet cvii.*

Age, old, infirmities of, *Comedy of Errors, v. 1; Measure for Measure, iii. 1;* wit out in, *Much Ado about Nothing, iii. 5; Comedy of Errors, v. 1;* spirit in, *Much Ado about Nothing, iv. 1,* "Time hath not yet," etc.; frosty, but kindly, *As You Like It, ii. 3;* full of wise saws, *As You Like It, ii. 7;* not desired, *All's Well that Ends Well, i. 2;* avarice inseparable from, *II. Henry IV., i. 2;* characters of, *II. Henry IV., v. 5;* alacrity and cheerfulness declined in, *Richard III., v. 3;* conduct becoming, *II. Henry IV., v. 5;* weary, *Henry VIII., iv. 2;* mimicry of, *Troilus and Cressida, i. 3;* good opinion purchased by, *Julius Cæsar, ii. 1;* ingratitude in, *Timon of Athens, ii. 2,* "You gods, reward," etc.; what should accompany, *Macbeth, v. 3;* too politic, slanders on, *Hamlet, ii. 2;* declined into the vale of years, *Othello, iii. 3;* infirmities of, *Lear, i. 1, 3; ii. 4;* reverence for, *Lear, i. 2, letter;* unnecessary, *Lear, ii. 4;* full of grief, *Lear, ii. 4;* cannot wither, *Antony and Cleopatra, ii. 2;* vigour in, *Antony and Cleopatra, iv. 8;* childless, *Sonnets ii., v., vii., xi.;* marks of, *Sonnets ii., v., xxii., lxii., lxiii., lxvii.;* the autumn, *Sonnet lxxiii.;* in love, *Sonnet cxxxix.;* cannot live with youth, *The Passionate Pilgrim, xii.;* traces of beauty in, *Lover's Complaint, l. 10.*

Aged, movements of the, *Romeo and Juliet, ii. 5.*

Ages, the seven, *As You Like It, ii. 7.*

Agenor, daughter of, (Europa,) *Taming of the Shrew, i. 1.* See EUROPA.

Agincourt, battle of (October 25, 1415), *Henry V., iv. 4, 5, 6, 7;* allusion to, *Henry V., i., chorus;* before, *Henry V., iii. 7; iv. 1, 2, 3;* dead and prisoners of, *Henry V., iv. 8;* thanksgiving for victory after, *Henry V., iv. 8.*

Aglet-baby (ornament carved like the human form for a pendant), *Taming of the Shrew, i. 2.*

Agnize (acknowledge), *Othello, i. 3.*

Agrippa, character in *Antony and Cleopatra;* introduced in *ii. 2,* a friend of Cæsar.

Aguecheek, Sir Andrew, character in *Twelfth Night.* He is a fool and a coward of an original type, so conscious of his folly and cowardice that the effect is almost pathetic. He is the boon companion of Sir Toby Belch, who makes a butt and a tool of him. See SLENDER.

Agues, in March, *1. Henry IV., iv. 1.*

Ahitophel. See BIBLE.

Aim, to cry, *Merry Wives of Windsor, ii. 3; iii. 1; King John, ii. 1.* An archery term, meaning to encourage.

Air, a spirit all of, *The Tempest, v. 1;* the empty, vast, and wandering, *Richard III., i. 4.*

Ajax, one of the Grecian commanders, of great size and courage, but dull and brutish in mind, a character in *Troilus and Cressida,* introduced in *ii. 1.* In *i. 2,* Pandarus describes him ; in *i. 3,* Ulysses speaks of his insubordination ; in *ii. 1,* he is railed at by Thersites ; flattered by Agamemnon in *ii. 3 ;* in *iii. 3,* it is decided that he shall fight with Hector, and in *iv. 5* they fight.

" The hand is masterly with which, in the delineation of Ajax, physical strength is exhibited intensified at the expense of mental power ; the abundance of similes and images with which the rare but simple nature is described is inexhaustible ; the discernment is wonderful with which all animal qualities are gathered together to form this man, at once both more and less than human ; Mars's idiot, a purblind Argus, and a gouty Briareus."—GERVINUS.

Allusions to Ajax: one of the Nine Worthies, *Love's Labour's Lost, v. 2;* allusions to his anger when the armour of Achilles was given to Ulysses, *Love's Labour's Lost, iv. 3; II. Henry VI., v. 1;* other allusions, *Taming of the Shrew, iii. 1; Lear, ii. 2; Antony and Cleopatra, iv. 12* or *14; Cymbeline, iv. 2;* in a painting, *The Rape of Lucrece, l. 1394.* See also TELAMON.

Alarbus, son of Tamora in *Titus Andronicus,* appears in *i. 1* or *2,* as a prisoner of the Romans, only to be taken away and sacrificed to the shades of the dead sons of Titus. He does not speak.

Albany, Duke of, Goneril's husband, in *King Lear,* introduced in the first scene. He is shocked and grieved at the treatment of the old king, but is too weak to interfere.

Albret, Charles d'. See CONSTABLE OF FRANCE.

Alchemist, *Timon of Athens, v. 2 ;* the sun an, *King John, iii. 1.*

Alchemy, *Julius Cæsar, i. 3, end.*

Alcibiades (B. C. 454–404), an Athenian general, character in

Timon of Athens, introduced in *i. 1;* banished, *iii. 5;* before the walls of Athens, *v. 4.* Having conquered the enemies of Athens and been repaid only with ingratitude and banishment, he takes up arms against his country and forces it to render him justice. His mode of revenge is distinctly contrasted with that of the less robust nature of Timon.

Alcides (Hercules), *Taming of the Shrew, iii. 2; The Merchant of Venice, ii. 1; iii. 2; King John, ii. 1; I. Henry VI., iv. 7; Antony and Cleopatra, iv. 10* or *12.* See HERCULES.

Alderliefest (dearest of all), *II. Henry VI., i. 1.*

Ale, cakes and, *Twelfth Night, ii. 3.*

Ale, quibble on the word, *Two Gentlemen of Verona, ii. 5.* Minor church festivals were called ales.

Alecto (one of the Furies), *II. Henry IV., v. 5.*

Alençon, the Duke of, a character in *I. Henry VI.*, spoken of in *i. 1,* first appears in *i. 2.* In *v. 4,* York calls him a "notorious Machiavel." He is mentioned in *Henry V., iii. 5;* his (supposed) glove, *Henry V., iv. 7, 8.*

Alexander, one of the Nine Worthies in *Love's Labour's Lost, v. 2.* The jests on the player, "Your nose," etc., are allusions to the traditions that his head was set obliquely, and that his body gave out a sweet fragrance; his crown, *A Winter's Tale, v. 1;* the king likened to, *Henry V., iv. 7.*

Alexander, character in *Troilus and Cressida*, Cressida's servant, introduced in *i. 2.*

Alexandria, a city of Egypt, scene of a part of *Antony and Cleopatra*.

Alexas, an attendant of the queen in *Antony and Cleopatra*, introduced in *i. 2;* his revolt, *iv. 6.*

Algiers. See ARGIER.

Alice, a lady attending on the Princess Katharine in *Henry V.*, first appears in *iii. 4,* an amusing scene, where she is teaching the princess English.

Aliena, name assumed by Celia in *As You Like It, i. 3.*

Alisander. See ALEXANDER.

Alla nostra casa, etc., *Taming of the Shrew, i. 2.* (Welcome to our house, much-honoured Signor Petruchio.)

Allegiance, offers of, *King John, v. 7;* pluck, from men's hearts, *I. Henry IV., iii. 2;* crowned with faith and constant loyalty, *Henry V., ii. 2;* cold hearts freeze, *I. Henry VI., v. 5;* to a fallen lord, *Antony and Cleopatra, iii. 11.* See also LOYALTY.

All-hallowmas summer, *I. Henry IV.,* *i. 2;* Indian summer.

All hid, all hid, *Love's Labour's Lost, iv. 3.* A children's game, perhaps hoodman-blind, or hide-and-seek.

Alliance, sought with France, *III. Henry VI., iii. 3;* of Cæsar and Antony, *Antony and Cleopatra, ii. 2.*

Alliteration, the use of, *Love's Labour's Lost, iv. 2,* "to affect the letter."

Allons (let us go), *Love's Labour's Lost, iv. 3.*

Allow (approve), *II. Henry IV., iii. 2; Troilus and Cressida, iii. 2.*

All-Saints' Day. See HALLOWMAS.

All-Souls' Day, *Richard III., v. 1.*

All's Well that Ends Well, a comedy first published in 1623, and judged to have been written in its present form about 1601 or 1602. But it is supposed to be a re-cast of an earlier play entitled "Love's Labour's Won," mentioned by Meres in 1598, though some editors have sought to identify that play with *Much Ado about Nothing,* others with *Taming of the Shrew,* and one at least with *The Tempest.* The general opinion, however, identifies it with this play. The story is from Boccaccio's "Decameron," where it is entitled "Giglietta di Nerbona," and was published in an English translation in Paynter's "Palace of Pleasure," where Shakspere may have got it. The tale is followed quite closely in the principal incidents, but Shakspere has added several important characters—Lafeu, Parolles, and the Countess. The scene is laid partly in France and partly in Italy, and the time is perhaps the fourteenth century. Although repellent in its plot, this play has some of Shakspere's finest passages and some of his best creations of character.

Allycholly (melancholy), *Two Gentlemen of Verona, iv. 2.*

Almanac, of my true date, *Comedy of Errors, i. 2.* One by whose birth he knew the date of his own.

Almanacs, allusions to weather prognostications in, *II. Henry IV., ii. 4; Antony and Cleopatra, i. 2; Sonnet xiv.*

Alms-drink, *Antony and Cleopatra, ii. 7.* The portion of one's share taken by others to relieve him. Perhaps here only the leavings, which would be given as alms.

Alonso, King of Naples, character in *The Tempest,* introduced in the first scene. He and his son, with the usurping Duke of Milan, whom he had aided in the usurpation, are shipwrecked in the storm raised by Prospero. He afterward repents of the wrong, and consents to the marriage of his son Ferdinand with Miranda.

Alphabet, the, called Absey. See ABSEY-BOOK; called the cross-row (or Christ-cross row, because it was often headed with a cross), *Richard III., i. 1.*

Althea, dreamed she was delivered of a firebrand, *II. Henry IV., ii. 2.* It was Hecuba that had that dream before the birth of Paris; burning the brand, *II. Henry VI., i. 1.* The destinies fore-told that the life of her son Meleager should last no longer than a brand then burning upon the hearth. She caught up the brand, ex-tinguished, and saved it. But when her son grew to manhood he slew her two brothers in a sudden passion; and Althea, to avenge their death, threw the brand upon the fire, and, as it burned, the life of Meleager wasted away with it.

Amaimon, *Merry Wives of Windsor, ii. 2, end; I. Henry IV., ii. 4.* One of the four demon-kings. His realm is in the north, the quarter most haunted by evil spirits.

Amazement (consternation), *The Tempest, i. 2; Hamlet, iii. 4.* See ASTONISHMENT.

Ambassadors, from France, *Henry V.* The chief speaker was the Archbishop of Bourges.

Ambition, growth of, *The Tempest, i. 2;* to expel remorse, *The Tempest, v. 1;* shrunk, *I. Henry VI., v. 4;* the object of, glory, like a circle in water, *I. Henry IV., i. 2;* of the Plantagenets, *III. Henry VI., i. 4;* charge to fling away, *Henry VIII., iii. 2;* a beastly, *Timon, iv. 3;* our own fault if we are underlings, *Julius Cæsar, i. 2;* ladder of, *Julius Cæsar, ii. 1;* of Cæsar, *iii. 2;* with scruples, *Macbeth, i. 5;* vaulting, *Macbeth, i. 7;* is but dreams and a shadow's shadow, *Hamlet, ii. 2;* the soldier's virtue, *Antony and Cleopatra, iii. 1.*

Amen, *The Tempest, v. 1;* say amen betimes, lest the devil cross the prayer, *Merchant of Venice, iii. 1;* could not say, *Macbeth, ii. 2.*

America, *Comedy of Errors, iii. 2;* allusion to, *Henry VIII., v. 3,* "Make new nations," etc.

Ames-ace, *All's Well that Ends Well, ii. 3.* The lowest throw upon two dice—two aces.

Amiens, one of the lords attending the banished duke in *As You Like It,* introduced in *ii. 1.*

Amity. See FRIENDSHIP.

Amnesty, offer of, *I. Henry IV., iv. 3; v. 1.*

Amort (dispirited), *Taming of the Shrew, iv. 3; I. Henry VI., iii. 2.*

Amphion, harp of, *The Tempest, ii. 1.*

Amulets. See CHARMS, PERIAPTS.

Amurath, *II. Henry IV., v. 2.* Amurath V., who, succeeding his father, Amurath IV., caused all his brothers to be strangled.

Amyntas, King of Lycaonia, *Antony and Cleopatra, iii. 6.*

Anarchy, prayer for, *II. Henry IV., i. 1;* danger of, *Richard III., ii. 2.*

Anatomize (analyze), *As You Like It, i. 1; ii. 7; II. Henry VI., v. 2.*

Anatomy, a mere, *Comedy of Errors, v. 1;* I'll eat the rest of the, *Twelfth Night, iii. 2;* that fell, which cannot heal, *King John, iii. 4;* in what part of the, does the name lodge, *Romeo and Juliet, iii. 3.*

Anchises, *Julius Cæsar, i. 2.* The father of Æneas, whom Æneas bore away on his back from burning Troy.

Ancient (a standard, or standard-bearer, or ensign). Pistol and Iago were ancients ; an old-faced (flag), *I. Henry IV., iv. 2;* of war (experienced), *King Lear, v. 1.*

Ancients, whether better than moderns, *Sonnet ix.*

Andirons, *Cymbeline, ii. 4.*

And let the canakin, song, *Othello, ii. 3.*

Andren (Arde), vale of, in Picardy, the meeting-place of the Kings Francis I. and Henry VIII., *Henry VIII., i. 1.* The Field of the Cloth of Gold.

Andrew, my wealthy, *Merchant of Venice, i. 1.* A merchant-man, supposed to be called so after the great admiral, Andrew Doria.

Andromache, Hector's wife, a character in *Troilus and Cressida,* introduced in *v. 3.*

Andronici, tomb of the, *Titus Andronicus, i. 1* or *2.* Titus brings home those of his twenty-five sons who have fallen, to be buried in the tomb of his ancestors.

· **Anemone,** the flower that sprang from the blood of Adonis, *V. and A., 195.* Purple was used for any bright color. Bion makes the rose to spring from the blood, the anemone from the tears of Venus.

Angelo, the deputy of the duke in *Measure for Measure,* introduced in the first scene—a cold-hearted, self-righteous man, who not only falls into the wickedness which he is making a great display of punishing, but aggravates it by cruelty and breach of faith. The development of the worse elements of his character, the existence of which he had never suspected, his surprise at his own fall, and the rapidity with which one baseness follows another in a life that was all selfishness and show even in its virtues, are brought out in the play with great skill and subtlety.

Angelo, a goldsmith, character in *Comedy of Errors,* introduced in *iii. 1.*

Angel(s), made to weep, *Measure for Measure, ii. 2;* blessed ministers above, *Measure for Measure, v. 1;* guardian, *II. Henry IV., ii. 2;* attending evil, *II. Henry IV., i. 2; Macbeth, iii. 1; Antony and Cleopatra, ii. 3;* fell by ambition, *Henry VIII., iii. 2;* love good men, *Henry VIII., ii. 2;* visions of, *Henry VIII., iv. 2;* beauty of, *Romeo and Juliet, ii. 2;* are bright still, *Macbeth, iv. 3;* and ministers of grace, *Hamlet, i. 4;* heavenly guards, *Hamlet, iii. 4;* sing thee to thy rest, *Hamlet, v. 2.*

Angel(s), (gold coins with the figure of an angel or saint), *Merry Wives of Windsor, i. 3; Merchant of Venice, ii. 7; King John, iii, 3; II. Henry IV., i. 2;* an ancient, *Taming of the Shrew, iv. 2.* The meaning of the last is obscure, but perhaps one of the old stamp, a true coin. Some understand it to be a word cognate to *angle,* and to mean either the bait or the victim—that angled with or that angled for.

Anger, in a woman, *Taming of the Shrew, v. 2,* "A woman moved," etc. ; the king's, *I. Henry IV., i. 3;* like a full horse, *Henry VIII., i. 1;* sudden, *Henry VIII., iii. 2;* my meat, *Coriolanus, iv. 2;* a short madness, *Timon of Athens, i. 2;* of Cassius, *Julius Cæsar, iv. 3;* more in sorrow than in, *Hamlet, i. 2;* righteous, *Lear, ii. 2,* "hath a privilege" ; *Othello, iii. 4,* "There's matter in't," etc.; never made good guard for itself, *Antony and Cleopatra, iv. 1.*

Angiers, scene of part of *King John* and of *I. Henry VI., v. 3;* addresses to citizens of, *King John, ii. 1* or *2.*

Angling, *Much Ado about Nothing, iii. 1; Antony and Cleopatra, ii. 5;* for hearts, *1. Henry IV., iv. 3.*

Angus, a thane of Scotland, character in *Macbeth,* appears in *i. 3.*

Angus, Earl of, *I. Henry IV., i. 1.*

Animals, souls of, in men, *The Merchant of Venice, iv. 1;* cruelty to, *As You Like It, ii. 1; Cymbeline, i. 5;* defend their young, *III. Henry VI., ii. 2;* know their friends, *Coriolanus, ii. 1;* strife among, *Timon of Athens, iv. 3.*

Anjou, scene of *I. Henry VI., v. 2, 4;* lost to England, *II. Henry VI., i. 1; iv. 1.*

Anjou, Margaret of. See MARGARET.

Anna, the confidant of Dido, *Taming of the Shrew, i. 1.*

Anne, Princess of Wales, widow of the son of Henry VI., and daughter of Warwick, a character in *Richard III.*, where she appears first in *i. 2*, and is successfully wooed in the street, while following the coffin of Henry VI., by Gloster (Richard III.), his murderer and the murderer of her husband. In *iv. 2*, he resolves that she shall die, so that he may marry his brother's daughter, and her death is announced in *iv. 3* (March 16, 1485). Her ghost appears to Richard in *v. 3.*

Anne Boleyn. See BOLEYN.

Annotanize (stilted for annotate), *Love's Labour's Lost, iv. 1.*

Annoy, farewell to, *III. Henry VI., v. 7.*

An old hare hoar (an old song), *Romeo and Juliet, ii. 4.*

Anon, *Merry Wives of Windsor, iii. 3; I. Henry IV., ii. 4.* A waiter's usual answer, used as " coming " is now.

Answer, you shall never take her without her answer, unless you take her without her tongue, *As You Like It, iv. 1;* to fit all questions, *All's Well that Ends Well, ii. 2.*

Antenor, a Trojan commander, character in *Troilus and Cressida*, passes through in *i. 2*, and is described by Pandarus. In *iii. 3* it is proposed to exchange him for Cressida, which is done, *iv. 1.*

Antenorides (name of a gate of Troy), *Troilus and Cressida*, prologue.

Anthropophagi, and men whose heads, etc., *Othello i. 3.* Raleigh described such men in the account of his voyage to Guiana; there is another allusion in *The Tempest, iii. 3*, to men whose heads stood in their breasts.

Anthropophaginian (cannibal), used in fun by the Host, *Merry Wives of Windsor, iv. 5.*

Antiates (of Antium), *Coriolanus, i. 6.*

Antic (buffoon in a farce), *Much Ado about Nothing, iii. 1*, and in other passages. The word antic, or antique, is also used as the name of a dance, *Macbeth, iv. 1; Love's Labour's Lost, v. 1.*

Anticipation, *Merchant of Venice, ii. 6;* pleasure of, *All's Well that Ends Well, ii. 4; Richard II., ii. 3;* the imaginary relish, *Troilus and Cressida, iii. 2.*

Antigonus, a character in *A Winter's Tale,* a lord at the court of Leontes, introduced in *ii. 1.* Like his wife, Paulina, he is at first an outspoken advocate of the suspected queen ; but he afterward weakens and is sent by the king to dispose of Perdita. He is killed by a bear, *iii. 1*, when on the way to his ship after leaving her on the desolate coast of Bohemia (!).

Antioch, scene of a part of *Pericles.*

Antiochus, King of Antioch, character in *Pericles,* Prince of Tyre, introduced in *i. 1;* his death, *ii. 4.* His daughter, also a character in the play, a beautiful woman whose many suitors were given the alternative of guessing a riddle or having their heads set on the palace-gate, is introduced in *i. 1;* her death, *ii. 4.*

Antiopa, *Midsummer - Night's Dream, ii. 1.* An Amazon, daughter of Mars.

Antipathies, instinctive, *Merchant of Venice, iv. 1;* of contraries, *Lear, ii. 2.*

Antipholus, the name of twin brothers in the *Comedy of Errors,* who were separated in infancy, one being taken to Ephesus, the other to Syracuse. The resemblance between them and that between their servants, the Dromios, is the source of the errors. Antipholus of Ephesus is introduced in *iii. 1,* Antipholus of Syracuse in *i. 2.*

Antipodes, the, *Much Ado about Nothing, ii. 1; Merchant of Venice, v. 1; Richard II., iii. 2; III. Henry VI., i. 4.*

Antiquity, *Hamlet, iv. 5; Sonnet lxviii;* the service of the antique world, *As You Like It, ii. 3.* In the sense of age, see AGE.

Antium, the Volscian capital, scene of *Coriolanus, iv. 4, 5.*

Antoniad, the, Cleopatra's ship, *Antony and Cleopatra, iii. 8* or *10.*

Antonio, brother of Prospero, in *The Tempest,* whose place and title as Duke of Milan he has usurped, first appears in *i. 1.* So far from repenting of his crime, he urges Sebastian, brother of the King of Naples, to commit a similar crime, and is willing himself to be the assassin.

Antonio, father of Proteus in the *Two Gentlemen of Verona,* appears in *i. 3.*

Antonio, brother of Leonato, in *Much Ado about Nothing,* introduced in *i. 2.*

Antonio, the merchant who is to lose the pound of flesh in *The Merchant of Venice.* He is the first speaker in the play. Although possessed of great wealth, he seems to care neither for hoarding nor spending it. The only passion he seems to have shown is his hatred of Shylock's usurious practices, intensified by the Christian hatred of his age for Shylock's race. Quiet, melancholy, and somewhat negative in character, he stands among the more lively personages of the play a sufferer rather than an actor.

Antonio, a sea-captain in *Twelfth Night,* introduced in *ii. 1,* a constant friend of Sebastian.

Antonius, Marcus, Marc Antony, character in *Julius Cæsar*, introduced in *i. 2;* Cassius proposes that he shall die with Cæsar, *ii. 1;* his message to Brutus, and lament over Cæsar, *iii. 1;* his funeral oration, *iii. 2.*

Also a character in *Antony and Cleopatra*, introduced in *i. 1;* his soldierly endurance, *i. 4;* Lepidus's praise of, travestied, *iii. 2;* in defeat, *iii. 2;* complaint against Cæsar, *iii. 4;* his division of his kingdoms, *iii. 6;* resolved to fight by sea, *iii. 7;* at Actium, *iii. 8–10;* shame and despair, *iii. 9* or *11, 11* or *13;* challenge to Cæsar, *iii. 11* or *13, iv. 1;* parting with his followers, *iv. 2;* portent of his fall, *iv. 3;* in supposed victory, *iv. 8;* in despair, *iv. 10* or *12; 12* or *14;* his death, *iv. 12* or *14; 13* or *15;* lamented by Cæsar, *v. 1;* by Cleopatra, *v. 2.*

" He refined the rough features of Marc Antony into the character of an Alcibiades. He passed silently over the youth of his hero, he took from him his tendency to cruelty, covered the misdeeds of the triumvirate with a veil, showed only the best side of his rapacity and lavish prodigality, spoke loudly of his warlike past, his victory over Brutus and Cassius, his heroic endurance of hunger and want after his defeat at Modena, and strove especially to make his hero interesting on the score of brilliant natural gifts. It is not to be disputed that Shakspere by these touches brought out the most attractive side of Antony. Even in the voluptuary and the profligate there is an alluring charm in the ready versatility, the natural superiority, the variety of talent, the abundance of resources, and in the natural aptness to fill any part. Antony was indeed a man thus variously endowed."—GERVINUS.

" Antony is a man of genius, with many splendid and some generous qualities, but self-indulgent, pleasure-loving, and a daring adventurer, rather than a great leader of the state."—DOWDEN.

Antony and Cleopatra, a tragedy, first published in the folio of 1623, is supposed to have been written in or near the year 1607, both from internal evidence and from the fact that in 1608 a book bearing the name was registered for publication, though for some reason it was not published, by Edward Blount, publisher of the first folio. It follows Plutarch's "Life of Antony" closely, beginning in the year 40 B. C., when Fulvia died, and covering a period of about ten years. The scenes are laid in Alexandria, Rome, Misenum, Athens, near Actium, Messina, and on a plain in Syria. White calls this, poetically, the most splendid creation of Shakspere's genius, an opinion in which he follows Coleridge, who says:

" Of all Shakspere's historical plays, *Antony and Cleopatra* is by far the most wonderful. There is not one in which he has followed history so minutely, and yet there are few in which he impresses the notion of angelic strength so much, perhaps none in which he impresses it more strongly. This is greatly owing to the manner in which the fiery force is sustained throughout, and to the numerous momentary flashes of nature counteracting the historic abstraction."

Antres (caves), *Othello, i. 3.*

Ape(s), the famous, *Hamlet, iii. 4,* allusion to some forgotten story; foreheads of, *The Tempest, iv. 1;* lead, in hell, *Much Ado about Nothing, ii. 1; Taming of the Shrew, ii. 1.* The proverbial future punishment of old maids was to lead apes in hell.

Apemantus, a cynic, character in *Timon of Athens,* introduced in *i. 1.*

"Diogenes, in Lily's 'Alexander and Campaspe,' sat to the poet for Timon's contrast, the cynic Apemantus; the quick, striking, epigrammatic answers to questions, which seem to be inserted here and there too much for the sake of eliciting witty replies, are quite on this model. The description of this antique fool is so perfect in its way that it is supposed Shakspere must have seen the short sketch of a cynic, which, in Lucian's 'Public Sale of Philosophers,' is put into the mouth of Diogenes. It is there said that, in order to belong to this sect, a man must be bold and shameless, and revile every one from the king to the beggar; thus he will draw all eyes upon him, and appear manly. His speech must be barbarous, his voice dissonant, and exactly like a dog's; his face rigid, his expression the same, and altogether he must be brutish and rough. Shame, equity, and moderation must be dispensed with, and blushes must be wholly banished from his countenance."—GERVINUS.

Aphrodisiacs, the potato, eringo, *Merry Wives of Windsor, v. 5.*

Apollo, lute of, *Love's Labour's Lost, iv. 3;* and Daphne, *Midsummer-Night's Dream, ii. 1; Troilus and Cressida, i. 1;* plays, *Taming of the Shrew, Induction, 2;* oracle of, consulted, *A Winter's Tale, ii. 1; iii. 1, 2; v. 1.*

Apologies: Proteus's to Valentine, *Two Gentlemen of Verona, v. 4;* Antony's to Octavius, *Antony and Cleopatra, ii. 2.*

Apostle-spoons. See SPOONS.

Apothecary, and his shop, *Romeo and Juliet, v. 1.*

Apparel, honour in the meanest, *Taming of the Shrew, iv. 3;* oft proclaims the man, *Hamlet, i. 3;* vices appear through mean, *King Lear, iv. 6.*

Apparitions: of hunters and hounds, *The Tempest, iv. 1;* of Cæsar, *Julius Cæsar, iv. 3;* of Macduff, Malcolm, and the eight kings, *Macbeth, iv. 1.* These are the Stuart kings to James V., said to have been descended from Banquo. The many more, some with twofold balls and treble sceptres, James VI. (James I. of England)

and his posterity, who were to reign over the united kingdom; of Hamlet's father, *Hamlet, i. 1, 4, 5.* See also GHOSTS.

Appeached (accused), *All's Well that Ends Well, i. 3.*

Appeal, the boisterous late, *Richard II., i. 1.* The accusation made against Norfolk of high treason.

Appearance, judging by the, *Merchant of Venice, ii. 7; iii. 2; Twelfth Night, i. 2,* "There is a fair behaviour," etc.; *Pericles, ii. 2.*

Apperil (endanger), *Timon of Athens, i. 2.*

Appetite, of her eye, *Merry Wives of Windsor, i. 3;* digestion wait on, *Macbeth, iii. 4;* grown with what it fed on, *Hamlet, i. 2;* and judgment, *Lover's Complaint, l. 166.*

Applause, *Henry VIII., iv. 1,* "Such a noise arose," etc.

Apple-Johns (apples with wrinkled skin), that would keep two years, *II. Henry IV., ii. 4.*

Apply (ply), *Taming of the Shrew, i. 1.*

Appreciation, after loss, *All's Well that Ends Well, v. 3.*

Approbation, receive her (enter on her probation), *Measure for Measure, i. 3.*

Apricock (apricot), *Midsummer-Night's Dream, iii. 1; Richard II., iii. 4.*

April, spongy, *The Tempest, iv. 1;* love like, *Two Gentlemen of Verona, i. 3.*

Aquitaine (a duchy in southwestern France), surrender of, *Love's Labour's Lost, i. 1 · ii. 1.*

Arabia, wilds of, *Merchant of Venice, ii. 7;* perfumes of, *Macbeth, v. 1;* trees of, *Othello, v. 2;* bird of, *Antony and Cleopatra, iii. 2; Cymbeline, i. 7.*

Arch (chief), *King Lear, ii. 1.*

Archbishop, an, rebuked for rebellion, *II. Henry IV., iv. 2.*

Archbishops of Canterbury. See BOURCHIER, CANTERBURY, CRANMER.

Archbishops of York. See ROTHERHAM, SCROOP, YORK.

Archelaus, King of Cappadocia, *Antony and Cleopatra, iii. 6.*

Archery, allusions to: wide o' the bow-hand (far from the mark), *Love's Labour's Lost, iv. 1;* flight and bird bolt (long and short shot)—to cry aim (to encourage), *Merry Wives of Windsor, ii. 3; iii. 1; King John, ii. 1;* in a bottle like a cat, *Much Ado about Nothing, i. 1;* the very pin of his heart cleft, etc., *Romeo and Juliet, ii. 4.* The clout, which was the pin, the very centre of the target, is spoken of in many places, *Love's Labour's Lost, iv. 1; II. Henry IV., iii. 2; King Lear, iv. 6.*

Archibald, Earl of Douglas. See DOUGLAS.

Archidamus, an unimportant character in *A Winter's Tale*, an attendant of Polixenes, appears in *i. 1.*

Arde, in Picardy, *Henry VIII., i. 1.*

Ardea (a city south of Rome), siege of, *Lucrece, argument,* and *l. 1.*

Arden, the forest of. See AS YOU LIKE IT.

Argier (old English name of Algiers), *The Tempest, i. 2.*

Argosy(ies), Antonio's, *Merchant of Venice, i. 1, 3; iii. 2;* choked with an, *Taming of the Shrew, v. 1.*

Argument (cause), *Henry V., iii. 1; Troilus and Cressida, i. 1; Hamlet, iv. 4.*

Argus, the hundred-eyed, *Love's Labour's Lost, iii. 1; Troilus and Cressida, i. 2.*

Ariachne (Arachne, the spider), *Troilus and Cressida, v. 2.*

Ariadne (daughter of Minos, King of Crete; she was deserted by her lover Theseus, whom she had rescued from the labyrinth), *Two Gentlemen of Verona, iv. 4; Midsummer-Night's Dream, ii. 1.*

Ariel, an airy spirit in *The Tempest*, whose service Prospero has secured by the exercise of his magic power.

" Grace, tenderness, speed, and especially freedom and lightness, the properties of his element, are peculiar to him. . . . Whilst the other spirits hate the magician, yet are compelled to serve him, Ariel obeys him thankfully and truly, without lies, without mistakes, without a murmur; for this, his perfect freedom, his all, is promised him within a certain time, and of this time, for good service, one year is abated. But even to wait this abridged time is painful to him. It is exquisitely conceived and very beautiful. What a peculiarly melancholic character the poet has cast over the being and relations of this creature, divided as he is between a superior nature and the aspirings of higher feelings! . . . His lord will miss him when he has given him his freedom; but he, the airy creature, will feel no longing after his dear master, whom he only seems to love for the sake of his promised freedom. He asks for more, for speedier freedom, and Prospero must, once in a month, recount to the quickly forgetting spirit the benefit he has received of his hands; then the variable servant struggles with his fluctuating nature, and is again all obedience, fidelity, and promptness."—GERVINUS.

Aries (the ram), *Titus Andronicus, iv. 3.*

Arion, rescued by the dolphin, *Twelfth Night, i. 2.*

Aristotle, *Taming of the Shrew, i. 1;* quoted by Hector, *Troilus and Cressida, ii. 2.* Aristotle lived 800 years after the Trojan war.

Ark, couples coming to the, *As You Like It, v. 4.*

Armado, Don Adriano de, a character in *Love's Labour's Lost.*

introduced in *i. 2*, a fantastical Spaniard, full of sounding words and boastings, but cowardly and of low instincts, chosen by the king to amuse him and his fellow-students in their seclusion.

Armagnac, Earl of, *I. Henry VI., v. 5.*

Arm-gaunt, *Antony and Cleopatra, i. 5.* There is no satisfactory explanation of this word. It is sometimes read "arm-girt," covered with armour.

Armigero (armiger), *Merry Wives of Windsor, i. 1.* One who bears arms, a gentleman. Written after the name in law-papers.

Arms, coats of. See HERALDRY.

Army, composition of an, *King John, ii. 1;* coming of an, *King John, iv. 4;* appeal to an, *Henry V., iii. 1;* embarkation of an, *Henry V., iii., chorus;* spoiled trappings of an, *Henry V., iv. 3;* a ragged, *II. Henry VI., iv. 4;* contempt for an opposing, *Richard III., v. 3.*

Aroint (avaunt), *Macbeth, i. 3; King Lear, iii. 4.* Said to be still used in the north of England, in some places pronounced *rynt.*

Aragon, the Prince of, one of the suitors of Portia in *Merchant of Venice,* appears in *ii. 9,* and loses her by choosing the silver casket.

Arras, hide behind the, *I. Henry IV., ii. 4,* and in many other places. It was placed on wooden frames or on hooks far enough from the wall to keep it from dampness; figures on, *Cymbeline, ii. 2.*

Arrogance, fed by supple knees, *Troilus and Cressida, iii. 3.*

Art, magic, *The Tempest, i. 2;* modifying nature, *A Winter's Tale, iv. 3* or *4;* in painting, *Lucrece, l. 1373.* See PAINTING and PICTURES.

Artemidorus, a sophist of Cnidos, character in *Julius Cæsar,* appears in *ii. 3* and *iii. 1,* with a warning for Cæsar. Plutarch says he was a doctor of Greek rhetoric, and, knowing the designs of the conspirators, with whom the practice of his profession had brought him into contact, tried to warn Cæsar. His warning, *ii. 3; iii. 1.*

Arteries and Veins, *Merchant of Venice, iii. 2; Love's Labour's Lost, iv. 3; King John, iii. 3; Richard III., i. 2; Troilus and Cressida, iv. 1; Coriolanus, v. 1; Romeo and Juliet, v. 1; Hamlet, i. 4.* See also BLOOD, CIRCULATION OF THE.

Arthur, Duke of Brittany, a character in *King John,* was the nephew of John and of Richard I., and by the latter designed, at one time at least, as his successor. Arthur was born in 1188, and is supposed to have been put to death at John's orders after being made prisoner by him in 1202. He was imprisoned at the castle of Falaise in Normandy, and afterwards in the castle of Rouen, where he is supposed to have met his death—not, as in the play, in England. He was undisputed heir to Anjou, Touraine, and Maine, and Duke of Brittany. As such he was a vassal of Philip, who took up his cause for his own interest, and went to war with John. Arthur first appears in *ii. 1.* He is gentle, innocent, and unambitious, yet in the scene with Hubert shows a high degree of childish wisdom. This scene is one of the finest in the play. His death, *iv. 3.*

Arthur's Show, *II. Henry IV., iii. 2.* An exhibition of archers, who took the names of Arthur's knights. Sir Dagonet was a sort of fool to the king.

Arundel, Archbishop. See CANTERBURY.

Arviragus, son of Cymbeline, disguised under the name of Cadwal. See GUIDERIUS.

Ascanius (son of Æneas), *II. Henry VI., iii. 2.* It was Cupid disguised as Ascanius that talked to Dido.

Ascapart (a legendary giant), *II. Henry VI., ii. 3.*

Asher House, *Henry VIII., iii. 2.* See ESHER HOUSE.

Ashes, as the phœnix, *III. Henry VI., i. 4;* show cinders through, *Antony and Cleopatra, v. 2.*

Asmath, a spirit, *II. Henry VI., i. 4.*

Asp, the, *Antony and Cleopatra, v. 2.*

Aspiration, shown by the gait, *Troilus and Cressida, iv. 5.*

Ass, a thrice double, *Tempest, v. 1;* Dogberry would be writ down an, *Much Ado about Nothing, iv. 2;* Bottom transformed into an, *Midsummer-Night's Dream, iii. 1, 2;* more captain than the lion, *Timon of Athens, iii. 5;* beating an, *Hamlet, v. 1;* allusion to the fable of the old man and the ass, *King Lear, i. 4,* "Thou borest thine ass," etc.

Assinego (little ass), *Troilus and Cressida, ii. 1.*

Associates, influence of, *Merchant of Venice, iii. 4,* "In companions," etc.; pitch doth defile, *I. Henry IV., ii. 4;* let men take heed of their company, *II. Henry IV., v. 1;* keep where wit is stirring, *Troilus and Cressida, ii. 1;* thou art noble, *Julius Cæsar, i. 2;* converse with him that is wise, *King Lear, i. 4.*

Assurance, made doubly sure, *Macbeth, iv. 1.*

Astonishment, signs of, *A Winter's Tale, v. 2;* "They spake not a word," etc., *Richard III., iii. 7;* at prodigies, *Julius Cæsar, i. 3.*

Astringer, a Gentle, character in *All's Well that Ends Well,* introduced in *v. 1.* A falconer that kept goshawks was so called.

Astrology, allusions to, *The Tempest, i. 2; Two Gentlemen of Verona, ii. 7;* born under Saturn, *Much Ado about Nothing, i. 3;* un-

der a dancing star, *Much Ado about Nothing, ii. 1;* under a rhyming
planet, *Much Ado about Nothing, v. 2;* under Mars, *All's Well that
Ends Well, i. 1;* the luckiest stars, *All's Well that Ends Well, i. 3;*
the most received star, *All's Well that Ends Well, ii. 1;* born under
Taurus, *Twelfth Night, i. 3;* constellation right apt, *Twelfth Night,
i. 4;* stars shine darkly, *Twelfth Night, ii. 1;* in my stars I am,
Twelfth Night, ii. 5; a bawdy planet, *A Winter's Tale, i. 2;* some
ill planet, *A Winter's Tale, ii. 1;* dishonour my fair stars, *Richard
II., iv. 1;* malevolent to you, *I. Henry IV., i. 1;* Glendower's nativity, *I. Henry IV., iii. 1;* ruled like a wandering planet, *II. Henry
VI., iv. 4;* my thwarting stars, *III. Henry VI., iv. 6;* star-crossed
lovers, *Romeo and Juliet, i., prologue;* yet hanging in the stars, *Romeo and Juliet, i. 4;* inauspicious stars, *Romeo and Juliet, v. 3;* not
in our stars, *Julius Cæsar, i. 2;* fortune's star, *Hamlet, i. 4;* out of
thy star, *Hamlet, ii. 2;* orbs from whom we exist, *King Lear, i. 1;*
eclipses, *King Lear, i. 2;* the stars blamed for the vices of men,
King Lear, i. 2; your great aspect, *King Lear, ii. 2;* it is the stars,
King Lear, iv. 3; my good stars, *Antony and Cleopatra, iii. 11* or
13; our bloods obey, *Cymbeline, i. 1;* O learned indeed, *Cymbeline,
iii. 2;* senate-house of planets, *Pericles, i. 1;* stars that frown, *Pericles, i. 4;* a chiding nativity, *Pericles, iii. 1;* mortal stars, *Lucrece,
l. 13;* not from the stars, *Sonnets xiv., xv.;* in favour with their
stars, *Sonnet xxv.;* whatsoever star, *Sonnet xxvi.;* crooked eclipses,
Sonnet ix.

Astronomers, have no more profit, *Love's Labour's Lost, i. 1.*

Astronomy (astrology), *Sonnet xiv.*

As You Like It, a comedy first printed in 1623, though it was
entered in the "Stationers' Register" for publication in 1600. It
must have been written between 1598 and 1600. The story is taken
from a tale by Thomas Lodge, "Rosalynde: Euphues' Golden Legacie," first published in 1590, and reprinted at least ten times before
1642. The characters of Jaques, Touchstone, and Audrey are not in
the story; and Shakspere changed the names of those he took, excepting Rosalind, Phœbe, Charles, and Adam (Adam Spencer in the
story). The scene of the play is in the Forest of Arden and in
France, though it does not correspond to Ardennes, and both place
and time are indefinite, intentionally so, as the character of the play
does not require definiteness in these respects.

Atalanta, the better part of, *As You Like It, iii. 2, verses.*

Ate (goddess of Discord), *Much Ado about Nothing, ii. 1; King
John, ii. 1; Julius Cæsar, iii. 1.*

Ates, more, *Love's Labour's Lost, v. 2.*

Athens, scene of the *Midsummer-Night's Dream, Timon of Athens,* and part of *Antony and Cleopatra.*

Athol, Earl of, *I. Henry IV., i. 1.*

Atlas (the Titan supposed to support the heavens), *III. Henry VI., v. 1; Antony and Cleopatra, i. 5.*

Atomies, shut coward gates on, *As You Like It, iii. 5;* a team of, *Romeo and Juliet, i. 4.*

Atone (to reconcile or be reconciled), *Coriolanus, iv. 6; Othello, iv. 1.*

Atonement of Christ, reference to the, *Measure for Measure, ii. 2,* "Why, all the souls," etc.

Atropos (one of the Fates, the one that cut off the thread), *II. Henry IV., ii. 4.*

Attempt, the, confounds us, *Macbeth, ii. 2.*

Attorney (substitute), *Comedy of Errors, v. 1.*

Audacious (spirited), *Love's Labour's Lost, v. 1.*

Audacity, arm me, *Cymbeline, i. 7.*

Audit, *Coriolanus, i. 1; Sonnets iv., xlix.* See ACCOUNT.

Audrey, an honest and ugly country girl in *As You Like It,* married to the clown Touchstone, introduced in *iii. 3.*

Aufidius, Tullus, general of the Volscians, character in *Coriolanus,* introduced in *i. 2;* his bravery, *i. 1;* fights with Marcius (*Coriolanus*), *i. 8;* his hatred to him, *i. 10;* joins him, *iv. 5;* his jealousy, *iv. 7.* He has the same desire for military glory that Coriolanus has; but he is of a much smaller and meaner nature. His great ambition is to conquer Coriolanus, and for this he is willing to use any means, however dishonourable; and Coriolanus falls at last through his malicious trickery.

Augurer. See SOOTHSAYER.

Auguries, of success, *Cymbeline, iv. 2;* "Last night the very gods," etc. See OMENS.

Augustus Cæsar, demands tribute, *Cymbeline, iii. 1;* character in *Antony and Cleopatra.* See CÆSAR.

Aumerle, Edward, Duke of, son of the Duke of York, character in *Richard II.,* first appears in *i. 3.* He was high constable, and was deprived of his dukedom for adhering to Richard, but allowed to retain the earldom of Rutland, "Call him Rutland" (*v. 2*). In *Henry V.* he is again spoken of, now an old man and Duke of York, as dying on the field of Agincourt (*Henry V., iv. 6*).

" The character of the Duke of Aumerle, who plays no brilliant part in *Richard II.* after his mother had saved him from the punishment of high treason, and has prayed to God to make 'her old son new,' is again silently brought forward by the poet in *Henry V.*, a new man indeed, who has become great with the heroic age, and dies the death of a hero at Agincourt."—GERVINUS.

Aunt, an old, *Troilus and Cressida, ii. 2.* Hesione, sister of Priam.

Austria, Leopold, Archduke of, a character in *King John*, where he is made identical with Vidomar, Viscount of Lymoges, in a quarrel with whom Richard I. of England fell, having been shot by one of the viscount's vassals while besieging the castle of Chaluz. The archduke died before Richard.

Authority, the demigod,—new, *Measure for Measure, i. 3;* "Whether it be the fault," etc.; a little brief,—hath a medicine in itself, *Measure for Measure, ii. 2;* abuse of, *Measure for Measure, ii. 4;* vice in, *Measure for Measure, iv. 2;* danger of divided, *Coriolanus, iii. 1;* a dog in office—great image of, *King Lear, iv. 6.*

Authorship. Following is a summary of the plays that are generally supposed to have been written in part by other hands than Shakspere's:

Titus Andronicus is thought by most critics to have been the work of an earlier dramatist and merely touched up by Shakspere, though some suppose it to be mainly his own work, and attribute its inferiority to the fact of its being his earliest play.

The three parts of *King Henry VI.*, which are recasts of two older plays, show other hands than Shakspere's. The general opinion seems to be that Marlowe, Greene, Peele, and possibly Shakspere wrote the old plays, and that they were revised by Shakspere, with possibly the help of Marlowe.

King Richard III. is referred in part to Marlowe by some critics; others suppose that the passages ascribed to Marlowe were written by Shakspere under the influence of Marlowe, his probable collaborator on *King Henry VI.*

A large part of *Henry VIII.* is judged to be by Fletcher, viz., *act i., scenes 3* and *4;* the first two scenes of *act ii.;* all of the third act except the second scene to the exit of the king; and all the remainder except the first scene of *act v.*

The first and second acts of *Pericles*, and the second, fifth, and sixth scenes of the fourth act, and the choruses, are attributed to some other author or authors.

Shakspere's part in *Taming of the Shrew* is limited by some critics to those parts in which Petruchio, Katherine, and Grumio appear prominently.

Parts of the witch-scenes in *Macbeth* have been conjectured to be the work of Thomas Middleton, author of the play "The Witch," who is supposed to have assisted in preparing *Macbeth* for the stage.

Others have seen traces of other hands in small portions of the *Comedy of Errors, Much Ado about Nothing*, the part of Hymen in *As You Like It, Romeo and Juliet*, and *Timon of Athens;* and the passage at the end of *act iii.* in *Measure for Measure*, the song beginning *act iv.*, and the fool's rhymes at the end of *King Lear, iii. 2*, are supposed to be interpolations.

Many plays have been ascribed to Shakspere that are not included in the ordinary editions of his works. Of these *The Two Noble Kinsmen* has the greatest weight of opinion in its favour. It purports to be the work of Fletcher and Shakspere. A part of the first and all of the second act of *Edward III.* have been attributed to him, and he is also supposed by some to have had a hand in *The Yorkshire Tragedy*. Other plays that have been thought to bear traces of his hand are *Arden of Feversham, The Birth of Merlin, Fair Emm, George a Green, 'Larum for London, The Merry Devil of Edmonton, Mucedorus*, and *Warning for Fair Women*.

Autolycus, an amusing and unique character in *A Winter's Tale*, a pedlar, thievish and witty.

"The art of thieving as practised by him is no crime, but the gift of some knavish god. He does not trample on the laws of morality, but dances or leaps over them with so nimble a foot that we forbear to stay him."—DOWDEN.

Auvergne, Countess of, a character in *I. Henry VI.*, first appears in *ii. 3*, having sent for Talbot (*ii. 2*), in hopes to keep him as a prisoner. This incident is not in history.

Avarice, Malcolm accuses himself of, *Macbeth, iv. 3.*

Aversions, instinctive, *Merchant of Venice, iv. 1.*

Avoid (avaunt), *Comedy of Errors, iv. 3.*

Away with, cannot (cannot endure), *II. Henry IV., iii. 2.*

Awful (law-abiding), *Two Gentlemen of Verona, iv. 1;* (respectful toward authority), *II. Henry IV., iv. 1.*

Awkward (perverse), *Pericles, v. 1.*

Aye-word, gull him into an (make a by-word of him by gulling him ?), *Twelfth Night, ii. 3.*

Babe, a cast-away, *A Winter's Tale, ii. 3*, near the end; love for a, *Macbeth, i. 7;* at my breast (the asp), *Antony and Cleopatra, v. 2.*

Baccare (to check over-forwardness), *Taming of the Shrew, ii. 1.*

Bacchus, song to, *Antony and Cleopatra, ii. 7.*

Bachelor, of threescore, a, *Much Ado about Nothing, i. 1;* determination to live a, *Much Ado about Nothing, i. 1, ii. 3;* less honourable, *As You Like It, iii. 3.*

Backgammon, spoken of under its old name "tables" in *Love's Labour's Lost, v. 2.*

Baffle, *1. Henry IV., i. 2.* To hang up by the heels; punishment of a recreant knight, probably alluded to again in *II. Henry IV., i. 2,* "to punish him by the heels," and in *All's Well that Ends Well, iv. 3,* "his heels have deserved it," etc.

Baffled (abused), *Richard II., i. 1.*

Bagot, Sir William, a character in *Richard II.,* introduced in *i. 3,* a parasite of the king.

Bag-pipe, the melancholy, *A Winter's Tale, iv. 3; I. Henry IV., i. 2.*

Baille (give), *Merry Wives of Windsor, i. 4.*

Bajazet's mute, *All's Well that Ends Well, iv. 1.* Meaning unknown.

Balcony-scene, *Romeo and Juliet, ii. 2.*

Balked (heaped or buried), *1. Henry IV., i. 1.* A balk is a little mound or ridge.

Ballad(s): of the king (Cophetua) and the beggar, *Love's Labour's Lost, i. 2;* Quince to write a, *Midsummer-Night's Dream, iv. 1;* sale of, *A Winter's Tale, iv. 3* or *4;* as a means of revenge, *I. Henry IV., ii. 2;* dread of being the subject of, *Antony and Cleopatra, v. 2,* "And scaled rhymers," etc.

Ballad-mongers, *I. Henry IV., iii. 1.*

Ballow (staff), *King Lear, iv. 6.*

Balm, healing of wounds by, *III. Henry VI., iv. 8; Timon of Athens, iii. 5; Macbeth, ii. 2;* meaning the oil for anointing kings, *Richard II., iii. 2; III. Henry VI., iii. 1;* medicinal gum, *Othello, v. 2.*

Balthasar, a servant of Portia in *Merchant of Venice, iii. 4.*

Balthasar, Romeo's servant, appears in *Romeo and Juliet, i. 1* and *v. 3.*

Balthazar, a merchant in *Comedy of Errors,* appears in *iii. 1.*

Balthazar, a servant of Don Pedro in *Much Ado about Nothing,* introduced in *i. 1.*

Banbury cheese, Slender called, *Merry Wives of Windsor, i. 1.* It was poor and thin.

Bangor, in Wales, scene of part of *I. Henru IV.*

Banishment, *Two Gentlemen of Verona, iii. 1; iv. 1;* of Rosalind, *As You Like It, i. 3;* of Bolingbroke and Norfolk, *Richard II., i. 3;* the bitter bread of, *Richard II., iii. 1;* of Coriolanus, *iii. 3;* of Romeo, *iii. 2, 3;* of Alcibiades, *Timon of Athens, iii. 5;* of Kent, *King Lear, i. 1;* real, *King Lear, i. 1.*

Bank'd, their towns (passed by the towns on the banks of rivers), *King John, v. 2.*

Bankrupt, a poor and broken, *As You Like It, ii. 1;* heart, a, *Romeo and Juliet, iii. 2;* servants of a, *Timon of Athens, iv. 2.*

Bankruptcy, *Timon of Athens, ii. 2; iii. 2.*

Banners, on outer walls, *Macbeth, v. 5.*

Banquet, served by spirits, *The Tempest, iii. 3;* of the Capulets, *Romeo and Juliet, i. 5;* for a mother, of her son's flesh, *Titus Andronicus, v. 2, 3.*

Banquo, an important character in *Macbeth,* a general in the army that suppressed the revolt, *i. 2.* The witches prophesy, in *i. 3,* that he shall be the father of a line of kings. See APPARITIONS. Like Macbeth, he is tempted to take measures for realizing the prophecy, *ii. 1,* "Restrain in me the cursed thoughts," etc., but he thrusts aside the temptation, and preserves his integrity and his loyalty. He is described by Macbeth, in *iii. 1,* and his murder planned; murdered, *iii. 3;* his ghost appears to Macbeth, *iii. 4.*

Baptism, of Elizabeth, *Henry VIII., v. 5;* symbol of, *Henry V., i. 2; Othello, ii. 3.*

Baptista, the player-queen in *Hamlet, iii. 2.* A man's name, though with the feminine ending.

Baptista Minola, father of Katherina and Bianca in *Taming of the Shrew,* introduced in *i. 1*—a "narrow-prying father."

Bar, Duke of, mentioned, *Henry V., iii. 5; iv. 8.*

Barabbas, *Merchant of Venice, iv. 1.* (See Matthew, xxvii. 20.)

Barbarians, Roman, *Coriolanus, iii. 1.*

Barbary, Bolingbroke's horse, *Richard II., v. 5.*

Barbason (a demon), *Merry Wives of Windsor, ii. 2, end; Henry V., ii. 1.*

Barber-monger (companion of barbers?), *King Lear, ii. 2.*

Barber's shop, forfeits in a, *Measure for Measure, v. 1.* Alluding to the custom of imposing forfeits for bad conduct on the loungers in barber-shops.

Barbury hen, a, *II. Henry IV., ii. 4.*

Bardolph, Lord, character in *II. Henry IV.,* appears in *i. 1.*

where he brings false news to Northumberland, and in *i. 3*, where he meets the other leaders of the rebellion.

Bardolph, one of the disreputable companions of Falstaff, character in the *Merry Wives of Windsor*, the two parts of *Henry IV.*, and *Henry V.* In the first three he is a corporal, in the last lieutenant. He is introduced in the first scene of the *Merry Wives of Windsor*, and in the second acts of the other plays. He is a great drunkard, and his red nose is the inspiration of continual jests (*Henry V.*, *i. 2, 3*). Falstaff calls him the "Knight of the Burning Lamp." His character is described in *Henry V.*, *iii. 2;* his face, *iii. 6.* He is sentenced for stealing a pyx, *iii. 6*, and hanged, *iv. 4, end.*

Barefoot, I must dance, *Taming of the Shrew, ii. 1.* Alluding to the notion that, if a younger sister were married first, the elder must dance barefoot at her wedding, or surely be an old maid.

Bargain, sold him a (taken him in), *Love's Labour's Lost, iii. 1;* close at a, *I. Henry IV., iii. 1.*

Barge, Cleopatra's, *Antony and Cleopatra, ii. 2.*

Bargulus (or Bardylis), *II. Henry VI., iv. 1.* Mentioned by Cicero. He was a pirate, and rose to be King of Illyria.

Barkloughly Castle, *Richard II., iii. 2.* No such castle is known.

Barm (yeast), *Midsummer-Night's Dream, ii. 1.*

Barnacles, we shall be turned to, *The Tempest, iv. 1.* There was a notion prevalent that the barnacle-goose was a transformation of the barnacle, an idea which gave rise to the custom in France of eating the bird on fast-days, as being of fishy substance.

Barnardine, a brutish prisoner in *Measure for Measure*, introduced in *iv. 3.*

Barnet, battle of (April 14, 1471), *III. Henry VI., v. 2, 3.*

Barrenness, supposed cure for, *Julius Cæsar, i. 2.*

Bartholomew, a page who plays the part of Sly's wife in the induction to the *Taming of the Shrew.*

Bartholomew-pig, *II. Henry IV., ii. 4.* Allusion to the roasted pigs which were a feature of the Smithfield Fair on Saint Bartholomew's Day.

Bartholomew-tide (August 24), *Henry V., v. 2.*

Basan, the hill of, *Antony and Cleopatra, iii. 11* or *13.* (See Psalm xxii., 12.)

Base, prisoner's, allusions to, *Two Gentlemen of Verona, i. 2;* the country, *Cymbeline, v. 4; Venus and Adonis, l. 303:* to bid the wind a base, to challenge it to run a race.

Basilisco-like, *King John, i. 1.* Name of a character, a braggart knight, in an old play, *Soliman and Perseda,* who insists on being addressed by his title.

Basilisk, the (or cockatrice), allusions to its supposed power of poisoning by its look, *Twelfth Night, iii. 4; A Winter's Tale, i. 2; II. Henry VI., iii. 2; III. Henry VI., iii. 2; Richard III., i. 2; iv. 1; Romeo and Juliet, iii. 2; Cymbeline, ii. 4; Lucrece, l. 540.*

Basilisks (pieces of ordnance), *I. Henry IV., ii. 3; Henry V., v. 2.*

Bassanio, a character in the *Merchant of Venice,* introduced in the first scene. It is to furnish him with the means to go as a suitor to the rich Portia that Antonio has borrowed from Shylock. In the early part of the play Bassanio appears a selfish and criminally careless fellow, a fortune-hunter, and hunting fortune at a fearful risk to his friend, whom he expects to repay with the money of his future wife. But in the later scenes of the play, when he makes his choice of the caskets, and particularly when Antonio is in danger and he is ready to sacrifice everything to his obligations to his friend, the more manly and genuine qualities of his nature are revealed, and justify the love in which he is held by Antonio and Portia.

Basset, a character in *I. Henry VI.,* a Lancastrian, appears in *iii. 4,* in a quarrel with Vernon, and again in *iv. 1.*

Bassianus, character in *Titus Andronicus,* brother of Saturninus, introduced in *i. 1,* where he offers himself as a candidate for the crown, and in the same scene he speaks of his love for Lavinia; his murder, *ii. 3.*

Basta (enough), *Taming of the Shrew, i. 1.*

Bastard (wine), *Measure for Measure, iii. 2; I. Henry IV., ii. 4.*

Bastard of Orleans. See ORLEANS.

Bastard(s), Perdita branded as a, *A Winter's Tale, ii. 3;* I love, *Troilus and Cressida, v. 8;* Edmund's soliloquy on, *King Lear, i. 2;* all, *Cymbeline, ii. 4;* in flowers, *A Winter's Tale, iv. 3.*

Bat, the, Ariel's steed, *The Tempest, v. 1;* flight of the, *Macbeth, iii. 2;* wool of the, in the witches' cauldron, *Macbeth, iv. 1.*

Bate (to blunt), *Love's Labour's Lost, i. 1;* (to flutter as a falcon preparing for flight), *Taming of the Shrew, iv. 1.*

Bates, a soldier in the king's army in *Henry V.,* first appears in *iv. 1,* where he speaks his mind about the king to the king himself in disguise.

Bath, a seething, *Sonnets cliii., cliv.*

Batler (used for beating soiled clothes in water), *As You Like It,* *ii. 4.*

Battle, orders in, criticised, *All's Well that Ends Well, iii. 6;* the dead in, *King John, ii. 2;* eagerness for, *I. Henry IV., iv. 1, 3,* "No more, no more"; conference before, *I. Henry IV., v. 1;* the sun on the morning of, *I. Henry IV., v. 1;* before a, *Henry V., iii. 7; iv., chorus; iv. 2, 3;* field of, *Henry V., iv. 7;* varying fortunes of, *III. Henry VI., ii. 5;* address to soldiers before, *Richard III., v. 3.*

Battle (often used instead of army), *Julius Cæsar, v. 1.*

Battles, *Cymbeline, v. 2, 3;* in France, *I. Henry VI., iv. 6;* between Greeks and Trojans, *Troilus and Cressida, v. 4, 5, 6;* between Glendower and Mortimer, *I. Henry IV., i. 1;* in France, *I. Henry VI., iv. 6.* See ACTIUM, AGINCOURT, BARNET, BOSWORTH, CORIOLI, DUNSINANE, MORTIMER'S CROSS, PHILIPPI, ST. ALBAN'S, SHREWSBURY, TEWKSBURY, TOWTON, WAKEFIELD.

Bavin (kindling or brush-wood), *I. Henry IV., iii. 2.*

Bawcock (beau coq), used for brave boy, *Twelfth Night, iii. 4; A Winter's Tale, i. 2.*

Bay, three pence a, *Measure for Measure, ii. 1;* the distance between the beams of a house, by the number of which the sizes of houses were reckoned.

Baynard's Castle, *Richard III., iii. 5.* A house where Richard had lived, on the bank of the river in Thames Street, London, said to have been built by a nobleman, Baynard, who came in with the Conqueror; it was burned twice, the second time in 1666.

Bayonne, Bishop of, *Henry VIII., ii. 4.*

Bay-trees, are withered, *Richard II., ii. 4.* The bay-tree was supposed to keep off sickness and the devil, so that its withering was an evil omen.

Beads (rosary), *Comedy of Errors, ii. 2; Richard II., iii. 3; Richard III., iii. 7.*

Beadsman, I will be thy (will pray for thee), *Two Gentlemen of Verona, i. 1.*

Beadsmen, *Richard II., ii. 2.*

Bear, Antigonus killed by a, *A Winter's Tale, iii. 3;* Sackerson, a famous, *Merry Wives of Windsor, i. 1;* a bush supposed a, *Midsummer-Night's Dream, v. 1;* and ragged staff, arms of Warwick, *II. Henry VI., v. 1;* unlicked whelp of a, *III. Henry VI., iii. 2;* betrayed with glasses, *Julius Cæsar, ii. 1.*

Bear, the (constellation), *Othello, ii. 1.*

Bear-baiting, allusion to, "fight the course," *Macbeth, v. 5.*

Beard, a cain-coloured (red), *Merry Wives of Windsor, i. 4;* on a woman, *Merry Wives of Windsor, iv. 2;* for an actor, *Midsummer-Night's Dream, i. 2;* Jove send thee a, *Twelfth Night, iii. 1;* greater than Dobbin's tail, *Merchant of Venice, ii. 2;* turned white with the news, *I. Henry IV., ii. 4;* a youth's, *Troilus and Cressida, i. 2;* of witches, *Macbeth, i. 3;* the insult of plucking the, *Hamlet, ii. 2;* "many a wart," etc., *King Lear, iii. 7;* shaving the, in respect, *Antony and Cleopatra, ii. 2.*

Bearing-cloth (christening-robe), *A Winter's Tale, iii. 3; I. Henry VI., i. 3.*

Bear in hand (keep along in expectation), *Measure for Measure, i. 5; II. Henry IV., i. 2; Macbeth, iii. 1.*

Beast(s), a, of good conscience, *Midsummer-Night's Dream, v. 1;* particular additions (attributes) of, *Troilus and Cressida, i. 2;* know their friends, *Coriolanus, ii. 1;* how betrayed, *Julius Cæsar, ii. 1;* strife among, *Timon of Athens, iv. 3;* would have mourned longer, *Hamlet, i. 2;* let a beast be lord of beasts, *Hamlet, v. 2;* since men prove, *Lucrece, l. 1148.*

Beatrice, the principal female character in *Much Ado about Nothing,* introduced in the first scene. She is perhaps the wittiest of Shakspere's women. Her raillery is unsparing, especially toward Benedick, whom she singles out from the first for special attack. But she is at the same time warm-hearted and affectionate, as shown by her faithful and generous defence of Hero, when every one else, even Hero's father, believed in her guilt.

"Her true love for Hero, her deep conviction of her innocence, her anger at the designed malice of her public dishonour, stir up her whole soul and convert it into a perfect contrast to that which we have seen in her hitherto. This scene (*iv. 1*) possesses infinite effect when performed without the least caricature, displaying those acutely sensitive natures in all their agitation of feeling, yet without falling into a sentimental tone, of which they are incapable. Sorrow for Hero and for the honour of her house makes Beatrice gentle, tender, and weakened into tears; this 'happy hour' facilitates to both their serious confession. But, at the same time, this hour of misfortune tests them [Benedick and Beatrice], accustomed as they are only to jest and raillery, by a heavy trial, in the sustaining of which we are convinced that these gifted natures are not devoid of that seriousness of life which regards no earnest situation with frivolity."—GERVINUS.

Beauchamp. See WARWICK.

Beaufort, Edmund and John. See SOMERSET.

Beaufort, Henry, Cardinal. See WINCHESTER.

Beaufort, Thomas. See Exeter.

Beaumond, Lord Henry, mentioned in *Richard II., ii. 2,* as one of Bolingbroke's adherents.

Beaumont, a French noble, killed at Agincourt, mentioned, *Henry V., iii. 5; iv. 8.*

Beautified, a vile phrase, *Hamlet, ii. 2.*

Beauty, that nothing ill can dwell in, *The Tempest, i. 2;* holiday time of, *Merry Wives of Windsor, ii. 1;* is a witch, *Much Ado about Nothing, ii. 1;* bought by judgment of eyes, *Love's Labour's Lost, ii. 1;* makes young, *Love's Labour's Lost, iv. 3;* praise of, *Love's Labour's Lost, iv. 3; Midsummer-Night's Dream, iii. 2; Cymbeline, v. 5; Merchant of Venice, i. 1;* deceitfulness of, *Merchant of Venice, iii. 2;* Portia's, *Merchant of Venice, iii. 2;* provoketh thieves, *As You Like It, i. 3;* with honesty, *As You Like It, iii. 3;* no more than may go dark to bed, *As You Like It, iii. 5;* of Helena, *All's Well that Ends Well, v. 3;* all by God, *Twelfth Night, i. 5;* scheduled, *Twelfth Night, i. 5;* purged pestilence, *Twelfth Night, i. 1;* virtue is, *Twelfth Night, iii. 4;* of a low-born lass, *A Winter's Tale, iv. 3;* short-lived, *Henry V., v. 2;* to be wooed, *I. Henry VI., v. 3;* if beauty have a soul, *Troilus and Cressida, v. 2;* without renown, *Coriolanus, i. 3;* unapproachable, *Romeo and Juliet, i. 1;* in comparison, *Romeo and Juliet, i. 2, end;* manly, *Romeo and Juliet, i. 3;* upon the cheek of night, *Romeo and Juliet, i. 5;* light of, *Romeo and Juliet, ii. 2;* with wickedness, *Romeo and Juliet, iii. 2;* and honesty, *Hamlet, iii. 1;* sense of, in inanimate objects, *Othello, ii. 1,* speech of Cassio; and ugliness, *Cymbeline, i. 6;* Imogen's, *Cymbeline, ii. 2; iii. 5, 6;* of the daughter of Antiochus, *Pericles, i. 1, 2;* child of, *Pericles, ii. 2; Venus and Adonis, l. 7;* dead, *Venus and Adonis, l. 1076;* effect of, on animals, *l. 1093;* needs no orator, *Lucrece, l. 29;* of Lucretia, *Lucrece, l. 52;* made more beauteous with truth, *Sonnet liv.;* the mark of slander, *Sonnet lxx.;* and flowers, *Sonnet xcix.;* unchanged, *Sonnet civ.;* descriptions of, *Sonnet cvi.;* traces of, *Lover's Complaint, l. 10;* manly, *Lover's Complaint, l. 85;* fleeting, *The Passionate Pilgrim, xiii.;* should be perpetuated in children, *Twelfth Night, i. 5; Sonnets i. to xvii.;* inspiration of poetry, *Sonnets lxxviii. to lxxx., lxxxiv.;* made richer by truth, *Sonnet liv.;* decay of, *Sonnets lx., lxv., lxvii.;* living in poetry, *Sonnets xv. to xix., lxiii., lxv., ci., cvii.;* change in, *Sonnets lxvii., lxviii.;* of the mind, *Sonnet lxix.*

Bedlam, the (lunatic), *II. Henry VI., iii. 1; King Lear, iii. 7, end.*
Bedlam beggar, tricks of a, *King Lear, ii. 3.*

Bedford, John, Duke of, third son of Henry IV., known as Prince John of Lancaster in *II. Henry IV.*, and as Duke of Bedford in *Henry V.* and *I. Henry VI.*, introduced in the second scene of the former, and first of the latter. He is represented in the play as having been at Harfleur and Agincourt, though he really stayed at home as lieutenant of the whole realm of England. Henry V., on his death-bed, made him Regent of France. He was prudent, patriotic, and skilful; the greatest blot on his record is his treatment of Joan of Arc, whom he caused to be burned as a witch. He is said to have died of grief for the Treaty of Arras, which united the Duke of Burgundy and Charles VII. His death (*I. Henry VI.*, *iii. 2*) occurred in 1435.

Beef, not good for the wit, *Twelfth Night, i. 3;* beef-witted, *Troilus and Cressida, ii. 1.* See MEATS.

Beelzebub, *Twelfth Night, v. 1.*

Beer, small, *II. Henry IV., ii. 2; Othello ii. 1.*

Bees, the, *The Tempest, v. 1, song;* murdered for their pains, *II. Henry IV., iv. 4;* commonwealth of, *Henry V., i. 2.*

Beetle, the, sufferings of, in death, *Measure for Measure, iii. 1;* shard-borne, *Macbeth, iii. 2; Antony and Cleopatra, iii. 2; Cymbeline, iii. 3.*

Beetle, a three-man (a pile-driver with three handles), *II. Henry IV., i. 2.*

Beggar(s), how a, should be answered, *Merchant of Venice, iv. 1;* a, made to think himself a king, *Taming of the Shrew, induction, i. ;* railing on the rich, *King John, ii. 2;* mounted, *III. Henry VI., i. 4;* book (learning) of, *Henry VIII., i. 1;* no comets seen at death of, *Julius Cæsar, ii. 1.*

Beggary, Falstaff on, *II. Henry IV., i. 2;* led by delay, *Richard III., iv. 3.*

Behaviour, what wert thou till this man showed thee? *Love's Labour's Lost, v. 2;* advice on, *Merchant of Venice, ii. 2; King Lear, i. 4,* "Have more than thou showest," etc.; an index of character, *Twelfth Night, i. 2;* advice to a young man on, *Hamlet, i. 3.*

Belarius, a banished lord in *Cymbeline,* introduced in *iii. 3.* He goes by the name of Morgan; tells his own story, *iii. 3;* his bravery, *v. 3;* avows his identity, *v. 5.*

Belch, Sir Toby, uncle of Olivia in *Twelfth Night,* introduced in *i. 3.*

"A drunkard, a coarse realist of the lowest sort, he yet possesses a slyness in seeing through the weaknesses of men who do not lie beyond his range of vision; rough and awkward in his manners, he yet so far knows how to assume the fashions of the town as to impose upon Sir Andrew; impudent enough to make an alehouse of Olivia's palace, and to take no heed when she orders him to leave, he yet knows how to keep on good footing with the servants of the house."

Belgia, *Comedy of Errors, iii. 2.*

Bellario, Doctor, Portia's cousin in Padua, *Merchant of Venice, iii. 4, iv. 1.*

Bellona's bridegroom (Macbeth), *Macbeth, i. 2.* Bellona was a Roman war goddess.

Bell(s), curfew, *The Tempest, v. 1; Measure for Measure, iv. 2; Romeo and Juliet, iv. 4; King Lear, iii. 4;* church, *As You Like It, ii. 7; Twelfth Night, v. 1;* book and candle, *King John, iii. 3;* passing, *II. Henry IV., i. 1; Romeo and Juliet, v. 3;* sweet, jangled, *Hamlet, iii. 1;* the funeral, *Hamlet, v. 1.*

Belly, the, and the members, fable of, *Coriolanus, i. 1.* A very old fable, perhaps by Æsop.

Belman, a dog, *Taming of the Shrew, induction, i.*

Belmont, scene of a part of the *Merchant of Venice.* It was the name of the residence of the heroine in the original tale, where it is only described as being on a gulf.

Benedick, an important character in *Much Ado about Nothing,* introduced in the first scene. The war of wit between him and Beatrice constitutes the great attractiveness of the play, and the plot by which each is made to believe in the infatuation of the other, and by which they are brought together, relieves the more serious plot against the honour of Hero. See BEATRICE.

Benedictions. See BLESSINGS.

Benefits, forgot, *As You Like It, ii. 7,* song.

Bennet, St., Church of, in Upper Thames Street, London, *Twelfth Night, v. 1.*

Bentivolii, family of Lucentio in *Taming of the Shrew, i. 1.*

Benvenuto (welcome), *Love's Labour's Lost, iv. 2; Taming of the Shrew, i. 2.*

Benvolio, character in *Romeo and Juliet,* first appearing in *i. 1,* Romeo's cousin and friend.

Berkeley, Thomes, fifth baron, character in *Richard II.,* introduced in *ii. 3.* He was one of the commission sent to notify Richard of his deposition.

Berkeley, a gentleman attending on Lady Anne in *Richard III.,* introduced in *i. 2.*

Berkeley Castle, in Gloucestershire, *Richard II., ii. 2, 3; I. Henry IV., i. 3.*

Bermoothes. See BERMUDAS.

Bermudas, the, *The Tempest, i. 2.* Spelled Bermoothes according to the Spanish pronunciation. One Silvester Jourdan had published, not long before this play was written, " A Discovery of the Bermudas, otherwise called the Isle of Divels," giving an account of the wreck of a ship of Sir George Somers. Purchas, too, in his " Pilgrimage," spoke of the Bermudas as " rent with tempests."

Bernardo, an officer in *Hamlet,* introduced in *i. 1.*

Berowne, or Biron(e), one of the lords attending on the king in *Love's Labour's Lost,* the most sharply characterized among them, a wit who, as Coleridge says, is " evidently the pre-existent state of Benedick" in *Much Ado about Nothing.* He is introduced in the first scene.

Berri, Duke of, *Henry V., iii. 5.*

Bertram, Count of Rousillon, character in *All's Well that Ends Well,* introduced in *i. 1,* a character very differently estimated by critics. Dr. Johnson says of it : " I cannot reconcile my heart to Bertram, a man noble without generosity, and young without truth ; who marries Helena as a coward, and leaves her as a profligate." Gervinus says : " The nobility of a fine nature is innate in Bertram ; his degeneracy into pride is only youthful error. . . . No inner mental life has yet penetrated his years of churlishness." While it is difficult to avoid regarding Bertram as something of a sneak, yet it seems evident that Shakspere meant to portray him as one whose errors spring from an overweening pride of birth excusable to the heir of a name and fortune like his, from the natural thoughtlessness of youth, and from the influence of the vile Parolles, and by no means unredeemable by the influence of a woman like Helena, when once he is brought to appreciate her worth.

Besort (attendance), *Othello, i. 3.*

Bestraught (distraught), *Taming of the Shrew, induction, 2.*

Beteem, to pour out, or to afford, *Midsummer-Night's Dream, i. 1;* to permit, *Hamlet, i. 2.*

Betrayal, of Antony, *iv. 10* or *12.*

Betrothals, *The Tempest, iii. 1; iv. 1; A Winter's Tale, iv. 8; Merchant of Venice, iii. 2;* violation of, *Measure for Measure, iii. 1;* secret, *Twelfth Night, iv. 3; v. 1;* proposed, *King John, ii. 1* or *2.*

Bevel (not morally upright), *Sonnet cxxi.*

Bevis, George, a follower of Jack Cade, *II. Henry VI., iv. 2.*

Bevis (of Hampton), *Henry VIII., i. 1.* Made Earl of Southampton by the Conqueror. There were wonderful stories of his bravery.

Bewilderment, like madness, *Twelfth Night, iv. 3; Venus and Adonis, l. 894.*

Bezonian (Italian *bisogno,* a beggar, or a raw recruit), *II. Henry IV., v. 3; II. Henry VI., iv. 1.*

Bianca, sister of the Shrew in the *Taming of the Shrew,* introduced in the first scene—a contrast to her sister.

Bianca, Cassio's mistress in *Othello,* introduced in *iii. 4.*

Bias, *Taming of the Shrew, iv. 5; Richard II., iii. 4.* A weight on one side of a bowl to incline it in running. Anything that ran against it was a rub.

Bible, the, allusions to: Adam, *Comedy of Errors, iv. 3; Love's Labour's Lost, iv. 2; Much Ado about Nothing, ii. 1; As You Like It, ii. 1; I. Henry IV., iii. 3; Henry V., i. 1; II. Henry VI., iv. 2; Hamlet, v. 1;* and Eve, *Love's Labour's Lost, v. 2; Richard II., iii. 4.* Eve, *Two Gentlemen of Verona, iii. 1; Merry Wives of Windsor, iv. 2; Love's Labour's Lost, i. 1; Twelfth Night, i. 5.* Cain, *Love's Labour's Lost, iv. 2; King John, iii. 4; Richard II., v. 6; II. Henry IV., i. 1; I. Henry VI., i. 3; Hamlet, v. 1.* Abel, *Richard II., i. 1; I. Henry VI., i. 3.* Abraham, *Merchant of Venice, i. 3; Richard II., iv. 1; Richard III., iv. 3.* Jacob, *Merchant of Venice, i. 3; ii. 5.* Laban, *Merchant of Venice, i. 3.* Hagar, *Merchant of Venice, ii. 5.* Noah, *Twelfth Night, iii. 2.* Japheth, *II. Henry IV., ii. 2.* The deluge, *Comedy of Errors, iii. 2.* The ark, *As You Like It, v. 4.* Pharaoh, *Much Ado about Nothing, iii. 3; I. Henry IV., ii. 4.* Jael, *The Tempest, iii. 2,* "Where thou mayst knock a nail into his head." Job, *Merry Wives of Windsor, v. 5; II. Henry IV., i. 2.* Deborah, *I. Henry VI., i. 2.* Daniel, *Merchant of Venice, iv. 1.* Nebuchadnezzar, *All's Well that Ends Well, iv. 5.* Samson, *Love's Labour's Lost, i. 2; I. Henry VI., i. 2; Henry VIII., v. 4.* Goliath, *Merry Wives of Windsor, v. 1; I. Henry VI., i. 2.* David, *II. Henry IV., iii. 2.* Achitophel, *II. Henry IV., i. 2.* Solomon, *Love's Labour's Lost, i. 2; iv. 3.* The Queen of Sheba, *Henry VIII., v. 5.* Jezebel, *Twelfth Night, ii. 5.* Jephthah, *II. Henry VI., iii. 2; III. Henry VI., v. 1; Hamlet, ii. 2.* Herod, *Henry V., iii. 3; Hamlet, iii. 2; Antony and Cleopatra, i. 2; iii. 3, 6; iv. 6.* Dives and Lazarus, *Richard II., iv. 1; I. Henry IV., iii. 3; iv. 2; Richard III., iv. 3.* The prodigal son, *Two Gentlemen*

*of Verona, ii. 3; Merry Wives of Windsor, iv. 5; Comedy of Errors,
iv. 3; As You Like It, i. 1; I. Henry IV., iv. 2; II. Henry IV., i.
2.* The legion of devils, *Merchant of Venice, i. 3; Twelfth Night,
iii. 4.* The house divided against itself, *Richard II., v. 5;* a camel
through a needle's eye, *Richard II., v. 5.* Judas, *Love's Labour's
Lost, v. 2; As You Like It, iii. 4; Richard II., iii. 2; iv. 1; III.
Henry VI., v. 7.* Pilate, *Richard II., iv. 1; Richard III., i. 4.*
Barabbas, *Merchant of Venice, iv. 1.* Golgotha, *Richard II., iv. 1;
Macbeth, i. 2.* The keys of Saint Peter, *Othello, iv. 2.* Saint Philip's
daughters, *I. Henry VI., i. 2.* Will have mercy on whom he will
have mercy, *Measure for Measure, i. 3.* Lead into temptation,
Measure for Measure, ii. 2. Spirits in prison, *Measure for Measure,
ii. 3.* Call brothers fools, *Merchant of Venice, i. 1.* The Nazarite,
Merchant of Venice, i. 3. The prayer for mercy, *Merchant of Venice,
iv. 1.* He that feeds the ravens, *As You Like It, ii. 3.* So holy writ
in babes hath judgment shown, etc., *All's Well that Ends Well, ii. 1.*
The canon of the law, etc., *King John, ii. 1,* an allusion to the second
commandment. The leopard change his spots, *Richard II., i. 1.*
Wisdom cries, *I. Henry IV., i. 2.* Return to vomit, *II. Henry IV.,
i. 3; Henry V., iii. 7.* Book of Numbers quoted, *Henry V., i. 2.*
Demon with lion gait, *Henry V., ii. 2.* Another fall of man, *Henry
V., ii. 2.* Wolf in sheep's clothing, *I. Henry VI., i. 3.* "*Medice te,*"
etc., *II. Henry VI., ii. 1.* Prayer for enemies, *Richard III., i. 3.*
As snow in harvest, *Richard III., i. 4.* Woe to that land, etc.,
Richard III., ii. 3. Of better luck than your master, *Henry VIII.,
v. 1.* The hill of Basan, *Antony and Cleopatra, iii. 11 or 13.*

Biggin, *II. Henry IV., iv. 4.* A head-band or cap of coarse linen.

Bigot, Robert (correctly Roger), second Earl of Norfolk, a character in *King John,* introduced in *iv. 3.* He was one of the twenty-five barons opposed to the king. See NORFOLK.

Bilbo (sword), *Merry Wives of Windsor, i. 1; iii. 5.* Fine swords were made at Bilboa in Spain.

Billiards, *Antony and Cleopatra, ii. 5.* An anachronism, as it is a modern game.

Bills, on their necks, *As You Like It, ii. 1.* Alluding to the weapon called a bill.

Biondello, one of the servants of Lucentio in *Taming of the
Shrew,* introduced in *i. 1.*

Birds, singing of, dependent on the listener, *Merchant of Venice,
v. i.* The ousel, throstle, wren, etc., *A Midsummer-Night's Dream,
iii. 1, song.* For other references, see under names of species.

Birnam Wood, prophecy concerning, *Macbeth, iv. 1;* its fulfilment, *v. 4, 5.*

Biron or Birone. See Berowne.

Birth, crying at, *King Lear, iv. 6.*

Birth. See Blood and Rank.

Bis coctus (twice cooked), *Love's Labour's Lost, iv. 2.*

Bisson (blinding), *Hamlet, ii. 2; Coriolanus, ii. 1; iii. 1.*

Blackbird, the. See Ousel.

Black-Friars, London, scene of *Henry VIII., ii. 4.*

Blackheath, in Kent, six miles southeast of London, scene of *II. Henry VI., iv, 2* and *3.*

Black Monday, *Merchant of Venice, ii. 5.* Easter Monday, so called from the violent storm of wind, hail, and lightning, April 14, 1360, to which King Edward III., with his army, was exposed on that day, near Chartres in France.

Blanch of Spain, daughter of Alphonso, King of Castile, and niece of King John, appears in *King John, ii. 1.*

Blasphemy, in the lowly and in the great, *Measure for Measure, ii. 2;* Sebastian called, *The Tempest, v. 1.*

Blench (move), *Measure for Measure, iv. 5.*

Blessedness, single, *A Midsummer-Night's Dream, i. 1.*

Blessings, invoked, *The Tempest, v. 1; Two Gentlemen of Verona, i. 1; Twelfth Night, iii. 1; Richard III., ii. 2; Coriolanus, i. 5; Othello, ii. 1.*

Blind man, a pretended, *II. Henry VI., ii. 1.*

Blindness, the best use of one's eyes, to see the way of, *Cymbeline, v. 4.*

Blindworm, *A Midsummer-Night's Dream, ii. 2; Macbeth, iv. 1.* A little snake with very small eyes, supposed to be very venomous.

Blood, swooning at sight of, *As You Like It, iv. 3;* drunk by the earth, *I. Henry IV., i. 1;* stains of, *Macbeth, ii. 2; v. 1;* will have blood—"I am stept in so far," *Macbeth, iii. 4;* circulation of the, *Measure for Measure, ii. 4; King John, iii. 3; II. Henry IV., v. 2; II. Henry VI., iii. 2; Coriolanus, i. 1; Romeo and Juliet, iv. 1; Julius Cæsar, ii. 1; Macbeth, ii. 2; Hamlet, i. 5; Othello, iv. 2; Lucrece, l. 1747.*

Blood (in the sense of ancestry), claims of, *As You Like It, i. 1;* distinctions of, *All's Well that Ends Well, ii. 3;* no sure foundation of, *King John, iv. 2;* sacredness of royal, *Richard II., i. 2;* conduct unworthy royal, *I. Henry IV., iii. 2;* weighed against learning (a beggar's book), *Henry VIII., i. 1;* a boil, etc., in my, *King Lear, ii. 4;* ties of, and evidence of good, *Cymbeline, iv. 2, 4.*

Blood-boltered (clotted), *Macbeth, iv. 1.*

Blow, blow, thou winter wind—song, *As You Like It, ii. 7.*

Blue-caps (Scotchmen, so called from their blue bonnets), *I. Henry IV., ii. 4.*

Blunt, Sir James, character in *Richard III.,* first appears in *v. 2,* a partisan of Richmond. He was a great-grandson of the Sir Walter Blunt in *I. Henry IV.*

Blunt, Sir Thomas, mentioned in *Richard II., v. 6,* as having been executed.

Blunt, Sir Walter, character in *I. Henry IV.,* introduced in *i. 1,* where the king calls him "a dear, a true industrious friend." In the battle of Shrewsbury, *act v., scene 3,* he is dressed in one of the king's coats, and Douglas, mistaking him for the king, kills him. His son, Sir John Blunt, is mentioned in the next play, *iv. 3.*

Bluntness, *Julius Cæsar, iii. 2,* "I have neither wit," etc.; *King Lear, ii. 2.*

Blushes, *Much Ado about Nothing, iv. 1; All's Well that Ends Well, ii. 3; Lucrece, l. 59.*

Boar, the (Richard III., whose device was a boar), *Richard III., iii. 2;* of Thessaly, *Antony and Cleopatra, v. 2; iv. 13;* hunting the wild, *Venus and Adonis, lines 614, 1105.*

Boar's Head Tavern. See EASTCHEAP.

Boasters. See BRAGGARTS.

Boasting, *Merry Wives of Windsor, ii. 3; As You Like It, i. 2; King John, ii. 1; ii. 2; Henry V., iii. 7; iv. 3, 4;* foolish, *Lucrece, l. 33.*

Boatswain, a, character in *The Tempest, i. 1.*

Bobbed (got by cheating), *Othello, v. 1.*

Bocchus, King of Lydia, *Antony and Cleopatra, iii. 6.*

Bodies, our, our gardens, *Othello, i. 3,* Iago; over-care of, *Sonnet cxlvi.*

Bohemia, scene of part of *A Winter's Tale.*

Bohun, Edward, *Henry VIII., ii. 1.* See BUCKINGHAM, EDWARD STAFFORD, DUKE OF.

Boldness, in a subject, *I. Henry IV., i. 3.*

Boleyn (or Bullen), Anne, maid of honour to Queen Katherine and afterward queen, a character in *Henry VIII.,* introduced in *i. 4,* where she dances with the king, an incident that took place at a banquet given by the king in 1527 to ambassadors from Francis I.

She would not be a queen, *ii. 3 ;* made a marchioness, *ii. 3 ;* married, *iii. 2.* This was January 25, 1533, or, according to some writers, November 14, 1532. In *iii. 2,* Suffolk says, "I persuade me, from her will fall some blessing to this land, which shall in it be memorized," a reference to her daughter Elizabeth. In the same scene, Wolsey speaks of her as the weight that pulled him down, he having planned that the king should marry the sister of the King of France after being divorced from Katherine. Anne's coronation and beauty, *iv. 1 ;* the birth of Elizabeth, *v. 1.* Anne was beheaded in 1536.

"With what a delicate and yet luxuriant grace is she sketched off, with her gaiety and her beauty, her levity, her extreme mobility, her sweetness of disposition, her tenderness of heart, and, in short, all her femalities! How characteristic that she should first express unbounded pity for her mistress, insisting chiefly on her fall from her regal state and worldly pomp, thus betraying her own disposition!"—MRS. JAMESON.

Bolingbroke, Henry of, Duke of Hereford, and afterward Henry IV. See HENRY IV.

Bolingbroke, Roger, a conjuror in *II. Henry VI. ;* first appears in *i. 4.*

Bolt, the fool's. See PROVERBS.

Bolting-hutch, *I. Henry IV., ii. 4.* A bin where meal is bolted.

Bombast (cotton used for wadding garments), *Love's Labour's Lost, v. 2 ; I. Henry IV., ii. 4.*

Bombard (a leather drinking-vessel), *1. Henry IV., ii. 4 ; Henry VIII., v. 4.*

Bona, Lady, the Princess Bonne of Savoy, a sister of the French queen, character in *III. Henry VI.,* introduced in *iii. 3.* In *ii. 6,* Warwick proposes to ask her in marriage for Edward, which he does in *iii. 3,* just before the news of Edward's marriage with the Lady Grey is announced by post. Edward's treatment of her is used against his heir by Richard in *Richard III., iii. 7.* The story of Edward's suit to her is not well authenticated.

Bona-robas (courtesans), *II. Henry IV., iii. 2.*

Bona terra, etc., *II. Henry VI., iv. 7.* Good land, bad people.

Bond(s), his words are, *Two Gentlemen of Verona, ii. 7 ;* for a pound of flesh, a, *Merchant of Venice, iii. 2, 3, 5 ; iv. 1 ;* of heaven, *Troilus and Cressida, v. 2 ;* of life, the, *Macbeth, iii. 2.*

Bondage, is hoarse, *Romeo and Juliet, ii. 2 ;* deliverance from, *Julius Cæsar, i. 3 ;* a way to liberty, *Cymbeline, v. 4.*

Bonfire, the everlasting, *Macbeth, ii. 3.*

Book, of songs and sonnets, *Merry Wives of Windsor, i. 1;* quarrelling by, *As You Like It, v. 4;* advice for a, *Sonnet lxvii.*

Book (magic), *The Tempest, v. 1.*

Book (learning), *II. Henry VI., iv. 7; Henry VIII., i. 1.*

Book (writing on a tablet), *Cymbeline, v. 4.*

Book-knowledge, ridiculed in Armado, in *Love's Labour's Lost.*

Book of Life, the, *Richard II., i. 3.*

Books, women are the, *Love's Labour's Lost, iv. 3,* near the end; in brooks, *As You Like It, ii. 1;* of our forefathers, *II. Henry VI., iv. 7;* binding of, *Romeo and Juliet, i. 3; iii. 2;* love in, *Sonnet xxiii.*

Books (favour), in one's, *Much Ado about Nothing, i. 1.*

Boot (advantage), *I. Henry VI., iv. 6.*

Borachio, the villainous follower of Don John in *Much Ado about Nothing,* who invents the plot against Hero and acts the part of her pretended lover; first appears in *i. 3.*

Bore, a, *I. Henry IV., iii. 1,* "O he's as tedious," etc.; *Venus and Adonis, l. 845.*

Boreas (the north wind), *Troilus and Cressida, i. 3.*

Bores (stabs), *Henry VIII., i. 1.*

Borough, the head (in some modern editions the third). Verges in *Much Ado about Nothing.* The former was an officer of the borough; the third borough was a constable.

Borrowing, dulls husbandry, *Hamlet, i. 3.*

Bosworth Field, battle of, August 22, 1485. This battle, where Richmond, afterward Henry VII., defeated Richard III., was the last of the Wars of the Roses. The field, or moor, is in Leicestershire. It is the scene of *Richard III., v. 3, 4.*

Botcher (cobbler), *All's Well that Ends Well, iv. 3.*

Bottle (bundle), of hay, *Midsummer-Night's Dream, iv. 1.*

Bottom (spool, shuttle), of thread, *Two Gentlemen of Verona, iii. 2; Taming of the Shrew, iv. 3.*

Bottom, Nick, a weaver, character in *A Midsummer-Night's Dream,* introduced in *i. 2.* In the play before the duke he takes the part of Pyramus.

"Bottom, in his broad-blown self-importance, his all but impenetrable self-satisfaction, stands a head and shoulders higher in absurdity than any other comic personage in Shakspere's early plays. He is the admitted king of his company, the cock of his walk, and he has a consciousness that his gifts are more than equal to his opportunities."—DOWDEN.

Bouciqualt, mentioned, *Henry V., iii. 5; iv. 8.*

Boult, a servant, in *Pericles*; first appears in *iv. 3.*

Bounds. See LIMITS.

Bounty, should have eyes behind, *Timon of Athens, i. 2;* mars men, *Timon of Athens, iv. 2;* that begs to be asked, *Antony and Cleopatra, iii. 11;* no winter in, *Antony and Cleopatra, v. 2.*

Bourbon, John, Duke of, character in *Henry V.*; first appears in *iii. 5,* where he talks vaingloriously of the easy conquest that will be made of the English.

Bourbon, Lord High Admiral, addressed in *III. Henry VI., iii. 3.* He was a grandson of the preceding.

Bourchier, Thomas, Archbishop of Canterbury and Cardinal, character in *Richard III.*, first appears in *iii. 1.* His mother was a daughter of the Duchess of Gloucester in *Richard II.* He had taken sides with the Yorkists, and crowned Edward IV., Richard III., and Henry VII. (Richmond).

Bourdeaux, scene of *I. Henry VI., iv. 2, 5.*

Bourn (burn, rivulet, or boundary), *Troilus and Cressida, ii. 3;* this chalky, *King Lear, iv. 6;* of the undiscovered country, *Hamlet, iii. 1.*

Bowling, allusions to, *Taming of the Shrew, iv. 5; Richard II., iii. 4; Coriolanus, v. ii;* rub on, etc., *Troilus and Cressida, iii. 2;* kissed the jack, *Cymbeline, ii. 1.*

Bow, the, is bent and drawn, *King Lear, i. 1.*

Boyet, a lord attending on the Princess of France in *Love's Labour's Lost,* an accomplished courtier wittily described by Berowne (Biron) in *act v., scene 2.* He first appears in *ii. 1.*

Boy(s), the whining schoolboy, *As You Like It, ii. 7;* life and ideas of, *A Winter's Tale, i. 2;* demureness in, *II. Henry VI., ii. 3;* a bright, *Richard III., iii. 1;* unrespective, *Richard III., iv. 2;* sacrifice to present pleasure, *Antony and Cleopatra, i. 4.*

Brabant, Duke of, mentioned, *Henry V., iii. 5; iv. 8.*

Brabantio, a Venetian senator, character in *Othello,* introduced in *i. 1,* the father of Desdemona. His death, *v. 2.*

Brach (a hound), *Taming of the Shrew, Induction i.*

Bracy, Sir John, mentioned in *I. Henry IV., ii. 4.*

Braggarts, *Much Ado about Nothing, v. 1; Two Gentlemen of Verona, ii. 4; All's Well that Ends Well,* Parolles in, *iv. 3,* etc.; tediousness of, *I. Henry IV., iii. 1;* I cannot choose, etc., *Romeo and Juliet, ii. 6;* They are but beggars, etc.; wear their daggers in their mouth, *Cymbeline, iv. 2.*

Braid (deceitful), *All's Well that Ends Well, iv. 2.*

Brains, boiled, *The Tempest, v. 1;* dry, *As You Like It, ii.* 7; idle comments of—dwelling of the soul, *King John, v. 7;* when the brains were out, the man would die, *Macbeth, iii. 4;* diminution of, restores heart, or courage, *Antony and Cleopatra, iii. 11* or *13, end;* forgeries of the, *Lucrece, l. 460.* See VENTRICLE OF MEMORY.

Brakenbury, Sir Robert, Lieutenant of the Tower, character in *Richard III.;* first appears in *i. 1;* his death, *v. 5.*

Brakes (thickets), of vice, *Measure for Measure, ii. 1.*

Brandon, Sir William, character in *Richard III.,* first appears in *v. 3,* in Richmond's army. He fell at Bosworth, *v. 5.*

Brandon, character in *Henry VIII.,* introduced in *i. 1.* The Duke of Buckingham was arrested by one Sir Henry Marney.

Brave, address to the, *Coriolanus, i. 6,* "Those are they," etc.

Bravery, of the princes, *I. Henry IV., v. 4;* of Talbot and his son, *I. Henry VI., iv. 5;* in war, *Coriolanus, i. 4, 5; ii. 2; Cymbeline, v. 3;* of Posthumus, *Cymbeline, v. 5.*

Bravery (fine apparel), *Taming of the Shrew, iv. 3.*

Brawl (a dance), *Love's Labour's Lost, iii. 1.*

Brawl, a, *Othello, ii. 3.*

Brazier, a, *Henry VIII., v. 4.*

Breach, once more unto the, *Henry V., iii. 1.*

Breast (voice), *Twelfth Night, ii. 3.*

Brecknock, *Richard III., iv. 2.* Buckingham's castle in South Wales, built in the time of the Conqueror, destroyed during the Civil War. The keep is still standing.

Breeches, *Two Gentlemen of Verona, ii. 7.*

Breeching scholar, *Taming of the Shrew, iii. 1.* To breech was an old term meaning to whip, used in *Merry Wives of Windsor, iv. 1,* "You must be breeched." A breeching scholar was a boy subject to whipping.

Breeding, of Orlando, *As You Like It, i. 1.*

Breese, or brize, *Antony and Cleopatra, iii. 8–10.* The gadfly.

Brentford, fat woman, or witch of, *Merry Wives of Windsor, iv. 2, 5.* Supposed to be a well-known personage of Shakspere's day, named Gillian.

Bretagne, John de Montfort, Duke of, mentioned in *Richard II., ii. 1,* as furnishing Bolingbroke with ships. Henry IV. afterward married his widow, Joan of Navarre.

Bretagnes, *Richard III., v. 3.*

Brevity, of fair things, *Midsummer-Night's Dream, i. 1;* the soul of wit, *Hamlet, ii. 2.*

Brewer's Horse, a, *I. Henry IV., iii. 3.* He carried the liquor on his back.

Bribery, attempt at, *Merry Wives of Windsor, iv. 6;* openness to, *All's Well that Ends Well, iv. 3;* used, *II. Henry IV., iii. 2;* contempt for, *Julius Cæsar, iv. 3;* defeats justice, *Hamlet, iii. 3,* speech of the king; *Cymbeline, ii. 3; iii. 3.*

Bribe-Buck (a stolen one), *Merry Wives of Windsor, v. 5.*

Bridegroom, dress of a, *Taming of the Shrew, iii. 2.*

Bridewell, palace at, scene of *Henry VIII., iii. 1, 2.*

Bridge, what need the, much broader than the flood, *Much Ado about Nothing, i. 1.*

Bridge, defence of the, *Henry V., iii. 6.* Over the Ternois, at Blangi. The French tried to break it down, but the English seized and held it till the army passed over on the way to Calais.

Bridget, Mistress, alluded to, *Merry Wives of Windsor, ii. 2.*

Bridgnorth, in Salopshire, twenty miles from Shrewsbury, forces to meet at, *I. Henry IV., iii. 2, end.*

Brief (betrothal), *All's Well that Ends Well, ii. 3.*

Brief (inventory), *Antony and Cleopatra, v. 2.*

Briers, world full of, *As You Like It, i. 3.*

Bring in (call to the tapster), *I. Henry IV., i. 2.*

Britain, scene of part of *Cymbeline;* its natural strength, *Cymbeline, iii. 1;* a swan's nest, *Cymbeline, iii. 4.* See ENGLAND.

British, bravery of the, *Cymbeline, ii. 4.*

Brocas, Sir Bernard, mentioned in *Richard II., v. 6,* as having been beheaded for adherence to Richard.

Broker, a crafty knave, *II. Henry VI., i. 2,*

Brooding, on what's done, *Macbeth, iii. 2.*

Brook, or Broom, name by which Ford gets himself introduced to Falstaff, *Merry Wives of Windsor, ii. 2.*

Brooks, books in the running, *As You Like It, ii. 1.*

Broom. See BROOK.

Brothers, fight between, *As You Like It, i. 1;* duty to avenge the death of, *Richard II., i. 2.*

Brownist, a (one of a sect of Puritans), *Twelfth Night, iii. 2.*

Bruit (report), *III. Henry VI., iv. 7.*

Brunette, a, *Sonnets cxxvii., cxxx., cxxxi., cxxxii., cxlviii.*

Brutus, Junius, a tribune of the people, character in *Coriolanus,* introduced in *i. 1;* Menenius on, *ii. 1.* See SICINIUS.

Brutus, there was a, once, *Julius Cæsar, i. 2.* Lucius Junius Brutus, prominent in the expulsion of the Tarquins and in turning the kingdom into a republic. When consul afterward, he condemned his sons to death for an attempt to restore the kingdom. He is again alluded to in *ii. 1,* " My ancestors did from the streets of Rome," in the argument to Lucrece, and at *lines 1734, 1807.*

Brutus, Marcus Junius, the most important character in the play *Julius Cæsar;* first appears in *i. 2,* talking with Cassius of the danger to the republic from Cæsar; his struggles, *ii. 1;* regretful thoughts of, *ii. 2, end ;* the assassination, *iii. 1 ;* justifies it, *iii. 1 ;* his speech, *iii. 2 ;* his love of books and music, *iv. 3 ;* sees Cæsar's ghost, *iv. 3 ;* on self-murder, *v. 1 ;* farewell to Cassius, *v. 1 ;* his death, *v. 5.*

" I do not at present see into Shakspere's motive, his *rationale,* or in what point of view he meant Brutus's character to appear. . . . Surely, nothing can seem more discordant with our historical preconceptions of Brutus, or more lowering to the intellect of the Stoico-Platonic tyrannicide, than the tenets here attributed to him—to him, the stern Roman republican—namely, that he would have no objection to a king, or to Cæsar, monarch in Rome, would Cæsar but be as good a monarch as he now seems disposed to be ! How, too, could Brutus say that he found no personal cause—none in Cæsar's past conduct as a man ? Had he not passed the Rubicon ? Had he not entered Rome as a conqueror ? Had he not placed his Gauls in the Senate ? . . . What character did Shakspere mean his Brutus to be ?"—Coleridge.

Brutus " acts as an idealist and theorizer might, with no eye for the actual bearing of facts, and no sense of the true importance of persons. Intellectual doctrines and moral ideas rule the life of Brutus; and his life is most noble, high, and stainless, but his public action is a series of practical mistakes. Yet, even while he errs, we admire him, for all his errors are those of a pure and lofty spirit. He fails to see how full of power Antony is, because Antony loves pleasure, and is not a Stoic like himself; he addresses calm arguments to the excited Roman mob; he spares the life of Antony, and allows him to address the people; he advises ill in military matters. All the practical gifts, insight, and tact which Brutus lacks are possessed by Cassius ; but of Brutus's moral purity, veneration of ideals, disinterestedness, and freedom from unworthy personal motive, Cassius possesses little. And the moral power of Brutus has in it something magisterial, which enables it to oversway the practical judgment of Cassius."—Dowden.

He is spoken of in *II. Henry VI., iv. 1 ;* in *Antony and Cleopatra ii. 6,* Pompey speaks of his motive; and in *iii. 9* or *11,* Antony calls him the mad Brutus.

Bubbles, the earth hath, *Macbeth, i. 3.*

Bubukles (pimples), *Henry V., iii. 6.*

Buckingham, Edward Stafford, Duke of. He calls himself Edward Bohun (*ii. 1*), as he was descended from the Bohuns, and from them inherited his office of constable, an office forfeited at his death, and never again revived in England. A character in *Henry VIII.*, introduced in the first scene, where he is arrested for treason. His surveyor's testimony against him is given in *i. 2*, where the king admits his learning and eloquence. He is condemned in *ii. 1*, and speaks to the people. He was accused of aspiring to the throne, and was executed in 1521. The Buckingham of *Richard III.* was his father.

Buckingham, Henry Stafford, Duke of, character in *Richard III.*, first appears in *i. 3*. He was one of Richard's most powerful friends; in *iii. 7*, he tries to make the people declare him king, and offers him the crown. But he became disaffected because Richard would not grant him the earldom of Hereford, to which he had a claim, *iv. 2*, and joined in the conspiracy to place Richmond on the throne. He headed an insurrection in Wales, *iv. 3;* but his army was broken up by sudden floods, and deserted. He fled, but was taken, *iv. 4*, and executed at Salisbury, *v. 1.* His ghost appears to Richard, *v. 3*. He was a grandson of the Buckingham of *II. Henry VI.*, and son of Sir Humphrey Stafford.

Buckingham, Humphrey Stafford, Duke of, character in *II. Henry VI.;* first appears in *i. 1.* He is on the side of the king. In *III. Henry VI.*, *i. 1*, Edward, Earl of March, boasts of having wounded him at St. Alban's, where his son, Lord Stafford, was slain. He fell at the battle of Northampton in 1460. He was the son of the Lord Stafford mentioned in *I. Henry IV.*, *v. 3*, as having been slain for the king, and the Buckingham of *Richard III.* was his grandson, son of the Lord Stafford who fell at St. Alban's.

Buckle (bend), *II. Henry IV., i. 1.*

Bucklers, give the (surrender), *Much Ado about Nothing, v. 2.*

Bucklersbury, a place in the outskirts of London where herbs and drugs were sold, *Merry Wives of Windsor, iii. 3.*

Buckram, cases of (oversuits), *I. Henry IV., i. 2.*

Buckram Scene, the, *I. Henry IV., ii. 4.*

Bucks (household washing), *II. Henry VI., iv. 2;* buck-basket, *Merry Wives of Windsor, iii. 5.*

Bug (bugbear), *Taming of the Shrew, i. 2*, and elsewhere; **War-**wick was the bug that feared us all, *III. Henry VI., v. 2.*

Builder, the strongest, *Hamlet, v. 1.*

Bulks (projecting show-windows or outside stalls), *Coriolunus*, *ii. 1; Othello, v. 1.*

Bull, the savage, etc., *Much Ado about Nothing, i. 1;* line from "The Spanish Tragedy," by Thomas Kyd, printed in 1603, but played before that time. It was much ridiculed by Kyd's contemporaries.

Bull-Baiting, allusions to, *Troilus and Cressida, v. 8; v. 7,* "Now bull, now dog!"

Bullcalf, one of the recruits in *II. Henry IV.*, appears in *iii. 2.*

Bullets, paper, *Much Ado about Nothing, ii. 3;* leaden messengers, *All's Well that Ends Well, iii. 2.*

Bully Monster, *The Tempest, v. 1.*

Bully Rook (a bold, bluff, rollicking fellow), *Merry Wives of Windsor, ii. 1.*

Bully Stale, *Merry Wives of Windsor, ii. 3.* Bully was a favourite word with the host of the Garter.

Bunch of Grapes, the, *Measure for Measure, ii.* 1. It was customary to give such names to rooms in taverns. See DOLPHIN CHAMBER, and JERUSALEM CHAMBER.

Bung (cant for purse, here cutpurse), *II. Henry IV., ii. 4.*

Bunting, took this lark for a, *All's Well that Ends Well, ii. 3.* A bird like the lark, but songless.

Burgh, Hubert de. See HUBERT DE BURGH.

Burgonet (helmet), *II. Henry VI., v. 1; Antony and Cleopatra, i. 5.* An anachronism.

Burgundy, Duchess of, *III. Henry VI., ii. 1.* She was third cousin to the young Plantagenets, though she is spoken of as their "kind aunt."

Burgundy, Duke of, character in *King Lear*, appears in *i. 1*, a suitor for Cordelia; but he withdraws the suit when she is disinherited. He is called "waterish Burgundy."

Burgundy, Philip the Good, Duke of, a character in *Henry V.*, where he appears in the last scene, and in *Henry VI.*, first appearing in *ii. 1.* His sister was married to Bedford, and he was in alliance with the English till 1435, when he was reconciled to the Dauphin through the mediation of the pope. In *iii. 3* he is represented as won over by Joan of Arc. His letter to Henry, announcing his change of alliance, *iv. 1.*

Burial, Christian, given to a suicide, *Hamlet, v. 1;* with the head to the east, *Cymbeline, iv. 2.*

Burn, burning out a, *Romeo and Juliet, i. 2.*

Burs, in the heart, *As You Like It, i. 3.*

Burton-Heath (Barton-on-the-Heath), in Warwickshire, *Taming of the Shrew, induction, 2.*

Bury St. Edmund's, abbey of, in Suffolk, scene of *II. Henry VI., i. 2.*

Bush, the thief doth fear each, *III. Henry VI., v. 1;* good wine needs no, *As You Like It, v. 4.* A bush of ivy was used at a vintner's door, ivy being sacred to Bacchus.

Bushy, Sir John, a character in *Richard II.,* introduced in *i. 3.* He is a parasite of the king's. "In this 22 year of King Richard the common fame ran that the King had letten to farm the realm unto Sir William Scrope, Earl of Wiltshire, and then Treasurer of England, to Sir John Bushy, Sir John Bagot, and Sir Henry Green, Knights." In the play only the Earl of Wiltshire is mentioned as having the realm in farm.

Business, promptness in that, which we love, *Antony and Cleopatra, iv. 4.*

Butcher, privilege to a, *II. Henry VI., iv. 3.* Referring to the practice of favouring some butchers by permits to kill a certain number of cattle every week in Lent.

But shall I go mourn, song, *A Winter's Tale, iv. 3.*

Butter, pitiful-hearted, *I. Henry IV., ii. 4.*

Butterfly(ies), painted, *Midsummer Night's Dream, iii. 1;* your, was a grub, *Coriolanus, v. 4;* show not their mealy wings but to the summer, *Troilus and Cressida, iii. 3.*

Buttery-bar, *Twelfth Night, i. 3.*

Buttons, 'tis in his (he can do it), *Merry Wives of Windsor, iii. 1;* (buds) *Hamlet, i. 3.*

Butts, Sir William, the king's physician in *Henry VIII.,* introduced in *v. 2.* He was a friend of Cranmer and adherent of the Protestant cause.

Butt-shaft (arrow to be shot at a butt or mark), *Love's Labour's Lost, i. 2, end.*

" But yet," dislike for, *Antony and Cleopatra, ii. 5.*

By (aby, abide, pay for), *III. Henry VI., v. 1.*

Cabin'd, cribb'd, confin'd, *Macbeth, iii. 4.*

Cacodæmon (an evil spirit), *Richard III., i. 3.*

Caddises (crewels or braid), *A Winter's Tale, iv. 3 or 4.*

Cade, Jack, leader of Cade's rebellion in 1450, who called himself

Mortimer. The murder of Suffolk at Dover was followed by a rumor that the king would take vengeance on the people of Kent, and this was the immediate cause of the insurrection, though under the king's weak rule there were real grievances to be redressed. Cade is a character in *II. Henry VI.*, introduced in *iv. 2.* History says nothing of York's agency as spoken of in *iii. 1.* In *iv. 6*, he takes possession of the capital by striking his staff on London stone (*q. v.*). He is killed by Iden, *iv. 10.*

Cadmus (the legendary founder of Thebes, who introduced the alphabet into Greece), *Midsummer-Night's Dream, iv. 1.*

Caduceus (Mercury's rod), *Troilus and Cressida, ii. 3.*

Cadwal. See ARVIRAGUS.

Cadwallader, *Henry V., v. 1.* The last Welsh king.

Cæsar, Julius, appears first in the second scene of the play that bears his name; his physical feebleness described by Cassius, *i. 2 ;* his fearlessness, *ii. 2 ;* his refusal of the suit of Metellus, and his death, *iii. 1 ;* his ghost, *iv. 3 ;* Octavius promises to avenge him, *v. 1 ;* avenged, *v. 3,* "Thy spirit walks abroad," etc.

"The character of Cæsar is conceived in a curious and almost irritating manner. Shakspere (as passages in other plays show) was certainly not ignorant of the character of one of the world's greatest men. But here it is his weaknesses that are insisted on. He is failing in body and mind, influenced by superstition, yields to flattery, thinks of himself as almost superhuman, has lost some of his insight into character, and his sureness and swiftness of action. Yet the play is rightly named *Julius Cæsar.* His bodily presence is weak, but his spirit rules throughout the play, and rises after death in all its might, towering over the little band of conspirators, who at length fall before the spirit of Cæsar as it ranges for revenge."— DOWDEN.

Allusions to Cæsar: The hook-nosed fellow, *II. Henry IV., iv. 2 ;* quoted, *II. Henry VI., iv. 7 ;* began the Tower, *Richard II., v. 1 ; Richard III., iii. 1.* He did not build any part of it. Ship that bare, *I. Henry VI., i. 2 ;* commentaries of, *II. Henry VI., iv. 7 ;* they that stabbed, *III. Henry VI., v. 5 ;* Mark Antony and, *Macbeth, iii. 1 ;* the dust of, *Hamlet, v. 1 ;* Cleopatra's praise of, *Antony and Cleopatra, i. 5 ;* death of, *Antony and Cleopatra, ii. 6 ;* in Britain, *Cymbeline, iii. 1.*

Cæsar, Octavius (Augustus), who was triumvir after the death of Julius Cæsar, is introduced in *iv. 1* of *Julius Cæsar ;* at Philippi, *v. 1.* He is also a character in *Antony and Cleopatra*, introduced in *i. 4.* His fortune, *ii. 3 ;* Lepidus's praise of, travestied, *iii. 2 ;* Antony's complaint of, *iii. 4 ;* laments Antony's death, *v. 1.*

In Julius Cæsar, Antony " was placed beside a man, the young Octavius, who even then treated him, the elder in politics and war, with haughtiness; in whose vicinity his genius (that is, the practical, actively disposed part of his genius) felt itself oppressed, and before whom his courage, his nobility, his magnanimity bowed, although unwillingly. An inward misgiving warned the more profound Julius Cæsar against Cassius; it needed a soothsayer to warn this superficial being against Octavius [*ii. 3*]. . . . Octavius owes his success more to Antony's luxuriousness, idleness, and frenzy than to his own merits. . . . Where [Antony] is genial and wanton, Octavius is full of petty carefulness; where the one idly, voluptuously, and madly puts off, neglects, and forgets every public duty, the other is all conscientiousness, economy, activity, and thoughtful quickness, and is prompted at least as much by the common interests of the state as by personal ambition."—GERVINUS.

Cæsars, there be many ere such another Julius, *Cymbeline*, *iii. 1.*

Cage (for vagabonds and criminals), *II. Henry VI., iv. 2.*

Cain, the curse of, *Hamlet, iii. 3*, "The primal eldest." See BIBLE.

Cain-coloured beard, *Merry Wives of Windsor, i. 4.* Cain was represented in old tapestry with a yellow beard. Some editors read cane-coloured.

Caithness, a thane of Scotland, character in *Macbeth*, appears in *v. 2.* Torfin, the son of Sigurd, affected to be independent Earl of Caithness during the whole reign of Duncan and of Macbeth.

Caius, Dr., character in the *Merry Wives of Windsor*, first spoken of in *i. 1*, introduced in *i. 4.* He is an irascible French physician, uses amusing English, is a suitor to Anne Page, and sends a challenge to Parson Evans, *i. 4.*

Caius, kinsman of Titus, in *Titus Andronicus*, addressed in *iv. 3* and *v. 2.*

Caius, name assumed by Kent in *King Lear*.

Cake, he that would have a, *Troilus and Cressida, i. 1;* is dough, *Taming of the Shrew, i. 1; v. 1.*

Cakes and ale, *Twelfth Night, ii. 3.* The usual entertainment on holidays and saints' days.

Calamity, sticking together in, *King John, iii. 4;* prepared for, *Richard II., iii. 2;* full of words, *Richard III., iv. 4;* wedded to, *Romeo and Juliet, iii. 3.*

Calchas, a Trojan priest who was sent by Priam to consult the oracle at Delphi as to the result of the war. Being warned not to return, as Troy was to be destroyed, he took part with the Greeks.

Cressida was his daughter. He is introduced in *iii. 3* of *Troilus and Cressida.*

Calendar(s), of nativity, *Comedy of Errors, v. 1;* of gentry, *Hamlet, v. 2.*

Caliban, a deformed monster in *The Tempest,* half-human, half-demon, whom Prospero has made his slave.

He is "all earth, all condensed, and gross in feelings and images; he has the dawnings of understanding without reason or the moral sense, and in him as in some brute animals this advance to the intellectual faculties, without the moral sense, is marked by the appearance of vice."—COLERIDGE.

Calipolis, feed and be fat, my fair, *II. Henry IV., ii. 4.* Travesty of a line in Peele's "Battle of Alcazar."

Callat (wanton), *A Winter's Tale, ii. 3; Othello, iv. 2.*

Calpurnia, Cæsar's wife, first appears in *i. 2* of *Julius Cæsar;* her dreams and fears, *ii. 2.*

Calumny, none can escape, *Measure for Measure, iii. 2;* will sear virtue itself, *A Winter's Tale, ii. 1;* the fate of place, *Henry VIII., i. 2;* not to be escaped, *Hamlet, iii. 1.* See also SLANDER.

Calydon (a city of Ætolia in Greece), the prince in, *II. Henry VI., i. 1.* Meleager. See ALTHEA.

Cambio, name assumed by Lucentio in *Taming of the Shrew, ii. 1.*

Cambridge, Richard, Earl of, character in *Henry V.* His part in the conspiracy to kill the king is mentioned in the prologue to the second act. In the second scene of the same act his treachery is exposed and he is ordered to execution. He was son of Edmund Langley, Duke of York, and brother of the York in this play. He is spoken of in *I. Henry VI., ii. 5,* in connection with the claim of the house of York to the throne. His wife was the sister of Mortimer; and the Duke of York, their son and the father of Edward IV. and Richard III., inherited from his mother the claim of the Mortimers. Cambridge was beheaded in 1415.

Cambyses, King, *I. Henry IV., ii. 4.* Allusion to a play by Thomas Preston, written about 1561, entitled "A Lamentable Tragedy, mixed ful of pleasant Mirth, conteyning the Life of Cambises, King of Percia, from the beginning of his Kingdome unto his Death, his one good Deed of Execution after the many wicked Deeds and tirannous Murders committed by and through him, and, last of all, his odious Death by God's Justice appointed, doon in such order as foloweth." The story is from Herodotus and Justin. It was Langbaine's conjecture that the direct allusion was to the opening speech of Cambyses, of which these lines are a specimen:

> " My counsaile grave and sapient,
>   With lords of legal train,
>   Attentive eares towards us bend,
>   And mark what shall be sain.
>   My sapient words, I say, perpend,
>   And so your skil delate :
>   You know that Mors vanquishèd **hath**
>   Cirus, the king of state;
>   And I, by due inheritance,
>   Possess that princely crown,
>   Ruling by sword of mighty force,
>   In place of great renown."

Camelot (in Somersetshire, where many geese are said to have been kept), *King Lear, ii. 2.*

Camillo, a character in *A Winter's Tale*, introduced in *i. 1.* He is a lord of Sicilia, who, at the command of the king to poison his guest, gives Polixenes warning, and flees with him to Bohemia. Later in the play, he protects and advises Florizel and Perdita.

Camomile, the, grows faster for being trodden upon, *I. Henry IV., ii. 4.*

Campeius (Laurence Campeggio), cardinal and legate, character in *Henry VIII.*, introduced in *ii. 2.* He was Bishop of Salisbury, but was deprived of his bishopric by Henry, who was irritated at his conduct concerning the divorce from Queen Katherine.

Canary, name of a lively dance and also of a wine, *Love's Labour's Lost, iii. 1 ; Merry Wives of Windsor, iii. 2, end ; All's Well that Ends Well, ii. 2.* The dance is said to have originated in the Canary Isles.

Cancer, more coals to, *Troilus and Cressida, ii. 3.*

Candle, how far that little, *Merchant of Venice, v. 1 ;* out, brief candle, *Macbeth, v. 5.*

Candle-wasters (book-worms), *Much Ado about Nothing, v. 1.*

Canidius, Antony's lieutenant-general, introduced in *iii. 7,* of *Antony and Cleopatra ;* his desertion, *iv. 6.*

Canis (dog), *Love's Labour's Lost, v. 2.*

Canker, in the bud, *Two Gentlemen of Verona, i. 1 ;* hath not thy rose a, Somerset, *I. Henry VI., ii. 4 ;* (the dog-rose), *Much Ado about Nothing, i. 3 ; I. Henry IV., i. 3 ; Sonnet liv.*

Cannibals, *II. Henry IV., ii. 4 ; Othello, i. 3 ; King Lear, i. 1,* " Make his generation messes." See ANTHROPOPHAGI.

Cannon, *King John, i. 1.* Gunpowder was not used until nearly a hundred years later. Cannons are said to have been first used by the English at the battle of Cressy in 1346, though the Moors used them in the year 1280. Another allusion is in *Macbeth*, *i. 2.*

Cannon-balls (gun-stones), *Henry V.*, *i. 2.* In the earliest days of the use of artillery, stone balls were fired from the guns.

Canterbury, Arundel, Archbishop of, mentioned in *Richard II.*, *ii. 1*, as one of those with Bolingbroke. He crowned Bolingbroke as Henry IV. in 1399.

Canterbury, Henry Chicheley, Archbishop of, character in *Henry V.*, enters in the first scene, where he describes the change in the king, and hopes to induce him to repeal the order passed in the last reign for seizing property of the Church, by offering a large sum for the wars in France. In the second scene he explains the claim of the king to the crown of France, and eloquently urges Henry to enforce his claim. He was the founder of All Souls' College, Oxford.

Canterbury, Thomas Bourchier, Archbishop of. See BOURCHIER.

Canterbury Pilgrims, *I. Henry IV.*, *i. 2.* Pilgrimages were made to the shrine of St. Thomas à Becket at Canterbury.

Cantle (corner or part), *I. Henry IV.*, *iii. 1; Antony and Cleopatra, iii. 8 or 10.*

Cantons (cantos), *Twelfth Night, i. 5.*

Canvass, *I. Henry VI.*, *i. 3.* To trap, as wild fowl were taken in a canvass or net.

Cap, order for a woman's, *Taming of the Shrew, iv. 3.*

Caper, Master, a prisoner, *Merry Wives of Windsor, iv. 3.*

Capet, Hugh, his title to the crown of France, *Henry V., i. 2.*

Caphis, servant of one of the creditors of *Timon of Athens,* introduced in *ii. 1,* where he is sent to dun for his master's due.

Capilet, family of, *All's Well that Ends Well, v. 3.*

Capilet, my horse, grey, *Twelfth Night, iii. 5.*

Capocchia (fool), *Troilus and Cressida, iv. 2.*

Capon, *Love's Labour's Lost, iv. 1.* The French poulet means both a young fowl and a love-letter.

Captain, the title of, *II. Henry IV.*, *ii. 4.*

Captious, and intenible (taking in, not holding), *All's Well that Ends Well, i. 3.*

Capucius, Eustachius, ambassador from Charles V., character in *Henry VIII.*, introduced in *iv. 2.* He was present at the death of Queen Katherine in 1536.

Capulet, character in *Romeo and Juliet*, introduced in *i. 1,*

Juliet's father, an irascible, tyrannical, meddlesome old man, unsteady in his feelings, and illogical in his actions and conversation.

Capulet, Lady, introduced in *Romeo and Juliet, i. 1,* a cold-hearted, conventional, unimpressible person, for whom Juliet in quiet times shows a decent filial regard, but from whom she expects no sympathy with her stronger feelings or in her troubles.

Car, John de la, the Duke of Buckingham's confessor, *Henry VIII., i. 1; ii. 1.*

Carack(s), *Comedy of Errors, iii. 2; Othello, i. 2.* Large ships of burden.

Caraway, eaten with apples, *II. Henry IV., v. 3.*

Carbonado (a slice cut for frying), *All's Well that Ends Well, iv. 5; I. Henry IV., v. 3; Coriolanus, iv. 5; King Lear, ii. 2.*

Carbuncle, the; allusions to its supposed power of giving out unreflected light, *Titus Andronicus, ii. 3; Henry VIII., ii. 3; Hamlet, ii. 2.*

Carded (mixed), *I. Henry IV., iii. 2.*

Cards, games of: Primero, *Merry Wives of Windsor, iv. 5; Henry VIII., v. 1;* a card of ten (possibly also an allusion to primero), *Taming of the Shrew, ii. 1;* the best cards, *King John, v. 2;* the king was fingered from the deck, *III. Henry VI., v. 1;* he lurched all swords, *Coriolanus, ii. 2.* (To lurch was to win easily); hardly shall I carry out my side (get the game), *King Lear, v. 1.*

Carduus Benedictus (holy thistle, a medicinal herb, thought good for heart-diseases), *Much Ado about Nothing, iii. 4.*

Care, business, *Merchant of Venice, i. 1;* killed a cat, *Much Ado about Nothing, v. 1;* an enemy to life, *Twelfth Night, i. 3;* on earth, *Richard II., ii. 2;* premature aging by, *I. Henry VI., ii. 5;* no cure, *I. Henry VI., iii. 3;* in the aged, *Romeo and Juliet, ii. 3.*

Careires (short turning of a horse from side to side), *Merry Wives of Windsor, i. 1.*

Carkanet (necklace), *Comedy of Errors, iii. 1; iv. 1.*

Carl (churl), *Cymbeline, v. 2.*

Carlisle, Thomas Merks, Bishop of, character in *Richard II.,* introduced in *iii. 2.* He was arrested for treason, *iv. 1,* but pardoned by Henry IV., *v. 6.*

" The grand type of genuine loyalty who stands faithfully by the side of the lawful king, without concealing from him the stern voice of truth ; who defies the unlawful usurper in the public assembly, but still elicits, even from the latter, true honour, favour, and esteem."

Carnations, *A Winter's Tale, iv. 3* or *4.*

Carp, of truth, *Hamlet, ii. 1.* The carp was proverbially the wisest of fishes. Its brain is said to be six times as large as the average fish-brain.

Carpets (tapestry table-cloths), *Taming of the Shrew, iv. 1.*

Carping, not commendable, *Much Ado about Nothing, iii. 1.*

Carriage (load), *The Tempest, v. 1; King John, v. 7.*

Carriers, conversation between, *I. Henry IV., ii. 1.*

Cart, the horse drawn by the, *King Lear, i. 4.*

Carthage, Dido, the Queen of, *Merchant of Venice, v. 1; The Tempest, ii. 1.*

Carve (to make gestures), *Love's Labour's Lost, v. 2; Merry Wives of Windsor, i. 3.*

Casca, character in *Julius Cæsar,* first appears in *i. 2.* He is bitter and sarcastic, and, though a friend of Cæsar, is drawn into the conspiracy by Cassius, and is one of the assassins, *iii. 1,* the first to strike. Antony calls him "the envious Casca," *iii. 2.*

Case (pair or box?), of lives, *Henry V., iii. 2.*

Cashiered (relieved of cash), *Merry Wives of Windsor, i. 1.*

Caskets, choice of the, *Merchant of Venice, ii. 7, 9; iii. 2.*

Cassandra, Priam's daughter, character in *Troilus and Cressida,* introduced in *ii. 2.* Apollo gave her the gift of prophecy, but afterward ordained that her prophecies should never be believed. In *v. 3* she foretells the death of Hector.

Cassibelan, *Cymbeline, i. 1; iii. 1.* He was King of Britain before Tenantius, the father of Cymbeline, and, being conquered by the Romans, agreed to pay tribute, B. C. 54.

Cassio, Michael, a Florentine, Othello's lieutenant, introduced in *i. 2.* Iago, who hates him for having been promoted above himself, contemptuously describes him in *i. 1* as an arithmetician, the Florentines being noted for banking and accounting. He is frank, simple, and straightforward, enthusiastically devoted to Othello, and a reverent admirer of Desdemona (*ii. 1*). He is disgraced, *ii. 3;* attacked by Roderigo and wounded by Iago, *v. 1.*

Cassius, Caius, character in *Julius Cæsar,* first appears in *i. 2.* He was married to Brutus's sister Junia. His leanness, *i. 2;* talks of Cæsar with Brutus, *i. 2;* quarrel with Brutus, *iv. 3;* farewell to him, *v. 1;* his death, *iv. 3.* The character of Cassius is sharply contrasted with that of Brutus. "He is keen, practical, prompt, energetic, severe, and inexorable; his hatred for tyranny is mingled with envy of the man whose life he had once saved, and for whose physical powers he feels contempt, and yet who seems about to 'bestride the narrow world like a Colossus.' A keen politician, he knows the special means to employ in influencing each of the confederates. He is less noble, less pure and disinterested than Brutus, less a man of thought and principle, more a man of action." His motive, *Antony and Cleopatra, ii. 6;* struck, *Antony and Cleopatra, iii. 9* or *11.* See also BRUTUS.

Cassocks (soldiers' cloaks), *All's Well that Ends Well, iv. 3.*

Castilian (then used as a term of reproach), *Merry Wives of Windsor, ii. 3.*

Castiliano vulgo (probably a blunder for *volto*), with a Spanish, or sober, face, *Twelfth Night, i. 3.*

Castle (a strong helmet), *Troilus and Cressida, v. 2; Titus Andronicus, iii. 1.*

Castle, old lad of the, *I. Henry IV., i. 2.* Allusion to Oldcastle, the name first given to Falstaff, *q. v.*

Casuistry, of the legate, *King John, iii. 1.*

Cat(s), *The Tempest, ii. 1; Midsummer-Night's Dream, iii. 2; Coriolanus, iv. 2;* in a bottle like a, *Much Ado about Nothing, i. 1;* allusion to the sport of hanging up a cat in a bottle of soot and striking it; the winner was the one who could break the bottle and escape the soot. In some places the cat was afterward tortured to death. Care killed a, *Much Ado about Nothing, v. 1;* a traitor, a, *All's Well that Ends Well, iv. 3;* aversion to, *Merchant of Venice, iv. 1; All's Well that Ends Well, iv. 3;* prince of cats. See TYBALT. Nine lives of, *Romeo and Juliet, iii. 1;* in the adage, *Macbeth, i. 7;* familiar of witches, *Macbeth, i. 1; iv. 1;* melancholy, *I. Henry IV., i. 2.*

Cataian (Chinaman, cheat), *Merry Wives of Windsor, ii. 1; Twelfth Night, ii. 3.*

Cataract (on the eye, called the web and pin), *A Winter's Tale, i. 2; King Lear, iii. 4.*

Catechism, Falstaff's, on honour, *I. Henry IV., v. 1.*

Cater-cousins, *Merchant of Venice, ii. 2.* Quater or quarter-cousins.

Caterpillars, of the commonwealth, *Richard II., ii. 3; II. Henry VI., iii. 1;* scholars, etc., called, *II. Henry VI., iv. 4.*

Catesby, Sir William, character in *Richard III.,* first appears in *i. 3.* He was unscrupulous in his devotion to the cause of Richard, was taken prisoner at Bosworth, and executed by order of Henry VII., August 25, 1485. His name is played upon in the rhyme :

"The Cat, the Rat, and Lovel the Dog,
Rule all England under the Hog."

Catling, Simon, a musician in *Romeo and Juliet, iv. 4,* named from a string of catgut.

Catlings (catgut strings), *Troilus and Cressida, iii. 3.*

Cato, mentioned, *Coriolanus, i. 4.* So in Plutarch, where it is the author's comment, not that of a character, as here. Cato was much later than Coriolanus. His suicide, *Julius Cæsar, v. 1.*

Cato, young, character in *Julius Cæsar,* appears in *v. 3,* and is slain in the following scene.

Cat o' mountain, pinch-spotted, *The Tempest, iv. 1.*

Causeless (supernatural), *All's Well that Ends Well, ii. 3.*

Cause(s), a common, *Troilus and Cressida, ii. 2;* good or bad, *II. Henry IV., iv. 1; Henry V., iv. 1; II. Henry VI., iii. 2.*

Causes, inquiry into, *A Winter's Tale, i. 2.* "How should this grow," etc.

Cautels, cautelous (deceptions, deceitful), *Coriolanus, iv. 1; Julius Cæsar, ii. 1; Hamlet, i. 3; Lover's Complaint, l. 303.*

Caution, in war, *II. Henry IV., i. 3;* in trusting men, *Henry V., ii. 3;* in observing signs of evil, *Richard III., ii. 3;* an adder in the path craves wary walking, *Julius Cæsar, ii. 1;* of age, *Hamlet, ii. 1.*

Cavaleiro-Justice, applied to Shallow by the Host, *Merry Wives of Windsor, ii. 1.*

Caviare to the general, *Hamlet, ii. 2.* Caviare was a dish made from sturgeons' roes, not liked by many.

Cawdor, Thane of, his revolt and the title given to *Macbeth, i. 2;* Macbeth hailed as, *i. 3;* death of the former thane, *i. 4.* The account corresponds with that by Stowe of the death of the Earl of Essex.

Cecily. See YORK, DUCHESS OF.

Celerity, most admired by the negligent, *Antony and Cleopatra, iii. 7.*

Celia, character in *As You Like It,* introduced in the second scene, cousin of Rosalind, and her companion in the forest under the name of Aliena. "Celia is more quiet and retired; but she rather yields to Rosalind than is eclipsed by her. She is as full of sweetness, kindness, and intelligence, quite as susceptible, and almost as witty, though she makes less display of wit. She is described as less fair and less gifted; yet the attempt [by her father] to excite in her mind a jealousy of her lovelier friend . . . fails to awaken in the generous heart of Celia any other feeling than increased tenderness and sympathy for her cousin."

Celibacy. See MAIDENHOOD and MARRIAGE.

Censure, taken to one's self, *As You Like It, ii. 7;* take each man's, *Hamlet, i. 3.*

Censures (advice), *Richard III., ii. 2.*

Censurers, of those in power, *Henry VIII., i. 2.*

Centaur, the (inn), *Comedy of Errors, i. 2.*

Centaurs (monsters, half man, half horse), *Midsummer-Night's Dream, v. 1; King Lear, iv. 6 ; Titus Andronicus, v. 2.*

Century (a hundred), *King Lear, iv. 4; Coriolanus, i. 7; Cymbeline, iv. 2.*

Cerberus (the three-headed dog at the entrance to Tartarus), *Love's Labour's Lost, v. 2; II. Henry IV., ii. 4; Titus Andronicus, ii. 4* or *5 ; Troilus and Cressida, ii. 1.*

Ceremony, the idol, *Henry V., iv. 1;* not needed in true friendship, *Timon of Athens, i. 2;* an indication of cooling friendship, *Julius Cæsar, iv. 2;* sauce to meat, *Macbeth, iii. 4;* mere mechanic compliment, *Antony and Cleopatra, iv. 4.*

Ceremonies (interpretation of omens), *Julius Cæsar, ii. 1, 2.*

Ceres (goddess of the harvest), *The Tempest, iv. 1; II. Henry VI., i. 2.*

Cerimon, a lord of Ephesus, in *Pericles,* introduced in *iii. 2;* his healing art, *iii. 2; v. 3.* "Cerimon, who is master of the secrets of nature, who is liberal in his 'learned charity,' . . . is like a first study for Prospero."—DOWDEN.

Cesario, name assumed by Viola in *Twelfth Night.*

Cess (measure), out of all, *I. Henry IV., ii. 1.*

Chafe, the carriage of (bearing of anger), *Antony and Cleopatra, i. 3.*

Chain, speech like a tangled, *Midsummer-Night's Dream, v, 1;* rub your chain with crumbs, *Twelfth Night, ii. 3.* Stewards and other upper servants wore chains of gold or silver.

Challenge(s), from Caius to Evans, *Merry Wives of Windsor, i. 4;* directions for a, *Twelfth Night, iii. 2;* sent, *Twelfth Night, iii. 4;* of Bolingbroke to Norfolk, *Richard II., i. 1;* Aumerle to Bagot, *Richard II., iv. 1;* of the prince to Hotspur, *I. Henry IV., v. 1, 2;* Hector's, *Troilus and Cressida, i. 3 ;* Laertes to Hamlet, *Hamlet, v. 2 ;* Albany's to Edmund, *King Lear, v. 3 ;* Antony's to Cæsar, *Antony and Cleopatra, iii. 11* or *13.* See GLOVES.

Cham, the great (sovereign of Tartary), *Much Ado about Nothing, ii. 1.*

Chamber, to your, *Richard III., iii. 1.* London was called the king's chamber.

Chamberlain, the, a character in *I. Henry IV.,* in league with the highwaymen, *ii. 1.*

Chamberlain, the lord, character in *Henry VIII.,* introduced in *i. 3.* Sir Charles Somerset, Earl of Worcester.

Chambers, *Henry VIII., i. 4.* Short pieces of ordnance, used chiefly on festive occasions.

Chameleon, the, *Two Gentlemen of Verona, ii. 1, 4; Hamlet, iii. 2;* referring to the supposed fact that it lived on air; its changes of colour, *III. Henry VI., iii. 2.*

Champ, Richard du, a modern French name oddly used in *Cymbeline, iv. 2.*

Champions, encounter of, in the lists, *Richard II., i. 3;* honours of, affect the reputation of the whole, *Troilus and Cressida, i. 3;* near the end like a bold, *Pericles, i. 1.*

Chance, staking on, *Merchant of Venice, i. 1,* "In my schooldays," etc.; *Richard III., v. 4,* "I have set my life," etc.; fulfilment of prophecy to be left to, *Macbeth, i. 3; iii. 1.* See also FORTUNE.

Chancellor, the lord, character in *Henry VIII.,* introduced in *v. 2.* Sir Thomas More.

Change, in a man's disposition, *Coriolanus, v. 4;* the lamentable, *King Lear, iv. 1;* of sovereigns, *King John, iii. 4.*

Changeling (child supposed to be left by fairies in place of another), *Midsummer-Night's Dream, ii. 1; A Winter's Tale, iii. 3; iv. 3; I. Henry IV., i. 1.*

Changes, wrought by time, *II. Henry IV., iii. 1.*

Channel, called the sea, *III. Henry VI., ii. 2.*

Chanticleer, *The Tempest, i. 2, song.*

Chantries, little chapels where masses were said for the dead founders of churches, *Twelfth Night, iv. 3; Henry V., iv. 1.*

Chapeless (chape, catch of the scabbard), *Taming of the Shrew, iii. 2.*

Character, a high, *Two Gentlemen of Verona, ii. 7,* "His words are bonds," etc.; manifested, *Measure for Measure, i. 1;* tests of, *Measure for Measure, i. 4, end;* of Wolsey, *Henry VIII., iv. 2;* change in, *Coriolanus, v. 4;* obscured by one defect, *Hamlet, i. 4;* sudden change in, *King Lear, i. 1,* "This is most strange," etc.; beauty of, a reproof to sin, *Othello, v. 1.*

Charactery (writing), *Julius Cæsar, ii. 1,* and elsewhere.

Characts (appellations), *Measure for Measure, v. 1.*

Chares (chores), *Antony and Cleopatra, iv., end; v. 2.*

Charge-House (free school), *Love's Labour's Lost, v. 1.*

Charing-Cross, *I. Henry IV., ii. 1.* Regarded as the central point of London.

Charity, a neighbourly, *Merchant of Venice, i. 2;* fulfils the law, *Love's Labour's Lost, iv. 3;* capricious, *II. Henry IV., iv. 4.* See also BOUNTY.

Charity, St., *Hamlet, iv. 5.*

Charlemagne, a physician that could raise, *All's Well that Ends Well, ii. 1;* and the Salic law, *Henry V., i. 2.*

Charles, the wrestler thrown by Orlando in *As You Like It,* introduced in *i. 1;* the wrestling-match is in *i. 2.*

Charles V., Emperor of Germany, *Henry VIII., i. 1;* Wolsey's revenge on, *ii. 1.*

Charles VI., of France, character in *Henry V.,* first appears in *ii. 4.* He shows a more just idea of the strength of the English than do his nobles.

Charles VII., of France, character in *I. Henry VI.,* introduced in *i. 2,* but spoken of in the first scene. His success began with the advent of Joan of Arc, *i. 2;* his compact with the English, *v. 4.*

Charles's Wain, *I. Henry IV., ii. 1.* Said to be a corruption of Chorl's or Churl's Wain—the Great Bear. Some, however, suppose the constellation to have been named in honour of Charlemagne.

Charmian, character in *Antony and Cleopatra,* introduced in *i. 2,* an attendant and confidante of Cleopatra.

Charms, magic, *The Tempest, i. 2; ii. 1, 2; iii. 2; iv. 1; v. 1; Richard III., iii. 4; Macbeth, iv. 1; King Lear, ii. 1;* love, *Othello, i. 1, 2, 3;* allusion to charms against death, *Cymbeline, v. 3,* "In mine own woe charmed," etc.; silence for a, *Othello, v. 2.*

Charneco, *II. Henry VI., ii. 3.* A kind of sweet wine made in Charneco, Portugal.

Charnel-house, horrors of a, *Romeo and Juliet, iv. 3.*

Charolois, mentioned, *Henry V., iii. 5.*

Charon, who ferried the dead over the river Acheron, *Richard III., i. 4; Troilus and Cressida, iii. 2.*

Chartreux, monk of the, *Henry VIII., i. 1.*

Charybdis, *Merchant of Venice, iii. 5.*

Chase, the, *Venus and Adonis, l. 3.*

Chase, terms of the. See HUNTING TERMS.

Chastity, *Romeo and Juliet, i. 1;* more than life, *Measure for*

Measure, ii. 4; ice of, *As You Like It, iii. 4;* as the icicle, *Coriolanus, v. 3; Cymbeline, ii. 3.*

Chatham, clerk of, a character in *II. Henry VI.*, introduced in *iv. 2.*

Chatillon, Hugh de, French ambassador in *King John,* introduced in the first scene.

Chatillon, Jaques, mentioned in *Henry V., iii. 5; iv. 8.*

Chaudron (entrails). *Macbeth, iv. 1.*

Cheapside, *II. Henry VI., iv. 2, 7.*

Cheater (or escheater, an officer that looked after reversions), *Merry Wives of Windsor, i. 3.*

Check, *Hamlet, iv. 7* (or *4*), and elsewhere. Said of a hawk that starts away from the lure.

Cheerfulness, *Merchant of Venice, i. 1,* " Let me play the fool," etc.; conduces to longevity, *Love's Labour's Lost, v. 2;* a merry heart goes all the day, *A Winter's Tale, iv. 2.*

Cheese, allusion to the love of the Welsh for, *Merry Wives of Windsor, v. 5;* Thersites called, *Troilus and Cressida, ii. 3.*

Cherry-pit (a game of pitching cherry-stones), *Twelfth Night, iii. 4.*

Chertsey, monastery, *Richard III., i. 2.*

Cherubin (old form of the word cherub), *The Tempest, i. 2,* and elsewhere.

Chess, allusions to: *Taming of the Shrew, i. 1,* " To make a stale of me," etc.; *The Tempest, v. 1; King John, ii. 1,* " Mayst be a queen and check the world;" *II. Henry VI., iii. 1,* " Mates," etc.

Chester, *II. Henry IV., i. 1.*

Chests, or caskets, the choice in, *Merchant of Venice, i. 2.*

Cheveril (kid), *Twelfth Night, iii. 1; Romeo and Juliet, ii. 4;* a conscience of, *Henry VIII, ii. 3.*

Chewet, *I. Henry IV., v. 1.* Probably the same as chough, jackdaw.

Chicheley, Henry. See CANTERBURY.

Chiding, of lovers, *Two Gentlemen of Verona, iii. 1;* of children, *Othello, iv. 2; II. Henry IV., iv. 4.*

Child (used for girl?), *A Winter's Tale, iii. 3.* Perhaps it should read " a *god* or a child," as the shepherd thought in Greene's story. Likeness of a, to its father, *A Winter's Tale, ii. 3;* pleadings of a, *King John, iv. 1;* government by a, *Richard III., ii. 3;* a discarded, *King Lear, i. 1;* a thankless, *King Lear, i. 4; ii. 4.*

Childeric, mentioned, *Henry V., i. 2.*

Childhood, second, *As You Like It, ii. 7; Hamlet, ii. 2.*

Childish-foolish, too, for this world, *Richard III., i. 3.*

Children, should not know wickedness, *Merry Wives of Windsor, ii. 2;* ingratitude of, *Measure for Measure, iii. 1,* "Friend hast thou none," etc.; innocence and influence of, *A Winter's Tale, i. 2;* cast away, *ii. 3;* wise, live not long, *Richard III., iii. 1;* on the stage, *Hamlet, ii. 2.* Children as actors were much in fashion at the time the play was written. A company of them played at the Blackfriars Theatre, and were called Children of the Revels; unfilial, *King Lear, ii. 4;* dying before their parents, *Lucrece, l. 1756;* the beautiful should leave, *Sonnets i.* to *xvii.* See also INGRATITUDE.

Child Roland, *King Lear, iii. 4.* A fragment of an old ballad.

Chine, mourning in the (mumps), *Taming of the Shrew, iii. 2;* (variorum, "mose in the chine," not explained); of beef, *Henry VIII., v. 4.*

Chiron, son of Tamora, in *Titus Andronicus,* introduced in *i. 1* (or *2*), as a prisoner of the Romans. He is released by the emperor; plots against Lavinia, *ii. 1, 3, 4;* is killed, *v. 2.* A brutal and disgusting character.

Chisel, what, could cut breath, *A Winter's Tale, iv. 3.*

Chivalry, *I. Henry IV., v. 1; Henry V., iv. 6;* in the vein of, *Troilus and Cressida, v. 3.*

Choice, obligation to stand by one's, *Troilus and Cressida, ii. 2.*

Choler, like gunpowder, *Henry V., iv. 7;* let reason question with, *Henry VIII., i. 1.*

Chopine, *Hamlet, ii. 2.* A very thick-soled shoe or clog worn by Spanish and Italian ladies.

Choplogic (to bandy words, quibble), *Romeo and Juliet, iii. 5.*

Chopping (changeable), *Richard II., v. 3.*

Choruses, are introduced at the beginning of each act in *Henry V.,* and first and second acts of *Romeo and Juliet.*

Chough (jackdaw), *The Tempest, ii. 1; Hamlet, v. 2;* and elsewhere.

Christ, atonement by, *Measure for Measure, ii. 2,* "He that might the vantage," etc.; *II. Henry VI., iii. 2,* "To free us from his Father's wrathful curse"; the captain, *Richard II., iv. 1;* "those blessed feet," *I. Henry IV., i. 1;* redemption by his blood, *Richard III., i. 4.*

Christendoms (Christian names), *All's Well that Ends Well, i. 1; King John, iv. 1.*

Christenings. See GOSSIPS, SPOONS, and ELIZABETH.

Christians, hatred toward, *Merchant of Venice, i. 3;* "mean to be saved," etc., *Twelfth Night, iii. 2;* war between, *King John, v. 2; I. Henry IV., v. 1;* crusade of, *Richard II., iv. 1.*

Christmas-tide, *Hamlet, i. 1, end;* comedy for, *Love's Labour's Lost, v. 2;* gambold for, *Taming of the Shrew, induction, 2.*

Christom-child, *Henry V., ii. 3.* One that dies soon after its baptism.

Chronicle, of day by day, *The Tempest, v. 1;* players are chronicles of the time, *Hamlet, ii. 2.*

Chrysolite, one entire and perfect, *Othello, v. 2.* An old Jewish writer is said to have mentioned a chrysolite, a stone having supernatural virtues, which was in the form of a woman, and had power against all charms.

Chuffs (coarse, fat fellows), *I. Henry IV., ii. 2.*

Church, plain as the way to, where bells have knolled to, *As You Like It, ii. 7;* headship of the, in England, *King John, iii. 1;* ransacking the, *King John, iii. 4;* forgotten the inside of a, *I. Henry IV., iii. 3;* proposal to convert its property to uses of the state, *Henry V., i. 1;* attack on the, *I. Henry VI., i. 1.*

Churchman, qualities becoming a, *Henry VIII., iii. 2; v. 3; I. Henry VI., iii. 1.*

Churchyards, scenes in, *Romeo and Juliet, v. 3; Hamlet, v. 1.*

Churlishness, *As You Like It, ii. 4.*

Cicely Hacket, *Taming of the Shrew, induction, 2.*

Cicero (106–43 B. C.), introduced as a character in *Julius Cæsar, i. 2;* his eyes, *i. 2;* his reputation, *ii. 1;* would never follow a thing begun by others, *ii. 1;* his death reported, *iv. 3.* Allusion to his murder, *II. Henry VI., iv. 1.*

Cicester, or Chichester, *Richard II., v. 6.*

Cinna, one of the conspirators in *Julius Cæsar,* first appears in *i. 3.* After his exit his worth and popularity are spoken of.

Cinna, a poet, character in *Julius Cæsar,* to be distinguished from the conspirator of the same name, appears in *iii. 3.* Plutarch says he was mistaken for Cinna the conspirator, and slain by the people.

Cinque-pace, *Much Ado about Nothing, ii. 1.* A dance in measures of five.

Cinque-ports, the, *Henry VIII., iv. 1.* The five ports were Dover, Hastings, Hythe, Romney, and Sandwich. They had enjoyed special privileges since the days of Edward the Confessor (*circa* 1050), on condition of providing a certain number of ships in time of war.

Cipher, a, in a rich place, *A Winter's Tale, i. 2;* value of, *Henry V., i., chorus;* without a figure, *King Lear, i. 4.*

Circe (a fabled sorceress), cup of, *Comedy of Errors, v. 1; Henry VI., v. 2.*

Circum circa (round about), *Love's Labour's Lost, v. 1.*

Circumlocution, *Measure for Measure, ii. 1,* Pompey's account; Armado's letter, *Love's Labour's Lost, i. 1; Romeo and Juliet, iii. 2,* the nurse; *II. Henry IV., ii. 1,* the hostess.

Circum-mured (walled about), *Measure for Measure, iv. 1.*

Circumspection, a tyrant's hatred of, *Richard III., iv. 2;* recommended, *Othello, iii. 3.*

Circumstanced (content with circumstances), *Othello, iii. 4.*

Citizens, fat and greasy, *As You Like It, ii. 1.*

City, the people are the, *Coriolanus, iii. 1.*

City woman, dress of the, *As You Like It, ii. 7.*

Civet, *Much Ado about Nothing, iii. 2; As You Like It, iii. 2;* to sweeten imagination, *King Lear, iv. 6.*

Civility, *Merchant of Venice, ii. 2;* empty of, *As You Like It, ii. 7.* See COURTESY.

Clack-dish (a rattling dish used by beggars), *Measure for Measure, iii. 2.*

Claims, ancient, *Henry V., ii. 4.*

Clamour your tongues (set them all off together like a peal of bells to close the ringing), *A Winter's Tale, iv. 3 or 4.*

Clare, St., sisterhood of, *Measure for Measure, i. 5.*

Clarence, George, Duke of, son of the Duke of York, and brother of Edward IV. and Richard III. He is a character in *III. Henry VI.*, introduced in *ii. 6,* where he is named Duke of Clarence. In *iv. 1,* he takes part with Warwick, ostensibly on account of Edward's marriage, and in *v. 1* again changes sides. Richard's designs toward him are expressed at the end of *v. 6.* He is also introduced in *Richard III., i. 1;* imprisoned in the Tower and secretly murdered, *i. 4;* Edward's sorrow for his death, *ii. 1.* His ghost appears to Richard, *v. 3.* His children, *ii. 2; iv. 1, 2, 3.* The boy was Edward, Earl of Warwick. He was kept a prisoner after Bosworth, and put to death in 1499, on a charge of being an accomplice of Perkin Warbeck. He was the last Plantagenet. The character of Clarence seems to have deserved the epithets heard in his dream, *i. 2,* "false, fleeting, perjured Clarence."

Clarence, Thomas, Duke of, son of Henry IV., character in second part, introduced in *iv. 4.*

Claribel, daughter of the King of Naples, mentioned in *The Tempest, ii. 1 ; v. 1.*

Claudio, character in *Measure for Measure,* introduced in *i. 3.* He is a young noble under sentence of death, on which sentence the plot of the drama depends. He is of light disposition, fickle, mercurial, and of lively imagination, far inferior to his sister Isabella in strength and elevation of character.

Claudio, the lover of Hero in *Much Ado about Nothing,* introduced in the first scene. He is a young Florentine, who has been in the wars with Don Pedro of Aragon, and his bravery is spoken of before he enters.

" With regard to Claudio's character, Shakspere has so blended the elements in his nature, he has given such a good foundation of honour and self-reliance to his unstable mind and fickle youth, that we cannot, with all our disapprobation of his conduct, be doubtful as to his character. Changeable as he is, he continues stable in no choice of friends and loved ones, since he had never continuously tested them ; at the slightest convulsion of events he is overpowered by first impressions, and he is without the strength of will to search to the bottom of things. This would be an odious and despicable character, if the changeableness were not tempered by the excitability of a tender feeling of honour."—GERVINUS.

Claudius, Brutus's servant in *Julius Cæsar,* appears in *iv. 3.*

Claudius, King of Denmark, Hamlet's step-father, introduced in *i. 2.* In the original history he is called Fengo. He has poisoned Hamlet's father, *i. 5,* and possessed himself of his dominions and his widow. His remorse, *iii. 1,* leads him to prayer, *iii. 4,* but not to restitution or open repentance. He seeks Hamlet's life, *v. 2,* and after the failure of his first scheme, plots with Laertes, *iv. 7,* that Hamlet shall die by the poisoned foil, or afterward by the poisoned cup, *iv. 7 ;* and he himself receives them both, *v. 2.*

Claw (flatter), *Much Ado about Nothing, i. 3.*

Clay, differs in dignity, *Cymbeline, iv. 2.*

Clean kam (nothing to the purpose), *Coriolanus, iii. 1.*

Clearness (from suspicion), that I require, *Macbeth, iii. 1.*

Cleomenes, an unimportant character in *A Winter's Tale,* sent by Leontes to the oracle at Delphos, *ii. 3 ; iii. 1.*

Cleon, Governor of Tharsus, character in *Pericles,* first appears in *i. 4 ;* he is an accomplice after the fact in the supposed murder of Marina, *iv. 3* (or *4*) ; his punishment, *v., end.*

Cleopatra, Queen of Egypt, introduced in the first scene of *Antony and Cleopatra.* Her complexion, *i. 1, 5* (she was of Greek extraction, and probably therefore not black) ; her age, *i. 5* (she was then twenty-eight); her splendor, *ii. 2;* anger and jealousy, *ii. 5;* carried in a mattress, *ii. 6;* Queen of Syria, *iii. 6;* purpose to go into the war, *iii. 7;* at Actium, *iii. 8–10;* her submission to Cæsar, *iii. 11* or *13;* charged by Antony with betraying him, *iv. 10* or *12;* feigns death, *iv. 11, 12* or *13, 14;* her grief for Antony, *iv. 13* or *15;* her horror of being carried to Rome, her message to Cæsar, and her death, *v. 2.*

"I have not the slightest doubt that Shakspere's Cleopatra is the real historical Cleopatra, the 'rare Egyptian,' individualized and placed before us. Her mental accomplishments, her unequalled grace, her woman's wit and woman's wiles, her irresistible allurements, her starts of ungovernable temper, her vivacity of imagination, her petulant caprice, her fickleness and her falsehood, her tenderness and her truth, her childish susceptibility to flattery, her magnificent spirit, her royal pride, the gorgeous Eastern colouring of the character—all these contradictory elements has Shakspere seized, mingled them in their extremes, and fused them into one brilliant impersonation of classical elegance, Oriental voluptuousness, and gipsy sorcery. What better proof can we have of the individual truth of the character than the admission that Shakspere's Cleopatra produces exactly the same effect on us that is recorded of the real Cleopatra? She dazzles our faculties, perplexes our judgment, bewilders and bewitches our fancy; from the beginning to the end of the drama, we are conscious of a kind of fascination against which our moral sense rebels, but from which there is no escape."—Mrs. Jameson.

Allusions to Cleopatra: *As You Like It, iii. 2, song;* a gipsy, *Romeo and Juliet, ii. 4;* her figure on tapestry, *Cymbeline, ii. 4.*

Clepe (call), *Hamlet, i. 4,* and elsewhere.

Clergy, the, like an effeminate prince, *I. Henry VI., i. 1;* robbed, *II. Henry VI., i. 3.*

Clergyman(men), good-humoured ridicule of, *Merry Wives of Windsor, iii. 1;* reproaches against a, *I. Henry III., iii. 1;* in war, *II. Henry IV., i. 2;* office of, *II. Henry IV., iv. 2.*

Cliff (clef), *Troilus and Cressida, v. 2.*

Clifford, John, Lord, son of Thomas, character in *II. Henry VI.,* where he appears in *v. 1* and *2* as "young Clifford," and in *III. Henry VI.,* introduced in the first scene. In revenge for his father's death, he kills the young Earl of Rutland in cold blood, *i. 3,* and for his cruelty he receives the name of "the butcher," *act ii., scene 2.* In *i. 4* he is represented as stabbing York, and in *ii. 3,* Warwick's brother, and fighting with Richard, *ii. 4.* His death at the battle of Towton, *ii. 6.* He was in reality slain shortly before that battle, at Ferrybridge (March 28, 1461), where he first defeated the Yorkists,

and was then defeated by them under Lord Falconberg. His **murder** of Rutland is again spoken of in *Richard III., i. 2.*

Clifford, Thomas, Lord, character in *II. Henry VI.,* introduced in *v. 1.* He was a grandson of Hotspur, and a partisan of Henry. He was killed at the battle of St. Albans (February 17, 1461), *v. 2.*

Cliffs, at Elsinore, *Hamlet, i. 4;* at Dover, *King Lear, iv. 6; Comedy of Errors, iii. 2; II. Henry VI., iii. 2.*

Clifton, Sir John, at Shrewsbury, *I. Henry IV., v. 4.*

Cling (wither), *Macbeth, v. 5.*

Clinquant, tinsel, *Henry VIII., i. 1.*

Clip (to clasp, embrace), *II. Henry VI., iv. 1,* and elsewhere.

Clitus, a servant of Brutus in *Julius Cæsar,* appears in *v. 5.*

Cloak, an old, makes a new jerkin, *Merry Wives of Windsor, i. 3;* on a horse, *II. Henry VI., iv. 7;* my inky, *Hamlet, i. 2.*

Clock(s), a woman like a German, *Love's Labour's Lost, iii. 1, end;* time hath made me his, *Richard II., v. 5;* their arms are set to strike on like, *Henry VI., i. 2.*

Cloten, son of the queen in *Cymbeline,* introduced in *i. 2.* He was intended by the king and queen for Imogen's husband. His wickedness, *i. 1;* encounter with Posthumus, *i. 1, 2;* Imogen's opinion of, *iii. 4;* his death, *iv. 2.*

" The character of Cloten, the conceited, booby lord, and rejected lover of Imogen, though not very agreeable in itself, and at present obsolete, is drawn with great humour and knowledge of character." —Hazlitt.

Clothair, *Henry V., i. 2; Henry VIII., i. 3.*

Clothes, the soul of a man, *All's Well that Ends Well, ii. 5;* tattered clothes, *King Lear, iv. 6;* but one suit of, *Taming of the Shrew, induction, 2,* " What raiment I'll wear," etc.

Clotpolt(s) (blockheads), Oswald a, *King Lear, i. 4; Troilus and Cressida, ii. 1; Cymbeline, iv. 2.*

Cloud, in the face, *Antony and Cleopatra, iii. 2.* A horse is said to have a cloud in his face when he has a dark spot between the eyes.

Cloud(s), when, appear, wise men put on their cloaks, *Richard III., ii. 3;* overcome us, like a summer, *Macbeth iii. 4;* forms of, *The Tempest, ii. 2; Hamlet, iii. 2; Antony and Cleopatra, iv. 12* or *14.*

Clout, the, *Love's Labour's Lost, iv. 1; King Lear, iv. 6,* and elsewhere. The bull's-eye of the target, a piece of white cloth.

Clowder, name of a dog, *Taming of the Shrew, induction, 1.*

Clown, a, character in *All's Well that Ends Well,* introduced in the third scene.

Clown, a character in *A Winter's Tale,* appears first in *iii. 3.*

Clown(s), acting by, *Midsummer-Night's Dream, v. 1;* meat and drink to see a, *As You Like It, v. 1; Hamlet, iii. 2.* See JESTERS.

Clubs, cry of, *I. Henry VI., i. 3; Henry VIII., v. 4.* A rallying-cry among apprentices.

Clytus, mentioned, *Henry V., iv. 7.*

Coals, carry, *Henry V., iii. 2; Romeo and Juliet, i. 1.* To bear insults.

Coat(s) of arms, the dozen white luces in their, *Merry Wives of Windsor, i. 1;* lions of England's, *I. Henry VI., i. 5;* in heraldry, *Midsummer-Night's Dream, iii. 2.*

Cobbler, a, *Julius Cæsar, i. 1.*

Cobham, Edward Brooke, Lord, mentioned in *III. Henry VI.,* in the second scene.

Cobham, Eleanor. See GLOUCESTER, DUCHESS OF.

Cobham, Reginald, Lord, mentioned in *Richard II., ii. 1,* as one of the adherents of Bolingbroke. He was the grandfather of the Duchess of Gloucester in *II. Henry VI.*

Cobloaf (a small, misshapen loaf), *Troilus and Cressida, ii. 1.* Alluding to the misshapen head of Thersites.

Cobweb, a fairy in the *Midsummer-Night's Dream, iii. 1.*

Cock, the word sometimes used as a corruption of "God," *Hamlet, iv. 5,* and elsewhere.

Cockatrice, or basilisk, *Richard III., iv. 1.* It was fabled to be hatched by a toad or serpent from the egg of a cock; kills by a look, *Twelfth Night, iii. 4; Romeo and Juliet, iii. 2; Lucrece, l. 540.* See also BASILISK.

Cock-a-whoop, set (begin a fight), *Romeo and Juliet, i. 5.*

Cock-crow, *The Tempest, i. 2, song; Richard III., v. 3;* ghosts vanish at, *Hamlet, i. 1, 2;* at Christmas, *Hamlet, i. 1.*

Cock-fighting, allusions to, *Antony and Cleopatra, ii. 3; Hamlet, v. 2,* "The potent poison quite o'ercrows," etc.

Cockle-hat, *Hamlet, iv. 5, song.* Hat with a cockle-shell, the pilgrim's badge, on it.

Cockney (perhaps an under-cook, originally), *Twelfth Night, iv. 1; King Lear, ii. 4.*

Cock-shut time, *Richard III., v. 3.* Evening twilight, when nets, called cock-shuts, were set in the woods for woodcocks.

Cocytus, *Titus Andronicus, ii. 3 or 4.* The river of lament.

Codling (an unripe apple), *Twelfth Night, i. 5.*

Cod's head, to change the, for the salmon's tail, *Othello, ii. 1.*

Cœur de Lion (Richard I.), *King John, i. 1; I. Henry VI., iii. 2.*

Cog (to load dice, to cheat), *Love's Labour's Lost, v. 2; Richard III., i. 3; Troilus and Cressida, v. 6,* and elsewhere.

Coigne of vantage (jutting point of a wall), *Macbeth, i. 6.*

Coil, *Two Gentlemen of Verona, i. 2;* I am not worth this, *King John, ii. 1;* this mortal, *Hamlet, iii. 1.*

Colbrand, *King John, i. 1: Henry VIII., v. 3.* A Danish giant with whom Guy of Warwick fought before King Athelstane.

Colchos, or Colchis, on the eastern shore of the Black Sea, where was the Golden Fleece, *Merchant of Venice, i. 1.*

Coleville, Sir John, character in *II. Henry IV.,* introduced in *iv. 3.* He is a rebel, surrenders to Falstaff, and is ordered to execution at York by Prince John of Lancaster.

Collatinus, husband of *Lucrece, argument* and *l. 7.*

Collatium, southeast of Rome, scene of *Lucrece.*

Collector(s), of knowledge, *As You Like It, ii. 7;* of trifles, *As You Like It, v. 4; A Winter's Tale, iv. 2.*

Collied (black, as in the collieries), *Midsummer-Night's Dream, i. 1; Othello, ii. 3.*

Collier (term of reproach), *Twelfth Night, iii. 4; Romeo and Juliet, i. 1.*

Collop (a slice of flesh; figuratively, a child), *A Winter's Tale, i. 2; I. Henry VI., v. 4.*

Colme-Kill (Colomb's Cell), *Macbeth, ii. 4.* The island Icolm-kill or Iona, one of the Hebrides, where Saint Colomb landed in the sixth century. The cathedral was a burial-place for kings. Forty-eight Scotch, four Irish, and eight Norwegian kings, besides many lords of the isles, are said to be buried there.

Colossus, like a, *Julius Cæsar, i. 2; Troilus and Cressida, v. 5.*

Colours, colourable (those not fast?), *Love's Labour's Lost, iv. 2.*

Colt (trick), *I. Henry IV., ii. 2.*

Columbine, *Hamlet, iv. 5.* It was emblematic of lovers forsaken.

Combat, clapper-clawing, *Troilus and Cressida, v. 5;* challenge to single, *I. Henry IV., i. 3; v. 1; Troilus and Cressida, i. 3.* See CHALLENGES.

Combined, combinate (pledged), *Measure for Measure, iii. 1; iv. 3.*

Come away, come away, Death, song, *Twelfth Night, ii. 4.*

Come-off (come down, pay), *Merry Wives of Windsor, iv. 3.*

Come, thou monarch of the vine, song, *Antony and Cleopatra, ii. 7.*

Come unto the yellow sands, song, *The Tempest, i. 2.*

Comedy, the most lamentable, *Midsummer-Night's Dream, i. 2;* a sweet, *iv. 2;* catastrophe of the old, *King Lear, i. 2.*

Comedy of Errors, the, might be called a farce, so glaringly improbable are the incidents; was first published in the folio of 1623, but written long before, probably among the earliest of the plays. (See Henry IV. of France.) It is known to have been acted at the Christmas Revels at Gray's Inn in 1594. The plot is from a translation by W. W. (William Warner) of the "Menæchmi" of Plautus, published in 1595, but made and circulated in manuscript some time before, or from an earlier English play, "The Historie of Error," acted at Hampton Court in 1576. A similar story is told in Goularb's "Admirable and Memorable Histories," 1607; and Dryden's play, "The Two Sosias," is founded on that of Plautus. In the original there is but one pair of twins. The play is full of anachronisms, and the time of action is indefinite. The scene is in Ephesus, a city that had a bad reputation for sorcery and all kinds of villainy.

Comet(s), omens of evil, *Taming of the Shrew, iii. 2; 1. Henry VI., i. 1; iii. 2; Julius Cæsar, ii. 2;* wondered at like a, *1. Henry IV., iii. 2.*

Comfort, made of losses, *All's Well that Ends Well, iv. 3;* cold, *King John, v. 7;* in heaven, *Richard II., ii. 2;* in thoughts of others' misfortunes, *Richard II., v. 5;* hateful to the despairing, *Richard II., iii. 2;* too late, *Henry VIII., iv. 2.*

Comforters, profitless, *Much Ado about Nothing, v. ι.*

Cominius, a general, character in *Coriolanus,* introduced in *i. 1.*

Commandments, the ten, *Measure for Measure, i. 2;* (the fingers) *II. Henry VI., i. 3.*

Commentaries, Cæsar's, *II. Henry VI., iv. 7.*

Commentary, fearful, is servitor to dull delay, *Richard III., iv. 3.*

Commission, Angelo's, *Measure for Measure, i. 1;* to right wrongs, a, *King John, ii. 1;* an altered, *Hamlet, v. 2.*

Commodity (law or justice), *Merchant of Venice, iii. 3;* (self-interest), power of, *King John,* end of *act ii.*

Commons, the, love in their purses, *Richard II., ii. 2.*

Commonty (comedy), *Taming of the Shrew, induction, 2.*

Commonwealth, an ideal, *The Tempest, ii. 1.* This is taken from Montaigne; the king's, *Love's Labour's Lost, iv. 1;* disease of the, *II. Henry IV., iv. 1.*

Companions, young, *A Winter's Tale, i. 2;* evil, *II. Henry IV., iv. 4.*

Company (companion), *All's Well that Ends Well, iv. 3.*

Company, too lavish of one's, *I. Henry IV., iii. 2,* "God pardon thee," etc.; caution concerning one's, *I. Henry IV., ii. 4; II. Henry IV., v. 1.*

Comparative (one that makes comparisons, a would-be wit), *I. Henry IV., i. 2; iii. 2.*

Comparisons, are odorous, *Much Ado about Nothing, iii. 5.*

Compassed (circular) window, *Troilus and Cressida, i. 2.*

Compassion, *III. Henry VI., i. 4,* had he been slaughterman, etc.; a grace of the gods, *Coriolanus, v. 3.*

Compensations, for losses, *All's Well that Ends Well, iv. 3; Richard III., iv. 4,* "The liquid drops," etc.; *Cymbeline, iv. 2,* "Some falls," etc.

Competency, advantage of a moderate, *Merchant of Venice, i. 2.*

Competitors (confederates), *Love's Labour's Lost, ii. 1; Twelfth Night, iv. 2.*

Complexion, fair, *Twelfth Night, i. 5,* " 'Tis beauty truly blent," etc.; a dark, *Merchant of Venice, ii. 1; Comedy of Errors, iii. 2;* "Mislike me not for my," etc., *Othello, i. 2; Sonnets cxxvii., cxxx., cxxxi., cxxxii.*

Compliment(s), *Two Gentlemen of Verona, ii. 4; Love's Labour's Lost, i. 1;* like the encounter of dog-apes, *As You Like It, ii. 5;* exchange of, *As You Like It, iii. 2;* lowly feigning called, *Twelfth Night, iii. 1;* Heaven walks on earth, *Twelfth Night, v. 1; A Winter's Tale, iv. 3* or *4.* See also FLATTERY.

Composition (what was compounded for), *Measure for Measure, v. 1;* (consistency), *Othello, i. 3.*

Compromise, inglorious, *King John, v. 1; Richard II., ii. 1.*

Compt (judgment), *Othello, v. 2.*

Comptible (accountable, sensitive), *Twelfth Night, i. 5.*

Concealment, like a worm i' the bud, *Twelfth Night, ii. 4.*

Concealments (mystic arts), *I. Henry IV., iii. 1.*

Conceit(s), winged, *Love's Labour's Lost, v. 2;* nearer death than the powers, *As You Like It, ii. 6;* derived from some forefather grief, *Richard II., ii. 2;* strongest in weakest bodies, *Hamlet. iii. 4;* may rob the treasury of life, *King Lear, iv. 6.*

Conclusion, lame and impotent, *Othello, ii. 1;* a foregone, *Othello, iii. 3.*

Conclusions (experiments), to try, *Hamlet, iii. 4; Cymbeline, i. 5.*

Concolinel, *Love's Labour's Lost, iii. 1.* Probably the beginning of a forgotten song.

Condition (disposition), *Merchant of Venice, i. 2; I. Henry IV., i. 3;* (art) *Timon of Athens, i. 1.*

Conduct. See BEHAVIOUR.

Coney-catching (poaching, cheating), *Merry Wives of Windsor, i. 1, 3; Taming of the Shrew, iv. 1; v. 1.*

Confect, Count, applied by Beatrice to Benedick, *Much Ado about Nothing, iv. 1.*

Confession, of Borachio, *Much Ado about Nothing, v. 1;* of Leontes, *A Winter's Tale, iii. 2;* exhortation to, *Richard II., i. 3;* riddling, *Romeo and Juliet, ii. 3.*

Confidence, in a leader, *Julius Cæsar, ii. 1;* in one's cause, *Richard II., i. 3;* rash, *All's Well that Ends Well, iii. 6.*

Confiners (borderers), *Cymbeline, iv. 2.*

Confiscation, threatened, *As You Like It, iii. 1; Merchant of Venice, iv. 1; Comedy of Errors, i. 2;* of John of Gaunt's property, *Richard II., ii. 1.*

Confound (consume), *I. Henry IV., i. 3; Coriolanus, i. 6.*

Confusion, how soon bright things come to, *Midsummer-Night's Dream, i. 1;* like a raven, *King John, iv. 3;* let confusion live, *Timon of Athens, iv. 1.*

Conjurer (exorciser), Pinch in *Comedy of Errors, v. 1.*

Conqueror, noise before and tears behind a, *Coriolanus, ii. 1;* afraid to speak, a, *Love's Labour's Lost, v. 2;* came over with the, *Taming of the Shrew, induction, i.* Sly calls him Richard.

Conquest, a, with no profit in but the name, *Hamlet, iv. 4.*

Conrade, one of the followers of Don John in *Much Ado about Nothing,* introduced in *i. 3.*

Conscience, *The Tempest, ii. 1; iii. 3;* examination of, *Measure for Measure, ii. 2, 3;* and the fiend, *Merchant of Venice, ii. 2;* silenced by interest, *King John, iv. 2;* tumult in, *King John, iv. 2;* clog of, *Richard II., v. 6;* a good, *II. Henry IV., v. 5;* outward, *Henry V., iv. 1;* a corrupted, *II. Henry VI., iii. 2,* "Thrice is he armed," etc.; fears of a guilty, *III. Henry VI., v. 6,* "The thief doth fear," etc.; in a purse—makes cowards, *Richard III., i. 4;* hath a thousand tongues—is a coward and a word that cowards use, *Richard III., v. 3;* a tender place, *Henry VIII., ii. 2;* accusations of, *Henry*

VIII., ii. 4; a still and quiet, *Henry VIII., iii. 2;* tortures of, *Macbeth, iii. 2; v. 3;* those thorns that in the bosom lodge, *Hamlet, i. 5;* makes cowards, *Hamlet, iii. 1; ii. 4;* a fettered, *Cymbeline, v. 4;* whose is entirely free, *Othello, iii. 3;* warning of, *Lucrece, l. 190;* in love, *Sonnet cli.* See also REMORSE and GUILT.

Consequence, yet hanging in the stars, *Romeo and Juliet, i. 4;* cannot be trammelled up, *Macbeth, i. 7.*

Consideration, *Julius Cæsar, i. 2;* like an angel came, *Henry V., i. 1.*

Consort (concert), *Two Gentlemen of Verona, iii. 2;* (company), *Two Gentlemen of Verona, iv. 1.*

Conspectuities (perceptions), *Coriolanus, ii. 1.*

Conspiracies: *The Tempest, ii. 1;* of the Percys, *1. Henry IV., v. 3; ii. 3, 4; iii. 1; iv. 1;* against the king's life, *Henry V., ii. 2; II. Henry VI., i. 4;* of Richard and Buckingham, *Richard III., iii. 1;* against Cæsar, *Julius Cæsar, ii. 1.*

Conspiracy, beginning of, *Julius Cæsar, i. 2;* in darkness—ripened, *Julius Cæsar, ii. 1;* popular, *Coriolanus, iii. 1.*

Conspirators, *Henry V., ii., chorus;* leanness of, *Julius Cæsar, i. 2;* justifying themselves and anticipating their fame, *Julius Cæsar, iii. 1.*

Constable of France, Charles Delabreth or D'Albret, the, character in *Henry V.,* first appears in *ii. 4.* He is perhaps the finest character among the French nobles introduced into the play. He fell at Agincourt. October 25, 1415, *iv. 8.*

Constance of Brittany, mother of Arthur in *King John,* introduced in *ii. 1.* After the death of Geoffrey Plantagenet, her husband, she was married by her father-in-law against her will to Randal de Blondeville, whom she afterward separated from and then married Guy of Thouars. She died in 1201, before John gained possession of Arthur. though she is represented in the play as still living at that time and still a widow. Dramatically, Constance is a fine character. Her whole nature is dominated by her love for her son and her ambition for him. Without much principle or any fairness of mind, she is impassioned, imaginative, and eloquent where his rights are concerned, and some of the highest strains of poetry in the plays are uttered by her. See especially the scolding scene between her and Elinor, *act ii., scene 1,* and also *act iii., scenes 1* and *4.*

Constancy, want of, *Two Gentlemen of Verona, v. 4;* protestation of, *A Winter's Tale, iv. 3* or *4; v. 1;* persistent, *Troilus and Cressida, i. 3;* Troilus a name for, *Troilus and Cressida, iii. 2;*

Julius Cæsar, iii. 1; vows of, *Cymbeline, i. 1;* of wives, *Henry VIII., ii. 2; Othello, iv. 2; Romeo and Juliet, iv. 1.* See LOVE, CONSTANCY IN.

Constantine, *I. Henry VI., i. 2.*

Constantinople, *Henry V., v. 2.*

Consulship, election to the, *Coriolanus, ii. 2; iii. 3.*

Consumption, of the purse, *II. Henry IV., i. 2.*

Contagion, pretended fear of, *Measure for Measure, i. 2.*

Contain (retain), *Merchant of Venice, v. 1.*

Contemporaries, judging one's self by his, *Sonnet xxii.*

Contempt, consequences of, *I. Henry IV., iii. 1,* "In faith, my lord," etc.; epithets of, *I. Henry IV., ii. 4; III. Henry VI., i. 4.*

Contemptible (contemptuous), *Much Ado about Nothing, ii. 3.*

Content, commend you to your own, *Comedy of Errors, i. 2;* sleep of, *II. Henry IV., iv. 5;* a life of, *III. Henry VI., ii. 5;* a crown, *III. Henry VI., iii. 1;* lowly birth with, the best having, *Henry VIII., ii. 3;* the best state, without, *Timon of Athens, iv. 3;* one's desire obtained without, *Macbeth, iii. 2;* farewell to,—with poverty, *Othello, iii. 3;* blessedness of, *Cymbeline, i. 7.*

Contention, broke loose, *II. Henry IV., i. 1.* See QUARRELS.

Continent (container), *Antony and Cleopatra, iv. 12,* and elsewhere.

Contriving (sojourning), *Antony and Cleopatra, i. 2.*

Con tutto il core, etc. (with all my heart, well met), *Taming of the Shrew, i. 2.*

Convent, a, the scene of *Measure for Measure, i. 5.*

Convent (summon), *Measure for Measure, v. 1; Henry VIII., v. 1; Coriolanus, ii. 2;* (to be convenient), *Twelfth Night, v. i.*

Conversation, *Love's Labour's Lost, v. 1;* on a journey, *Richard II., ii. 3;* soft parts of, *Othello, iii. 3.*

Convertites (converts), *As You Like It, v. 4; King John, v. 1; Lucrece, l. 743.*

Convey, conveyance (stealing craft), *Merry Wives of Windsor, i. 3,* and elsewhere; (manage), *King Lear, i. 2.*

Convulsions, caused by magic, *The Tempest, iv. 1.*

Cookery, fine Egyptian, *Antony and Cleopatra, ii. 6;* Imogen's, *Cymbeline, iv. 2.*

Copatain hat (sugar-loaf hat), *Taming of the Shrew, v. 1.*

Cope (reward), *Merchant of Venice, v. 1.*

Cophetua, King, *Love's Labour's Lost, iv. 1; II. Henry IV., v. 3; Romeo and Juliet, ii. 1.*

Copper-spur (a prisoner), *Measure for Measure, iv. 3.*

Copy (burden), of conference, *Comedy of Errors, v. 1.*

Coram, used by Slender as a title of Shallow, *Merry Wives of Windsor, i. 1,* eithor for *quorum,* because he was a justice of *quorum,* or quoted like armigero from a phrase used in warrants, *coram me* ——, *armigero,* before me ——, knight.

Coranto, *All's Well that Ends Well, ii. 3; Twelfth Night, i. 3,* and elsewhere. A lively Italian dance.

Cord, charity of a penny, *Cymbeline, v. 4.*

Cordelia, the youngest daughter of King Lear. She refuses to make professions of love to her father, as her sisters do, is disinherited, and betrothed to the King of France, *i. 1;* returns with an army to restore her father, *iii. 7; iv. 2, 3, 4;* the battle, *iv. 6, 7; v. 1, 2;* she is defeated and taken, *v. 2;* put to death in prison, *v. 3.*

"Everything in her seems to lie beyond our view, and affects us in a manner which we feel rather than perceive. The character appears to have no surface, no salient points upon which the fancy can readily seize; there is little external development of intellect, less of passion, and still less of imagination. It is completely made out in the course of a few scenes. . . . It is not to be comprehended at once or easily. . . . The impression it leaves is beautiful and deep, but vague. Speak of Cordelia to a critic or to a general reader, all agree in the beauty of the portrait, for all must feel it; but when we come to details, I have heard more various and opposite opinions relative to her than any other of Shakspere's characters. . . . What is it, then, which lends to Cordelia that peculiar and individual truth of character, which distinguishes her from every other human being? It is a natural reserve, a tardiness of disposition, 'which often leaves the history unspoke which it intends to do;' a subdued quietness of deportment and expression, a veiled shyness thrown over all her emotions, her language, and her manner; making the outward demonstration invariably fall short of what we know to be the feeling within."—MRS. JAMESON.

Corin, the old shepherd in *As You Like It*, introduced in *ii. 4,* for whom Rosalind and Celia buy his master's flock and pasture.

Corinth, in Greece, *Comedy of Errors, i. 1; v. 1; Timon of Athens, ii. 2.*

Corinthian, *I. Henry IV., ii. 4.* Slang for a wild roystering fellow.

Coriolanus, a tragedy first published in 1623, and from the evidences of style supposed to have been written at a late period of the author's work, 1608–1610. The material was drawn from the translation of Plutarch by Sir Thomas North, many passages and expressions being copied literally, though there are variations from the story. The time of action fills about four years—494 to 490 B. C. It is one of the finest of the plays, dealing with the struggles between the patricians and the plebeians of Rome.

Coriolanus, Caius Marcius, surnamed, enters in the first scene of the drama that bears his name. His pride and disdain of the poor, *i. 1;* bravery, *i. 4, 6, 8, 9; iii. 2;* his sincerity, *iii. 1;* wounded, *i. 5;* fights with Aufidius, *i. 8;* refuses spoils, *i. 9;* receives his surname, *i. 9;* the people's hatred of him, *ii. 1;* his triumph and wounds, *ii. 1;* made consul, *ii. 2;* the tribunes' treachery, *ii. 3;* his arrest and sentence, *iii. 1;* will not sue to the people, *iii. 2;* goes to Aufidius, *iv. 4, 5;* marches against Rome, *iv. 6;* Aufidius's opinion of him, *iv. 7;* besought to return to Rome, *v. 1;* he is accused, *v. 6;* his death, *v. 6.*

Coriolanus is a noble and heroic character, ruined by his haughty, contemptuous, unbending spirit. When he is banished he goes away in bitterness and takes up arms against his country, but lays them down at the suit of his wife and mother. His relations with them form a relief to his hateful pride of rank and contempt for the people.

Corioli, the city taken by Coriolanus from the Volscians, about 494 B. C., *act i., scene 10,* from which his surname was taken; scene of a part of the play.

Cormorant, the, allusions to its voracity, *Love's Labour's Lost, i. 1; Troilus and Cressida, ii. 2; Coriolanus, i. 1.*

Cornelia, mother of the Gracchi, *Titus Andronicus, iv. 1.*

Cornelius, a courtier in *Hamlet,* introduced in *i. 2.*

Cornelius, a physician in *Cymbeline,* introduced in *i. 5,* to whom the queen applies for poisons to administer to Imogen.

Cornwall, Duke of, Regan's husband, in *King Lear,* introduced in the first scene. He is slain by his servant when "going to put out the other eye of Gloucester," *iv. 2.*

Coronation, a second, *King John, iv. 2;* of Bolingbroke, *Richard II., v. 2;* procession, *Henry VIII., iv. 1.*

Corpse(s), like a flower-strewn, *A Winter's Tale, iv. 3* or *4;* an unhandsome, *I. Henry IV., i. 3;* decay of, *Hamlet, v. 1;* the sailor's superstition that it is unlucky to have one on board, *Pericles, iii. 1;* regarding one bleeding, *Richard III., i. 2.*

Correction, degrading, *King Lear, ii. 2;* difficulties of, *II. Henry IV., iv. 1.*

Corruption, through bad company, *I. Henry IV., i. 2.*

Corruption, in Vienna, *Measure for Measure, v. 1;* wins not more than honesty, *Henry VIII., iii. 2;* honoured by the name of Cassius, *Julius Cæsar, iv. 3;* rank, *Hamlet, iii. 4.* See also BRIBERY.

Corvinus, King of Hungary, who took Vienna in 1485, *Measure for Measure, i. 2.*

Corydon, lament of, *Passionate Pilgrim, xviii.*

Cost, fashion to avoid, *Much Ado about Nothing, i. 1;* counting the, *II. Henry IV., i. 3.*

Costard, a clown in *Love's Labour's Lost,* introduced in *i. 1,* a blunderer in the use of long words in imitation of the pedantry of his superiors, but blundering into some shrewd sayings.

Costumes, brought from France, *Henry VIII., i. 3.*

Coted, come to the side of, *Hamlet, ii. 2.*

Cot-quean, *Romeo and Juliet, iv. 4.* A man meddling with kitchen affairs.

Cotsall, *Merry Wives of Windsor, i. 1.* See COTSWOLD MAN.

Cotswold man, a (an athlete), *II. Henry IV., iii. 2.* The Cotswold Hills, in Gloucestershire, were the scene of rural sports on Thursday in Whitsun-week, the Cotswold games.

Counsel, to the sorrowing, *Much Ado about Nothing, v. 1;* the cripple, *Merchant of Venice, i. 2;* friendly, *I. Henry VI., iii. 1;* is a shield, *Richard III., iv. 3;* Christian, *Henry VIII., iii. 1;* too late, *Julius Cæsar, ii. 4;* two may keep, *Romeo and Juliet, ii. 4.* See also ADVICE.

Counsellors, the winds truthful, *As You Like It, ii. 1;* good, lack no clients, *Measure for Measure, i. 2;* love's, *Cymbeline, iii. 2.*

Countenance(s), lay my, to pawn, *Merry Wives of Windsor, ii. 2;* almost chide God for making you that, you are, *As You Like It, iv. 1;* one more in sorrow than in anger, *Hamlet, i. 2.*

Counter. See HUNTING.

Counter-caster, *Othello, i. 1.* Allusion to the use of counters in casting accounts.

Counter-check, quarrels in. See DUELLING.

Counterfeit, to die is to be a, *I. Henry IV., v. 4;* of passion, *Much Ado about Nothing, ii. 3.*

Counter-gate, love to walk the (a prison-gate), *Merry Wives of Windsor, iii. 3.*

Counterpoints (counterpanes), *Taming of the Shrew, ii. 1.*

Countries, on a fat woman, *Comedy of Errors, iii. 2.*

Country, the, manner of, at court, *As You Like It, iii. 2.*

Country, an unsettled, *King John, iv. 3; v. 1;* the undiscovered, *Hamlet, iii. 1;* disease of a, *Macbeth, v. 3.* See also PATRIOTISM.

Courage, boasts of, *Merry Wives of Windsor, i. 1;* ironical praise for, *Merry Wives of Windsor, iii. 1;* boasted, *Merchant of Venice, ii. 1; Much Ado about Nothing, i. 1;* mounteth with occasion, *King John, ii. 1;* exhortation to, *King John, v. 1;* of feeble, *II. Henry IV., iii. 2;* the dauphin's, *Henry V., iii. 7;* French boasts of, *Henry V., iii. 7; iv. 2;* prayer for, *Henry V., iv. 1;* of Fluellen, *Henry V., iv. 7;* of the English, *Henry V., iv. 3;* after loss, *III. Henry VI., v. 4; Coriolanus, ii. 2, iii. 1,* "His nature is too noble," etc., *iii. 3;* true, *Timon of Athens, iii. 5;* sticking point of, *Macbeth, i. 7;* for anything material, *Macbeth, iii. 4;* boasts of, *Macbeth, v. 3;* Goneril's boasts of, *King Lear, iv. 2.* See also BRAVERY and VALOUR.

Course, the holy, *Julius Cæsar, i. 2.*

"That day [the feast Lupercalia] there are divers noble mens sons, yong men, which run naked through the citie, striking in sport them they meete in their way, with leather thongs, hair and all on, to make them give place."—NORTH'S "PLUTARCH."

Court, a soldier in the king's army in *Henry V.,* who first appears in *iv. 1.*

Court, a beauty of the, *Merry Wives of Windsor, iii. 3;* life at, *As You Like It, ii. 1; All's Well that Ends Well, i. 1; iii. 2;* manners of, *As You Like It, iii. 2; All's Well that Ends Well, ii. 2;* do you take the court for Paris garden, *Henry VIII., v. 3;* holy-water of the (flattery), *King Lear, iii. 2;* news of, *King Lear, v. 3;* folly of seeking preferment at, *Cymbeline, iii. 3.*

Court-cupboard (a sideboard), *Romeo and Juliet, i. 5.*

Courtenay, Sir Edward, mentioned in *Richard III., iv. 4,* together with his brother Peter, Bishop of Exeter.

Courtesan, a, a character in the *Comedy of Errors, iv. 3.*

Courtesy, advice concerning, *All's Well that Ends Well, ii. 1;* to an oyster-wench, *Richard II., i. 4;* without love, *Timon of Athens, i. 1,* speech of Apemantus; dissembling, *Cymbeline, i. 2;* to cover sin, *Pericles, i. 1;* of the wrong breed, *Hamlet, iii. 2.*

Courtier(s), a model for, *All's Well that Ends Well, i. 1, 2;* the curse of kings to be attended by, *King John, iv. 2;* inconstancy of, *Richard II., iv. 1;* description of a, *I. Henry IV., i. 3;* discord among, *I. Henry IV., iv. 1;* hypocrisy of, *Cymbeline, i. 1;* poor wretches, *Cymbeline, v. 4.*

Courtney, Sir Edward, in arms, *Richard III., iv. 4.*

Courtship. See LOVE and LOVERS.

Covent (old form for convent), *Measure for Measure, iv. 3.*

Coventry, a city in Warwickshire, and roads near, scene of the meeting of Bolingbroke and Norfolk in *Richard II.,* of part of *I. Henry IV.,* and *III. Henry VI., v. 1.*

Coventry, a mayor of, *III. Henry VI., v. 1.*

Covetous, the, *Lucrece, l. 134.*

Covetousness, skill confounded in, *King John, iv. 2.*

Cow, a curst, has short horns, *Much Ado about Nothing, ii. 1.*

Cowardice, hated by women, *Two Gentlemen of Verona, iii. 1;* of a parson, *Merry Wives of Windsor, iii. 1;* of preferring life to honour, *Measure for Measure, iii. 1;* refuge of, *As You Like It, v. 4;* All's Well that Ends Well, i. 1;* religious in, *Twelfth Night, iii. 4;* hoxes (cuts the hamstrings of) honesty, *A Winter's Tale, i. 2;* a calf's skin for—strong on the stronger side, *King John, iii. 1;* in the noble, *Richard II., i. 2; I. Henry IV., ii. 3, 4; iv. 3;* of suicide, *Romeo and Juliet, iii. 3;* the gods shame, *Julius Cæsar, ii. 2;* accusations of, *King Lear, iv. 2;* self-accusation of, *Hamlet, ii. 2;* of procrastination, *Hamlet, iv. 4; Antony and Cleopatra, iii. 9* or *11; Cymbeline, iii. 6;* slanderous, *Much Ado about Nothing, v. 1; Henry V., iv. 5; I. Henry VI., i. 5;* infectious, *III. Henry VI., v. 4; i. 4.*

Coward(s), a, that hath drunk, *The Tempest, iii. 2;* boast of a, *Merry Wives of Windsor, i. 1; Merchant of Venice, iii. 2;* with martial outside, *As You Like It, i. 3;* a high-born, *Taming of the Shrew, induction, 2;* description of a, *All's Well that Ends Well, iii. 6; iv. 3;* the gift of a, *Twelfth Night, i. 3;* like the hare in the proverb, *King John, ii. 1;* three, *I. Henry IV., i. 2;* on instinct a, *I. Henry IV., ii. 4;* description of a, *Henry V., iii. 2; iv. 3;* souls of geese, *Coriolanus, i. 4, 6;* die many times, *Julius Cæsar, ii. 2;* to live a, *Macbeth, i. 7;* made by tailors, *King Lear, ii. 2;* milk-livered, *King Lear, iv. 2;* bred by plenty, *Cymbeline, iii. 6;* father cowards, *Cymbeline, iv. 2;* brave by example, *Cymbeline, v. 3.*

Cowish (cowardly), *King Lear, iv. 2.*

Cowl-staff (for carrying a burden on the shoulders of two men), *Merry Wives of Windsor, iii. 3.*

Cowslips, *The Tempest, v. 1, song; Midsummer-Night's Dream, ii. 1;* freckled, *Henry V.. v. 2; Cymbeline, ii. 2.*

Coxcombs. See DANDY.

Coyness, *Much Ado about Nothing, iii. 1.*

Coystril (an army-follower), *Twelfth Night, ii. 3.*

Cozened, would all the world might be, *Merry Wives of Windsor, iv. 5.*

Coziers (botchers), *Twelfth Night, ii. 3.*

Crab, name of a dog, *Two Gentlemen of Verona, ii. 3.*

Crab, backward like a, *Hamlet, ii. 2.*

Crabs (apples), roasted, *Love's Labour's Lost, v. 2 ; Midsummer-Night's Dream, ii. 1.* A favourite drink for winter nights, especially at Christmas-time, was "lamb's wool," made of ale with crabs roasted in it, and flavoured with nutmeg.

Crack of doom, *Macbeth, iv. 1.*

Crack (a bold boy), *Coriolanus, i. 3 ; II. Henry IV., iii. 2.*

Crack (to load), *Macbeth, i. 2.*

Cracker (a braggart), *King John, ii. 1.*

Crack-hemp (gallows-bird), *Taming of the Shrew, v. 1.*

Craft, richer than innocency, *Measure for Measure, iii. 2 ;* denunciation of, *Twelfth Night, v. 1 ;* of the fox, *III. Henry VI., iv. 7 ;* met with craft, *Hamlet, iii. 4, end.*

Craftsmen, wooed with craft, *Richard II., i. 4.*

Cramps, invoked by magic, *The Tempest, iv. 1 ; v. 1.*

Crants (*Krantz,* garlands), *Hamlet, v. 1.* The only instance known of the use of the word in English.

Cranmer, Thomas, Archbishop of Canterbury, character in *Henry VIII.,* introduced in *v. 1 ;* spoken of by Henry, *ii. 4, end ;* his zeal for the divorce, *iii. 2 ;* a heretic, *iii. 2 ;* his accusation by Gardiner and interview with the king, *v. 1 ;* disgraced and tried for heresy, and championed by the king, *v. 2 ;* the popular opinion of, *v. 2 ;* his prophecy concerning Elizabeth, *v. 4.* He was put to death in 1556, (æt. sixty-six) during the reign of Mary, who hated him both as a Protestant and for his agency in the divorce of her mother.

Crare (or crayer, a small, clumsy ship), *Cymbeline, iv. 2.*

Crassus, a gentleman mentioned in *Measure for Measure, iv. 5.*

Crassus, Marcus, his death avenged, *Antony and Cleopatra, iii. 1.*

Crécy, battle of (Aug. 3, 1346), mentioned, *Henry V., i. 2 ; ii. 4.*

Credent (unquestionable), *Measure for Measure, iv. 4.*

Credit (credulity), *Comedy of Errors, iii. 2.*

Credit, give no, *Henry V., ii. 3.*

Creditor(s), duns of, *Timon of Athens, ii. 1, 2 ; iii. 4 ;* nature a, *Measure for Measure, i. 1.*

Credulity, *Othello, iv. 4 ; Antony and Cleopatra, v. 5 ; Cymbeline, v. 5.*

Cressets (torches), *I. Henry IV., iii. 1.*

Cressida, daughter of Calchas, heroine of *Troilus and Cressida,* first appears in *i. 2.* In her, Coleridge says, Shakspere "has drawn the portrait of a vehement passion, that, having its true origin and proper cause in warmth of temperament, fastens on, rather than fixes to, some one object by liking and temporary preference." Cressida is introduced in *i. 2* of *Troilus and Cressida.* Her beauty and wit, *i. 1.* She is exchanged (*iv. 1, 2, 3*) for Antenor and sent to the Greek camp; forgets Troilus and loves Diomedes. Ulysses divines her character, *iv. 5;* her inconstancy discovered by Troilus, *v. 2.* She is artful and coquettish, passionate but not affectionate, and therefore ardent and inconstant. Ulysses says of her:

" . . . Her wanton spirits look out
At every joint and motive of her body."

Allusions to Cressida: Cressida's uncle (Pandarus), *All's Well that Ends Well, ii. 1;* Cressida to this Troilus, *Twelfth Night, iii. 1.*

Cressy. See CRÉCY.

Crest, the devil's, *Measure for Measure, ii. 4;* prouder than blue Iris, *Troilus and Cressida, i. 3.*

Crete, the desperate sire of, *I. Henry VI., iv. 6;* fool of, *III. Henry VI., v. 6.* Dædalus, who made wings for himself and his son Icarus.

Crickets, merry as, *I. Henry IV., ii. 4;* cry of, ominous, *Macbeth, ii. 2;* song of, at night, *Cymbeline, ii. 2.*

Crime, suggestions of, *The Tempest, ii. 1; iii. 2, 3;* petty, *Two Gentlemen of Verona, iv. 1;* unpunished, *Measure for Measure, i. 4;* cherished by virtues, *All's Well that Ends Well, iv. 3;* plans for, *As You Like It, i. 1; ii. 3; A Winter's Tale, i. 2;* hints for, *King John, iii. 3;* effects of, *King John, iii. 4;* results of declaring the purpose to commit and the sight of means, *King John, iv. 2;* not inherited, *Timon of Athens, v. 5;* the mind before a, *Julius Cæsar, ii. 1;* first suggestion of, *Macbeth, i. 3;* for naught, *Macbeth, iii. 1;* to secure results of crime, *Macbeth, iii. 2, 4;* will out, *Hamlet, i. 2, end;* a gross, *Hamlet, iii. 4;* revelations of, *King Lear, iii. 2;* planned, *King Lear, iv. 6;* accusation of, *Othello, i. 3;* time for shrift of, *Othello, v. 2.*

Crisis, the, *King John, iii. 4; Macbeth, iv. 2,* "Things at the worst," etc.

Crispian (Crispin and Crispianus), Saint, feast of, October 25th, *Henry V., iv. 3.* Saint Crispin made shoes to render himself independent while preaching Christianity, and is the tutelar saint of shoemakers.

Critical, nothing if not, *Othello, ii. 1.*

Criticism, on men, *Much Ado about Nothing, iii. 1.*

Critics, satire on, *Love's Labour's Lost, iv. 2,* speech of Holofernes, near the end.

Croaker, a, *Troilus and Cressida, v. 2.*

Crocodile, the mournful, *II. Henry VI., iii. 1;* Antony's description of the, *Antony and Cleopatra, ii. 7;* tears of the, *Othello, iv. 1;* eat a, *Hamlet, v. 1.*

Cromer, Sir James, *II. Henry VI., iv. 7.*

Cromwell, Thomas, subordinate of Wolsey in *Henry VIII.,* introduced in *iii. 2.* Wolsey's advice to him, *iii. 2;* preferments of, *iv. 1; v. 1.* He entered Parliament and defended Wolsey; the king made him Earl of Essex, and he became chancellor and vicar-general. He was the most influential adviser of the king, and it was through his policy that the Church of England separated from the Papacy. After Henry's marriage with Anne of Cleves, however, which he brought about, he fell in favour, and was finally arrested on a charge of treason and beheaded in 1540.

Crosby Place, *Richard III., i. 2, 3.* A house still standing in Bishopsgate Street, London.

Cross, the bitter, *I. Henry IV., i. 1;* you Pilates have delivered me to my, *Richard II., iv. 1.*

Crosses, wayside, *Merchant of Venice, v. 1;* (coins which had crosses on the back), *Love's Labour's Lost, i. 2.*

Cross-row, the alphabet in the primer, called so because headed by a cross, *Richard III., i. 1.*

Cross-ways, suicides buried at, where stakes were driven through the bodies, *Midsummer-Night's Dream, iii. 2.*

Crow(s), singing of the, *Merchant of Venice, v. 1;* over a battle-field, *Henry V., iv. 2;* ominous, *Julius Cæsar, v. 1; Macbeth, iii. 2; Troilus and Cressida, iv. 2;* the treble-dated, the Phœnix and the Turtle.

Crow-flowers, *Hamlet, iv. 7.* Said to have been the ragged robin.

Crow-keeper, *Romeo and Juliet, i. 4; King Lear, iv. 6.* A man or boy who drives crows from fields, or a scarecrow.

Crowd, a, foolishness of, *Measure for Measure, i. 4;* in London, *Henry VIII., v. 4.*

Crown, the imperial, *A Winter's Tale, iv. 3 or 4;* cares go with —like a well—resigning a, *Richard II., iv. 1;* uneasy lies the head that wears a, *II. Henry IV., iii. 1;* an ill-gotten—weight of a—the prince takes the, *II. Henry IV., iv. 4;* would the, were red-hot steel,

Richard III., iv. 1. This may be an allusion to the punishment of a burning crown for regicides and usurpers. Sweet to wear, *III. Henry VI., i. 2;* for York, *III. Henry VI., i. 4;* of content, *III. Henry VI., iii. 1;* ambition for, *III. Henry VI., iii. 2;* offered, *Julius Cæsar, i. 2; iii. 2;* might change the nature, *Julius Cæsar, ii. 1;* gift of a, *King Lear, i. 1, 4;* a thousand flatterers in a, *Richard II., ii. 1; iii. 2, 3;* a fruitless, *Macbeth, iii. 1.*

Crowner (coroner), *Twelfth Night, i. 5; Hamlet, v. 1.*

Crucifixion of Christ, the, *I. Henry IV., i. 1.*

Cruels (cruelties), *King Lear, iii. 7.*

Cruelty, *Merchant of Venice, iv. 1,* "A stony adversary," etc., prayer for, *Macbeth, i. 5; Hamlet, iii. 2, 4;* in a woman, *III. Henry VI., i. 4,* "O tiger's heart," etc.; inhuman, *King Lear, iii. 7,* "Because I would not see," etc.; toward Lear, *iv. 7;* to the falling, *Henry VIII., v. 2; Othello, v. 2.*

Crusades, the, *Richard II., iv. 1; I. Henry IV., i. 1; II. Henry IV., iii. 1; iv. 4.*

Crusadoes (Portuguese coins of gold stamped with a cross), *Othello, iii. 4.*

Cry, They come, *Macbeth, v. 5;* you and your, *Coriolanus, iv. 6;* of players, a, *Hamlet, iii. 2.* A cry was a pack of hounds; aim (give encouragement), *Merry Wives of Windsor, iii. 2.*

Cubiculo (chamber, lodging), *Twelfth Night, iii. 2.*

Cuckold(s), *Merry Wives of Windsor, ii. 2; iii. 5; v. 5; Measure for Measure, v. 1; Much Ado about Nothing, ii. 1; Merchant of Venice, v. 1; All's Well that Ends Well, i. 3; A Winter's Tale, i. 2; Coriolanus, iv. 5; Antony and Cleopatra, i. 2; Troilus and Cressida, iv. 1; Cymbeline, ii. 4; Othello, iii. 3; iv. 3;* calamity the only true, *Twelfth Night, i. 5.*

Cuckoo, the, *Merry Wives of Windsor, ii. 1; Love's Labour's Lost, v. 2, song;* voice of, *Midsummer-Night's Dream, iii. 1; Merchant of Venice, v. 1;* in June, *I. Henry IV., iii. 2;* in the sparrow's nest, *I. Henry IV., v. 1; Antony and Cleopatra, ii. 6; King Lear, i. 4;* sings in kind, *All's Well that Ends Well, ii. 1.*

Cuckoo-buds, *Love's Labour's Lost, v. 2.* Variously supposed to be the cowslip, crowfoot, and pile-wort.

Cuckoo-flower, *King Lear, iv. 4.* Probably ragged robin.

Cucullus non facit monachum (the cowl does not make the monk), *Measure for Measure, v. 1; Twelfth Night, i. 5.*

Cullion, -ly (scullion), *Taming of the Shrew, iv. 2; King Lear, ii. 2; Henry V., iii. 2.; II. Henry VI., i. 3.*

Cum privilegio, etc., the words of an old grant of privilege for printing a book with the sole right of putting to press, *Taming of the Shrew, iv. 4.*

Cunning, bashful, *The Tempest, iii. 1;* skilled, *Taming of the Shrew, i. 1; ii. 1;* to be strange, *Romeo and Juliet, ii. 2;* plaited, *King Lear, i. 1;* errs in ignorance, not in, *Othello, iii. 3.*

Cupid, introduced as a character in *Timon of Athens, i. 2.*

Cupid, foiled, *The Tempest, iv. 1; Merry Wives of Windsor, v. 5;* challenged, *Much Ado about Nothing, i. 1; ii. 1; iii. 1, 2; Love's Labour's Lost, i. 2; ii. 1; iii. 1; iv. 3; v. 2; Midsummer-Night's Dream, i. 1; ii. 1, 2; iii. 2; Merchant of Venice, ii. 6. 9; As You Like It, iv. 1, end; All's Well that Ends Well, i. 1; iii. 2; Troilus and Cressida, iii. 2, 3; Romeo and Juliet, i. 1, 4; ii. 1, 5; Othello, i. 3; King Lear, iv. 6;* his brand in a boiling spring, *Sonnets cliii., cliv.*

Cur(s), small, *I. Henry VI., iii. 1;* bark when their fellows do, *Henry VIII., ii. 4;* that like nor peace nor war, *Coriolanus, i. 1;* Casca like a, *Julius Cæsar, v. 1;* Ajax and Achilles, *Troilus and Cressida, v. 4.*

Curan, a courtier in *King Lear,* introduced in *ii. 1.*

Curds and cream, queen of, *A Winter's Tale, iv. 3* or *4.*

Curfew, the solemn, *The Tempest, v. 1; Measure for Measure, iv. 2; Romeo and Juliet, iv. 4*—a slip for matin, probably.

Curio, a gentleman attending on the duke in *Twelfth Night,* introduced in the first scene, an unimportant character.

Curiosity, woman's, *Two Gentlemen of Verona, i. 2; As You Like It, iii. 2;* (exact scrutiny), *King Lear, i. 1;* (fastidiousness), *Timon of Athens, iv. 3;* (fine distinctions), *King Lear, i. 2.*

Current(s), course of an unhindered, *Two Gentlemen of Verona, ii. 7;* corrupted, of this world, *Hamlet, iii. 3;* of the sea, *Othello, iii. 3.*

Curses, on Prospero, *The Tempest, ii. 2;* of the church, *King John, iii. 1, 3;* for murder, *King John, iv. 3;* on Judases, *Richard II., iii. 2;* of Suffolk—recoil of, *II. Henry VI., iii. 2; v. 1;* Anne's, *Richard III., i. 2;* Margaret's, *Richard III., i. 3; iii. 3, 4; iv. 1;* teaching of, *Richard III., iv. 4;* of a mother on her son, *Richard III., iv. 4;* York's on Margaret, *Richard III., i. 3;* of Thersites, *Troilus and Cressida, v. 1;* on Romans, *Coriolanus, i. 4; iv. 1, 2; Timon of Athens, iii. 6; iv. 1, 3; Julius Cæsar, iii. 1;* not loud but deep, *Macbeth, v. 2;* a father's, *King Lear, i. 1, 4; ii. 4;* on a liar, *Othello, v. 2; Lucrece, l. 967.* See also MALEDICTIONS.

Curst (cross, scolding, ill-tempered), *Two Gentlemen of Verona,* *iii. 1; Taming of the Shrew, i. 1, 2; Richard III., i. 2;* and others.

Curtal, name of a horse, *All's Well that Ends Well, ii. 3.*

Curtal dog (curtail), a, *Merry Wives of Windsor, ii. 1.*

Curtis, one of the servants of Petruchio in the *Taming of the Shrew,* introduced in *iv. 1.*

Curtle-axe (cutlass), *As You Like It, i. 3.*

Custard, leaped into the, *All's Well that Ends Well, ii. 5.* An allusion to the custom of having a clown leap into a custard at a feast.

Custard coffin (the crust of a pie was called a coffin), *Taming of the Shrew, iv. 2.*

Custom(s), if obeyed in all things, *Coriolanus, ii. 3;* one honoured in the breach, *Hamlet, i. 4;* that monster, *Hamlet, iii. 4;* makes insensible, *Hamlet, v. 1;* nice, courtesy to kings, *Hamlet, v. 2;* the plague of, *King Lear, i. 2;* new, *Henry VIII., i. 3.* See HABIT, FASHION.

Cut, the unkindest, *Julius Cæsar, iii. 2.*

Cut, *Twelfth Night, ii. 3.* A name applied to a horse.

Cut and long tail (short- and long-tailed dogs—that is, people of all ranks), *Merry Wives of Windsor, iii. 4.*

Cutpurse, requisites for a, *A Winter's Tale, iv. 3 or 4.*

Cuttle, play the saucy, *II. Henry IV., ii. 4.* Perhaps an allusion to the cuttle-fish, which hides itself by throwing out a black juice from its mouth.

Cyclops, *Titus Andronicus, iv. 3; Hamlet, ii. 2.*

Cydnus River, the, in Cilicia, *Antony and Cleopatra, ii. 2; v. 2; Cymbeline, ii. 4.*

Cymbals, *Coriolanus, v. 4.*

Cymbeline, a play classed with the tragedies, though not tragic in its ending. It was first printed in 1623, and is supposed to have been written in 1609 or 1610. The historic material for it, that regarding the Roman tribute, is taken from Holinshed. The story of Posthumus and his wife is from one of the novels of the "Decameron." The time, as nearly as can be determined of a play that utterly disregards consistency in time as well as in other regards, is shortly before the Christian era. The vision or dream of Posthumus, in *iv. 4,* is supposed to be by some other hand than Shakspere's. Hazlitt calls *Cymbeline* "one of the most delightful of Shakspere's historical plays," and Swinburne says of it, "I may say I have always loved this one above all other children of Shakspere." The greatest charm of the play is in the character of Imogen.

Cymbeline, King of Britain, first appears in the drama that bears his name, toward the close of the first scene. He is weak, and entirely under the influence of his queen.

Cynic(s), Timon and Apemantus in *Timon of Athens;* curses of a, *Timon of Athens, iv. 1, 3;* quarrel of, *Timon of Athens, iv. 3;* epitaph on a, *Timon of Athens, v. 4;* vile rhymes of a, *Julius Cæsar, iv. 3.*

Cynicism, of Cassius, *Julius Cæsar, i. 2,* "I do not know the man," etc.; *Sonnet lxvi.*

Cynthia, *Venus and Adonis, l. 727.* The moon, or Diana.

Cypress, let me be laid in, *Twelfth Night, ii. 4.* Coffins were made of cypress-wood.

Cyprus, an island in the Mediterranean, scene of the last four acts of *Othello.*

Cyprus (a veil of crape), *Twelfth Night, iii. 1.*

Cytherea (Venus), *Taming of the Shrew, induction, 2; A Winter's Tale, iv. 3 or 4; Cymbeline, ii. 2; Passionate Pilgrim, iv., vi., ix., xi.*

Daff (doff, put off), *Much Ado about Nothing, v. 1; Othello, iv. 2.*

Daffodils, *A Winter's Tale, iv. 3, 4.*

Dagger(s), a phantom, *Macbeth, ii. 1; iii. 4;* in thoughts, *II. Henry IV., iv. 4;* speak, *Hamlet, iii. 2;* worn in the mouth, *Cymbeline, iv. 2.*

Dagonet, Sir, King Arthur's jester, whom he made a knight, *II. Henry IV., iii. 2.*

Daintry (Daventry in Northamptonshire), *III. Henry VI., v. 1.*

Daisies, pied, *Love's Labour's Lost, v. 2.*

Dalliance, *The Tempest, iv. 1;* the primrose path of, *Hamlet, i. 3;* in time of action, *I. Henry IV., v. 2; Troilus and Cressida, iii. 3; Othello, i. 3.*

Dalmatians, *Cymbeline, iii. 1, 7.*

Damascus, in Syria, *I. Henry VI., i. 3.* Damascus was said to be on the spot where Cain killed Abel.

Damnation, *Merry Wives of Windsor, iii. 2; Much Ado about Nothing, iv. 1; King John, iv. 2; Othello, iii. 3;* a more delicate way than by drowning, *Othello, i. 3;* ancient, *Romeo and Juliet, iii. 3;* by not being at court, *As You Like It, iii. 2;* no warrant can defend from, *Richard III., i. 4;* of his taking off, *Macbeth, i. 7.*

Damned, torment for the. *The Tempest, i. 2.*

Damon, *Hamlet, iii. 2.* Applied to Horatio.

Dances, Bergomask, *Midsummer - Night's Dream, v. 1.* See BRAWL, CANARY, CINQUE-PACE, CORANTO, HAY, JIG, LAVOLTA, MEASURE, PAVAN, ROUNDEL, SWORD-DANCE, TRIP-AND-GO, UPSPRING.

Dances, of shepherds, *A Winter's Tale, iv. 3 or 4.*

Dancing, *Twelfth Night, i. 3 ; A Winter's Tale, iv. 3 or 4 ; Romeo and Juliet, i. 5 ; Venus and Adonis, l. 146.*

Dandy(ies), a, *Love's Labour's Lost, i. 1 ; iv. 3 ; v. 2,* "This is he that," etc.; Hotspur's description of a, *I. Henry IV., i. 3,* "He was perfumed," etc., *Hamlet, v. 2 ; Othello, v. 2.*

Danes, drinking habits of the, *Hamlet, i. 4 ; Othello, ii. 3.*

Danger, makes unscrupulous, *King John, iii. 4 ; Richard II., ii. 1 ;* the nettle, *I. Henry IV., ii. 3 ;* of the great, *Richard III., i. 3,* "They that stand high," etc. ; subtly taints, *Troilus and Cressida, iii. 3 ;* more dangerous than, *Julius Cæsar, ii. 2 ;* in, of the scotched snake, *Macbeth, iii. 2 ;* to be too busy is some, *Hamlet, iii. 4 ;* deviseth shifts, *Venus and Adonis, l. 690 ;* lurking, *I. Henry VI., v. 3 ; II. Henry VI., iii. 1 ;* of pride when in power, *Troilus and Cressida, i. 3.* See OMENS.

Daniel, a, come to judgment, *Merchant of Venice, iv. 1.*

Danskers (Danes), *Hamlet, ii. 1.*

Dante, imagery reminding of, *Measure for Measure, iii. 1,* "To bathe in fiery floods," etc.

Daphne, the nymph that was changed into a laurel-tree when flying from Apollo, *Taming of the Shrew, induction, 2 ; Midsummer-Night's Dream, ii. 1.*

Dardan (Troy, Trojan), *Lucrece, l. 1436 ;* Dardanian wives, *Merchant of Venice, iii. 2.*

Dardanius, a servant of Brutus in *Julius Cæsar*, appears in *v. 5.*

Daring, becoming a man, *Macbeth, i. 7 ;* of an adventurous spirit, *I. Henry IV., i. 3 ;* damnation, *Hamlet, iv. 5.*

Darius, King of Persia, *I. Henry VI., i. 5.*

Darkness, makes hearing more acute, *Midsummer - Night's Dream, iii. 2.*

Darlings, curled, *Othello, i. 2.*

Darnel, *I. Henry VI., iii. 2 ; King Lear, iv. 4 ; Henry V., v. 2.*

Darraign (arrange), *II. Henry VI., ii. 2.*

Dartford, a town in Kent, seventeen miles from London, *II. Henry VI., v. 1.*

Datchet-mead (bleaching-place), *Merry Wives of Windsor,*
iii. 3. Datchet is a hamlet adjoining Windsor.

Dates, pies of, *All's Well that Ends Well, i. 1; Troilus and*
Cressida, i. 2.

Dates at which the plays were written and published. See OR-
DER AND DATES.

Daub (keep up the pretence), *King Lear, iv. 1.*

Daughter(s), still harping on my, *Hamlet, ii. 2;* unkind, *King*
Lear, ii. 4; iii. 4; trust not, *Othello, i. 1.*

Dauphin, the (afterward Louis VIII.), treachery of, *King John,*
v. 4. See MELUN.

Dauphin, the, crowned Charles VII., *I. Henry VI., i. 1.*

David's (St.) Day (March 1st), the leek worn upon, *Henry V.,*
iv. 7. See LEEK.

Davy, servant of Justice Shallow in *II. Henry IV.,* first appears
in *v. 1.*

Dawn, *Much Ado about Nothing, v. 3.* "The gentle day," etc.
See MORNING.

Day, the time of, *I. Henry IV., i. 2;* the tell-tale, *II. Henry VI.,*
iv. 1; Lucrece, l. 806; prying, *Lucrece, l. 1088;* jocund, *Romeo and*
Juliet, iii. 5; stirring passage of the, *Comedy of Errors, iii. 1;* who
dares not stir by, *King John, i. 1.*

Day(s), better, *As You Like It, ii. 7; Timon of Athens, iv. 2;*
an unseasonable, *All's Well that Ends Well, v. 3;* of reconciliation
—of ill omen, *King John, iii. 1;* evil, *Sonnets lxvi.* to *lxviii.;* never
such a, since Cæsar, *II. Henry IV., i. 1.*

Day-woman (dairy), *Love's Labour's Lost, i. 2.* Day is supposed to be an old word for milk.

Dead, the, appreciation of, *All's Well that Ends Well, v. 3,*
"well excused," etc.; spirits of, *A Winter's Tale, iii. 3;* indignities
to, *I. Henry IV., i. 1;* of this year, quit for the next, *II. Henry IV.,*
iii. 2; eulogy on, *I. Henry VI., i. 1;* appeasing of, by vengeance,
Titus Andronicus, i. 1 or *2;* flowers for the, *Henry VIII., iv. 2;*
Romeo and Juliet, iv. 5; v. 3; Hamlet, iv. 5; v. 1; Cymbeline, iv.
2; Pericles, iv. 1; arms hung over the, *Hamlet, iv. 5; Titus An-*
dronicus, i. 1; borne with uncovered face, *Romeo and Juliet, iv. 1;*
Hamlet, iv. 5, song; among the, *Romeo and Juliet, iii. 5;* base uses
of, *Hamlet, v. 1;* sorrow for, *Sonnets xxx., xxxi., lxxi.;* hair of, *Son-*
net lxviii.; praise of, *Sonnet lxxii.*

Dead men's fingers, a plant, *Hamlet, iv. 7.* Supposed to be
the purple orchis, spoken of in the same sentence as long purples.

Deafness, a tale to cure, *The Tempest, i. 2.*

Dear, so bloody and so, *Twelfth Night, v. i.* Dear and dearth from *dere,* to hurt.

Dearn (lonely), *Pericles, iii., prologue.*

Death, preparation for, *Measure for Measure, ii. 2;* better than dishonour, *Measure for Measure, ii. 4;* the fool of, see LIFE; terrors of, *Measure for Measure, iii. 1;* a great disguiser, *Measure for Measure, iv. 2;* life that is past fearing, *Measure for Measure, v. 1;* the end of woes, *Comedy of Errors, i. 1;* penalty of, for traffic between cities, *Comedy of Errors, i. 1;* effect of, *Much Ado about Nothing, iv. 1;* good inspirations at, *Merchant of Venice, i. 2;* sought, *As You Like It, i. 2;* conceit nearer to it than the powers, *As You Like It, ii. 6;* and sleep, *Taming of the Shrew, induction, 1;* tests of, *A Winter's Tale, iii. 2;* feasts by quarrels of kings, *King John, ii. 1 or 2;* order for Arthur's, *King John, iii. 3;* welcome, *King John, iii. 4;* effect of report of Arthur's, *King John, iv. 2;* no life achieved by others', *King John, iv. 4;* truth in, *King John, v. 4;* besieging the mind, *King John, v. 7;* value of words at, *Richard II., ii. 1;* prophecy before, *Richard II., ii. 1; I. Henry IV., v. 4;* nothing our own but—an antic throned in the crown, *Richard II., iii. 2;* owed to God, *I. Henry IV., v. 1;* counterfeited, *I. Henry IV., v. 4;* allusion to the notion that it takes place at ebb-tide, *Henry V., ii. 3;* friendship in, *Henry V., iv. 6;* the umpire of men's miseries, *I. Henry VI., ii. 5;* like the removal of a court, *I. Henry VI., ii. 5;* the end of misery, *I. Henry VI., iii. 2;* thou antic (harlequin), *I. Henry VI., iv. 7;* signs of a violent, *II. Henry VI., iii. 2;* fear of, *II. Henry VI., iii. 3;* coming of, *III. Henry VI., i. 4,* "The sands are numbered," etc.; summons to, *Troilus and Cressida, iv. 4;* defiance of, *Coriolanus, iii. 2, 3;* apparent, *Romeo and Juliet, iv. 5; v. 3;* lamentation for, *Romeo and Juliet, iv. 5;* merriment at, *Romeo and Juliet, v. 3;* beauty in, *Romeo and Juliet, v. 3;* and honour, *Julius Cæsar, i. 2;* fear of, *Julius Cæsar, ii. 2; iii. 1;* lament for, *Julius Cæsar, iii. 1;* time of, the only anxiety, *Julius Cæsar, iii. 1;* a becoming, *Macbeth, i. 4;* omens of, *Macbeth, ii. 3,* see also OMENS; peace of, *Macbeth, iii. 2;* in life, *Macbeth, iv. 3,* "The quean, etc.; dusty, *Macbeth, v. 5;* a soldier's, *Macbeth, v. 7;* common, *Hamlet, i. 2;* without absolution, *Hamlet, i. 5;* what may come after, *Hamlet, iii. 1;* proud—a fell sergeant—why should, be shunned, *Hamlet, v. 2,* "Not a whit," etc.; men must await their, *King Lear, v. 2;* suffered hourly, *King Lear, v. 3;* effect of, *Antony and Cleopatra, i. 2;* lament for, *Antony and Cleopatra, iv., end;* study for an easy,

Antony and Cleopatra, v. 2; end of fear, *Cymbeline, iv. 2, song;* sought, *Cymbeline, v. 3;* the sure physician—the after-inquiry, *Cymbeline, v. 4;* like a mirror, *Pericles, i. 1;* apparent, *Pericles, iii. 2;* apostrophe to, *Venus and Adonis, lines 931, 997;* preferred to dishonour, *Lucrece, l. 1723;* of the childless, *Sonnets i., iii., iv., vi., x., xii., xiii., xiv.;* defeated by verse, *Sonnets xviii., cvii.;* the churl, *Sonnet xxxii.;* longing for, *Sonnet lxvi.;* knell of, *II. Henry IV., i. 1; Sonnet lxxi.; Venus and Adonis, l. 701;* a fell arrest, *Sonnet lxxvi.;* feeds on men, *Sonnet cxlvi.;* of a youth, *Passionate Pilgrim, x.*

Deaths, pangs of three several, *Measure for Measure, iii. 5.*

Deborah, the sword of, *I. Henry VI., i. 2.*

Deboshed, in many passages for debauched.

Debts, paid by death, *Tempest, iii. 2;* desperate, *Timon of Athens, iii. 4.*

Decay, this muddy vesture of, *Merchant of Venice, v. 1.*

Deceit, justified, *Measure for Measure, iii. 1; iv. 1;* of men, *Much Ado about Nothing, ii. 3, song;* under smiles, *Merchant of Venice, i. 3; Hamlet, i. 5;* of a traitor, *II. Henry VI., iii. 1;* steals gentle shapes, *Richard III., ii. 2;* in a gorgeous palace, *Romeo and Juliet, iii. 2;* in friendship, *Julius Cæsar, iv. 2;* in prophecy, *Macbeth, v. 7,* "And be these juggling," etc.; commended, *Othello, i. 1; Macbeth, i. 5, 7;* in a face, *Lucrece, l. 1506 Midsummer-Night's Dream, iii. 2; A Winter's Tale, i. 2; II. Henry VI., iii. 2; III. Henry VI., iii. 2.*

Decimation, and a tithed death, *Timon of Athens, v. 5.*

Decision. See PROMPTNESS.

Decius Brutus, one of the conspirators in *Julius Cæsar,* first appears in *i. 2.* His real name was Decimus Junius Brutus Albanus. Shakspere took this form of the name from his English Plutarch.

Decline (incline), *Comedy of Errors, iii. 2.*

Deed(s), ill, double, *Comedy of Errors, iii. 2;* high and worthy, *Much Ado about Nothing, v. 1;* light of a good, *Merchant of Venice, v. 1;* dying tongueless, *A Winter's Tale, i. 2;* without a name, *Macbeth, iv. 1;* foul, will rise, *Hamlet, i. 2;* must go with the purpose, *Macbeth, iv. 1.*

Deep-vow, a prisoner, *Measure for Measure, iv. 3.*

Deer, killed my, *Merry Wives of Windsor, i. 1;* see SHALLOW; the killing of, *As You Like It, ii. 1;* let the stricken, go weep, *Hamlet, iii. 2;* the frightened, *Lucrece, l. 1149;* England's timorous, *I. Henry VI., iv. 2.* See also HUNTING.

Defeat, everlasting shame, *Henry V.*, *iv. 5.*

Defeatures (disfigurement), *Comedy of Errors*, *ii. 1; v. 1.*

Defect(s), influence of one, *Hamlet, i. 4;* sometimes prove commodities (advantages), *King Lear, iv. 1;* made perfections, *Antony and Cleopatra, ii. 2.*

Defence, in cases of, weigh the enemy more mighty than he seems, *Henry V.*, *ii. 4.*

Defiance (refusal), *Measure for Measure, iii. 1.*

Defiance, *King John, i. 1; iv. 3; v. 2; Richard II., i. 1; iv. 1; Henry V., i. 2; ii. 4; iii. 6; iv. 3; Julius Cæsar, iv. 3; v. 1; The Tempest, iii. 3; Much Ado about Nothing, v. 1; I. Henry IV., i. 3; iv. 1; II. Henry IV., v. 2; Coriolanus, iii. 3; Macbeth, iii. 4; Troilus and Cressida, iv. 1.*

Deformed, the, in shape and manners, *Tempest, v. 1;* talk of one, *Much Ado about Nothing, v. 1;* only ambition left for the, *III. Henry VI., iii. 2;* called stigmatics, *II. Henry VI., v. 1; III. Henry VI., ii. 2.*

Deformity, *Richard III., i. 1–3; iii. 1; King Lear, iv. 2.*

Defuse (disorder), *King Lear, i. 4.*

Degeneracy, of descendants of the great, *Taming of the Shrew, induction, 2; Julius Cæsar, i. 3; Coriolanus, iii. 1; I. Henry IV., i. 3;* of the world, *Measure for Measure, iii. 2; Richard III., i. 3.*

Degree, observance of, *Troilus and Cressida, i. 3.*

Deign (to honour), *Two Gentlemen of Verona, i. 1.*

Deiphobus, son of Priam, character in *Troilus and Cressida*, introduced in *iv. 1.*

Deity, used in the sense of an attribute of deity, ubiquity, *Twelfth Night, v. 1*, "Nor can there be that deity," etc.

Delabreth, Charles, Constable of France. See CONSTABLE.

De la Pole. See SUFFOLK.

Delations, close (secret accusations?), *Othello, iii. 3.*

Delay(s), danger of, *All's Well that Ends Well, v. 3*, "Let's take the instant by the forward top," etc.; *I. Henry IV., iii. 2, end; I. Henry VI., iii. 2;* leads to beggary, *Richard III., iv. 3;* take swift advantage of the hours, *Richard III., iv. 1; Troilus and Cressida, iii. 3; Timon of Athens, v. 1; Julius Cæsar, iv. 3*, "We must take the current," etc.; *Hamlet, iv. 7*, "That we would do," etc.; *Henry VIII., iv. 2; Romeo and Juliet, i. 4;* the flighty purpose never is o'ertook unless the deed go with it, *Macbeth, iv. 1.*

Deliberation. See DELAY.

Delighted spirit, the, *Measure for Measure, iii. 1.*

"A difficult word to explain in this connection. It is variously understood as referring to the previous condition of the spirit, as being used in the sense of delightful, as in *Othello, i. 3*, ' If virtue no delighted beauty lack '; and as meaning de-lighted, deprived of light, a manner of using the prefix not uncommon among writers of Shakspere's time."—HUDSON.

Delights, the vainest, *Love's Labour's Lost, i. 1;* violent, *Romeo and Juliet, ii. 6.*

Delirium, *King John, v. 7.*

Delphos, oracle at, consulted, *A Winter's Tale, ii. 1; iii. 1, 2.* It is spoken of as an island in *iii. 1*, as it is in the story on which the play was founded.

Delusion, *Hamlet, iii. 4; Cymbeline, iv. 2.*

Demerits (merits), *Coriolanus, i. 1.*

Demetrius, character in *Midsummer-Night's Dream*, introduced in *i. 1;* a lover of Hermia at first, afterward of Helena.

Demetrius, son of Tamora in *Titus Andronicus;* is introduced in *i. 1* or *2* as a prisoner of the Romans, and is set free by the emperor; plots against Lavinia, *ii. 1, 3, 4;* is killed, *iv. 2.* Like his brother, he is pure brute.

Demetrius, character in *Antony and Cleopatra;* introduced in *i. 1*, a friend of Antony.

Demon, thy, thy spirit which keeps thee, *Antony and Cleopatra, ii. 3.* Demon here is used in the sense of guardian angel.

Demureness, in boys, *II. Henry IV., iv. 3.*

Denayed (denied), *II. Henry VI., i. 3.*

Denis, Saint, patron of France, *Henry V., v. 2; I. Henry VI., iii. 2.*

Denmark, something rotten in, *Hamlet, i. 4.*

Dennis, one of Oliver's servants in *As You Like It, i. 1.*

Denny, Sir Anthony, character in *Henry VIII.;* introduced in *v. 1.*

Denny, Lady, the name sometimes given as that of the old lady, friend to Anne Boleyn, in *Henry VIII.*

Denunciation, of Leontes by Paulina, *A Winter's Tale, ii. 3;* of Perdita and Florizel, *iv. 3* or *4.*

Denunciation (proclamation), *Measure for Measure, i. 3.*

Depart (rather part with), *Love's Labour's Lost, ii. 1.*

Deputy, power entrusted to a, *Measure for Measure i. 1;* state of a, *Merchant of Venice, v. 1.*

Derby, Earl of. See STANLEY, THOMAS, LORD.

Dercetas, character in *Antony and Cleopatra;* introduced in *iv. 14*, friend of Antony; his desertion, *iv. 12* or *14.*

Derivative (inheritance), *A Winter's Tale, iii. 2.*

Descant (part added to a song), *Two Gentlemen of Verona, i. 2.*

Descent, poor, hated by women, *Two Gentlemen of Verona, iii. 2.*

Desdemona, wife of Othello, first appears in *i. 3;* described, *ii. 1;* the story of her marriage, *iii. 1;* she intercedes for Cassio, *iii. 3, 4;* is murdered, *v. 2.*

"In Desdemona we cannot but feel that the slightest manifestation of intellectual power or active will would have injured the dramatic effect. She is a victim consecrated from the first—'an offering without blemish,' alone worthy of the grand final sacrifice; all harmony, all grace, all purity, all tenderness, all truth!"—MRS. JAMESON. See also IMOGEN.

Desert, an inaccessible, *As You Like It, ii. 7.*

Desert, your, speaks loud, *Measure for Measure, v. 1;* used after one's, *Hamlet, ii. 2.*

Desertion, remorse for, *Antony and Cleopatra, iv. 6, 9;* in misfortune, *Antony and Cleopatra, iv. 10 or 12.*

Desire, gratified, without content, *Macbeth, iii. 2; Cymbeline, i. 7.*

Desolation, *King John, ii. 2; Richard II., i. 2; Henry VIII., iii. 1; Cymbeline, iii. 3.*

Despair, *King John, iii. 4; iv. 3; Hamlet, i. 2,* "That this too, too solid flesh would melt," etc.; trifling with, to cure, *King Lear, iv. 6; Cymbeline, i. 1; Antony and Cleopatra, iii., end; iv. 10 or 12, 12 or 14; Comedy of Errors, v. 1; Richard II., ii. 2; Richard III., v. 3; Titus Andronicus, iii. 1; Macbeth, v. 5; Merchant of Venice, iii. 2.*

Desperate (magic) studies, *As You Like It, v. 4.*

Desperation, *Macbeth, iii. 1; v. 7; III. Henry VI., i. 4; King John, iii. 4; Romeo and Juliet, v. 3; Othello, v. 2; Julius Cæsar, v. 5; Antony and Cleopatra, iii. 9; iv. 13.*

Despondency, *Richard II., iii. 2; Richard III., v. 3; Timon of Athens, iv. 3.*

Destiny, *The Tempest, iii. 3; Richard III., iv. 4; Othello, iii. 3;* hanging and wiving go by, *Merchant of Venice, ii. 9.*

Determination. See RESOLUTION.

Detraction. See CALUMNY, SLANDER.

Detractions, they that hear their, *Much Ado about Nothing, ii. 3.*

Deucalion, *A Winter's Tale, iv. 3 or 4.* The Noah of Greek mythology.

De Vere, John. See OXFORD.

Devil, the, will not have me damned, *Merry Wives of Windsor*, *v. 5;* a cunning enemy, *Measure for Measure, ii. 2;* write good angel on his horn (that is, give a false seeming), *Measure for Measure, ii. 4;* crest of, *Measure for Measure, ii. 4;* seek redemption of the, *Measure for Measure, v. 1;* his burning throne, *Measure for Measure, v. 1;* a long spoon to eat with the, *Comedy of Errors, iv. 3;* can cite Scripture, *Merchant of Venice, i. 3;* in the likeness of a Jew, *Merchant of Venice, iii. 1; All's Well that Ends Well, iv. 5;* lead the measure (of fashion), *All's Well that Ends Well, ii. 1;* thy master, *All's Well that Ends Well, ii. 3;* possession by, *Twelfth Night, iii. 4;* treated with courtesy, *Twelfth Night, iv. 2;* in likeness of a bride, *King John, iii. 1;* selling the soul to—due of, *I. Henry IV., i. 2;* Glendower's league with, *I. Henry IV., ii. 2;* command—tell truth and shame the, *I. Henry IV., iii. 1;* seem a saint and play the, *Richard III., i. 3;* mistake of, *Timon of Athens, iii. 3; Julius Cæsar, i. 2;* "'can the, speak true?" *Macbeth, i. 3;* a painted, *Macbeth, ii. 2;* sold to, for Banquo's children, *Macbeth, iii. 1;* hath power to assume a pleasing shape, *Hamlet, ii. 2;* with visage of devotion, *Hamlet, iii. 1;* prince of darkness, *King Lear, iii. 4;* in the voice of a nightingale, *King Lear, iii. 6;* reference to the cloven foot of, *Othello, v. 2,* "I look down toward his feet," etc.

Devil(s), a born, *The Tempest, iv. 1;* speaking, *The Tempest, v. 1;* a demi-devil, *The Tempest, v. 1;* crime too inhuman for a, *A Winter's Tale, iii. 2;* affect sanctity, *Othello, ii. 3;* names of, *King Lear, iii. 4.* See FIENDS.

Devotion, *Two Gentlemen of Verona, ii. 7; Henry VIII., iv. 1;* pretence of, *Merchant of Venice, ii. 2; Othello, ii. 3;* the devil sugared over with the visage of, *Hamlet, iii. 1.*

Dew, from Bermuda's wicked, *The Tempest, i. 2;* tears of flowers, *Midsummer-Night's Dream, iii. 1;* the, *Midsummer-Night's Dream, iv. 1;* falling, *King John, ii. 1;* the air doth drizzle, *Romeo and Juliet, iii. 5;* honey-dew, *Titus Andronicus, iii. 1.* Pliny says that honey-dew is the saliva of the stars, or a liquid produced by the purgation of the air.

Diana, the goddess, introduced in *Pericles, v. 1* (or *2*), where she appears to the king in a vision. Her livery, *ii. 5;* in the fountain, *As You Like It, iv. 1.* Dianas at fountains were not uncommon; one set up in 1596 at West Cheap, London, poured water from the breasts; seemed as, *Much Ado about Nothing, iv. 1;* chaste as, *Merchant of Venice, i. 2;* bud of (Agnus Castus, chaste tree), *Midsummer-Night's Dream, iv. 1;* knights of, *All's Well that Ends*

Well, i. 3; from thy altar fly, *All's Well that Ends Well, ii. 3;* her foresters, *I. Henry IV., i. 2;* the stars her waiting-women, *Troilus and Cressida, v. 2.*

Diana, a young girl, daughter of a widow in Florence, character in *All's Well that Ends Well,* introduced in *iii. 5.*

Dice, *Henry V., iv., prologue; King Lear, iii. 4; Antony and Cleopatra, ii. 3.* See GOURD.

Dick, a butcher, follower of Jack Cade in *II. Henry VI., iv. 2, 3.*

Dickens, the, *Merry Wives of Windsor, iii. 2.*

Dickon (Richard III.), *Richard III., v. 3.*

Dictator, a, *Antony and Cleopatra, ii. 6.*

Dictynna (Diana), *Love's Labour's Lost, iv. 2.*

Dido, Queen of Carthage, *The Tempest, ii. 1; Merchant of Venice, v. 1; Midsummer-Night's Dream, i. 1; II. Henry VI., iii. 2; Titus Andronicus, ii. 3; Antony and Cleopatra, iv. 12 or 14.*

Die, to, is to be a counterfeit, *I. Henry IV., v. 4;* without a sign, *II. Henry VI., iii. 3;* when the brains were out, the man would, *Macbeth, iii. 4.*

Dieu vous garde, etc. (God guard you, sir, and you also your servant), *Twelfth Night, iii. 1.*

Di faciant, etc. (the gods grant this may be the last triumph), *III. Henry VI., i. 3.*

Difficulty, as great as for a camel, etc., *Richard II., v. 5.*

Diffused (wild, elf-like), *Merry Wives of Windsor, iv. 4.*

Digest (? dissolve or receive), *King Lear, i. 1.*

Digestion, described, *Coriolanus, i. 1, fable;* of unquiet meals, *Comedy of Errors, v. 1; Troilus and Cressida, ii. 3;* wait on appetite, *Macbeth, iii. 4.*

Dighton, John, a murderer, *Richard III., iv. 3.*

Dignity(ies), of office, *II. Henry IV., v. 3; Henry VIII., iii. 1;* clay and clay differ in, *Cymbeline, iv. 2.*

Dildos and fadings, refrains of songs, *A Winter's Tale, iv. 3 or 4.*

Dilemmas (plans), *All's Well that Ends Well, iii. 6.*

Diluculo surgere, etc. (to rise early is most healthful), *Twelfth Night, ii. 3,* from Lily's Latin Grammar.

Dimples, *A Winter's Tale, ii. 3; Venus and Adonis, l. 242.*

Dinner, a man is unforgiving before, *Coriolanus, v. 1;* haste for, *King Lear, i. 4.*

Diomedes, Grecian general, character in *Troilus and Cressida,* introduced in *ii. 3.* Cressida deserts Troilus for him, and they fight in *v. 6.* Alluded to in *III. Henry VI., iv. 2.*

Diomedes, an attendant of Cleopatra in *Antony and Cleopatra,* introduced in *iv. 14.*

Dion, one of the lords sent to consult the oracle in *A Winter's Tale, ii. 1; iii. 1, 2.*

Dionyza, wife of Cleon, in *Pericles,* introduced in *i. 4;* plots against Marina, *iv., prologue, 1, 3* or *4;* burned in the palace, *v. 3.*

Dirges, *Cymbeline, iv. 2,* "Notes of sorrow out of tune."

Dis, *The Tempest, iv. 1;* wagon of, *A Winter's Tale, iv. 3* or *4.* Pluto, god of the realms of the dead.

Disappointment, in one beloved, *Sonnets xxxiv.* to *xlii.*

Disasters, attributed to planets, *King Lear, i. 2; Hamlet, i. 1; Julius Cæsar, iii. 1;* in lofty actions, *Troilus and Cressida, i. 3.*

Discipline, of war, *Henry V., iii. 2; iv. 1; Richard III., v. 3; Troilus and Cressida, ii. 3.*

Discomfort, from the seeming spring of comfort, *Macbeth, i. 2.*

Discontent, brows full of, *Richard II., iv. 1;* with the present, *II. Henry IV., i. 3;* popular, *King John, iii. 4; Henry VIII., i. 2;* winter of, *Richard III., i. 1;* in poverty, *Richard III., iv. 2;* with one's talents, *Sonnet xxix.; Romeo and Juliet, iii. 3.*

Discord, civil, *II. Henry IV., i. 1.*

Discord, gives strength to the enemy, *Troilus and Cressida. i. 3.*

Discretion, the better part of valour is, *I. Henry IV., v. 4;* want of, in age, *King Lear, ii. 4,* "You are old," etc.; honourable not to outsport, *Othello, ii. 3.*

Discrimination, of man, *Cymbeline, i. 6.*

Discussion, keen encounter of wits, *Richard III., i. 2.*

Disdain, Lady, applied to Beatrice by Benedick, *Much Ado about Nothing, i. 1.*

Disease(s), *Measure for Measure, i. 2;* worst before cure, *King John, iii. 4;* vanity of sickness, *King John, v. 7;* (anxiety) *I. Henry VI., ii. 5; King Lear, i. 1;* turn to commodity—of not listening, *II. Henry IV., i. 2;* of the mind, *Macbeth, v. 3;* concealed, *Hamlet, iv. 1;* desperate, need desperate remedies, *Hamlet, iv. 3;* bestow the fee upon the, *King Lear, i. 1; Venus and Adonis, l. 739.*

Diseases, rotten, of the south, *Troilus and Cressida, v. 1;* list of, *Venus and Adonis, l. 739;* ague, *The Tempest, ii. 2; King John, iii. 4; Richard II., ii. 1; I. Henry IV., iii. 1; Henry VIII., i. 1; Troilus and Cressida, iii. 3; Macbeth, v. 5;* apoplexy, allusions to, *II. Henry IV., i. 2; iv. 4; II. Henry VI., iii. 2; Coriolanus, iv. 5;* cataract, or pin-and-web, *A Winter's Tale, i. 2; King Lear, iii. 4;*

consumption, *Timon of Athens, iv. 3; King Lear, iv. 6;* dropsy, *The Tempest, iv. 1; I. Henry IV., ii. 4;* epilepsy, the, allusions to, *Julius Cæsar, i. 2; Othello, iv. 1;* fevers, *Comedy of Errors, v. 1; Measure for Measure, v. 1; King John, v. 3; II. Henry IV., iv. 1; Henry V., ii. 1; Julius Cæsar, i. 2* (see ague, above); fistula, *All's Well that Ends Well, i. 1;* green-sickness, *II. Henry IV., iv. 3; Romeo and Juliet, iii. 5; Antony and Cleopatra, iii. 2; Pericles, iv. 6;* gout, *As You Like It, iii. 2; Cymbeline, v. 4;* heart-break, *A Winter's Tale, iii. 2; Richard III., i. 3; Macbeth, iv. 3;* hysteria, *King Lear, ii. 4;* indigestion, *The Tempest, ii. 2,* "My stomach is not constant;" *Comedy of Errors, v. 1; Love's Labour's Lost, i. 1; Midsummer-Night's Dream, ii. 2; iv. 1,* "Like a sickness," etc.; jaundice, *Troilus and Cressida, i. 3;* leprosy (see measles); malady of France, *Measure for Measure, i. 2; Henry V., v. 1; Pericles, iv. 2, 6;* measles (leprosy), *Coriolanus, iii. 1; Timon of Athens, iv. 1, 3;* nightmare, *King Lear, iii. 4;* palsy, allusions to, *Richard II., ii. 3; II. Henry VI., iv. 7; Troilus and Cressida, i. 3;* plague or pestilence, *Love's Labour's Lost, v. 2; Troilus and Cressida, ii. 3; Coriolanus, i. 4; iv. 1; Romeo and Juliet, v. 2; King Lear, ii. 4;* plurisy (plethora), *Hamlet, iv. 7;* rheumatism, *Midsummer-Night's Dream, ii. 1; Julius Cæsar, ii. 1;* sciatica, the, *Measure for Measure, i. 2; Timon of Athens, iv. 1;* scrofula or king's evil, *Timon of Athens, iv. 3,* "Consumptions sow," etc.; *Macbeth, iv. 3;* serpigo, *Measure for Measure, iii. 1; Troilus and Cressida, ii. 3;* swooning, *Measure for Measure, ii. 4; As You Like It, iv. 3;* toothache, *Much Ado about Nothing, iii. 2; v. 1; Othello, iii. 3; Cymbeline, v. 4.*

Disedged, satiated, a term in falconry, *Cymbeline, iii. 4.*

Disguise, wickedness of, *Twelfth Night, ii. 2.*

Disguises, of Julia, *Two Gentlemen of Verona;* of Portia, *Merchant of Venice;* of Rosalind and Celia, *As You Like It;* of Viola, *Twelfth Night, i. 2;* of Feste, *Twelfth Night, iv. 2;* of Edgar, *King Lear, ii. 3;* of Kent, *King Lear, i. 4;* of Falstaff, *Merry Wives of Windsor, iv. 4;* of Imogen, *Cymbeline, iii. 6.*

Dishonour, compared with death, *Measure for Measure, iii. 1; Lucrece, l. 1723;* unconsciousness of one's own, *Othello, iv. 1.* See HONOUR.

Dislike (displease), *Romeo and Juliet, ii. 2.* See MISLIKE.

Disloyalty, rebuke of, *Two Gentlemen of Verona, iv. 2, 4.*

Dismes (tens), *Troilus and Cressida, ii. 2.*

Disobedience, *Two Gentlemen of Verona, iii. 1; Midsummer-Night's Dream, i. 1; Merchant of Venice, iii. 1.*

King Lear, iv. 6; not a word to throw at a, *As You Like It, i. 3;* of war, *Julius Cæsar, iii. 1.*

Dogberry, a blundering and conceited constable in *Much Ado about Nothing,* introduced in *iii. 3.* " It is a charming incongruity to find, while Leonato rages and Benedick offers his challenge, that the solemn ass, Dogberry, is the one to unravel the tangle of threads." —DOWDEN.

Dog-days, *Romeo and Juliet, iii. 1,* " For now, these hot days," etc.; *Henry VIII., v. 3.*

Doing, if doing were as easy as knowing what to do, *Merchant of Venice, i. 2.*

Doit, John, *II. Henry IV., iii. 2.*

Doit, *Merchant of Venice, i. 3.* Equal to about half a farthing.

Dolabella, a friend of Cæsar in *Antony and Cleopatra,* introduced in *iii. 12;* his message to Cleopatra, *v. 2.*

Dole (portion, lot), happy man be his, *Merry Wives of Windsor, iii. 4; A Winter's Tale, i. 2,* and elsewhere.

Dole (wailing), *As You Like It, i. 2.*

Doll Tearsheet, a low woman, character in *II. Henry IV.,* first appears in *ii. 4.* In *Henry V., ii. 1,* Pistol recommends her to Nym. It has been suggested that her name is corrupted from Tear-Street, which would explain the remark of the prince, " This Doll Tearsheet should be some road " (*II. Henry IV., ii. 3*).

Dolphin, the. See DAUPHIN.

Dolphin chamber, the, *II. Henry IV., ii. 1.*

Domineer (bluster), *Taming of the Shrew, iii. 2.*

Donalbain (Donald Bane), younger son of King Duncan in *Macbeth.* He escapes to Ireland after the murder of his father. He succeeded his brother Malcolm on the throne of Scotland in 1093.

Don Pedro. See PEDRO.

Doom, the crack of, *Macbeth, iv. 1;* the general, *Romeo and Juliet, iii. 2.*

Doomsday, *Richard III., v. 1; Julius Cæsar, iii. 1;* is near, *1 Henry IV., iv. 1, end; Hamlet, ii. 2.*

Dorcas, a shepherdess, introduced in *A Winter's Tale, iv. 4.*

Doricles, name assumed by Florizel, *A Winter's Tale, iv. 3 or 4.*

Dorset, Thomas Grey, first Marquis of, character in *Richard III.,* son of Queen Elizabeth, first appears in *i. 3.* He joined Buckingham's rebellion, but escaped to Brittany after its failure. His marriage with the daughter of William Bonville, Lord Harrington, is spoken of in *III. Henry VI., iv. 1.* Lady Jane Grey was his great-granddaughter.

Double meanings, *Macbeth, v. 7,* "Keep the word of promise to our ear and break it to our hope."

Doublet and hose, courage due from, *As You Like It, ii. 4;* in my disposition, *As You Like It, iii. 2.*

Doubt, beacon of the wise, *Troilus and Cressida, ii. 2;* worse than certainty of evil, *Cymbeline, i. 6.*

Doubts, are traitors, *Measure for Measure, i. 5.*

Doubts (suspicions), the noble cast away, *Henry VIII., iii. 1.*

Dough, the cake is, *Taming of the Shrew, i. 1; v. 1.*

Douglas, Archibald, Earl of, character in *I. Henry IV.,* introduced in *iv. 1.* His defeat at Holmedon or Homildon Hill, September 14, 1402, by Hotspur, is described in *i. 1.* He afterward became the ally of the Percys when they rebelled against Henry IV. On the field of Shrewsbury, July 23, 1403, he kills Lord Stafford and Sir Walter Blunt, mistaking them for the king. When he meets the king at last, the prince comes to his father's rescue, and Douglas flies. Taken prisoner afterward, he is set free by the prince, *v. 5.* He is brave, fearless, and faithful.

Dove(s), allusions to: Modest as, *Taming of the Shrew, ii. 1; A Winter's Tale, iv. 4* (turtles); spirit of peace, *II. Henry IV., iv. 1;* Mahomet's, *I. Henry VI., i. 2* (see MAHOMET); like a pair of, *I. Henry VI., ii. 2;* innocence of, *II. Henry VI., iii. 1;* faithfulness of, *Troilus and Cressida, iii. 2* (turtle); love and, *Romeo and Juliet, ii. 1;* young of, *Hamlet, v. 1;* doves of Venus, *The Tempest, iv. 1;* presents of, *Merchant of Venice, ii. 2; Midsummer-Night's Dream, i. 1; Venus and Adonis, l. 1190;* of Paphos, *Pericles, iv., prologue.* Paphos is on the island of Cyprus, where Venus was worshipped.

Dover, England, scene of part of *King Lear;* cliffs of, *King Lear, iv. 1, end; iv. 6.*

Dowland, John, an English musician (1562–1626), who called himself a "lutenist," and published song-books, *Passionate Pilgrim, viii.* Wood says, "We are assured that John Dowland was the rarest musician that his age did behold."

Dowry, a curse for a, *King Lear, i. 1; Hamlet, iii. 1.*

Dowsabel, name applied to a fat woman, *Comedy of Errors, iv. 1.*

Drachma (about sevenpence), *Julius Cæsar, iii. 2.*

Draft, of soldiers, *I. Henry IV., iv. 2.*

Dragon(s), on the chariot of night, *Midsummer-Night's Dream,*

Drowning-mark, *The Tempest, i. 1; v. 1.*

Drum, let him fetch off his, *All's Well that Ends Well, iii. 6.*

Drum, John, entertainment of (a beating), *All's Well that Ends Well, iii. 6.*

Drunk, in godly company, *Merry Wives of Windsor, i. 1.*

Drunkard, one loves another, *Love's Labour's Lost, iv. 3.*

Drunken man, what like, *Twelfth Night, i. 5.*

Drunkenness, *The Tempest, iii. 2; iv. 1; v. 1;* folly of, *Othello, ii. 3; Merry Wives of Windsor, i. 1, 2; Taming of the Shrew, induction, 1; Much Ado about Nothing, iii. 3.*

Dry-beat (beat soundly), *Romeo and Juliet, iii. 1.*

Dry-foot, draws (follows the scent), *Comedy of Errors, iv. 2.*

Ducats, gild myself with, *Merchant of Venice, ii. 6;* my daughter and my, *Merchant of Venice, ii. 8;* fourscore spent, *Merchant of Venice, iii. 1.*

Ducdame, *As You Like It, ii. 5.* Of uncertain meaning. Some read it *Duc ad me,* lead to me.

Duck, swim like a, *The Tempest, ii. 2.*

Dudgeon (handle), *Macbeth, ii. 1.*

Duel(s), contemplated, *Merry Wives of Windsor, i. 4; ii. 1, 3; iii. 1; Much Ado about Nothing, v. 1; Twelfth Night, iii. 4;* threats of a, *All's Well that Ends Well, ii. 3;* between Horner and Peter, *II. Henry VI., ii. 3; Hamlet, i. 1.* See CHALLENGES.

Duelling, causes for, *Love's Labour's Lost, i. 2, end;* satire on rules of, *As You Like It, v. 4.* The passage is supposed to have been suggested by a book on the punctilio of duelling, by Vincentio Saviolo, published in 1596. Terms of, *Romeo and Juliet, ii. 4; iii. 1; Taming of the Shrew, iii. 5.*

Duke, the, in *As You Like It,* who is living in the Forest of Arden, his brother having usurped his place. He is introduced in *ii. 1.* He is just and moderate, unembittered by the wrong he has suffered, and as happy in the forest as at the court.

Duke of Dark Corners, the, *Measure for Measure, iv. 3.*

Dull, a stupid constable in *Love's Labour's Lost,* introduced in *i. 1.*

Dulness, *Hamlet, iv. 1.*

Dumbleton, a merchant spoken of in *II. Henry IV., i. 2.*

Dumain, one of the lords attending on the king in *Love's Labour's Lost,* introduced in the first scene —

"For he hath wit to make an ill shape good,
And shape to win grace though he had no wit."

Dumain, Captain, slanderously described by Parolles in *All's Well that Ends Well, iv. 3.*

Dumps (sad music), *Two Gentlemen of Verona, iii. 2; Lucrece, l. 1127,* and elsewhere.

Dun, if thou art, *Romeo and Juliet, i. 4.* Allusion to the game Dun-is-in-the-Mire. Dun was a log of wood, which stood for a horse and was said to be in the mire. Two of the company tried to pull him out, calling one after another of the rest to their assistance, until all were helping, and Dun was at length pulled out.

Dunbar, George, Earl of March, in Scotland called Lord Mortimer, letter from, *I. Henry IV., ii. 3; iii. 2.* His title March led to the mistake of calling him Mortimer.

Duncan, King of Scotland, character in *Macbeth,* described by Macbeth in *i. 7.* He first appears in *i. 2,* visits Macbeth's castle, *i. 6,* and is murdered, *ii. 1.* The circumstances of the murder are taken from the account of the assassination of King Duff. In other respects, the play follows the traditional story, as told in Holinshed, quite closely. The real Duncan, whose death took place by the treachery of Macbeth, Mormaer of Moray, in 1040, is said to have been an unjust and somewhat weak sovereign. The gracious character ascribed to him in the play is according to the chronicle.

Duns, of creditors, *Timon of Athens, ii. 1, 2; iii. 4.*

Dunsinane, a hill nine miles northeast of Perth, *Macbeth, iv. 1,* scene of *act v.;* battle of, *v. 6, 7, 8.*

Dunsmore, *III. Henry VI., v. 1.*

Dunstable, *Henry VIII., iv. 1.*

Dupe, an easy, *King Lear, i. 2.*

Duplicity. See DECEIT, FALSEHOOD.

Duty, to make virtue known, *Measure for Measure, i. 1;* service sweat for, *As You Like It, ii. 3;* promptings of, *Midsummer-Night's Dream, v. 1;* did never want his meed, *Two Gentlemen of Verona, ii. 4;* unswerving, *Henry VIII., iii. 2; Hamlet, ii. 2;* cannot be silent, *King Lear, i. 1, 4.*

Eagle(s), the sight of, *Love's Labour's Lost, iv. 3; III. Henry VI., ii. 1;* flight of, *Timon of Athens, i. 1;* age of, *Timon of Athens, iv. 3;* suffer little birds to sing, *Titus Andronicus, iv. 4;* omens of victory, *Julius Cæsar, v. 1; Cymbeline, i. 1; iv. 2;* a hungry, *Venus and Adonis, l. 55;* eye of, *Romeo and Juliet, iii. 5; Richard II., iii. 3;* England the, *Henry V., i. 2;* the holy, *Cymbeline, v. 4.*

Ear (to plough), *Antony and Cleopatra, i. 2, 4.*

Ear(s), what fire is in my, *Much Ado about Nothing, iii. 1.* Allusion to the supposed burning of the ears when one is talked of. Locks worn by the, *Much Ado about Nothing, iii. 3 ; v. 1 ;* biting the, *Romeo and Juliet, ii. 4 ;* thy fair, large, *Midsummer-Night's Dream, iv. 1 ;* ear of man hath not seen, *Midsummer-Night's Dream, iv. 1 ;* deaf to counsel, not to flattery, *Timon of Athens, i. 2 ;* promise kept to the, *Macbeth, v. 8 ;* give every man thine, *Hamlet, i. 3 ;* light of (ready to hear scandal), *King Lear, iii. 4.*

Early rising, *Twelfth Night, ii. 3.*

Early training, *II. Henry VI., iii. 1,* "Now 'tis the spring," etc.; *Hamlet, i. 3,* "The canker galls," etc.

Earth, the, I task (throw down my gage), *Richard II., iv. 1 ;* curse on, *Timon of Athens, iv. 3,* "That nature," etc.; mother and tomb of nature, *Romeo and Juliet, ii. 3 ;* a sterile promontory, *Hamlet, ii. 2 ;* a girdle round the, *Midsummer-Night's Dream, ii. 1 ;* nothing lives on, but crosses, *Richard II., ii. 2 ;* more things in heaven and, *Hamlet, i. 5.*

Earthquake(s), *As You Like It, iii. 2 ;* explanation of, *I. Henry IV., iii. 1 ; Romeo and Juliet, i. 3.* Perhaps an allusion to one felt in England, April 6, 1580. The earth feverous, *Macbeth, ii. 3.*

Eastcheap, in London, scene of parts of *I.* and *II. Henry IV.,* and *Henry V.,* which are at the Boar's Head Tavern, kept by Mrs. Quickly. A tavern with that sign stood near Blackfriars Playhouse. Eastcheap was near the mansion assigned to the Prince of Wales.

Easter, allusion to the custom of wearing new clothes at, *Romeo and Juliet, iii. 1,* "Wearing his new doublet before Easter."

Eater, a hearty, *Much Ado about Nothing, i. 1,* "A valiant trencher-man."

Eating. See APPETITE, DIGESTION, DINNER.

Ebony, black as, *Love's Labour's Lost, iv. 3.*

Eaves, made of reeds, *The Tempest, v. 1.*

Eaves-dropper, play the, *Richard III., v. 3.*

Ecce signum (behold the sign), *I. Henry IV., ii. 4.*

Eche (eke), *Pericles, iii., prologue.*

Echo, babbling gossip, *Twelfth Night, i. 5 ;* cave of, *Romeo and Juliet, ii. 2 ; Taming of the Shrew, induction, 2 ; Titus Andronicus, ii. 3.*

Echo, name of a dog, *Taming of the Shrew, induction, 1.*

Eclipses, ominous, *Macbeth, ii. 3 ; iv. 1 ; Hamlet, i. 1 ; King Lear, i. 2 ; Othello, v. 2 ; Antony and Cleopatra, iii. 13.*

Ecstasy (madness), *The Tempest, iii. 3; Hamlet, iii. 4,* and elsewhere.

Edgar, son of Gloucester, in *King Lear,* introduced in *i. 2;* his brother's plot against him, *i. 2; ii. 1;* his flight, *ii. 1;* his feigned madness, *ii. 3; iii. 4, 6; iv. 1;* fights with Oswald, *iv. 6;* is restored to his place, *v. 3.* The character of Edgar is contrasted with that of Edmund; both are able, but Edgar's uprightness and unsuspiciousness make him at first an easy prey to his brother's scheme; yet he carries out his own designs with patience and skill.

Edmund, Earl of Rutland. See RUTLAND.

Edmund, an important character in *King Lear,* illegitimate son of Gloucester, introduced in the first scene. He is able, bold, and wicked, his wickedness finding some excuse in the fact that he is embittered by the stain upon his birth, and the consequent injustice which he feels he labours under, and some mitigation in the fact that he is not a hypocrite to his own conscience, but writes himself down "plain villain." His plot against Edgar, *i. 2; ii. 1;* his double-dealing with Regan and Goneril, *iv. 5, 6; v. 1, 3.*

Education, for a gentleman, *As You Like It, i. 1.* See GRAMMAR.

Edward, the Confessor (1004–1066), *Macbeth, iii. 6.*

Edward III. (1312–1377), *Henry V., ii. 4;* at Crécy, *i. 2.*

Edward, the Black Prince (1330–1376), *Richard II., ii. 1,* "In war was never," etc.; *Henry V., i. 2; ii. 4.*

Edward, Prince of Wales (1453–1471), son of Henry VI., character in *III. Henry VI.,* introduced in *i. 1;* disinherited, *ii. 2;* knighted, *ii. 2;* captured and killed, *v. 5.* It is not certain whether he fell in battle or was put to death afterward.

Edward IV. (1442–1483), character in *II.* and *III. Henry VI.,* and *Richard III.* In the first he appears as Edward, son of the Duke of York, only in *v. 1.* In *III. Henry VI.* he is introduced in *i. 1,* as Earl of March. On the death of his father at Wakefield, *i. 4,* he becomes Duke of York and claimant to the throne. He defeats the Lancastrians at Mortimer's Cross, *ii. 1.* This scene gives the traditional origin of his device of the three suns. He went to London and was proclaimed king, then went north and won the battle of Towton (March 29, 1461), *ii. 4,* and returning to London was crowned king. His marriage with Lady Grey gives offence in France and turns the Earl of Warwick against him, *iii. 3; iv. 1.* His capture and rescue are in *iv. 3, 5, 6;* in *v. 2,* the battle of Barnet (April 14, 1471), where Warwick was killed, and in *v. 4* that of Tewksbury (May 4, 1471), where Margaret's forces were defeated. These victories and the death of Henry VI. made him secure on the throne. The profligate character attributed to him in the play is matter of history. In *Richard III.* he is introduced in *ii. 1;* his remorse for the fate of Clarence, *ii. 1;* his death, *ii. 2.* .

Edward, Prince of Wales (Edward V.), son of Edward IV., character in *Richard III.*, appears first in *iii. 1*, where he is sent to the Tower. His beauty, *iii. 1, 2;* declared illegitimate by Buckingham, *iii. 7;* his death, *iv. 2, 3;* his ghost, *v. 3.* In the mere hints given of his character he appears as having a delicate tact, with precocity of discretion and caution, quite in contrast with the saucy wit of his younger brother, little Richard of York (1470-1483).

Eels, *King Lear, ii. 4.* Allusion to the opinion that they were roused by thunder, *Pericles, iv. 3.*

Effeminacy, loathed, *Troilus and Cressida, iii. 3;* of Antony, *Antony and Cleopatra, i. 4.*

Egeus, father of Hermia, in *Midsummer-Night's Dream,* introduced in *i. 1.*

Eggs, to steal, from a cloister, *All's Well that Ends Well, iv. 3;* for money (proverb), *A Winter's Tale, i. 2.*

Eglamour, a character in the *Two Gentlemen of Verona,* who helps Silvia to escape, *iv. 3.*

Egypt, name applied to Cleopatra in *Antony and Cleopatra.*

Egyptian fog, *Twelfth Night, iv. 2.*

Egyptian thief, *Twelfth Night, v. 1.* Thyamis, chief of a band of robbers, who killed his mistress when surprised by a stronger band, that he might have her company in the other world.

Eisel (vinegar), *Sonnet cxi.* See also ESILL.

Elbow, rub the, *I. Henry IV., v. 1.* Allusion to the notion that an itching elbow was a precursor of change.

Elbow, an ignorant and amusing constable in *Measure for Measure,* introduced in *ii. 1,* whose use of English is much like Dogberry's. He arrests " two notorious benefactors" who are "void of all profanation in the world that good Christians ought to have."

Elder-tree, allusion to the belief that it grows where blood has been shed, *Titus Andronicus, ii. 4;* emblem of grief, *Cymbeline, iv. 2.* Judas was said to have hanged himself on an elder, *Love's Labour's Lost, v. 2.*

Eleanor, Duchess of Gloucester, in *Richard II.* See GLOUCESTER.

Eleanor, wife of Humphrey, Duke of Gloucester. She was the daughter of Reginald, Lord Cobham, and celebrated for her beauty and bad morals. She is a character in *II. Henry VI.*, introduced in *i. 2*, where her ambition to become queen is expressed, and her determination to resort to witchcraft; her meeting with the witch, *i. 4;* charge against her, *ii. 1;* sentenced to banishment, *ii. 3;* led barefoot through the streets, *ii. 4.* It was charged that she or her accomplices melted before the fire a waxen image of the king, that his life might waste away as the wax melted. Her trial took place in 1441, and Queen Margaret did not arrive in England till 1445, so that their meeting in *i. 3* is by dramatic license. The "Hall of Justice" is St. Stephen's Chapel, Westminster. Eleanor was imprisoned in Chester Castle, and afterward in Kenilworth, where she died in 1454.

Election, the doctrine of, *Measure for Measure, i. 3,* "On whom it will, it will," etc.

Elements, a word over-worn, *Twelfth Night, iii. 1;* the four, *Twelfth Night, ii. 3; Antony and Cleopatra, v. 2; Sonnets xliv., xlv.;* so mixed, *Julius Cæsar, v. 5;* alluding to the idea that the body is composed of the four elements, and that health and ability depend on their due proportion; Lear's appeal to the, *King Lear, iii. 2.*

Elephant, the, an inn, *Twelfth Night, iii. 3.*

Elephant, the, *Troilus and Cressida, ii. 3.* Alluding to the notion that the elephant had no joints, and could not bend its knees or lie down. Betrayed with holes (pitfalls), *Julius Cæsar, ii. 1.*

Elf-locks, *Romeo and Juliet, i. 4.* Fairies were supposed to mat and tangle the manes of horses into "elf-locks."

Elinor of Aquitaine, widow of King Henry II., character in *King John,* introduced in the first scene. She is the inspirer of the worst deeds of her son John. Constance, whom she hates and torments through Arthur, calls her an offence to morality. She had before incited her sons against their father, Henry II. (1122–1204).

Elizabeth Woodville (Lady Grey), queen of Edward IV., character in *Richard III.,* introduced in *i. 3.* In *iv. 4,* she entertains the proposal for her daughter's hand, of the king, the enemy of her house, and the one responsible for the murder of her sons. She was the daughter of Richard Woodville, Earl Rivers, and the first English woman that was raised from the rank of subject to that of royalty after the Conquest. Her first husband was Sir John Grey, who was slain at St. Albans fighting for the House of Lancaster. His estate was confiscated when the Yorkists came into power. Tradition says that she first met Edward IV. in a forest near Grafton, her father's residence, where he was hunting, and where she sought him to petition for the restoration of her husband's estate to her and her children. The tree under which they were said to have met was known for centuries as the Queen's Oak. For other members of her family, see EDWARD V., ELIZABETH, RICHARD, RIVERS, and SCALES.

Elizabeth, the princess, daughter of Edward IV. Richard III. resolves to marry her, *iv. 2, 3,* and proposes it to her mother, *iv. 4,* who professes to entertain the proposal while secretly planning to marry her to Richmond in case of his success. She is betrothed to Richmond, *v. 5.* This united the title of the House of York to that of Henry VII., which was very slight.

Elizabeth, Queen, her birth, *Henry VIII., v. 1;* christening, *v. 2, 3, 4;* Cranmer's prophecy concerning her, *v. 4.* In *iii. 2,* Suffolk makes something like a prophecy of her reign when speaking of her mother, "There's order given," etc. See BOLEYN. The passage in *Midsummer-Night's Dream, ii. 1,* beginning "That very time I saw," is supposed to be an allusion to Elizabeth (1533–1603).

Elm and vine, figure of the, *Comedy of Errors, ii. 2; Midsummer-Night's Dream, iv. 1.*

Elopements, *Two Gentlemen of Verona, ii. 4; iii. 1; v. 2; Merry Wives of Windsor, iv. 6; v. 5; Merchant of Venice, ii. 6, 8; Midsummer-Night's Dream, i. 1; iv. 1; A Winter's Tale, iv. 3* or *4; Othello, i. 1–3.*

Eloquence, *Love's Labour's Lost, ii. 1,* "Aged ears play truant," etc.; *Henry V., i. 1,* "The air, a chartered," etc.; *Lover's Complaint, l. 120;* a tapster's, *I. Henry IV., ii. 4.*

Elsinore, in the island of Seeland, Denmark, scene of a part of *Hamlet;* cliff at, *i. 4.*

Elves, offices of, *The Tempest, v. 1.* See FAIRIES.

Elvish-marked, *Richard III., i. 3.* Allusion to the notion that deformity was due to evil fairies.

Ely, John Fordham, Bishop of, from 1388 to 1425, character in *Henry V.,* enters in scene first in conference with the Archbishop of Canterbury, to whom he plays second throughout.

Ely, John Morton, Bishop of, character in *Richard III.,* first appears in *iii. 4;* the strawberries in his garden, *iii. 4.* In *iv. 3* he flees to Richmond. He was made Bishop of Ely in 1478, and of Canterbury in 1486, and Lord Chancellor in 1487. The marriage of Richmond and Elizabeth was his suggestion. Sir Thomas More was a member of the bishop's household in his youth, and doubtless used information received from him in the life he afterward wrote of Richard in Latin, which furnished the chroniclers with a part of their material regarding his reign.

Ely House, London, scene of a part of *Richard II.*

Elysium, *Two Gentlemen of Verona, ii. 7; Twelfth Night, i. 2; II. Henry VI., i. 2; Cymbeline, v. 4.*

Emballing, *Henry VIII., ii. 3.* Receiving the ball given to sovereigns at coronation.

Emblems, at coronation, *Henry VIII., iv. 1.* See ROSES.

Embossed (foaming at the mouth from hard running—hence. run nearly to death), *Taming of the Shrew, induction, 1; All's Well that Ends Well, iii. 6; Antony and Cleopatra, iv. 13.*

Embowelled (embalmed), *I. Henry IV., v. 4.*

Embrace, before battle, *I. Henry IV., v. 2, end.*

Emilia, an attendant of the queen in *A Winter's Tale, ii. 2.*

Emilia, Iago's wife, in *Othello,* introduced in *ii. 1.*

"Emilia is a perfect portrait from common life, a masterpiece in the Flemish style; and though not necessary as a contrast, it cannot be but that the thorough vulgarity, the loose principles of this plebeian woman, united to a high degree of spirit, energetic feeling, strong sense, and low cunning, serve to place in brighter relief the exquisite refinement, the moral grace, the unblemished truth, and the soft submission of Desdemona."—MRS. JAMESON.

Emmanuel, clerk of Chatham, *II. Henry VI., iv. 2,* "They use to write it on the top of letters." The name was written at the head of public papers.

Emmew (keep in a cage or mew by terror, as a falcon does a fowl), *Measure for Measure, iii. 1,* "And follies doth emmew."

Emotions, *All's Well that Ends Well, iii. 2;* silent, *Much Ado about Nothing, ii. 1; Henry VIII., v. 1;* conflicting, *A Winter's Tale, v. 2; King Lear, iv. 3;* of joy, *Pericles, v. 1.*

Empericeutic (empiric), *Coriolanus, ii. 1.* In some old texts it is "empyric qutique."

Emperor of Rome, candidates for the office of, *Titus Andronicus, i. 1 or 2.*

Empirics, *All's Well that Ends Well, ii. 1,* "We thank you."

Employment, affects nature. *Sonnet cxi.*

Empress, station of an, *Titus Andronicus, ii. 1.*

Emulation (rivalry), *Troilus and Cressida, ii. 2, end;* hath a thousand sons, *Troilus and Cressida, iii. 3;* virtue cannot live out of the teeth of, *Julius Cæsar, ii. 3.*

Enceladus, *Titus Andronicus, iv. 2.* The fabled giant under Mount Ætna.

End, the, justifies the means, *Lucrece, l. 528;* crowns all, *King John, i. 1; Troilus and Cressida, iv. 5.*

Endurance. See FORTITUDE.

Endymion, a beautiful shepherd, beloved by Diana, *Merchant of Venice, v. 1.*

Enemy(ies), at my mercy, *The Tempest, iv. 1;* during a truce, *Troilus and Cressida, iv. 1;* dearest, *I. Henry.IV., iii. 2;* praise of an, *I. Henry IV., iv. 1,* "No more," etc.; wisdom of accounting him strong, *Henry V., ii. 4;* combination against, *King Lear, v. 1;* union before a common, *Antony and Cleopatra, ii. 1, 2;* folly of imitating an, *Henry V., iv. 1;* causeless, *Henry VIII., ii. 4;* drink is an enemy in the mouth, *Othello, ii. 3.*

Engaged (held as a hostage), *I. Henry IV., iv. 4; v. 2.*

Engine (instrument of torture), *King Lear, i. 4.*

Engineer, hoist with his own petar, *Hamlet, iii. 4, end.*

England, curiosity in, *The Tempest, ii. 2; Comedy of Errors, iii. 2;* white-faced shore of, *King John, ii. 1;* if only true to itself, *King John, v. 7;* praise of—evil times in, *Richard II., ii. 1;* an untended garden, *Richard II., iii. 4;* claim of kings of, to France, *Henry V., i. 2;* a little body with a mighty heart, *Henry V., ii., chorus;* the defence of, *III. Henry VI., iv. 1;* in Elizabeth's time, *Henry VIII., v. 5.* See BRITAIN.

English, the, bravery of, *Henry V., iii. 5, 6;* French opinion of, *Henry V., iii. 7; iv. 1, 2;* diet of, *I. Henry VI., i. 2;* Froissart's account of, *I. Henry VI., i. 2;* tenacity of, *I. Henry VI., i. 2,* "Rather with their teeth," etc.; have angels' faces, *Henry VIII., iii. 1;* epicures, *Macbeth, v. 3;* drinking habits of, *Othello, ii. 3;* dress of one of the, *Merchant of Venice, i. 2.*

English (language), the king's, *Merry Wives of Windsor, i. 4;* a fellow that frights it out of his wits, *Merry Wives of Windsor, ii. 1;* let them hack our, *Merry Wives of Windsor, iii. 1;* makes fritters of, *Merry Wives of Windsor, v. 5;* a lesson in, *Henry V., iii. 4.*

Enlarge (set at liberty), *Twelfth Night, v. 1, and elsewhere.*

Enmity. See HATRED.

Enobarbus, Domitius, character in *Antony and Cleopatra,* introduced in *i. 2;* his desertion, *iv. 5;* remorse, *iv. 6, 9;* death, *iv. 9.*

"Enobarbus, who sees through every wile and guile of the queen, is, as it were, a chorus to the play, a looker-on at the game; he stands clear of the golden haze which makes up the atmosphere around Cleopatra; and yet he is not a mere critic or commentator (Shakspere never permitting the presence of a person in his drama who is not a true portion of it). Enobarbus himself is under the influence of the charm of Antony, and slays himself because he has wronged his master."—DOWDEN.

Enskied (in heaven), *Measure for Measure, i. 5.*

Enterprise(s), want of, *All's Well that Ends Well, i. 1;* a desperate, *I. Henry VI., ii. 1;* failure of great, by irresolution, *Hamlet, iii. 1.*

Entertain (take into service), *Julius Cæsar, v. 5.*

Entrails, as if, were hairs, *Henry V., iii. 7.* Alluding to the bounding of a tennis-ball, which was stuffed with hair.

Envoy (a stanza, first or last, conveying the moral of a poem, or addressing it to some person), *Love's Labour's Lost, iii. 1.*

Envy (generally in the sense of malice), *Merchant of Venice, iv. 1; As You Like It, i. 2;* of the world, *As You Like It, ii. 3;* of a father, *I. Henry IV., i. 1; Richard III., iv. 1; Henry VIII., iii. 2,* "Follow your envious courses," etc.; *v. 2;* lean-faced, *II. Henry VI., iii. 2; Troilus and Cressida, ii. 1; Lucrece, l. 39.*

Ephesians (slang for carousers), *II. Henry IV., ii. 2.*

Ephesus, scene of the *Comedy of Errors.* Its quarrel with Syracuse and its bad name for sorcery adapted it for the scene of the extravagant incidents of the play. It is also the scene of a part of *Pericles.*

Epicurean, Cassius an, *Julius Cæsar, v. 1.*

Epidamnum, in Illyria, *Comedy of Errors, i. 1, 2; v. 1.*

Epidaurus, *Comedy of Errors, i. 1.*

Epilepsy, or falling-sickness, *Julius Cæsar, i. 2; Othello, iv. 1.*

Epilogues, to *The Tempest* (not by Shakspere, probably, perhaps by Ben Jonson); to *As You Like It;* to *All's Well that Ends Well,* probably not by Shakspere; to *II. Henry IV.,* probably not by Shakspere; to *Henry V.;* to *Henry VIII.,* probably not by Shakspere.

Epitaph(s), on Hero, *Much Ado about Nothing, v. 3;* on the deer, *Love's Labour's Lost, iv. 2;* lying, *All's Well that Ends Well, ii. 3,* "And these breed honour," etc.; on Timon, *Timon of Athens, v. 4.* This is made up of two, one said to have been written by Timon himself, the other by the poet Callimachus. Better have a bad, than, etc., *Hamlet, ii. 2.*

Epitheton (epithet), *Love's Labour's Lost, i. 2.*

Epithets, sweetly varied, *Love's Labour's Lost, v. 2;* pretty, fond, adoptious Christendoms, *All's Well that Ends Well, i. 1.*

Equality, of man, *A Winter's Tale, iv. 3,* "Once or twice I was about to speak," etc.; *Henry V., iv. 1,* "The king is but a man," etc.; *Richard III., i. 4,* "Princes have but," etc.; *Coriolanus, i. 1,* "The gods sent not corn," etc.

Equinox, storms at the vernal, *Macbeth, i. 2,* "As whence the sun," etc.

Equinox (opposite, counterpart), *Othello, ii. 3.*

Equipage (slang for stolen goods), *Merry Wives of Windsor, ii. 2.*

Equivocator, here's an, *Macbeth, ii. 3.* Supposed allusion to the doctrine of equivocation, as professed by the Superior of the Jesuits, on trial for complicity in the gunpowder plot, in 1606.

Ercles (Hercules), *Midsummer-Night's Dream, i. 2.*

Erebus (the passage to Hades), *Merchant of Venice, v. 1; Julius Cæsar, ii. 1.*

Eringo, the (held to be an aphrodisiac), *Merry Wives of Windsor, v. 5.*

Eros, friend of Antony, introduced in *iii. 5* of *Antony and Cleopatra.* In *iv. 12* or *14* he kills himself rather than be the instrument of Antony's death.

Erpingham, Sir Thomas, mentioned, *Richard II., ii. 1.*

Erpingham, Sir Thomas, character in *Henry V.,* first appears in *iv. 1,* an old man, treated with great reverence by the king. It was he who set the English army in order for battle at Agincourt, and gave the signal for the attack by throwing his truncheon in the air, calling, "Now strike!" He built the Erpingham Gate at Norwich. He was a Lollard. The first mention of him is in *Richard II., ii. 1,* where he is mentioned among the companions of Bolingbroke.

Error, melancholy's child, *Julius Cæsar, v. 3;* translated to truth, *Sonnet xcvi;* unavoidable, *A Winter's Tale, i. 2;* popular, *King Lear, iv. 1.*

Errors, of men. See FAULTS.

Escalus, an ancient lord, character in *Measure for Measure,* introduced in the first scene. He is wise, moderate, and merciful in his unregarded counsel to Angelo.

Escalus, Prince of Verona, character in *Romeo and Juliet,* introduced in *i. 1,* where he appears in the scene of the quarrel and disperses the combatants, and in *iii. 1* banishes Romeo.

Escanes, a lord of Tyre, in *Pericles,* introduced in *i. 3.*

Escapes, hair-breadth, *Othello, i. 3.*

Escoted (paid), *Hamlet, ii. 2.*

Esher House, or Asher House, residence of the bishops of Winchester, once occupied by Cardinal Wolsey, who is ordered to retire to it in *Henry VIII., iii. 2.* Esher is in Surrey, southwest of London, on the river Mole. An old Gothic building on Esher Place, with a castellated gateway, is known as "Wolsey's Tower." It was tenanted, but not built by the cardinal, and is said to have been erected by a bishop of Winchester nearly a century before Wolsey's time.

Esill (or eisel), *Hamlet, v. i.* A word not understood; by some supposed to be the river Yesel, by others vinegar.

Esperance (hope), *I. Henry IV., ii. 3; King Lear, iv. 1,* and elsewhere. It was the motto of the Percys.

Essex, Countess of. See MAIDENHOOD.

Essex, Geoffrey Fitz-Peter, Earl of, a character in *King John,* introduced in the first scene.

Essex, Robert Devereaux, Earl of, allusion to his expedition to Ireland, *Henry V., v., prologue.* He was sent over in April, 1599, to suppress Tyrone's rebellion. For his conduct of the war, and the terms on which he made peace, he was tried and dismissed from all offices. He formed a conspiracy to force his way to the queen's presence and remove his enemies by force of arms, for which he was tried and condemned for high treason, and executed February 25, 1601. This passage was written, of course, during the summer, before his failure in Ireland.

Estate (bestow), *The Tempest, iv. 1;* dispute his own (debate about his property), *A Winter's Tale, iv. 3* or *4.*

Estimate, is the worth in the, *Troilus and Cressida, ii. 2.*

Estimation (conjecture), *I. Henry IV., i. 3.*

Estridges (ostriches), *I. Henry IV., iv. 1; Ant. and Cleo., iii. 13.*

Et bonum, etc., the older the better, *Pericles, i., prologue.*

Ethiop, a swarthy, *Two Gentlemen of Verona, ii. 6;* jewels of an, *Romeo and Juliet, i. 5.*

Et tu, Brute? *Julius Cæsar, iii.,* and thou, too, Brutus? There is no record that Cæsar uttered these words; but Suetonius, who wrote about one hundred and seventy-five years later, has it that tradition reported him as saying in Greek, "Thou too, my son?"

Euphonius, character in *Antony and Cleopatra,* introduced in *iii. 10* or *12,* where he is called Antony's schoolmaster.

Euphuisms, *Hamlet, v. 2,* speech of Osric; *Love's Labour's Lost.*

Europa, daughter of Agenor, *Taming of the Shrew, i. 1; Merry Wives of Windsor, v. 5; Much Ado about Nothing, v. 4.*

Evans, Sir Hugh, a Welsh parson and schoolmaster, character in the *Merry Wives of Windsor,* introduced in the first scene. "The title Sir was applied to the inferior clergy; such as had it were not graduates at the university, being in orders, not in degrees." His bad English and his simplicity, which is not without a touch of shrewdness, make him a very amusing character. He is challenged by Doctor Caius, and prepares to meet him, in a very funny scene, the first of Act III.

Evasion, *I. Henry IV.*, *ii. 4; iv. 1;* exhausted, *All's Well that Ends Well*, *ii. 2;* Falstaff's, with the chief justice, *II. Henry IV.*, *i. 2; ii. 4*, "I dispraised him before the wicked," etc.

Eve, *Richard II.*, *iii. 4;* the legacy of, *Two Gentlemen of Verona*, *iii. 1;* our grandmother, *Love's Labour's Lost*, *i. 1.*

Even-Christian (fellow-Christian), *Hamlet*, *v. 1.*

Evening, *Venus and Adonis*, *l. 529; Macbeth*, *iii. 2, 3.*

Evidence, circumstantial, *Cymbeline*, *ii. 2, 4.*

Evil, to allow, is to order, *Measure for Measure*, *i. 4;* the beauteous, *Twelfth Night*, *iii. 4;* the sight of means for, *King John*, *iv. 2;* some soul of goodness in, *Henry V.*, *iv. 1;* lives in brass, *Henry VIII.*, *iv. 2;* doing, for good, *Troilus and Cressida*, *v. 3;* some good in, *Romeo and Juliet*, *ii. 3*, "Nought is so vile," etc.; none wholly free from, *Othello*, *iii. 3;* playing with, *Othello*, *iv. 1;* mending evil by, *Othello*, *iv. 3, end;* that men do lives after them, *Julius Cæsar*, *iii. 2;* attributed to a divine thrusting on, *King Lear*, *i. 2.*

Evils, of age and hunger, *As You Like It*, *ii. 7;* worst before departure, *King John*, *iii. 4;* of the age, *Sonnet lxvi.*

Examination, an, *Hamlet*, *iii. 4;* of Prince Hal, *I. Henry IV.*, *ii. 4.*

Example, of our virtues, *Measure for Measure*, *i. 1;* powerlessness of, *All's Well that Ends Well*, *iii. 3;* and precept, *Hamlet*, *i. 3*, "Do not, as some ungracious pastors," etc.; of vice, *Measure for Measure*, *ii. 2.*

Excellence, modesty a witness of, *Much Ado about Nothing*, *ii. 3;* attributed, *Tempest*, *iii. 1; Cymbeline*, *v. 5.*

Except before excepted (an unmeaning use of a law-term), *Twelfth Night*, *i. 3.*

Excess, *Measure for Measure*, *i. 3*, "From too much liberty," etc.; *Midsummer-Night's Dream*, *ii. 3*, "A surfeit of the sweetest things," etc.; in ornamentation, *King John*, *iv. 2;* advice concerning, *Richard II.*, *ii. 1; Henry VIII.*, *i. 1*, Norfolk to Buckingham; *Romeo and Juliet*, *ii. 6; iii. 3;* consequences of, *King Lear*, *iv. 1*, near *end;* allow not nature more than nature needs, *King Lear*, *ii. 4.*

Exclamations. See OATHS and EXCLAMATIONS.

Excommunication, *King John*, *iii. 1.*

Excuses, often make faults worse, *King John, iv. 2.*

Executioner, *Measure for Measure, iv. 2;* the common, *As You Like It, iii. 5.*

Exempt (separated), *Comedy of Errors, ii. 2.*

Exeter, Thomas Beaufort, Duke of, character in *Henry V.,* entering in *i. 2,* and in *I. Henry VI.,* entering in the first scene. He was uncle of Henry V., and was appointed governor of Henry VI. after his father's death. He was Earl of Dorset only, and not Duke of Exeter, until after Agincourt, and was not present at that battle, being at that time Governor of Harfleur, *iii. 3,* where he displayed great prowess in defending the place in two attacks by the French. He died in 1427.

Exeter, Henry Holland, Duke of, character in *III. Henry VI.,* introduced in *i. 1.* He was a son of the Earl of Huntingdon, mentioned in *Henry V., v. 2,* was a faithful Lancastrian, and served at the battles of Wakefield, Towton, and Barnet. He was attainted in 1461 under Edward IV., and became so poor that Commines saw him, as he says (*Memoirs, iii. 4*), begging for bread. He was found dead in the Straits of Dover in 1473.

Exeter, Peter Courtenay, Bishop of, mentioned in *Richard III., iv. 4.*

Exeter, castle at, *Richard III., iv. 2.* Built in the time of William I., destroyed in the Civil War.

Exhalations (meteors or flashes of lightning), *Henry VIII., iii. 2; Julius Cæsar, ii. 1.*

Exhibition (allowance of money, still used for pensions allowed to scholars in English colleges), *Two Gentlemen of Verona, i. 3; King Lear, i. 2; Othello, i. 3.*

Exile, *As You Like It, ii. 1;* a speechless death, *Richard II., i. 3;* worse than death, *Romeo and Juliet, iii. 3.* See BANISHMENT.

Exorcisms (summoning spirits), *II. Henry VI., i. 4.* Exorciser and exorcist used in a like sense, *All's Well that Ends Well, v. 3; Julius Cæsar, ii. 1; Cymbeline, iv. 2.*

Expectation, mistaken, *All's Well that Ends Well, ii. 1;* of evil, disappointed, *I. Henry IV., i. 2, end;* to a child, *Romeo and Juliet, iii. 2;* in war-time, *Troilus and Cressida, prologue; Othello, ii. 1.*

Expedience (expedition), *Antony and Cleopatra, i. 2.*

Expedient (expeditious), *King John, ii. 1.*

Experience, achieved by industry, *Two Gentlemen of Verona, i. 3;* a jewel, *Merry Wives of Windsor, ii. 2,* want of, *Romeo and*

Juliet, ii. 2, " He jests at scars," etc.; must be schoolmaster to the wilful, *King Lear, ii. 4;* learning by others', *Lover's Complaint, l. 155.*

Experiments, deep, *I. Henry IV., iii. 1.*

Expiate (expired, or, to end), *Richard III., iii. 3; Sonnet xxii.*

Explosion, a threatened, *Hamlet, iii. 4.*

Expression, in the whole body, *Troilus and Cressida, iv. 5,* " There's a language," etc. See FACES, LANGUAGE, WORDS.

Expulsed (expelled), *I. Henry VI., iii. 3.*

Exsufflicate (swollen), *Othello, iii. 3.*

Extended, extent (seized, attachment, a law-term), *As You Like It, iii. 1; Antony and Cleopatra, i. 2.*

Extenuation, begged for youthful errors, *I. Henry IV., iii. 2;* intention of, disclaimed, *Othello, v. 2.*

Extirped (extirpated), *I. Henry VI., iii. 3.*

Exton, Sir Pierce of, character in *Richard II.,* first appears in *v. 4;* murders Richard, *v. 5;* and is condemned for it by Henry, *v. 6.* Some historians are of opinion that Richard was starved to death in captivity, others that he starved himself in grief, though many follow the story as Shakspere has it. Henry IV. executed several who said that Richard had escaped. A remarkable resemblance between him and his chaplain, Mandelain, led some to believe that it was the chaplain who suffered death and whose body was shown.

Extravagance, *Timon of Athens, ii. 1, 2.*

Extravagant (wandering), *Othello, i. 1.*

Extremes, *As You Like It, iv. 1.*

Eyas, or eyas-musket (a young hawk), *Merry Wives of Windsor, iii. 3.*

Eye(s), a blue and sunken, *As You Like It, iii. 2;* blueness about the eyes was thought a sign of being in love; all senses locked in the, *Love's Labour's Lost, ii. 1,* near the *end;* a still-soliciting, *King Lear, i. 1;* the evil eye, referred to in the word " o'erlook," which means to cast the evil eye upon, in *Merry Wives of Windsor, v. 5; Merchant of Venice, iii. 2;* like Mars, *Hamlet, iii. 2;* doth not behold itself, *Troilus and Cressida, iii. 3;* spies, *The Tempest, v. 1;* coward gates of, *As You Like It, iii. 5;* woman's, *Love's Labour's Lost, iv. 3;* crystal, *Two Gentlemen of Verona, ii. 4;* to be put out, *King John, iv. 1; King Lear, iii. 7;* praise of, *Romeo and Juliet, ii. 2;* green (hazel), *Romeo and Juliet, iii. 5,* the nurse's speech; closing in death, *Antony and Cleopatra, v. 2;* blue, *Venus and Adonis, l. 481;* like the moon in water, *Venus and Adonis, l. 491;*

darkened, *Venus and Adonis, l. 1037;* beauty of, *Sonnet xvii.;* hearing with, *Sonnet xxiii.;* the painter, *Sonnet xxiv.;* dark, *Sonnets cxxvii., cxxxii.;* in distraction, *Lover's Complaint, l. 22.*

Eyebrows, ladies', *A Winter's Tale, ii. 1.*

Eyelids, fringed curtains, *The Tempest, i. 2;* advanced, *The Tempest, iv. 1.*

Fabian, a witty fellow, servant in the house of Olivia, in *Twelfth Night,* introduced in *ii. 5.*

Fable, of the fox and the grapes, *All's Well that Ends Well, ii. 1;* of the belly and the other members, *Coriolanus, i. 1.*

Face (to pretend), *I. Henry VI., v. 3.*

Face(s), jest on a, *Love's Labour's Lost, v. 2,* "A cittern head," etc.; was this the, *Richard II., iv. 1;* a red, *I. Henry IV., iii. 3;* a royal, *II. Henry IV., i. 2;* commanding, *Coriolanus, iv. 5;* of Paris, *Romeo and Juliet, i. 3;* no art to read the mind in, like a book, *Macbeth, i. 4, 5;* round, are foolish, *Antony and Cleopatra, iii. 3;* expression of, *Sonnets xciii., xciv;* of men and of women, *Antony and Cleopatra, ii. 6;* judgment of, *Othello, iii. 3;* pleasant, *Pericles, i. 1.*

Facinorous (atrocious), *All's Well that Ends Well, ii. 3.*

Fact, those of your (of the same deed as you), *A Winter's Tale, iii. 2.*

Factions, cause weakness, *Troilus and Cressida, i. 3.*

Faculties, use of, *Measure for Measure, i. 1,* "Heaven doth with us," etc.; *Hamlet, iv. 4,* "What is a man," etc.; *Othello, i. 3,* "Our bodies are our gardens," etc.

Fadge (to fit, or be suitable), *Love's Labour's Lost, v. 1; Twelfth Night, ii. 2.*

Fadings. See DILDOS.

Failure, the result of striving for better than well, *King John, iv. 2;* of a soldier to prosper in time of peace, *Coriolanus, iv. 7;* possible, *Macbeth, i. 7.*

Fair, was the morn, *Passionate Pilgrim, vii.;* is my love, *ix.*

Fairies, forms assumed by, and pranks of, *The Tempest, i. 2; ii. 2; v. 1; Midsummer-Night's Dream, ii. 1; Romeo and Juliet, i. 4;* offices of, *The Tempest, v. 1;* rings made by the dances of, *The Tempest, v. 1;* see RINGLETS; superstitions regarding, *Merry Wives of Windsor, iv. 4;* a personation of, *Merry Wives of Windsor, iv. 4, 5;* death the penalty of speaking to, *Merry Wives of Windsor, v. 5;* land of, *Comedy of Errors, ii. 2;* malevolent, *Comedy of Errors, iv. 2;* introduced as characters in the *Midsummer-Night's Dream;* lore of, *Midsummer-Night's Dream, ii. 1;* swiftness of—offices of, *Midsummer-Night's Dream, iii. 1;* gold of, *A Winter's Tale, iii. 3;* changelings of, *1. Henry IV., i. 1;* description of Queen Mab—her chariot, *Romeo and Juliet, i. 4;* allusion to their office in keeping away worms from the dead, *Cymbeline, iv. 2; Midsummer-Night's Dream, ii. 2.*

Faith, plural, in love, *Two Gentlemen of Verona, v. 4;* a charm against witchcraft, *Comedy of Errors, iii. 2;* worn as the fashion, *Much Ado about Nothing, i. 1;* speaks from need, not from faith, *King John, iii. 1;* want of, see FRIENDS, LOVERS, TREACHERY.

Faitours (traitors), *II. Henry IV., ii. 4.*

Falconry, or hawking, allusions to, sometimes called birding, *Merry Wives of Windsor, iii. 3, 5; iv. 2;* the staniel (kestrel-hawk), *Twelfth Night, ii. 5;* the tercel-gentle or tassel-gentle, *Romeo and Juliet, ii. 1;* this is a male goss-hawk, which is gentle and easily tamed; the gentle astringer (hawk-tamer), *All's Well that Ends Well, v. i;* the falcon's bells, *As You Like It, iii. 3; III. Henry VI., i. 1; Lucrece, l. 511;* jesses (straps on the falcon's legs by which it was held), *Othello, iii. 3;* hood my unmanned blood, *Romeo and Juliet, iii. 2;* an unmanned hawk, one not used to man, was hooded to prevent fright; haggards (wild hawks), *Much Ado about Nothing, iii. 1, end; Twelfth Night, iii. 1; Othello, iii. 3;* a hooded valour, *Henry V., iii. 7;* to check (start away from the lure), *Twelfth Night, iii. 1; Hamlet, iv. 7;* the method of taming hawks, *Taming of the Shrew, iv. 1;* to seel up the eyes, as was done to the hawk in training by sewing the eyelids up, *II. Henry IV., iii. 1; Macbeth, iii. 2; Othello, i. 3; iii. 3;* imp, *Richard II., ii. 1;* to imp a hawk was to mend broken feathers by grafting or piecing them out; mailed up (wrapped), *II. Henry VI., ii. 4;* mew up or emmew, *Measure for Measure, iii. 1; Taming of the Shrew, i. 1; Romeo and Juliet, iii. 4;* to tower, *II. Henry VI., ii. 1; Macbeth, ii. 4; Lucrece, l. 506;* baiting (fluttering), *Romeo and Juliet, iii. 2;* to tire (feed ravenously), *III. Henry VI., i. 1; Timon of Athens, iii. 6; Cymbeline, iii. 4;* disedged (satiated), *Cymbeline, iii. 4;* whistle her off and let her down the wind, *Othello, iii. 3;* will coast (hover about) my crown, *III. Henry VI., i. 1;* quarry, *Coriolanus, i. 1; Macbeth, iv. 3; Hamlet, v. 2.*

Fall (let fall), *Comedy of Errors, ii. 2,* and elsewhere.

Fall, of Cæsar, the, *Julius Cæsar, iii. 2,* Antony's speech; of Percy, *I. Henry IV., v. 4;* of a queen, *Richard III., iv. 4;* of a king, *Richard II., iii. 2;* of man, *Henry V., ii. 2;* of Wolsey, *Henry*

VIII., *iii. 2;* of the great, *Macbeth, ii. 4; Antony and Cleopatra, iii. 10; iv. 10, 13.*

Falling, the, cruelty to, *Henry VIII., iii. 2; v. 2.*

Falling-sickness. See EPILEPSY, under DISEASES.

Falsehood, caused by trust, *The Tempest, i. 2;* hated by women, *Two Gentlemen of Verona, iii. 2;* in love, *Two Gentlemen of Verona, iv. 2;* goodly outside of, *Merchant of Venice, i. 1;* cures falsehood, *King John, iii. 1;* hidden, *Richard III., ii. 1;* Cressida a name for, *Troilus and Cressida, iii. 2;* of Diomed, *Troilus and Cressida, v. 1.*

Falsity, of women, *A Winter's Tale, i. 2,* " Were they as false as o'er dyed blacks."

Falstaff, Sir John, appears in the two parts of *Henry IV.* and the *Merry Wives of Windsor.* He is the leader of the dissolute band that surround the Prince of Wales. In *I. Henry IV.* he first appears in *i. 2.* This scene and *ii. 4* are full of bantering epithets and allusions to his size, directed against him by his companions. His adventure at Gadshill, *ii. 2;* takes the character of Henry IV., *ii. 4;* his account of his soldiers, *iv. 2;* he counterfeits death at the battle of Shrewsbury, *v. 4.* In the *Merry Wives of Windsor* he is introduced in the first scene. His character in this play appears much more degraded than in *Henry IV.* The time is probably shortly before the death of the king. His wit, or at least his shrewdness, seems to have deserted him, and he is outwitted by simple people whom he despises. Gervinus, who finds a moral design in everything, thinks that Shakspere exhibited the deterioration of his character, and threw it into contrast with the ennoblement of the prince's, to show his essential baseness, and do away with whatever bad impression may have been made by the glamour that his wit throws over his moral qualities. However that may be, the reader is prepared by this play for the disgrace that overtakes him, which otherwise would seem cruel and not altogether deserved. His hypocrisy and inconsistency, *ii. 1;* ridicule of his size, *ii. 1; iii. 5; iv. 4, 5;* his honour, *ii. 2;* epithets applied to him, *i. 3; iii. 1; v. 5;* his adventure in the buck-basket, *iii. 3;* in a woman's clothes, *iv. 2;* at Herne's oak with the fairies, *v. 5.* See MERRY WIVES OF WINDSOR. He is introduced in *II. Henry IV.*, in *i. 2,* where he talks with the chief justice; arrested at the instance of Mrs. Quickly, *ii. 1;* overheard by the prince in disguise, *ii. 4;* ridiculed, *ii. 2, 4; iv. 3;* his recruits for the army, *iii. 2;* his expectations from the prince, *v. 3;* disappointed, *v. 5;* banished from the prince, *v. 5.* His death is described by Mrs. Quickly in

Henry V., *ii. 3*, and he is spoken of by Fluellen in *iv. 7* of the same play. The name of this character was at first Sir John Oldcastle, *q. v.*

"Falstaff, not a degraded man of genius, like Burns, but a man of degraded genius, with the same consciousness of superiority to his companions [as Iago and Richard III.], fastened himself on a young prince, to prove how much his influence on an heir-apparent would exceed that of a statesman. With this view he hesitated not to adopt the most contemptible of all characters, that of an open and professed liar; even his sensuality was subservient to his intellect; for he appeared to drink sack that he might have occasion to show off his wit. One thing, however, worthy of observation, is the perpetual contrast of labour in Falstaff to produce wit with the ease with which Prince Henry parries his shafts; and the final contempt which such a character deserves and receives from the young king, when Falstaff exhibits the struggle of inward determination with an outward show of humility."—COLERIDGE.

Fame, all men hunt after, *Love's Labour's Lost, i. 1;* anticipated, *Henry V., iv. 3;* living in, *Richard III., iii. 1;* of heroes, *Troilus and Cressida, ii. 2, end;* best gained in second place, *Coriolanus, i. 1, end;* fold in this orb, *Coriolanus, v. 6;* of good and evil deeds, *Julius Cæsar, iii. 2;* danger of acquiring too high a, *Antony and Cleopatra, iii. 1;* undying, *Measure for Measure, v. 1; Richard III., iii. 1;* brevity of, *Much Ado about Nothing, v. 2;* effect of, *Troilus and Cressida, i. 3; I. Henry IV., v. 4; Henry VIII., iv., 2;* would be exchanged for a pot of ale, *Henry V., iii. 2.*

Familiarity, with an inferior, *Comedy of Errors, ii. 2;* too great, *Hamlet, i. 3.*

Family pride, of Sly, *Taming of the Shrew, induction, 1.*

Famine, *Pericles, i. 4;* makes valiant, *Cymbeline, iii. 6.*

Fancies, the humour of forty, stuck for a feather in an old hat, *Taming of the Shrew, iii. 2.*

Fancy, where bred, *Merchant of Venice, iii. 2, song;* sweet and bitter, *As You Like It, iv. 3;* (love) followers of, *Midsummer-Night's Dream, i. 1;* full of shapes, *Twelfth Night, i. 1;* nature wants stuff to vie with, *Antony and Cleopatra, v. 2;* every one to his own, *All's Well that Ends Well, iv. 1.*

Fancy-free, *Midsummer-Night's Dream, ii. 2.*

Fang, one of the sheriff's officers in *II. Henry IV.*, who appears in *ii. 1.*

Fangled (capricious), *Cymbeline, v. 4.*

Fap (tipsy), *Merry Wives of Windsor, i. 1.*

Farewell(s), to greatness, *Henry VIII., iii. 2; Troilus and*

Cressida, iv. 4; an everlasting, *Julius Cæsar, v. 1; Antony and Cleopatra, iii. 2; Sonnet lxxxvii.* See PARTING.

Farmer, the, that hanged himself, *Macbeth, ii. 3.*

Farthingale, *Two Gentlemen of Verona, ii. 7; Merry Wives of Windsor, iii. 3; Taming of the Shrew, iv. 3.*

Fashion, wears out more apparel than the man—a deformed thief, *Much Ado about Nothing, iii. 3;* infected with, *Taming of the Shrew, iii. 2;* following the, *All's Well that Ends Well, ii. 1;* from Italy, *Richard II., ii. 1,* common in Shakspere's time but not at time of the play; of France, *Henry VIII., i. 3;* behind the, *Julius Cæsar, iv. 1,* Antony speaking on Lepidus; the glass of, *Hamlet, iii. 1;* in speech, *Hamlet, v. 2;* garments out of, *Cymbeline, iii. 4;* less without, and more within, a new, *Cymbeline, v. 1.*

Fast and Loose, *Antony and Cleopatra, iv. 10* or *12,* a game played by gypsies. A belt was folded and knotted up and placed on a table, and the victim made a wager that he could hold it fast to the table ; he would then place a skewer through what seemed to be the central fold, when the gypsy would take hold of the two ends and pull it away.

Fastidiousness, the extreme of, *I. Henry IV., i. 3,* Hotspur's description.

Fasting, oath concerning, *Love's Labour's Lost, i. 1;* effect of, on the disposition, *Coriolanus, v. 1.*

Fastolfe, Sir John, character in *I. Henry VI.* He was lieutenant-general to Bedford in Normandy, and deputy regent. His cowardice at the siege of Orleans is spoken of in *i. 1,* and Talbot execrates him in *i. 4.* He first appears in *iii. 2,* and is deprived of the garter and banished in *iv. 1.* He died in 1469.

Fat, to be, to be hated, *I. Henry IV., ii. 4;* men, *Merry Wives of Windsor, ii. 1;* men, not dangerous, *Julius Cæsar, i. 2;* woman, description of a, *Comedy of Errors, iii. 2.*

Fatality, *Measure for Measure,* "The words of heaven," etc.; *Hamlet, v. 2,* "There's a divinity," etc.; *King Lear, i. 2,* "This is the excellent foppery," etc. See also FREE WILL.

Fate, *The Tempest, iii. 3;* no escape from, *Love's Labour's Lost, iv. 3,* "The sea will ebb." etc.; malignancy of, *Twelfth Night, ii. 1;* the book of, *II. Henry IV., iii. 1;* no resisting, *III. Henry VI., iv. 3;* men masters of their, *Julius Cæsar, i. 2;* unavoidable, *Julius Cæsar, ii. 2; Othello, v. 2; Hamlet, iii. 2; v. 2;* in an auger-hole, *Macbeth, ii. 3;* challenge to, *Macbeth, iii. 1;* makes desperate, *Hamlet, i. 4;* bewailing one's, *Sonnet xxix.*

Father, praise by a, *The Tempest, iv. 1;* an angry, *Two Gentlemen of Verona, iii. 1;* shame of a, *Much Ado about Nothing, iv. 1;* that knows his child, *Merchant of Venice, ii. 2;* right of a, *Midsummer-Night's Dream, i. 1;* at his son's nuptial, *A Winter's Tale, iv. 3;* anger of a, *A Winter's Tale, iv. 4;* vote of, against a son, *Richard II., i. 3;* judgment on a, *I. Henry IV., iii. 2;* desperation of a, *II. Henry IV., i. 1;* cares of a, *II. Henry IV., iv. 4;* grief of a, *Titus Andronicus, iii. 1;* anger of a, *King Lear, i. 1;* in rags, *King Lear, ii. 4;* who would be a, *Othello, i. 1;* an infirm, *Sonnet xxxvii;* duty to a, and to a husband, *Othello, i. 3.*

Fauconberg, mentioned, *Henry V., iii. 5; iv. 8.*

Faulconbridge, an English baron, one of the suitors of Portia, mentioned in *Merchant of Venice, i. 2.*

Faulconbridge, Philip, half-brother of Robert F., in *King John*, and natural son of Richard I., enters in the first scene. His name is changed by John to Richard Plantagenet. He is cynical, coarse, and skeptical in conversation, but brave, straightforward, and patriotic in action. He revolts at the murder of Arthur, *iv. 3*, but will not on that account turn against his country as Salisbury does.

Faulconbridge, Robert, son of Sir Robert Faulconbridge, character in *King John*, first appears in *i. 1.*

Faulconbridge, Lady, character in *King John*, introduced in the first scene.

Faulconbridge, William Neville, Lord, mentioned in the third part of *King Henry VI.*

Fault, sometimes used for misfortune.

Fault(s), condemn the, *Measure for Measure, ii. 2;* best moulded out of, *Measure for Measure, v. 1;* hearing one's, *Much Ado about Nothing, ii. 3;* excuses make worse, *King John, iv. 2;* turned to good, *II. Henry IV., i. 2,* "I will turn diseases to commodity"; of the rich, *Timon of Athens, i. 2;* one, *Hamlet, i. 4;* truth about, *Antony and Cleopatra, i. 2;* made glaring by virtues, *Antony and Cleopatra, i. 4;* punishment of, *Cymbeline, v. 1,* "You snatch some hence," etc.; all men make, *Sonnet xxxv.;* made graces, *Sonnet xcvi;* his worst is, that he is given to prayer, *Merry Wives of Windsor, i. 4;* abundance of, *As You Like It, iii. 2;* of men, *Much Ado about Nothing, iv. 1; Coriolanus, i. 1;* a headstrong, *Twelfth Night, iii. 4;* a man is the abstract of all, *Antony and Cleopatra, i. 4.*

Fauste, precor, etc. (Faustus, I pray when the herd chews the cud in the cool shade), *Love's Labour's Lost, iv. 2.* A quotation from Battista Spagnolus, of Mantua.

Faustus, Dr., *Merry Wives of Windsor, iv. 5.*

Favour, of the great, *Richard III., iii. 4; Cymbeline, v. 4.*

Favour, defeat thy (disguise thy face), *Othello, i. 3.*

Favourites, that abuse their privilege, *II. Henry IV., iv. 2; Much Ado about Nothing, iii. 1.*

Fawning, *Julius Cæsar, i. 2; iii. 1; Richard II., ii. 3;* "Grace me no grace," etc.

Fay (faith), *Hamlet, ii. 2.*

Fear (to frighten), *Taming of the Shrew, i. 2,* and elsewhere.

Fear, gives the foe strength, *Richard II., iii. 2;* this living, *Richard II., v. 4;* not spoken of in Scotland, *I. Henry IV., iv. 1;* of death, *Julius Cæsar, ii. 2; Hamlet, i. 4;* impostors to true, *Macbeth, iii. 4;* pale-hearted, *Macbeth, iv. 1; v. 3;* expression of, *Cymbeline, iii. 4;* extreme, *Lucrece, l. 230;* most accursed of all base passions, *I. Henry VI., v. 2;* a sin in war, *Cymbeline, v. 3;* leads to hate, *Antony and Cleopatra, i. 3;* led by reason, *Troilus and Cressida, iii. 2.*

Fear no more the heat of the sun, song, *Cymbeline, iv. 2.*

Fears, of a woman, *King John, iii. 1;* make devils of cherubins, *Troilus and Cressida, iii. 2;* make traitors, *Macbeth, iv. 2;* taste of, forgotten, *Macbeth, v. 5.*

Feast(s), beginning of, suits a keen guest, *I. Henry IV., iv. 2;* to false friends a, *Timon of Athens, iii. 6;* must be given with welcome, *Macbeth, iii. 4;* a good man's, *As You Like It, v. 1;* sheep-shearing, *A Winter's Tale, iv. 4;* Capulet's, *Romeo and Juliet, i. 2.*

Feated (moulded), *Cymbeline, i. 1.*

Feather, life tested by a, *King Lear, v. 3; II. Henry IV., iv. 4.*

Federary (confederate), *A Winter's Tale, ii. 1.*

Feeble, a recruit in *II. Henry IV.,* appears in *iii. 2.*

Feeders (dependents), *Antony and Cleopatra, iii. 11* or *13.*

Feeding (pasture tract), *A Winter's Tale, iv. 3* or *4.*

Feint, a, *Othello, i. 3.*

Fellow-feeling, *Merry Wives of Windsor, ii. 2,* "Sir, I hear," etc.; *Measure for Measure, ii. 2; iii. 2.*

Fencing, allusions to, and terms of, *Merry Wives of Windsor, i. 1; ii. 3; iii. 2; Love's Labour's Lost, i. 2; v. 1;* description of, *Hamlet, iv. 7* or *4.* "Feney" or "venue" and "staccato" signify a quick, sharp stroke; "montant" or "montanto," an upward thrust; "punto reverso," a backward, and "passado," a forward thrust.

Fennel, *II. Henry IV., ii. 4; Hamlet, iv. 5.* Fennel was hot, and therefore deemed exciting; it was also emblematic of a flatterer

Fenton, a gentleman in the *Merry Wives of Windsor,* a suitor and afterward the husband of Anne Page. He has formerly been one of the prince's roguish companions, but through the influence of Anne Page, whom he at first seeks for her money, his character is transformed. He first appears in *i. 4.*

Feodary (companion), *Measure for Measure, ii. 4; Cymbeline, iii. 2.*

Ferdinand, son of the King of Naples in *The Tempest,* introduced in *i. 2,* and the lover of Miranda.

Ferdinand, King of Navarre, character in *Love's Labour's Lost,* introduced in the first scene. He has set up a "little Academe," a school of culture for himself and three companions. That for women in Tennyson's "Princess" is somewhat after the same plan.

Fere (mate), *Titus Andronicus, iv. 1; Pericles, i., prologue.*

Fern-seed, *I. Henry IV., ii. 1.* It was supposed to render one invisible.

Ferrers, Walter, Lord, his death, *Richard III., v. 5.*

Feste, the fool in *Twelfth Night,* introduced in *i. 5,* one of Shakspere's airiest and most delicate clowns.

Festinate, -ly (speedy, speedily), *Love's Labour's Lost, iii. 1; King Lear, iii. 1.*

Festival, a Roman, *Julius Cæsar, i. 2.*

Fet (fetched), *Henry V., iii. 1.*

Fettle (prepare), *Romeo and Juliet, iii. 5.*

Feuds, between Somerset and Plantagenet, *I. Henry VI., ii. 4;* between their adherents, *iii. 4; iv. 1, 3;* between Gloucester and Winchester, *I. Henry VI., i. 3; iii. 1; v. 1; II. Henry VI., i. 1; ii. 1;* between Wolsey and Buckingham, *Henry VIII., i. 1;* of Montague and Capulet, *Romeo and Juliet, i. 1, 5; iii. 1; v. 3.*

Fever, a fit of madness, *Comedy of Errors, v. 1;* sensations of, *King John, v. 7.*

Fewness (few words), *Measure for Measure, i. 5.*

Fickleness, *Two Gentlemen of Verona, ii. 4; Twelfth Night, ii. 4.* See INCONSTANCY.

Fico (fig), *Merry Wives of Windsor, i. 3; Henry V., iii. 6.*

Fidelity. See CONSTANCY, FAITH, LOYALTY.

Fie on sinful fantasy, song, *Merry Wives of Windsor, v. 5.*

Field of the Cloth of Gold, expense of, *Henry VIII., i. 1.*

Fiend(s), temptations of, *Merchant of Venice, ii. 2;* summoned by Joan, *I. Henry VI., v. 3;* lies like truth, *Macbeth, v. 5;* description of a, *King Lear, iv. 6.* See MAHU.

Fife, the wry-necked, *Merchant of Venice, ii. 5.*

Fife, in Scotland, scene of a part of *Macbeth.* Macduff was Thane of Fife.

Fife, Mordake, Earl of, spoken of in *I. Henry IV., i. 1,* as son of Douglas, was son of the Duke of Albany. The mistake was occasioned by an ambiguity in Holinshed, caused by defective punctuation.

Fifteens (fifteenths of the personal property), one-and-twenty, *II. Henry VI., iv. 7.*

Fighting, by book, *Romeo and Juliet, iii. 1.*

Fights (pieces of cloth hung around a ship to keep men out of sight during an engagement), *Merry Wives of Windsor, ii. 2.*

Fights, *As You Like It, i. 1; Twelfth Night, iv. 1; v. 1; Troilus and Cressida, iv. 5.*

Filberts, *The Tempest, ii. 2.*

File (number), *Measure for Measure, iii. 2.*

File, the valued (list with estimates of value), *Macbeth, iii. 1.*

Filed (polished), *Love's Labour's Lost, v. 1.*

Filial love and duty, *Two Gentlemen of Verona, iii. 1; A Winter's Tale, iv. 4; King Lear, i. 4; ii. 1, 4; iv. 2, 7.*

Fineless (endless), *Othello, iii. 3.*

Finsbury, *I. Henry IV., iii. 1.* Then open fields and a favourite resort, now a part of London.

Fire, that's closest kept, *Two Gentlemen of Verona, i. 2;* shunned, *Two Gentlemen of Verona, i. 3;* cannot melt out of me, *Much Ado about Nothing, i. 1;* drives out fire, *Coriolanus, iv. 7;* a mighty, *Julius Cæsar, i. 3;* a wheel of, *King Lear, iv. 7.*

Fire-drake (variously explained as the Will o' the wisp, a sort of firework, and a mild form of lightning), *Henry VIII., v. 4.*

Fire-new (brand-new), *Love's Labour's Lost, i. 1, and elsewhere.*

Fire out, *Sonnet cxliv.*

Fires (a disease like the strangles), *Taming of the Shrew, iii. 2.*

Firmament, the, *Hamlet, ii. 2,* "I will tell you why," etc.

Firmness, *Julius Cæsar, iii. 1.*

Fish, to eat no, *King Lear, i. 4;* of fortune's buttering, *All's Well that Ends Well, v. 2;* finless, *Comedy of Errors, iii. 1; I. Henry IV., iii. 1.*

Fishermen, moralizing by, *Pericles, ii. 1.*

Fishes, the great eat the little, *Pericles, ii. 1.*

Fishing, nothing to be got nowadays except by, *Pericles, ii. 1.*

Fistula, disease of the kit_, *All's Well that Ends Well, i. 1.*

Fitchew (pole-cat), *Othello, iv. 1, and elsewhere.*

Fitzwalter, a character in *Richard II.*, introduced in *iv. 1.*

Flaminius, a servant of *Timon of Athens*, introduced in *ii. 2.* Owing to confusion in the original copy, where the steward is sometimes known as Flavius, and that name is also given to this servant, later editions vary. See FLAVIUS.

Flannel, made in Wales, *Merry Wives of Windsor, v. 5.*

Flap-dragons, *Love's Labour's Lost, v. 1; A Winter's Tale, iii. 3; II. Henry IV., ii. 4.* Substances set on fire and placed on the top of liquor, skill being required to drink without being burned. Sometimes they were candle-ends.

Flatterers, of a king, *Richard II., ii. 1;* of the rich, *Timon of Athens, i. 1, 2;* ingratitude of, *Timon of Athens, ii. 2; iii. 2, 5;* all men are, *Timon of Athens, iv. 3; Julius Cæsar, ii. 1; iv. 3; v. 1; Passionate Pilgrim, xx.*

Flattery, of Falstaff, *Merry Wives of Windsor, ii. 2; iii. 3;* of Evans, *Merry Wives of Windsor, iii. 1;* of Mrs. Ford, *Merry Wives of Windsor, iii. 3;* conquers strife, *Comedy of Errors, iii. 2; Love's Labour's Lost, ii. 1;* of Hero, *Much Ado about Nothing, iii. 4; As You Like It, ii. 1;* of a king, *Richard II., i. 1; iii. 2;* thought truth, *I. Henry IV., iv. 1;* of King James I., *Henry VIII., v. 5;* poured on Ajax, *Troilus and Cressida, ii. 3;* of the people, *Coriolanus, ii. 2; iii. 2;* contempt for, *Coriolanus, iii. 1,* "Neptune for his trident," etc.; men deaf to counsel, but not to, *Timon of Athens, i. 2; iii. 3;* necessity for, *Macbeth, iii. 2;* profitable, *Hamlet, iii. 2,* to Horatio; *Othello, iv. 2,* "I grant, indeed," etc.; *King Lear, i, 1;* fault contrary to — sarcastic, *King Lear, ii. 2; Cymbeline, i. 6; Pericles, i. 2; iv. 4;* which melteth fools, *Julius Cæsar, iii. 1.*

Flavius, a gentleman, mentioned in *Measure for Measure, iv. 5.*

Flavius, one of the tribunes in *Julius Cæsar*, first appears in *i. 1.* See MARULLUS.

Flavius, steward of *Timon of Athens*, introduced in *i. 2.* In some editions he is mentioned simply as the steward, and those copies have the name Flavius for the servant Flaminius. The difference arises from some confusion in the original copy. The steward remained faithful and disinterested after Timon's false friends had deserted him, *iv. 3, end.*

Flaws (sudden gusts of wind), *II. Henry IV., iv. 4; II. Henry VI., iii. 1; Venus and Adonis, l. 456.*

Fleance, son of Banquo, in *Macbeth*, first appears in *ii. 1.* In *iii. 3*, he escapes from the murderers that are set upon him and his father.

Fleece, hair like a golden, *Merchant of Venice, i. 1; iii. 2.*

Fleet, description of a, *Henry V., iii., chorus.*

Fleet (the prison), *II. Henry IV., v. 5.*

Flemish drunkard, a, *Merry Wives of Windsor, ii. 1.*

Flesh, the pound of, *Merchant of Venice, i. 3; iii. 1, 3, 5; iv. 1;* as regards the original story, see under MERCHANT OF VENICE; and blood, my own, *Merchant of Venice, iii. 1;* more, more frailty, *I. Henry IV., iii. 3;* this too solid, *Hamlet, i. 2.*

Fleur-de-lys. See FLOWER-DE-LUCE.

Flew'd (with flews or large chaps), *Midsummer-Night's Dream, iv. 1.*

Flibbertigibbet, a fiend, *King Lear, iii. 4; iv. 1.* See MAHU.

Flight, of Hotspur's soldiers, *II. Henry IV., i. 1;* of Antony at Actium, *Antony and Cleopatra, iii. 8 or 10, 11 or 13; Macbeth, v. 3.*

Flint Castle, in Wales, scene of *Richard II., iii. 3.*

Flirtation, *Hamlet, i. 3,* "The trifling of his favours," etc.

Flood, the great, *Julius Cæsar, i. 2.* Deucalion's (*q. v.*).

Flood, loss by, *King John, v. 6, 7.* John once lost his baggage and treasure by a flood while on his way from Lynn to Lincolnshire.

Florence, Italy, scene of a part of *All's Well that Ends Well.*

Florence, Duke of, an unimportant character in *All's Well that Ends Well*, introduced in *iii. 1.*

Florentius, *Taming of the Shrew, i. 2.* Allusion to an old story told by Gower in "Confessio Amantis." Florentius bound himself to marry a deformed hag if she would solve for him a riddle on which his life depended.

Florizel, character in *A Winter's Tale*, first appears in *iv. 4.* He is the son of the King of Bohemia and lover of Perdita, to whom he is first known as Doricles. His character is pure, disinterested, and romantic.

Flote (wave), *The Tempest, i. 2.*

Flout 'em and scout 'em, song, *The Tempest, iii. 2.*

Flower-de-luce, *A Winter's Tale, iv. 3 or 4; I. Henry VI., i. 2; II. Henry VI., v. 1;* cropped on the, *I. Henry VI., i. 1*, alluding to the losses in France; the three fleurs-de-lis of France were on the arms of England until the beginning of this century. It is a corruption of "Fleur de Louis," from Louis VII., who chose it for his emblem when about to start on his crusade.

Flower(s), *Two Gentlemen of Verona, ii. 4; Midsummer-Night's*

Dream, ii. 1, 2; A Winter's Tale, iv. 4; significance of, *Hamlet, iv. 5* (or *2*); *Romeo and Juliet, iv. 5; Hamlet, v. 1;* for the dead, *Cymbeline, iv. 2; Pericles, iv. 1;* from the blood of Adonis, *Venus and Adonis, l. 1168.*

Fluellen, a Welshman, character in *Henry V.,* introduced in *iii. 2.* He talks with an affectation of learning, but is in reality straightforward, simple, true, and serious. In *iv. 1* the king says of him:

> " Though it appear a little out of fashion,
> There is much care and valour in this Welshman."

The name is found among those of contemporaries of Shakspere at Stratford.

Flute, Francis, a bellows-mender, character in *Midsummer-Night's Dream,* introduced in *i. 2.* He takes the part of Thisbe in the play before the duke.

Fly, killing of a, *Titus Andronicus, iii. 2.* Perhaps an allusion to the belief that evil spirits sometimes took the form of a fly.

Foe, a furnace heated for a, *Henry VIII., i. 1;* my dearest, *Hamlet, i. 2.*

Foes, profit by, in self-knowledge, *Twelfth Night, v. 1.*

Foil, use of a, *I. Henry IV., i. 2, end.*

Foins (passes in fencing), *Much Ado about Nothing, v. i; King Lear, iv. 6.*

Foison (abundance), *The Tempest, iv. 1; Macbeth, iv. 3.*

Foix, a French lord, killed at Agincourt, mentioned, *Henry V., iii. 5; iv. 8.*

Folly, of love, *Two Gentlemen of Verona, i. 1; ii. 1;* of the wise, *As You Like It, ii. 7; Love's Labour's Lost, v. 2;* waited on by wisdom, *All's Well that Ends Well, i. 1;* of fools and wise, *Twelfth Night, iii. 1.*

Food, influence of, *Comedy of Errors, ii. 2; Love's Labour's Lost, i. 1.* See BEEF.

Fool, of *King Lear,* the, introduced in *i. 4,* of the play.

"The fool is no comic buffoon to make the groundlings laugh. . . . He is as wonderful a creation as Caliban; his wild babblings and inspired idiocy articulate and gauge the horrors of the scene." —COLERIDGE.

Fool-begg'd patience, *Comedy of Errors, ii. 1.* Supposed allusion to the custom of begging the king for the guardianship of rich idiots.

Foolhardiness, *Cymbeline, iv. 2,* "Being scarce made up," etc.

Fooling, *Twelfth Night, ii. 3; Troilus and Cressida, v. 2, Hamlet, iii. 2.*

Foolishness, monopoly of, *King Lear, i. 4.*

Fool(s), let me play the, *Merchant of Venice, i. 1;* whetstones of wit, *As You Like It, i. 2;* wit of, *As You Like It, i. 2;* to call, *As You Like It, ii. 5;* a motley, *As You Like It, ii. 7;* liberty of, *As You Like It, ii. 7;* thinks he is wise, *As You Like It, v. 1;* made better by infirmity, *Twelfth Night, i. 5;* wise men that crow at, *Twelfth Night, i. 5;* no slander in, *Twelfth Night, i. 5;* wit required for playing the, *Twelfth Night, iii. 1; Troilus and Cressida, ii. 3;* livery of, white and green, *Romeo and Juliet, ii. 2;* old, *King Lear, i. 3;* constancy for, *King Lear, ii. 4;* of fortune, *King Lear, iv. 6;* to suckle, *Othello, ii. 1;* a son of a crafty devil, *Cymbeline, ii. 1;* bolt of, soon shot (proverb), *Henry V., iii. 7;* paradise of, *Romeo and Juliet, ii. 4;* let him play the fool nowhere but in his own house, *Hamlet, iii. 1.*

Football, allusions, *Comedy of Errors, ii. 1; King Lear, i. 4.*

Foot land-rakers (footpads), *I. Henry IV., ii. 1.*

Footsteps, light, *Venus and Adonis, l. 1028.*

Fop, a, *All's Well that Ends Well, ii. 5,* "The soul of this man is in his clothes." See DANDY.

Fopp'd (fooled), *Othello, iv. 2.*

Forbid (bewitched, set apart), *Macbeth, i. 3.*

Ford, Frank, a character in the *Merry Wives of Windsor*, introduced in *ii. 1.* Pistol arouses his jealousy toward Falstaff, and he disguises himself, and is introduced to the knight as Mr. Brook.

Ford, Mistress, one of the *Merry Wives of Windsor*. Incensed by Falstaff's outrageous love-making, she and Mrs. Page, to whom he had sent the "twin brother" of the love-letter he sent to her, combine to punish him, and their scheme forms the plot of the play.

Fordham, John. See ELY, BISHOP OF.

Fordoes (undoes), *Hamlet, ii. 1; Othello, v. 1.*

Foreboding, *A Winter's Tale, iii. 3,* "The skies look grimly;" *Richard II., ii. 2,* "Some unborn sorrow is coming toward me;' *Henry V., iv. 1,* "Even as wrecked men;" *Romeo and Juliet, i. 4,* "Some consequence yet hanging in the stars;" *iii. 5,* "I have an ill-divining soul;" *Macbeth, ii. 1,* "A heavy summons lies like lead upon me." See OMENS.

Foreheads, low, *The Tempest, iv. 1; Two Gentlemen of Verona, iv. 4; Antony and Cleopatra, iii. 3;* armed and reverted, *Comedy of Errors, iii. 2.*

Forester, a character in *Love's Labour's Lost*, introduced in *iv. 1.*

Forfeit, all souls were once, *Measure for Measure, ii. 2.*

Forfeits (fines on loungers), *Measure for Measure, v. 1.*

Forgery (imagination), *Hamlet, iv. 7* (or *4*).

Forgetfulness, like a dull actor now, I have forgot my part *Coriolanus, v. 3.*

Forgiveness, *Tempest, v. 1; All's Well that Ends Well, v. 3; Hamlet, iii. 3; Cymbeline, v. 5; Two Gentlemen of Verona, v. 4; All's Well that Ends Well, v. 3.* It was an old custom for the executioner to ask forgiveness of the condemned before inflicting the penalty. See also MERCY and PARDON.

Formal (normal), *Comedy of Errors, v. 1; Antony and Cleopatra, ii. 5; Twelfth Night, ii. 5.*

Forms, effect of changing old, *King John, iv. 2.*

Forres, a town about twenty-five miles from Inverness, on the Moray Frith, scene of a part of *Macbeth.*

Forrest, Miles, a murderer, *Richard III., iv. 3.*

Forslow (delay), *III. Henry VI., ii. 3.*

Forthcoming (in custody), *II. Henry VI., ii. 1.*

For shame! deny that thou bear'st love, *Sonnet x.*

Forthright, a prisoner, *Measure for Measure, iv. 3.*

Fortinbras, King of Norway, slain by *Hamlet, i. 1,* father of the prince of that name in the play.

Fortinbras, Prince, nephew of the King of Norway, *Hamlet, i. 2;* character in *Hamlet,* appears in *iv. 4* (or *1*), and *v. 2.*

Fortitude, *Timon of Athens, iii. 5,* "He's truly valiant," etc.; *Troilus and Cressida, i. 3,* "In the reproof of chance," etc.; *Antony and Cleopatra, iv. 12,* "Nay, good my fellows," etc.

Fortune, all is but, *The Tempest, v. 1;* girl that flies her, *Two Gentlemen of Verona, v. 2;* with her wheel, *As You Like It, i. 2; III. Henry VI., iv. 3; King Lear, ii. 2, end; v. 3; Lucrece, l. 952;* out of suits with, *As You Like It, i. 2;* railed on, *As You Like It, ii. 7,* "Call me not fool till," etc.; play upon thy helm, *All's Well that Ends Well, iii. 3;* displeasure of, *All's Well that Ends Well, v. 2;* a good lady, *All's Well that Ends Well, v. 2;* accident and flood of, *Twelfth Night, iv. 3;* fickleness of, *King John, iii. 1; Macbeth, i. 2; Romeo and Juliet, iii. 5; Passionate Pilgrim, xxi.;* most threatening before favoring, *King John, iii. 4;* never has both hands full, *II. Henry IV., iv. 4;* the blind goddess, *Henry V., iii. 6;* proves men, *Troilus and Cressida, i. 3;* men fallen out with, *Troilus and Cressida, iii. 3;* blows of, to the noble, *Coriolanus, iv. 1;* fool of,

Romeo and Juliet, iii. 1; King Lear, iv. 6; changes of, *Timon of Athens, i. 1;* every step (grise) of, *Timon of Athens, iv. 3;* at odds with, *Timon of Athens, iv. 3;* in a merry mood, *Julius Cæsar, iii. 2;* a tide that leads to, *Julius Cæsar, iv. 3;* we are not the button on the cap of, *Hamlet, ii. 2;* turn Turk, *Hamlet, iii. 2;* men that are not a pipe for, *Hamlet, iii. 2;* a good man's, *King Lear, ii. 2;* ne'er turns the key to the poor, *King Lear, ii. 4;* friends in good, *King Lear, ii. 4;* the worst, *King Lear, iv. 1;* tame to blows of, *King Lear, iv. 6;* two loved and hated by, *King Lear, v. 3;* mark of harsh, *Antony and Cleopatra, ii. 6;* laughed away, *Antony and Cleopatra, ii. 6;* scorned most, *Antony and Cleopatra, iii. 9 or 11;* and Antony part, *Antony and Cleopatra, iv. 10 or 12;* false house-wife, *Antony and Cleopatra, iv. 13 or 15;* knave of, *Antony and Cleopatra, v. 2;* uncertainty of, *Cymbeline, iii. 3;* brings in boats not steered, *Cymbeline, iv. 3;* spite of, *Sonnets xxxvii., xc.;* responsibility of, *Sonnet cxi.*

Fortune-hunter, not a, *Twelfth Night, ii. 4.*

Fortune, my foe, an old song, alluded to, *Merry Wives of Windsor, iii. 3.*

Fortune-telling, *Merry Wives of Windsor, iv. 2; Comedy of Errors, v. 1; Antony and Cleopatra, i. 2;* allusions to the use of a glass in, *Measure for Measure, ii. 2; Macbeth, iv. 1.*

Forum, Roman, scene of *Coriolanus, ii. 3.*

Fountain, a warm, *Sonnets cliii., cliv.*

Fowling, allusions to, stale (decoy), *The Tempest, iv. 1;* stalk on, *Much Ado about Nothing, ii. 3;* limed a bush, *II. Henry VI., i. 3; ii. 4;* dare with his cap like larks, *Henry VIII., iii. 2.* Larks were "dared by small mirrors on scarlet cloth, which dazed them while the net was thrown over them." The allusion here is to the cardinal's red hat.

Fox, a drawn, *I. Henry IV., iii. 3,* drawn from cover; never trusted, *I. Henry IV., v. 2;* thou diest on point of, *Henry V., iv. 4.* The last alludes to a sword with the figure of a fox on it, originally used by Ferrara as a trade-mark. Allusions to the cunning of the, *II. Henry VI., iii. 1; III. Henry VI., iv. 7; Henry VIII., i. 1; Timon of Athens, iv. 3; Lear, iii. 4;* this lion is a fox for his valour, *Midsummer Night's Dream, v. 1.*

Fox and grapes, the, *All's Well that Ends Well, ii. 1.*

Frailty, of women, *Measure for Measure, ii. 4; Hamlet, i. 2;* human, *Henry VIII., v. 3;* we are devils to ourselves when we tempt the frailty of our powers, *Troilus and Cressida, iv. 4.*

Frampold (uncomfortable), *Merry Wives of Windsor, ii. 2.*

France, scene of parts of *King John, Henry V., I.* and *III. Henry VI., All's Well that Ends Well.* Allusion to the war in, in 1589, against Henry IV., *Comedy of Errors, iii. 2 ;* the Salique law in, *Henry V., i. 2.* The errors in the passage where the bishop states the case, are taken, with all the other statements, from Holinshed. Besides the evident mistake in the number of years, Charlemain is spoken of instead of Charles the Bald as father of the Lady Lingare, and Louis X. is mentioned in place of Louis IX., St. Louis. English claim to the crown of, *Henry V., i. 1; ii. 4;* boasting in the air of, *Henry V., iii. 6;* English losses in, *I. Henry VI., i. 1;* wounds of, *I. Henry VI., iii. 3;* compact of, with England, *I. Henry VI., v. 4;* English wars and losses in, *II. Henry VI., i. 1; iii. 1;* better using than trusting, *III. Henry VI., iv. 1;* following the fashions of, *Henry VIII., i. 3.*

France, King of, a fine and noble character in *All's Well that Ends Well,* introduced in the second scene.

France, King of, character in *King Lear,* introduced in *i. 1,* as a suitor for Cordelia, afterward her husband.

France, Kings of. See CHARLES VII.. LOUIS XI.

France, Princess of, one of the principal characters in *Love's Labour's Lost,* introduced in *ii. 1.* She comes to ask Aquitaine from the young King of Navarre in his "Academe." She and her ladies are lively if not altogether refined, full of drollery and mischief.

Francis, a friar in *Much Ado about Nothing,* introduced in *iv. 1,* "a near spiritual kinsman of Friar Laurence in *Romeo and Juliet.*"

Francisca, a nun, character in *Measure for Measure,* appears in *i. 5.*

Francisco, a lord, character in *The Tempest,* introduced in *ii. 1.*

Francisco, a soldier in *Hamlet,* introduced in *i. 1,* as a sentinel.

Frank (stye), *II. Henry IV., ii. 2.*

Franked (penned), *Richard III., i. 3; iv. 5.*

Frateretto, a fiend, *King Lear, iii. 6.* See MAHU.

Frederick, brother of Mariana in *Measure for Measure,* who had been shipwrecked with his sister's dowry in his charge, mentioned in *iii. 1.*

Frederick, the usurping duke in *As You Like It,* first appears in *i. 2.* He "is called, even by his daughter, a man of harsh and envious mind ; he appears to be perpetually actuated by gloomy fancies, by suspicion and mistrust, and to be urged on by covetousness." He repents in the end, and becomes a hermit.

Free (pure), *Twelfth Night, ii. 4; A Winter's Tale, ii. 3.*

Freedom, with foppery, *Measure for Measure, i. 3;* of spirit, *Julius Cæsar, i. 3;* real, *King Lear, i. 1.*

Freetown, *Romeo and Juliet, i. 1.* Literal translation of *Villa Franca.*

Free will, of men, *All's Well that Ends Well, i. 1,* " Our remedies oft in ourselves," etc.; *Julius Cæsar, i. 2,* "Men at some time are masters," etc.; *Othello, i. 3,* "'Tis in ourselves," etc.

French, the, *II. Henry IV., i. 3.* A large French force was sent over during this rebellion to Milford Haven in aid of Glendower. Defeat of, *Henry V., iv. 5;* those killed at Agincourt, *iv. 8;* inconstancy of, *I. Henry VI., iii. 3;* supposed fear of Henry V. of, *I. Henry VI., i. 1;* fashions from, *Romeo and Juliet, ii. 4;* characteristics of, *Merchant of Venice, i. 2;* lack language to deny if girls of Italy demand, *All's Well that End's Well, ii. 1.*

French language, scenes or parts of scenes in, *Henry V., iii. 4; iv. 4; v. 2.*

Frenzy, humours his, *Comedy of Errors, iv. 4;* melancholy the nurse of, *Taming of the Shrew, induction, 2.*

Frets, the stops on lutes, guitars, and viols, *Taming of the Shrew, ii. 1; Hamlet, iii. 2.*

Friar, the duke disguised as a, *Measure for Measure, ii. 3.*

Friars, not allowed to go alone, *Romeo and Juliet, v. 2.*

Friend remembered not, song, *As You Like It, ii. 7.*

Friend(s), must needs be proportion in, *Merchant of Venice, iii. 4;* keep thy, *All's Well that Ends Well, i. 1;* in misery, *As You Like It, ii. 1;* abused by praise of, *Twelfth Night, v. 1;* happiness in remembering, *Richard II., ii. 3;* backing of, *I. Henry IV., ii. 4;* desertion of, *Henry VIII., ii. 1; Troilus and Cressida, iii. 3,* " 'Tis certain greatness," etc.; praise of, *Coriolanus, v. 2;* need the opportunity of, *Timon of Athens, i. 2;* an over-generous, *Timon of Athens, ii. 1;* reliance on, *Timon of Athens, ii. 2;* false, *Timon of Athens, i. 1; iii. 1, 3; iv. 2, 3;* "Not by his breath," etc.; old and new, *Hamlet, i. 3;* who needs not shall never lack a, *Hamlet, iii. 2,* speech of the player king; in misfortune, *Antony and Cleopatra, iv. 10* or *12;* be not last to desert a, *Sonnet xc.;* a true, *Passionate Pilgrim, xxi.;* duty of a, *Othello, iii. 3; Julius Cæsar, iv. 3;* description of, *Hamlet, iii. 2; Merchant of Venice, iii. 2; As You Like It, i. 3.*

Friendship, of Valentine and Proteus, *Two Gentlemen of Ve-*

rona; treachery to, *Two Gentlemen of Verona, ii. 6; iii. 1; v. 4;* constant in all but, *Much Ado about Nothing, ii. 1;* of Helena and Hermia, *Midsummer-Night's Dream, iii. 2;* of Rosalind and Celia, *As You Like It, i. 2, 3;* of the kings, *A Winter's Tale, i. 1;* of York and Suffolk, *Henry V., iv. 6;* not knit by wisdom, *Troilus and Cressida, ii. 3;* needs no ceremony, *Timon of Athens, i. 2;* coolness in, *Julius Cæsar, i. 2; iv. 2;* caution and constancy in, *Hamlet, i. 3;* brittleness of, *Coriolanus, v. 4;* falsehood to, *Sonnet xxxiv.*

Friendship is feigning, song, *As You Like It, ii. 7.*

Frieze, made in Wales, *Merry Wives of Windsor, v. 5.*

Fright, appearance of, *Hamlet, iii. 4,* "Alas! how is't?"

Frippery (a second-hand shop), *The Tempest, iv. 5.*

Frogmore, *Merry Wives of Windsor, ii. 3.* Frogmore House is half a mile east of Windsor.

Froissart, Jean, *I. Henry VI., i. 2.* Author of the "Chronicles," who lived from 1337 to 1410.

Frontiers (forts on the frontiers), *I. Henry IV., ii. 3.*

From east to western Ind, love-verses, *As You Like It, iii. 2.*

Froth, a foolish man in *Measure for Measure,* introduced in *ii. 1,* where he is under arrest, but is discharged on account of his evident incapacity.

Froth and lime, let me see thee, *Merry Wives of Windsor, i. 3.* Froth beer and lime sack, to make it sparkle.

Frown, a, *Henry VIII., ii. 2; v. 1;* of majesty, *King John, iv. 2.*

Frush (break to pieces), *Troilus and Cressida, v. 6.*

Full fathom five, song, *The Tempest, i. 2.*

Fullam. See GOURD.

Full many a glorious morning, *Sonnet, xxxiii.*

Fulvia, Antony's first wife, spoken of in *Antony and Cleopatra, i. 1, 2; ii. 2.*

Function (ability to act), *Macbeth, i. 3.*

Funeral(s), of Henry V., *I. Henry VI., i. 1;* of Cæsar, *Julius Cæsar, iii. 1, 2;* followed by marriage, *Hamlet, i. 2;* of Ophelia, *Hamlet, v. 1;* of Cleopatra, *Antony and Cleopatra, v. 2;* of the sons of Titus, *Titus Andronicus, i. 1;* music for a, the Phœnix and the Turtle; song for a, *Cymbeline, iv. 2.*

Furs, of foxes, and lamb-skins, significance of, *Measure for Measure, iii. 2.*

Fury, *Henry V., iv. 4; III. Henry VI., i. 4; Troilus and Cressida, ii. 3;* fire-eyed, *Romeo and Juliet, iii. 1;* I understand a fury in your words, *Othello, iv 2;* a noble, *Cymbeline v. 5.*

Fury, the apparition of a hound, *The Tempest, iv. 1.*

Furze, *The Tempest, i. 1.*

Fust (mould), *Hamlet, iv. 4* (or *1*).

Future, the, if it were known, *II. Henry IV., iii. 1; Julius Cæsar, v. 1;* if you can look into, *Macbeth, i. 3;* dread of, *Hamlet, iii. 1; Measure for Measure, iii. 2 ;* we know not, *Hamlet, v. 5.* See PROPHECIES.

G., the letter, prophecy regarding, *Richard III., i. 1.*

Gaberdine, *The Tempest, ii. 2; Merchant of Venice, i. 3.* A long, frock-like coat.

Gadfly. See BREESE.

Gads-Hill, scene of a part of *I. Henry IV.* On the Kentish road near Rochester.

Gadshill, a character in *I. Henry IV.*, introduced in *ii. 1.* He is one of Falstaff's company, and so disreputable that the carriers are afraid to trust him with their lanterns. In *ii. 2* he takes part in the robbery, and in the lying in *ii. 4.*

Gage. See CHALLENGE.

Gain, be my lord, *King John,* end of *act ii.;* seekers of, *King Lear, ii. 4.*

Gaingiving (misgiving), *Hamlet, v. 2.*

Gait, a springing, *Troilus and Cressida, iv. 5 ;* a majestic, *Love's Labour's Lost, v. 1; Antony and Cleopatra, iii, 3; Lear, v. 3; A Winter's Tale, iv. 3;* of a shuffling nag, *I. Henry IV., iii. 1.*

Galathe, Hector's horse, *Troilus and Cressida, v. 5.*

Galen, *Merry Wives of Windsor, ii. 3; iii. 1; All's Well that Ends Well, ii. 3; II. Henry IV., i. 2; Coriolanus, ii. 1.*

Gall, in ink, *Twelfth Night, iii. 2.*

Galliard (a sprightly dance), *Twelfth Night, i. 3; Henry V., i. 2.*

Galliass, *Taming of the Shrew, ii. 1.* A large galley with three masts and seats for thirty-two rowers.

Gallimaufry (medley), *Merry Wives of Windsor, ii. 1; A Winter's Tale, iv. 4.*

Gallow (frighten), *King Lear, iii. 2.*

Gallowglasses (troops each "armed with a scull, a shirt of mail, and a galloglas-axe"), *Macbeth, i. 2; II. Henry VI., iv. 9.*

Gallows, born for the, *The Tempest, i. 1; v. 1; Love's Labour's Lost, v. 2 ; I. Henry IV., i. 2;* abolition of the, *I. Henry IV., i. 2;* a fat pair, *I. Henry IV.. ii. 1: Hamlet, v. 1.* See HANGING.

Gallus, character in *Antony and Cleopatra*, introduced in *v. 1*, a friend of Cæsar.

Gam, Davy, his death, *Henry V.*, *iv. 8.*

Gaming, the varnish of a complete man, *Love's Labour's Lost*, *i. 2.*

Gamut, Hortensio's, *Taming of the Shrew*, *iii. 1.*

Ganymede, name assumed by Rosalind, *As You Like It*, *i. 3.*

Garboils (tumult), *Antony and Cleopatra*, *i. 3; ii. 2.*

Garden, order in a, *Richard II.*, *iii. 4.*

Gardener, a, *Richard II.*, *iii. 4.*

Gardening, *II. Henry VI.*, *iii. 1,* "Now 'tis the spring," etc.; *Henry V.*, *ii. 4;* Adam's profession, *Richard II.*, *iii. 4; II. Henry VI.*, *iv. 2; Hamlet v. 1.*

Gardiner, Stephen, Bishop of Winchester, character in *Henry VIII.*, introduced in *ii. 2;* his unscrupulousness, *ii. 2.* In *v. 1,* he expresses enmity to Cromwell and Cranmer. He favored the divorce and the Anglican Church under Henry, but became a papist again under Mary, in whose reign he was chancellor, and whose measures against the Protestants he was largely concerned in.

Gargantua, *As You Like It*, *iii. 2.* A giant in the writings of Rabelais, who swallowed five pilgrims with their staves in a salad.

Gargrave, Sir Thomas, character in *I. Henry VI.*, appears in *i. 4*, at the siege of Orleans, and is killed.

Garlands, *A Winter's Tale*, *iv. 3* or *4;* oaken, *Coriolanus*, *ii. 1;* wheaten, *Hamlet*, *v. 2;* willow, *Othello*, *iv. 3, song.*

Garment, the everlasting, *Comedy of Errors*, *iv. 2.*

Garter, Knights of the, *Merry Wives of Windsor*, *v. 5.*

Garter, Order of the, *I. Henry VI.*, *iv. 1; Richard III.*, *iv. 4.*

Garter king at arms, *Henry VIII.*, *iv. 1,* order of the coronation. Thomas Wriothesley, grandfather of Henry Wriothesley, to whom *Venus and Adonis* and *Lucrece* were dedicated.

Garter Inn, the, scene of a part of the *Merry Wives of Windsor.* The Host, one of the characters, first appears in *i. 3.*

Gascoigne, Sir William, Lord Chief Justice, character in *II. Henry IV.*, first appears in *i. 2.* One of the legends about the wild Prince Hal is that he gave the chief justice a cuff on the ear, and was sent to prison for it by the justice. In *v. 2,* Sir William defends his action, and is unexpectedly praised for it and retained in office by the young king.

Gascony, in southwestern France, scene of *I. Henry VI.*, *iv. 3, 4.*

Gate, the strait, *All's Well that Ends Well, iv. 5.*

Gaudy night, one other, *Antony and Cleopatra, iii. 13.* Gaudy days—that is, days of joy—is a term for feast-days.

Gaunt, John of, Duke of Lancaster, character in *Richard II.,* enters in the first scene. He was born in 1339 in Ghent, whence his name. At the opening of the play he was fifty-eight, though addressed as a very old man. He is a fine and stately character. His patriotism is shown in his reproaches to Richard for his sins against his country, and his eulogy on England in *ii. 1,* just before his death (1399). His line, *III. Henry VI., i. 1;* his wisdom, *III. Henry VI., iii. 4.*

Gawsey (Gausel or Goushill), Sir Nicholas, *I. Henry IV., v. 4.*

Gear (business), *Merchant of Venice, i. 1; II. Henry VI., i. 4; Troilus and Cressida, i. 1.*

Geck (fool, fop), *Twelfth Night, v. 1; Cymbeline, v. 4.*

Gelidus timor, etc., *II. Henry VI., iv. 1.* Cold fear seizes my limbs.

Gender (sort), *Hamlet, iv. 7 (or 4).*

General (the common people), *Measure for Measure, ii. 4;* caviare to the. See CAVIARE.

General (the public weal), *Julius Cæsar, ii. 1.*

General, fame of a, *Coriolanus, i. 1, end.*

Generation (children), *King Lear, i. 1.*

Generation, to yonder (or the under), *Measure for Measure, iv. 3.* The under would mean the antipodes; yonder may mean those outside the prison.

Genius, the (the soul), *Julius Cæsar, ii. 1; Twelfth Night, iii. 4;* (the tutelar angel), *Troilus and Cressida, iv. 4.*

Gentility, law against—the influence of women, *Love's Labour's Lost, i. 1.*

Gentleman, characteristics of a, *Two Gentlemen of Verona, ii. 4;* a fine, *Love's Labour's Lost, v. 2;* signs of a, *Twelfth Night, i. 5;* born a, *Merry Wives of Windsor, i. 1; A Winter's Tale, v. 2;* a brave, *I. Henry IV., v. 1;* a, framed in the prodigality of nature, *Richard III., i. 2;* bears him like a, *Romeo and Juliet, i. 5;* the most ancient, *Hamlet, v. 1.*

Gentlemen, who neither envy the great nor despise the low, *Pericles, ii. 3.*

Gentleness, a strong enforcement, *As You Like It, ii. 7;* necessary for success, *Coriolanus, iii. 1.*

Gentry (courtesy), *Hamlet, ii. 2.*

Gentry, degrees of, *Merry Wives of Windsor, ii. 1,* "Not alter the article," etc.; inheritance of, *A Winter's Tale, i. 2.*

Geoffrey Plantagenet, the father of Prince Arthur, mentioned in *King John.*

Geography, *Merchant of Venice, i. 1,* "Peering in maps for ports and piers and roads."

Geologic changes, *II. Henry IV., iii. 1,* "O God, that one might read," etc.

George, look on my, *II. Henry VI., iv. 1; Richard III., iv. 4.* The Knights of the Garter wore a figure of St. George on horseback.

George, St., battle-cry of English soldiers, *Henry V., iii. 1; I. Henry VI., iv. 2; Richard III., v. 3;* feast of, April 23d, *I. Henry VI., i. 1;* and the dragon, *King John, ii. 1.* Allusion to the picture used as an innkeeper's sign.

Germans, the, *Merry Wives of Windsor, iv. 3, 5.* It has been found by Mr. Knight that the Duke of Würtemberg travelled in England with a retinue in 1592, and went to Windsor, under the name of Count Mombeliard (Mumplegart), his title at the time, and no doubt this is a reminiscence of that event. Garmomble, almost an anagram of Mumplegart, appears in the copy of 1602. An order was found from the lord chamberlain that the count should have post-horses free. Apparently the host intends to take it out of the rest of the company. Germans are honest men, *Merry Wives of Windsor, iv. 5;* all slops (loose breeches) from the waist downward like, *Much Ado about Nothing, iii. 2;* are hasty, *III. Henry VI., iv. 8.*

Germany, the heresies in Upper, *Henry VIII., v. 3.* Alluding to the "following of Thomas Muncer in Thuringia in 1521."

Gertrude, Queen of Denmark and mother of *Hamlet*, first appears in *i. 2.* In the history her name is Geruth or Gerutha. It is left doubtful whether she knew of the poisoning of Hamlet's father, but her affection for Hamlet and for Ophelia make it probable that she was weak rather than cruel. She dies, *v. 2,* of the poison intended for Hamlet.

Gest, *A Winter's Tale, t. 2.* An appointed stage in a royal progress; sometimes used for an appointed limit of time.

Get you hence, song, *A Winter's Tale, iv. 3* or *4.*

Ghost (corpse), *II. Henry VI., iii. 2.*

Ghost (soul), vex not his, *King Lear, v. 3.*

Ghost(s), returning, *Midsummer-Night's Dream, iii. 2;* appear to Richard and Richmond, *Richard III., v. 3;* of Cæsar, *Julius Cæsar, iv. 3; v. 5;* of Banquo, *Macbeth, iii. 3, 4;* of Hamlet's father, *Hamlet, i. 1, 2, 4, 5; ii. 2, end; iii. 4;* make the, gaze, *Antony and Cleopatra, iv. 12* or *14;* disbelief in, *A Winter's Tale, iii. 3.*

Giant, a, *Twelfth Night, i. 5,* meaning a guardian giant; strength of, *Measure for Measure, ii. 2;* pangs of, in death, *Measure for Measure, iii. 1;* robe of a, *Macbeth, v. 2.*

Gib-cat (an old cat), *I. Henry IV., i. 2.*

Gifts, slight, *As You Like It, i. 2,* "Wear this for me," etc.; that are locked in the heart, *A Winter's Tale, iv. 3;* win with, *Two Gentlemen of Verona, iii. 1;* of love, *Midsummer-Night's Dream, i. 1;* returned, *Hamlet, iii. 1;* gain praise, *Love's Labour's Lost, iv. 1;* seven hundred pounds and possibilities is good, *Merry Wives of Windsor, i. 1;* of rich men, *Timon of Athens, v. 1.*

Gig (a kind of top), *Love's Labour's Lost, iv. 3; v. 1.*

Giglot (giddy, inconstant), *I. Henry VI., iv. 7; Cymbeline, iii. 1.*

Gilded, by liquor, *The Tempest, v. 1, 2.*

Gillyvors (gillyflowers), *A Winter's Tale, iv. 3* or *4.*

Gimmals, or gimmers, machinery or jointing of an automaton, *I. Henry VI., i. 2.* A gimmal-ring was a jointed one, two or three fastened together, used by lovers. "Gimmal-bit" is used in *Henry V., iv. 2.*

Ginger, shall be hot i' the mouth, *Twelfth Night, ii. 3.*

Gipsy, Cleopatra called a, *Antony and Cleopatra, i. 1; iv. 10* or *12.*

Gird (rail at), *Coriolanus, i. 1;* a kindly, *I. Henry VI., iii. 1.* The right kind of reproof.

Girdle, turn his (challenge by turning the buckle to the back), *Much Ado about Nothing, v. 1.*

Girdle, round the earth. *Midsummer-Night's Dream, ii. 1.*

Gis, *Hamlet, iv. 5* (or *2*). Meaning unknown.

Giving vein, the, *Richard III., iv. 2.*

Glamis, Macbeth made thane of, by the death of his father, Sinel, Finel, or Finlay, *Macbeth, i. 3.*

Glansdale, Sir William, character in *I. Henry VI.,* appears in *i. 4,* and is killed in the same scene.

Glass, a prophet looks in a, *Measure for Measure, ii. 2.* Allusion to fortune-tellers that prophesied from looking into a beryl or crystal glass.—HUDSON.

Gleek(s), jests or gibes, *Midsummer-Night's Dream, iii. 1; I. Henry VI., iii. 2; Romeo and Juliet, iv. 5.*

Glendower, Owen, a Welsh nobleman, character in *I. Henry IV.,* introduced in *iii. 1.* His victory over Mortimer is reported in *i. 1.*

He joins in rebellion with the Percys. He believes himself to be possessed of supernatural power, and talks pompously (*iii. 1*) of the portents at his birth, and, Hotspur says, kept him at least nine hours "in reckoning up the several devils' names that were his lackeys." His death, *II. Henry IV., iii. 1.* As a matter of fact, he did not die till 1415, after Henry's death. Allusions to, *Richard II., iii. 1; II. Henry VI., ii. 2.* It was Lord Grey, of Ruthven, who was held captive as described in the last passage.

Globe, this, shall dissolve, *The Tempest, iv. 1.*

Globe Theatre, called "this wooden O," in the chorus to *act i., Henry V.*

Glory, guilty of crimes, *Love's Labour's Lost, iv. 1;* the greater dims the less, *Merchant of Venice, v. 1;* departure of, *Richard II., ii. 4;* like a circle in water, *I. Henry VI., i. 2;* view of earthly (Field of the Cloth of Gold), *Henry VIII., i. 1;* of the world, *Henry VIII., iii. 2;* of this life, madness, *Timon of Athens, i. 2.* See also FAME.

Gloucester, Thomas of Woodstock, Duke of, uncle of Richard II. He was arrested for treason in 1397, condemned, and given into the charge of Norfolk, who, it was said, by order of the king, secretly made away with him. In *Richard II., i. 1,* Bolingbroke charges Norfolk with his death. In *iv. 1,* Aumerle is accused of being the instrument of it.

Gloucester, Richard, Duke of. See PLANTAGENET, RICHARD, and RICHARD III. In *III. Henry VI., iii. 2,* he is first called Gloucester.

Gloucester, Duke of, character in *King Lear,* introduced in the first scene. He is coarse in conversation and hot and fiery in his condemnation of Edgar; but the better points of his character come out afterward in his manifestation of loyalty, *iii. 3, 7,* and his bearing in the sufferings it brings upon him, *iii. 7.*

Gloucester, dukedom of, ominous, *III. Henry VI., ii. 6.* It was thought to be unlucky on account of the deaths of three of the dukes.

Gloucester, Eleanor de Bohun, Duchess of, a character in *Richard II.,* enters in *i. 2.* Her death, *ii. 2,* supposed in the play to be at the duke's castle of Plashy or Pleshy, really occurred at Barking Abbey, one of the most ancient abbeys of England, founded by St. Erkenwald, about 675 A. D. It was seven miles east of London, on the Roding. Nothing now remains of its once fine buildings but a gateway with a tower, called the "Fire-Bell Tower," from a tradition that curfew and fire-alarms were rung from it.

Gloucester, Eleanor Cobham, Duchess of. See ELEANOR.

Gloucester, Humphrey, Duke of. See HUMPHREY.

Gloucestershire, scene of a part of *Richard II.* and a part of *II. Henry IV.* Shallow's residence was there.

Gloves, lovers on, *Two Gentlemen of Verona, ii. 1; Romeo and Juliet, ii. 2;* used as gages, *Richard II., i. 1; iv. 1; Henry V., iv. 1; Troilus and Cressida, iv. 4; v. 2; Timon of Athens, v. 4; King Lear, v. 2;* perfumed, *Much Ado about Nothing, iii. 4.*

Glow-worm, the, *Hamlet, i. 5; Midsummer-Night's Dream, iii. 1.*

Glutton, the (Dives), *II. Henry IV., i. 2.*

Gluttony, bankrupts the wits, *Love's Labour's Lost, i. 1.*

Gobbo, an old man, father of Launcelot Gobbo, in the *Merchant of Venice,* introduced in *ii. 2.*

Gobbo, Launcelot. See LAUNCELOT.

Go-between, denunciation of a, *Two Gentlemen of Verona, i. 2;* a zealous, *Merry Wives of Windsor, i. 1; ii. 2; Troil. and Cress., iii. 2.*

God, his mercy, *Measure for Measure, ii. 2; Merchant of Venice, iv. 1; II. Henry VI., iv. 8;* and the rope-maker, *Comedy of Errors, iv. 3;* the tuition of, *Much Ado about Nothing, i. 1;* they hope they serve, *Much Ado about Nothing, iv. 2;* feeds the raven and the sparrow, *As You Like It, ii. 3;* chooses weak ministers, *All's Well that Ends Well, ii. 1;* the widow's champion, *Richard II., i. 2;* guards his anointed, *Richard II., iii. 2, 3;* is mustering armies of pestilence, *Richard II., iii. 3;* King of kings, *Henry V., i. 1;* we are in his hand, *Henry V., iii. 6;* cannot be escaped, *Henry V., iv. 1; Hamlet, iii. 3,* "There is no shuffling," etc.; gives light in darkness, *II. Henry VI., ii. 1;* a stay and guide, *II. Henry VI., ii. 3;* works in all his creatures, *II. Henry VI., ii. 1;* the judge, *II. Henry VI., iii. 2; Henry VIII., iii. 1; King Lear, iv. 2;* the all-seeing, *Richard III., v. 1;* the omniscient, *All's Well that Ends Well, ii. 1; Henry VIII., iii. 1;* is just, *Richard III., i. 2; Macbeth, iv. 3;* rewards service, *Henry VIII., iii. 2;* his spies, *King Lear, v. 3.*

God(s), the, a thousand knees could not move, *A Winter's Tale, iii. 2;* in shapes of beasts, *A Winter's Tale, iv. 3* or *4;* the service greater than, *Troilus and Cressida, ii. 2;* Cæsar as a, *Julius Cæsar, i. 2;* threatenings of the, *Julius Cæsar, i. 3;* wants nothing of a, out eternity and a heaven, *Coriolanus, v. 4;* prayer to, *Timon of Athens, i. 2;* let them find their enemies, *King Lear, iii. 2;* sport of, *King Lear, iv. 1;* opposeless wills of, *King Lear, iv. 6;* are just, *King Lear, v. 3;* justice and delays of, *Antony and Cleopatra, ii. 1;*

seel our eyes, *Antony and Cleopatra, iii. 11* or *13;* detest baseness, *Antony and Cleopatra, iv. 12* or *14;* injurious, *Antony and Cleopatra, iv., end;* partiality of, *Cymbeline, v. 1;* cross whom they love —their clemency, *Cymbeline, v. 4;* incense to, *Cymbeline, v. 5, end;* recall their gifts, *Pericles, iii. 1.*

God save her (a charm), *Henry VIII., v. 4.*

God ye good even (God give you), *As You Like It, v. 1.* See GOOD DEN.

Goffe, Matthew, character in *II. Henry VI.,* first appears in *iv. 7,* mentioned in *iv. 5.* He was a foster-brother of Talbot, Earl of Shrewsbury, and led the Londoners against Jack Cade in 1450.

Going, stay not upon the order of, *Macbeth, iii. 4.*

Gold, *Comedy of Errors, ii. 1;* all that glisters is not, *Merchant of Venice, ii. 7;* hard food for Midas, *Merchant of Venice, iii. 2;* fairy gold, *A Winter's Tale, iii. 3;* authority led by, *A Winter's Tale, iv. 3* or *4;* to gild refined, *King John, iv. 2;* greed for, *II. Henry IV., iv. 4;* allusion to the notion that potable gold was a powerful medicine, *II. Henry IV., iv. 4;* corrupting, *Richard III., iv. 2;* o'erdusted, *Troilus and Cressida, iii. 3;* worse poison, *Romeo and Juliet, v. 1;* allusion to the punishment in hell of the avaricious by molten gold poured down the throat, *Timon of Athens, iii. 1;* power of, *Timon of Athens, iv. 3;* what a god it is!—brings back friends, *Timon of Athens, v. 1;* sin plated with, *King Lear, iv. 6;* power of, *Cymbeline, ii. 3;* worthlessness of, *Cymbeline, iii. 6;* saint-seducing, *Romeo and Juliet, i. 1.*

Golden age, or world, *The Tempest, ii. 1; As You Like It, i. 1.*

Goldsmiths' wives, sentiments from, *As You Like It, iii. 2.*

Golgotha, *Richard II., iv. 1;* memorize (make memorable), another, *Macbeth, i. 2.*

Goliases, *I. Henry VI., i. 2.* Goliaths.

Goliath, with a weaver's beam, *Merry Wives of Windsor, v. 1.*

Goneril, one of the daughters of King Lear, introduced in the first scene. Her professions of love, *i. 1;* treatment of her father, *i. 3, 4;* intrigue with Edmund, *iv. 2, 5; v. 1;* plots against her husband's life, *iv. 6;* poisons Regan and dies, *v. 3.*

"The monsters Goneril and Regan are gorgons rather than women, such as Shakspere has nowhere else conceived. The aspect of Goneril can almost turn to stone; in Regan's tongue there is a viperous hiss. Goneril is the more formidable, because the more incaple of any hatred which is not solid and four-square. Regan acts under her sister's influence, but has an eager venomousness of her own."—DOWDEN.

Gonzago. See MURDER OF GONZAGO.

Gonzalo, a loyal and faithful subject of Prospero in *The Tempest*, introduced in *i. 5.*

Good, render, for evil, *The Tempest, v. 1,* "The rarer action," etc.; *As You Like It, iv. 3; All's Well that Ends Well, ii. 5; Richard III., i. 3; Timon of Athens, iii. 3;* to do, sometimes folly, *Macbeth, iv. 2;* apparent, *Cymbeline, iii. 4;* light of deeds of, *Merchant of Venice, v. 1.*

Good den (evening), *King John, i. 1,* and elsewhere.

Goodfellow, Robin. See PUCK.

Good Friday, allusions to fasting on, *King John, i. 1; 1. Henry IV., i. 2.*

Goodness, a fever in, *Measure for Measure, iii. 2;* may goodness and he fill up one monument, *Henry VIII., ii. 1;* a kind of, in speaking well, *Henry VIII., iii. 2;* brighter after ill behaviour, *I. Henry IV., i. 2, end;* a soul of, in things evil, *Henry V., iv. 1;* made a net for destruction, *Othello, ii. 3,* "And what's he," etc.

Good-night, *Passionate Pilgrim, xiv.;* a hurried, *Macbeth, iii. 4;* lovers', *Romeo and Juliet, ii. 2; Venus and Adonis, l. 529.*

Good things, made too common, *II. Henry IV., i. 2.*

Goodwins, *Merchant of Venice, iii. 1; King John, v. 3, 5.* Sands off the coast of Kent, where the castle of Earl Goodwin was said to have been engulfed.

Good year (supposed corruption of gougères, a disease), *Much Ado about Nothing, i. 3; King Lear, v. 3.*

Goose, the tailor's, *Macbeth, ii. 3.*

Goose-quills, many wearing rapiers afraid of, *Hamlet, ii. 2.* Those who wrote plays for children to act.

Gorboduc, King of Britain (perhaps), *Twelfth Night, iv. 2.*

Gordian knot, the, *Cymbeline, ii. 2; Henry V.; i. 1.* Gordius was a peasant, who was made King of Phrygia because the oracle had said that the future king should come in a wagon, and Gordius came driving into the public square in one just after the oracle had been received. He dedicated his wagon to Jupiter, and tied it up so that the ends of the knot could not be seen. It was believed that he who should untie the knot should be king of all Asia. No one succeeded in untying it, but Alexander the Great cut it with his sword.

Gorgon, a new, *Macbeth, ii. 3;* one way like a, *Antony and Cleopatra, ii. 5.*

Gormandizing, *Love's Labour's Lost, i. 1; Merchant of Venice, ii 5; II. Henry IV., v. 5.*

Gosford Green, near Coventry, scene of part of *Richard II.*

Gossamer, symbol of lightness, *Romeo and Juliet, ii. 6; King Lear, iv. 6.*

Gossips (sponsors), *All's Well that Ends Well, i. 1; Midsummer-Night's Dream, ii. 1; Henry VIII., v. 5; Romeo and Juliet, iii. 5.*

Goths, wars of Rome against the, *Titus Andronicus, i. 1.*

Gough. See GOFFE.

Gourd and fullam (false dice), *Merry Wives of Windsor, i. 3.* Fullam is conjectured to be from Fulham, either because they were made there, or because gamblers made that place a resort. They were loaded on one side, while the gourds were hollowed out, making a secret cavity.

Government(s), deputed, *Measure for Measure, i. 1;* order in, like that of bees, *Henry V., i. 2;* that makes women seem divine, *III. Henry VI., i. 4;* resigned, *III. Henry VI., iv. 6.*

Gower, an officer in the army, character in *II. Henry IV.,* introduced in *ii. 1,* and in *Henry V.,* introduced in *iii. 2.*

Gower, John, the poet, author of "Confessio Amantis," from which the story of *Pericles, Prince of Tyre,* was taken, and therefore introduced as the chorus in that play. He died in 1408.

Grace, forgot, makes all go wrong, *Measure for Measure, iv. 4;* special, *Love's Labour's Lost, i. 1;* of men, more sought than God's, *Richard III., iii. 4;* opposed to rude will, *Romeo and Juliet, ii. 3;* must look so, *Macbeth, iv. 3.*

Grace before meat, *Measure for Measure, i. 2; Merry Wives, i. 1;* not enough for a prologue to egg and butter, *I. Henry IV., i. 2;* used as the, *Coriolanus, iv. 7;* by cynics, *Timon of Athens, i. 2; iii. 6.*

Graceful (gracious), *Antony and Cleopatra, ii. 2.*

Gracefulness, *A Winter's Tale, iv. 3* or *4.*

Graces, some men's, are their enemies, *As You Like It, ii. 3;* a dumb discursive devil in, *Titus Andronicus, iv. 4;* in herbs, *Romeo and Juliet, ii. 3;* her subjects, *Pericles, i. 1.*

Grained (wrinkled), *Comedy of Errors, v. 1.*

Grammar, sin of understanding, *II. Henry VI., iv. 7.*

Grandam, give, kingdom, *King John, ii. 1.*

Grandchildren, *Richard III., iv. 4.*

Grandpré, a French lord in *Henry V.,* first appears in *iv. 2;* his death, *iv. 8.*

Grange (a large country house), Mariana in the moated, *Measure for Measure, iii. 1; iv. 1.*

Grass, grows fastest by night, *Henry V., i. 1.*

Gratiano, a character in the *Merchant of Venice*, introduced in the first scene, a merry, talkative fellow, who, Bassanio says, "speaks an infinite deal of nothing, more than any man in all Venice" (*i. 2*).

Gratiano, an unimportant character in *Othello*, introduced in *v. 2.*

Gratitude, *Macbeth, i. 3*, "Your pains are registered"; *King Lear, iv. 7;* for the poorest service, *Taming of the Shrew, iv. 3;* of an old servant, *As You Like It, ii. 3;* to heaven, *II. Henry VI., ii. 1.* See THANKS.

Gratuity, indirect begging for a, *Two Gentlemen of Verona, i. 1.*

Grave-diggers, characters in *Hamlet, v. 1.*

Gravel-heart (stony heart), *Measure for Measure, iv. 3.*

Grave(s), opened by magic—every third thought a, *The Tempest, v. 1;* with sorrow to the, *Two Gentlemen of Verona, iii. 1;* opened, *Midsummer-Night's Dream, iii. 2; v. 2; Hamlet, iii. 2;* an old man asks a, *Henry VIII., iv. 2; Julius Cæsar, ii. 2; Hamlet, i. 1; iii. 2;* wrestling in a, *Hamlet, v. 1;* silence of the, *Titus Andronicus, i. 1;* by the sea, a, *Timon of Athens, iv. 3; v. 1, 3, 4;* lovers at a, *Romeo and Juliet, v. 3;* position of, east and west, *Cymbeline, iv. 2.*

Gravity, revolted to wantonness, *Love's Labour's Lost, v. 2;* affectation of, *Merchant of Venice, i. 1.*

Graymalkin, the quasi-personal name for the cat, *Macbeth, i. 1.*

Great, the, mercy in—privileges of—wit in, to jest with saints, *Measure for Measure, ii. 2;* have many blasts to shake them, *Richard III., i. 3;* favour of, *Richard III., iii. 4;* criticism of, *Henry VIII., i. 2;* griefs of, *Henry VIII., ii. 3;* one of, like a colossus, *Julius Cæsar, i. 2;* have countenance to suicide, *Hamlet, v. 1;* servants of, *King Lear, iii. 1;* ebb and flow of, *King Lear, v. 3;* pay for demerit of others, *Antony and Cleopatra, v. 2.*

Greatness, rumours concerning, *Measure for Measure, iv. 1;* some achieve, *Twelfth Night, ii. 5; iii. 4; v. 1;* needs pruning *Richard II., iii. 4;* ingratitude of, *I. Henry IV., iv. 3; v. 1;* out of love with, *II. Henry IV., ii. 2;* unsought, *II. Henry IV., iii. 1;* highest point of, *Henry VIII., ii. 2;* farewell to, *Henry VIII., iii. 2;* fall of, *Richard III., iv. 4;* fallen out with fortune, *Troilus and Cressida, iii. 3;* dangers of, *Julius Cæsar, ii. 1;* not independent, *Hamlet, i. 3;* the fall of, *Hamlet, iii. 3;* the right, *Hamlet, iv. 4;* departing, *Antony and Cleopatra, iv. 11 or 13;* magnifies faults and merits, *Lucrece, l. 1004.*

Greek (good fellow), *Twelfth Night, iv. 1.*

Greeks, the, war of, with the Trojans, *Troilus and Cressida;* their ships, *prologue;* strength and skill, *i. 1;* discord among, *i. 3.*

Green, Sir Henry, a character in *Richard II.,* first introduced in *i. 3;* his death, *iii. 2.*

Green, the colour of lovers, *Love's Labour's Lost, i. 2.*

Greene, Robert. The name of the play, "The thrice three Muses mourning for the Death of Learning, late deceased in Beggary," offered to Theseus in *Midsummer-Night's Dream, v. 1,* is by some supposed to refer to his death. See SOURCES.

Green Sleeves, tune of, *Merry Wives of Windsor, ii. 1; v. 5.* The words of this old song are lost, but they are judged, from contemporary allusions, to have been indecent.

Greenwood Tree, Under the, song, *As You Like It, ii. 5.*

Greeting. See SALUTATION.

Gregory, one of Capulet's servants, character in *Romeo and Juliet,* appears in *i. 1.*

Gregory, St., *Two Gentlemen of Verona, iv. 2.* Three popes of the name were canonized.

Gregory, Turk, *I. Henry IV., v. 3.* Pope Gregory VII.

Gremio, an ill-natured old man, suitor of Bianca in the *Taming of the Shrew,* introduced in *i. 1.*

Grey, Elizabeth Woodville, Lady, afterward queen of Edward IV. See ELIZABETH.

Grey, Sir Richard (correctly John), spoken of in *III. Henry VI., iii. 2,* as having lost his life in the cause of the house of York, and in *Richard III., i. 3,* as a partisan of Lancaster. The latter is correct. He fell at the first battle of St. Albans in 1455. His widow married Edward IV.

Grey, Richard, Lord, son of Lady Elizabeth Grey, character in *Richard III.,* first appears in *i. 3;* sent to execution, *iii. 3, 4;* his ghost, *v. 3.* The Greys were hated as upstarts by the family of York, and the favour shown them by Edward IV. intensified the feeling.

Grey, Sir Thomas, character in *Henry V.* He conspires with Cambridge and Scroop to murder the king, and is exposed and ordered to execution in *ii. 2.* The conspiracy is mentioned in the prologue to the act.

Grey, Thomas. See DORSET.

Greyhounds, race by, *Merry Wives of Windsor, i. 1.*

Grief(s), beauty's canker, *The Tempest, i. 2;* unspeakable, *Comedy of Errors, i. 1;* every one can master a, but he that has it, *Much Ado about Nothing, iii. 2;* one in, easily led, *Much Ado about Noth-*

ing, iv. 1; comfort in—patch with proverbs, *Much Ado about Nothing, v. 1;* that burns worse than tears drown, *A Winter's Tale, ii. 1;* what's past help, should be past, *A Winter's Tale, iii. 2; I. Henry IV., iii. 3; III. Henry VI., v. 4; Macbeth, iii. 2; Othello, i. 3;* a throne, *King John, iii. 1;* fills the room of the absent, *King John, iii. 4;* boundeth, *Richard II., i. 2;* counterfeit, *Richard II., i. 4;* shadows of, *Richard II., ii. 2;* king of my, *Richard II., iv. 1;* eased by speech, *Richard III., iv. 4; Macbeth, iv. 3;* a glistering, *Henry VIII., ii. 3;* overflowing, *Titus Andronicus, iii. 1;* one, cured by another, *Romeo and Juliet, i. 2;* much of, shows some want of wit, *Romeo and Juliet, iii. 5;* sin of excessive, *Hamlet, i. 2; iii. 2;* expression of, *Hamlet, v. 1;* fellowship in, *King Lear, iii. 6;* full of, as age, *King Lear, ii. 4;* to deal alone with, *King Lear, iv. 3;* folly of, for cureless ills, *Othello, i. 3;* great, medicine the less, *Cymbeline, iv. 2;* our own forgotten in others', *Pericles, i. 4;* hath two tongues, *Venus and Adonis, l. 1007;* testy, *Lucrece, l. 1094;* best society for, *Lucrece, l. 1111;* dallied with, *Lucrece, l. 1120;* at grievances foregone, *Sonnet xxx.;* the greatest first, *Sonnet xc;* blows a man up, *I. Henry IV., ii. 4;* weighed with wrongs, *II. Henry IV., iv. 1;* softens the mind, *II. Henry IV., iv. 4;* moderation in, *Troilus and Cressida, iv. 4;* speechless, *Macbeth, iv. 3.* See SORROW and TEARS.

Griffith, Richard, Queen Katherine's gentleman usher in *Henry VIII.,* introduced in *ii. 4;* his eulogy on Wolsey, *iv. 2.*

Grise (step, degree), *Othello, i. 3, and elsewhere.*

Grissel, *Taming of the Shrew, ii. 1.* The patient Griselda, whose story is told by Boccaccio and by Chaucer.

Groans, *Richard II., i. 2; v. 1; Lear, iii. 2;* of a deer, *As You Like It, ii. 1.*

Groat, a half-faced, *King John, i. 1.* A coin first issued in the reign of Henry VII., having a profile on it.

Groom, of *Richard II.,* a faithful servant who comes to the deposed king in prison, and expresses his grief because Richard's horse had carried Henry on his coronation-day.

Groundlings, split the ears of, *Hamlet, iii. 2.*

Grudge, to feed an ancient, *Merchant of Venice, i. 3.*

Grumio, an oddly witty servant of Petruchio in the *Taming of the Shrew,* introduced in *i. 2.*

Gualtree Forest, *II. Henry IV., iv. 1.*

Guarded (trimmed), *Merchant of Venice, ii. 2, and elsewhere.*

Guards, priestly, princely, or precise, *Measure for Measure, iii. 1.* The original reads prenzie, variously supposed to be a mistake for the three words above. Guards were facings or trimmings, and the passage refers to the decorousness of the deputy's dress. Precise was used in the sense of puritanical.

Guiana, a region in, *Merry Wives of Windsor, i. 3.*

Guiderius and Arviragus, sons of *Cymbeline,* introduced in *iii. 3.* They pass under the names of Polydore and Cadwal as sons of Belarius, who stole them in their infancy in revenge for his banishment. Their longing for war, *iv. 4;* bravery, *v. 3;* they are discovered and knighted, *v. 5.*

Guildenstern, a courtier in *Hamlet,* introduced in *ii. 2.* See ROSENCRANTZ.

Guildford, Sir Henry, character in *Henry VIII.,* introduced in *i. 4,* son of one of the Guildfords mentioned in *Richard III.*

Guildfords, the, *Richard III., iv. 4.* Sir John and his son Sir Richard.

Guildhall, *Richard III., iii. 5.*

Guilt, consciousness of, *King John, iv. 2;* jealousy of, *Hamlet, iv. 5* (or *2*)*;* revelations of, in the tempest, *King Lear, iii. 2;* who is quite free from, *Othello, iii. 3;* to be read in the face, *Othello, v. 1;* makes cowardly, *Cymbeline, v. 2.* See CONSCIENCE, REMORSE.

Guines, in Picardy, *Henry VIII., i. 1.*

Guinevere, *Love's Labour's Lost, iv. 1.* The wife of King Arthur.

Gulls (fools), *Twelfth Night, v. 1; Henry V., iii. 6; Timon of Athens, ii. 1; Othello, v. 2;* also used for a trick, as in *Much Ado about Nothing, ii. 3; I. Henry IV., v. 1,* "That ungentle gull." Gull is a provincial name for a nestling.

Gun-stones. See CANNON-BALLS.

Gurnet, a soused, *I. Henry IV., iv. 2.* Used as a term of contempt. A gurnet is a sea-fish used for food.

Gurney, James, servant of Lady Faulconbridge in *King John,* appears in the first scene.

Guy, Sir, *Henry VIII., v. 3.* Sir Guy of Warwick, a crusader of the tenth century, of whose prowess fabulous stories were told.

Haberdasher, a, a character in *The Taming of the Shrew, iv. 3.*

Habit, *Two Gentlemen of Verona, v. 4; Hamlet, vii. 4; Othello, i. 3.*

Hack. See KNIGHTHOOD.

Hacket, Marian and Cicely, an alewife and her maid, mentioned, *Taming of the Shrew, induction, 2.*

Haggards (wild hawks), *Much Ado about Nothing, iii. 1; Taming of the Shrew, iv. 1; Twelfth Night, iii. 1; Othello, iii. 3.*

Hair, the, raised with fright, *The Tempest, i. 2; II. Henry VI., iii. 2; Richard III., i. 3; Macbeth, i. 3; v. 5; Hamlet, iii. 4;* of professions, *Merry Wives of Windsor, ii. 3;* why time takes, more, than wit, *Comedy of Errors, ii. 2; Two Gentlemen of Verona, iii. 2;* golden, *Merchant of Venice, i. 1;* false, *Merchant of Venice, iii. 2; Henry V., iii. 7; Timon of Athens, iv. 3,* "Thatch your poor, thin roofs," etc.; *Sonnet lxviii.;* flaxen, *Twelfth Night, i. 3;* conceit of friendship in, *King John, iii. 4;* used for character, complexion, *I. Henry IV., iv. 1;* of Judas, *As You Like It, iii. 4;* allusion to the belief that a hair turns to a snake in water, *Antony and Cleopatra, i. 2;* dishevelled, *Lover's Complaint, l. 29.*

Hal, Prince. See HENRY V.

Halcyon beaks, *King Lear, ii. 2.* Allusion to the belief that the turns of the halcyon's beak indicate changes in the weather.

Halcyon days, *I. Henry VI., i. 2.* These were fourteen days in winter, when, as was supposed, the halcyon builds its nest, and the sea is calm. Hence it is used for days of peace.

Half Can, a prisoner, *Measure for Measure, iv. 3.*

Half Moon, a room in an inn, *I. Henry IV., ii. 4.*

Halidom (holy dame or holy dom?), *Henry VIII., v. 1.*

Hallowmas (All-Saints' Day), *Richard II., v. 1;* a beggar at, *Two Gentlemen of Verona ii. 1, 2.*

Hamlet is introduced in *i. 2* of the play of the name. Amlettus, Amleth, and Hamblet are older forms of the name. In *i. 4* he sees the ghost of his father, and in *i. 5* learns the manner of his death and vows revenge; his soliloquy, *iii. 1;* he learns by his artifice with the players, *iii. 2,* that there is no mistake about the king's guilt; feigns madness, kills Polonius by mistake for the king, *iii. 4;* is sent to England, *iv. 3;* returns, *iv. 6;* at Ophelia's grave, *v. 1;* fights with Laertes and dies, *v. 2.*

"I believe the character of Hamlet may be traced to Shakspere's deep and accurate science in mental philosophy. Indeed, that this character must have some connection with the common fundamental laws of our nature may be assumed from the fact that Hamlet has been the darling of every country in which the literature of England has been fostered. . . . In Hamlet he seems to have wished to exemplify the moral necessity of a due balance between our attention to the objects of our senses, and our meditation on the workings of our minds, an equilibrium between the real and the imaginary worlds. In Hamlet this balance is disturbed; his thoughts and the images of his fancy are far more vivid than his actual impressions, and his very perceptions, instantly passing through the medium of his contemplations, acquire as they pass a form and a colour not naturally their own. Hence we see a great, an almost enormous intellectual activity, and a proportionate aversion to real action consequent upon it, with all its symptoms and accompanying qualities. This character Shakspere places in circumstances where it is obliged to act on the spur of the moment; Hamlet is brave and careless of death; but he vacillates from sensibility and procrastinates from thought, and loses the power of action in the energy of resolve. . . . Shakspere seems to mean all Hamlet's character to be brought together before his final disappearance from the scene; his meditative excess in the grave-digging, his yielding to passion with Laertes, his love for Ophelia blazing out, his tendency to generalize on all occasions in the dialogue with Horatio, his fine gentlemanly manners with Osric, and his and Shakspere's own fondness for presentiment: ' But thou wouldst not think how ill all's here about my heart: but it is no matter.' "— COLERIDGE.

Hamlet, Prince of Denmark, a tragedy first published in 1603 in a meagre form, either Shakspere's first draft of the play, or an unauthorized version made up from parts supplied to actors, probably the former. In its enlarged form it appeared in 1604, and in two or three later editions before the folio of 1623 was published. The first appearance of the story of Hamlet, so far as is known, was in the " Historia Danica " of Saxo Grammaticus, a Danish historian, who wrote it about 1204. A version of the story in Italian by Bandello was translated into French by Belleforest, from which it was rendered into English, though no earlier edition of the English translation is known than one of 1608. Besides these there was an older play in English on the subject, which has not come down to us. In the " Hystorie of Hamblet " the time is placed before the introduction of Christianity into Denmark, and in fact before Christ. Shakspere leaves the time indefinite, though the characters are Christians. The period of action seems to be but a few months. None of the plays has excited more interest or more study and criticism. There is an opinion that the main characters were intended for portraits more or less exact of personages of Shakspere's own time, Hamlet himself being referred to Sir Philip Sidney.

Hames Castle, *III. Henry VI., v. 5.*

Hampton, *Henry V., ii. 2.*

Hand, in any (at any rate), *All's Well that Ends Well, iii. 6.*

Hand-fast (troth-plight), *Cymbeline, i. 5.*

Hand(s), Cressida's, *Troilus and Cressida, i. 1;* indications in, *Comedy of Errors, iii. 2; Merchant of Venice, ii. 2; Othello, iii. 4; Antony and Cleopatra, i. 2;* beauty of, *Venus and Adonis, l. 361;*

Lucrece, l. 393; blood on, *Macbeth, ii. 2 ; v. 1 ; Richard II., ii. 1;* proper fellow of my (tall and well made), *II. Henry IV., ii. 2 ; Winter's Tale, v. 2.*

Handkerchief, Desdemona's, *Othello, iii. 3, 4.*

Handwriting, a fair, held base, *Hamlet, v. 2.*

Hanged, born to be, *The Tempest, i. 1 ; v. 1 ; Two Gentlemen of Verona, i. 1 ;* never undone till, *Two Gentlemen of Verona, ii. 5.*

Hanger-on, a, *Much Ado about Nothing, i. 1.*

Hanging, comfort in, *Cymbeline, v. 4 ;* many a good, prevents a bad marriage, *Twelfth Night, i. 5.*

Hannibal, *Measure for Measure, ii. 1 ; I. Henry VI., i. 5.*

Happiness, seen through another's eyes, *As You Like It, v. 2 ;* achieved in not being over-happy, *Hamlet, ii. 2 ;* by virtue, *Taming of the Shrew, i. 1 ;* brevity of, *Lucrece, l. 22 ;* of kings, *Henry V., iv. 1 ;* absolute, *Othello, ii. 1.*

Happy man be his dole, proverbial expression, *Taming of the Shrew, i. 1,* and elsewhere.

Harcourt, character in *II. Henry IV.,* first appears in *iv. 4.* He is on the side of the king, and brings news of Northumberland's defeat. Perhaps Sir Thomas Harcourt. who was Sheriff of Berkshire.

Hardships, cheerful acceptance of, *Henry V., iv. 1.*

Hare, the melancholy, *I. Henry IV., i. 2 ;* the hunted, *Venus and Adonis, l. 679, et seq.*

Harebell, the, *Cymbeline, iv. 2.*

Hare-lip, *Midsummer-Night's Dream, v. 2 ; Lear, iii. 4.* Supposed to be caused by malignant fairies.

Harfleur, in France, six miles from Havre, scene of a part of *Henry V. ;* its surrender, *iii. 3.*

Harfleur, Governor of, a character in *Henry V.,* first appears in *iii. 3,* where he surrenders the town to the English (1415).

Ha'rford West (Haverford West), *Richard III., iv. 5.*

Hark, hark, the lark, song, *Cymbeline, ii. 3.*

Harm, to do, is often laudable, *Macbeth, iv. 2.*

Harmony, in parts working to one end, *Henry V., i. 2 ;* of the spheres, *Merchant of Venice, v. 1.*

Harpy, like the, *Pericles, iv. 3* (or *4*).

Haste, too great, *Coriolanus, iii. 1,* "unscanned swiftness."

Hastings, Lord, character in *II. Henry IV.,* first appears in *i. 3.* He is one of the party opposed to the king. He was not Lord but Sir Ralph Hastings.

Hastings, William, Lord, character in *III. Henry VI.,* introduced in *iv. 1;* and again in *Richard III.*, introduced in *i. 1.* He was a favourite of Edward IV., and supposed himself to be in favour with Richard, who, however, ordered him to execution, *iii. 4*, probably because he saw that Hastings would not go with him in his intended crimes against his nephews. The accusations made against him are in *iii. 5, 6;* his ghost appears to Richard, *v. 3.* The character of Hastings in the play is frank, open, and unsuspicious; on his way to execution he recalls the curses invoked on him by Queen Margaret for looking on at the murder of her son, *i. 3.* It was not he, but his son, Edward Hastings, who married the daughter of Sir Thomas Hungerford (*iv. 1*). Lord William Hastings rebuilt the castle of Ashby de la Zouch, mentioned in "Ivanhoe."

Hat, a fantastic, *Taming of the Shrew, iii. 2.*

Hatched, in silver, *Troilus and Cressida, i. 3.* Inlaid with fine lines of silver.

Hatred, Shylock's, for Antonio, *Merchant of Venice, i. 3; iii. 3;* of a tyrant, *Richard III., i. 1; iv. 4;* of Aufidius, *Coriolanus, i. 10; iii. 1;* of the plebeians, *Coriolanus, ii. 1;* of the race, *Macbeth, iv. 3*, "Had I power," etc.; nought in, *Othello, v. 2;* not for you, *Sonnet cxlv;* Margaret's, for York, *III. Henry VI., i. 4.*

Haud credo (I do not believe), *Love's Labour's Lost, iv. 2.*

Have I caught my heavenly jewel? *Merry Wives of Windsor, iii. 3.* Quotation from Sidney's "Arcadia."

Havoc, cry, *King John, ii. 1; Coriolanus, iii. 1; Julius Cæsar, iii. 1;* a signal for slaughter.

Hawking, allusions to: prune herself and bristle up the crest, *I. Henry IV., i. 1;* you must be watched, *Troilus and Cressida, iii. 2;* hawks were tamed by being kept from sleeping. See also FAL-CONRY.

Hawthorn-buds (ladies' men), *Merry Wives of Windsor, iii. 3.*

Hay (a boisterous dance), *Love's Labour's Lost, v. 1.*

Hazard, edge of, *All's Well that Ends Well, iii. 3.*

Head, the gate of the mind, *King Lear, v. 4.*

Head, of the first (in its fifth year), *Love's Labour's Lost, iv. 2.*

Heart, a merry, goes all the way, song, *A Winter's Tale, iv. 2.*

Heart-break, *Antony and Cleopatra, iv. 12 or 14.*

Heart(s), how won, *I. Henry IV., iii. 2;* a good, *Henry V., v. 2;* flinty, *Richard III., i. 3;* a thousand, *Richard III., v. 3;* seat of the brains (an old belief), *Coriolanus, i. 1;* for the event, *Coriolanus, ii. 1;* ruddy drops that visit my sad, *Julius Cæsar, ii. 1;* throw away the worser part, *Hamlet, iii. 4;* now cracks a noble.

Hamlet, v. 2; cause in nature for hard, *King Lear, iii. 6;* burst smilingly, *King Lear, v. 3;* wear my, upon my sleeve, *Othello, ı. 1;* pursed up his, *Antony and Cleopatra, ii. 2;* empty of all but grief, *Cymbeline, iii. 4;* a quiet cabinet—seat of sensation, *Lucrece, l. 442;* a light, lives long, *Love's Labour's Lost, v. 2;* courage of an innocent, *II. Henry VI., iii. 1, 2.*

Heaven, served worse than self, *Measure for Measure, ii. 2;* splits the oak rather than the myrtle, *Measure for Measure, ii. 2;* in the mouth, evil in the heart, *Measure for Measure, ii. 4;* an ambassador to, *Measure for Measure, iii. 1;* the sword of, *Measure for Measure, iii. 2;* appeal to the justice of, *Measure for Measure, v. 1;* help of, *All's Well that Ends Well, i. 1, last paragraph; ii. 1;* recognition in, *King John, iii. 4;* comfort in, *Richard II., ii. 2;* aids given by, *Richard II., iii. 2, 3;* help of, *III. Henry VI., iv. 1; Pericles, i. 4;* o'er our heads, *Richard II., iii. 3;* above all yet, *Henry VIII., iii. 1;* deaf to sorrow, *Titus Andronicus, iv. 1;* tempting, *Julius Cæsar, i. 3;* no bribery before, *Hamlet, iii. 3;* appeal to, *King Lear, ii. 4;* judgment of, *King Lear, v. 3;* fire from, *Pericles, ii. 4.*

Hebenon (henbane ?), *Hamlet, i. 5.*

Hecate, in *Macbeth,* appears in *iii. 5; iv. 1;* that railing, *1. Henry VI., iii. 2;* ban of, *Hamlet, iii. 2; King Lear, i. 1.*

Hector, son of Priam, the great Trojan hero, and one of the most exalted characters in classic literature, is introduced in *Troilus and Cressida, i. 2,* where he is described, and said to have been struck down by Ajax. His challenge to the Greeks, *i. 3;* fight with Ajax, *iv. 5;* bravery in the field, *v. 5;* his death, *v. 9;* dragged by Achilles, *v. 10;* mentioned, *Merry Wives of Windsor, i. 3; ii. 3; Love's Labour's Lost, v. 2; II. Henry IV., ii. 4; Coriolanus, i. 3, 8; I. Henry VI., ii. 3; III. Henry VI., iv. 8; Antony and Cleopatra, iv. 8;* in a painting, *Lucrece, lines 1430, 1486.*

Hecuba, Queen, *Troilus and Cressida, i. 2; Coriolanus, i. 3; Titus Andronicus, iv. 1; Cymbeline, iv. 2;* witnessing Priam's death —an actor's grief for, *Hamlet, ii. 2;* in a painting, *Lucrece, lines 1447, 1450, 1485.*

Hedge (as a verb), *Merry Wives of Windsor, ii. 2, and elsewhere.*

Hedgehogs, or urchins, *Midsummer-Night's Dream, ii. 2; Richard III., i. 2; Macbeth, iv. 1; Tempest, ii. 2.*

Hedge-priest, *Love's Labour's Lost, v. 2,* "The pedant, the braggart," etc.

Hefts (heavings), *A Winter's Tale, ii. 1.*

Heigh-ho ! (refrain of a song), *As You Like It, ii. 7.*

Heirloom, an, *All's Well that Ends Well, iv. 2 ; v. 2.*

Helen, wife of Menelaus, King of Sparta. She chose **him** from among many suitors, all of whom took an oath, before her decision was made, to defend and avenge her if necessary, whatever her choice might be. Paris persuaded her to elope with him to Troy, and from this arose the Trojan war. She is talked of in *Troilus and Cressida, i. 2 ;* the question of giving her up discussed in *ii. 2 ;* she is introduced in *iii. 1 ;* at the end of *iv. 1,* Diomedes bitterly estimates her cost to Greece and Troy; mentioned, *As You Like It, iii. 2, song ; All's Well that Ends Well, i. 3, song ; III. Henry VI., ii. 2 ; Lucrece, l. 1368 ; Sonnet liii ; Midsummer - Night's Dream, v. 1.*

Helen, Imogen's attendant in *Cymbeline,* introduced in *ii. 2.*

Helena, character in *Midsummer-Night's Dream,* introduced in *i. 1.* She is in love with Demetrius, who loves Hermia, who again is in love with Lysander. Lysander returns Hermia's love, except for a short time, when he is under the enchantment produced by the fairies, when he loves Helena. In her self-distrust she thinks it is a jest put upon her by Hermia and her lover. In character she is gentler than Hermia, but not altogether generous, as she runs off to tell of Hermia's elopement. The smaller girl, in her jealousy, calls Helena a " painted Maypole."

Helena, heroine of *All's Well that Ends Well,* introduced in the first scene. Taking the repulsive *rôle* of the heroine of the original tale, Shakspere has portrayed a character of great sweetness and strength. Helena is at the same time clever and self-sacrificing, meek and high-spirited, willing to renounce if necessary, and yet quick to see the way to win, and firm and clear-headed in availing herself of it. Many of the most beautiful passages of the play are put into her mouth and express her "pious trust and persevering, steadfast nature, which from her youth up, on account of her lowly position, has rendered her self-dependent," the depth and at the same time the straightforward simplicity of her character.

Helenus, son of Priam, character in *Troilus and Cressida,* introduced in *i. 2 ;* satirized by Troilus, *ii. 2.*

Helicanus, a lord of Tyre, in *Pericles,* introduced in *i. 2.* He is an adviser of the prince; refuses the crown, *ii. 4.* " A figure of truth, of faith, of loyalty."

Helicons, *II. Henry IV., v. 3.* Helicon was the mountain of the Muses.

Hell, set on fire, *Merry Wives of Windsor, v. 5;* cunning livery of, *Measure for Measure, iii. 1;* gate of, *Much Ado about Nothing, ii. 1;* what hole in, hot enough, *I. Henry IV., i. 2;* a fate to remind of, *I. Henry IV., iii. 3;* dream of, *Richard III., i. 4;* the porter imagines himself keeper of the gate of, *Macbeth, ii. 3.*

Hell (cant for prison), *Comedy of Errors, iv. 2.*

Hellespont, the, *Two Gentlemen of Verona, i. 1.* The strait between the Mediterranean and the Sea of Marmora.

Hemlock, *Macbeth, iv. 1;* perhaps the "insane root" mentioned in *Macbeth, i. 3.*

Henry, Kings, IV., V., VI., and VIII., dramas of. See KING HENRY IV., etc.

Henry, Prince, son of King John, appears in the last scene of *King John,* speaking as a man. In truth, he was but nine years old when his father died in 1216. He reigned under the title of Henry III.

Henry IV., first of the Lancastrian kings. He was the son of John of Gaunt, Duke of Lancaster, and was born in 1366, died in 1413. He is a character in *Richard II.,* as well as in the plays that bear his name. In the former play he is called Bolingbroke, a title given him from the name of the town where he was born. He was Duke of Hereford during Richard's reign. In *Richard II.* he appears in the first scene in a quarrel with Norfolk concerning the murder of his uncle, the Duke of Gloucester. His meeting with Norfolk, *i. 3.* His intended marriage is spoken of in *ii. 1.* He was to marry the cousin of the French king, but Richard hearing of it sent Salisbury to prevent it. Richard was forced to resign the crown, and Henry was proclamed, *iv. 1.* A plot against his life was discovered by York, *v. 2.* In *I. Henry IV.* he is introduced in the first scene; in *II. Henry IV.* in *iii. 1.* The rebellion of the Percys and their party embittered his reign, and the wildness of his eldest son was a continual grief to him—evils which he believed sent on him in punishment of his usurpation and in fulfilment of the curse of *Richard II.* He intended to go on a crusade, but was prevented by the rebellion. A prophecy had told him he was to die in Jerusalem—a prophecy he understood when he found that the chamber where he was taken with his last illness was called the Jerusalem Chamber, after a fashion of naming the rooms of inns. Henry IV. is brave and wise in action, but at times morbid, distrustful, and suspicious; prompt and noble at decisive moments, he frets away his leisure with remorse and apprehension.

Henry V., called Henry of Monmouth and Prince Hal, son of Henry IV., born at Monmouth in 1388, reigned from 1413 to 1422. He is a character in the two parts of *Henry IV.*, as well as in the play that bears his name. His dissoluteness is spoken of in *Richard II., v. 3*, where he is mentioned as a young man, though in reality only eleven years of age at that time. In *I. Henry IV.* he is introduced in *i. 2*, and his mad pranks with his wild comrades are represented in that play. In *act v.* he shows unexpected bravery in the battle of Shrewsbury. In *II. Henry IV.* he appears first in *ii. 2*. In the close of that scene he soliloquizes on the company he keeps and his reasons and intentions. He is described by Falstaff in *ii. 4*. His father's forebodings as to his reign are expressed in *iv. 4;* those of the Chief Justice, in *v. 2*. At his father's death he reforms, *v. 2* and *5;* dismisses his low companions, and becomes one of the most successful and the best loved of English sovereigns. His versatility, *Henry V., i. 1;* his reputation, *ii. 4;* among his soldiers, *iv., chorus;* his piety, *iv. 1, 8; v., chorus;* at Agincourt, *act iv.;* his wooing, *v. 2;* his funeral, *I. Henry VI., i. 1;* his wars in France, *II. Henry VI., i. 1*.

" The prince, whom Shakspere admires and loves more than any other person in English history, afterward to become Shakspere's ideal King of England, cares little for mere reputation. He does not think much of himself and of his own honour; and while there is nothing to do, and his great father holds all power in his own right hand, Prince Hal escapes from the cold proprieties of the court to the boisterous life and mirth of the tavern. He is, however, only waiting for a call to action, and Shakspere declares that from the first he was conscious of his great destiny, and, while seeming to scatter his force in frivolity, was holding his true self, well guarded, in reserve."—DOWDEN.

Henry VI., King (1421–1471), character in the three plays that bear his name. He was but nine months old when his father died, though in the first part, *iii. 4*, he speaks of remembering what his father said of Talbot. He is introduced in *iii. 1;* his coronation at Paris (December 17, 1431), first part, *iv. 1;* his marriage with Margaret of Anjou (1445), second part, *i. 1;* his bookish rule, second part, *i. 1, end;* his piety, *i. 3;* York's opinion of him, *v. i;* his cowardice, third part, *i. 1;* his leniency and conscientiousness, *ii. 2;* his ill success in the field, *ii. 2, 5;* his weakness, *ii. 6;* his return from Scotland (1465) and capture, *iii. 1, 2*. In *iv. 6*, he makes a prophecy concerning Richmond (Henry VII.), who when he became king asked the pope to canonize Henry VI. on account of it; but the pope re-

fused, on the ground that Henry's saintliness was united with so
much weakness that to canonize him would bring saintship into contempt. His kindness to his subjects, third part, *iv. 8;* his death, *v.
6.* During his reign England lost all that she had gained in France
under Henry V., and all that was done to save his crown at home
was done by his queen—who, however, was very unpopular—and by
the partisans of his house. They were successful in the battle of
Wakefield, but were defeated at St. Albans, Bloreheath, Northampton,
Towton, Hexham, Barnet, and Tewksbury. It was commonly believed that Henry was killed by Gloucester, as in the play. The removal of his body to Chertsey, *Richard III., i. 2;* his ghost, *v. 3.*

Henry VII. See RICHMOND.

Henry VIII. (1491–1547), King, enters in the second scene of
the play that bears his name. The divorce from Katherine is talked
of in *ii. 1,* is the subject of *ii. 2,* and is tried in *ii. 4;* his marriage
with Anne Boleyn, *iii. 2;* befriending of Cranmer, *v. 3.*

"Henry, if we judge him sternly, is cruel and self-indulgent; but
Shakspere will hardly allow us to judge Henry sternly. He is a
lordly figure, with a full, abounding strength of nature, a self-confidence, an ease and mastery of life, a power of effortless sway, and
seems born to pass on in triumph over those who have fallen and are
afflicted."—DOWDEN.

Henry IV., of France, *Comedy of Errors, iii. 2.* Allusion to
the war in regard to his succession, 1589–'93.

Hent, a more horrid, *Hamlet, iii. 3.* Hold, opportunity, or to
take hold, *Measure for Measure, iv. 6.*

Henton (or Hopkins), Nicholas, *Henry VIII., i. 1, 2; ii. 1.* His
name was Hopkins, the name of the monastery Henton.

Herald, at a masquerade, *Love's Labour's Lost, v. 2.*

Heraldry, allusions to: bear for a difference. A difference is
a mark added to a coat of arms to distinguish branches of a family
or the sons of one family, *Much Ado about Nothing, i. 1;* my golden
coat, *Lucrece, l. 205,* an anachronism; our new, *Othello, iii. 4.* Allusion to the red hand on the arms of Ulster, which were placed on
the escutcheon of baronets of a new order instituted by James I.
for the purpose of subduing Ulster; the dozen white luces in their
coat, *Merry Wives of Windsor, i. 1.* The arms of the Lucy family
(*q. v.*) bore three pikes or luces.

Herbert, Sir Walter, character in *Richard III.,* first appears in
v. 2; mentioned in *iv. 5* as having gone to Richmond. He was a
son of the Earl of Pembroke in *III. Henry VI.*

Herbert, William, Earl of Pembroke. See PEMBROKE.

Herb of grace, or rue, *Richard II., iii. 4; Hamlet, iv. 5.*

Herbs, to remove error, *Midsummer-Night's Dream, iii. 2;* salad and nose, *All's Well that Ends Well, iv. 5;* virtues of, *Romeo and Juliet, ii. 3.*

Hercules, bully, *Merry Wives of Windsor, i. 3;* labours of, *Much Ado about Nothing, ii. 1,* near the *end;* made to turn a spit, *Much Ado about Nothing, ii. 1; Love's Labour's Lost, i. 2;* whipping a top—love a, *Love's Labour's Lost, iv. 3;* incorrectly placed among the nine worthies, *Love's Labour's Lost, v. 1, 2;* alluded to, *Midsummer-Night's Dream, iv. 1; v. 1; Merchant of Venice, ii. 1;* invoked, *As You Like It, iv. 3; I. Henry IV., ii. 4; III. Henry VI., ii. 1;* if you had been the wife of, *Coriolanus, iv. 1;* did shake down mellow fruit, *Coriolanus, iv. 6,* allusion to the gardens of the Hesperides; and his load, *Hamlet, ii. 2;* Hercules bearing the globe was the sign of the Globe Theatre; leaving Antony, *Antony and Cleopatra, iv. 3.*

Hereafter, the all-hail, *Macbeth, i. 5.*

Heredity, none of treason, *As You Like It, i. 3; All's Well that Ends Well, i. 1,* "His sole child," etc., and "Be thou blest, Bertram, and succeed thy father," etc.

Hereford, earldom of, promised to Buckingham, who claimed it as his by right of inheritance from his ancestor, Thomas of Woodstock, *Richard III., iii. 1;* the promise urged, *iv. 2.*

Hereford, Henry of (Bolingbroke, afterward Henry IV.), *Richard II., i. 1.*

Heretics, could not die by drowning, *Romeo and Juliet, i. 2.*

Heresy, hated most by the deceived, *Midsummer-Night's Dream, ii. 2;* Cranmer accused of, *Henry VIII., v. 1, 2.*

Hermia, a character in the *Midsummer-Night's Dream.* She is beloved by Lysander and Demetrius, and loves Lysander. Her vixenish spirit comes out principally in her quarrels with the taller and gentler Helena. She is introduced in the first scene.

Hermione, heroine of the first part of *A Winter's Tale,* wife of Leontes and daughter of the Emperor of Russia. Her character is one of the noblest among Shakspere's women, of mingled sweetness, forbearance, and dignity, strong and calm. See IMOGEN.

Hermits, your (beadsmen to pray for you), *Macbeth, i. 6; Cymbeline, iii. 6,* "Great men," etc.

Hermit-life, *Timon of Athens, iv. 3.*

Herne, the hunter, his oak in Windsor Forest, *Merry Wives of*

Windsor, iv. 4; v. 5. The tree shown as Herne's oak was so decayed in 1795 that it was cut down by the king's order.

Hero, of war, a, his defects shown in peace, *Coriolanus, iv. 7;* a pretended, *Henry V., iii. 6;* a true, *II. Henry IV., ii. 3; Henry V., i. 2; Troilus and Cressida, iv. 5.*

Hero, of Sestos, *As You Like It, iv. 1;* her tower, *Two Gentlemen of Verona, iii. 1; Romeo and Juliet, ii. 4.*

Hero, daughter of Leonato, Governor of Messina, one of the principal characters in *Much Ado about Nothing,* introduced in the first scene. Benedick describes her appearance at about the middle of the scene. Her mildness and gentleness are sharply contrasted with the fire and spirit of Beatrice, but her wit and power of expression are shown in the scene, *iii. 1,* where she is exaggerating her cousin's faults, to be overheard by her, and to carry out the trick against her and Benedick.

Herod, of Jewry, *Merry Wives of Windsor, ii. 1; Henry V., iii. 2; Antony and Cleopatra, i. 2; iii. 3, 6; iv. 6;* out-Herods, *Hamlet, iii. 2.* Herod was a frequent character in the miracle-plays.

Heroines, of poetry, *Romeo and Juliet, ii. 4.*

Heronshaw, or hernshaw, perhaps the "hand-saw" of the proverb, *Hamlet, ii. 2.*

Herring, a shotten, *I. Henry IV., ii. 4.* One that has cast its spawn and looks thin.

Hesperides, gardens of the, *Love's Labour's Lost, iv. 3; Pericles, i. 1.* In those gardens were the golden apples given to Juno at her marriage by the goddess of the Earth, which were under the care of the daughters of Hesperis, assisted by a watchful dragon.

Hesperus, sleepy lamp of, *All's Well that Ends Well, ii. 1.*

He that has and a little, song, *King Lear, iii. 2.*

Hey Robin, song by Sir Thomas Wyatt, *Twelfth Night, iv. 2.*

Hic et ubique (here and everywhere), *Hamlet, i. 5.*

Hic ibat Simois, etc., from Ovid, *Taming of the Shrew, iii. 1.* "Here Simois flowed; here was the Sigeian land; here stood the lofty realm of old Priam."

Hic jacet, or, *All's Well that Ends Well, iii. 6.* "Here lies."

Hide, your, and you, *King John, ii. 1.* Austria was represented as wearing the lion's skin taken from Richard.

Highwaymen, St. Nicholas's clerks—Trojans, *I. Henry IV., ii. 1;* gentlemen of the shade, minions of the moon, *I. Henry IV., i. 2.* See OUTLAWS.

Highway robbery, *I. Henry IV., ii. 2; As You Like It, ii. 3.*

Hilding (cowardly), *II. Henry IV.*, *i. 1; Henry V.*, *iv. 2.*

Hilding (a coarse girl), *Taming of the Shrew, ii. 1.*

Hill, perpendicular, o' horseback up a, *I. Henry IV.*, *ii. 4.*

Hind, the, that would mate with the lion, *All's Well that Ends Well, i. 1.*

Hip, to have upon the (a hunting phrase), *Merchant of Venice, i. 3; iv. 1.*

Hippocrates, *Merry Wives of Windsor, iii. 1.* A Greek physician, born about 460 B. C., called the father of medicine.

Hippolyta, Queen of the Amazons, character in the *Midsummer-Night's Dream,* introduced in the first scene. Her marriage to Theseus is the occasion of the festivities. In classic story Hippolyta was slain by Hercules, who came to obtain her girdle. She would have given it, but, under a false impression of treachery on her part, he slew her and took it. Antiope is the name of the Queen of the Amazons whom Theseus carried off.

Hippopotamus, supposed to be the "sea monster," mentioned in *King Lear, i. 4.*

Hisperia, an attendant of the princess, mentioned in *As You Like It, ii. 2.*

Historical Plays, the.

"It certainly seems that Shakspere's historic dramas produced a very deep effect on the minds of the English people, and in earlier times they were familiar even to the least informed of all ranks, according to the relation of Bishop Corbett. Marlborough, we know, was not ashamed to confess that his principal acquaintance with English history was derived from them: and I believe that a large part of the information as to our old names and achievements even now abroad is due, directly or indirectly, to Shakspere."—COLE-RIDGE.

Hit, a palpable, *Hamlet, v. 2.*

Hobbididence, a fiend, *King Lear, iv. 1.* See MAHU.

Hobby-horse, *Hamlet, iii. 2.* The figure of a horse fastened to a man, used in the morris-dance.

Hobby-horse is forgot, *Love's Labour's Lost, iii. 1.* A line of an old song.

Hob nob, is his word, *Twelfth Night, iii. 4.* Have or not have.

Hogs, shall I keep your, *As You Like It, i. 1.* Allusion to the parable of the prodigal son. This making of Christians will raise the price of, *Merchant of Venice, iii. 5.*

Hold you there (keep yourself in that mind), *Measure for Measure, iii. 1.*

Holiday(s), if all the year were, *I. Henry IV., i. 2;* a beautiful, *King John, iii. 1.*

Holland, John, a follower of Jack Cade, *II. Henry VI., iv. 2.*

Holmedon, or Homildon Hill, September 14, 1402, battle at, *I. Henry IV., i. 1, 3,* between the Scots under Douglas and the king's troops under Hotspur.

Holofernes, a character in *Love's Labour's Lost,* introduced in *iv. 2,* an empty, wordy pedant, characterized by the page and the clown as having "been at a great feast of languages and stolen the scraps," and "lived long on the alms-basket of words." He has been supposed to be a caricature of an Italian teacher in London named Florio, who translated Montaigne and published in 1598 a dictionary called "A World of Words," and who had criticised the English dramas as being "neither right comedies nor right tragedies, but perverted histories without decorum."

Holy Land, the, *I. Henry IV., i. 1.*

Holy-rood day, *I. Henry IV., i. 1.* September 14th, feast of the Exaltation of the Cross.

Holy thistle, *Much Ado about Nothing, iii. 4.* It was used as a specific for heart diseases.

Holy water, court (flattery), *King Lear, iii. 2.*

Homage, a duke's, to a king, *The Tempest, i. 1.*

Home-keeping youth, *Two Gentlemen of Verona, i. 1; Cymbeline, iii. 3.*

Homildon Hill. See HOLMEDON.

Honesty, wrangle with one's own, *Merry Wives of Windsor, ii. 1;* description of Duncan's, *All's Well that Ends Well, iv. 3;* is a fool, *A Winter's Tale, iv. 3* or *4;* pretence of, *Richard III., i. 3,* "Because I cannot flatter," etc.; armed strong in, *Julius Cæsar, iv. 3;* rarity of, *Hamlet, ii. 2; iii. 1; A Winter's Tale, ii. 1; Timon of Athens, iv. 3;* honesty his fault, *Timon of Athens, iii. 1;* no puritan, *All's Well that Ends Well, i. 3;* unsafe, *Othello, iii. 3;* a man of, *Othello, v. 2.*

Honeymoon, a, *Taming of the Shrew, iv. 1.*

Honey-stalks, *Titus Andronicus, iv. 4.* Supposed to be clover.

Honi soit, etc., *Merry Wives of Windsor, v. 5.* "Shame to him that thinks evil of it," the motto of the Order of the Garter.

Honorificabilitudinitatibus, not so long as, *Love's Labour's Lost, v. 1.*

Honour(s), take the, *Merry Wives of Windsor, ii. 1;* hidden in necessity, *Merry Wives of Windsor, ii. 2;* that it were purchased by merit, *Merchant of Venice, ii. 9;* the knight that swore by his, *As You Like It, i. 2;* perfect, *All's Well that Ends Well, i. 2;* real, *All's Well that Ends Well, ii. 3;* wins but a scar, or, *All's Well that Ends Well, iii. 2;* a woman's, *The Tempest, i. 2; All's Well that Ends Well, iii. 5; iv. 2;* life loved more than, *Measure for Measure, iii. 1;* I stand for, *A Winter's Tale, iii. 2;* signs of new-made, *King John, i. 1;* value of, *Richard II., i. 1;* shows in the meanest habit, *Taming of the Shrew, iv. 3;* sets him off more than a mortal seeming, *Cymbeline, i. 7;* in war and in peace, *Coriolanus, iii. 2;* who hates, hates the gods, *Pericles, ii. 3;* to pluck or bring up—shared with others, *I. Henry IV., i. 3;* Falstaff's opinion of, *I. Henry IV., v. 1, end;* lost, *II. Henry IV., ii. 3;* covetous of, *Henry V., iv. 3;* new, *Richard III., i. 3; Macbeth, i. 3;* depths and shoals of, *Henry VIII., iii. 2;* for accidental advantages—travels in a narrow strait, *Troilus and Cressida, iii. 3;* dearer than life, *Troilus and Cressida, v. 3;* desire of, *Coriolanus, i. 3;* at difference with mercy, *Coriolanus, v. 3;* a brow, a throne for, *Romeo and Juliet, iii. 2;* love of, *Julius Cæsar, i. 2;* justice of a quarrel for, *Hamlet, iv. 4* or *1;* an essence not seen, *Othello, iv. 1;* all in, *Othello, v. 2;* in love, *Antony and Cleopatra, i. 3;* before profit, *Antony and Cleopatra, ii. 7;* if born to, show it, *Pericles, iv. 6;* appeal to, *Lucrece, l. 568;* and death, *Lucrece, lines 1032, 1051;* fleeting, *Sonnet xxv.* See Truth, Reputation.

Honour, riches, marriage blessing, song, *The Tempest, iv. 1.*

Hood, Robin, *Two Gentlemen of Verona, iv. 1; As You Like It, i. 1.* An English outlaw, supposed to have lived at the close of the twelfth and beginning of the thirteenth century.

Hoodman blind (blind-man's-buff), *All's Well that Ends Well, iv. 3; Hamlet, iii. 4.*

Hopdance, a fiend, *King Lear, iii. 6.* See Mahu.

Hope, put off, *The Tempest, iii. 3;* a lover's staff, *Two Gentlemen of Verona, iii. 1;* a curtal (tailless) dog, *Merry Wives of Windsor, ii. 1;* medicine for the miserable, *Measure for Measure, iii. 1;* fulfilment oft comes when it is coldest, *All's Well that Ends Well, ii. 1;* lined himself with, *II. Henry IV., i. 3;* is swift, *Richard III., v. 2;* never wholly fulfilled, *Troilus and Cressida, i. 3;* against evidence, *Troilus and Cressida, v. 2;* was the, drunk, *Macbeth, i. 7;* at the darkest time, *Macbeth, iv. 2, 3;* cozening, *Richard II., ii. 2;* far off, *III. Henry VI., iii. 2;* one worth fighting for. *III. Henry VI., v. 4.*

Hopkins, Nicholas. See HENTON.

Horace, quoted, *Titus Andronicus, iv. 2.*

Horatio, character in *Hamlet,* first appears in *i. 1.* He is Hamlet's most intimate friend, and the only one to whom he confides the revelations made by his father's ghost. A fine and noble character, the ideal of a friend, warm-hearted, true, and judicious.

Horn, is dry, the, *King Lear, iii. 6.* The horn cup of the beggar, to be filled by charity with beer.

Horns, of the cuckold, allusions to, *Much Ado about Nothing, i. 1; As You Like It, iii. 3; iv. 1, 2; Troilus and Cressida, i. 1;* and in various other passages.

Horner, Thomas, an armourer in *II. Henry VI.,* introduced in *i. 3,* accused by his man of treason, and sentenced to single combat with him. They fight in *ii. 3.* The armourer's real name was William Catur.

Horror, a tale of, *Hamlet, i. 5.* ·

Horrors, supped full of, *Macbeth, v. 5.*

Horse(s), the dancing, *Love's Labour's Lost, i. 2.* A learned horse belonging to one Bankes was exhibited in London in 1589. In France he was near being taken as a sorcerer at the instance of the Capuchins; description of a diseased, *Taming of the Shrew, iii. 2;* of that colour, *Twelfth Night, ii. 3;* praise of a, *Henry V., iii. 7;* my kingdom for a, *Richard III., v. 4;* ate each other, *Macbeth, ii. 4;* buttered hay for, *King Lear, ii. 4;* beauty of a, *Venus and Adonis, l. 295;* roan Barbary, *Richard II., v. 5.*

Horsemanship, good, *Hamlet, iv. 7* (or *4*); *I. Henry IV., iv. 1; Lover's Complaint, l. 106.*

Hortensio, one of the unsuccessful suitors for Bianca in the *Taming of the Shrew,* introduced in *i. 1.* He gains admission to her as a teacher of music under the assumed name of Licio.

Hortensius, servant of one of the creditors of Timon of Athens, introduced in *iii. 4.*

Hospitality, want of, *As You Like It, ii. 4;* extended, *A Winter's Tale, i. 1, 2; v. 1; Timon of Athens, iii. 4;* abuse of, *King Lear, iii. 7; Lucrece, lines 575, 842.*

Host, trust of a, *Macbeth, i. 7.*

Host of the Garter Inn, a witty character in *The Merry Wives of Windsor,* introduced in *i. 3.*

Hostess, a character in the *induction* to the *Taming of the Shrew.*

Hotspur, Henry Percy, so surnamed from his quick and fiery temper, son of the Earl of Northumberland, character in *Richard II.*, introduced in *ii. 3*, and in *I. Henry IV.*, introduced in *i. 3*. He engages in the rebellion and is killed at Shrewsbury by Prince Henry, *v. 4*. He is brave, rash, high-spirited, devoted to honour, contemptuous toward all sentimentality and insincerity, impatient of vanity and pretentiousness, and as impolitic as his father is crafty and smooth. At the last moment he is deserted by his father and deceived by his uncle Worcester, and falls in a fruitless attempt. In *I. Henry IV.*, *iii. 2*, he is described by the king, and there represented as of about the same age as the prince, though really twenty years older.

Hounds, description of, *Midsummer-Night's Dream, iv. 1;* fell and cruel, *Twelfth Night, i. 1*, allusion to the story of Actæon (*q. v.*); *Venus and Adonis, l. 913.* See HUNTING.

Hour-glass, allusions to the, *The Tempest, i. 2; Merchant of Venice, i. 1; Henry V., i., chorus; Cymbeline, iii. 2.*

Hours, of youth and age, *Sonnet v.;* lovers', *Othello, iii. 4.*

House, taken when the prop is taken, *Merchant of Venice, iv. 1;* a desolate, *Richard II., ii. 2;* an unfinished, *II. Henry IV., i. 3;* a rich, *II. Henry IV., v. 3;* in the rocks, *Cymbeline, iii. 3.*

Howard, John. See NORFOLK.

Howard, Thomas. See SURREY.

How can I then return in happy plight, *Sonnet xxviii.*

How can my muse want subject to invent, *Sonnet xxxviii.*

How careful was I, *Sonnet xlviii.*

How heavy do I journey, *Sonnet l.*

How like a winter hath my absence been, *Sonnet xcvii.*

How oft, when thou, my music, *Sonnet cxxviii.*

How sweet and lovely, *Sonnet xcv.*

How should I your true love, song, *Hamlet, iv. 5* or *2.*

Hoxes (cuts the hamstrings of), *A Winter's Tale, i. 2.*

Hubert de Burgh, a character in *King John*, introduced in *iii. 3*. He was the king's chamberlain, and in point of descent and of power was regarded as the greatest subject in Europe during this and the succeeding reigns The scene between him and Prince Arthur is exquisitely pathetic, *iv. 1.*

Hugger-mugger in (stealthily), *Hamlet, iv. 5* (or *2*).

Humanity, must prey upon itself, *King Lear, iv. 2.*

Human nature, *Love's Labour's Lost, iv. 3,* "God amend us," etc.; depravity of, *Henry VIII., v. 2,* "We all are man's," etc.; *Timon of Athens, i. 2; iv. 3,* "All is oblique," etc.

Hume, John, a priest in *II. Henry VI.,* introduced in *i. 2.* He is playing a double part for money.

Humility, *Measure for Measure, ii. 4,* "Let me be ignorant," etc.; the witness of excellency, *Much Ado about Nothing, ii. 3;* of a great man, *All's Well that Ends Well, i. 2;* the base string of, *I. Henry IV., ii. 4;* becoming in time of peace, *Henry V., iii. 1; Henry V., v. 1,* "Being free from vainness," etc.; God thanked for, *Richard III., ii. 1;* the ladder of ambition, *Julius Cæsar, ii. 1;* despised, *Othello, i. 1,* "You shall mark many," etc.; base, *Richard II. v. 1;* refusal to assume, *Coriolanus, ii. 1;* the beetle often safer than the eagle, *Cymbeline, iii. 3.*

Humour of Forty Fancies, *Taming of the Shrew, iii. 2.* Thought to be a collection of ballads.

Humour(s), all, from Adam to this pupil age, *I. Henry IV., ii. 4;* every, has his adjunct pleasure, *Sonnet xci.;* claw no man in his, *Much Ado about Nothing, i. 3.* The favourite catchword of Nym.

Humourous (capricious or ill-natured), *As You Like It, i. 2; ii. 3.*

Humphrey, Duke, of Gloucester, called the good Duke Humphrey, character in *II. Henry IV.,* where he is Prince Humphrey and takes little part in the play, and in the first and second parts of *Henry VI.,* introduced in the opening scene of each. He was uncle of the infant king, and protector. His quarrel with the Cardinal of Winchester, *I. Henry VI., i. 1, 3.* His ambition for England's glory in foreign war, which made him a favorite with the people, is expressed in *II. Henry VI., i. 1.* His death resolved upon, *iii. 1;* accomplished, *iii. 2;* his ghost, *iii. 2, 3.*

"Duke Humphrey, of Gloucester, who appears in the second part totally different from the Gloucester of the first, is invested with the great qualities of consummate mildness and benevolence, with a Solomon-like wisdom, with freedom from all ambition, and with severe, Brutus-like justice toward every one, even his wife, in whose last dishonour he notwithstanding shares as a private character. . . . There is too much noble and quiet grandeur in Humphrey for us not to be grieved at his fall, which appears merely an exemplification of the fable of the lamb that had troubled the wolf's water. . . . At the moment of his fall he too late becomes keen-sighted, and predicts his own ruin and that of his king."—Gervinus.

Humphrey Hour (or Hower), *Richard III., iv. 4.* A puzzle to the commentators. No satisfactory explanation has been given.

"Hundred Merry Tales," *Much Ado about Nothing, ii. 1.* Name of a jest-book.

Hungarian wight (gipsy), *Merry Wives of Windsor, i. 3.*

Hungary, King of. See CORVINUS.

Hunger, *Coriolanus, i. 1;* makes food savoury, *Cymbeline, iii. 6.*

Hungerford, Lord, *I. Henry VI., i. 1.*

Hunt, a, *Titus Andronicus, ii. 2; Venus and Adonis, l. 870, et seq.*

Hunting, terms of, and allusions to: uncape (let loose), *Merry Wives of Windsor, iii. 3;* trail—open, *Merry Wives of Windsor, iv. 2;* counter—dry foot, *Comedy of Errors, iv. 2;* recheat, *Much Ado about Nothing, i. 1;* hunting-scenes, *Love's Labour's Lost, iv. 1; Midsummer-Night's Dream, iv. 1;* on the hip, *Merchant of Venice, i. 3;* cruelty of, *As You Like It, ii. 1;* dogs for, *Taming of the Shrew, induction, 1, 2;* embossed (foaming at the mouth), *All's Well that Ends Well, iii. 6;* and elsewhere; metaphors from, *Twelfth Night, i. 1;* "all with purpled hands," *King John, ii. 1* or *2*, allusion to the custom for all in the chase to dye their hands in the blood of the game; before the game's afoot, thou still let'st slip, *I. Henry IV., i. 3;* hunt-counter (hunter going backward on the trace), *II. Henry IV., i. 2;* coward dogs, *Henry V., ii. 4;* a little herd, etc., *I. Henry VI., iv. 2;* razed, *Richard III., iii. 2;* rascal, worst in blood, *Coriolanus, i. 1;* full of vent (eager, as at first scent), *Coriolanus, iv. 5;* hunt's-up (a reveille on the morning of a hunt), *Romeo and Juliet, iii. 5;* recover the wind of one (get the animal to run with the wind, that it may not know it is pursued), *Hamlet, iii. 2;* this is counter, *Hamlet, iv. 5* (or *2*); "This quarry cries on havoc," *Hamlet, v. 2*, an unnecessary amount of game killed by raw huntsmen; putting on (inciting)—trash (hold back by a trash or halter). *Othello, ii. 1;* fills up the cry, *Othello, ii. 3;* to be unbent, *Cymbeline, iii. 4;* dangers of, *Venus and Adonis, lines 673, 883.*

Huntingdon, John Holland, Earl of, addressed in *Henry V., v. 2,* one of the king's council.

Husband(s), reproaches to a, *Comedy of Errors, ii. 2; v. 1;* compared to an elm, *Comedy of Errors, ii. 2;* duty of a, *Comedy of Errors, iii. 2;* Christian, *Merchant of Venice, iv. 1;* duty to a, *Taming of the Shrew, v. 2; Othello, i. 3;* should be older than their wives—like fools, *Twelfth Night, iii. 1;* that cannot stay the tongues of their wives, *A Winter's Tale, ii. 3,* "Hang all the," etc.; treachery to a—contrast between a first and second, *Hamlet, iii. 4;* injustice of, *Othello, iv. 3, end.*

Husbandry (economy), in heaven, *Macbeth, ii. 1;* borrowing dulls the edge of, *Hamlet, i. 3.*

Hybla, bees of, *I. Henry IV., i. 2; Julius Cæsar, v. 1.* Hybla, in Sicily, noted for its honey.

Hydra (hundred-headed monster), *Coriolanus, iii. 1; Othello, ii 3; and elsewhere.*

Hyems (winter), *Midsummer-Night's Dream, ii. 2.*

Hymen, *The Tempest, iv. 1; Much Ado about Nothing, v. 3;* personated in *As You Like It,* last scene. Some critics think this an interpolation by some other hand than Shakspere's.

Hyperbole(s), *Love's Labour's Lost, v. 2;* three-piled, *Troilus and Cressida, i. 3.*

Hyperion (Apollo), *Henry V., iv. 1; Timon of Athens, iv. 3; Titus Andronicus, v. 2; Troilus and Cressida, ii. 3;* to a satyr, *Hamlet, i. 2;* curls of, *Hamlet, iii. 4.*

Hypocrisy, of Proteus and Valentine, *Two Gentlemen of Verona, iii. 1, 2;* of Falstaff, *Merry Wives of Windsor, ii. 1;* of Angelo, *Measure for Measure, i. 4, 5; iii. 1, 2; v. 1;* recommended to a husband, *Comedy of Errors, iii. 2;* no vice but practises, *Merchant of Venice, iii. 2;* long experience in, *King John, iv. 3;* the evil done by, *Henry V., ii. 2; II. Henry VI., iii. 1;* of Richard (Gloucester), *III. Henry VI., iii. 2; Richard III., i. 1–6; ii. 1, 2; iii. 5, 7;* Anne accused of, *Henry VIII., ii. 3;* Wolsey accused of, *Henry VIII., iii. 1;* denounced, *Romeo and Juliet, iii. 2,* "O serpent heart," etc.; recommended, *Macbeth, i. 3,* to beguile the time, etc.; the devil sugared over, *Hamlet, iii. 1;* time shall uncover, *King Lear, i. 1;* of simpering dames, *King Lear, iv. 6;* mere, *Othello, ii. 1;* of devils, *Othello, ii. 3,* "And what's he," etc.; of Iago, *Othello, iii. 3;* of a woman, *Othello, iv. 1; Lucrece, lines 846, 1514;* cunning of, *Much Ado about Nothing, iv. 1.*

Hyrcan deserts, *Merchant of Venice, ii. 7.* Hyrcania, a wilderness south of the Caspian Sea.

Hyrcan tiger, *Macbeth, iii. 4;* Hyrcanian beast, *Hamlet, ii. 2.*

Hysterica passio (hysteric passion), *King Lear, ii. 4.*

Iachimo, an Italian, friend of Philario in *Cymbeline,* introduced in *i. 4;* his wager, *i. 4;* his stratagem, *ii. 2;* his confession, *v. 5.*

Iago, ancient or ensign of *Othello,* one of the principal characters in the play, and one of the most remarkable of all in the dramas, introduced in *i. 1.* He hates Cassio for having been promoted to an office above him, and Othello for having promoted him, and he devises and carries out the plot that culminates in the murder of Desdemona. See under OTHELLO.

"Some persons, more nice than wise, have thought this whole character unnatural because his villainy is *without a sufficient mo-*

tive. . . . Iago, in fact, belongs to a class of characters common to Shakspere, and at the same time peculiar to him ; whose heads are as acute and active as their hearts are hard and callous. Iago is, to be sure, an extreme instance of the kind—that is to say, of diseased intellectual activity, with an almost perfect indifference to moral good or evil, or rather with a decided preference for the latter, because it falls more readily in with his favourite propensity, gives greater zest to his thoughts and scope to his actions."—HAZLITT.

Icarus, *I. Henry VI., iv. 6, 7 ; II. Henry VI., v. 6.* Dædalus made wings for himself and his son Icarus, on which they rose from Crete ; but the boy flew too near the sun, the wax that held the feathers together melted, and he fell into the sea.

Ice, thrilling region of thick-ribbed, *Measure for Measure, iii. 1.*

Iceland dog, *Henry V., ii. 1.*

Icicle(s), on a Dutchman's beard, *Twelfth Night, iii. 2 ;* roping, *Henry V., iii. 5 ;* chaste as the, *Coriolanus, v. 3.*

Iden, Alexander, character in *II. Henry VI.,* introduced in *iv. 10.* He was Sheriff of Kent, and captured Jack Cade, who, struggling against capture, was mortally wounded.

Identity, mistaken, plot of *Comedy of Errors* founded on ; and Viola is mistaken for Sebastian in *Twelfth Night, iii. 4 ; iv. 1.*

Ides of March, *Julius Cæsar, iii. 1.* The fifteenth.

Idiot(s), a blinking, *Merchant of Venice, ii. 9 ;* play the, in fortune's eyes, *Troilus and Cressida, iii. 3 ;* holds his bauble for a god, *Titus Andronicus, v. 1 ;* life a tale told by an, *Macbeth, v. 5 ;* would be wisely definite, *Cymbeline, i. 6.*

Idleness, to mar with, *As You Like It, i. 1 ;* makes man a beast, *Hamlet, iv. 4 ;* evils of, *Antony and Cleopatra, i. 2.*

Idolatry, in making the service greater than the god, *Troilus and Cressida, ii. 2 ;* pure, *Love's Labour's Lost, iv. 3.*

Ield, or ild (yield, shield), *As You Like It, iii. 3 ; Hamlet, iv. 5.*

If(s), traitorous to talk of, *Richard III., iii. 4 ;* virtues of an, *As You Like It, v. 4.*

If a hart do lack a hind, travesty on Orlando's love-verses, *As You Like It, iii. 2.*

If love make me forsworn, poem, *Love's Labour's Lost, iv. 2 ; Passionate Pilgrim, v.*

If music and sweet poetry agree, *Passionate Pilgrim, viii.*

If my dear love were but the child of state, *Sonnet cxxiv.*

If the dull substance of my flesh, *Sonnet xliv.*

If there be nothing new, *Sonnet lix.*

If thou survive my well-contented day, *Sonnet xxxii.*

If thy soul check thee, *Sonnet cxxxvi.*

Ignominy, to ransom life, *Measure for Measure, ii. 4;* with thee in the grave, *I. Henry IV., v. 4.*

Ignorance, no darkness but, *Twelfth Night, iv. 2;* bliss of, *A Winter's Tale, ii. 1,* "How blest am I," etc.; the curse of God, *II. Henry VI., iv. 7;* a valiant, *Troilus and Cressida, iii. 3;* finds not till it feels, *Coriolanus, iii. 3;* of one's losses, *Othello, iii. 3;* makes us pray for what would harm us, *Antony and Cleopatra, ii. 1;* of books, a monster, *Love's Labour's Lost, iv. 2;* dull, unfeeling, barren, *Richard II., i. 3;* short-armed, *Troilus and Cressida, ii. 3.*

Ignorant, the, their eyes more learned than their ears, *Coriolanus, iii. 2.*

I grant thou wert not married to my Muse, *Sonnet lxxxii.*

Ilium, a name of Troy, but in *Troilus and Cressida, i. 1,* used as the name of the palace.

Illness, allowances for, *King Lear, ii. 4,* "Infirmity doth still neglect all office whereto our health is bound," etc.

Ills, heightened by the thought of good, *Richard II., i. 3;* known preferred to unknown, *Hamlet, iii. 1.*

Illyria, on the eastern coast of the Adriatic Sea, scene of *Twelfth Night.*

Imagination, effect of death on, *Much Ado about Nothing, iv. 1;* of lunatics, lovers, and poets, *Midsummer-Night's Dream, v. 1;* of greatness, *Twelfth Night, ii. 5;* impotence of, *Richard II., i. 3,* "O who can tell," etc.; help of, at the theatre, *Henry V., i., chorus;* of riches, *Lover's Complaint, l. 136;* desperate with, *Hamlet, i. 4.*

Imbare (make bare, expose), *Henry V., i. 2.*

Imitation, even of faults, *II. Henry IV., ii. 3.*

Imitator, an, *Julius Cæsar, iv. 1,* "A barren-spirited fellow."

Immanity (inhumanity), *I. Henry VI., v. 1.*

Immortality of the soul. See SOUL.

Imogen, daughter of *Cymbeline,* introduced in the first scene of the play. The wager concerning her, *i. 4;* her interview with Iachimo, *i. 6;* his stratagem, *ii. 2;* the command for her death, *iii. 2;* her journey, *iii. 4;* her beauty, *iii. 6;* her apparent death, *iv. 2.*

"The very crown and flower of all her father's daughters. I do not speak here of her human father, but her divine—the woman above all Shakspere's women is Imogen. As in Cleopatra we found the incarnate sex, the woman everlasting, so in Imogen we find half glorified already the immortal godhead of womanhood. I would fain have some honey in my words at parting—with Shakspere never, but forever with these notes on Shakspere; and I am there-

fore something more than fain to close my book upon the name of
the woman best beloved in all the world of song and all the tide of
time, upon the name of Shakspere's Imogen."—SWINBURNE.

"Imogen, Desdemona, and Hermione are three women placed in
situations nearly similar and equally endowed with all the qualities
which can render that situation striking and interesting. They are
all gentle, beautiful, and innocent; all are models of conjugal submission, truth, and tenderness; and all are victims of the unfounded
jealousy of their husbands. So far the parallel is close, but here the
resemblance ceases. . . . Critically speaking, the character of Hermione is the most simple in point of dramatic effect, that of Imogen
is the most varied and complex. Hermione is most distinguished by
her magnanimity and her fortitude, Desdemona by her gentleness
and refined grace, while Imogen combines all the best qualities of
both with others which they do not possess; consequently she is, as
a character, superior to either; but, considered as women, I suppose
the preference would depend on individual taste."—MRS. JAMESON.

Imp, *Love's Labour's Lost, i. 2.* A graff or shoot of a tree, and
so used for child in a good sense.

Imp, *Richard II., ii. 1.* To imp a hawk was to supply missing
wing-feathers.

Impartiality, the king's profession of, *Richard II., i. 1.*

Impatience, to hear news, *As You Like It, iii. 2; Romeo and
Juliet, ii. 5;* does become a dog that's mad, *Antony and Cleopatra,
iv., end;* waiteth on true sorrow, *III. Henry VI., iii. 3.*

Impeachment (impediment), *Henry V., iii. 6.*

Imperceiverant (unperceiving), *Cymbeline, iv. 1.*

Imperfection(s), piece out our, *Henry V., i., chorus;* in everything, *Lucrece, l. 869;* in fair things, *Sonnet xxxv.*

Implacability, *Richard III., i. 4,* "Not to relent," etc. See
HATRED and INFLEXIBILITY.

Impleached (intertwined), *Lover's Complaint, l. 205.*

Imponed (impawned, staked), *Hamlet, v. 2.*

Import (imply), *Antony and Cleopatra, ii. 2.*

Importance (import), *A Winter's Tale, v. 2.*

Importance (importunity), *King John, ii. 1; Twelfth Night,
v. 1.*

Important (importunate), *Comedy of Errors, v. 1; Much Ado
about Nothing, ii. 1; All's Well that Ends Well, iii. 7; King Lear,
iv. 4.*

Imposition, hereditary ours, the, *A Winter's Tale, i. 2.* Meaning original or transmitted sin.

Impossibility, *Coriolanus, v. 3;* seeming, *All's Well that Ends
Well, ii. 1,* "Methinks in thee some blessed spirit speaks," etc.

Imprecations, *Merry Wives of Windsor, i. 3,* "Let vultures gripe," etc.; *Troilus and Cressida, ii. 3; Coriolanus, iv. 2,* "The hoarded plagues," etc.; *Timon of Athens, iii. 5, end, 6; iv. 1, 3; Lucrece, l. 967.* See CURSES.

Imprisonment, *King John, iv. 1;* of Hermione, *A Winter's Tale, ii. 1;* long, *I. Henry VI., ii. 5.*

Impudence, of vice, *A Winter's Tale, iii. 2; Titus Andronicus, v. 1.*

Incantations, *Macbeth, i. 3; iv. 1.*

Incapable (insensible), *Hamlet, iv. 7* or *4.*

Inchide (restrain), *Two Gentlemen of Verona, v. 4.*

Incivilities, between Jaques and Orlando, *As You Like It, iii. 2.*

Inconstancy, in love, *Two Gentlemen of Verona, ii. 4; v. 4; Romeo and Juliet, ii. 3;* Falstaff's, *Merry Wives of Windsor, ii. 1;* of men, *Much Ado about Nothing, ii. 3, song;* of common men, *III. Henry VI., iii. 1,* "Look, as I blow this feather," etc.; novelty only is in request, *Measure for Measure, iii. 2.*

Incony (unlearned, artless), *Love's Labour's Lost, iii. 1; iv. 1.*

Indecision, *II. Henry IV., ii. 3; Macbeth, i. 7; Hamlet, iii. 1; iv. 4, 7.* See OPPORTUNITY.

Indent, with fears, *I. Henry IV., i. 3.* Make bargains with those who would be objects of fears.

Indenture, tripartite, *I. Henry IV., iii. 1.* Division of England into three parts by the conspirators.

Independence, *Julius Cæsar, i. 2;* of fortune's caprices, *Hamlet, iii. 2.*

Index (beginning), *Richard III., ii. 2; iv. 4, and elsewhere.*

India, metal of (gold), *Twelfth Night, ii. 5.*

Indictment, of Hermione, *A Winter's Tale, iii. 2.*

Indies, the, *Comedy of Errors, iii. 2;* East and West, *Merry Wives of Windsor, i. 3;* the, *Twelfth Night, iii. 2.* See MAP.

Indifferent (impartial), *Richard II., ii. 3.*

Indigest (chaos), *King John, v. 7.*

Indirection (crookedness), *Julius Cæsar, iv. 3.*

Indirection, finding out by, *Hamlet, ii. 1.*

Indiscretion, sometimes serves well, *Hamlet, v. 2.*

Induction, *Taming of the Shrew.* The play is a play within a play, acted before the characters of the induction. See LORD, a.

Induction(s) (preparations), *Richard III., i. 1;* (beginning), *Richard III., iv. 4; I. Henry IV., iii. 1.*

Industry, *King Lear, ii. 4,* "To school to an ant;" must have an end to work to, *Cymbeline, iii. 6;* his industry is to go up and down stairs, *I. Henry IV., ii. 4.*

I never saw that you did painting need, *Sonnet lxxxiii.*

In faith I do not love thee with mine eyes, *Sonnet cxli.*

Infant, the, *As You Like It, ii. 7.*

Infatuation, of Antony, *Antony and Cleopatra, i. 1;* laughed at by the gods, *Antony and Cleopatra, iii. 2;* of Hotspur, *II. Henry IV., i. 3.*

Inflexibility, *Merchant of Venice, iii. 3; iv. 1; A Winter's Tale, i. 2; Coriolanus, i. 10.*

Influence, of associates, *Merchant of Venice, iii. 4; I. Henry IV., ii. 4; II. Henry IV., v. 1; Troilus and Cressida, ii. 1; Julius Cæsar, i. 2; King Lear, i. 4.*

Informal (incoherent), *Measure for Measure, v. 1.*

Ingener (artist), *Othello, ii. 1.* "Does tire the ingener" is the reading of the folio, "Does bear all excellency" of the quarto.

Ingratitude, *Twelfth Night, iii. 4; v. 1;* song on, *As You Like It, ii. 7;* charged on the king, *I. Henry IV., iv. 3; v. 1;* toward God, *Richard III., ii. 2;* of the king, *Henry VIII., iii. 2,* "Had I but served," etc.; for good deeds past, *Troilus and Cressida, iii. 3,* "Time hath a wallet," etc.; *Coriolanus, ii. 3;* in Rome, *Titus Andronicus, i. 1* or *2; Romeo and Juliet, iii. 3; Timon of Athens, ii. 2; iii. 1–4, 6; v. 1;* of the populace, *Julius Cæsar, i. 1;* of Brutus, *Julius Cæsar, iii. 2;* of children, *King Lear, i. 4; iii. 2, 4;* of Seleucus, *Antony and Cleopatra, v. 2; Pericles, i. 4.*

In hoc spe vivo, *Pericles, ii. 2.* In this hope I live.

Inherit (possess), *Richard II., i. 1, and elsewhere.*

Inheritance, waiting for an, *Midsummer-Night's Dream, i. 1;* quarrel concerning an, *King John, i. 1;* seizure of an, *Richard II., ii. 1;* haste to receive an, *II. Henry IV., iv. 4.*

Iniquity, I lack, *Othello, i. 2;* the formal vice, *Richard III., iii. 1.*

Injointed (united), *Othello, i. 3.*

Injury, knowledge of, *A Winter's Tale, ii. 1,* "How blest am I," etc.; the jailor to pity, *Coriolanus, v. 1;* complaints of, *Sonnets xxxiv.—xlii; Twelfth Night, v. 1;* the jailor to pity, *Coriolanus, i. 1.*

Injustice, blacker by contrast, *A Winter's Tale, iii. 2,* "How he glisters," etc.

Ink, let gall enough be in, *Twelfth Night, iii. 2; Cymbeline, i 2;* a pit of, *Much Ado about Nothing, iv. 1.*

Inkhorn mate (scholar), *I. Henry VI., iii. 1.*

Inkle (used in embroidery, silk, or braid), *A Winter's Tale, iv. 4; Pericles, v., prologue.*

In loving thee thou knowst I am forsworn, *Sonnet clii.*

Innocence, plain and holy, *The Tempest, iii. 1;* of children, *A Winter's Tale, i. 2;* persuades, *A Winter's Tale, ii. 2;* silence of, *A Winter's Tale, iii. 2,* "If powers divine," etc.; protestations of, *Othello, iv. 2;* unsuspecting, *Lucrece, l. 99;* trust in, *II. Henry IV., iv. 4;* appearance of, *Much Ado about Nothing, iv. 1.*

Innocent III. See POPE.

Innocents, escape not, *Antony and Cleopatra, ii. 5.*

Inns, the Porpentine (porcupine), *Comedy of Errors, iii. 1; v. 1;* the Tiger, *Comedy of Errors, iii. 1;* the Garter, *Merry Wives of Windsor;* the Boar's Head at Eastcheap, *I. Henry IV.* It was the custom to name chambers in inns, as the Bunch of Grapes, Pomegranate, Half-Moon, Jerusalem Chamber, etc. See *I. Henry IV., ii. 4;* mine ease in mine inn, *I. Henry IV., iii. 3.*

Insane, liberty of the, *Hamlet, iv. 1* or *iii. 5.*

Insane root, the, *Macbeth, i. 3.* Henbane or hemlock.

Insanity, affected by music, *Richard II., v. 5; King Lear, iv. 7;* restraints for, *As You Like It, iii. 2; Twelfth Night, v. 1;* gradual coming on of, *Hamlet, ii. 2;* symptoms of, *Hamlet, ii. 1; iii. 1, 4;* betrays secrets, *Macbeth, v. 1;* medicine for, *Macbeth, v. 3;* the mind suffering with the body, *King Lear, ii. 4;* caused by the moon, *Othello, v. 2.*

Insinuations, of evil, *Othello, iii. 3.*

Inspiration, of poetry. See MUSE, the.

Instances, modern (trivial or trite examples of?), *As You Like It, ii. 7;* (motives) to second marriage, *Hamlet, iii. 2.*

Instinct, of beasts, in knowing their friends, *Coriolanus, ii. 1;* of royalty, *Cymbeline, iv. 2,* "O thou goddess," etc.

Instructions, a good divine that follows his own, *Merchant of Venice, i. 2.*

Instrument(s), a poor, may do a noble deed, *Antony and Cleopatra, v. 2;* of darkness, *Macbeth, i. 3;* the mortal, *Julius Cæsar, ii. 1.*

Insubordination, results of, *Troilus and Cressida, i. 3.*

Insults, to a coward, *Hamlet, ii. 2,* end of the soliloquy.

Insurrection, cause of, *I. Henry IV., v. 1;* turned to religion, *II. Henry IV., i. 1.*

Integer vitæ, etc., *Titus Andronicus, iv. 2.*

"He who is upright in life and pure from sin,
Needs neither the spear nor bow of the Moor."—HORACE.

Integrity. See HONESTY, HONOUR.

Intellect, degrees of, *A Winter's Tale, i. 2,* "For thy conceit."

Intemperance, *Twelfth Night, i. 5;* fury in, *Timon of Athens, iii. 5;* of the Danes, *Hamlet, i. 4;* folly of, *Othello, ii. 3; v. 1;* boundless, is a tyranny, *Macbeth, iv. 3.*

Intend (pretend), *Much Ado about Nothing, ii. 2; Lucrece, l. 121; Richard III., iii. 7.*

Intentions, bad, cannot be punished, *Measure for Measure, v. 1,* "Most bounteous sir," etc.; between the, and the act, *Julius Cæsar, ii. 1;* good, baulked, *King Lear, v. 3.*

Intercession, *The Tempest, iii. 1; Two Gentlemen of Verona, i. 1; Henry VIII., ii. 1; Richard III., i. 3; Macbeth, iii. 1.*

Interest, *Merchant of Venice, i. 3.* In the same sense as usury.

Interjections, *Much Ado about Nothing, iv. 1.*

Intermediate state, the, in Abraham's bosom, *Richard II., iv. 1; Richard III., iv. 4.*

In the old age black was not counted fair, *Sonnet cxxvii.*

Invasion, *King John, v. 1; King Lear, iii. 1.*

Invention (imagination), *Measure for Measure, ii. 4.*

Inventions, return to plague the inventor, *Macbeth, i. 7.*

Inventory, of Wolsey's possessions, *Henry VIII., iii. 2;* Cleopatra's, *Antony and Cleopatra, v. 2.*

Inverness, in Scotland, seat of Macbeth's castle and scene of a part of the drama.

Invised (unseen), *Lover's Complaint, l. 212.*

Invitis nubibus (in spite of clouds), *II. Henry VI., iv. 1.*

Invisibility, of Ariel, *The Tempest, i. 2;* produced by fernseed, *I. Henry IV., ii. 1.*

Invulnerability, *The Tempest, iii. 3;* supposed, *Macbeth, iv. 1; v. 7, 8.*

Inward (intimate, confidential), *Measure for Measure, iii. 2; Love's Labour's Lost, v. 1.*

Inward quality, the, drawn after the outward, *Antony and Cleopatra, iii. 11 or 13.*

Io, *Taming of the Shrew, induction, 2.* The daughter of the river-god Inachus, changed by Jupiter into a heifer, and persecuted by Juno.

Ipswich, college at, *Henry VIII., iv. 2.*

Ira furor brevis est, *Timon of Athens, i. 2.* Anger is a short madness.

Iras, an attendant of Cleopatra in *Antony and Cleopatra,* introduced in *i. 2.*

Ireland, bogs of, *Comedy of Errors, iii. 2;* rebellion in, *Richard II., i. 4; I. Henry IV., iv. 4; v. 1; II. Henry VI., i. 1; iii. 1;* no snakes in, *Richard II., ii. 1.*

Iris, goddess of the rainbow and messenger of Juno, *The Tempest, iv. 1; All's Well that Ends Well, i. 3; II. Henry VI., iii. 2.*

Irish, the, *Richard II., ii. 1,* "Rough, rug-headed kerns."

Irish rat, an, *As You Like It, iii. 2.*

Irish wolves, howling of, *As You Like It, v. 2.*

Irony, of the Host, *Merry Wives of Windsor, ii. 3; iii. 1; Measure for Measure, v. 1,* in the duke's praise of Angelo; suspected, *Midsummer-Night's Dream, iii. 2;* in flattery, *Taming of the Shrew, ii. 1.*

Irregulous (lawless), *Cymbeline, iv. 2.*

Irresolution. See DOUBT, DELAY, INDECISION.

Isabel, Queen of France, character in *Henry V.,* first appears in *v. 2;* she is the mother of the Princess Katherine, who becomes the queen of Henry V.

Isabella, character in *Measure for Measure,* introduced in *i. 5,* one of the noblest of Shakspere's heroines.

Her character is marked by a lofty severity, which has caused some critics to call her unwomanly; but her purity is unaccompanied by any Pharisaic harshness toward the follies of others; and, indeed, she seems to have no pride of character whatever, but simply unaffected devotion to goodness as goodness; and this perfect sincerity is united with a clear and strong intellect and a persistent though modest force of will.

Isabella, queen of Richard II., is introduced in the play, *ii. 1;* her sorrow when he is taken to the Tower, and indignation at his want of spirit, *v. 1.*

I shall no more to sea, song, *The Tempest, ii. 2.*

Isis (chief goddess of the Egyptians, wife of Osiris), invoked, *Antony and Cleopatra, i. 2;* habiliments of, *Antony and Cleopatra, iii. 6.*

Is it for fear to wet a widow's eye, *Sonnet ix.*

Is it thy will, *Sonnet lxi.*

Island, scenes in an, *The Tempest;* Delphos spoken of as an, *A Winter's Tale, iii. 1,* "The fertile isle."

Issues, spirits are not finely touched but to fine, *Measure for Measure, i. 1.*

Italy, scene of part of *Cymbeline;* fashions of, see FASHIONS.

Iteration, damnable, *I. Henry IV., i. 2;* truth tired with, *Troilus and Cressida, iii. 2.*

It was a friar of orders grey, *Taming of the Shrew, iv. 1.* A line of an old ballad, other lines of which are scattered through the play. From these Percy constructed the ballad, with additions.

It was a lording's daughter, *Passionate Pilgrim, xvi.*

Ivy, allusion to the custom of using a bush of, as a vintner's sign, *As You Like It, epilogue.*

Jack, played the, *The Tempest, iv. 1;* term of reproach, *Merry Wives of Windsor, ii. 3; iii. 1, 2;* and Jill, *Love's Labour's Lost, v. 2; Midsummer-Night's Dream, iii. 2.*

Jack-a-Lent, *Merry Wives of Windsor, iii. 3; v. 5.* A puppet to be thrown at as an amusement in Lent.

Jack-an-apes (Jack o' lantern), *Merry Wives of Windsor, iv. 4.*

Jackdaws. See CHOUGHS.

Jack o' the clock, *Richard II., v. 5; Richard III., iv. 2.* The automaton that struck the hours.

Jacks, *Taming of the Shrew, iv. 1.* Leather drinking-vessels.

Jacob, *Merchant of Venice, i. 3.*

Jacques, Saint, pilgrim of, *All's Well that Ends Well, iii. 4.* Pilgrimages were made to the shrine of St. James at Compostella, Spain.

Jade, let the galled, wince, *Hamlet, iii. 2.*

Jaded (degraded by menial labor), *II. Henry VI., iv. 1;* (beaten), *Henry VIII., iii. 2.*

Jailer, the, character in the *Comedy of Errors, i. 1.*

James I., of England, flattery of, see KING'S EVIL; prophecy concerning, *Henry VIII., v. 4; Macbeth, iv. 1,* "That twofold balls," etc. The passages in *Measure for Measure* beginning, "I love the people" (*i. 1*), "How I have ever loved the life removed" (*i. 4*), and "The general subject to a well-wished king" (*ii. 4*), are supposed to refer to his dislike to being the centre of a pageant.

Jamy, a Scottish captain in *Henry V.,* first appears in *iii. 2.*

Janus, two-headed, *Merchant of Venice, i. 1.*

Jape (coarse joke), *A Winter's Tale, iv. 3* or *4.*

Japhet, *II. Henry IV., ii. 2.*

Jaquenetta, a country wench in *Love's Labour's Lost,* beloved by Costard and Don Adriano, first appears in the first scene.

Jaques, the melancholy, one of the lords attending the banished duke in *As You Like It.*

"Jaques is not a bad-hearted egoist, like Don John, but he is a perfectly idle seeker for new sensations, and an observer of his own feelings; he is weary of all that he has found, and especially professes to despise the artificial society, which yet he never really escapes from, as the others do. His wisdom is half foolery, as Touchstone's foolery is half wisdom."—DOWDEN.

Jaques de Bois, a brother of Oliver and Orlando in *As You Like It.*

Jasons, many, *Merchant of Venice, i. 1; iii. 2.* Jason went after the Golden Fleece.

Jay(s), *Tempest, ii. 2 ; Taming of the Shrew, iv. 3.*

Jealousy, of Adriana, *Comedy of Errors, ii. 1, 2; iii. 1, end; iv. 2; v. 1;* of Ford, *Merry Wives of Windsor, ii. 1, 2; iii. 2, 5; iv. 1, 4;* love full of, *Two Gentlemen of Verona, ii. 4; iv. 4;* a ruse, to excite, *Twelfth Night, iii. 2;* savage, *Twelfth Night, v. 1;* of Leontes, *A Winter's Tale, i. 2; ii. 1, 3; iii. 2;* Elinor's, of Constance, *King John, i. 1;* godly, *Troilus and Cressida, iv. 4;* aroused, *Coriolanus, iv. 7;* of Cassius, *Julius Cæsar, i. 2;* guilt full of, *Hamlet, iv. 5;* Goneril's, *King Lear, iv. 2,* "But being widow," etc.; Regan's, *King Lear, v. 1, 3;* green-eyed monster—trifles to, *Othello, iii. 3;* self-made, *Othello, iii. 4;* one wrought up to, *Othello, v. 2;* of Cleopatra, *Antony and Cleopatra, i. 1, 3; ii. 5; iii. 3;* toward superior officers, *Antony and Cleopatra, iii. 1;* of Posthumus, *Cymbeline, i. 6; ii. 4; Venus and Adonis, l. 649;* the forgeries of, *Midsummer-Night's Dream, ii. 2; Romeo and Juliet, iv. 4.*

Jephthah, *III. Henry VI., v. 1; Hamlet, ii. 2.*

Jerkin, a buff (sheriff's coat), *I. Henry IV., i. 2;* an old cloak makes a new, *Merry Wives of Windsor, i. 3.*

Jeronimy, Saint, *Taming of the Shrew, induction, 1.* Supposed to be Sly's blunder for a phrase from Thomas Kyd's play "The Spanish Tragedy; or, Hieronimo is Mad again," published in 1603, but acted before that time. Ben Jonson played Hieronimo. "Go by, Hieronymo," was much quoted in fun in Shakspere's day.

Jerusalem, *King John, ii. 2; III. Henry VI., v. 4;* King of. See REIGNIER.

Jerusalem Chamber, the, *II. Henry IV., iv. 4.*

Jessica, daughter of Shylock in the *Merchant of Venice,* introduced in *ii. 3.*

"The little Jessica is placed by the poet no higher than she could be; brought up, as she was, without a mother, in the society of Shylock and Launcelot, with a mind entirely child-like, *naïve,* true, and spotless; and, if we may trust Lorenzo's words and her sure perception of the greatness of Portia, with a capacity for true wisdom. . . . Launcelot also bears a relation to the common idea of the piece.

Greedy and rough as he is, he also is inclined to lack economy. . . .
Otherwise the scene with his father is exhibited in parodic contrast
to Jessica's relation with hers. The emphasis of the scene lies in the
words that the son of a father must ever come to light, that child-
like feeling can never be renounced, not even by so coarse and blunt
a fellow as this. How much more should this be the case with a being so ethereal as Jessica! But that it is not so is the strongest
shadow thrown by the poet upon Shylock; he has not designed by it
to cast any upon Jessica. 'She is damn'd,' says Shylock. 'That's
certain, if the devil may be her judge,' answers Salarino."—Gervinus.

Jest(s), an unseen, *Two Gentlemen of Verona, ii. 1;* the prosperity of a, *Love's Labour's Lost, v. 2,* "Why, that's the way," etc.; a,
in a fool's ear, *Hamlet, iv. 2* (or *v. 6*); at scars, *Romeo and Juliet, ii.
2;* effect of a, *II. Henry IV., v. 1.* See JOKES, WIT.

Jest (masque), *Richard II., i. 3.*

Jesters do oft prove prophets, *King Lear, v. 3;* drive off melancholy, *Comedy of Errors, i, 2.*

Jester(s), reform for a, *Love's Labour's Lost, v. 2;* oft prove
prophets, *King Lear, v. 3.*

Jesters. Touchstone in *As You Like It,* Feste in *Twelfth
Night,* the clown in *All's Well that Ends Well,* and the fool in
King Lear, are the most noteworthy jesters in the plays.

Jet (strut), *Cymbeline, iii. 3,* and elsewhere.

Jewel(s), move a woman's mind, *Two Gentlemen of Verona, iii.
1;* best enamelled, *Comedy of Errors, ii. 1 ·* in the toad's head, *As
You Like It, ii. 1;* mine eternal, *Macbeth, iii. 1;* my heavenly.
See HAVE I CAUGHT, etc.

Jeweller, a, in *Timon of Athens, i. 1,* seeking patronage.

Jewess's eye, *Merchant of Venice, ii. 5.* The Jews were forced
to pay the price of an eye—that is, a ransom—to save themselves
from mutilation, hence the proverb, "Worth a Jew's eye." Another
explanation, however, makes the expression a corruption of the
Italian for jewel, *gioia.*

Jewry, the sepulchre in, *Richard II., ii. 1.*

Jew(s), would have wept, *Two Gentlemen of Verona, ii. 3;* used
opprobriously, *Two Gentlemen of Verona, ii. 5;* I am a, if, *Much Ado
about Nothing, ii. 3;* treatment of, *Merchant of Venice, i. 3; ii. 2;*
of like nature with Christians, *Merchant of Venice, iii. 1;* an Ebrew,
I. Henry IV., ii. 4; blaspheming, *Macbeth, iv. 1.*

Jezebel, *Twelfth Night, ii. 5.*

Jig (a dance), *Much Ado about Nothing, ii. 1; Twelfth Night,
i. 3.* The name was also applied to a comic recitation or song, given

by the clown and accompanied with dancing and playing on the pipe or tabor, *Hamlet, ii. 2;* your only (only your) jig-maker, *Hamlet, iii. 2.*

Joan of Arc, La Pucelle, character in *I. Henry VI.,* first appears in *i. 2,* where she convinces the dauphin of her mission by fighting with and conquering him. In *v. 3,* she summons fiends to her aid, but is taken by York; in *v. 4,* she denies her father, and is ordered to execution. Joan was burned at the stake in Rouen, May 30, 1431. History bears undisputed testimony to the purity, lofty enthusiasm, and disinterestedness of her character. In drawing her as a vile sorceress the authors of the play followed the English prejudice of the time.

Job, allusion to the Book of, *Merry Wives of Windsor, v. 1;* poor as, *Merry Wives of Windsor, v. 5.*

Jog on, jog on, the footpath way, *A Winter's Tale, iv. 2* or *3.* Part of an old round for three voices.

John, King, drama of. See KING JOHN.

John, King of England from 1199 to 1216, succeeded his brother Richard I., or *Cœur de Lion,* according to a will that he brought forward after Richard's death, though Richard had named his nephew Arthur his successor in 1190. John's title was further confirmed by an election, the hereditary principle in succession not having been established at that time. The story, in *v. 6,* that he was poisoned by a monk, is not found in the histories of the time, but is mentioned by Holinshed. Of the character of John as delineated in the play, Gervinus says:

" He is not the image of a brutal tyrant, but only the type of the hard, manly nature, without any of the enamel of finer feelings, and without any other motives for action than those arising from the instinct of this same inflexible nature and of personal interest. Severe and earnest, an enemy to cheerfulness and merry laughter, conversant with dark thoughts, of a restless, excitable temperament, he quickly rises to daring resolves. . . . No higher principle sustains the man and his energetic designs in time of danger; the great idea at the outset of his career leaves him during its progress and at its end. After his power, thus displayed against France, has risen even to the defiance of the Pope and the Church, and to the inconsiderate design upon the life of a child whose temper was not to be feared, and had not even been tried by him, it sinks down, struck by conscience, by curses, and by prophecies, by dangers without and within; he becomes anxious, mistrustful, superstitious, fearful to absolute weakness and to a degree of faint-heartedness, in which he sells his country as cheap as once, in his self-confidence, he had held it dear and defended it boldly."

John of Gaunt. See GAUNT.

John of Lancaster. See LANCASTER.

John, Don, bastard brother of Don Pedro in *Much Ado about Nothing*, introduced in *i. 1.* He is of black and sour disposition, and the villain of the play. His jealousy at the honour Claudio has brought from the wars, and of Don Pedro's love for him, leads him to prepare the plot against Hero to destroy her happiness and that of Claudio.

John, a Franciscan friar in *Romeo and Juliet*, introduced in *v. 2.*

John-a-dreams, *Hamlet, ii. 2.* A sleepy or absent-minded fellow.

Joint ring (a double ring used as a lover's token), *Othello, iv. 3.*

Jokes, practical, on the tinker, *Taming of the Shrew, induction;* on Malvolio, *Twelfth Night, ii. 3;* on Aguecheek, *Twelfth Night, iii. 4;* on Falstaff, *Merry Wives of Windsor, iii. 3; v. 3–5; I. Henry IV., i. 2; ii. 2, 4.*

Joshua, one of the nine worthies (*q. v.*), *Love's Labour's Lost, v. 1.*

Jourdain, Margery, a witch in *II. Henry VI.*, introduced in *i. 4.*

Journeys, from and toward one loved, *Sonnets l., li.*

Joust, a, *Pericles ii. 2.*

Jove, *Troilus and Cressida, ii. 3;* lightnings of, *The Tempest, i. 2;* oak of, *The Tempest, v. 1;* thunder of, *Measure for Measure, ii. 2;* would swear Juno an Ethiope, *Love's Labour's Lost, iv. 3;* the page of, *As You Like It, i. 3;* in a thatched house, see OVID; doing of, *Twelfth Night, iii. 4;* his forehead, *Hamlet, iii. 4;* bless thee, *Twelfth Night, iv. 2.* Used here for God, because of the law against the use of God's name on the stage. Laughs at lover's perjuries, *Romeo and Juliet, ii. 2;* thunder-darter, *Troilus and Cressida, ii. 3;* bird of, *Cymbeline, iv. 2.*

Joy, shown by tears—better to weep at, than, etc., *Much Ado about Nothing, i. 1;* silence the herald of, *Much Ado about Nothing, ii. 1;* description of, *A Winter's Tale, v. 2;* from wondering—to weeping, *II. Henry VI., i. 1;* sudden, *Pericles, v. 1;* expression of, *Coriolanus, ii. 1; iv. 5; v. 4;* subtle, *Troilus and Cressida, iii. 2.*

Judas, hanged on an elder-tree, *Love's Labour's Lost, v. 2;* his hair, *As You Like It, iii. 4.* It was believed to have been red. His kiss, *III. Henry VI., v. 7;* three Judases, *Richard II., iii. 2; iv. 1.*

Judas Maccabæus, one of the nine worthies (*q. v.*), *Love's Labour's Lost, v. 1, 2.*

Judge(s), what 'twere to be a, *Measure for Measure, ii. 2;* a wise and upright, *Merchant of Venice, iv. 1;* the incorruptible, *Henry VIII., iii. 1;* delaying, *Coriolanus, ii. 1.*

Judgment, conceit of one's own, corrected, *All's Well that Ends Well, iv. 3;* of heaven, *I. Henry IV., iii. 2;* a grand juryman since Noah, *Twelfth Night, iii. 2;* fled to beasts, *Julius Cæsar, iii. 2;* on earth, *Macbeth, i. 7;* of men, a parcel of their fortunes, *Antony and Cleopatra, iii. 11* or *13;* a Daniel come to, *Merchant of Venice, iv. 1;* hath bred a kind of remorse, *Richard III., i. 4;* repented of, *Measure for Measure, ii. 2;* without which (reason) we are pictures or mere beasts, *Hamlet, iv. 5.* See JUSTICE.

Judgment-day, the, *Richard III., i. 4; I. Henry VI., i. 1,* See DOOMSDAY.

Julia, a sweet, unselfish character, the first love of Proteus, in the *Two Gentlemen of Verona,* introduced in *i. 2.*

Juliet, a character in *Measure for Measure,* appears in *ii. 3,* betrothed to Claudio. She is meek, weak, and patient.

Juliet, heroine of *Romeo and Juliet,* introduced in *i. 3;* her beauty, *ii. 2;* her wit and dignity, *iii. 5;* meets Romeo, *i. 5;* is married, *ii. 6;* drinks the potion, *iv. 3;* stabs herself, *v. 3.* See under MIRANDA.

"Juliet is love itself. The passion is her state of being, and out of it she has no existence. . . . Such, in fact, are the simplicity, the truth, and the loveliness of Juliet's character, that we are not at first aware of its complexity, its depth, and its variety. There are in it an intensity of passion, a singleness of purpose, a completeness of effect, which we feel as a whole."—MRS. JAMESON.

Julius Cæsar, an historic tragedy, first published in 1623. The date of writing is not certainly known, but the critics assign it to the year 1600 or 1601, judging from internal evidence as well as from an allusion to Antony's speech in a poem printed in 1601. Sir Thomas North's translation of Plutarch furnished the materials, which are taken from the lives of Cæsar, Brutus, and Antony. The action covers the space from the feast of Lupercalia, February 13, B. C. 44, to the battle of Philippi, in the autumn of 42, a period of about two and a half years. There is an allusion to a play called "Julius Cæsar" in *Hamlet, iii. 2,* which by some is supposed to refer to this drama. But it may refer to a Latin drama on the subject, by Richard Eades, which was played at Oxford in 1582.

"Everything is wrought out in the play with great care and completeness; it is well planned and well proportioned; there is no tempestuousness of passion, and no artistic mystery. The style is full, but not overburdened with thought or imagery; this is one of the most perfect of Shakspere's plays; greater tragedies are less perfect, perhaps for the very reason that they try to grasp greater, more terrible, or more piteous themes."—DOWDEN.

Julius Cæsar. See CÆSAR.

Jump (risk) the life to come, *Macbeth, i. 7 ;* a body with a dangerous physic, *Coriolanus, iii. 1;* fortune lies upon this jump, *Antony and Cleopatra, iii. 8.*

Jump (opportunely), *Hamlet, i. 1 ; Othello, ii. 3.*

Juno, *The Tempest, iv. 1;* an Ethiope, *Love's Labour's Lost, iv. 3;* swans of, *As You Like It, i. 3;* his despiteful, *All's Well that Ends Well, iii. 4,* alluding to the story of Hercules or that of Æneas; *A Winter's Tale, iv. 3 or 4; Antony and Cleopatra, iv. 13.*

Jupiter, *Merry Wives of Windsor, v. 5; As You Like It, iii. 2; A Winter's Tale, iv. 3 or 4;* in a vision, *Cymbeline, v. 4; Antony and Cleopatra, iii. 2; Titus Andronicus, iv. 3; v. 2; Troilus and Cressida, iv. 5; v. 1.* See JOVE and PHILEMON.

Jury, the, may have one guiltier than the prisoner, *Measure for Measure, ii. 1.*

Justice, sleeping, *Measure for Measure, i. 4;* seizes what it sees, *Measure for Measure, ii. 1;* and mercy, *Measure for Measure, ii. 2;* innocence with, *Measure for Measure, iv. 2;* "His life is paralleled," etc., *Merchant of Venice, iv. 1;* of condemning by surmises, *A Winter's Tale, iii. 2;* course of Shallow's, *II. Henry IV., v. 1;* scales of, *II. Henry VI., ii. 1;* not to be judged by results, *Troilus and Cressida, ii. 2;* gone from earth, *Titus Andronicus, iv. 3;* even-handed, *Macbeth, i. 7;* against gold, *King Lear, iv. 6;* of the gods, *King Lear, v. 3;* delays of, *Lucrece, l. 906;* impartial, *Richard II., i. 1;* of Heaven, *Hamlet, iii. 3.*

Justice, description of a, *As You Like It, ii. 7;* of the peace, *II. Henry VI., iv. 7.*

Justicer (judge), *King Lear, iii. 6; iv. 2; Cymbeline, v. 5.*

Justify (prove), *The Tempest, v. 1.*

Juvenal (youth), *Love's Labour's Lost, i. 2; iii. 1; II. Henry IV., i. 2; Midsummer-Night's Dream, iii. 1.*

Kam, clean (all crooked), *Coriolanus, iii. 1.*

Kate, name given to Hotspur's wife, whose real name was Elizabeth; play on the name, *Taming of the Shrew, ii. 1.*

Katharine, one of the ladies attending the princess in *Love's Labour's Lost,* introduced in *ii. 1.* She is sought in marriage by

Dumain, but puts him off for a twelvemonth and a day. She was pock-marked, as appears by a jest of Rosalind in *v. 2.*

Katherina, the heroine of the *Taming of the Shrew*, introduced in *i. 1*, "Like a wasp, like a foal that kicks from its halter—pert, quick, and determined, but full of good heart."

Katherine, daughter of Charles VI. of France, character in *Henry V.*, first appears, *iii. 4.* She afterward became the wife of the English king; the betrothal, *v. 2.*

Katherine of Aragon, Queen, character in *Henry VIII.*, introduced in *i. 2.* The subject of her divorce from Henry is discussed in *ii. 1, 2;* her goodness, *ii. 2, 4;* her petition to the king, the trial, and her reproaches to Wolsey, *ii. 4;* interview with the cardinals, *iii. 1;* the divorce, *iv. 1;* her vision, letter to the king, and approaching death, *iv. 2.* The character of Katherine in the play is very noble; her pride of birth and station never deserts her, but it is united with religious meekness and long-enduring affection, and gives a noble dignity and pathos to her words and the struggle to maintain the position to which she feels she has a right. In the scenes where she appears, Shakspere has followed the chronicles in the main, only giving poetic grouping and colouring to their accounts. The scene in which the vision appears to the queen is attributed to Fletcher.

Kecksies. See KEXES.

Keech (a lump of fat), *Henry VIII., i. 1.* Alluding to Wolsey's corpulence, and his being reputed a butcher's son; *I. Henry IV., i. 4.*

Keel (cool), *Love's Labour's Lost, v. 2.*

Keisar, *Merry Wives of Windsor, i. 3.* Emperor.

Kendal Green, *I. Henry IV., ii. 4,* colour worn by Robin Hood's men. Cloth was made at Kendal in Westmoreland.

Kenilworth Castle, *II. Henry VI., iv. 4;* scene of *II. Henry VI., iv. 9.* An ancient castle, now in ruins, about five miles from War-wick and the same distance from Coventry. The first castle, which was destroyed in the eleventh century in the wars between Edmund Ironside and Canute the Dane, is supposed by some antiquaries to have been founded in the time of Kenelph, a King of Mercia, and to have taken its name from him. The present castle was built by Geoffrey de Clinton in the reign of Henry I. It belonged successively to many of the greatest subjects of the Kings of England—including Simon de Montfort, John of Gaunt, and Dudley, Earl of Leicester—and several times reverted to the crown. John of Gaunt made many additions to the castle, which are still known as Lançæster's Buildings, and the celebrated Earl of Leicester, Elizabeth's favorite, many more, called Leicester's Buildings. Cromwell's soldiers plundered the castle and left it in ruins. Some parts have since been repaired, and excavations have revealed underground apartments and passages long hidden. During the Wars of the Roses the castle was sometimes in the possession of one party, sometimes in that of the other. Henry VI. retired to it in some times of adversity, as in the text.

Kennel (gutter), *II. Henry VI.; iv. 1.*

Kent, a southeastern county of England, scene of *II. Henry VI., iv. 1;* Cæsar on the people of, *II. Henry VI., iv. 7;* men of, *III. Henry VI., i. 2;* rebellion in, *Richard III., iv. 4.*

Kent, Thomas Holland, Earl of, beheaded, *Richard II., v. 6.*

Kent, the Earl of, character in *King Lear*, introduced in *i. 1,* where he is banished by Lear for remonstrating against the treatment of Cordelia; he follows the king, however, in his misfortune, acting as his servant under the name of Caius, and brings about the meeting with Cordelia in the last scene. See under KING LEAR.

"Kent is perhaps the nearest to perfect goodness in all Shakspere's characters, and yet the most individualized. There is an extraordinary charm in his bluntness, which is that only of a nobleman arising from a contempt of overstrained courtesy, and combined with easy placability where goodness of heart is apparent."—COLERIDGE.

Kerns (light-armed troops from Ireland), *Macbeth, i. 2, and elsewhere.*

Ketly, Sir Richard, his death, *Henry V., iv. 8.*

Kexes (hollow-stemmed weeds), *Henry V., v. 2.*

Kildare, Earl of, *Henry VIII., ii. 1.*

Killing, a trifle, *I. Henry IV., ii. 4;* in defense, *Timon of Athens, iii. 5;* do all men kill the things they do not love? *Merchant of Venice, iv. 1;* I promised to eat all of his, *Much Ado about Nothing, i. 1.*

Killingworth. See KENILWORTH.

Kiln-hole (fireplace), *A Winter's Tale, iv. 3 or 4.*

Kimbolton, a castle in Huntingdonshire belonging to the Duke of Manchester, the scene of *Henry VIII., iv. 2.* Katherine's jewel-chest and some of her clothing are still shown there.

Kin, a little more than, *Hamlet, i. 2;* one touch of nature makes the whole world, *Troilus and Cressida, iii. 3.*

Kind, kindless, kindly (nature, unnatural, naturally), *All's Well*

*that Ends Well, i. 3 ; Taming of the Shrew, induction, 1 ; Hamlet,
ii. 2 ; Antony and Cleopatra, v. 2, and elsewhere.*

Kindness, *Twelfth Night, i. 5,* " What is yours to oestow," etc. ;
Timon of Athens, i. 1, 2, " We are born to do benefits," etc. ; to kill
with, *Taming of the Shrew, iv. 1 ;* in women, wins love, *Taming of
the Shrew, iv. 2 ;* nobler than revenge, *As You Like It, iv. 3 ;* power
of, *A Winter's Tale. i. 2 ;* recalled, *King John, iv. 1.*

King, On the, a quatrain attributed to Shakspere, and usually
placed at the end of the miscellaneous poems. If it is his, it of
course refers to James I., who liked to be flattered about his learning. It exists in a manuscript written in the time of his successor,
in which the verses are entitled " Shakspere on the King."

King Cophetua, ballad of, *Love's Labour's Lost, i. 2.*

Kingdom, a diseased, *II. Henry IV., iii. 1 ;* partition of a, *King
Lear, i. 1 ;* divisions in a, *King Lear, iii. 1, 3 ;* any oath may be
broken for a, *III. Henry VI., v. 2 ;* a, for a grave, *Richard II., iii.
3 ;* for a horse, *Richard III., v. 4 ;* for a mirth, *Antony and Cleopatra, i. 4.*

King Henry the Fourth, Parts I. and II. These two plays
may be regarded as essentially one. The first part was written in
1596-'97, the second in 1597-'98. The first part was published in
1598, the second in 1600. The sources from which it was in part
drawn were the " Chronicles " of Holinshed and an older play, " The
Famous Victories of Henry the Fifth, containing the Honourable
Battell of Agincourt." From the play were gathered the hints for
the wild pranks of the prince and his low companions. Among them
was one Sir John Oldcastle, the name borne by Falstaff in the first
editions of Shakspere's play, though he has little to say or do in the
old drama. (See OLDCASTLE.) The period of action of Part I. extends from the battle of Holmedon Hill, September 14, 1402, to the
battle of Shrewsbury, July 21, 1403. Part II. extends from that
time to the death of Henry IV. in 1413. These two plays, with *Henry V.,* which is a continuation of them, are the finest of the English
historical plays. See HENRY IV.

" None of Shakspere's plays are more read than the First and
Second Parts of Henry the Fourth. Perhaps no author has ever, in
two plays, afforded so much delight. The great events are interesting, for the fate of kingdoms depends on them ; the slighter occur-
rences are diverting, and, except one or two, sufficiently probable ;
the incidents are multiplied with wonderful fertility of invention,
and the characters diversified with the utmost nicety of discernment
and the profoundest skill in the nature of man. . . . The character

[of the prince] is great, original, and just. Percy is a rugged soldier, choleric and quarrelsome, and has only the soldier's virtues, generosity and courage. But Falstaff! unimitated, unimitable Falstaff! how shall I describe thee? thou compound of sense and vice; of sense which may be admired, but not esteemed; of vice which may be despised, but hardly detested. Falstaff is a character loaded with faults, and with those faults which naturally produce contempt. He is a thief and a glutton, a coward and a boaster; always ready to cheat the weak and prey upon the poor; to terrify the timorous and insult the defenseless. . . . Yet the man thus corrupt, thus despicable, makes himself necessary to the prince that despises him, by the most pleasing of all qualities, perpetual gaiety, by an unfailing power of exciting laughter, which is the more freely indulged, as his wit is not of the splendid or ambitious kind, but consists in easy scapes and sallies of levity, which make sport, but raise no envy."— JOHNSON.

King Henry the Fifth, which, as promised in the epilogue to the second part of *Henry IV.*, continues the story, was probably written in 1598 or 1599; the prologue or chorus to *Act v.* has a reference to the absence of Essex in Ireland, the time of which was between March and September, 1599. There is also a reference to "this wooden O," the Globe Theatre, built in 1599. An unauthorized and imperfect edition was published in 1600, and the full text in 1623. For the source drawn upon, see KING HENRY IV. The time of action is from 1414 to 1420. See HENRY V. Dowden says:

"In this play Shakspere bade farewell in trumpet tones to the history of England. It was a fitting climax to the great series of works which told of the sorrow and the glory of his country, embodying as it did the purest patriotism of the days of Elizabeth."

King Henry the Sixth. The three plays that bear this name were produced early in Shakspere's career, the first from 1590 to 1592, the second and third from 1592 to 1594, probably.

The first part is held to be mostly from other hands than Shakspere's, an old play, perhaps, by Marlowe, with the assistance of Greene or Peele, touched up by Shakspere, to whom are attributed the fourth scene of *Act ii.*, and that between Margaret and Suffolk, *v. 3.* The time of action is 1422 to 1444. The facts are drawn from Holinshed. The second and third parts are rewritten from two older plays: "The First Part of the Contention betwixt the Two Famous Houses of York and Lancaster," etc., and "The True Tragedie of Richard Duke of York and the Death of Good King Henrie the Sixt." Critics differ about these plays; some holding that Shakspere had a hand in them, others that they were written by Greene, Marlowe, and Peele, one or more of them; and some attributing the

entire revision to Shakspere, others supposing that Marlowe assisted
him. The period of action of the second part is 1445 to 1455; that
of the third part, 1455 to 1471. The events connected with Dame
Eleanor in the second part really took place some years before the
opening of the play. With this exception the events generally follow in historical order.

King Henry the Eighth was first published in the folio of
1623. It is supposed to have been written in 1612 or 1613, last of
all the plays, after Shakspere had left the theatre. It is mentioned
under the present title, and also under that of " All is True," as having been on the stage the night the Globe Theatre was burned, June
26, 1613, the fire having been caused by the discharge of some chambers during the play. Sir Henry Wotton speaks of it in this connection as a new play. The material is taken from the " Chronicles " of
Holinshed and Stowe, and from Foxe's " Acts and Monuments of
the Church." Some critics think they find evidence that Fletcher
had a hand in the writing of the play. The action covers the period
from 1521 to 1533. Some of the events are moved from their actual
sequence in the history, as the death of Katherine, which took place
in 1536. The prologue and epilogue are generally believed to be
the work of another hand. See HENRY VIII.

King John, the earliest of the historic dramas as to the period
of action, was written probably later than *Richard II.*, *Richard III.*,
and *Henry VI.* The date assigned for the writing is 1595. The first
known drama founded on the reign of John is " The Pageant of
Kynge Johan," by Bishop Bale, supposed to have been written in
the reign of Edward VI. It has a distinct religious purpose, being
full of ferocious anti-popish bigotry, and it introduces among real
historical characters allegorical figures, such as Treason, Verity,
England, Sedition, after the fashion of the old moralities. This
play was succeeded by " The Troublesome Reign of King John,"
published in 1591 and by a few critics supposed to be from Shakspere's hand. Upon it the present play is founded. *King John* follows the truth of history less closely than the other English historical plays: the king's unpopularity and troubles are made to result
from his treatment of Arthur; Constance is represented as a widow
and living at the time Arthur fell into the hands of John (see CON-
STANCE); and the Archduke of Austria and the Viscount of Lymoges are united in the same person (see AUSTRIA); the imprisonment
and death of Arthur are represented as taking place in England instead of France; the quarrel between John and the Pope is ante-

dated by several years. Most of these departures from fact were in the older play. See JOHN.

King Lear, one of the greatest of the tragedies, was first published in 1608, three editions having appeared in that year. The evidence points to the year 1605 as the date of writing. The story of Lear was first told, so far as is known, by Geoffrey of Monmouth, who wrote a history of Britain in the twelfth century. Holinshed also tells it, and there was an older play on the subject which was published in 1594. The story is also told in Higgins's "Mirror for Magistrates" and Spenser's "Faerie Queene." The part of Gloucester and his sons Shakspere found in Sidney's "Arcadia," "The Paphlagonian Unkind King." The time of action is about 800 B. C., the date given by Geoffrey of Monmouth. See LEAR.

"This firm faith in filial piety, and the giddy anarchy and whirling tumult of the thoughts at finding this prop failing it, the contrast between the fixed, immovable basis of natural affection and the rapid, irregular starts of imagination, suddenly wrenched from all its accustomed holds and resting-places in the soul—this is what Shakspere has given, and what nobody else could give."—HAZLITT.

"So ends King Lear, the most stupendous of the Shaksperean dramas; and Kent, the noblest feature of the conceptions of his divine mind. This is the magnanimity of authorship, when a writer, having a topic presented to him, fruitful of beauties for common minds, waives his privilege and trusts to the judicious few for understanding the reason of his abstinence. What a pudder would a common dramatist have raised here of a reconciliation-scene, a perfect recognition between the assumed Caius and his master!—to the suffusing of fair eyes and the moistening of cambric handkerchiefs. The old, dying king partially catching at the truth, and immediately lapsing into obliviousness, with the high-minded carelessness of the other to have his services appreciated, as one that—

'Served not for gain,
Or followed out of form'—

are among the most judicious, not to say heart-touching, strokes in Shakspere."—CHARLES LAMB.

King Richard the Second, second of the historical plays as to the period of action, was written before *King John,* and perhaps earlier than any other of the histories except *I. Henry VI.*—that is, in 1593 or 1594. The play was first published in 1597, a second edition appeared in 1598, and in 1608 a third, with the following added to the title: "With new additions of the Parliament sceane and the deposing of King Richard." The additions were in *iv. 1,* one hundred and sixty-four lines. There is evidence that they were originally in the play; and they were presumably omitted in deference to Elizabeth, who was sensitive on the subject of the deposition of sovereigns. There were two other plays on the same subject, but the source from which Shakspere drew was Holinshed's "Chronicles." There are some few departures from fact in the play, mostly in the age of the characters. The queen, for instance, was but nine years old at the time of Bolingbroke's banishment (1398); John of Gaunt, spoken of repeatedly as a very old man, was fifty-eight; Prince Henry was but eleven (*v. 3*); and Norfolk was but thirty when he speaks (*i. 3*) of "the language I have learned these forty years." The period of action is from September, 1398, to February, 1400. The scene is in different parts of England and in Wales. See RICHARD II.

"In itself, and for the closet, I feel no hesitation in placing it as the first and most admirable of all Shakspere's purely historical plays. . . . But, however unsuited to the stage this drama may be, God forbid that even there it should fall dead on the hearts of jacobinized Englishmen ! . . . For the spirit of patriotic reminiscence is the all-permeating soul of this noble work."—COLERIDGE.

King Richard the Third, the best known and most popular of the histories, was first published in 1597, and is held to have been written about 1592-'94, directly after *Henry VI.* In the opinion of some critics, Marlowe had a hand in its production. The facts were drawn from the "Chronicles" of Holinshed and Hall. There were two older plays on the subject, one in English, "The True Tragedie of Richard the Third," and one in Latin by Thomas Legge, "Richardus Tertius;" but Shakspere took nothing from them. The play takes up English history where *III. Henry VI.* leaves it, after the battle of Tewksbury in 1471, and brings it to that of Bosworth and the fall of Richard in 1485. Although far from being one of Shakspere's best plays, *Richard III.* has always been popular, especially on the stage—where, however, Colley Cibber's version has usually been given—from the singular and intense character of the king and the rapid action of the plot. By the English of Elizabeth's time it was especially liked, because it brought in the first Tudor king as the saviour of his country. See RICHARD III.

King(s), murder of, *A Winter's Tale, i. 2,* "If I can find example," etc.; prerogative of, *ii. 1,* "Why, what need we," etc.; children of, *iv. 1* or *2 ;* quarrels of, *King John, ii. 1* or *2 ;* conduct becoming, *King John, v. 1 ;* the curse of, *King John, iv. 2 ;* sacredness of, *Richard II., i. 2 ; iii. 2 ;* power of words of, *Richard II., i. 3 ;* advice to, *Richard II., ii. 1 ;* reverence due to, *Richard II., iii. 3 ;* deposition of, *Richard II., iii. 2, 3 ; iv. 1 ; v. 1 ;* woe's slaves, *Richard II., iii. 2 ;* sentenced by subjects, *Richard II., iv. 1 ;* confession demanded of, *Richard II., iv. 1;* treatment of a, deposed by the populace, *Richard II., v. 2;* remorse of a, *Richard II., iii. 2;* rights of, *I. Henry IV., i. 3;* too lavish of his company. *I. Henry IV., iii. 2,* murder of the wardrobe of the, *I. Henry IV., v. 3;* fickleness of the populace toward, *II. Henry IV., i. 3;* kin to, *II. Henry IV., ii. 2;* uneasiness of, *II. Henry IV., iii. 1;* majesty of, like heavy armour, *II. Henry IV., iv. 4;* what have, that privates have not—cares of—but a man—responsibility of, *Henry V., iv. 1;* presence of a, *I. Henry VI., iii. 1;* troubles of a, *II. Henry VI., iv. 9;* cares of a, *III. Henry VI., ii. 5;* prophecy concerning a future (Richmond), *III. Henry VI., iv. 6;* his name a tower of strength, *Richard III., v. 3;* danger of crossing the pleasure of, *Henry VIII., iii. 1;* honour of a, *Troilus and Cressida, ii. 2;* the Lord's anointed temple, *Macbeth, ii. 3;* graces becoming a, *Macbeth, iv. 3;* many lives dependent on a, *Hamlet, iii. 3;* divinity doth hedge a, *Hamlet, iv. 5* (or *2*); progress of, *Hamlet, iv. 3* (or *v. 7*); every inch a, *King Lear, iv. 6;* smiles and frowns of, reflected, *Cymbeline, i. 1;* vices of, *Pericles, i. 1;* secrets of, *Pericles, i. 3;* misdeeds of, *Lucrece, l. 609;* like the sea, *Lucrece, l. 652;* their baseness worse, *Lucrece, l. 1002;* knowledge in a, *On the King;* annoyed by crowds, see JAMES I.; adviser of a, *II. Henry IV., iv. 2;* a versatile, *Henry V., v. 1;* troubles of a, *Richard III., i. 4;* Mulmutius, the first, of Britain, *Cymbeline, iii. 1;* flattery of, *Pericles, i. 2.* See CROWN.

King Stephen was a worthy peer, song, *Othello, ii. 3.*

King's evil, the, *Macbeth, iv. 3.* A compliment to James I., who revived the old superstitious ceremony of touching the scrofulous, who were supposed to be healed by the touch of a king.

Kinship, claims of, *As You Like It, i. 1;* power of, *Coriolanus, v. 3;* instinct of, *Cymbeline, iv. 2.* See BLOOD.

Kisses, to shadows, *Merchant of Venice, ii. 9;* religious, *As You Like It, iii. 4;* to fill pauses, *As You Like It, iv. 1;* at marriage, *Taming of the Shrew, iii. 2; Richard II., v. 1;* four negatives, *Twelfth Night, v. 1;* women influenced by, *A Winter's Tale, i. 2;* given to a partner, *Henry VIII., i. 4;* of pilgrims—by the book, *Romeo and Juliet, i. 5;* hard, *Othello, iii. 3; Venus and Adonis,* lines 18, 54, 84, 96, 115, 207, 479, 511, 536; *I. Henry IV., iii. 1; Coriolanus, v. 3; Othello, ii. 1;* comfortless, as frozen water to a starved snake, *Titus Andronicus, iii. 1;* to every sedge, *Two Gentlemen of Verona, ii. 7;* kingdoms and provinces kissed away. *Antony and Cleopatra, iii. 8.*

Knapped (snapped), *Merchant of Venice, iii. 1.*

Knave(s), or fool, *All's Well that Ends Well, iv. 5;* some most villainous, *Othello, iv. 2;* pleading for a, *II. Henry IV., v. 1;* will backbite, *II. Henry IV.. v. 1;* description of a, *King Lear, ii. 2;* a slippery and subtle, *Othello, ii. 1.*

Knell, it is a, *Macbeth, ii. 1; iv. 3; v. 7;* talks like a, *Coriolanus, v. 4.*

Knife, inscription on a, *Merchant of Venice, v. 1.*

Knight, a carpet, *Twelfth Night, iii. 4,* "on carpet consideration."

Knighthood, will become hackneyed, *Merry Wives of Windsor, ii. 2,* "These knights will hack." A supposed allusion to the liberality with which James I. bestowed the honour of knighthood. If so, the passage must have been inserted some time after the play was first presented. Another meaning has been suggested—namely, these knights will be degraded, "hack" being the term for taking off a knight's spurs.

Knight of the Burning Lamp, *I. Henry IV., iii. 3.*

Knights, encounter of, *Richard II., i. 3;* at a tournament, *Pericles, ii. 2.*

Knights of the Garter. See GARTER, ORDER OF THE.

Knocking, at the gate, the, *Macbeth, ii. 2, 3.*

Knot-grass, hinders growth, *Midsummer-Night's Dream, iii. 2.* It was supposed that an infusion of knot-grass taken by a child would retard its growth.

Knots, in trees, *Troilus and Cressida, i. 3.*

Knowledge, too much, *Love's Labour's Lost, i. 1;* seeming, *All's Well that Ends Well, ii. 3;* accursed, *A Winter's Tale, ii. 1;* ill-inhabited (ill-housed), *As You Like It, iii. 3;* the wing, wherewith we fly to heaven, *II. Henry VI., iv. 7;* limited, *Hamlet, i. 5,* "There are more things in heaven and earth," etc.; of the present only, *Hamlet, iv. 5 or 2,* "We know what we are, but," etc.

Kyd, Thomas. See JERONIMY.

Laban, *Merchant of Venice, i. 3.*

Labienus, mentioned in *Antony and Cleopatra, i. 2.*

Labour, menial, made pleasure, *The Tempest, iii. 1;* physics pain, when delighted in, *Macbeth, ii. 3;* vain, *Richard II., ii. 2; Henry V., iv. 1; III. Henry VI., i. 4.*

Labras (lips), *Merry Wives of Windsor, i. 1.*

Lackbeard, my lord, *Much Ado about Nothing, iv. 1.*

Ladies, know if they be fair, *As You Like It, ii. 7.* See WOMEN.

Ladies' men, called lisping hawthorn-buds, *Merry Wives of Windsor, iii. 3.*

Lady, attending the queen in *Richard II.* Eleanor Holland, widow of the fourth Earl of March.

Lady, an old friend of Anne Boleyn in *Henry VIII.*, sometimes called Lady Denny.

Lady-smocks, *Love's Labour's Lost, v. 2.*

" A white field-flower, called also mayflower and Canterbury bell. Growing in masses, it looks like linen bleaching."—WHITE.

Laertes, son of Polonius and brother of Ophelia, in *Hamlet*, introduced in *i. 2.* He is sent to Paris, and his father despatches Reynaldo to watch him, *ii. 1.* He seeks vengeance for his father's death, *iv. 5* or *2*, and the mob proclaim him king. He dies by his own treacherous weapons, *v. 2.*

" Yet I acknowledge that Shakspere evidently wishes, as much as possible, to spare the character of Laertes—to break the extreme turpitude of his consent to become an agent and accomplice of the king's treachery ; and to this end he reintroduces Ophelia at the close of this scene to afford a probable stimulus of passion in her brother."—COLERIDGE.

" And Laertes, who takes violent measures at the shortest notice to revenge *his* father's murder, is in another way a contrast [to Hamlet] ; but Laertes is the young gallant of the period, and his capacity for action arises in part from the absence of those moral checks of which Hamlet is sensible."—DOWDEN.

Lafeu, an old lord in *All's Well that Ends Well*, introduced in *i. 1*, courtier-like and wordy, characterized by the king's words in *ii. 1*, " Thus he his special nothing ever prologues," but sound, true, and of quick discernment, the first to discover the true character of Parolles (*ii. 3*), " So, my good window of lattice, fare thee well ; thy casement I need not open, for I look through thee."

La fin, etc., *II. Henry VI., v. 2.* The end crowns the work.

Lakin (ladykin), *The Tempest, iii. 3.* Little lady, the Virgin Mary.

Lamb, the, entreats the butcher, *Cymbeline, iii. 4 ;* and the fox, *Measure for Measure, v. 1 ; Timon of Athens, iv. 3 ;* and the wolf, *III. Henry VI., i. 1, 4 ;* in a borrowed skin, *III. Henry VI., iii. 1 ;* follows the lion, *III. Henry VI. iv. 8 ;* doing the feats of a lion in the figure of a, *Much Ado about Nothing, i, 1 ;* offered up, *Macbeth, iv. 3.*

Lambert's (St.) day (September 17th), *Richard II., i. 1.*

Lamentations, moderate, for the dead, *All's Well that Ends*

Well, i. 1; the wise do not indulge in, *III. Henry VI., v. 4;* why should calamity be full of words, *Richard III., iv. 4;* ease the heart, *Richard III., iv. 4;* called for in advance, *Troilus and Cressida, ii. 2.*

Lammas-tide (August 1st), *Romeo and Juliet, i. 3.*

Lamont (or Lamond), a fencer spoken of in *Hamlet, iv. 7* (or *4*). This character is supposed to be intended for Raleigh. See under the name of the play.

Lamps, aye-remaining, *Pericles, iii. 1.* The perpetual lamps lighted for the dead.

Lancaster, House of, its wars with the House of York. See WARS OF THE ROSES.

Lancaster, John of Gaunt, Duke of. See GAUNT.

Lancaster, John, Prince of, character in both parts of *Henry IV.,* and, under the title of Duke of Bedford, in *Henry V.* and *I. Henry VI.* In *I. Henry IV.* he is introduced in *i. 1,* and in *II. Henry IV.* in *iv. 2.* In *II. Henry IV., iv. 3,* Falstaff describes him contemptuously as a demure and sober-blooded boy, and probably a coward. His father and brother, however, praise his bravery on the field of Shrewsbury. See BEDFORD.

Land-damn, *A Winter's Tale, ii. 1.* Conjectured to be an allusion to the punishment of being half buried and left to starve. Perhaps it means to be forced to quit the land.

Land(s), an owner of, spacious in the possession of dirt, *Hamlet, v. 2;* you have sold your own to see other men's, *As You Like It, iv. 1;* cheap, *I. Henry IV., ii. 4;* nothing left of all my, but my body's length, *III. Henry VI., v. 2;* to be gained by wit, if not by birth, *King Lear, i. 2.*

Langley, scene of *Richard II., iii. 4.* There are fifteen places named Langley in England, widely separated, and it is difficult to say which is intended.

Langton, Stephen, Archbishop of Canterbury, *King John, iii. 1.*

Language, taught to Caliban, *The Tempest, i. 2;* stilted, *Love's Labour's Lost, iv. 2; v. 1;* travesty on high-flown, *Love's Labour's Lost, i. 1; iv. 1; Hamlet, v. 2;* pretended, *All's Well that Ends Well, iv. 1;* bolted, *Coriolanus, iii. 1;* he speaks holiday, *Merry Wives of Windsor, iii. 2;* in movement, *Troilus and Cressida, iv. 5.*

Lantern, *Romeo and Juliet, v. 3.* A lanternium, a high turret full of windows.

Lanthorn, of the man in the moon, the, *Midsummer-Night's Dream, iii. 1; v. 1;* in the nose, *I. Henry IV., iii. 3; II. Henry IV., i. 2.*

Lapland, sorcerers of, *Comedy of Errors, iv. 3.* That country was thought to be a favourite home of witches.

Lapwing, the, *Measure for Measure, i. 5; Comedy of Errors, iv. 2.* Alluding to the habit of the bird of crying far away from her nest to divert pursuers, and used figuratively in reference to those who pretend interest in some certain place in order to divert attention from their real object. In *Hamlet, v. 2,* is an allusion to the notion that the young bird runs out of the shell in such haste that it carries part of it on its head; runs close by the ground, *Much Ado about Nothing, iii. 1.*

Lard, to, the lean earth, *I. Henry IV., ii. 2.*

Lark, the, dared like, see FOWLING; changed eyes with the toad, *Romeo and Juliet, iii. 5;* the ploughman's clock, *Love's Labour's Lost, v. 2, song;* the shrill-gorged, *King Lear, iv. 6;* at heaven's gate, *Cymbeline, ii. 3; Venus and Adonis, l. 853; Sonnet xxix.; Passionate Pilgrim, xv;* when not attended, *Merchant of Venice, v. 1;* its song, *Romeo and Juliet, iii. 5.*

Larron (thief), *Merry Wives of Windsor, i. 4.*

Lartius, Titus, character in *Coriolanus,* first appears in *i. 1.* He is one of the generals, an old man, who will "lean upon one crutch and fight with t'other."

Latch (catch), *Macbeth, iv. 3.*

Late, too, *Measure for Measure, ii. 2; All's Well that Ends Well, v. 3; Much Ado about Nothing, v. 1; A Winter's Tale, iii. 2.*

Late hours, *Twelfth Night, i. 3; I. Henry IV. ii. 4.*

Lath, a dagger of, *I. Henry IV., ii. 4; Titus Andronicus, ii. 1.*

Latin, no, *Henry VIII., iii. 1;* in conversation, *Love's Labour's Lost, iv. 2; v. 1, 2; II. Henry VI., iv. 2;* lessons in, *Merry Wives of Windsor, iv. 1; Taming of the Shrew, iii. 1.*

Latten (a kind of pewter), *Merry Wives of Windsor, i. 1.*

Laughter, connected with the spleen, *Love's Labour's Lost, v. 2;* that idiot, *King John, iii. 3;* of those that win, *Othello, iv. 1;* excessive, *Love's Labour's Lost, v. 2; Midsummer-Night's Dream, v. 1; II. Henry IV. v. 1; Cymbeline, i. 7;* fortune laughed away, *Antony and Cleopatra, ii. 6.*

Launce, servant of Proteus in the *Two Gentlemen of Verona,* a great punster, first appears in *ii. 3;* addresses his dog Crab, *ii. 3; iv. 4.*

Launcelot Gobbo, the clown, Shylock's servant in the *Merchant of Venice,* introduced in *ii. 2.* See JESSICA.

Laura, Petrarch's, *Romeo and Juliet, ii. 4.*

Laurence, a Franciscan friar in *Romeo and Juliet*, introduced in *ii. 3.* He marries the lovers, *ii. 6*, and gives Juliet the potion, *iv. 1.*

" The reverend character of the friar, like all Shakspere's representations of the great professions, is very delightful and tranquillizing, yet it is no digression, but immediately necessary to the carrying on of the plot."—COLERIDGE.

Laus Deo, bone intelligo (Praise to God, I understand well), *Love's Labour's Lost, v. 1.*

Lavinia, character in *Titus Andronicus*, daughter of Titus, first appears in *i. 1* or *2.* She is claimed by the emperor and his brother Bassianus. Titus favours the emperor's claim, but his sons that of Bassianus, to whom she was first promised, and she becomes his wife; plot of the Goths against her. *ii. 1;* dishonoured and mutilated, *ii. 3–5;* pitied by Marcus, *ii. 4* or *5;* writes the names of the Goths, *iv. 1;* avenged, *v. 2;* killed by her father, *v. 3.*

Lavolta, an Italian dance, *Henry V., iii. 5; Troilus and Cressida, iv. 4.*

Law(s), revival of old, *Measure for Measure, i. 3–5;* unenforced, *Measure for Measure, ii. 1, 2;* not dead but sleeping, *Measure for Measure, ii. 2;* bitten by the enforcer, *Measure for Measure, iii. 1;* a wise fellow that knows the, *Much Ado about Nothing, iv. 2;* tainted and corrupt pleas in, *Merchant of Venice, iii. 2;* as adversaries do in, *Taming of the Shrew, i. 2;* on the windy side of the, *Twelfth Night, iii. 4;* reliability of witnesses in, *A Winter's Tale, iv. 3;* when it can do no right, *King John, iii. 1;* called old father antic, *I. Henry IV., i. 2;* framed to the will—sharp quillets of the, *I. Henry VI., ii. 4;* as administered by the tribunes, *Coriolanus, ii. 1;* pity is the virtue of the, *Timon of Athens, iii. 5;* in hot blood, hath stept into the, *Timon of Athens, iii. 5;* one who goes to, called an action-taking knave, *King Lear, ii. 2;* the bloody book of the, *Othello, i. 3;* the brain may devise laws for the blood, *Merchant of Venice, i. 2;* no power to alter those of Venice, *Merchant of Venice, iv. 1;* a poor man's right in the, *Pericles, ii. 1;* broken by those that enforce them, *Lear iv. 6,* " The usurer hangs the cozener."

Law, allusions to, and terms of the : cheater (escheater), *Merry Wives of Windsor, i. 3;* lost my edifice by mistaking the place, *Merry Wives of Windsor, ii. 2;* a star-chamber matter, *Merry Wives of Windsor, i. 1;* fee simple—fine and recovery, *Merry Wives of Windsor, iv. 2; Comedy of Errors, ii. 2;* arrested in the case, *Comedy of Errors, iv. 2;* wards of the king, given by him in marriage,

Comedy of Errors, v. 1; All's Well that Ends Well, i. 1; recorded for a precedent—formerly (above), *Merchant of Venice, iv. 1;* charge upon interrogatories—answer faithfully, *Merchant of Venice, v., end;* taken with the manner, *Love's Labour's Lost, i. 1; I. Henry IV., ii. 4;* make an extent (attachment), *As You Like It, iii. 1;* videlicet, *As You Like It, iv. 1;* present her at the Leet, *Taming of the Shrew, induction, 2;* specialties—covenants, *Taming of the Shrew, ii. 1;* pass assurance, *Taming of the Shrew, iv. 3;* fee-simple—entail—perpetual succession, *All's Well that Ends Well, iv. 3;* except before excepted, *Twelfth Night, i. 3;* common—several, *Twelfth Night, ii. 1;* grand-jurymen, *Twelfth Night, iii. 2;* an action of battery, *Twelfth Night, iv. 1;* fees of acquitted prisoners to the jailer, *A Winter's Tale, i. 2; III. Henry VI., iv. 6;* indictment, *A Winter's Tale, iii. 2; II. Henry VI., iv. 7;* hand-fast (out on bail), *A Winter's Tale, iv. 3;* to sue out livery, *Richard II.. ii. 1, 3; I. Henry IV., iv. 3;* enfeoffed (disposed of absolutely), *I. Henry IV., iii. 2;* advised by my counsel—to lay by the heels (send to prison), *II. Henry IV., i. 2; Henry VIII., v. 3;* absque hoc, *II. Henry IV., v. 5;* attainder, *I. Henry VI., ii. 4;* writ of præmunire, *Henry VIII., iii. 2;* in fee-farm—in witness whereof, *Troilus and Cressida, iii. 2;* amerce, *Romeo and Juliet, iii. 1;* utter (to pass or sell at retail) *Romeo and Juliet, v. 1;* affeered (confirmed), *Macbeth, iv. 3;* countenance, *Hamlet, iv. 2;* the clown's argument, and Hamlet's speech on the skull, *Hamlet, v. 1;* capable (of inheriting), *King Lear, ii. 1;* comforting, *King Lear, iii. 5;* witness suborned, *Othello, iii. 4;* purchased (obtained otherwise than by inheriting), *Antony and Cleopatra, i. 4;* pray in aid (asking help from another person interested in the claim), *Antony and Cleopatra, v. 2;* oversee this will, *Lucrece, l. 1205;* overseers as well as executors were sometimes appointed; sessions—summon, *Sonnet xxx.;* defendant, *Sonnet xlvi.;* determinate (ended), *Sonnet lxxxvii.*

Lawn as white as driven snow, song, *A Winter's Tale, iv. 4.*

Lawyer(s), the melancholy of the, *As You Like It, iv. 1;* let's kill all the, *II. Henry VI., iv. 2;* crack the voice of the, *Timon of Athens, iv. 3;* dreams of, *Romeo and Juliet, i. 4;* skull of a, *Hamlet, v. 1;* an unfeed, *King Lear, i. 4.*

Lay by, *I. Henry IV., i. 2.* Supposed to be the highwayman's summons, equivalent to "Stand and deliver."

Lay on, Macduff, *Macbeth, v. 7.*

Lazarus, in the painted cloth (tapestry), *I. Henry IV., iv. 2.*

Lead. slow, *Love's Labour's Lost, iii. 1;* prayer to have it kept out, *I. Henry IV.*, *v. 3;* heavy, *II. Henry IV.*, *i. 1; Richard III.*, *v. 3; Coriolanus, i. 1; Romeo and Juliet, i. 1.*

Leaf, the sear, the yellow, *Macbeth, v. 3.*

Leaguer (camp), *All's Well that Ends Well, iii. 6.*

Leah, Shylock's wife, *Merchant of Venice, iii. 1.*

Leander, *Two Gentlemen of Verona, i. 1; iii. 1; As You Like It, iv. 1; Much Ado about Nothing, v. 2.* He was drowned swimming the Hellespont to Hero's tower at Sestos. When she became aware of it, Hero cast herself from her tower, and perished in the sea. The celebrated poem on the subject, written by Musæus, a Greek author of the sixth century, was discovered in the thirteenth.

Leanness, of Pinch, *Comedy of Errors, v. 1,* "My liege, I am advised," etc.; of Robert Faulconbridge, *King John, i. 1;* Falstaff's, *I. Henry IV., iii. 3;* dangerous—of Cassius, *Julius Cæsar, i. 2.*

Leap-frog, allusion to the game of, *Henry V., v. 2.*

Lear, King of Britain, according to Geoffrey of Monmouth, about 800 years before Christ. In *King Lear, i. 1,* he divides his kingdom according to the professions of love to him made by his daughters. Of his character, as revealed in this scene, Coleridge says:

"The strange, yet by no means unnatural, mixture of selfishness, sensibility, and habit of feeling derived from and fostered by the particular rank and usages of the individual; the intense desire of being intensely beloved—selfish, and yet characteristic of the selfishness of a loving and kindly nature alone; the self-supportless leaning for all pleasure on another's breast; the craving after sympathy with a prodigal disinterestedness, frustrated by its own ostentation and the mode and nature of its claims; the anxiety, the distrust, the jealousy which more or less accompany all selfish affections, and are among the surest contradistinctions of mere fondness from true love, and which originate Lear's eager wish to enjoy his daughters' violent professions, while the inveterate habits of sovereignty convert the wish into claim and positive right, and an incompliance with it into crime and treason—these facts, these passions, these moral verities, on which the whole tragedy is founded, are all prepared for, and will to the retrospect be found implied in the first four or five lines in the play. They let us know that the trial is but a trick; and that the grossness of the old king's rage is in part the natural result of a silly trick suddenly and most unexpectedly baffled and disappointed."

Lear disowns Cordelia, *i. 1;* is criticised by the other daughters at the end of the same scene; leaves Goneril's house in a passion, *i. 4;* leaves Regan's, *ii. 4;* on the heath, *iii. 2, 4, 6;* his madness, *iv. 6; v. 3;* his death, *v. 3.*

Learning, in a woman's eye, *Love's Labour's Lost, iv. 3;* plodding for, *Love's Labour's Lost, i. 1; iv. 3;* late deceased in beggary, *Midsummer-Night's Dream, v. 1.* Supposed to refer to the death of the dramatist Robert Greene in poverty in 1592; though Dowden thinks it more likely to refer to Spenser's " The Tears of the Muses; " what a thing it is, *Taming of the Shrew, i. 2;* under ban, *II. Henry VI., iv. 2;* in comparison with blood, *Henry VIII., i. 1,* " A beggar's book," etc.; what, is, *Romeo and Juliet, iii. 3;* a mere hoard of gold till sack sets it in use, *II. Henry IV., iv. 3;* of the king, *Henry V., i. 1;* little will die the day thou art hanged, *Timon of Athens, ii. 2.*

Leasing (lying), *Twelfth Night, i. 5; Coriolanus, v. 2.*

Leather-coats (russet apples), *II. Henry IV., v. 3.*

Leave-taking, *Hamlet, i. 3;* " nothing I would so willingly part withal," *Hamlet, ii. 2;* the last, *Richard II., v. 1;* of youth, *III. Henry VI., iii. 2.* See PARTING.

Le Beau, a courtier attending the usurping duke in *As You Like It,* introduced in *i. 2.*

Le Bon, Monsieur, one of the suitors of Portia mentioned in the *Merchant of Venice, i. 2.*

Leda, *Merry Wives of Windsor, v. 5;* the daughter of (Helen), *Taming of the Shrew, i. 2.*

Leek, wearing the, *Henry V., iv. 1, 7; v. 1.* A leek is worn by Welshmen on St. David's Day, March 1, because. it is said, St. David ordered his soldiers to wear it in battle to distinguish them from their enemies.

Leer (face, look), *As You Like It, iv. 1.*

Leet (a petty criminal court), *Taming of the Shrew, induction, 1; Othello, iii. 3.*

Leg (cant for obeisance), make a, *All's Well that Ends Well, ii. 2; I. Henry IV., ii. 4.*

Legion, possessed him, *Twelfth Night, iii. 4.* Meaning the legion of devils.

Legitimacy, *King John, i. 1; ii. 1; King Lear, i. 2.*

Leicester, *Henry VIII., iv. 2.*

Leicester, Earl of. See MAIDENHOOD.

Lendings (clothes), *King Lear, iii. 4.*

Lenity, in war, *Henry V., iii. 6;* makes robbers bold, *III. Henry VI., ii. 2, 6;* away to heaven, respective, *Romeo and Juliet, iii. 1.*

Lenox, a thane of Scotland, and character in *Macbeth,* introduced in *i. 2.* In *iii. 6,* he expresses his suspicions of Macbeth. He is keen, but dissembling and cowardly.

Lent, a joint of mutton or two in a whole, *II. Henry IV., ii. 4;* shall be as long again, *II. Henry VI., iv. 3.* Butchers were forbidden to sell meat in Lent; but some few were excepted from the general rule by special favour, and it is this license that is referred to. A hare for a pie in, *Romeo and Juliet, ii. 4.*

Lenten answer (dry or short answer), *Twelfth Night, i. 5.*

Lenten entertainment, *Hamlet, ii. 2.*

Leonardo, the servant of Bassanio in the *Merchant of Venice,* appears in *ii. 2.*

Leonato, governor of Messina, father of Hero in *Much Ado about Nothing,* is introduced in the first scene. He is merry, lighthearted, and indulgent, but weakly credulous of the slander against his daughter.

Leonine, servant of Dionyza in *Pericles,* first appears in *iv. 1,* as the intended murderer of Marina.

Leontes, King of Sicilia, character in *A Winter's Tale,* introduced in the second scene. His jealousy is the prime cause of the action throughout the plot. Both Coleridge and Gervinus have, in somewhat different ways, drawn contrasts between his jealousy and that of the nobler Othello. His disposition is passionate, obstinate, and tyrannical, his imagination gross, and his judgment weak.

Leopards, lions make, tame, *Richard II., i. 1.* The crest of Norfolk was a golden leopard.

Lepidus, M. Æmilius, one of the triumvirs after Cæsar's death, character in *Julius Cæsar,* introduced in *iii. 1;* Antony's opinion of, *iv. 1.* Also a character in *Antony and Cleopatra,* introduced in *i. 4.* Enobarbus travesties his praise of Cæsar and Antony. In *iii. 5,* he is seized by Cæsar's order.

Lestrale, mentioned, *Henry V., iii. 5; iv. 8.*

Let (stay, stop), *Comedy of Errors, ii. 1,* and elsewhere.

Lethe, *Richard III., iv. 4; Julius Cæsar, iii. 1; Antony and Cleopatra, ii. 7; Hamlet, i. 5; Twelfth Night, iv. 1; II. Henry IV., v. 2.* In mythology, a river of the lower world. The shades of the dead drank of it and forgot the sorrows of life.

Let me confess that we two must be twain, *Sonnet xxxvi.*

Let me not to the marriage of true minds, *Sonnet cxvi.*

Let not my love be called idolatry, *Sonnet cv.*

Letter, affect the (use alliteration), *Love's Labour's Lost, iv. 2.*

Letter(s), of love, see LOVE-LETTERS; allusions to the custom of addressing letters to "the bosom" of a lady, *Two Gentlemen of Verona, iii. 1; Hamlet, ii. 2;* Armado's, *Love's Labour's Lost, i. 1:*

old ends of, *Much Ado about Nothing, i. 1;* unpleasant, *Merchant of Venice, iii. 2;* allusion to the custom of writing Emmanuel at the head of, *II. Henry VI., iv. 2;* appetite after reading, *Henry VIII., iii. 2;* forged, *King Lear, i. 2;* of Goneril, *King Lear, iv. 6;* a, *Lucrece, l. 1296;* destroyed, *Lover's Complaint, l. 43;* patents, *Richard II., ii. 1;* effect of a, *Henry V, ii. 2.*

Let those who are in favor with their stars, *Sonnet xxv.*

Leviathan, *Midsummer-Night's Dream, ii. 2; Henry V., iii. 3.*

Liar(s), believe themselves at length, *The Tempest, i. 2,* "Like one who having unto truth," etc.; an accomplished, *Love's Labour's Lost, i. 1;* an infinite and endless, *All's Well that Ends Well, iii. 6;* God and good men hate, *Richard II., i. 1;* one that lies three-thirds, *All's Well that Ends Well, ii. 5;* one that would make you think truth a fool, *All's Well that Ends Well, iv. 3;* old men apt to be, *II. Henry IV., iii. 4;* go to hell, *Othello, v. 2.*

Liberality, in offers, *Merchant of Venice, iv. 1;* prodigal, *Timon of Athens, i. 1, 2; ii. 1, 2.*

Liberty, headstrong, *Comedy of Errors, ii. 1;* too much, *Measure for Measure, i. 3, 4;* of fools, *As You Like It, ii. 7;* enough, *King John, iv. 1;* blessing of, *Cymbeline, i. 7;* fighting for, *II. Henry VI., iv. 2.*

Library, *Titus And., iv. 1;* Prospero's, *The Tempest, i. 2; iii. 2.*

Lichas, *Merchant of Venice, ii. 1; Antony and Cleopatra, iv. 10* or *12.* The attendant that brought the poisoned shirt to Hercules from Dejanira.

Licio, name assumed by Hortensio in *Taming of the Shrew, ii. 1.*

Liefest (dearest), *II. Henry VI., iii. 1.*

Lieger (citizen), an everlasting, *Measure for Measure, iii. 1.*

Lie(s), repeated, *The Tempest, i. 2;* invention of, *All's Well that Ends Well, iv. 1;* charges of, *Richard II., i. 1; iv. 1;* Falstaff's anticipated, *I. Henry IV., i. 2;* gross, *I. Henry IV., ii. 4;* for a friend, *Coriolanus, v. 2;* an odious, damned, *Othello, v. 2;* by the poor, *Cymbeline, iii. 6;* of lovers, *Sonnet cxxxviii.;* only become tradesmen, *A Winter's Tale, iv. 3;* women should not tell, *Antony and Cleopatra, v. 2;* every third word a, *II. Henry IV., iii. 2;* circumstantial, direct, etc., see DUELLING.

Lieutenant, to Aufidius, character in *Coriolanus, iv. 7.*

Lieutenant of the Tower, *III. Henry VI., iv. 6.* Supposed to have been John Tibetoft, first Earl of Worcester.

Lieutenantry, dealt on, *Antony and Cleopatra, iii. 9* or *11.* Allowed his lieutenants to do the fighting.

Life, rounded with a sleep, *The Tempest, iv. 1;* a shuttle, *Merry Wives of Windsor, v. 1;* brevity and worthlessness of, *Measure for Measure, iii. 1;* death's fool, *Measure for Measure, iii. 1;* allusion to death and his fool in an old play; any, better than death—compared with honour, *Measure for Measure, iii. 1;* past fear of death, *Measure for Measure, v. 1;* the idea of a, in imagination, *Much Ado about Nothing, iv. 1;* taken when the means are taken, *Merchant of Venice, iv. 1;* brevity of, *As You Like It, ii. 7; iii. 2, song;* web of a mingled yarn, *All's Well that Ends Well, iv. 3;* to come, *A Winter's Tale, iv. 3;* a twice-told tale, *King John, iii. 4;* the bloody house of, *King John, iv. 2;* not to be lengthened, *Richard II., i. 3;* shortness of, *I. Henry IV., v. 2,* Hotspur's speech; better than honour, *I. Henry IV., v. 3;* less than honour, *I. Henry IV., v. 4;* time's fool, *I. Henry IV., v. 4;* thought the slave of, *I. Henry IV., v. 4;* set upon a cast, *Richard III., v. 4;* its wine drawn, *Macbeth, ii. 3;* its fitful fever, *Macbeth, iii. 2;* its brevity—a tale told by an idiot—a poor player, *Macbeth, v. 5;* a charmed, *Macbeth, v. 7;* cheapness of man's, *King Lear, ii. 4;* yields to age, *King Lear, iv. 1;* treasury of, *King Lear, iv. 6;* why should a dog have, *King Lear, v. 3;* the light of, *Othello, v. 2;* nobleness of, *Antony and Cleopatra, i. 1;* bears the stamp of the gods, *Cymbeline, v. 4;* shortness of, *Sonnet lx.;* autumn and twilight of, *Sonnet lxxiii.;* man's, is tedious, *Cymbeline, iii. 6;* love of long, *Antony and Cleopatra, i. 2;* brevity of its greatness, *Henry VIII., prologue;* when it is a torment, *Othello i. 3;* its glory like madness, *Timon of Athens, i. 2.*

Ligarius, a conspirator in *Julius Cæsar,* first appears in *ii. 1.*

Light, sought in books, *Love's Labour's Lost, i. 1.* See STUDY.

Lightly (usually), *Richard III., iii. 1.*

Lightning, its swiftness, *Midsummer-Night's Dream, i. 1; Richard II., i. 3; King Lear, iv. 7; Romeo and Juliet, ii. 2;* before death, a, *Romeo and Juliet, v. 3.*

Light o' Love, a dance-tune, *Two Gentlemen of Verona, i. 2; Much Ado about Nothing, iii. 4.*

Like as the waves, *Sonnet lx.*

Like as, to make our appetites more keen, *Sonnet cxviii.*

Lilly (or Lyly), John (about 1553–1600), quotations and allusions to his Latin Grammar, *Twelfth Night, ii. 3.*

Lily (ies), *A Winter's Tale, iv. 3* or *4; Sonnet xcix.;* festering, *Sonnet xciv.;* to paint the, *King John, iv. 2;* perish like the, *Henry VIII., iii. 1.*

Limander (Leander ?), *Midsummer-Night's Dream, v. 1.*

Limbo Patrum, place where the souls of the patriarchs remained till the descent of Christ, *Henry VIII., v. 4.*

Limbo, Tartar, *Comedy of Errors, iv. 2.*

Lime, in sack (to make it sparkle), *Merry Wives of Windsor, i. 3; I. Henry IV., ii. 4.*

Limed (caught as with bird-lime), *Twelfth Night, iii. 4.*

Limehouse, limbs of (in some editions Limbo), *Henry VIII., v. 4.* Limehouse was near Tower Hill, and the tribulation of Tower Hill and the limbs of Limehouse may refer to the roughs that infested the neighborhood.

Limits, everything has, *Comedy of Errors, ii. 1.*

Lincoln, John Langland, Bishop of, character in *Henry VIII.,* introduced in *ii. 4.* He is said to have made the first suggestion of the divorce. There is a chapel in Lincoln Cathedral planned by him, and named for him, Langland Chapel.

Line, the equinoctial, *The Tempest, iv. 1.* Quibbling allusion to the supposed fact that the heat there caused loss of hair.

Line (strengthen), *I. Henry IV., ii. 3.*

Lineage, evidence of good, *Cymbeline, iv. 2,* "O thou goddess," etc.; *I. Henry IV., i. 2.* See BLOOD AND RANK.

Linen, Poins's, *II. Henry IV., ii. 2.*

Linguist, a, Sir Andrew, *Twelfth Night, i. 3; iv. 1; All's Well that Ends Well, iv. 3.*

Link (torch), hats blackened with a, *Taming of the Shrew, iv. 1.*

Lion(s), royal disposition of the, *As You Like It, iv. 3;* in Arden, *As You Like It, iv. 3;* better to fall before the, than the wolf, *Twelfth Night, iii. 1;* the dying, *Richard II., v. 1;* will not touch a true prince. *I. Henry IV., ii. 4;* the man that sold the skin of a, *Henry V., iv. 3;* allusions to the story that Richard I. tore out the heart of one sent to devour him, *King John, i. 1; ii. 1.*

Lion, a character in the interlude in *Midsummer-Night's Dream, v. 1,* taken by Snug the joiner.

Lion-skin, doff the, *King John, iii. 1.*

Lips, pretty, *Midsummer-Night's Dream, iii. 2; Measure for Measure, iv. 1; Richard III., iv. 3;* coward, *Julius Cæsar, i. 2.*

Lipsbury Pinfold, *King Lear, ii. 2.* Of unknown meaning.

Liquors, hot and rebellious, *As You Like It, ii. 3.* See DRUNKENNESS.

List (limit, edge of cloth), *Measure for Measure, i. 1, 2; Twelfth Night, iii. 1; Hamlet, iv. 5 or 2.*

Liver, the, seat of love, *Merry Wives of Windsor, ii. 1; Much*

Ado about Nothing, iv. 1; Twelfth Night, i. 1; ii. 4; Love's Labour's Lost, iv. 3; As You Like It, iii. 2; white, *Merchant of Venice, iii. 2; Twelfth Night, iii. 2.*

Livery, sue his, *I. Henry IV., iv. 3; Richard II., ii. 1, 3.* Sue delivery of his lands, as an heir who was of age sued for custody of his own property.

Living, Falstaff's plan to get a, *Merry Wives of Windsor, i. 3.*

Lizard, sting of the, *II. Henry VI., iii. 2; III. Henry VI., ii. 2;* leg of, *Macbeth, iv. 1.*

Loan(s), to an enemy—without interest, *Merchant of Venice, i. 3;* a, oft loses both itself and friend, *Hamlet. i. 3.*

Lo! as a careful housewife, *Sonnet cxliii.*

Lo! in the orient, *Sonnet vii.*

Lob (lubber), *Midsummer-Night's Dream, ii. 1.*

Lock (love-lock), *Much Ado about Nothing, iii. 3; v. 1.*

Lodovico, a kinsman of Othello's father-in-law, introduced in *iv. 1* of the play.

Lodowick, Friar, name assumed by the duke in *Measure for Measure, v. 1.*

Loggats, *Hamlet, v. 1.* A game played with loggats or pieces of wood, which are thrown at a jack. It is somewhat like bowls or skittles.

Logic, of the schools, travesty on, *Twelfth Night, iv. 2,* "What is that but that?"

Lombardy, garden of Italy, *Taming of the Shrew, i. 1.*

London, scene of parts of the historical plays. See LUD'S TOWN.

London Bridge, order for the burning of, *II. Henry VI., iv. 6* In Shakspere's day there was but the one bridge over the Thames at London.

London-stone, *II. Henry VI., iv. 6.* A stone supposed to have been set up in the time of the Romans, and now built into the wall of St. Swithin's Church. Distances were measured from it.

Longaville, one of the lords attending on the king in *Love's Labour's Lost*, introduced in the first scene.

> "The only soil of his fair virtue's gloss,
> If virtue's gloss will stain with any soil,
> Is a sharp wit matched with too blunt a will."

Longing, immortal, *Antony and Cleopatra, v. 2.*

Looker-on in Vienna, a, *Measure for Measure, v. 1.*

Looking-glass, a, *Richard II., iv. 1;* to court an amorous,

Richard III., *i. 1*; at charges for a, *Richard III.*, *i. 2*; to test life, *King Lear*, *v. 3*.

Look in thy glass, *Sonnet iii.*

Looks, a war of, *Venus and Adonis*, *l. 355*; foreboding, *III. Henry VI.*, *ii. 1*.

Lop (branches), *Henry VIII.*, *i. 2*.

Lord, a, a character in the *Taming of the Shrew*. The trick he played upon Sly is said to have been played upon an artisan by Philip the Good, Duke of Burgundy. An account of it is in "Admirable and Memorable Histories," by Goulart, translated by E. Grimstone, 1607, though it had appeared in English in 1570 in a collection of stories by Richard Edwards. It was also in the old play.

Lord Chief-Justice Gascoigne. See GASCOIGNE.

Lord have mercy upon us, *Love's Labour's Lost*, *v. 2.* An inscription on houses infected with the plague.

Lord, how mine eyes, *Passionate Pilgrim*, *xv.*

Lord Mayor of London, the, a character in *III. Henry VI.*

Lord of my love, *Sonnet xxvi.*

Lord's Prayer, the, *Merchant of Venice*, *iv. 1,* "And that same prayer," etc.

Lord's sake, for the, *Measure for Measure*, *iv. 3*, an allusion to the practice of prisoners for debt begging from the window of passers-by, "For the Lord's sake."

Lorenzo, the lover of Jessica, in the *Merchant of Venice*, enters in the first scene, a thoughtless, boyish, romantic personage.

Loss, racks the estimation of value, *Much Ado about Nothing*, *iv. 1;* make comfort of, *All's Well that Ends Well*, *iv. 3;* appreciation after, *All's Well that Ends Well*, *v. 3;* how men should bear, *Julius Cæsar*, *iv. 3;* at sea, *Merchant of Venice*, *iv. 1.*

Lottery, of the caskets, *Merchant of Venice*, *i. 2; ii. 1.*

Louis, the Dauphin, afterward Louis VIII. of France, a character in *King John*, introduced in *ii. 1.*

Louis, the Dauphin of France, character in *Henry V.*, first appears in *ii. 4.* He is a rash and confident young braggart. In *i. 2,* he sends tennis-balls to Henry to intimate that Henry is more fit for that game than for war.

Louis X. of France, his title, *Henry V.*, *i. 2.*

Louis XI. of France, character in *III. Henry VI.*, introduced in *iii. 3;* Henry's opinion of his susceptibility, *iii. 1.*

Louted (treated as a lout, mocked), *I. Henry VI.*, *iv. 3.*

Louvre, your Paris, *Henry V.*, *ii. 4; Henry VIII.*, *i. 3.*

ever died of, *As You Like It*, *iv. 1;* what 'tis—sudden, *As You Like It*, *v. 2;* *Taming of the Shrew*, *i. 1;* rough, *Taming of the Shrew*, *ii. 1;* lectures on—pleading for another in, *Taming of the Shrew*, *i. 2;* despairing, *All's Well that Ends Well*, *i. 1, 3;* of one in higher rank—belongs to youth—evidences of, *All's Well that Ends Well*, *i. 3;* ambition in, *All's Well that Ends Well*, *i. 1;* *iii. 4;* without, *All's Well that Ends Well*, *iv. 2;* come too late, *All's Well that Ends Well*, *v. 2;* music the food of—like the sea—one sovereign, *Twelfth Night*, *i. 1;* and flowers, *Twelfth Night*, *i. 1*, *end;* messenger of, *Twelfth Night*, *i. 4, 5;* refused, *Twelfth Night*, *i. 5;* hungry—never told, *Twelfth Night*, *ii. 4;* offered by a lady, *Twelfth Night*, *iii. 1;* shows itself, *Twelfth Night*, *iii. 1;* unsought, *Twelfth Night*, *iii. 1, 4;* declaration of, *Twelfth Night*, *v. 1;* indications of, *A Winter's Tale*, *i. 2;* *iv. 3* or *4;* prosperity the bond of, *A Winter's Tale*, *iv. 3;* turns to hate, *Richard II.*, *iii. 2;* this no world for, *I. Henry IV.*, *ii. 3;* worth a million, *I. Henry IV.*, *iii. 3;* protestations of, *I. Henry IV.*, *iv. 1;* sincerity in, *Henry V.*, *v. 2;* sudden, *I. Henry VI.*, *v. 3;* to Clarence, *Richard III.*, *i. 1;* suing for, *Richard III.*, *i. 2;* of Troilus, *Troilus and Cressida*, *i. 1;* before gained, *Troilus and Cressida*, *i. 2*, *end;* nothing but (song), *Troilus and Cressida*, *iii. 1;* enchantment of—will is infinite, *Troilus and Cressida*, *iii. 2;* comes with lack, *Coriolanus*, *iv. 1;* tyrannous and paradoxical, *Romeo and Juliet*, *i. 1;* sprung from hate, *Romeo and Juliet*, *i. 5;* infinite—daring of, *Romeo and Juliet*, *ii. 2;* in the eyes, *Romeo and Juliet*, *ii. 3;* like a natural—slain by, *Romeo and Juliet*, *ii. 4;* heralds of, *Romeo and Juliet*, *ii. 5;* moderate—lightness of, *Romeo and Juliet*, *ii. 6;* shadows of, *Romeo and Juliet*, *v. 1;* cooling, *Julius Cæsar*, *iv. 2;* caution in, *Hamlet*, *i. 3;* madness in, *Hamlet*, *ii. 1, 2;* inconstant, *Hamlet*, *iii. 2,* player king; nature is fine (sensitive) in, *Hamlet*, *iv. 5* or *2;* effect of time on, *Hamlet*, *iv. 7* (or *4*); undemonstrative—in misfortune, *King Lear*, *i. 1;* penalty for giving charms for, *Othello*, *i. 2, 3;* unnatural, *Othello*, *i. 3;* doting, *Othello*, *ii. 3,* "And what's he," etc.; its crown and hearted throne, *Othello*, *iii. 3;* deceived, *Othello*, *iv. 2;* finds grace in frowns, *Othello*, *iv. 3;* not wise, *Othello*, *v. 2;* *Antony and Cleopatra*, *i. 1, 3, 5;* *iii. 9* or *11;* protestations of, *Cymbeline*, *i. 1, 3;* impatience of, *Cymbeline*, *iii. 2;* reason of, *Cymbeline*, *iv. 2;* repelled, *Venus and Adonis*, *lines 31, 130, 137;* compact of fire, *Venus and Adonis*, *l. 149;* surfeits not, *Venus and Adonis*, *l. 799;* ridiculous, *Venus and Adonis*, *l. 985;* prophecy concerning, *Venus and Adonis*, *l. 1136;* want of, *Sonnets viii.-x.;* poetry of, *Sonnet xxi.;* hears with eyes,

Love-broker, report of valour the best, *Twelfth Night, iii. 2.*

Love-in-idleness, *Midsummer-Night's Dream, ii. 1.* The pansy.

Love is my sin and thy dear virtue hate, *Sonnet cxlii.*

Love is too young to know what conscience is, *Sonnet cli.*

Lovel, Francis, Lord, character in *Richard III.,* first appears in *iii. 4.* He was one of Richard's chief supporters, fled to France after Bosworth, but returned and took the side of Lambert Simnel.

Love-Letters, *Two Gentlemen of Verona, i. 2; ii. 1; iii. 1; Merry Wives of Windsor, ii. 1; Love's Labour's Lost, iv. 1, 2; v. 2; As You Like It, iv. 3; Twelfth Night, ii. 3, 5; Hamlet, ii. 2; Cymbeline, iii. 4;* blanks for, *Merry Wives of Windsor, ii. 1.*

Lovell, Sir Thomas, character in *Henry VIII.,* introduced in *i. 2.* He was a favourite with both Henry VII. and Henry VIII., was a devout Catholic, endowed the priory at Halliwell, Shoreditch, and built a chapel there, where he was buried. An inscription reads:

> "All ye nunns of Halliwell,
>   Pray ye both day and night
>   For the soul of Sir Thomas Lovell,
>   Whom Harry the Seventh made Knight."

Sir Thomas Lovell is mentioned in *Richard III., iv. 4.*

Love-making, *Comedy of Errors, iii. 2; iv. 2; Merry Wives of Windsor, ii. 1, 2; iii. 4; Midsummer-Night's Dream, i. 1; iii. 2; Twelfth Night, i. 5; v. 1; Richard III., i. 2; Antony and Cleopatra, i. 3; Cymbeline, ii. 3; Troilus and Cressida, iii. 2; iv. 2; v. 2; Romeo and Juliet, ii. 1; The Tempest, iii. 1; Much Ado about Nothing, iv. 1; v. 3; Taming of the Shrew, iii. 1; A Winter's Tale, iv. 4; Venus and Adonis, lines 1–768.*

Lover(s), mercenary, *Measure for Measure, iii. 1,* "She should this Angelo have married," etc.; keen faculties of, *Love's Labour's Lost, iv. 3;* trusting a, *Love's Labour's Lost, v. 2;* fantasies of—all compact of imagination, *Midsummer-Night's Dream, v. 1;* sighs of, *As You Like It, ii. 7;* propositions of a, *As You Like It, iii. 2;* given to poetry, *As You Like It, iii. 4;* fickle in everything but love, *Twelfth Night, ii. 4;* generosity in, *A Winter's Tale, iv. 3* or *4;* vows of, *Troilus and Cressida, iii. 2;* sighs of, *Romeo and Juliet, i. 1;* chaffing a, *Romeo and Juliet, ii. 1;* ravings of, *Romeo and Juliet, ii. 2;* impatience of, *Romeo and Juliet, ii. 5;* exiled, *Romeo and Juliet, iii. 3;* partings of, *Romeo and Juliet, iii. 5; Two Gentlemen of Verona, ii. 2; Antony and Cleopatra, i. 3;* mêeting of, *Othello, ii. 1,* "O my fair," etc.; exaggerations of, *Antony and Cleopatra, i. 5;* tedious, *Venus and Adonis, l. 841;* gifts of, *Lover's Complaint, lines 197, 232;* like misers, *Sonnet lxxv.;* see only the beloved, *Sonnets cxiii., cxiv.*

Lover's Complaint, A, a poem first published in 1609, with the first edition of the Sonnets. From its style it is judged to have been written before the Sonnets and after the other poems.

Loves, of the poets, *Romeo and Juliet, ii. 4.*

Love-songs, *Hamlet, iv. 5* or *2; Troilus and Cressida, iii. 1.*

Love-Sonnets, addressed to a man, *i.–cxxvi.;* to a woman, *cxxvii.–clii.*

Love's Labour's Lost, one of the earliest, if not the very earliest, of the comedies, the date commonly assigned to it being the poet's twenty-fifth year. It was first published in 1598 in an edition "corrected and augmented." Shakspere's work on *Titus Andronicus* is alone thought to be earlier than this in its original form. No play or story is known on which this comedy could have been founded. Editors have discovered only a passage in Monstrelet, concerning a negotiation between the Kings of Navarre and France, by which Navarre gave up the castle of Cherbourg, the county of Evreux, and all the other lordships he possessed within the kingdom of France, and received the duchy of Nemours and two hundred thousand gold crowns. The scene is Navarre. Coleridge says of the play:

"The satire is chiefly on follies of words. . . . The frequency of the rhymes, the sweetness as well as the smoothness of the metre, and the number of acute and fancifully illustrated aphorisms, are all as they ought to be in a poet's youth. True genius begins by generalizing and condensing; it ends in realizing and expanding."

Love's Labour's Won. See ALL'S WELL THAT END'S WELL.

Love-verses, *Two Gentlemen of Verona, ii. 1; iii. 1; iv. 2; Love's Labour's Lost. iv. 2, 3; As You Like It, iii. 2; Twelfth Night, ii. 5;* directions for writing, *Two Gentlemen of Verona, iii. 2.*

Lowly, better to be. *Henry VIII., ii. 3; Cymbeline, i. 6.*

Loyalty, in service, *As You Like It, i. 3; ii. 3;* professions of, *Richard II., i. 3; Henry VIII., iii. 2; King John, iv. 2; Macbeth, i. 4;* difficult, of York, *Richard II., ii. 2;* Kent's, *King Lear, i. 4;* pretended, *King Lear, iii. 5;* to the fallen, *Antony and Cleopatra, iii. 11* or *13;* where shall it find a harbour in the earth? *II. Henry VI., v. 1.*

Lozel (good-for-nothing), *A Winter's Tale, ii. 3.*

Lubber, the world a great, *Twelfth Night, iv. 1.*

Lubber's Head (leopard's), an inn, *II. Henry IV., ii. 1.*

Lucentio, the successful suitor of Bianca in the *Taming of the Shrew,* introduced in *i. 1,* who goes into her father's family as a teacher under the assumed name of Cambio.

Luce, servant of Adriana in the *Comedy of Errors.*

Luces, the dozen white, *Merry Wives of Windsor, i. 1.* A supposed allusion to the arms of the Lucy family, in which there were three pike, luce being another name for that fish. See SHALLOW.

Lucetta, Julia's maid in the *Two Gentlemen of Verona,* who is keen-sighted enough to discover the true character of Proteus, appears in *i. 2.*

Luciana, sister of the wife of Antipholus of Ephesus in *Comedy of Errors.* She is mild-tempered and gentle, forming a contrast to her vixenish sister, and advocating the theory of wifely submission to which Katherine is brought in the *Taming of the Shrew.*

Lucianus, nephew of the player king. *Hamlet, iii. 2.*

Lucifer, *Merry Wives of Windsor, ii. 2, end;* falls like, *Henry VIII., iii. 2; King John, iv. 3.*

Lucilius, a servant of *Timon of Athens,* introduced in *i. 1.*

Lucilius, a friend of Brutus in *Julius Cæsar,* appears in *iv. 2;* made prisoner. *v. 4.*

Lucio, a fantastic in *Measure for Measure,* introduced in *i. 2,* a witty but vile and shameless character.

Lucius, one of the flattering lords in *Timon of Athens,* introduced in *iii. 2,* where he mentions the presents he has received from Timon, and makes an excuse for not lending him money in his need.

Lucius, servant of Brutus in *Julius Cæsar,* introduced in *ii. 1.*

Lucius, character in *Titus Andronicus,* son of Titus, introduced in *i. 1* or *2,* where he demands the sacrifice of a prisoner to the shades of his brothers; banished, *iii. 1;* general of the Goths, *iv. 4; v. 1;* made emperor, *v. 3.*

Lucius, Young, a brave child, son of Lucius in *Titus Andronicus,* introduced in *iii. 2.*

Lucius, brother of Antony, mentioned in *Antony and Cleopatra, i. 2,* as in alliance with Fulvia.

Lucius, Caius, general of the Roman forces in *Cymbeline,* introduced in *iii. 1,* where he demands payment of the tribute.

Lucius Pella, condemned for taking bribes, *Julius Cæsar, iv. 3.*

Luck, bad, an indication of want of piety, *Merry Wives of Windsor, iv. 5;* good, in odd numbers, *Merry Wives of Windsor, v. 1.* See OMENS.

Lucrece, a poem published in 1594, dedicated to the Earl of Southampton. The story on which it is founded is told by Ovid and Livy, and is given in the argument that Shakspere prefixed to the poem. Coleridge says:

"In this poem ['Venus and Adonis'] and 'The Rape of Lucrece' Shakspere gave ample proof of his possession of a most profound, energetic, and philosophical mind, without which he might have pleased, but could not have been a great dramatic poet."

References to Lucrece, *As You Like It, iii. 2, song; Taming of the Shrew, ii. 1; Twelfth Night, ii. 5.*

Lucretius, *Lucrece, l. 1751.*

Lucullus, one of the flattering lords in *Timon of Athens,* introduced in *iii. 1.* When Timon sends to him for a loan in this scene, he tries to bribe the servant to say to Timon that he had not been seen. Timon's servant calls him "Thou disease of a friend."

Lucy, Lady Elizabeth, *Richard III., iii. 7.*

Lucy, Sir William, character in *I. Henry VI.,* first appears in *iv. 3,* seeking reënforcements for Talbot.

Lucy, Sir Thomas, supposed allusion to, in *Merry Wives of Windsor, i. 1.* See LUCES and SHALLOW.

Ludlow Castle, an ancient and celebrated castle in Shropshire, where the young prince (Edward V.) was living with his uncle, Earl Rivers, *Richard III., ii. 2.* In the time of Elizabeth, the castle was in possession of the Sidney family.

Lud's-town (London), *Cymbeline, iii. 1; iv. 2.*

Lunatic, the, imagination of, *Midsummer-Night's Dream, v. 1,* speech of, *Cymbeline, v. 4.* See INSANE, INSANITY, MADNESS.

Lunes (insane freaks), *Merry Wives of Windsor, iv. 2; A Winter's Tale, ii. 2; Troilus and Cressida, ii. 3; Hamlet, iii. 3.*

Lupercal, feast of, *Julius Cæsar, i. 1; iii. 2.* In honour of Lupercus, a god of the woods and of shepherds, who was supposed to keep away wolves. It fell on February 15th.

Lurched (robbed), *Coriolanus, ii. 2.*

Lust, wicked fire of, *Merry Wives of Windsor, ii. 1;* though to an angel linked, *Hamlet, i. 5; Venus and Adonis, l. 794; Sonnet cxxix.*

Lustick (*lustig,* merry), *All's Well that Ends Well, ii. 3.*

Lute, pleasing of a, *Richard III., i. 1;* melancholy as a lover's, *I. Henry IV., i. 2;* broken over the teacher, *Taming of the Shrew, ii. 1;* music of the, *Henry VIII., iii. 1.*

Lutheran, a spleeny, *Henry VIII., iii. 2.*

Lux tua, etc., *Pericles, ii. 2.* Thy light is my life.

Lying, the world given to, *I. Henry IV., v. 3;* as easy as, *Hamlet, iii. 2;* becomes only tradesmen, *A Winter's Tale, iv. 3;* old men subject to the vice of, *II. Henry IV., iii. 2.*

Lychorida, nurse of Marina, in *Pericles,* first appears in *iii., chorus;* her death, *iv. 1.*

Lymoges, Archduke of Austria. See AUSTRIA.

Lycurgeses, *Coriolanus, ii. 1.*

Lym, a hunting-dog, *King Lear, iii. 6.*

Lysander, character in *Midsummer-Night's Dream,* introduced in *i. 1,* a lover of Hermia.

Lysimachus, governor of Mitylene, character in *Pericles,* first appears in *iv. 6;* betrothed to Marina, *v. 1* or *2.*

Mab, Queen, *Romeo and Juliet, i. 4.*

Macbeth is a drama sometimes placed first among the histories, but usually with the tragedies. It was included in the folio of 1623: the earliest known allusion to it was made in 1610; and the date of writing is placed between 1604 and 1610. The story is given mainly as it appears in Holinshed's "Chronicles." The circumstances of the assassination are found in Holinshed's account of the murder of

King Duff by Donwald and his wife in their castle at Fores. The time of the historical action is from 1039 to 1057; but Shakspere has crowded the events together for dramatic effect. Many castles are designated as the one in which Macbeth killed Duncan. Glamis Castle, five miles from Forfar, is one; Cawdor Castle, six miles from Nairn, is another; Fores Castle a third, and Macbeth's castle at Inverness a fourth. In Macbeth's time there were no castles of stone and mortar; timber and sods were the materials used. A castle built of these materials stood on an eminence southeast of Inverness. This was razed by Malcolm Canmore, son of Duncan, and a new one was built on another part of the hill. It was this castle that Dr. Johnson visited in 1773, supposing it to be the identical castle in which Duncan was murdered.

"While in 'Romeo and Juliet' and in 'Hamlet' we feel that Shakspere now began and now left off, and refined upon or brooded over his thoughts, Macbeth seems as if struck out at a heat, and imagined from first to last with unabated fervour. It is like a sketch by a great master in which everything is executed with rapidity and power, and a subtlety of workmanship which has become instinctive."—Dowden.

Macbeth, King of Scotland, is introduced in *i. 3* of the play, in the scene on the witches' heath; murders Duncan, *ii. 1*, and is made king; causes Banquo to be murdered, *iii. 1;* and Macduff's family, *iv. 1, 2;* meets the English army at Dunsinane, *Act v.*, and is slain by Macduff, *v. 8.* As a matter of fact, he was not killed at Dunsinane, but at Lumphanan two years later, in 1057. He is described by his wife in the fifth scene of the first act; his ambition has to contend with conscientious scruples; "What thou wouldst highly, that wouldst thou holily;" he is "too full of the milk of human kindness to catch the nearest way." These in the beginning are very nearly balanced; he dwells on the prophecy and the means by which he might realize it; on the other hand, he dwells on Duncan's character and the honours he had received from him. The scale inclines to the side of right, when his wife's influence is again exerted, and Duncan's death is resolved upon. Struggling with remorse of conscience, he confuses it, as Coleridge says, with the feeling of insecurity, and plunges into more crime in order to make himself safe in the results of the first. But his is not a character to be contented or happy in infamy; his conscience and his imagination work upon him till he is as if driven on by an irresistible fate, having "stepped so far in blood that returning were as tedious as going over." So possessed is he with despair, that the news of

his wife's death only draws from him the philosophy of hopeless-
ness:

> " And all our yesterdays have lighted fools
> The way to dusty death."

" Although it is difficult to separate the Macbeth of history from
the Macbeth of Shakspere and tradition, he appears to have ruled
Scotland well, and to have benefited the church in no small degree."
—DICTIONARY OF ENGLISH HISTORY.

Macbeth, Lady, character in *Macbeth*, introduced in *i. 5*, where
she promptly plans the murder of Duncan on hearing that he is to
sleep at her house; spurs on Macbeth to it, *i. 7;* places the daggers
by the guards, *ii. 2;* in the banquet scene, *iii. 4;* in the sleep-walk-
ing scene, *v. 1;* the doctor's report, *v. 3;* her death, *v. 5.* The
wife of Macbeth in history was the Lady Guroch, granddaughter
of Kenneth IV., and was a widow before her marriage with Macbeth.

" Lady Macbeth is of a finer and more delicate nature [than Mac-
beth]. Having fixed her eye upon an end—the attainment for her
husband of Duncan's crown—she accepts the inevitable means; she
nerves herself for the terrible night's work by artificial stimulants;
yet she cannot strike the sleeping king who resembles her father.
Having sustained her weaker husband, her own strength gives way;
and in sleep, when her will cannot control her thoughts, she is pite-
ously afflicted by the memory of one stain of blood upon her little
hand."—DOWDEN.

Macdonwald, a rebel against Duncan, vanquished and killed,
Macbeth, i. 2.

Macduff, Thane of Fife, an important character in *Macbeth*, introduced in *i. 6;* he discovers the murdered king, *ii. 1;* has fled to
England, *iv. 1;* confers with Malcolm and hears of the murder of
his family, *iv. 3;* slays Macbeth, *v. 8.* Macduff is loyal, slow to
suspect, and unambitious; but, when roused, he is resolute, brave,
and unbending. The remains of Macduff's castle are said to exist
about three miles from Dysart, in Fifeshire. Other ruins are also
pointed out as his castle.

Macduff, Lady, character in *Macbeth*, introduced in *iv. 2*, where
she witnesses the murder of her little son, and is pursued by the
murderers and afterward killed. The news carried to Macduff by
Rosse, *iv. 3.*

Macduff, the little son of, *Macbeth, iv. 2.*

Macedon, compared with Monmouth, *Henry V., iv. 7.*

Machiavel, *Merry Wives of Windsor, iii. 1: 1. Henry VI., u*

4; III. Henry VI., iii. 2. He was born in Italy in 1469. Henry VI. died in 1471.

MacMorris, Captain, character in *Henry V.*, first appears in *iii. 2.* He is an Irish captain, described by Fluellen as having "no more directions in the true discipline of the wars, look you, of the Roman disciplines, than is a puppy dog!"

Madmen, speech of, *Cymbeline, v. 4,* "Tongue and brain not"; imagination of, *Midsummer-Night's Dream, v. 1.*

Madness, symptoms and treatment of, *Comedy of Errors, iv. 4; Measure for Measure, iv. 4;* cause of, *Comedy of Errors, v. 1;* sense in, *Measure for Measure, v. 1;* letters of, *Twelfth Night, v. 1;* prayed for, *King John, iii. 4;* method in, *Hamlet, ii. 2;* like sweet bells jangled, *Hamlet, iii. 1;* a test of, *Hamlet, iii. 4,* "Ecstasy! My pulse," etc.; Ophelia's, *Hamlet, iv. 5* or *2;* harm done in, *Hamlet, v. 2,* "Give me your pardon," etc.; prayer concerning, *King Lear, i. 5;* he's that way, *King Lear, iii. 4;* remedy for, *King Lear, iv. 4;* reason in, *King Lear, iv. 6;* recovery from, *King Lear, iv. 7;* the error of the moon, *Othello, v. 2;* the world mad, *King John, ii. 2.* See INSANITY.

Madonna, the, appears to Joan, *I. Henry VI., i. 2.*

Magic, *The Tempest, i. 2; iii. 1–3;* music by, *The Tempest, iii. 2;* graves opened by—Prospero abjures, *The Tempest, v. 1.* See WITCHCRAFT.

Magician, Rosalind claims to be a, *As You Like It, v. 2;* Glendower a, *I. Henry IV., i. 3.*

Magistrate(s), of the people, a, *Coriolanus, iii. 1,* "Who puts his shall," etc.; petty, *Coriolanus, ii. 1.*

Magnanimity, toward enemies, *I. Henry IV., v. 5;* of a soldier, *Coriolanus, ii. 2.*

Magne Dominator poli, etc., *Titus Andronicus, iv. 1.* Great lord of the heaven, dost thou so leniently hear of wickedness? so leniently look upon it?

Magnificoes, *Merchant of Venice, iv. 1; Othello, i. 2.*

Magpie, the (magot-pie), *Macbeth, iii. 4;* (pie) *III. Henry VI., v. 6.*

Mahomet, inspired with a dove, *I. Henry VI., i. 2.* Alluding to the story that Mahomet had a tame dove, which he used to feed with wheat from his ear, and which he led his followers to believe was the Holy Spirit.

Mahu, a fiend, *King Lear, iii. 4; iv. 1.* The names of fiends in these two scenes and in *iii. 6* are said to be taken from a book by

214

one Harsnet, published in 1603, entitled "Declaration of Popish Impostures," and giving many details about witchcraft.

Maidenhood, *Midsummer-Night's Dream, ii. 1.* See ELIZABETH. It has also been supposed that the "little western flower" may refer to Lettice, Countess of Essex, with whom Leicester carried on an intrigue during her husband's absence in Ireland. The "mermaid on a dolphin's back," once interpreted as referring to Mary Queen of Scots, is now known to refer to a part of the exhibition given by Leicester at Kenilworth for Elizabeth's entertainment, in 1575, a mermaid on a dolphin's back with shooting fires.

Maiden(s), to travel alone, *As You Like It, i. 3;* when they sue, *Measure for Measure, i. 5;* flowers for, *A Winter's Tale, iv. 3* or *4;* advice to a, *Hamlet, i. 3; iii. 1.*

Maine, an ancient province in France, lost to England, *II. Henry VI., i. 1; iv. 1, 7.*

Majesty, will not endure boldness in a subject, *I. Henry IV., i. 3;* weariness under, *II. Henry IV., iv. 4;* sits not so easy, *II. Henry IV., v. 2;* interests dependent on, *Hamlet, iii. 3;* stoops to folly, *King Lear, i. 1.*

Make (do), *As You Like It, i. 1; ii. 2,* and elsewhere.

Makeless (mateless), *Sonnet ix.*

Malady, the lesser dwarfed by the greater, *King Lear, iii. 4.*

Malchus, of Arabia, *Antony and Cleopatra, iii. 6.*

Malcolm, afterward Malcolm III., surnamed Canmore, son of Duncan in *Macbeth,* introduced in *i. 2.* In *i. 4* he is named Prince of Cumberland, which was equivalent to being appointed successor to the throne; flees to England, *ii. 1;* makes accusations against himself to test Macduff, *iv. 3;* returns with his uncle Siward to fight against Macbeth, *v. 2;* is hailed as king, *v. 8.* He is represented as able and brave, though cautious and prudent; and this seems to have been the character of Malcolm III. in history, whose reign extended from 1058 to 1093. Canmore signifies "Great Head."

Maledictions, *The Tempest, i. 2; ii. 2; iii. 2; iv. 1; v. 1; Troilus and Cressida, ii. 1, 3; v. 1.* See CURSES.

Malevolence, expressed, *Coriolanus, iv. 5; Macbeth, iv. 3.*

Malice, nothing set down in, *Othello, v. 2.* See ENVY.

Mall, Mistress, *Twelfth Night, i. 3.* A character of Shakspere's time usually known as Mall Cutpurse. She dressed in man's clothing, and was the heroine of a play by Middleton and Dekker, "The Roaring Girl," which was acted at the Fortune Theatre and was published in 1611. Her real name was Mary Frith, and her chief exploit was the robbery of General Fairfax on Hounslow Heath, for which she was sent to Newgate.

Malmsey-Butt, *Richard III., i. 4.* Clarence has been called from this " Malmsey Clarence."

Malt-worms (drunkards), *I. Henry IV., ii. 1.*

Malvolio, Olivia's steward in *Twelfth Night,* introduced in *i. 5.* He is a fool of the solemn pompous order; conceited and Pharisaical. His puritanical precision incites the conspirators in the household to play their cruel practical jokes upon him, to which his conceit makes him fall an easy prey.

Mamilius, the little prince in *A Winter's Tale,* introduced in *i. 2;* his talk with the queen's ladies, *ii. 1;* his illness, *ii. 3;* his death in consequence of his mother's disgrace, *iii, 2.*

" And to the very end I must confess that I have in me so much of the spirit of Rachel weeping in Ramah as will not be comforted because Mamilius is not. It is well for those whose hearts are light enough to take perfect comfort in the substitution of his sister Perdita for the boy who died of 'thoughts high for one so tender.' Even the beautiful suggestion that Shakspere as he wrote had in mind his own dead little son still fresh and living at his heart, can hardly add more than a touch of additional tenderness to our perfect and piteous delight in him."—SWINBURNE.

Mammering (hesitating), *Othello, iii. 3.*

Mammet (puppet), *Romeo and Juliet, iii. 5.*

Mammock (tear to pieces), *Coriolanus, i. 3.*

Man, varnish of a complete, *Love's Labour's Lost, i. 2;* place for every, *All's Well that Ends Well, iv. 3;* God made him; therefore let him pass for a, *Merchant of Venice, i. 2;* a better, better spared, *I. Henry IV., v. 4;* a model, *II. Henry IV., ii. 3;* grace of, sought, *Richard III., iii. 4;* a, not honoured as man, *Troilus and Cressida, iii. 3;* one honest, *Timon of Athens, iv. 3,* " Had I a steward," etc.; nature might say this was a, *Julius Cæsar, v. 5;* died like a, *Macbeth, v. 7;* taken for all in all, *Hamlet, i. 2;* you cannot play upon a, *Hamlet, iii. 2;* to give the world assurance of a. *Hamlet, iii. 4;* what a piece of work is, *Hamlet, ii. 2;* capability of, *Hamlet, iv. 4* or *1;* more than wit, *King Lear, ii. 4;* unaccommodated (uncivilized), *King Lear, iii. 4;* life of a, tedious, *Cymbeline, iii. 6;* a, with a woman's beauty, *Sonnet xx.* See MEN.

Manage (behaviour), *As You Like It, i. 1.*

Mandragora (mandrake), a soporific, *Othello, iii. 3; Antony and Cleopatra, i. 5.*

Mandrake, the, superstition concerning—that it gave a shriek when pulled from the ground, and that an evil fate pursued the one that rooted it up, *II. Henry VI., iii. 2; Romeo and Juliet, iv. 3.*

Mandrake (a small person), *II. Henry IV., i. 2.*

Manhood, forgot on earth. *I. Henry IV., ii. 4;* degenerated, *Much Ado about Nothing, iv. 1;* is called foolery when it stands against a falling fabric, *Coriolanus, iii. 1.*

Manner, taken with the (in the act), *Love's Labour's Lost, i. 1; I. Henry IV., ii. 4.*

Manner, born to the, *Hamlet, i. 4.* The persistent miswriting of this word in the familiar quotation (making it *manor*) arises from a neglect to consider the context, and also from ignoring the fact that Hamlet was born, not to a manor, but to a whole kingdom.

Manners, of the court, in the country, *As You Like It, iii. 2;* rude, *Twelfth Night, iv. 1;* defect of, *I. Henry IV., iii. 1.*

Manningtree ox, *I. Henry IV., ii. 4.* Manningtree was a place in Essex, noted for fairs, where probably an ox had been roasted whole.

Mannishness, in a woman, *Troilus and Cressida, iii. 3.*

Mantle, a magic, *The Tempest. i. 2.*

Mantua, a city in northern Italy, scene of *Romeo and Juliet, v. 1.*

Mantuan, good old, *Love's Labour's Lost, iv. 2.* Battista Spagnolus (1443–1516), a writer of Latin verse.

Many, converging in one, *Henry V., i. 2.*

Map, a new, with the Indies, *Twelfth Night. iii. 2.* "A map to accompany Linschoten's 'Voyage,' published in England in 1598, the first in which the eastern islands were shown."

Marcellus, an officer in *Hamlet*, introduced in *i. 1.* He was a friend of Hamlet, and to him the ghost appeared before Horatio or Hamlet saw it. In the interpretation of the characters of the play alluded to under the name of the play, the character of Marcellus is thought to be meant for that of Sir Edward Dyer, friend of Sir Philip Sidney. See under the name of the play.

March, Earl of. See Mortimer and Edward IV.

March, the Ides of, the 15th, *Julius Cæsar, i. 2; iv. 3; v. 1.*

Marcians, the house of the, *Coriolanus, ii. 3.*

Marcius, Caius, afterward Coriolanus, *q. v.*

Marcius, Young, son of Coriolanus, introduced in *v. 3* of the drama; discussed in *i. 3.*

Marcus Andronicus, character in *Titus Andronicus*, brother of Titus. He enters in *i. 1*, where he announces the choice of Titus as emperor; his grief and generosity, *ii. 4 or 5; iii. 1.*

Mardian, an attendant of Cleopatra in *Antony and Cleopatra*, introduced in *i. 5.*

Margarelon, Priam's natural son, introduced in *Troilus and Cressida, v. 8.*

Margaret, a gentlewoman attending on Hero in *Much Ado about Nothing*, introduced in *ii. 1*, who is mistaken by the watching prince and Claudio for Hero while she is talking to Borachio from the chamber-window of her mistress.

Margaret of Anjou, queen of Henry VI., and daughter of Regnier (René), King of Naples, Sicily, and Jerusalem, character in the three parts of *Henry VI.* and in *Richard III.*, first appearing in *I. Henry VI., v. 3*, where Suffolk has captured and fallen in love with her, and forms the plan of marrying her to Henry VI. The betrothal follows in *v. 5.* Her contempt for the king is expressed in the second part, *i. 3*, as well as her jealousy of the Duchess of Gloucester, to whom she gives in this scene a box on the ear; her affection for Suffolk, *iii. 2.* In the third part, *i. 1*, she resolves to raise an army, in her wrath at Henry for disinheriting their son. She defeated the Yorkists at Wakefield, *i. 3–5*, where York was slain, but suffered defeat at Mortimer's Cross, Towton, *ii. 3–6*, Barnet, *v. 2, 3*, and lastly at Tewksbury, *v. 4, 5*, where her son was killed. The Margaret of the play is coarse, fierce, revengeful, unprincipled. But her love for Suffolk is not in history, neither is there sufficient evidence that she had a hand in Gloucester's death, nor any that she stabbed York. She was confined in the Tower from 1471 to 1475, when she was ransomed by Louis XI., and lived in France till her death in 1482. It is therefore contrary to history to introduce her in the reign of Richard, which began in 1483; but her presence is dramatically effective, as she appears only to curse and watch with greedy eyes for the fulfilment of her curses, *Richard III., i. 3; iv. 4.*

Margery Jourdain. See JOURDAIN.

Maria, one of the ladies attending on the princess in *Love's Labour's Lost*, first appears in *ii. 1.*

Maria, Olivia's waiting-maid in *Twelfth Night*, introduced in *i. 3*, a keen, shrewd, witty woman, who captures Sir Toby Belch through her cleverness in putting up the practical joke on Malvolio.

Marian, Maid, *I. Henry IV., iii. 3.* The companion of Robin Hood, and a leading character in the morris-dance, where the part was generally taken by a man. Hence a name for a masculine woman.

Mariana, a character in *Measure for Measure*, first mentioned in *iii. 1*, introduced in *iv. 1*, at "the moated grange at St. Luke's," after she has been betrothed to Angelo and deserted by him—a pitiable character. In the original story, the part she takes in the play was united with that of Isabella.

Mariana, an unimportant character in *All's Well that Ends Well, iii. 5.*

Marigold (sunflower), *A Winter's Tale, iv. 3* or *4.*

Marina, daughter of Pericles and Thaisa, introduced in the chorus of the third act of *Pericles* as an infant; left at Tharsus, *iii. 3;* plot against her, prologue and first scene of *Act iv;* in Mitylene, *iv. 2* or *3, 6;* her epitaph, *iv. 4;* her accomplishments, prologue to *Act v.;* meets her father, *v. 1;* betrothed to Lysimachus, *v. 1* or *2.*

"She is indeed a nature that appears capable of remaining unsullied amid the impurest, and, as her persecutor says, 'of making a puritan of the devil.' "—GERVINUS.

Marjoram, *Sonnet xcix.*

Mark, God save the, *Romeo and Juliet, iii. 2, and elsewhere.* The meaning is doubtful. It has been suggested that mark may mean omen—save from the disaster threatened. Another suggestion is that it means the cross, the mark of the cross.

Mark Antony, his genius rebuked by Cæsar, *Macbeth, iii. 1.* See ANTONIUS.

Market, the, ended, *Love's Labour's Lost, iii. 1.* Alluding to the proverb, "Three women and a goose make a market."

Marle, a French earl, mentioned in *Henry V., iv. 8.*

Marlowe, Christopher (born in the same year with Shakspere, 1564, died in 1593), quoted, *Merry Wives of Windsor, iii. 1; As You Like It, iii. 5.* See AUTHORSHIP and PASSIONATE PILGRIM, THE.

Marmoset, the, *The Tempest, ii. 2.*

Marriage(s), rite of, *The Tempest, iv. 1; v. 1;* proposals of, *Merry Wives of Windsor, i. 1;* mercenary motives for, *Merry Wives of Windsor, iii. 2, 4;* without love, *Merry Wives of Windsor, v. 5, near the end;* railings against, *Much Ado about Nothing, i. 3; ii. 1, 3; v. 4;* goes by destiny, *Merchant of Venice, ii. 9; As You Like It, iii. 3;* coldness in, *As You Like It, iv. 1;* a world-without-end bargain, *Love's Labour's Lost, iv. 3;* a mad, *Taming of the Shrew, iii. 2;* disparity of years in, *Twelfth Night, ii. 4;* reasons for, *All's Well that Ends Well, i. 3;* offer of, from a lady, *All's Well that Ends Well, ii. 3;* a distasteful, *All's Well that Ends Well, ii. 3, end;* unfaithfulness in, *A Winter's Tale, i. 2;* a father's counsel concerning, *A Winter's Tale, iv. 3;* second, *A Winter's Tale, v. 1;* treaty of

King John, ii. 1 or *2;* promise of, *II. Henry IV., ii. 1;* God the best maker of, *Henry V., v.;* contract of, *I. Henry VI., v. 1, 5;* proposed, *I. Henry VI., v. 3;* forced, *I. Henry VI., v. 5;* by proxy, *II. Henry VI., i. 1;* hasty, *III. Henry VI., iv. 1;* with a sister-in-law, *Henry VIII., ii. 4;* of Romeo and Juliet, *ii. 6;* proposed, *Romeo and Juliet, iii. 5;* an abhorred, *Romeo and Juliet, iv. 1;* of a newly-made widow, *Hamlet, i. 2;* state considerations in, *Hamlet, i. 3;* no more, to be, *Hamlet, iii. 1;* second, *Hamlet, iii. 2,* player queen; motives in, *King Lear, i. 1;* justification of a secret, *Othello, i. 3;* of Antony and Octavia, *Antony and Cleopatra, ii. 2, 6;* of Imogen, *Cymbeline, i. 1;* urged, *Sonnets i.-xvii.;* of true minds, *Sonnet cxvi;* ceremony of, *Twelfth Night, v. 1;* hands, not hearts, *Othello, iii. 4.*

Married man, Benedick the, *Much Ado about Nothing, i. 1; v. 1.*

Marry, an exclamation used in numberless cases, said to be a corruption of Mary.

Marry-trap, *Merry Wives of Windsor, i. 1.* Hudson says it seems to have been a word of triumph in seeing one caught in his own snare.

Mars, of malcontents, *Merry Wives of Windsor, i. 3, end;* novices of, *All's Well that Ends Well, ii. 1;* the file of, *All's Well that Ends Well, iii. 3;* fear of, *All's Well that Ends Well, iv. 1;* in swaddling-clothes, *I. Henry IV., iii. 2;* drave, to faction, *Troilus and Cressida, iii. 3;* invoked, *Coriolanus, i. 4;* an eye like, *Hamlet, iii. 4;* in love, *Venus and Adonis, l. 98.* The Roman god of war.

Mars (planet), born under, *All's Well that Ends Well, i. 1;* his true moving, *I. Henry VI., i. 2.* The irregularities in the movements of the planet Mars, consequent on the eccentricity of his orbit, were puzzling to astronomers until Kepler's "New Astronomy; or, Commentaries on the Motions of Mars" appeared in 1609.

Marseilles, France, the scene of a part of *All's Well that Ends Well.*

Marshal, the lord, in *Richard II., i. 3,* was the Duke of Surrey, who temporarily filled the place, the office being held by Norfolk, one of the combatants.

Marshalsea, prison in Southwark, *Henry VIII., v. 4.*

Mart (bargain), *Hamlet, i. 1.*

Martext, Sir Oliver, a vicar in *As You Like It,* determined that "ne'er a fantastical knave of them all shall flout me out of my calling." For the use of the title Sir, see under EVANS.

Martin, St., summer of, *I. Henry VI., i. 2.* Fair weather in late autumn—Indian summer.

Martius, character in *Titus Andronicus,* son of Titus, introduced in *i. 1* or *2,* is taken for the murderer of Bassianus, *ii.* or *4;* executed, *iii. 1.*

Martlemas (Martinmas, November 11th), *II. Henry IV., ii. 2.* Applied to an old man given to gaiety, because it was the time of St. Martin's or Indian summer.

Martlet, the temple-haunting, chooses delicate air, *Macbeth, i. 6;* builds on the outward wall, *Merchant of Venice. ii. 9.*

Marullus, one of the tribunes in *Julius Cæsar.* first appears in *i. 1,* where he rebukes the people for forgetting Pompey. He and Flavius tore the scarfs and badges from Cæsar's images, and were put to silence, *i. 2.*

Mary, Princess, afterward queen (1553–'58). *Henry VIII., iv. 2.*

Mary, the Virgin, *Richard II., ii. 1; Henry VIII. v. 2.*

Mary, Queen of Scots. See MAIDENHOOD.

Mask(s), sun-expelling, *Two Gentlemen of Verona, iv. 4;* black, *Measure for Measure, ii. 4; Romeo and Juliet, i. 1.* They were worn by gentlewomen to protect their faces from the sun and at the theatre.

Masque, a, *Timon of Athens, i. 2.*

Masquerades, *Much Ado about Nothing, ii. 1; Love's Labour's Lost, v. 2; Romeo and Juliet, i. 4, 5; Merchant of Venice, ii. 6; Henry VIII., i. 4.*

Mass, evening, *Romeo and Juliet, iv. 1.*

Master and men, influence of, on one another, *II. Henry IV., v. 1,* "It is a wonderful thing," etc.

Master-gunner, of Orleans, and his son, characters in *I. Henry VI., i. 4.*

Masters, all cannot be, *Othello, i. 1.*

Match, set a (arranged an expedition ?), *I. Henry IV., i. 2.*

Mated (bewildered), *Comedy of Errors, iii. 2; v. 1;* my mind has, *Macbeth, v. 1.*

Material fool, a, *As You Like It, iii. 3.* A fool with matter in him, or a fool in what is material or essential.

Mathematics, *Taming of the Shrew, i. 1.*

Matron, evil passion in a, *Hamlet, iii. 4.*

Maund (a small basket), *Lover's Complaint, l. 36.*

May, as full of spirit as the month of, *I. Henry IV., iv. 1;* of life, fallen into the sere the yellow leaf, *Macbeth, v. 3;* of youth,

Henry V., i. 2; allusions to the sports of, *Midsummer-Night's Dream, i. 1; iv. 1; Twelfth Night, iii. 4; All's Well that Ends Well, ii. 2; Henry VIII., v. 3.*

Mayor of London, in *I. Henry VI.,* first appears in *i. 3.* His name was John Coventry.

Mayor of London, character in *Richard III.,* first appears in *iii. 1.* Sir Edward Shaw, brother of the Doctor Shaw that is mentioned in *iii. 5.*

Mayor of London, *Henry VIII., iv. 1; v. 4.* Sir Stephen Peacocke.

Mayors of York, Coventry, and St. Alban's. See YORK, COVENTRY, and ST. ALBAN'S.

Mean, advantage of being, in that of fortune, *Merchant of Venice, i. 2;* Nature makes the mean that makes her better, *A Winter's Tale, iv. 3.*

Mean (tenor), *Love's Labour's Lost, v. 2; A Winter's Tale, iv. 2 or 3; Two Gentlemen of Verona, i. 2.*

Means, living beyond one's, *Merchant of Venice, i. 1;* slender, *II. Henry IV., i. 2;* too humble for the mind, *Richard III., iv. 2;* wasted, *Othello, iv. 2.*

Meagreness, *II. Henry IV., iii. 2; v. 4.* See LEANNESS.

Mealed (sprinkled), *Measure for Measure, iv. 2.*

Measles (distemper), *Coriolanus, iii. 1.*

Measure, to tread a, *Love's Labour's Lost, v. 2; As You Like It, v. 4.* A slow, stately dance.

Measure for Measure, first published in 1623, is referred to the period that produced the greater plays, *Julius Cæsar, Hamlet, Othello, Macbeth,* and *King Lear,* and is supposed to have been written about the year 1603. The plot, originally from a story in the "Hecatommithi" of Giraldi Cinthio, was the foundation of a play, "Promos and Cassandra," published in 1578, by George Whetstone, who afterward translated the Italian story for his "Heptameron of Civil Discourses," 1582. The most notable change made by Shakspere in the plot was the introduction of the character of Mariana, thus doing away with a repulsive feature of the old plot, the marrying of Isabella (Cassandra) to Angelo (Promos). Notwithstanding the repellent story and the disgusting nature of most of the humour, this is in many respects a very noble play—in the general tone of thought in the serious scenes, the strength and purity of Isabella's character, the subtlety with which Angelo's is drawn, and the beauty of single passages. The scene is laid in Vienna, at about the year

1485, the date being fixed by the allusion to Corvinus, King of Hungary, in *i. 2*, who in that year took Vienna. Cinthio lays the scene in Innspruck; Whetstone in Julio, Hungary.

Meats, influence of, on temper, *Taming of the Shrew, iv. 1, 3.* An old book, "The Glasse of Humours," says that a choleric man should "abstain from all salt, scorched, dry meats, from mustard, and such things as will aggravate his malignant humours." See BEEF.

Mecænas, character in *Antony and Cleopatra*, introduced in *ii. 2*, a friend of Cæsar.

Mechanics, to wear the signs of their trades, *Julius Cæsar, i. 1.*

Medea, *Merchant of Venice, v. 1; II. Henry VI., v. 2.* Fleeing from Colchis with her lover Jason, she was pursued by her father; and to gain time she caused her little brother Absyrtus to be killed and his limbs to be thrown on the water, that her father, in stopping to collect them, might be detained long enough to allow of her escape.

Meddlers, *Timon of Athens, iv. 3; Hamlet, iii. 4; v. 2.*

Meddle nor make, *Troilus and Cressida, i. 1.*

Medice, etc., *Henry VI., ii. 1.* Physician, heal thyself.

Medicine, theory and practice of, allusions to: lives consist of the four elements, *Twelfth Night, ii. 3;* bleeding, *Love's Labour's Lost, ii. 1; Richard II., i. 1;* diagnosis by urine, *Two Gentlemen of Verona, ii. 1; Twelfth Night, iii. 4; II. Henry IV., i. 2; Macbeth, v. 3;* a miracle in, *All's Well that Ends Well, ii. 3;* read in Galen, *II. Henry IV., i. 2.* See under ARTERIES, BLOOD, CIRCULATION OF THE, DISEASES, DIGESTION, INSANITY, MEDICINES, PHYSICIANS, POISONS, SURGERY.

Medicine (physician), a, *All's Well that Ends Well, ii. 1.*

Medicines: narcotics, *Othello, iii. 3; Antony and Cleopatra, i. 5; Cymbeline, iv. 2;* aqua vitæ, *A Winter's Tale, iv. 3; Romeo and Juliet, iv. 5;* sherris, *II. Henry IV., iv. 3;* balm, *III. Henry VI., iv. 3; Troilus and Cressida, i. 1; Timon of Athens, iii. 5;* liquid gold, *The Tempest, v. 1* (grand liquor); *All's Well that Ends Well, v. 3; II. Henry IV., iv. 4;* mummy (a medicine made from embalmed bodies), *Othello, iii. 4;* eisel or vinegar (to prevent contagion), *Sonnet cxi.;* recipe for, *All's Well that Ends Well, i. 3; ii. 1;* plantain-leaf, *Love's Labour's Lost, iii. 1; Romeo and Juliet, i. 2;* parmaceti, *I. Henry IV., i. 3;* cobweb, *Midsummer-Night's Dream, iii. 1;* flax and whites of eggs, *King Lear, iii. 7;* catharucs, *As You Like It, iii. 2; Richard II., i. 1; Henry VI., i. 3; iii. 2; iv. 4; Coriolanus, iii. 1; Macbeth, v. 3; Sonnet cxviii.*

Mediterranean Sea, the, *Love's Labour's Lost, v. 1.*

Medlar, the true virtue of the, *As You Like It, iii. 2.*

Meeting, when shall we three meet again, *Macbeth, i. 1.* See WELCOME.

Mehercle (by Hercules?), *Love's Labour's Lost, iv. 2.*

Meiny (servants), *King Lear, ii. 4.*

Melancholy, kinsman to despair, *Comedy of Errors, v. 1;* Count John's, *Much Ado about Nothing, i. 3; ii. 1;* not conducive to long life, *Love's Labour's Lost, v. 2;* turn, to funerals, *Midsummer-Night's Dream, i. 1;* out of a song, *As You Like It, ii. 5;* kinds of, *As You Like It, iv. 1;* nurse of frenzy, *Taming of the Shrew, induction, 2;* trick of, *All's Well that Ends Well, iii. 2;* a surly spirit, *King John, iii. 3;* fashion of, *King John, iv. 1;* similes for, *I. Henry IV., i. 2;* cursed, *I. Henry IV., ii. 3;* effect of, *Hamlet, ii. 2; iii. 1;* power of, *Cymbeline, iv. 2;* constant, *Pericles, i. 2.*

Melford, commons of, *II. Henry VI., i. 3.*

Melun, a French lord in *King John,* introduced in *v. 2.* He is said by Matthew Paris to have disclosed to some of the English barons before his death, which took place in London, that Louis and sixteen earls and barons of France had secretly sworn, that if Louis should conquer England and be crowned king, all the English nobility should be killed, banished, or imprisoned as traitors and rebels, he himself being one of the sixteen. The dauphin's oath is in the old play.

Memory, made a sinner, *The Tempest, i. 2;* warder of the brain, *Macbeth. i. 7;* of things precious, *Macbeth, iv. 3;* devoted to one subject, *Hamlet, i. 5;* of old woes, *Sonnet xxx.;* of the beloved, *Sonnet cxxii.;* ventricle of the, see VENTRICLE.

Memory (memorial), *Coriolanus, v. 1.*

Memphis, pyramid of, *I. Henry VI., v. 6.*

Men, a bill for putting down, *Merry Wives of Windsor, ii. 1;* supremacy of, *Comedy of Errors, ii. 1;* why scanted of hair, *Comedy of Errors, ii. 2;* what they dare do, *Much Ado about Nothing, iv. 1;* should be thankful not to be beasts, *Love's Labour's Lost, iv. 2;* girls dressed like, *As You Like It, i. 3;* more fickle than women, *Twelfth Night, ii. 4;* not three good, unhanged, *I. Henry IV., ii. 4;* no faith in, *Romeo and Juliet, iii. 2;* summer-birds, *Timon of Athens, iii. 6;* ranks of, *Macbeth, iii. 1;* inconstancy of, *Othello, iii. 4,* "'Tis not a year or two," etc.: marble minds of, *Lucrece, l.*

1240; old, of less truth than tongue, *Sonnet xvii;* best are moulded out of faults, *Measure for Measure, v. 1;* are as the time is, *King Lear, v. 3.* See MAN.

Menaphon, Duke, mentioned in *Comedy of Errors, v. 1.*

Menas, character in *Antony and Cleopatra,* introduced in *ii. 1,* a friend of Pompey, a pirate.

Menecrates, character in *Antony and Cleopatra,* introduced in *ii. 1,* a friend of Pompey, a pirate.

Menelaus, brother of Agamemnon, character in *Troilus and Cressida,* introduced in *i. 3,* the husband of Helen. Spoken of also in *III. Henry VI., ii. 2.*

Menenius Agrippa, character in *Coriolanus,* appears in *i. 1,* as an ambassador from the patricians to the people; description of himself, *ii. 1;* refused, *v. 2.* In Plutarch, he is said to have been the pleasantest old man in the senate, but nothing further is given of him except the fact of his telling the fable in *i. 1.* He is an admiring friend of Coriolanus, a fluent talker, witty, good-humoured, discreet, and persuasive.

Menteith, Earl of, *I. Henry IV., i. 1.*

Menteith, a thane of Scotland, character in *Macbeth,* appears in *v. 2, 4,* and *7.*

Me perdonato, *Taming of the Shrew, i. 1.* I being pardoned, or *perdonate,* pardon me.

Mephistopheles, *Merry Wives of Windsor, i. 1.* Here used for an ugly fellow.

Me pompæ, etc., *Pericles, ii. 2.* Glory leads me on.

Mercade, a lord attending on the princess in *Love's Labour's Lost,* appears only in the last scene.

Mercatante (merchant), *Taming of the Shrew, iv. 2.*

Mercatio, the rich, mentioned in *Two Gentlemen of Verona, i. 2,* as one of Julia's suitors.

Merchant, a, character in the *Comedy of Errors,* introduced in *i. 2,* a friend to Antipholus of Syracuse.

Merchant, a, character in *Timon of Athens, i. 1,* where he is seeking patronage.

Merchant of Venice, the, a comedy known to have been acted before 1598, and probably the same as "The Venesyon Comedy," acted August 25, 1594. The internal indications are that it was written as early as the latter year, though the date has been placed as late as 1596. It was first published in 1600. No earlier tale or play is now known that unites the two stories contained in this play—that of the pound of flesh and that of the three caskets. But one Stephen Gosson, who published his "School of Abuse" in 1579, mentions a play, "The Jew," which represented "the greediness of worldly chusers, and bloody minds of usurers." So that Shakspere may have taken his plot directly from this forgotten drama. Both of the stories are very old. That of the pound of flesh, Mr. Collier says, is unquestionably of Oriental origin. It was told by Giovanni Fiorentino in 1378 in a collection of tales, "Il Pecorone," the circumstances very much resembling those of the play; in the "Orator," by Alexander Silvayn, translated into English in 1598, and in some old ballads, "The Northern Lord" and "Gernutus, the Jew of Venice." The story of the three caskets is in the Greek romance of "Barlaam and Josephat," about 800; and was again told in the "Gesta Romanorum," translated in 1577, where the story is entitled "Ancelmus the Emperour." The time of action is Shakspere's own day; the scene, Venice and Portia's house at Belmont, somewhere on the Continent, probably. The name Belmont is the same used in the story from "Il Pecorone."

Mercury, god of lying, commerce, and thievery, and messenger of Jupiter, *Twelfth Night, i. 5 ; King John, iv. 2 ; I. Henry IV., iv. 1 ; Troilus and Cressida, ii. 3 ; Hamlet, iii. 4 ; A Winter's Tale, iv. 2 ; Henry V., ii., chorus ; Richard III., ii. 1.*

Mercutio, friend of Romeo, first appears in *i. 4.* In *iii. 1* he is slain by Tybalt, who has been seeking a quarrel with Romeo. See ROMEO.

"Wit ever wakeful, fancy busy and procreative as an insect, courage, an easy mind that, without cares of its own, is at once disposed to laugh away those of others, and yet to be interested in them—these and all congenial qualities, melting into the common copula of them all, the man of rank and the gentleman, with all its excellences and its weaknesses, constitute the character of Mercutio!"—COLERIDGE.

Mercy, assaulted by prayer, *The Tempest, epilogue ;* obligation to, *The Tempest, v. 1,* "And shall not myself," etc.; mistaken, *Measure for Measure, ii. 1,* "Mercy is not itself," etc.; becomes the great—of Heaven, *Measure for Measure, ii. 2 ;* devilish, *Measure for Measure, iii. 1 ;* when made by vice, *Measure for Measure, iv. 2 ;* recommended to Shylock, *Merchant of Venice, iii. 3 ; iv. 1 ;* the better part made, *As You Like It, iii. 1 ;* beyond the infinite reach of, *King John, iv. 3 ;* for small and great offences, *Henry V., ii. 2 ;* a vice of, *Troilus and Cressida, v. 3 ;* at differences with honour, *Coriolanus, v. 3 ;* nobility's badge, *Titus Andronicus, i. 1 or 2 ;* to murderers, *Romeo and Juliet, iii. 1, end;* emboldens sin, *Timon of Athens, iii. 5;* show no, *Timon of Athens, iv. 3,* "That, by killing," etc.; whereto serves, but to confront the visage of offence, *Hamlet, iii. 3;* to the falling, *Henry VIII., iii. 2.*

Mered (limited), *Antony and Cleopatra, iii. 10* or *12.*

Merit, honours not purchased by, *Merchant of Venice, ii. 9;* value without, *Troilus and Cressida, ii. 2;* often overlooked, on account of one defect, *Hamlet, i. 4;* seldom justly attributed, *All's Well that Ends Well, iii. 6;* men of, sought after, *II. Henry IV., ii. 4;* far beyond recompense, *Macbeth, i. 4.*

Merlin, prophecies of, *I. Henry IV., iii. 1; King Lear, iii. 2, end.* See PROPHECIES.

Mermaid, music of a, *Comedy of Errors, iii. 2; Midsummer-Night's Dream, ii. 1; III. Henry VI., iii. 2; Hamlet, iv. 7; Venus and Adonis, l. 429.*

Merops, son of, *Two Gentlemen of Verona, iii. 1.* Phaethon.

Merriman, a hunting-dog, *Taming of the Shrew, induction, 1.*

Merry Wives of Windsor, The, a comedy written as we have it probably between 1598 and 1601, though an allusion in *iv. 3* has led some to suppose that it was written in or soon after 1592, because then free post-horses were given, by order of Lord Howard, to a German duke who passed through Windsor. There is no reason, however, for supposing that the event might not have been alluded to several years after its occurrence. A plausible explanation is that the play, in an early form which has come down to us, was written at the former date; while the amended form was later, perhaps even after the accession of James I. (See KNIGHTS.) One John Dennis, who remodelled the play in 1702 for the stage, says in the dedication that it was written in fourteen days at the request of Queen Elizabeth; and another writer adds that it was because she wished to see Falstaff as a lover. The plot is not known to have been drawn from any other, though some of the incidents had been used before. That between Falstaff and Ford in disguise is said to be in Fiorentino's "Art of Loving," and in Straparola's "Ring." The time is probably before the death of Henry IV., since Falstaff is spoken of as being still in favour at court. There has been considerable controversy, both as to the time when this play was written, and as to its place in the series that include the characters of Falstaff, Mrs. Quickly, Pistol, Nym, and Bardolph. Difficulties are met with under every supposition possible. Some, but few, have supposed the Falstaff of the *Merry Wives of Windsor* not to be the same as the Falstaff of the historical plays, who, as is well known, was at first called Oldcastle. There is more reason to suppose that there are two Mistress Quicklys. The question is of little importance.

Messes (grades), *A Winter's Tale, i. 2.*

Messala, a friend of Brutus and Cassius in *Julius Cæsar,* first appears in *iv. 3,* bringing news of Portia's death.

Messaline (Mitylene?), *Twelfth Night, ii. 1.*

Messenger, a, is what he knows, *Antony and Cleopatra, ii. 5;* of ill news, *The Tempest, ii. 1; II. Henry IV., i. 1; Antony and Cleopatra, ii. 5; Macbeth, v. 5;* of good news, *Merchant of Venice, ii. 9; I. Henry IV., i. 1.*

Messina, Sicily, scene of *Much Ado about Nothing,* and a part of *Antony and Cleopatra.* Pompey had a house there, *ii. 1.*

Metaphysical (supernatural), *Macbeth, i. 5.*

Metaphysics, *Taming of the Shrew, i. 1.*

Meteors, his heart's, *Comedy of Errors, iv. 2.* Allusion to meteors imagined to look like armies meeting; ominous, *Richard II., ii. 4; I. Henry IV., ii. 4;* over a ship, *The Tempest, i. 2,* "To every article," etc.; *Romeo and Juliet, iii. 5; King John, v. 2.*

Metellus Cimber, one of the conspirators in *Julius Cæsar,* first appears in *ii. 1.* His suit to Cæsar for the recall of his banished brother, *iii. 1,* was made the occasion for the assassins to gather about Cæsar.

Mettle, of the English, *Henry V., iii. 5;* undaunted, *Macbeth, i. 7;* of a king, *King John, ii. 2.*

Michael, Sir, a friend of the archbishop in *I. Henry IV.,* appears only in *iv. 4.*

Michael, one of the followers of Jack Cade in his insurrection, *II. Henry VI., iv. 2, 3.*

Michaelmas, *Merry Wives of Windsor, i. 1; I. Henry IV., ii. 4.* The feast of St. Michael, September 29th. The custom of eating roast goose on that day was at least as early as the fifteenth century. It was also the day for choosing civil magistrates.

Micher (truant), *I. Henry IV., ii. 4.*

Miching mallecho (sly mischief), *Hamlet, iii. 2.*

Middle-earth (the natural world), *Merry Wives of Windsor, v. 5.*

Midnight, almost fairy-time, *Midsummer-Night's Dream, v. 1;* business at, *Henry VIII., v. 1;* the witching time of night, *Hamlet, iii. 2;* going to bed after, *Twelfth Night, ii. 3.*

Midsummer madness, *Twelfth Night, iii. 4.*

Midsummer-Night's Dream, A, a comedy in which three sets of actors appear—the Duke of Athens and his friends, the Athenian handicraftsmen, and the fairy-people. It was first published in 1600, but was mentioned in 1598, and is thought to have been written between 1594 and 1598, and by some authorities even as early as 1592. Possibly some other dramatist assisted Shakspere in the scenes between the lovers. The life of Theseus in Plutarch may have given some suggestions for the play; and for the part of the fairies some hints may have been furnished by a little book mentioned under PUCK. The scene of the action is ostensibly Athens, and the time three days, ending at midnight of the 1st of May; but time and place are entirely disregarded.

"The epilogue expresses satisfaction if the spectator will regard the piece as a dream; for in a dream time and locality are obliterated; a certain twilight and dusk is spread over the whole. . . . We have before said that the piece appears designed to be treated as a dream; not merely in outer form and colouring, but also in inner signification. The errors of that blind intoxication of the senses, which form the main point of the play, appear to us to be an allegorical picture of the errors of a life of dreams."—GERVINUS.

Mighty, the, dead, *I. Henry VI., ii. 2; iii. 2; Julius Cæsar, iii. 1; v. 5; Coriolanus, v. 5; Antony and Cleopatra, v. 1, 2.*

Milan, Duke of, Prospero, in *The Tempest.*

Milan, Duke of, the father of Silvia in the *Two Gentlemen of Verona,* introduced in *ii. 4.*

Mile-End Green, *All's Well that Ends Well, iv. 3; II. Henry IV., iii. 2.* A place for sports and musters.

Milford-Haven, Wales, *Cymbeline, iii. 2;* scene of, *iii. 4.*

Milk of human kindness, the, *Macbeth, i. 5.*

Miller, Yead, mentioned in *Merry Wives of Windsor, i. 1.*

Milliner, *A Winter's Tale, iv. 3* or *4.* Men were milliners in Shakspere's time.

Mill-sixpences, *Merry Wives of Windsor, i. 1.* They were used as counters.

Millstones, wept, *Richard III., i. 3, 4; Troilus and Cressida, i. 2.*

Milo, *Troilus and Cressida, ii. 3.* An athlete of Crotona, a Greek city of southern Italy, one of whose feats was the carrying of a living bull on his shoulders through the race-course at Olympia. He was born about 520 B. C., and was therefore some hundreds of years before the Trojan war.

Mind, the, affected by food, *Love's Labour's Lost, i. 1;* makes the body rich, *Taming of the Shrew, iv. 3;* contempt for the work of the, *Troilus and Cressida, i. 3;* tempest in the, *King Lear, iii. 4;* infected, diseased, *Macbeth, v. 1, 3;* a noble, o'erthrown, *Hamlet, iii. 1;* no art to find its construction in the face, *Macbeth, i. 4;* fearless, climb soonest into crowns, *III. Henry VI., iv. 7.*

Mine eye and heart are at a mortal war, *Sonnet xlvi.*

Mine eye hath played the painter, *Sonnet xxiv.*

Mineral (mine), *Hamlet, iv. 1,* or *iii. 5.*

Minerva, goddess of wisdom, *Taming of the Shrew, i. 1.*

Mines (undermines), *As You Like It, i. 1.*

Minim's rest, a, *Merry Wives of Windsor, i. 3.* A minim is a half-note in music.

Minister, services of a king's, *A Winter's Tale, iv. 1* or *2.*

Minnows, *Love's Labour's Lost, i. 1;* Sicinius a Triton of the, *Coriolanus, iii. 1.*

Minola. See BAPTISTA.

Minos, King of Crete, *III. Henry VI., v. 6.*

Minotaurs, *I. Henry VI., v. 3.* The minotaur was a fabled monster in Crete, having a human head and the body of a bull. It roamed through a labyrinth made by Dædalus, and was fed with human victims.

Miracle-plays and Moralities, the, allusions to. See HEROD, TERMAGANT, VICE.

Miracle(s), past, *All's Well that Ends Well, ii. 1, 3; Henry V., i. 1;* a pretended, *II. Henry VI., ii. 1;* thy life's a, *King Lear, iv. 6.*

Miranda, the heroine of *The Tempest,* one of the most exquisite characters in the dramas. Brought up away from society and with no teacher but her father, she is natural, unconventional, but full of native grace and dignity.

"She is one of those quiet natures whose mental worth is closed as within a bud, whose depth of character is hidden, like the fire of the diamond, until the occasion comes which strips off the concealing husk, and reveals the richness and splendour of the inner life. Reared in solitude. she is like a blank leaf as regards all social gifts and conventional accomplishments. She is quiet and of few words, but her fancy is full of inward life and playfulness, and her pure soul uninjured by intercourse with mankind."

"I do not know a more wonderful instance of Shakspere's mastery in playing a distinctly rememberable variety on the same remembered air, than in the transporting love-confessions of Romeo and Juliet and Ferdinand and Miranda. There seems more passion in the one and more dignity in the other; yet you feel that the sweet girlish lingering and busy movement of Juliet, and the calmer and more maidenly fondness of Miranda, might easily pass into each other."—COLERIDGE.

Mirth, a man of, *Love's Labour's Lost, ii. 1;* tears of, *Midsummer-Night's Dream, v. 1;* goes all the day, *A Winter's Tale, iv. 2;* rather have a fool to make, *As You Like It, iv. 1;* away from home, *Henry V., i. 2;* exhortations to, *Merchant of Venice, i. 1; ii. 2; Midsummer-Night's Dream, i. 1; Taming of the Shrew, induction, 2; A Winter's Tale, iv. 3; I. Henry IV., ii. 4; Macbeth, iii. 4;* a light heart lives long, *Love's Labour's Lost, i. 2;* all, from the crown of the head to the sole of the foot, *Much Ado about Nothing, iii. 2;* of a child, *A Winter's Tale, i. 2.*

Misanthrope, a, *Timon of Athens, iv. 1, 3; v. 2.* See CYNICS.

Mischief, swift to enter the thoughts of the desperate, *Romeo and Juliet, v. 1;* mourning past mischief, draws new mischief on, *Othello, i. 3.*

Misenum, Italy, scene of a part of *Antony and Cleopatra.*

Misers, *Henry V., ii. 4;* like whales, *Pericles, ii. 1;* gold of, *Venus and Adonis, l. 767; Lucrece, l. 855.*

Miserable, the, hope the only medicine for, *Measure for Measure, iii. 1.*

Misery, makes strange bedfellows, *The Tempest, ii. 2;* parts the flux of company, *As You Like It, ii. 1;* willing, *Timon of Athens, iv. 3;* sees miracles, *King Lear, ii. 2;* of one's betters, *King Lear, iii. 6, end;* trodden on, *Venus and Adonis, l. 707;* makes sport to mock itself, *Richard II., ii. 1.* See also ADVERSITY, MISFORTUNE.

Misfortune, turned to advantage, *I. Henry IV., iv. 1,* "You strain too far," etc.; doomed to, *Romeo and Juliet, iii. 3;* friends who desert in, *King Lear, ii. 4; Timon of Athens, iii. 1, 3; iv. 2, 3.* See ADVERSITY, WOE, SORROW.

Misfortunes, come not singly, *Hamlet, iv. 5, 7; Pericles, i. 4.*

Mislike (dislike), *Merchant of Venice, ii. 1; II. Henry VI., i. 1.*

Miss (dispense with), *The Tempest, i. 2.*

Missive (messenger), *Antony and Cleopatra, ii. 2.*

Mistakes, a lark taken for a bunting, *All's Well that Ends Well, ii. 5;* a drunkard for a god, *The Tempest, v. 1.*

Mistletoe, baleful, *Titus Andronicus, ii. 3.*

Mistress (the jack at bowls), *Troilus and Cressida, iii. 2.*

Mistrust. See DOUBT, SUSPICION.

Mithridates, of Comagene, *Antony and Cleopatra, iii. 6.*

Mitylene, in Lesbos, scene of a part of *Pericles.*

Mob(s), a London, *Henry VIII., v. 4;* Roman, *Coriolanus, i. 1; ii. 1; iii. 1, 3; iv. 1, 2, 6; Antony and Cleopatra, v. 2;* the fool multitude, *Merchant of Venice, ii. 9.*

Mobled, *Hamlet, ii. 2.* Hastily dressed, or, perhaps, hooded or muffled. Mob-cap is from the same word.

Mockery, made serious, *Henry V., i. 2;* of Beatrice, *Much Ado about Nothing, iii. 1;* returned, *Love's Labour's Lost, v. 2;* solemn, *Hamlet, iii. 4;* of a man by his own achievements, *Troilus and Cressida, iv. 2.*

Model (platform?), *Much Ado about Nothing, i. 3.*

Moderation, *Midsummer-Night's Dream, ii. 3,* " A surfeit," etc.; commended, *Henry VIII., i. 1; Romeo and Juliet, ii. 6; iii. 3; Merchant of Venice, i. 2; Othello, ii. 3..* See EXCESS.

Modern (trivial or ordinary), *As You Like It, ii. 7; All's Well that Ends Well, ii. 3; Antony and Cleopatra, v. 2; King John, iii. 4.*

Modesty, may more betray our sense, etc., *Measure for Measure, ii. 2;* the witness of excellence, *Much Ado about Nothing, ii. 3;* shown in the face, *III. Henry VI., iii. 2;* too great, *Coriolanus, i. 9;* of a girl, *Othello, i. 3;* an excellent touch of, *Twelfth Night, ii. 1;* the crimson of, *Henry V., v. 2;* of women in men's apparel, *Two Gentlemen of Verona, v. 4; Cymbeline, iii. 4.*

Modesty (moderation), *Taming of the Shrew, induction, 1.*

Modo, a fiend, *King Lear, iii. 4; iv. 1.* See MAHU.

Module (model, outward show), *All's Well that Ends Well, iv. 3; King John, v. 7.*

Moe (more), *A Winter's Tale, i. 2; v. 2;* (to mow), *Tempest, ii. 2.*

Moiety (portion), *I. Henry IV., iii. 1.*

Moldwarp (mole), *I. Henry IV., iii. 1.*

Mole, the blind, *The Tempest, iv. 1; A Winter's Tale, iv. 3; Hamlet, i. 5.*

Mole(s) (marks), *Twelfth Night, v. 1; King John, iii. 1; Hamlet, i. 4; Cymbeline, ii. 2, 4; v. 5.*

Mome (fool), *Comedy of Errors, iii. 1.*

Momentany (an old form of momentary), *Midsummer-Night's Dream, i. 1.*

Monarcho, *Love's Labour's Lost, iv. 1.* The nickname of an Italian, a fantastic character of the time.

Monarchs, high-arched gates of, *Cymbeline, iii. 3; King John, iii. 1.* See KINGS.

Monasteries, to pay the cost of war, *King John, i. 1; iii. 3.*

Money, all ways lie open for, *Merry Wives of Windsor, ii. 2;* marrying for, *Merry Wives of Windsor, iii. 4; Taming of the Shrew, i. 2;* love of, *All's Well that Ends Well, iv. 3,* "Sir, for a quart d'ecu," etc.; *Richard II., ii. 2,* "Their love lies in their purses," etc.; raised by farming the realm, *Richard II., i. 4;* gained by vile means, *Julius Cæsar, iv. 3;* power of, *Timon of Athens, iv. 3;* put, in thy purse, *Othello, i. 3;* despised, *Cymbeline. iii. 6.* See also GOLD.

Monks, are not made by hoods, *Twelfth Night, i. 5; Henry VIII., iii. 1.*

Monmouth, Henry of. See HENRY V.

Monmouth, compared to Macedon, *Henry V., iv. 7.*

Monster(s), a shallow, weak, credulous, *The Tempest, ii. 2;* of the sea, *Merchant of Venice, iii. 2; Coriolanus, iv. 2;* in love with a, *Midsummer-Night's Dream, iii. 2.*

Montacute. See SALISBURY.

Montacute, Henry Pole, Lord, *Henry VIII., i. 1.* Son-in-law of Abergavenny, brother of Cardinal Pole. He was executed in the reign of Henry VIII. on another charge than the one here spoken of.

Montague, John Neville, Marquis of, character in *III. Henry VI.,* introduced in *i. 1.* He was a partisan of the House of York, but followed his brother, Warwick, to the other side. His death is described in *v. 2.*

Montague, and Lady Montague, father and mother of Romeo, introduced in *i. 1.*

Montaigne, Michel, a French author, 1533–1592. Gonzalo's ideal commonwealth, *The Tempest, ii. 1,* is after Montaigne.

Montano, governor of Cyprus, character in *Othello,* introduced in *ii. 1.*

Montgomery, Sir John, character in *III. Henry VI.,* introduced in *iv. 7.* His name should be given Thomas. He was a favourite of Edward IV., and one of his most intimate friends and advisers.

Month's mind, a, *Two Gentlemen of Verona, i. 2.* Strong desire, a proverbial expression, of doubtful origin.

Montjoy, a French herald in *Henry V.,* first appears in *iii. 6,* playing a quite important part. "Montjoie" was the battle-cry of the French.

Monument, a, in verse, *Sonnets lv., lxxxi., cvii.;* a living, *Hamlet, v. 1;* goodness and he shall fill up one, *Henry VIII., ii. 1.*

Monument, the, at Alexandria, *Antony and Cleopatra, iv. 11* and *13,* or *13–15; v. 2.*

Moods, must be indulged, *Much Ado about Nothing, i. 3; of* Jaques, *As You Like It, ii. 1.*

Moon, the, the man in, *The Tempest, ii. 2;* controlled by a witch, *The Tempest, v. 1;* like a silver bow, *Midsummer-Night's Dream, i. 1;* diseases caused by, *Midsummer-Night's Dream, ii. 1;* creep through the earth's centre, *Midsummer-Night's Dream, iii. 2;* the watery star, *A Winter's Tale, i. 2;* the sea governed by, *I. Henry IV., i. 2;* envious, *Romeo and Juliet, ii. 2;* change like, *Timon of Athens, iv. 3;* a drop from, distilled by witchcraft, *Macbeth, iii. 5;* eclipse of, portentous, *Macbeth, iv. 1; Antony and Cleopatra. iii. 13; Hamlet, i. 1;* to revisit the glimpses of, *Hamlet, i. 4;* error of (lunacy caused by), *Othello, v. 2;* mistress of melancholy, *Antony and Cleopatra, iv. 9;* visiting, *Antony and Cleopatra, iv. 13* or *15;* fleeting, *Antony and Cleopatra, v. 2;* eclipses of, *King Lear, i. 2;* conjuring, *King Lear, ii. 1;* age of, *Love's Labour's Lost, iv. 2.*

Moon-calf, *The Tempest, ii. 2; iii. 2.* A monster supposed to be formed under the moon's influence.

Moonlight, sleeping, *Merchant of Venice, v. 1.*

Moons, five, *King John, iv. 2.*

Moonshine, a character in the interlude in *Midsummer-Night's Dream, v. 1,* taken by Starveling. the tailor.

Moonshine, fairies in, *The Tempest, v. 1.*

Moorditch, *I. Henry IV., i. 2.* A part of the ditch about London, spread to an unwholesome morass, and therefore shunned and melancholy.

Moorfields, *Henry VIII., v. 4.* The train-bands were drilled there.

Moors, changeable in their wills, *Othello, i. 3.*

Mopsa, a shepherdess in *A Winter's Tale, iv. 4.*

Mordake, Earl of Fife, mentioned in *I. Henry IV.* as one of the prisoners taken by Hotspur. It was Murdach Stuart.

More, Sir Thomas, *Henry VIII., iii. 2.* Lord Chancellor of England, born 1480, executed 1535.

Morgan. See BELARIUS.

Morisco, *II. Henry VI., iii. 1.* Name applied to the Moors left in Spain after the fall of Granada.

Morning, *The Tempest, v. 1; Much Ado about Nothing, v. 3; Midsummer-Night's Dream, iii. 2,* "For night's swift dragons," etc.; *1. Henry VI., ii. 2; III. Henry VI., ii. 1; Richard III., v. 3; Romeo and Juliet, i. 1; ii. 3; iii. 5; Hamlet, i. 1, 5;* song on, *Cymbeline, ii. 3; Venus and Adonis, lines 2, 853; Sonnet xxxiii.; Pas-*

sionate Pilgrim, xv.; King John, iii. 3; Troilus and Cressida, iv. 2; Julius Cæsar, ii. 1; Antony and Cleopatra, iv. 4.

Morocco, the Prince of, one of the suitors of Portia in the *Merchant of Venice,* appears in *ii. 1* and *7,* and chooses the golden casket.

Morris, *All's Well that Ends Well, ii. 2; Henry V., ii. 4.* A dance, in which the characters were generally Robin Hood, Maid Marian, Little John, Scarlet, Stokesley, the Fool, and Tom the Piper.

Morris, nine men's, *Midsummer-Night's Dream, ii. 1.* A square of sod marked into squares like a chess-board for a game.

Morris-pike (Moorish pike), *Comedy of Errors, iv. 3.*

Morrow, never shall sun that, see, *Macbeth, i. 5.*

Mortality, *As You Like It, ii. 7,* " And so from hour to hour," etc.; *King John, v. 7,* " When this was now a king," etc.; *Sonnet lxv.;* this muddy vesture of decay, *Merchant of Venice, v. 1;* if knowledge could have been set up against, *All's Well that Ends Well, i. 1.* See DEATH, LIFE.

Mortals, thoughts beyond, *Hamlet, i. 4.*

Mort Dieu! (God's death), *II. Henry VI., i. 1.*

Mortimer, Edmund, Earl of March, character in *I. Henry IV.,* introduced in *iii. 1,* Glendower's son-in-law. In *i. 1,* his capture by Glendower is spoken of, and in *i. 3* Hotspur vows to

> " lift the down-trod Mortimer
> As high i' the air as this unthankful king."

The Mortimer that was Earl of March was in reality not the one that was Glendower's son-in-law. The latter was Sir Edmund Mortimer, uncle of the young Earl of March. who had a claim to the crown, and is the Earl of March in *I. Henry VI.* Mortimer in the play is a rather contemptible character, unwilling to do anything for himself, and basely failing at the critical moment.

Mortimer, Edmund, Earl of March, character in *I. Henry VI.,* first appears in *ii. 5.* He was not kept in confinement during the reign of Henry V., but held high honours under him, and went with him to the wars in France. He was made Lord Lieutenant of Ireland in 1422, and died at Trim Castle in 1424.

Mortimer, Lady, daughter of Owen Glendower, character in *I. Henry IV.,* introduced in *iii. 1.* She can speak no English, Mortimer no Welsh, and Glendower interprets, while Hotspur ridicules the absurd love-scene.

Mortimer of Scotland, Lord, *I. Henry IV., iii. 2.* Perhaps George Dunbar, Earl of March in Scotland.

Mortimer, Sir Hugh and Sir John, uncles of York in *III. Henry VI.*, introduced in *i. 2.*

Mortimer, John, the Duke of York's plan for having Jack Cade assume the name of, *II. Henry VI., iii. 1.* History does not impute to York any such connection with Cade's plot.

Mortimers, claim of the, to the throne, *I. Henry VI., ii. 5.*

Mortimer's Cross, scene of *III. Henry VI., ii. 1.* A battle was fought there February 2, 1461, between the Yorkists under Edward, Duke of York, afterward Edward IV., and the Lancastrians under the Earl of Pembroke, with victory to York.

Morton, a retainer of Northumberland, in *II. Henry IV.*, first appears in *i. 1.*

Morton, John, Bishop of Ely. See ELY.

Mot (word, motto), *Lucrece, l. 830.*

Moth, a fairy in the *Midsummer-Night's Dream, iii. 1.*

Moth, an airy, saucy, witty, little page serving the pompous Spaniard in *Love's Labour's Lost*, introduced in *i. 2.* The word was pronounced "Mote."

Mother, grief of a, *King John, iii. 4; III. Henry VI., v. 5;* ambition of a, *Coriolanus, i. 3;* one, pleading for her son, *Titus Andronicus, i. 1* or *2;* and her child, *Richard II., iii. 2; I. Henry VI., iii. 3; Julius Cæsar, iii. 1; Macbeth, i. 7.*

Motion, things in, catch the eye, *Troilus and Cressida, iii. 3.*

Motion (puppet-show), *Two Gentlemen of Verona, ii. 1; A Winter's Tale, iv. 2.*

Motley, to wear, in the brain, *Twelfth Night, i. 5;* motley-minded, *As You Like It, v. 4.*

Mouldy, a recruit, character in *II. Henry IV., iii. 2.*

Mountain, the apparition of a hound, *The Tempest, iv. 1.*

Mountaineers, dew-lapped like bulls, *The Tempest, iii. 3.*

Mountains, far off, *Midsummer-Night's Dream, iv. 1;* firmness of, *Taming of the Shrew, ii. 1; As You Like It, iii. 2; King John, ii. 2.*

Mountanto, or **Montanto,** Signior, a name applied to Benedick by Beatrice, meaning that he was a great fencer, or professed to be, *Much Ado about Nothing, i. 1.*

Mourning, excessive, *Twelfth Night, i. 1, 2, 5; All's Well that Ends Well, i. 1; Hamlet, i. 2.*

Mouse, the most magnanimous, *II. Henry VI., iii. 2;* in absence of the cat, *Henry V., i. 2.; Coriolanus, i. 6.*

Mouse-trap, the, *Hamlet, iii. 2.* Applied to the play he brings forward, because it was designed to entrap the king into the betrayal of his guilt.

Mouth, a beautiful, *Venus and Adonis, lines 451, 504.*

Mouthing, by actors, *Hamlet, iii. 2.*

Mowbray, Lord Thomas, character in *II. Henry IV.,* first appears in *i. 3.* He is on the side opposed to the king.

Mowbray. See NORFOLK.

Moyses, an outlaw metioned in the *Two Gentlemen of Verona, v. 2.*

Much Ado about Nothing, a comedy first published in 1600, and probably written in that or the previous year. The plot, so far as regards Hero and Claudio, had already been used by Ariosto, in the story of Ariodante and Ginevra, in the fifth canto of "Orlando Furioso," by an English playwright, who dramatized Ariosto's story, by Spenser in the "Faerie Queene," and by Bandello in his story "Timbreo di Cardona," translated by Belleforest into French. The last-named was probably the one used by Shakspere, who united with the serious plot the parts of Benedick and Beatrice. The scene is laid in Messina. Mr. White thinks that a pun is intended in the title of the play on *noting* and *nothing,* pronounced very much alike in Shakspere's time. The people in the play make much ado about noting—that is, watching one another—while at the same time much ado is made about the scandal regarding Hero, which rests on a basis of nothing. This is one of the most popular of the comedies, both for reading and for stage representation.

Mugs, a carrier in *I. Henry IV., ii. 1.*

Mulier (woman), from the Latin *mollis aer* (gentle air), *Cymbeline, v. 5.* This fanciful etymology is said to have been a favourite notion in Shakspere's time.

Mulmutius, first king of Britain, *Cymbeline, iii. 1.*

Multitude, the, rumour among, *II. Henry IV., induction;* fickleness of, *II. Henry IV., i. 3;* affections of, in their eyes, *Hamlet, iv. 3,* or *v. 7;* the fool, *Merchant of Venice, ii. 9;* many-headed, *Coriolanus, ii. 3.*

Mummy, dyed in (in spicy liquor from mummies, supposed to have magic or medicinal virtue), *Othello, iii. 4;* the witches', *Macbeth, iv. 1.*

Munificence, *Love's Labour's Lost, iii. 1,* "The best ward of mine honour is rewarding my dependents."

Murder, sin of, *Measure for Measure, ii. 4;* for love, *Twelfth Night, ii. 1;* see SUPERSTITION; suggestion of—of kings, *A Winter's*

Tale, *i. 2;* of Arthur—excuses for, *King John, iv. 2;* nature's aid to punish—crest of, *King John, iv. 3;* accusation of, *Richard II., i. 1;* of a deposed king, *Richard II., v. 5;* reward for, at a king's instance, *Richard II., v. 6;* sentence for, *Timon of Athens, iii. 5;* of Duncan, the: first suggested to Macbeth, *i. 3;* to Lady Macbeth, *i. 5;* planned, *i. 7;* accomplished, *ii. 3;* of the guards, *Macbeth, ii. 3;* of Banquo—will out, *Macbeth, iii. 4;* in old times, *Macbeth, iii. 4;* most foul, *Hamlet, ι. 5;* will speak, *Hamlet, ii. 2;* a brother's, *Hamlet, iii. 3;* during prayer, *Hamlet, iii. 3;* no place should sanctuarize, *Hamlet, iv. 7;* evidences of, *II. Henry VI., iii. 2;* against God's law, *Richard III., i. 4;* ruthless, *Richard III., iv. 3;* of Desdemona, thought sacrifice, *Othello, v. 2;* command to, *Cymbeline, iii. 2, 4.*

Murderer(s), of Clarence in *Richard III., i. 3* and *4;* fears of a, *Macbeth, ii. 1;* of Banquo, *Macbeth, iii. 1, 3, 4;* of Macduff's children, *Macbeth, iv. 2;* of the princes, *Richard III., iv. 3;* of Arthur, *King John, iv. 2;* of the king, *Richard II., v. 6;* denunciation of, *III. Henry VI., v. 5;* pardon of, *Romeo and Juliet, iii. 1.*

Murdering-piece, *Hamlet, iv. 5* or *2.* A small piece of artillery often used on ships.

Murder of Gonzago, *Hamlet, ii. 2.* The play selected by Hamlet for the actors.

Mure (wall), *II. Henry IV., iv. 4.*

Murray, Thomas Dunbar, Earl of, *I. Henry IV., i. 1.*

Muscles, fresh-brook, *The Tempest, i. 2.*

Muscovites (Russians), *Love's Labour's Lost, v. 2.*

Muse, the. See POETRY.

Muse (to wonder), *Two Gentlemen of Verona, i. 3, and elsewhere.*

Muses, the thrice three. See GREENE, ROBERT.

Musets (openings in hedges), *Venus and Adonis, l. 683.*

Mushrooms, made by fairies, *The Tempest, v. 1.*

Music, effects of, *The Tempest, i. 2; iv. 1;* magic, *The Tempest, iii. 2;* power of, *Two Gentlemen of Verona, iii. 2; Much Ado about Nothing, ii. 3;* a mermaid's, *Midsummer-Night's Dream, ii. 1;* by fairies, *Midsummer-Night's Dream, ii. 3; iii. 1;* broken (ribs), *As You Like It, i. 2;* at a marriage, *As You Like It, v. 4;* charm of, *As You Like It, iv. 1;* fading in, *Merchant of Venice, iii. 2;* a soul without, *Merchant of Venice, v. 1;* design of, *Taming of the Shrew, iii. 1;* the food of love, *Twelfth Night, i. 1;* without time, *Richard II., v. 5:* a composer of, *I. Henry IV., iii. 1;* for the sick, *II. Henry IV., iv. 5;* charm of, *Henry VIII., iii. 1, song;* discordant when it calls to parting, *Romeo and Juliet, iii. 5;* doth lend redress, *Romeo and Juliet, iv. 5;* for lovers, *Antony and Cleopatra, ii. 5;* in the air, *Antony and Cleopatra, iv. 3;* a master of, *Pericles, ii. 5;* of the spheres, *Pericles, v. 1; Merchant of Venice, v. 1;* at a burial, *Cymbeline, iv. 2;* family happiness like, *Sonnet viii.;* the player, *Sonnet cxxviii.;* and poetry, *Passionate Pilgrim, viii.;* stopped for the love of music, *Othello, iii. 1.*

Musicians, characters in *Romeo and Juliet* and in *Othello.*

Music to hear, why hear'st thou music sadly? *Sonnet viii.*

Muss (scramble), *Antony and Cleopatra, iii. 13.*

Mustard. See TEWKSBURY MUSTARD.

Mustard-seed, a fairy in the *Midsummer - Night's Dream, iii. 1.*

Mutability, of earthly things, *II. Henry IV., iii. 1; Romeo and Juliet, iv. 5; Hamlet, iii. 2; iv. 5; v. 1.* See TIME.

Mutius, character in *Titus Andronicus,* son of Titus, enters in *i. 1* or *2,* is stabbed by his father in the same scene, and dies.

Mutton, a laced (wanton), *Two Gentlemen of Verona, i. 1; Measure for Measure, iii. 2.*

Muzzle, trusted with a, *Much Ado about Nothing, i. 3.*

My flocks feed not, *Passionate Pilgrim, xviii.*

My glass shall not persuade me I am old, *Sonnet xxii.*

My love is as a fever, *Sonnet cxlvii.*

My love is strengthened, though more weak in seeming, *Sonnet cii.*

My mistress' eyes are nothing like the sun, *Sonnet cxxx.*

Mystery, a, in the soul of state, *Troilus and Cressida, iii. 3;* of things, *King Lear, v. 3.*

My thoughts do harbour, poem, *Two Gentlemen of Verona, iii. 1.*

My tongue-tied muse in manners holds her still, *Sonnet lxxxv.*

Naiads, *The Tempest, iv. 1.*

Nail, one, drives out another, *Two Gentlemen of Verona, ii. 4;* dead as nail in door, *II. Henry IV., v. 3.* See PROVERBS.

Name, a good, shamed by falsehood, *Comedy of Errors, ii. 1;* an enemy—what's in a, *Romeo and Juliet, ii. 2;* where lodges the, *Romeo and Juliet, iii. 3;* good, *Othello, ii. 3;* robbery of a good, *iii. 3; Lucrece, l. 820.* See also REPUTATION.

Names, forgetting of, *King John, i. 1;* comparison of, *Julius Cæsar, i. 2.*

Naples, Alonzo, King of. See ALONZO.

Naples, Reignier, King of. See REIGNIER.

Narbon, Gerard de, father of Helena in *All's Well that Ends Well,* mentioned in *i. 1; ii. 1.*

Narcissus, *Venus and Adonis, l. 161; Lucrece, l. 265; Antony and Cleopatra, ii. 5.* A beautiful youth, who fell in love with his own image in a fountain.

Nathaniel, Sir, a curate in *Love's Labour's Lost,* introduced in *iv. 2,* "a foolish, mild man, an honest man, look you, and soon dashed."

Nation, a miserable, *Macbeth, iv. 3.*

Nature, requires interest for her gifts, *Measure for Measure, i. 1;* office of, *As You Like It, i. 2;* sale-work of, *As You Like It, iii. 5;* brings together what Fortune separates, *All's Well that Ends Well, i. 1, end;* will betray folly, *A Winter's Tale, i. 2;* itself makes the art that improves it, *A Winter's Tale, iv. 3 or 4,* "Say there be," etc.; gifts of, *King John, iii. 1;* one touch of, *Troilus and Cressida, iii. 3;* horrible places of, *Titus Andronicus, iv. 1;* bounteous housewife and common mother, *Timon of Athens, iv. 3,* goddess, *King Lear, i. 2;* foster-nurse of, *King Lear, iv. 4;* redeems from curse, *King Lear, iv. 6;* needs of, *King Lear, ii. 4;* the sparks of, hard to hide, *Cymbeline, iii. 3;* against fancy, *Antony and Cleopatra, v. 2;* hath meal and bran, *Cymbeline, iv. 2;* a forger, *Venus and Adonis, l. 728;* lends, not gives, *Sonnet iv.;* bankrupt, *Sonnet lxvii.;* shows false art, *Sonnet lxviii.;* mistress over wrack, *Sonnet cxxvi.;* labouring art can never ransom, *All's Well that Ends Well, ii. 1;* the products of, good or evil, according as they are applied, *Romeo and Juliet, ii. 3.*

Naught awhile, be (be hanged to you?), *As You Like It, i. 1.*

Navarre, a province of Spain, once a kingdom, scene of *Love's Labour's Lost.*

Nay-word, or aye-word (watch-word, countersign), *Merry Wives of Windsor, ii. 2,* and others; by-word, *Twelfth Night, ii. 3.*

Nazarite, the, *Merchant of Venice, i. 2.* Nazarene, Jesus.

Neapolitan Prince, one of the suitors of Portia, mentioned in the *Merchant of Venice, i. 2.*

Near-legged (starting with the left, or interfering), *Taming of the Shrew, iii. 2.*

Neat-slave (one to take care of neat cattle), *King Lear, ii. 2.*

Nebuchadnezzar, *All's Well that Ends Well, iv. 5.*

Necessity, virtue of, *Two Gentlemen of Verona, iv. 1;* honour hidden in, *Merry Wives of Windsor, ii. 2;* the fairest grant, *Much Ado about Nothing, i. 1;* plea of, *Love's Labour's Lost, i. 1; All's Well that Ends Well, i. 3,* " He must needs go," etc.; no virtue like, *Richard II., i. 3;* sworn brother to, *Richard II., v. 1; Hamlet, v. 1,* "The cat will mew," etc.; sharp pinch of, *King Lear, ii. 4;* can make vile things precious, *King Lear, iii. 2.*

Nedar, father of Helena in *Midsummer-Night's Dream, iv. 1.*

Need, and faith, *King John, iii. 1.*

Negligence, fit for a fool to fall by, *Henry VIII., iii. 2;* danger of, *Troilus and Cressida, iii. 3;* omittance is no quittance, *As You Like It, iii. 5.*

Neif (fist), *Midsummer-Night's Dream, iv. 1; II. Henry IV., ii. 4.*

Neighbour, a bad, is an outward conscience, *Henry V., iv. 1.*

Ne intelligis (do you not understand?), *Love's Labour's Lost, v. 1.*

Nell, the fat cook in the *Comedy of Errors,* described in *iii. 2.*

Nemean lion, the, *Love's Labour's Lost, iv. 1; Hamlet, i. 4.* It was killed by Hercules.

Nemesis, avenging goddess, *I. Henry VI., iv. 7.*

Neoptolemus, *Troilus and Cressida, iv. 5.* Incorrectly used as a name of Achilles. He was a son of Achilles.

Neptune, *The Tempest, i. 2; v. 1; A Winter's Tale, iv. 3 or 4; II. Henry IV., iii. 1; Hamlet, iii. 2; Antony and Cleopatra, iv. 12 or 14; Midsummer-Night's Dream, ii. 2;* would not flatter him for his trident, *Coriolanus, iii. 1;* England his park, *Cymbeline, iii. 1.* The god of the ocean.

Nerissa, the waiting-maid of Portia in the *Merchant of Venice,* first appears in *i. 2,* a bright, pert imitator of Portia, somewhat resembling Lucetta in the *Two Gentlemen of Verona.*

Nero (Emperor of Rome, born 37, died 68 A. D.), *King John, v. 2; I. Henry VI., i. 4; III. Henry VI., iii. 1;* the soul of, *Hamlet, iii. 2.* He is said to have murdered his mother; an angler in the lake of darkness, *King Lear, iii. 6.* See SMULKIN. Lear was hundreds of years before Nero.

Neroes, ye bloody, *King John, v. 2.*

Nervii, the, *Julius Cæsar, iii. 2.* A tribe of the Belgæ, the victory over whom was one of Cæsar's greatest achievements.

Nessus, *All's Well that Ends Well, iv. 3; Antony and Cleopa-*

tra, iv. 10 or *12*. A centaur killed by Hercules, who told Dejanira, the wife of Hercules, to save some of his blood for a charm with which to keep the love of Hercules. This she did, and afterward unwittingly poisoned him by using it on the robe sent for by him.

Nestor, one of the Grecian generals, distinguished for his wisdom and experience and his powers of persuasion. His name has become a synonym for the wisdom of ripe experience. He is introduced in *i. 3* of *Troilus and Cressida*, and in the same scene Ulysses describes how Patroclus mimics the infirmities of age in him to amuse Achilles. Other allusions, *Love's Labour's Lost, iv. 3; Merchant of Venice, i. 1; I. Henry VI., ii. 5; III. Henry VI., iii. 2;* in a painting, *Lucrece, l. 1401.*

Netherlands, the, *Comedy of Errors, iii. 2.*

Nettle, from the, danger, pluck the flower, safety, *I. Henry IV., ii. 3.*

Neville. See WARWICK.

Neville, Ralph. See WESTMORELAND.

New, nothing, *Sonnet lix.*

Newness, in authority, zeal of, *Measure for Measure, i. 3.*

News, good and bad, *Two Gentlemen of Verona, iii. 1;* resentment toward the bearer of, *Much Ado about Nothing, ii. 1;* the bearer of ill, *King John, iii. 1; II. Henry IV., i. 1; Macbeth, iv. 3; Antony and Cleopatra, i. 2; ii. 5;* fitting to the night, *King John, v. 6;* bearer of good, *II. Henry IV., iv. 4,* "Thou art a summer bird," etc.; impatience for, *Romeo and Juliet, ii. 5; iii. 2;* bad, *Cymbeline, iii. 4;* of war, *II. Henry IV., i. 1; ii. 4;* of carnal, bloody, and unnatural acts, *Hamlet, v. 2; King John, iv. 2; Julius Cæsar, v. 3;* wonderful, *A Winter's Tale, v. 2;* fresh, every minute, *Antony and Cleopatra, iii. 7;* the bearer of strange, *Macbeth, i. 2;* stale, *Hamlet, i. 5;* old (great), *Taming of the Shrew, iii. 1.*

Nice (foolish or trivial), *Taming of the Shrew, iii. 1; Romeo and Juliet, v. 2.*

Nicholas, Saint, *Two Gentlemen of Verona, iii. 1;* clerks of, *I. Henry IV., ii. 1.* Robbers were so called.

Nick (reckoning made by notches in sticks), out of all, *Two Gentlemen of Verona, iv. 2.*

Nicks, like a fool (cuts his hair like a fool's or jester's), *Comedy of Errors, v. 1.*

Night, beauty of a, *Merchant of Venice, v. 1;* makes the ear more quick, *Midsummer-Night's Dream, iii. 2;* time for fairies and ghosts, *Midsummer-Night's Dream, v. 2,* "Now the hungry lion," etc.; for plotting crime, *King John, iii. 3;* crimes in the, *Richard II., iii. 2;* the tragic, *II. Henry VI., iv. 1;* sober-suited, *Romeo and Juliet, iii. 2;* a dark, *Macbeth, ii. 1,* "There's husbandry in heaven;" an unruly, *Macbeth, ii. 3, 4;* description of, *Macbeth, iii. 2;* is long that, *Macbeth, iv. 3;* the witching time of, *Hamlet, iii. 2; Lucrece, lines 117, 162, 764, 1081;* wakefulness in the, *Sonnet lxi.;* imagination at, *Sonnets xxvii., xxviii.;* unwelcome, *Passionate Pilgrim, xv.;* the dragon-wing of, *Troilus and Cressida, v. 9.* See also MIDNIGHT.

Night-crow, *III. Henry VI., v. 6.*

Nightingale, the, *Two Gentlemen of Verona, v. 4; Merchant of Venice, v. 1; Romeo and Juliet, iii. 5; Midsummer-Night's Dream, i. 3; Taming of the Shrew, induction, 2; ii. 1; Twelfth Night, iii. 4; Antony and Cleopatra, iv. 8; King Lear, iii. 6; Passionate Pilgrim, xxi.;* allusion to the belief that she sings with her breast against a thorn, *Lucrece, l. 1135.*

Night-mare, the, *King Lear, iii. 4.*

Night-raven, *Much Ado about Nothing, ii. 3.*

Nile, the, serpent of old, *Antony and Cleopatra, i. 5;* overflowing of, *Antony and Cleopatra, ii. 7;* presageth famine, *Antony and Cleopatra, i. 2.*

Nine Worthies, the. See WORTHIES.

Ninny (Ninus), tomb of, *Midsummer-Night's Dream, iii. 1; v. 1.*

Niobe, all tears, *Hamlet, i. 2; Troilus and Cressida, v. 2.* She wept herself into stone for the loss of her children.

No, meant for ay, *Two Gentlemen of Verona. i. 2.*

Noah, *Comedy of Errors, iii. 2; Twelfth Night, iii. 2;* his ark, *As You Like It, v. 4.*

Nobility, fearless, *II. Henry VI., iv. 1;* loss of, *Richard III., i. 3.* See BLOOD, RANK.

Noble, the, in adversity, *Coriolanus, iv. 1.*

Nobleman, a, *III. Henry VI., iii. 2.* The king was taken by the servants of Sir James Harrington.

Nobleman, as one should live, *I. Henry IV., v. 4, end;* blood of a, compared with learning, *Henry VIII.*

Nobleness, in the wilds, *Cymbeline, iv. 2.*

Nobody, picture of, *The Tempest, iii. 2.* A common sign.

No longer mourn for me when I am dead, *Sonnet lxxi.*

No more be grieved at that which thou hast done, *Sonnet xxxv.*

No more dams I'll make for fish, song, *The Tempest, ii. 2.*

Nook-shotten (shut into a nook, or diversified with nooks), *Henry V.,* *iii. 5.*

Noon, to bed at. See PROVERBS, etc.

Norbury, Sir John, is mentioned in *Richard II., ii. 1,* as one of the companions of Bolingbroke. Henry, after his accession, made him Governor of Guisnes and treasurer of the exchequer.

Norfolk, Robert (correctly Roger) Bigot, Earl of, character in *King John,* introduced in *iv. 3.* He was one of the twenty-five barons opposed to John.

Norfolk, Thomas Mowbray, Duke of, character in *Richard II.* He enters in the first scene, where he is unjustly accused of the murder of Gloucester, and challenged by Bolingbroke on that account. After their meeting, *i. 3,* he is sentenced by the king to perpetual exile, although he is a friend of the king, while Bolingbroke, whom the king hates and fears, receives but a limited term of banishment. His death at Venice, *iv. 1.* This occurred in 1400. His eldest son did not bear the title on account of the attainder, but was simply Lord Mowbray, under which name he appears in *II. Henry IV.* The title was, however, restored to the second son, John, and his grandson bears it in *III. Henry VI.*

Norfolk, John Mowbray, Duke of, character in *III. Henry VI.,* introduced in *i. 1.* He belongs to the York party. He was the last Mowbray that was Duke of Norfolk; the title descended to the Howards through his daughter, who married Sir Robert Howard, and her son, John Howard, is the Norfolk of *Richard III.*

Norfolk, John Howard, Duke of, character in *Richard III.,* first appears in *v. 3.* The incident in that scene of the warning rhyme placed on his tent the night before Bosworth is historical. He fell on Bosworth field, *v. 5.* He was the first Howard that became Duke of Norfolk; he was also Earl Marshal of England; both of which titles still remain in the Howard family.

Norfolk, Thomas Howard, Duke of, character in *Henry VIII.,* introduced in *i. 1.* He is an enemy of Wolsey. There were two Dukes of Norfolk during the time of this play. The first was the Surrey of *Richard III.,* son of the Norfolk who fell at Bosworth. He died in 1524, and was succeeded by his son of the same name, the Earl of Surrey in this play.

Normandy, the loss of, to England, *II. Henry VI., iv. 7.*

Normans, the English, called, *Henry V., iii. 5.*

North, of opinion, the, *Twelfth Night, iii. 2.*

North, monarch of the. See WITCHCRAFT.

Northampton, scene of a part of *King John.*

Northumberland, Henry Percy, Earl of, a powerful nobleman, character in *Richard II.*, introduced in *ii. 3*, and in the two parts of *Henry IV.*, introduced in *i. 3* and in *i. 1*. He joins in rebellion against Richard with Bolingbroke, and, after helping to seat the usurper on the throne, joins in rebellion against him. At Shrewsbury he is " crafty-sick," and fails to go to the aid of his son and allies. In *II. Henry IV.* he again fails his allies, and the rebellion is quelled. Warwick says [*Part II., iii. 1*]:

"King Richard might create a perfect guess,
That great Northumberland, then false to him,
Would, of that seed, grow to a greater falseness."

"It is Northumberland, now smooth and flexible, now rough and unfeeling, that first speaks of Richard with the omission of his title; he it is that repeats more solemnly and forcibly the oath of Bolingbroke that his coming is but for his own: he it is who, in the scene of deposition, maliciously torments Richard with the reading of his accusation; and he it is who would arbitrarily arrest the noble Carlisle for high treason after the outbreak of his feelings of right and his civic fidelity."—GERVINUS.

Northumberland, Lady, a character in *II. Henry IV.*, appears in *ii. 3* only. She was Hotspur's step-mother, the Lady Maud Lucy, who was the widow of the Earl of Angus before she married Northumberland.

Northumberland, third Earl of, character in *III. Henry VI.*, introduced in *i. 1*. He is a Lancastrian. His father, who fell at the first battle of St. Alban's, was the son of Hotspur. This earl fell at Towton, March 29, 1461.

Northumberland, the melancholy, *Richard III., v. 3.*

Norweyan lord, the (Sweno, King of Norway), *Macbeth, i. 2.*

Nose(s), an embellished, *Comedy of Errors, iii. 2;* a good, is requisite, *A Winter's Tale, iv. 3;* twenty of the dog-days in a, *Henry VIII., v. 3;* why it is in the middle of the face, *King Lear, i. 5;* liberty (license) plucks justice by the, *Measure for Measure, i. 4;* to be led by the, *Othello, i. 3;* Heaven stops the, *Othello, iv. 2;* Bardolph's, see BARDOLPH; Alexander's, see ALEXANDER.

Nose-bleed, the, ominous, *Merchant of Venice, ii. 5.*

Not from the stars do I my judgment pluck, *Sonnet xiv.*

Nothing, an infinite deal of, *Merchant of Venice, i. 1;* prologue to, *All's Well that Ends Well, ii. 1,* "Thus he his special nothing ever prologues"; all the world is, *A Winter's Tale, i. 2;* can come of nothing, *King Lear, i. 1.*

No, Time, thou shalt not boast that I do change, *Sonnet xxiii.*

Not marble, nor the gilded monuments, *Sonnet lv.*

Not mine own fears, nor the prophetic soul, *Sonnet cvii.*

Nott-pated (crop-headed), *I. Henry IV., ii. 4.*

Novelty, in request, *Measure for Measure, iii. 2; Henry VIII., i. 3; Troilus and Cressida, iii. 2,* " All praise new-born gauds."

Novem, or **novum** (a game at dice), *Love's Labour's Lost, v. 2.*

Novi hominem, etc., *Love's Labour's Lost, v. 1.* I know the man as well as you.

Nowl (head), *Midsummer-Night's Dream, iii. 2.*

Numbers, odd. See ODD NUMBERS.

Nunnery, advice to enter a, *Hamlet, iii. 1.*

Nuns, life of, *Midsummer-Night's Dream, i. 1; Measure for Measure, i. 5; Lover's Complaint, l. 232; As You Like It, iii. 4.*

Nurse, character in *Titus Andronicus,* first appears in *iv. 2,* and is killed in the same scene.

Nurse, Juliet's, in *Romeo and Juliet,* first appears in *i. 3.* She is coarse, garrulous, deceitful, and time-serving, first helping on the marriage of Juliet with Romeo, and then counselling her, after his banishment, to marry Paris, trusting to the chance of Romeo's never turning up again—a proposal that reveals her real baseness to Juliet, who calls her " ancient damnation."

Nuthook (used by thieves to take things out of windows), *Measure for Measure, i. 1;* (slang for bailiff), *II. Henry IV., v. 4.*

Nutmeg, a gilt, *Love's Labour's Lost, v. 2.* A common gift.

Nym, a character in the *Merry Wives of Windsor* and in *Henry V.,* a corporal under Falstaff, and a great rogue. His conversation is marked by the use of " humour" as a catch-word. In *Henry V.* he appears in *i. 1,* in a quarrel with Pistol, and he is described by the boy in *iii. 2,* and at the end of *iv. 4,* where he says that Bardolph and Nym are both hanged. His name is a word that means to filch, " Convey, the wise it call," as Pistol says in the *Merry Wives of Windsor, i. 3.*

Nymphs, cold, *The Tempest, iv. 1.*

O, this wooden, *Henry IV.,* chorus to *act i.* This was the Globe Theatre, which was circular inside. This little O, the earth, *Antony and Cleopatra, v. 2;* an O without a figure, *King Lear, i. 4;* the stars, fiery Oes, *Midsummer-Night's Dream, iii. 2;* so deep an, *Romeo and Juliet, iii. 3.*

Oak, Jove's tree, *The Tempest, v. 1; As You Like It, iii. 2;* an ancient, *As You Like It, ii. 1; iv. 3;* garland of, *Coriolanus, i. 3; ii. 1, 2;* Herne's, *Merry Wives of Windsor, iv. 4;* strength of, *Measure for Measure, ii. 2; Julius Cæsar, i. 3;* to hew down with rushes, *Coriolanus, i. 1.* See HERNE.

Oatcake, Hugh, mentioned in *Much Ado about Nothing, iii. 3.*

Oath(s), weakness of, *The Tempest, iv. 1;* his, are oracles, *Two Gentlemen of Verona, ii. 7;* lose our, to find ourselves, *Love's Labour's Lost, iv. 3, near end;* Celia's, to make restitution, *As You Like It, i. 2;* not the many, that make the truth, *All's Well that Ends Well, iv. 2;* administered, *A Winter's Tale, iii. 2;* never to marry, *A Winter's Tale, v. 1;* obligation of, *King John, iii. 1;* of vengeance, *King John, iv. 3;* of enemies not to be reconciled, *Richard II., i. 3;* of the king, *I. Henry IV., v. 1;* a sin to keep sinful, *II. Henry VI., v. 1; III. Henry VI., v. 1,* "To keep that oath were more impiety than Jephthah's," etc.; binding, *III. Henry VI., i. 2;* Henry's, *III. Henry VI., ii. 2;* needlessness of, *Julius Cæsar, ii. 1;* on a sword, *Hamlet, i. 5;* no better than the word, *Pericles, i. 2;* deep, *Sonnet clii;* are straws, *Henry V., ii. 3;* are in heaven, *Merchant of Venice, iv. 1;* stronger thnn Hercules in breaking, *All's Well that Ends Well, iv. 3.* See also Vows and PERJURY.

Oaths (exclamatory), face the matter out with, *Taming of the Shrew, ii. 1;* approve manhood, *Twelfth Night, iii. 4,* "Go, Sir Andrew," etc.; the right kind of, *I. Henry IV., iii. 1.*

Oaths and Exclamations: Richard III. swears by St. Paul, his favourite oath according to tradition (*Richard III., i. 2, 3; iii. 4; v. 3*), and "by my George" (*iv. 4*), that is, the figure of St. George on the badge of Knights of the Garter, though that was first used in the reign of Henry VII. A favourite exclamation with Henry VIII. was "Ha!" frequently used in the play; Hamlet swears by St. Patrick (*i. 5*), by our lady (*iv. 2*), and by the rood (*iii. 4*); Polonius, by the mass (*Hamlet, ii. 1*); Parson Evans, by God's lords and his ladies, 'od's (God's) plessed will, and the tevil and his tam (*Merry Wives of Windsor, i. 1*); Mrs. Page, by the dickens (*Merry Wives of Windsor, iii. 2*); Nym, by welkin and her star (*i. 3*); Dr. Caius, by gar (*i. 4; iii. 3*); Shallow and Page, by cock and pie (*Merry Wives of Windsor, i. 1; II. Henry IV., v. 1*), possibly referring to the cock and magpie, a common alehouse sign; by cock, *Taming of the Shrew, iv. 1; Hamlet, iv. 5;* perdy (*par Dieu*), *Comedy of Errors, iv. 4; Henry V., ii. 1;* 's lid (by God's lid), *Merry Wives of Windsor, iii. 4; Twelfth Night, iii. 4;* 'od's lifelings (God's dear life), *Twelfth*

Night, v. 1; by my halidom (holy dame, or holy dom, salvation ?), *Two Gentlemen of Verona, iv. 2; Taming of the Shrew, v. 2; Henry VIII., v. 1; Romeo and Juliet, i. 3;* holy Mary, *Henry VIII., v. 2;* 's death (God's death), *Coriolanus, i. 1;* by God's sonties (? sanctities), *Merchant of Venice, ii. 2;* 's blood (God's blood), *I. Henry IV., i. 3;* zounds (God's wounds), *King John, ii. 2; I. Henry IV., i. 3; ii. 3; iv. 1;* bodikins (little body), *Merry Wives of Windsor, ii. 3;* marry (supposed corruption of Mary), in numberless passages; rivo, a drinking exclamation of unknown meaning, *I. Henry IV., ii. 4;* by my hood (? manhood), *Merchant of Venice, ii. 6;* by the rood, *Love's Labour's Lost, iv. 3;* mort du vinaigre (a nonsensical expression, literally, death of the vinegar), *All's Well that Ends Well, ii. 3;* darkness and devils—life and death, *King Lear, i. 4;* vengeance, plague, death, confusion—my breath and blood—death on my state, O the blest gods, *King Lear, ii. 4;* by Cheshu (Jesu), *King Henry V., iii. 2;* by Chrish (Christ), *King Henry V., iii. 2;* by Apollo, *King Lear, i. 1;* by Jupiter, by Juno, *King Lear, ii. 4;* by two-headed Janus, *Merchant of Venice, i. 1;* by Pluto and hell, *Coriolanus, i. 4;* O immortal gods, *Taming of the Shrew, v. i;* Mehercle (? Hercules), *Love's Labour's Lost, iv. 2;* the good year, *Merry Wives of Windsor, i. 4;* by St. Jeronimy, *Taming of the Shrew, induction, 1;* by St. Jamy, *induction, 2;* gramercies, *Taming of the Shrew, i. 1;* St. Denis to St. Cupid, *Love's Labour's Lost, v. 2;* 'i fecks (? in effect)—grace to boot, *A Winter's Tale, i. 2;* by my fay (faith), *Taming of the Shrew, induction, 2.*

Oats, wild, *Hamlet, ii. 1.*

Ob (obolus, half-penny), *I. Henry IV., ii. 4.*

Obedience, to one's appointed work, *Henry V., i. 2,* " Therefore doth Heaven divide," etc.; is for those that cannot rule, *II. Henry VI., v. 1;* princes love, *Henry VIII., iii. 1.* See DISOBEDIENCE.

Oberon, king of the fairies, introduced in *ii. 1* of *Midsummer-Night's Dream.* The name is French. from Alberon or Alberich, a fairy dwarf in old German poems. In French it became Auberich and Auberon. See FAIRIES.

Obidicut, a fiend, *King Lear, iv. 1.* See MAHU.

Oblivion, alms for, *Troilus and Cressida, iii. 3;* formless ruins of, *Troilus and Cressida, iv. 5;* the gulf of, *Richard III., iii. 7.*

Observation, places crammed with, *As You Like It, ii. 7;* need of, in men of the time, *King John, i. 1;* prophecy from, *II. Henry IV., iii. 1.*

Obstinacy, in folly, *A Winter's Tale, i. 2,* "You may as well forbid," etc.

O call not me to justify the wrong, *Sonnet xxxix.*

Occupation, necessary to enjoyment, *I. Henry IV., i. 2,* "If all the year," etc.; *Troilus and Cressida, i. 2,* "Joy's soul lies in the doing;" gone, *Othello, iii. 3.*

Ocean, encroachments of the, *Sonnet lxiv.*

Octavia, Antony's wife, character in *Antony and Cleopatra,* introduced in *ii. 3;* her marriage proposed by Agrippa, *ii. 2;* parting with Cæsar, *iii. 2;* described to Cleopatra, *iii. 3;* attempts to reconcile Antony and Cæsar, *iii. 4;* her appearance at Rome, *iii. 6.*

"The character of Octavia is merely indicated in a few touches, but every stroke tells. We see her 'with downcast eyes sedate and sweet, and looks demure,' with her modest tenderness and dignified submission—the very antipodes of her rival."—MRS. JAMESON.

Octavius Cæsar. See CÆSAR.

Oddity, in dress, *Merchant of Venice, i. 2.*

Odd numbers, superstition about, *Merry Wives of Windsor, v. 1.*

Odds, foolhardiness of taking great, *Coriolanus, iii. 1.*

Ods pittikins (God's dear pity), *Cymbeline, iv. 2.*

Oeillades (glances), *Merry Wives of Windsor, i. 3; King Lear, iv. 5.*

O'erlooked (bewitched), *Merry Wives of Windsor, v. 5.*

O'erraught (overreached), *Comedy of Errors, i. 2;* (overtook), *Hamlet, iii. 1.*

Offence, a pardoned, may gall the innocent afterward, *Measure for Measure, ii. 2;* a man that is a general, *All's Well that Ends Well, ii. 3;* not a time to criticise every slight, *Julius Cæsar, iv. 3;* a rank, *Hamlet, iii. 3.*

Offender, sorrow of an, *Sonnet xxxiv.*

Office, abuse of those in, *Henry VIII., i. 2.* See AUTHORITY, GREATNESS.

Offices, sale of, *Julius Cæsar, iv. 3.*

O for my sake do you with fortune chide, *Sonnet cxi.*

O from what power hast thou this powerful might, *Sonnet cl.*

O how I faint when I of you do write, *Sonnet lxxx.*

O how much more doth beauty beauteous seem, *Sonnet liv.*

O how thy worth with manners may I sing, *Sonnet xxxix.*

Old age. See AGE.

Oldcastle, Sir John, was the name first given to Falstaff, as it was the name of the character in the old play that furnished the hint for him. It was changed because it was taken to be intended for a real Sir John Oldcastle, who had been page to the Duke of Norfolk (said of Falstaff in *II. Henry IV., iii. 2*), and was afterward, as Lord Cobham, a Lollard or Wickliffite, who fell a martyr to his faith. The Protestants were scandalized and the Catholics gratified by the supposed portrait of the Lollard martyr. Shakspere then changed the name, and in the epilogue to *II. Henry IV.* says, speaking of Falstaff, "For Oldcastle died a martyr, and this is not the man." In *I. Henry IV., i. 2*, the prince calls him "my old lad of the castle."

O lest the world should task you to recite, *Sonnet lxxii.*

Oliver, a character in *As You Like It*, elder brother of Orlando, appears in the first scene. "In this eldest son of the brave Rowland de Boys there flows the same vein of avarice and envy as in the duke. He strives to plunder his brother of his poor inheritance; he undermines his education and gentility; he first endeavors to stifle his mind, and then he lays snares for his life; all this he does from an undefined hatred of the youth who, he is obliged to confess, is 'full of noble device,' but who, for this very reason, draws away the love of all his people from Oliver to himself, and on this account excites his envious jealousy." On Orlando's saving his life, he "experiences a sudden change of heart, and proposes to give up all his possessions to Orlando, marry the supposed shepherdess Aliena, and live and die a shepherd."

Olivers, *I. Henry VI., i. 2.* Oliver was one of Charlemagne's twelve peers.

Olivia, character in *Twelfth Night*, introduced in *i. 5*, beloved by the duke, whom she rejects, and falls in love with his man Cesario, who comes to urge his master's suit. She anticipates Priscilla Mullens by telling the ambassador:

> "But would you undertake another suit,
> I had rather hear you to solicit that
> Than music from the spheres."

Olympian games, *III. Henry VI., ii. 3; Troilus and Cressida, iv. 5.*

Olympus, *Hamlet, v. 1; Coriolanus, v. 3; Titus Andronicus, ii. 1.* The mountain of the gods.

Omens, unnatural reasons, *Midsummer-Night's Dream, ii. 2;*

five moons, *King John, iv. 2;* of anarchy, *Richard II., ii. 4;* night-owls, *Richard II., iii. 3;* at Glendower's birth, *I. Henry IV., iii. 1;* of evil, *II. Henry IV., iv. 4;* Gloucester's dream, *II. Henry VI., i. 2;* at Richard's birth, *III. Henry VI., v. 6;* Stanley's dream, *Richard III., iii. 2;* a stumbling horse, *Richard III., iii. 4;* a tempest after a treaty of peace, *Henry VIII., i. 1;* irregularity of planets, *Troilus and Cressida, i. 3;* Andromache's dream, *Troilus and Cressida, v. 3;* stumbling at graves, *Romeo and Juliet, v. 3;* dreams, *Julius Cæsar, i. 3; ii. 2; v. 1;* the raven is hoarse that croaks, *Macbeth, i. 5;* the owl, *Macbeth, ii. 2, 3;* of death, *Macbeth, ii. 3, 4;* the ghost—of Cæsar's death. *Hamlet, i. 1;* swallows' building, *Antony and Cleopatra, iv. 10* or *12;* should have shown the death of Antony, *Antony and Cleopatra, v. 1;* of success, *Cymbeline, iv. 2,* " Last night the very gods," etc. ; fear caused by, *Venus and Adonis, l. 924;* the three suns. See SUNS. See also DREAMS and PORTENTS.

O me what eyes hath love put in my head, *Sonnet cxlviii.*

O mistress mine, song, *Twelfth Night, ii. 3.*

Omittance, is no quittance, *As You Like It, iii. v.*

Omne bene (all well), *Love's Labour's Lost, iv. 2.*

On a day, alack the day, *Passionate Pilgrim, xvii.*

One fair daughter, *Hamlet, ii. 2.* Part of an old ballad beginning:

> " I have read that many years agoe,
> When Jephtha, judge of Israel,
> Had one fair daughter and no moe."

One, the number, *Romeo and Juliet, i. 2; Sonnet cxxxvi.,* " One is no number."

O never say that I was false of heart, *Sonnet cix.*

Onions, to draw tears, *Taming of the Shrew, induction, 1; All's Well that Ends Well, v. 3, near end; Antony and Cleopatra, i. 3; iv. 2.*

Ooze, of the Nile, *Antony and Cleopatra, ii. 7.*

Opal, thy mind is a very, *Twelfth Night, ii. 4.*

Ophelia, heroine of *Hamlet,* introduced in *i. 3;* her madness, *iv. 5* or *2;* her death, *iv. 7* or *4;* burial, *v. 1.*

" Whenever we bring her to mind, it is with the same exclusive sense of her real existence, without reference to the wondrous power that called her into life. The effect—and what an effect !—is produced by means so simple, by strokes so few and so unobtrusive, that we take no thought of them. It is so purely natural and unsophisticated, yet so profound in its pathos, that, as Hazlitt observes, it

takes us back to the old ballads; we forget that, in its perfect art-lessness, it is the supreme and consummate triumph of art. . . . As the character of Hamlet has been compared, or rather contrasted with the Greek Orestes, being like him called on to avenge a crime by a crime, tormented by remorseful doubts, and pursued by distraction, so, to me, the character of Ophelia bears a certain relation to that of the Greek Iphigenia, with the same strong distinction between the classical and the romantic conception of the portrait. Iphigenia led forth to sacrifice, with her unresisting tenderness, her mournful sweetness, her virgin innocence, is doomed to perish by that relentless power which has linked her destiny with crimes and contests in which she has no part but as a sufferer; and even so poor Ophelia, 'divided from herself and her fair judgment,' appears here like a spotless victim offered up to the mysterious and inexorable Fates."
—Mrs. Jameson.

Opinion, may be worn on both sides, like a leather jerkin, *Troilus and Cressida, iii. 3;* if I bleed for my, *I. Henry VI., ii. 4;* sovereign mistress of effects, *Othello, i. 3;* fool's gudgeon, *Merchant of Venice, i. 1;* a fool, *Pericles, ii. 2;* (dogmatism), *Love's Labour's Lost, v. 1,* "Learned without opinion;" (reputation), lost, *I. Henry IV., v. 4.*

Opinions, holding popular, *II. Henry IV., ii. 2,* "Never a man's thought," etc.; golden, *Macbeth, i. 7;* caution in expressing, *Hamlet, i. 3;* influenced by conduct, *Antony and Cleopatra, iii. 11,* "When we in our viciousness," etc.; new and dangerous, *Henry VIII., v. 2;* depend on one's own character, *I. Henry VI., v. 4, Sonnet cxxi.;* on the time, *Coriolanus, iv. 7;* there's nothing good or bad but thinking makes it so, *Hamlet, ii. 2.*

Opportunity, *The Tempest, i. 2,* "I find my zenith," etc.; to sin, *Measure for Measure, ii. 1; King John, iv. 2;* let slip, *Twelfth Night, iii. 1,* "She did show," etc.; *Richard II., iii. 2; III. Henry VI., iv. 8,* "A little fire," etc.; *Julius Cæsar, iv. 3,* "There is a tide," etc.; once lost, *Antony and Cleopatra, ii. 7,* "Who seeks and will not take when once 'tis offered," etc.; guilt of, *Lucrece, l. 876.* See also Delay.

Oppression. See Tyranny.

Oppressors, league of, *King John, iii. 1.*

Oracle, I am Sir, *Merchant of Venice, i. 1.*

Oracle, the Delphic, appealed to, *A Winter's Tale, iii. 1;* the answer, *iii. 2;* fulfilled, *v. 2;* of Jupiter, *Cymbeline, v. 5.*

Oracles, ambiguous, *II. Henry VI., i. 4.*

Orator, I am no, *Julius Cæsar, iii. 2;* to play the, *III. Henry VI., i. 2; iii. 2; Richard. III., iii. 5.*

Oratory, popular, *Coriolanus, iii. 2.*

Orbs (orbits), *Pericles, i. 2.*

Orchard (garden), *Much Ado about Nothing, ii. 3; Romeo ana Juliet, ii. 1.*

Order, results of disregard of, *Troilus and Cressida, i. 3.*

Order and Dates of the Plays and Poems. The following table shows the dates of publication of the plays and poems, so far as is known, together with the order in which they were written and the dates of writing as nearly as can be determined from contemporary allusions, the decisions of critics on internal evidence, etc. The more or less sparing use of rhyme is one of the chief tests, the earlier plays abounding in it much more than the later.

PLAYS.	Supposed date of writing.	First publication.
Titus Andronicus,	1585–'90,	1600
Love's Labour's Lost,	1588–'90,	1598
Comedy of Errors,	1589–'93,	1623
Midsummer-Night's Dream,	1590–'92 (1593–'94),	1600
Two Gentlemen of Verona,	1590–'92 (1592–'93),	1623
I. Henry VI.,	1590–'92,	1623
II. and III. Henry VI.,	1590–'4 (worked over, 1600–'3),	1623
Romeo and Juliet,	1591–'93, revised 1596,	1597
Venus and Adonis,	1592–'93,	1593
Lucrece,	1593–'94,	1594
Richard II.,	1593–'97,	1597
Richard III.,	1593–'94,	1597
A Lover's Complaint,	1595–'97,	1609
Merchant of Venice,	1594–'96,	1600
King John,	1595–'96,	1623
Taming of the Shrew,	1596–'97,	1623
I. Henry IV.,	1596–'98,	1598
II. Henry IV.,	1597–'99,	1600
Merry Wives of Windsor,	1597–1601,	1602
Sonnets,	before 1598,	1609
Henry V.,	1599,	1600
Much Ado about Nothing,	1598–1600,	1600
As You Like It,	1599–1600,	1623
The Phœnix and the Turtle,	1600,	1601
Twelfth Night,	1600–'1,	1623
Julius Cæsar,	1600–'1,	1623
All's Well that Ends Well,	1601–'3 (in present form),	1623

PLAYS.	Supposed date of writing.	First publication.
Hamlet,	1600–'3,	1604
Measure for Measure,	1603–'4,	1623
Othello,	1604,	1622
King Lear,	1605–'6,	1608
Antony and Cleopatra,	1605–'8,	1623
Macbeth,	1605–'9,	1623
Troilus and Cressida,	1606–'8,	1609
Timon of Athens,	1607–'10,	1623
Coriolanus,	1607–'12,	1623
Pericles,	1608,	1609
The Tempest,	1610,	1623
Cymbeline,	1610–'12,	1623
A Winter's Tale,	1611,	1623
Henry VIII.,	1612–'13,	1623

Ordinaries, *All's Well that Ends Well, ii. 3.* Meals at an ordinary or inn.

Orgulous (proud). *Troilus and Cressida, prologue.*

Original sin, *A Winter's Tale, i. 2,* "The imputation hereditary ours."

Or I shall live your epitaph to make, *Sonnet lxxxi.*

Orisons, *Henry V., iv. 2; III. Henry VI., i. 4; Romeo and Juliet, iv, 3; Hamlet, iii. i; Cymbeline, i. 4.*

Orlando, hero of *As You Like It,* introduced at the beginning. He is foully wronged by his elder brother, who is jealous of his noble qualities and the love they gain for him, and, not satisfied with wronging him out of his patrimony, wishes to degrade him by neglect into a churl. "Throughout we see the healthful, self-contained, calm nature of a youth which promises a perfect man. . . . What a shaming contrast to the calumniator Jaques, whom he thus answers, when he invites him to rail with him against the deceitful world: 'I will chide no breather in the world but myself, against whom I know most faults!'"

Orleans, Charles d'Angoulême, Duke of, character in *Henry V.,* first appears in *iii. 7.* He was taken prisoner at Agincourt, and was kept in the Tower for twenty-five years. His son reigned as Louis XII.

Orleans, the Bastard of. character in *I. Henry VI.,* spoken of in *i. 1,* first appears in *i. 2.* He was Count of Dunois and Longueville, and is known under the former name as one of the greatest soldiers of his time.

Orleans, siege of (1428–'29), *I. Henry VI.*, *i. 1, 2, 4, 5; ii. 1.*

Ornament, the world deceived with, *Merchant of Venice, iii. 2.*

Ornaments, oft prove dangerous, *A Winter's Tale, i. 2.*

Orodes, *Antony and Cleopatra, iii. 1.*

Orpheus, the lute of, *Two Gentlemen of Verona, iii. 2;* legend of, *Merchant of Venice, v. 1;* song, *Henry VIII., iii. 1;* playing of, *Lucrece, l. 553.* A traditionary poet, musician, and philosopher of Greece, whose skill at the lyre was such that the wild beasts of the forests gathered around him to hear his playing. In his grief at the loss of his wife, Eurydice, he determined to descend to Hades to induce the powers there to release her. The music of his lyre so charmed the deities of the lower world that they agreed to let Eurydice follow him to the upper world, on condition that he should not look back on her till they had passed the borders of Hades. But he could not keep the condition, and she vanished.

Orsino, Duke of Illyria, character in *Twelfth Night*, introduced in the first scene, in love at first with Olivia after a sentimental and unconsciously insincere fashion, but of a refined and lovable nature—

" Of great estate, of fresh and stainless youth,
    In voices well divulged, free, learned, and valiant."

Orthography, rackers of, *Love's Labour's Lost, v. 1.*

Ort(s) (scraps, leavings), *Timon of Athens, iv. 3; Troilus and Cressida, v. 2.*

Or whether doth my mind, being crowned with you, *Sonnet cxiv.*

Osprey, the, *Coriolanus, iv. 7.* Allusion to a supposed fascination the osprey exercised over fish.

Osric, a courtier, character in *Hamlet*, appears in *v. 2.* His affected manner, which is ridiculed by Hamlet and Horatio, is probably a satire on the foppish gallants of Shakspere's own time.

Ossa, *Hamlet, v. 1.* A mountain in Thessaly, one of those that the giants were said to have piled upon Olympus in their war with the gods, in order to reach heaven.

Ostent (appearance, display), *Merchant of Venice, ii. 2, 8.*

Ostentation, *Love's Labour's Lost, v. 2; Coriolanus, i. 6; II. Henry IV., ii. 2; Hamlet, iv. 5;* of mourning, *Much Ado about Nothing, iv. 1.*

Ostrich, eat iron like an, *II. Henry VI., iv. 10.*

Oswald, the knavish steward of Goneril in *King Lear*, introduced in *i. 3;* Kent's opinion of him, *ii. 2;* his death, *iv. 6.*

"The only character of utter, irredeemable baseness in Shakspere."—COLERIDGE.

O that you were yourself, *Sonnet xiii.*

Othello, is introduced in the second scene of the play; his defence before the senate, *i. 3;* in Cyprus, *ii. 1;* his jealousy aroused, *iii. 3;* confirmed, *iv. 1;* kills Desdemona and himself, *v. 2.*

"He is of a free and noble nature, naturally trustful, with a kind of grand innocence, retaining some of his barbaric simpleness of soul in midst of the subtle and astute politicians of Venice. He is great in simple heroic action, but unversed in the complex affairs of life, and a stranger to the malignant deceits of the debased Italian character."—DOWDEN.

"The noblest man of man's making."—SWINBURNE.

"Between Iago and Othello the position of Desdemona is precisely that defined with such quaint sublimity of fancy in the old English by-word, 'Between the devil and the deep sea.' Deep and pure and strong and adorable always, and terrible and pitiless on occasion as the sea, is the great soul of the glorious hero to whom she has given herself; and what likeness of man's enemy, from Satan down to Mephistopheles, could be matched for danger and for dread against the good, bluff, soldierly, trustworthy figure of honest Iago?"—SWINBURNE.

Othello, the Moor of Venice. This play was first published in 1622, though it had been on the boards for years, and was a favourite play. The first authentic mention of it is in a diary kept by one Wurmsser, who was in the suite of the Duke of Würtemberg when he visited England in 1610. The allusion to the new heraldry in *iii. 4* is to the new order of baronetage established by the king in 1611, a red hand being on the arms of the order. But this may have been introduced long after the play was written. It is generally agreed that it is of the same period as *Hamlet, Macbeth,* and *King Lear.* The source whence Shakspere drew the outline of the plot and the name of the heroine was an Italian story by Giraldo Cinthio, published in 1565. The time of the play is the year 1570, when Cyprus was invaded by the Turks.

"The picturesque contrasts of character in this play are almost as remarkable as the depth of the passion. The Moor Othello, the gentle Desdemona, the villain Iago, the good-natured Cassio, the fool Roderigo, present a range and variety of character as striking and palpable as that produced by the opposition of costumes in a picture."—HAZLITT.

Othergates (otherwise), *Twelfth Night, v. 1.*

O thou my lovely boy, *Sonnet cxxvi.*

O truant Muse, what shall be thy amends, *Sonnet ci.*

Otter, the, neither fish nor flesh, *I. Henry IV., iii. 3.*

Ottomites, *Othello, i. 3; ii. 3.* Turks.

Ouches (bosses of gold), *II. Henry IV., ii. 4.*

Ouphes (elves), *Merry Wives of Windsor, iv. 4; v. 5.*

Ousel (blackbird), the, *Midsummer-Night's Dream, iii. 1; II. Henry IV., iii. 2.*

Outcast, an, *Macbeth, iii. 1; I. Henry IV., iv. 3.*

Outlaws, a band of, *Two Gentlemen of Verona, iv. 1; v. 3.*

Outside, a fair, *Romeo and Juliet, iii. 2,* " O serpent heart," etc., *Cymbeline, i. 1.*

Outward man, an, *All's Well that Ends Well, iii. 1.* One not in the secrets of state.

Overdone, Mistress, a procuress in *Measure for Measure,* introduced in *i. 2.*

Ovid, allusions to his story of Philemon and Baucis entertaining Jove in their thatched cottage, *Much Ado about Nothing, ii. 1; As You Like It, iii. 3;* as Ovid be an outcast, *Taming of the Shrew, i. 1;* Metamorphoses of, *Titus Andronicus, iv. 1;* quotations from, *Taming of the Shrew, iii. 1;* Hic ibat, etc., *Venus and Adonis,* motto; *Love's Labour's Lost, iv. 2.*

Owe (own), *All's Well that Ends Well, ii. 1, 5; King John, ii. 1; Macbeth, i. 4; Antony and Cleopatra, iv. 8,* and elsewhere.

Owl, the, *The Tempest, v. 1, song; Love's Labour's Lost, v. 2, song;* allusion to the superstition that it sucks the blood of infants and changes the favour of children, *Comedy of Errors, ii. 2;* of evil omen, *Midsummer-Night's Dream, v. 1; I. Henry VI., iv. 2; II. Henry VI., iii. 2; III. Henry VI., ii. 6; v. 6; Richard III., iv. 4; Julius Cæsar, i. 3; Macbeth, ii. 2; ii. 4; Richard II., iii. 3; Titus Andronicus, ii. 3; Lear, ii. 4;* mocked at by day, *III. Henry VI., v. 4;* was a baker's daughter, *Hamlet, iv. 5;* allusion to the story that a baker's daughter reproved her father for giving bread to Christ, crying, " Heugh! heugh!" in derision, and was turned into an owl as a judgment. An owlet's wing was placed in their cauldron by the witches, *Macbeth, iv. 1.*

Oxford, John de Vere, thirteenth Earl of, character in *III. Henry VI.* and in *Richard III.,* an adherent of the House of Lancaster, and one of the most powerful supporters of Richmond. In *Richard III., ii. 1,* he is spoken of as having been at Tewksbury, as he was not in reality, having fled to France after the battle of Barnet. He afterward seized St. Michael's Mount in Cornwall, was besieged, taken, and imprisoned at Hamnes Castle in Picardy, *III. Henry VI.,* *v. 5.* He went with the governor of the castle to join Richmond, and fought for him at Bosworth. Henry VII., with whom he was high in favour, bestowed various offices upon him. He is introduced in *iii. 3* of the former play; *v. 2* of the latter. His father and brother were attainted and beheaded on the accession of Edward IV. He speaks of it in *iii. 3.*

Oxford University, *Henry VIII., iv. 2.*

Oxlips, *A Winter's Tale, iv. 3* or *4; Midsummer-Night's Dream, ii. 2.*

Oyster, the world's my, *Merry Wives of Windsor, ii. 2.* There was a saying, "The Mayor of Northampton opens oysters with his dagger." Canst tell how an oyster makes his shell, *King Lear, i. 5;* love may transform me to an, *Much Ado about Nothing, ii. 3;* this treasure of an, *Antony and Cleopatra, i. 5;* as much as an apple doth resemble an oyster, *Taming of the Shrew, iv. 2;* off goes his bonnet to an oyster-wench, *Richard II., i. 4.*

Pace, Doctor Richard, *Henry VIII., ii. 2.* He was Vicar of Stepney, and one of Wolsey's secretaries.

Packing (plotting), *Taming of the Shrew, v. 1, and elsewhere.*

Pacorus, son of Orodes, King of Parthia, killed by Ventidius, *Antony and Cleopatra, iii. 1.*

Paddock, the toad, *Macbeth, i. 1.* Toads as well as cats were familiars of witches.

Padua, Italy, scene of the *Taming of the Shrew;* called the nursery of arts, *i. 1.*

Pagan(s), *I. Henry IV., ii. 3; II. Henry IV., ii. 2; Henry VIII., i. 3;* most beautiful, *Merchant of Venice, ii. 3.*

Page, a, in *Richard III., iv. 2,* supposed to be John Green, who was rewarded for his share in the murder of the princes by the receivership of the lordships of Porchester and the Isle of Wight.

Page, Anne, character in the *Merry Wives of Windsor,* introduced in *i. 1.* She has seven hundred pounds left her by her grandfather, and is sought by three suitors—one favoured by her father, one by her mother, and the third by herself.

Page, George, character in the *Merry Wives of Windsor,* introduced in *i. 1.* Unlike Ford, he has confidence in his wife. They are both outwitted by their daughter, who marries Fenton while they are trying to outwit each other and marry her, the one to Doctor Caius, the other to Slender.

Page, Mistress, one of the *Merry Wives of Windsor.* See FORD, MISTRESS.

Page, William, a school-boy in the *Merry Wives of Windsor,* examined in Latin by Parson Evans in *iv. 1.*

Pageant(s), *As You Like It, ii. 7; iii. 4; Richard III., iv. 4;* of spirits, *The Tempest, iv. 1;* of clouds, *Antony and Cleopatra, iv. 12* or *14; Two Gentlemen of Verona, iv. 3; Troilus and Cressida, iv. 3; Othello, i. 3.* The pageants were a kind of play like that of the Nine Worthies in *Love's Labour's Lost.*

Pages, characters in, *As You Like It, Taming of the Shrew,* and *Romeo and Juliet.*

Paid, he is well, that is well satisfied, *Merchant of Venice, iv. 1.*

Pain(s), delights that are purchased with, *Love's Labour's Lost, i. 1;* one lessened by another, *Romeo and Juliet, i. 2;* pays for every treasure, *Lucrece, l. 334.*

Painted cloth (tapestry), *As You Like It, iii. 2; Love's Labour's Lost, v. 2;* Lazarus in the, *I. Henry IV., iv. 2;* maxims on, *Lucrece, l. 245.* See also TAPESTRY.

Painter, a, character in *Timon of Athens,* introduced in the first scene, where he is seeking patronage from Timon. In *v. 1,* having heard that Timon has found a treasure, he returns to flatter him.

Painter, mine eyes have played the, *Sonnet xxiv.*

Painting, *Taming of the Shrew, induction, i.;* praise of a, *Timon of Athens, i. 1;* of the siege of Troy, *Lucrece, l. 1368.*

Painting, of the skin, *Cymbeline, iii. 4; Timon of Athens, iv. 3; Hamlet, iii. 1.*

Pajock (peacock), *Hamlet, iii. 2.* The peacock had a reputation for evil passion as well as vanity.

Palabras (words), *Much Ado about Nothing, iii. 4.*

Palace, full of tongues, etc., *Titus Andronicus, ii. 1.*

Palaces, gorgeous, *The Tempest, iv. 1.*

Palatine, the Count, one of the suitors of Portia, mentioned in the *Merchant of Venice, i. 2.*

Pale (encircle), *III. Henry VI., i. 4.*

Pallas, Minerva, goddess of wisdom, *Titus Andronicus, iv. 1.*

Palliament, *Titus Andronicus, i. 1* or *2.* The robe worn by the candidate, who was so called from *candidus,* white, its colour.

Palm, an itching, *Julius Cæsar, iv. 3.*

Palmer(s), *All's Well that Ends Well, iii. 5; Richard II., iii 1; II. Henry VI., v. 1; Romeo and Juliet, i. 5.*

Palmistry, *Merchant of Venice, ii. 2,* Launcelot's speech *Othello, iii. 4; Antony and Cleopatra, i. 2.*

Pandarus, a character in *Troilus and Cressida,* uncle of the latter, introduced in *i. 1.* His office was the origin of the noun pander. In *iii. 2,* at the end, he says, "Let all goers-between be called to the world's end after my name."

"Pandarus, in Chaucer's story, is a friendly sort of go-between, tolerably busy, officious, and forward in bringing matters to bear: but in Shakspere he has 'a stamp exclusive and professional'; he wears the badge of his trade; he is a regular knight of the game. The difference of the manner in which the subject is treated arises perhaps less from intention, than from the different genius of the two poets. There is no *double entendre* in the characters of Chaucer; they are either quite serious or quite comic. In Shakspere the ludicrous and ironical are constantly blended with the stately and impassioned."—HAZLITT.

Allusions to, *Measure for Measure, i. 3; Twelfth Night, iii. 1; Merry Wives of Windsor, i. 3; Much Ado about Nothing, v. 2; Hamlet, iii. 4.*

Panders, origin of the word, *Troilus and Cressida, iii. 2, end;* ill requited, *Troilus and Cressida, v. 11.*

Pandion, King, *Passionate Pilgrim, xxi.*

Pandulph (Pandulphus de Masca), Cardinal, legate of the pope in *King John,* introduced in *iii. 1,* a wily and subtle agent in the management of a difficult business. It was not he but Cardinal Gualo who tried to persuade the dauphin to wind up his "threatening colours," *v. 2.*

Pannonians, *Cymbeline, iii. 1, 7.* Pannonia was a Roman province, including in part what is now Hungary.

Pantaloon, the lean and slippered, *As You Like It, ii. 7;* the old, *Taming of the Shrew, iii. 1.*

"Pantaleone was a stereotyped character in old Italian comedy, always aged, lean, slippered, and wearing loose pantaloons."—WHITE.

Panthino, servant of Antonio, the *Two Gentlemen of Verona, i. 3.*

Pansy, the, *Hamlet, iv. 4;* called love-in-idleness, *Midsummer-Night's Dream, ii 1.*

Paper bullets, of the brain, *Much Ado about Nothing, ii. 3.*

Paphos, in Cyprus, *The Tempest, iv. 1; Pericles, iv., induction; Venus and Adonis, l. 1193.* Paphos was sacred to Venus.

Paracelsus, *All's Well that Ends Well, ii. 3.* A philosopher, physician, and reputed magician, 1493–1541, who used metallic medicines, while Galen preferred vegetable.

Paradise, the offending Adam out of, *Henry V., i. 1;* what fool is not so wise to lose an oath to win a, *Love's Labour's Lost, iv. 3.*

Paradox(es), *Timon of Athens, iii. 5; Troilus and Cressida, i. 3; Othello, ii. 1.*

Parasite(s), *Timon of Athens, i. 2; ii. 2; iii. 6; King Lear, ii. 4; A Winter's Tale, ii. 3; King John, iv. 2; Richard II., iii. 2;* hope is a, *Richard II., ii. 2.* See FLATTERERS.

Parchment, dangerousness of, *II. Henry VI., iv. 2.*

Pard, the, more pinch-spotted than, *The Tempest, iv. 1;* bearded like, *As You Like It, ii. 7.*

Pardon, nurse of second woe, *Measure for Measure, ii. 1;* goddess of the night, song, *Much Ado about Nothing, v. 3;* prayers for, *Richard II., v. 3;* offer of, to rebels, *I. Henry IV., iv. 3; v. 1; II. Henry IV., iv. 1; II. Henry VI., v. 8;* royal if given when least expected, *Coriolanus, v. 1;* when the offence is continued, *Hamlet, iii. 3.* See FORGIVENESS, MERCY.

Parent, a, suing to a son, *Coriolanus, v. 3.* See FATHER, MOTHER.

Parental love, *III. Henry VI., ii. 2; v. 5; A Winter's Tale, i. 2; Coriolanus, v. 3; Macbeth, iv. 2.*

Paris, scene of a part of *All's Well that Ends Well,* and of *1. Henry VI., iii. 4; iv. 1.*

Paris, son of Priam, King of Troy, whose elopement with Helen caused the Trojan war, character in *Troilus and Cressida,* introduced in *i. 2.* Alluded to in *Taming of the Shrew, i. 2; Lucrece, lines 1473, 1490; I. Henry VI., v. 6.*

Paris, a character in *Romeo and Juliet,* introduced in *i. 2.* He is a kinsman of the prince and a suitor for Juliet, who is commanded by her parents to accept him. He is killed by Romeo at Juliet's tomb, *v. 3.*

"The well-meaning bridegroom, who thinks that he has loved Juliet right tenderly, must do something out of the common way; his sensibility ventures out of its every-day circle, though fearfully, even to the very borders of the romantic. And yet how far different are his death-rites from those of the beloved! How quietly he scatters his flowers! Hence I cannot ask: 'Was it necessary that this honest soul, too, should be sacrificed? Must Romeo a second time shed blood against his will?' Paris belongs to those persons whom we commend in life, but do not immoderately lament in death; at his last moments he interests us especially by the request to be laid in Juliet's grave. Here Romeo's generosity breaks forth, like a flash of light from darksome clouds, when he utters the last words of blessing over one that has become his brother by misfortune."—SCHLEGEL.

Paris-garden, *Henry VIII., v. 4.* A bear-garden on the Bankside, London.

Parish-top, *Twelfth Night, i. 3.* A large top was usually kept in each village in England for the amusement of the villagers.

Paritors, *Love's Labour's Lost, iii. 1, end.* Officers of the spiritual court who serve citations.

Parle (talk), *Two Gentlemen of Verona, i. 2, and elsewhere.*

Parliament, at Westminster, *III. Henry VI., i. 1;* at Bury St. Edmund's, *II. Henry VI., iii. 1.*

Parlous (perilous), *As You Like It, iii. 2, and elsewhere.*

Parolles, a character in *All's Well that Ends Well,* introduced in the first scene. The name signifies "words," and Parolles is wordy, a braggart, and a treacherous coward. His duplicity is revealed to Bertram in an amusing scene, the third of the fourth act.

Parricides, *King Lear, ii. 1; Macbeth, iii. 1.*

Parrots, prophesy like the, *Comedy of Errors, iv. 4.* It was a custom to teach them phrases like the one in the above passage, and say they prophesied. Discourse will grow commendable in none but, *Merchant of Venice, iii. 5;* clamourous before rain, *As You Like It, iv. 1;* quaint wings of the popinjay, *I. Henry IV., i. 3;* of fewer words than a, *I. Henry IV., ii. 4.*

Parrying, skill in, *Twelfth Night, v. 1; I. Henry IV., ii. 4.*

Parson, dreams of a, *Romeo and Juliet, i. 4.*

Parted (endowed), *Troilus and Cressida, iii. 3.*

Parthians, *Antony and Cleopatra, iii. 1;* fight flying, *Cymbeline, i. 7.*

Parting, of lovers, *Two Gentlemen of Verona, ii. 2; Merchant of Venice, ii. 7; Romeo and Juliet, ii. 2; iii. 5; Troilus and Cressida, iv. 4; Antony and Cleopatra, i. 3; iv. 4, 12, 15; II. Henry VI., iii. 2;* of husband and wife, *I. Henry IV., iii. 1; Cymbeline, i. 4;* of brother and sister, *Hamlet, i. 3; Antony and Cleopatra, iii. 2;* of friends, *Merchant of Venice, ii. 8; Julius Cæsar, v. 1; Antony and Cleopatra, iv. 2;* of Launce from his family, *Two Gentlemen of Verona, ii. 3;* of Cromwell from Wolsey, *Henry VIII., v. 2.*

Partition, a witty, *Midsummer-Night's Dream, v. 1.*

Partition, of England among conspirators, *I. Henry IV., iii. 1.*

Partlet, Dame, *A Winter's Tale, ii. 3* or *4; I. Henry IV., 1; iii. 3.* The hen in "Reynard the Fox."

Partridge, the, in the puttock's nest, *II. Henry V., iii. 2.*

Pash (smash), *Troilus and Cressida, ii. 3.*

Pass (care), *II. Henry VI., iv. 2.*

Pass (thought), of pate, *The Tempest, iv. 1.*

Pass, defence of a, *Cymbeline, v. 3.*

Passado (pass in fencing), *Love's Labour's Lost, i. 2, end; Romeo and Juliet, ii. 4; iii. 1.*

Passes (doings or trespasses), *Measure for Measure, v. 1.*

Passing-bell, the, *II. Henry IV., i. 1; Venus and Adonis, l. 701; Sonnet lxxi.*

Passion, that hangs weights on the tongue, *As You Like It, i. 2;* dangers of, *II. Henry VI. v. 1,* "Take heed lest by your heat," etc.; *Henry VIII., i. 1;* man not the slave of, *Hamlet, iii. 2;* a, torn to tatters, *Hamlet, iii. 2;* of Lear, *King Lear, iii. 1, 2, 4;* between extremes of, *King Lear, v. 3.*

Passionate Pilgrim, The, the name given to a collection of poems usually included in Shakspere's works, though many of them are known not to be from his hand. They were collected and printed with his name in 1599 by a piratical publisher. Of the poems composing it, five are known to be Shakspere's—namely, those beginning, "When my love swears," "Two loves I have," "Did not the heavenly," "If love make me forsworn," "On a day, alack the day," the first two of which are in the *Sonnets (cxxxviii.* and *cxliv.),* and the others in *Love's Labour's Lost,* published in 1598. Two of them are by Richard Barnfield, those beginning, "If music and sweet poetry," "As it fell upon a day." The one beginning, "Live with me and be my love," is by Marlowe; and the answer, "If that the world," is generally attributed to Raleigh. No. *xviii.,* "My flocks feed not," is from Weelkes's "Madrigals," published in 1597. The authorship of the others is doubtful. Swinburne says of them:

"The rest of the ragman's gatherings [excepting the poems from Shakspere], with three most notable exceptions [Marlowe's and Barnfield's], is little better, for the most part, than dry rubbish or disgusting refuse; unless a plea may haply be put in for the pretty commonplaces of the lines on a 'sweet rose, fair flower,' and so forth; for the couple of thin and pallid, if tender and tolerable, copies of verse on 'Beauty' and 'Good-Night,' or the passably light and lively stray of song on 'Crabbed age and youth.'"

The second title given to the latter part of the collection, "Sonnets to Sundry Notes of Music," was in the original.

Passy-measures. See PAVAN.

Past, the, and the to-come. seem best, *II. Henry IV., i. 3;* good deeds of, forgotten, *Troilus and Cressida, iii. 3.*

Pastors, that do not practise what they preach, *Hamlet, i. 3.*

Pastry (room for pastry), *Romeo and Juliet, iii. 4.*

Patay, battle of, *I. Henry VI., iv. 1.*

Patch, *Comedy of Errors, iii. 1, 2; Macbeth, v. 3, and others.* Fool; originally a jester in a patched dress.

Patches, worse than rents, *King John, iv. 2.*

Patchery (roguery), *Troilus and Cressida, ii. 3; Timon of Athens, v. 1.*

Paths, walking in trodden, *As You Like It, i. 3.*

Patience, at others' troubles, *Comedy of Errors, ii. 1;* exhortation to, *Comedy of Errors, iii. 1,* Balthazar's speech; under sorrow, *Much Ado about Nothing, v. 1;* opposed to fury, *Merchant of Venice, iv. 1;* on a monument, *Twelfth Night, ii. 4;* is cowardice in nobles, *Richard II., i. 2;* what goddess she be, *Troilus and Cressida, i. 1;* cool, *Hamlet, iii. 4;* prayer for, *King Lear, ii. 4;* makes a mockery of injury, *Othello, i. 3;* they are poor that have not, *Othello, ii. 3;* past, *Othello, iv. 2;* is sottish, *Antony and Cleopatra, iv., end;* gazing on kings' graves, *Pericles, v. 1;* a tired mare, *Henry V., ii. 1;* grief and, *Cymbeline, iv. 2;* badge of the Jews, *Merchant of Venice, i. 3;* sovereign aid of, *Tempest, v. 1.*

Patience, an attendant of Queen Katharine in *Henry VIII.,* introduced in *iv. 2.*

Patines, *Merchant of Venice, v. 1.*

" A patine is a small, flat dish or plate (for holding the bread) used with the chalice in the administration of the sacrament."—DYCE.

Patricians, complaint against, *Coriolanus, i. 1;* dividing their power, *Coriolanus, iii. 1.*

Patrick, Saint, Hamlet swears by, *i. 5.*

Patriotism, *King John, v. 2; Richard II., ii. 1; iii. 2; I. Henry IV., iv. 3,* "The king is kind," etc.; a woman's, *Coriolanus, i. 3;* of Comenius, *Coriolanus, iii. 3;* of Macduff, *Macbeth, iv. 3;* and friendship, *Julius Cæsar, i. 2,* speech of Brutus, "Passions of some difference," etc.; professed, of Brutus, *Julius Cæsar, iii. 2.*

Patroclus, a Grecian general, character in *Troilus and Cressida,* introduced in *ii. 1.* In *i. 3* Ulysses describes his mimicry of the other Greek leaders for the amusement of Achilles.

Pauca verba (few words), *Love's Labour's Lost, iv. 2.*

Paucas pallabris (few words), *Taming of the Shrew, induction, 1.*

Paul, by Saint, a favourite oath of Richard III., *i. 1, 3; iii. 4; v. 3.*

Paulina, an important character in *A Winter's Tale*, a champion of the queen against the jealous king.

"Such are some of the words that boil over from the stout heart of Paulina, the noblest and most amiable termagant we shall anywhere find, when, with the new-born babe in charge, she confronts the furious king. He threatens to have her burnt, and she replies instantly:

> "'I care not;
> It is an heretic that makes the fire,
> Not she which burns in't.'

If her faults were a thousand times greater than they are, I could pardon them all for this one little speech; which proves that Shakspere was, I will not say a Protestant, but a true Christian intellectually, at least, and far deeper in the spirit of his religion than a large majority of the Church's official organs were in his day, or, let me add, have been any day since. . . . With a head to understand and a heart to reverence such a woman [Hermione], she unites a temper to fight and a generosity to die for her. . . . Loud, voluble, violent, and viraginous, with a tongue sharper than a sword, and an eloquence that fairly blisters where it hits, she has, therewithal, too much honour and magnanimity and kind feeling either to use them without good cause, or to forbear using them at all hazards when she has such cause."—HUDSON.

Paul's, I bought him in, *II. Henry IV., i. 2.* St. Paul's was a resort for all kinds of idlers, and men out of service were to be found there as at an intelligence-office. See under PROVERBS.

Pavan, *Twelfth Night, v. 1.* The pavan is a grave, formal dance. This word is in some texts *paynim*, in which case "a passy-measures paynim" is interpreted, a heathen past measure. With pavan, passy-measures may be understood to mean *pacing-measure*.

Payment, fair, for foul words, *Love's Labour's Lost, iv. 1.*

Peace, Heaven's, but not the King of Hungary's, *Measure for Measure, i. 2;* soldiers and, *Measure for Measure, i. 2;* to all that dare not fight, *Love's Labour's Lost, i. 1;* made, *King John, ii. 1; iii. 1;* fat ribs of, *King John, iii. 3;* attempt to make, between challenger and challenged, *Richard II., i. 1;* a breathing-space for, *I. Henry IV., i. 1;* made, *II. Henry IV., iv. 2; Henry V., v. 3; I. Henry VI., v. 1; II. Henry VI., i. 1; Henry VIII., i. 1;* virtues becoming in, *Henry V., iii. 1;* one unfitted for—the piping time of, *Richard III., i. 1;* desire for, *Richard III., ii. 1;* above earthly dignities, *Henry VIII., iii. 2;* prophesied in the time of Elizabeth, *Henry VIII., v. 4;* shallow boats in time of, *Troilus and Cressida, i. 3;* an apoplexy, etc., *Coriolanus, iv. 5;* made by women, *Coriolanus, v. 3;* ratified, *Cymbeline, v. 5, end.*

Peace-maker(s), King Edward as a, *Richard III., ii. 1;* God's blessing on, *Macbeth, ii. 4.*

Peacocks, Juno's, *The Tempest, iv. 1;* pride of, *Comedy of Errors, iv. 3; I. Henry VI., iii. 3; Troilus and Cressida, iii. 3; Hamlet, iii. 2.*

Pearls, in a foul oyster, *As You Like It, v. 4;* tears transformed to, *Richard III.. iv. 4;* alluding to the notion that pearl-oysters open on a certain day in the year to receive rain-drops, which then become pearls; in India, *Troilus and Cressida, i. 1;* a union (a large pearl), *Hamlet, v. 2;* a rich, thrown away, *Othello, v. 2.*

Pears, poperin, *Romeo and Juliet, ii. 1;* warden, *A Winter's Tale, iv. 3.*

Peas-blossom, a fairy in the *Midsummer-Night's Dream, iii. 1.*

Peascod, wooing a, *As You Like It, ii. 4.* Alluding to the custom of using the pods of peas in divinations of lovers.

Peat (pet), *Taming of the Shrew, i. 1.*

Peck, Gilbert, *Henry VIII., i. 1; ii. 1.*

Pedant, a, a character in the *Taming of the Shrew*, introduced in *iv. 2*, who takes the name of Vincentio. Another pedant in the plays is Holofernes in *Love's Labour's Lost.*

Pedantry, ridiculed in *Love's Labour's Lost.*

Pedascule (pedant), *Taming of the Shrew, iii. 1.*

Pedlar, a, Autolycus in *A Winter's Tale.*

Pedro, Don, Prince of Aragon, character in *Much Ado about Nothing*, introduced in *i. 1*, a good-humoured meddler.

Peeled (bald, tonsured), *I. Henry VI., i. 3.*

Peer out, *Merry Wives of Windsor, iv. 2.* Allusion to a children's rhyme to a snail—

      "Peer out, peer out, peer out of your hole,
        Or else I'll beat you as black as a coal."

Peevish (foolish), *Comedy of Errors, iv. 1, 4; Richard III., iv. 4;* (saucy), *Twelfth Night, i. 5.*

Peg-a-Ramsey, *Twelfth Night, ii. 3.* The heroine of an old song, mistress of James I. of Scotland.

Pegasus, *I. Henry IV., iv. 1; Henry V., iii. 7.* The winged horse of the Muses.

Pegasus, the, *Taming of the Shrew, iv. 4.* An inn in Genoa. The arms of the Middle Temple, and a popular sign.

Peise or peize (to weigh), *Merchant of Venice, iii. 2; King John, ii. 1.*

Pelican, the, *Richard II., ii. 1; Hamlet, iv. 5 or 2; King Lear,* *iii. 4.* Allusion to the notion that young pelicans were fed on their mother's blood.

Pelion, Mount (a range in Thessaly), *Merry Wives of Windsor, ii. 1; Hamlet, v. 1.* The giants piled Ossa upon Pelion in order to climb into heaven.

Pelting (paltry), *Richard II., ii. 1, and elsewhere.*

Pembroke, William Marshall, Earl of, character in *King John,* introduced in the first scene. He did not go over to the French interest, as represented in the play, but his son, of the same name, joined the Dauphin.

Pembroke, William Herbert, Earl of, character in *III. Henry VI.,* introduced in *iv. 1.* He was a partisan of York. He was beheaded in 1469. Sir Walter Herbert in *Richard III.* was his son.

Pembroke, Jasper Tudor, Earl of, *Richard III., iv. 5.* He was an uncle of Richmond.

Pembroke, Marchioness of, Anne Boleyn receives the title of, *Henry VIII., ii. 3.*

Penalties, unenforced, *Measure for Measure, i. 4.* See PARDON.

Penance, for a jealous tyrant, *A Winter's Tale, iii. 2,* "A thousand knees," etc.

Pendragon, *I. Henry VI., iii. 2.* Uther, father of Arthur.

Penelope, her spinning, *Coriolanus, i. 3.*

Penelophon (or Zenelophon), *Love's Labour's Lost, iv. 1.* The beggar-maid loved by King Cophetua.

Penitence, the signal for mercy, *The Tempest, v. 1;* enough, *Two Gentlemen of Verona, v. 4;* for another's fault, *Comedy of Errors, i. 2;* in ashes, *King John, iv. 1.*

Penker, Friar, *Richard III., iii. 5.* Provincial of the Augustine friars, and a popular preacher. See SHAW.

Pensioners, *Merry Wives of Windsor, ii. 2; Midsummer-Night's Dream, ii. 1.* Allusion to Elizabeth's tall gentlemen pensioners, who wore an abundance of gold lace.

Pentapolis, scene of a part of *Pericles.*

Pentecost, pageants at, *Two Gentlemen of Verona, iv. 4.*

Penthesilea, *Twelfth Night, ii. 3.* The queen of the Amazons.

People, dislike of being gazed at by the, *Measure for Measure, i. 1;* courting the common, *Richard II., i. 4;* liking of the, in their eyes, *Hamlet, iv. 3 or v. 7;* sympathy of the, *King Lear, iv. 3,* "To pluck the common bosom;" fickleness of the, *Antony and Cleopatra, i. 2, 4;* are the city, *Coriolanus, iii. 1.* See also PLEBEIANS.

Pepin, King, when he was a boy, *Love's Labour's Lost, iv. 1;* s physician that could raise, *All's Well that Ends Well, ii. 1;* his title to the throne, *Henry V., i. 2;* counsellors to, *Henry VIII., i. 3.*

Percy, Henry. See NORTHUMBERLAND, and HOTSPUR.

Percy, Lady, wife of Hotspur, character in *I. Henry IV.*, introduced in *ii. 3,* and as Hotspur's widow in *II. Henry IV., ii. 3,* where she upbraids Northumberland for sacrificing his son by his delay. Her name, called Kate in the play, was Elizabeth. She was a sister of Mortimer.

Percy, Thomas. See WORCESTER.

Perdita, the lost daughter of Leontes and Hermione in *A Winter's Tale,* is brought up as a shepherdess, but restored to her parents at the age of sixteen. Her natural grace and the delicacy and elevation of her nature, the strong features of her mother's softened by inexperience and girlish light-heartedness, make her one of the most attractive among the heroines of the plays. Her character is exhibited chiefly in *iv. 4.*

Perdu, *King Lear, iv. 7.* A soldier sent on a forlorn hope.

Perdy (par Dieu), *Comedy of Errors, iv. 4, and elsewhere.*

Peregrinate (of a foreign cast), *Love's Labour's Lost, v. 1.*

Perfect (certain), *A Winter's Tale, iii. 3 or 4, and elsewhere.*

Perfection, *All's Well that Ends Well, ii. 1,* "All that life can rate," etc.; *Othello, ii. 1,* "She that was ever fair," etc.; no absolute, *Lucrece, l. 853.*

Performance, *Henry VIII., i. 2;* a kind of testament, *Timon of Athens, v. 2.*

Perge (go on), *Love's Labour's Lost, iv. 2.*

Periapts, charms worn to guard from danger, *I. Henry VI., v. 3.*

Pericles, Prince of Tyre, a drama first published in 1609; it was not included in the folio of 1623. Some critics suppose it to be the joint production of Shakspere and another or others; that the first three acts were not his, and that this accounts for its omission from the folio. Others think he wrote it at an early period, and rewrote the better part in his maturer years. It is known to have been very popular on the stage. The plot is taken from an old story in the "Gesta Romanorum," translated into Anglo-Saxon, and afterward into English (1576), by Lawrence Twine, under the title, "The Pattern of Painful Adventures." Gower rendered it into English verse, and included it in his "Confessio Amantis." The play is apparently from the version of Gower, who appears as chorus in it. Apollonius is the name of the prince in those versions; and it has been conjectured that Pericles is a form for Pyrocles, name of the hero of Sidney's "Arcadia," published in 1590; the more so, as the character in the play, and some of the incidents and ideas, resemble those of Sidney's work. The period of action extends over from fifteen to twenty years. The play as a whole is not regarded as of any great value, but portions of it are in Shakspere's best manner. "No poetry of shipwreck and the sea has ever equalled the great scene of 'Pericles;' no such note of music was ever struck out of the clash and contention of tempestuous elements."

Pericles, Prince of Tyre, introduced in the first scene of the drama, where he solves the riddle of Antiochus, who seeks his life in revenge, and he, by the advice of Helicanus, goes away to travel; relieves Tharsus, *i. 4;* is shipwrecked, *ii. 1;* victor in a joust, *ii. 3;* marries Thaisa, *ii. 5;* is wrecked a second time, *iii., prologue;* finds his daughter, *v. 1;* his wife, *v. 3.*

"His depth of soul and intellect, and a touch of melancholy, produce in him that painful sensitiveness, which indeed, as long as he is unsuspicious, leaves him indifferent to danger; but, after he has once perceived the evil of men, renders him more faint-hearted than bold, and more agitated and uneasy than enterprising."—GERVINUS.

Perigenia, *Midsummer-Night's Dream, ii. 1.*

Perigort, Lord, *Love's Labour's Lost, ii. 1.*

Perjurer, wearing papers, *Love's Labour's Lost, iv. 3.* A perjurer was punished by being compelled to wear a paper on the breast naming his crime.

Perjury, *King John, iii. 1;* of lovers, *Romeo and Juliet, ii. 2;* plagues for, *Love's Labour's Lost, v. 2; Merchant of Venice, iv. 1; Much Ado about Nothing, iv. 1; As You Like It, i. 2.*

Perpend (consider), *Merry Wives of Windsor, ii. 1; Twelfth Night, v. 1; Hamlet, ii. 2.*

Perpetual motion, scoured to death with, *II. Henry IV., i. 2.*

Perplexity, expression of, *Cymbeline, iii. 4.*

Perseus, *Henry V., iii. 7; Troilus and Cressida, i. 3; iv. 5.* The hero that took the Gorgon's head.

Perseverance, keeps honour bright, *Troilus and Cressida, iii 3; Venus and Adonis, l. 565;* after repulse, *The Tempest, iii. 3.*

Perspective, *Twelfth Night, v. 1; Richard II., ii. 2.* The name was applied to all kinds of optical instruments, some of which produced illusions, and it was also a name for pictures painted so as to show the design only from a certain point of view at one side.

Perversion, from natural use, *Romeo and Juliet, ii. 3;* of the fairest things, *Sonnets xciv.-xcvi.*

Pestilence, *Coriolanus, iv. 1; Romeo and Juliet, v. 2; Antony and Cleopatra, iii. 8;* judgment of God, *Richard II., iii. 3;* "the Benedick," *Much Ado about Nothing, i. 1.*

Petar (petard), hoist with his own, *Hamlet, iii. 4, end.*

Peter, Saint, *Othello, iv. 2; Much Ado about Nothing, ii. 1; Romeo and Juliet, iii. 5.*

Peter of Pomfret, a character in *King John,* appears in *iv. 2.* He was a hermit reverenced ·by the common people as a seer. It is said that for his prophecy, which was really made in 1213, he was dragged at horses' tails and afterward hanged on a gibbet with his son. He was said to have been instigated to utter the prophecy against John by the pope's legate and the barons; it was supposed also that his words moved John to come to a speedier agreement with the pope.

Peter, a friar in *Measure for Measure,* introduced in *iv. 5.*

Peter, assistant of the armourer in *II. Henry VI.,* introduced in *i. 3;* his combat with his master, *ii. 3.*

Peter, servant of the nurse in *Romeo and Juliet,* appears in *ii. 4* and *iv. 5.*

Petitions, of maidens, *Measure for Measure, i. 5.*

Peto, one of the companions of Falstaff in the two parts of *Henry IV.,* introduced in the first part in *ii. 2,* and in the second in *ii. 4.* He was Falstaff's lieutenant in his "charge of horse."

Petrarch, *Romeo and Juliet, ii. 4.*

Petrifaction, *Hamlet, iv. 7* or *4.*

Petruchio, character in the *Taming of the Shrew,* who marries Katherina the shrew, first appears in *i. 2.*

"Petruchio appears the only rational character of the piece; yet even he is driven, by the pervading folly of all the rest, at least to play the part of a fool, and so becomes ridiculous, even though eventually the laugh is on his side. All the characters except Petruchio and Katherina are sketched with a light touch; the very composition of the piece forbids a nicer and more accurate delineation, and yet Shakspere has succeeded in giving to all the stamp of individuality. One trait in Katherina's conduct appears false: it is not easy to see how so self-willed and stubborn a disposition could have been so easily persuaded into a marriage with Petruchio. . . . The true motive, evidently, was the surprise and irresistible impression which an energetic mind and manly resolution made upon her. In Petruchio she meets for the first time in her life a man worthy of the name; hitherto she has been surrounded with mere women in male attire. A genuine man she cannot but admire, nay, more, love. The very pride and somewhat overweening energy of her womanly nature is a sufficient reason, psychologically, for her hearty submission."—ULRICI.

Pew-fellow (companion), *Richard III., iv. 4.*

Phaeton, *Two Gentlemen of Verona, iii. 1; Richard II., iii. 3; III. Henry VI., i. 4; ii. 6; Romeo and Juliet, iii. 2.* He attempted to drive for one day the chariot of his father, the Sun. The horses ran away. The world was set on fire, and Jove, at the petition of the Earth, hurled a thunderbolt at the unhappy charioteer, who fell headlong into the river Eridanus.

Pharamond, King, and the Salic law, *Henry V., i. 2.*

Pharaoh, lean kine of, *I. Henry IV., ii. 4;* soldiers of, *Much Ado about Nothing, iii. 3.*

Pheezar (conqueror), *Merry Wives of Windsor, i. 3.*

Pheeze (to chastise or humble), *Taming of the Shrew, induction, 1; Troilus and Cressida, ii. 3.*

Philadelphos, of Paphlagonia, *Antony and Cleopatra, iii. 6.*

Philario, an Italian, friend of Posthumus in *Cymbeline,* introduced in *i. 4.*

Philemon. See OVID.

Philemon, servant of Cerimon in *Pericles,* appears in *iii. 2.*

Philip, name for a sparrow, *King John, i. 1,* so called from its note, which is thought to sound like the name.

Philip and Jacob, Saints, *Measure for Measure, iii. 2.* A holiday falling on May 1st.

Philip (Augustus) II., King of France from 1180 to 1223, a character in *King John.* He is introduced at the beginning of the second act. He was the great enemy and rival of Cœur-de-Lion.

Philippi, the battles of: decision to give battle, *Julius Cæsar, iv. 3;* the action, *Julius Cæsar, v. 1–5;* they were separated by an interval of twenty days, though spoken of in *v. 3* as being on the same day; *Antony and Cleopatra, iii. 9 or 11.*

Philo, character in *Antony and Cleopatra,* introduced in *i. 1,* friend of Antony.

Philomel, *Titus Andronicus, ii. 4* or *5; iv. 1; Lucrece, lines 1079, 1128; Sonnet cii.; Passionate Pilgrim, xv; Cymbeline, ii. 2.* See TEREUS.

Philosopher, a, never could endure toothache, *Much Ado about Nothing, v. 1;* the weeping (Heraclitus), *Merchant of Venice, i. 2;* desiring to eat a grape, *As You Like It, v. 1.*

Philosopher's stone, the, *All's Well that Ends Well, v. 3,* "Plutus himself," etc.; two stones, *II. Henry IV., iii. 2;* alluded to as a great medicine, *Antony and Cleopatra, i. 5.*

Philosophy, a school of, *Love's Labour's Lost, i. 1;* a shepherd's, *As You Like It, iii. 2;* adversity's milk, *Romeo and Juliet, iii. 3;* make no use of, *Julius Cæsar, iv. 3;* things not dreamt of in, *Hamlet, i. 5;* pretended, *All's Well that Ends Well, ii. 3.*

Philostrate, character in the *Midsummer-Night's Dream,* introduced in *i. 1.* He is Theseus's master of the revels.

Philoten, daughter of Cleon, Governor of Tarsus, mentioned in *Pericles, iv., prologue.*

Philotus, servant of one of the creditors of *Timon of Athens,* introduced in *iii. 4.*

Phisnomy (physiognomy), *All's Well that Ends Well, iv. 5.*

Phœbe (the moon), *Midsummer-Night's Dream, i. 1; Titus Andronicus, i. 2.*

Phœbe, a shepherdess and rustic beauty in *As You Like It,* with "inky brows, black silk hair, bugle eyeballs, and cheeks of cream," beloved by Silvius, appears first in *iii. 5.* She "is quite an Arcadian coquette; she is a piece of pastoral poetry."

Phœbus Apollo, god of the sun, *The Tempest, iv. 1; Much Ado about Nothing, v. 3; A Winter's Tale, iv. 3 or 4; III. Henry VI., ii. 6; Hamlet, iii. 2; Antony and Cleopatra, iv. 8; v. 2; Cymbeline, ii. 3; I. Henry IV., i. 2; Romeo and Juliet, iii. 2.*

Phœnix, the, *The Tempest, iii. 3; Comedy of Errors, i. 2; III. Henry VI., i. 4; Henry VIII., v. 5; Cymbeline, i. 6; Sonnet xix.; Lover's Complaint, l. 93; As Yon Like It, iv. 3; I. Henry VI., v. 1; Timon of Athens, ii. 1.* A fabled Arabian bird, which, after living five hundred years, made for itself a funeral pyre, from the ashes of which rose a new phœnix.

Phœnix and the Turtle, The, was printed as Shakspere's in a book which appeared in 1601, "Love's Martyr, or Rosalin's Complaint." Its authorship is doubtful.

Phraseless (indescribable), *Lover's Complaint, l. 225.*

Phrases, red-lattice (alehouse), *Merry Wives of Windsor, v. 5;* not soldier-like, *Merry Wives of Windsor, ii. 1;* a mint of, *Love's Labour's Lost, i. 1.*

Phrygian Turk, base, *Merry Wives of Windsor, i. 3.*

Phrynia, a mistress to Alcibiades, character in *Timon of Athens,* introduced in *iv. 3.*

Physic, throw, to the dogs, *Macbeth, v. 3.* See MEDICINE.

Physical (medicinal), *Coriolanus, i. 4; Julius Cæsar, ii. 1.*

Physician(s), ridicule of, *Merry Wives of Windsor, ii. 3;* ironical praise of, *Merry Wives of Windsor, iii. 1;* skill of a, *All's Well that Ends Well, i. 1;* a woman, *All's Well that Ends Well, ii. 1;*

trust not the, *Timon of Athens, iv. 3;* kill the, and bestow the fee on the disease, *King Lear, i. 1;* give what they would not take, *Pericles, i. 2;* sleeps while the patient dies, *Lucrece, l. 904;* an angry, *Sonnet cxlvii.*

Physicians. See BUTTS, CAIUS, CERIMON, CORNELIUS, NARBON, and **Doctors** in MACBETH and KING LEAR.

Physiognomy, *Macbeth, i. 1,* "There is no art to find the mind's construction in the face."

Picardy, scene of a part of *Henry V.,* and mentioned in *II. Henry VI., iv. i.*

Picked (nice, fastidious), *Love's Labour's Lost, v. 1.*

Pickpocket, a, Autolycus in *A Winter's Tale.*

Pickthanks (parasites), *I. Henry IV., iii. 2.*

Pickt-hatch, *Merry Wives of Windsor, ii. 2.* "A disreputable neighbourhood in London, where the hatches or half-doors were protected against rogues by spikes or pickets."

Picture, of we three, *Twelfth Night, ii. 3.* Allusion to a common sign representing two fools and the legend beneath, "We three fools be."

Pictures, two contrasted, *Hamlet, iii. 4;* description of, *Taming of the Shrew, induction. 2;* the sleeping and the dead are as, *Macbeth, ii. 2.* See PERSPECTIVES and PAINTING.

Piedness, in flowers, *A Winter's Tale, iv. 3 or 4.*

Pierce of Exton, Sir. See EXTON.

Piety, rewards by fairies for, *Merry Wives of Windsor, v. 5;* cruel, irreligious, *Titus Andronicus, i. 2.*

Pigeons, carrier, *Titus Andronicus, iv. 3.*

Pight (pitched, set), *King Lear, ii. 1; Troilus and Cressida, v. 2.*

Pigrogromitus and the Vapians, *Twelfth Night, ii. 3.* This is probably an invention of Shakspere's, used in fun.

Pilate, Pontius, *Richard II., iv. 1; Richard III., i. 4.*

Pilcher (scabbard), *Romeo and Juliet, iii. 1.*

Pilgrim, a true devoted, *Two Gentlemen of Verona, iv. 7.*

Pilgrimage(s), *All's Well that Ends Well, iv.3;* to Canterbury, *I. Henry IV., i. 2;* to atone for guilt, *Richard II., v. 6.*

Pillage, forbidden to soldiers, *Henry V., iii. 6.*

Pillar of the world, the triple [or third], *Antony and Cleopatra, i. 1.* Alluding to the three triumvirs.

Pilled (despoiled, from the same root as *pillage*), *Richard II., ii. 1; Richard III., i. 3.*

Pillicock, sat on, etc., *King Lear, iii. 4.* A nursery rhyme.

Pillory, the, *Two Gentlemen of Verona, iv. 4; Taming of the Shrew, ii. 1.*

Pimpernell, Henry, mentioned, *Taming of the Shrew, induction, 2.*

Pin and web (cataract on the eye), *A Winter's Tale, i. 2; King Lear, iii. 4.*

Pinch, a schoolmaster in the *Comedy of Errors,* introduced in *iv. 4;* described by Antipholus in *v. 1.*

Pindarus, a servant of Cassius in *Julius Cæsar,* appears in *iv. 2.*

Pine-trees, knots in, *Troilus and Cressida, i. 3.*

Pioned (covered with peonies), *The Tempest, iv. 1.*

Pip out, a, *Taming of the Shrew, i. 2.* " A phrase applied to a drunken person, borrowed from a game of cards, Bone-ace, or One and Thirty."

Pipe, a, for Fortune's finger to sound what stop she pleases, *Hamlet, iii. 2;* of Hermes, *Henry V., iii. 7.*

Pirate(s), *Twelfth Night, v. 1; II. Henry VI., i. 1;* Suffolk dies by, *iv. 1; Hamlet, iv. 6* or *3; Antony and Cleopatra, i. 4; ii. 6;* the sanctimonious, *Measure for Measure, i. 2.*

Pisa, renowned, *Taming of the Shrew, i. 1; iv. 2.*

Pisanio, servant to Posthumus in *Cymbeline,* introduced in *i. 1;* ordered to kill Imogen, *iii. 2;* his scheme to save her, *iii. 4.*

Pistol, a swaggering bully, one of Falstaff's companions in *II. Henry IV.,* the *Merry Wives of Windsor,* and *Henry V.* He is at first ancient or ensign, afterward lieutenant, and marries Mistress Quickly, the tavern hostess. In the *Merry Wives of Windsor* he conspires with Nym to defeat Falstaff. His character is set forth by Falstaff in *ii. 2.* His conversation is distinguished by the use of classical allusions. He is introduced in *II. Henry IV.* in *ii. 4,* where he rants snatches of plays and ballads. In *Henry V., ii. 1,* he appears as the husband of Mistress Quickly, and quarrels with Bardolph, who had been troth-plight to her. He goes to the war in France, appearing on the battle-field in *iv. 4,* and is last seen in *v. 1.* The names of Bardoulph and Pistail are said to be on the muster-roll of artillerymen serving under the Earl of Arundel in 1435.

Pitch, they that touch, are defiled, *Much Ado about Nothing, iii. 3; I. Henry IV., ii. 4; II. Henry VI., ii. 1; Love's Labour's Lost, iv. 3.*

Pitchers, have ears, *Taming of the Shrew, iv. 4; Richard III., ii. 4.*

Pity, and justice, *Measure for Measure, ii. 2;* even beasts know

Richard III., *i. 2;* for the falling, *Henry VIII.*, *iii. 2;* leave, with our mothers, *Troilus and Cressida*, *v. 3;* the virtue of the law, *Timon of Athens*, *iii. 5;* like a new-born babe, *Macbeth*, *i. 7;* 'tis true, 'tis, *Hamlet*, *ii. 2;* for the poor, *King Lear*, *iii. 4*, " Poor naked wretches," etc. ; implored, *As You Like It*, *ii. 7;* *Cymbeline*, *iv. 2 ;* *Henry VIII.*, *prologue;* for a begging prince, *Richard III.*, *i. 4;* want of, *Richard II.*, *v. 2 ; Timon of Athens*, *iii. 2 ; iv. 3.*

Piu por dulzura, que por fuerza, *Pericles*, *ii. 2.* More by gentleness than by force.

Place and greatness, *Measure for Measure*, *iv. 1.*

Plague, the: inscription on infected houses, " Lord have mercy on us," *Love's Labour's Lost*, *v. 2 ;* of Greece, *Troilus and Cressida*, *ii. 1*, sent by Apollo on the Grecian army ; of both your houses, *Romeo and Juliet*, *iii. 1;* of custom (conventionality), *King Lear*, *i. 2.*

Plain-speaking, *Julius Cæsar*, *i. 2*, " Rudeness is a sauce," etc. ; *Julius Cæsar*, *iii. 2*, " I have neither wit nor words," etc. ; *King Lear*, *ii. 2*, " These kind of knaves I know," etc.

Planched (planked), *Measure for Measure*, *iv. 1.*

Planetary influence. See ASTROLOGY.

Planets, the, disorder of, *Troilus and Cressida*, *i. 3.*

Plantagenet. For Edmund, see RUTLAND. For Edward, see EDWARD IV. For George, see CLARENCE. For Richard, Duke of York, see YORK. For Richard, see RICHARD III.

Plantain, the herb, used for wounds, *Love's Labour's Lost*, *iii. 1; Romeo and Juliet*, *i. 2.*

Plashy, *Richard II.*, *i. 2; ii. 2.* Castle of the Duchess of Gloster in Essex.

Platforms (plans), *I. Henry VI.*, *ii. 1.*

Plautus, *Hamlet*, *ii. 2.* A Roman comic dramatist, died in the year 184 B. C.

Player(s), a strutting, *Troilus and Cressida*, *i. 3*, "The great Achilles," etc.; *Taming of the Shrew, induction*, *1; Hamlet*, *ii. 2 ;* life like a, *Macbeth*, *v. 5;* advice to, *Hamlet*, *iii. 1.* See ACTORS.

Play(s), life a, *As You Like It*, *ii. 7;* remorse oft aroused by, *Hamlet*, *ii. 2;* names of, *Midsummer-Night's Dream*, *v. 1;* good for · melancholy, *Taming of the Shrew, induction*, *2.*

Plea, of " not guilty," *A Winter's Tale*, *iii. 2.*

Pleached (intertwined), *Much Ado about Nothing*, *i. 2*, and elsewhere.

Pleasure, deaf to reason, *Troilus and Cressida*, *ii. 2;* turned ill, *Antony and Cleopatra*, *i. 2;* dearly bought, *Lucrece*, *l. 211.*

Plebeians, of Rome, revolt of, *Coriolanus, i. 1.* This incident in the play is placed in a street of Rome; but, according to Plutarch, the plebs withdrew to Mons Sacer, the holy hill. Wrongs and faults of, *Coriolanus, i. 1;* cowardice of, *Coriolanus, i. 4, 6;* abuse of, *Coriolanus, ii. 1;* flatterers of, *Coriolanus, ii. 2, 3; iii. 2;* wits of the, *Coriolanus, ii. 3;* denounced, *Coriolanus, iii. 1;* contempt for, *Coriolanus, iii. 1–3;* defied, *Coriolanus, iii. 3;* repent the banishment, *Coriolanus, iv. 6.* See PEOPLE, POPULACE.

Plenty, breeds cowards, *Cymbeline, iii. 6.*

Plodding, in books, *Love's Labour's Lost, i. 1;* prisons the spirits, *Love's Labour's Lost, iv. 3.*

Plots: against Falstaff, *Merry Wives of Windsor, ii. 1; iii. 3, 5; iv. 2, 4; v. 2–5;* Ford's, *Merry Wives of Windsor, ii. 2;* against Benedick and Beatrice, *Much Ado about Nothing, ii. 3; iii. 1;* against Hero, *Much Ado about Nothing, ii. 2;* of Hortensio and Petruchio, *Taming of the Shrew, i. 2;* of Lucentio and Tranio, *Taming of the Shrew, i. 1;* of Helena, *All's Well that Ends Well, iii. 7;* against Parolles, *All's Well that Ends Well, iii. 6; iv. 1;* to commit murder, *A Winter's Tale, i. 2;* to rob, *A Winter's Tale, iv. 2 or 3;* of the Abbot of Westminster, *Richard II., iv. 1; v. 2, 3, 6;* of the Percys, *I. Henry IV., i. 3; ii. 3;* against Clarence, *Richard III., i. 1;* against Hamlet, *Hamlet, iv. 7 or 4;* of Edmund against Edgar, *King Lear, i. 2; ii. 1;* of Iago, *Othello, ii. 1, last part;* of Pisanio, *Cymbeline, iii. 4;* of Cloten, *Cymbeline, iii. 5.*

Plunder, soldiers', *I. Henry IV., iv. 2,* "They'll find linen enough on every hedge;" wrangled over, *Richard III., i. 3.*

Plurisy (plethora, superabundance), *Hamlet, iv. 7.*

Pluto, god of the infernal regions, *Titus Andronicus, iv. 3; Lucrece, l. 553; II. Henry IV., ii. 4; Coriolanus, i. 4; Troilus and Cressida, v. 2.*

Plutus, god of riches, mine of, *Julius Cæsar, iv. 3;* alchemy of, *All's Well that Ends Well, v. 3;* god of gold, *Timon of Athens, i. 1.*

Po, the river, *King John, i. 1.*

Pocket-picking, Falstaff's charge of, *I. Henry IV., iii. 3.*

Poet(s), ink of the, *Love's Labour's Lost, iv. 3;* imagination of the, *Midsummer-Night's Dream, v. 1;* one early dead, *Sonnet xxxii.;* read for his love, *Sonnet xxxii.;* a rival, *Sonnets lxxx., lxxxiv., lxxxv.*

Poet, a, character in *Timon of Athens,* introduced in the first scene, seeking patronage from Timon. In *v. 1* he comes to get gold, having heard of the treasure Timon has found.

Poet (Marcus Favonius), a character in *Julius Cæsar,* who breaks in on the quarrel of Brutus and Cassius in *iv. 3*, and is thrust out by Brutus.

Poetry, the force of, *Two Gentlemen of Verona, iii. 2;* directions for making, *Two Gentlemen of Verona, iii. 2;* lovers given to, *As You Like It, iii. 3;* of love, *Twelfth Night, i. 5,* "Write loyal cantons," etc.; contempt for, *I. Henry IV., iii. 1;* spontaneous, *Timon of Athens, i. 1;* beauty perpetuated in, *Sonnets xv.-xix.; lxiii., lxv., ci., cvii.;* of love, *Sonnets xxi., xxxii., xxxviii., lv.;* enduring, *Sonnets lv., lx.;* sameness in, *Sonnet lxvi.;* immortality in, *Sonnet lxxxi.;* beauty the inspiration of, *Sonnets lxxviii.-lxxx.; lxxxiv.;* defeats time, *Sonnet c.;* inadequacy of, *Sonnet ciii.;* and music, *Passionate Pilgrim, viii.;* the muse of, invoked, *Love's Labour's Lost, i. 2;* golden cadence of, *Love's Labour's Lost, iv. 2;* bootless rhymes, *Love's Labour's Lost, v. 2.*

Poins, or Pointz, one of the companions of the prince, introduced in *I. Henry IV.,* in *i. 2,* and in *II. Henry IV.,* in *ii. 2.* In *ii. 4,* of the second part, Falstaff explains why the prince loves him.

Point-device (foppish, neat), *Love's Labour's Lost, v. 1; As You Like It, iii. 2; Twelfth Night, ii. 5.*

Points, *Taming of the Shrew, iii. 2; A Winter's Tale, iv. 3 or 4, and elsewhere.* Tags to fasten doublet and hose together.

Poison(s), *The Tempest, iii. 3;* alluding to the custom of having a taster for the food of the great, to prevent the administering of, *King John, v. 6;* effect of, *King John, v. 7;* physic in, *II. Henry IV., i. 1, 2;* mentioned, *I. Henry VI., v. 4; Romeo and Juliet, ii. 3; King Lear, iii. 4; Antony and Cleopatra, v. 2;* penalty for selling, *Romeo and Juliet, v. 1;* supposed to swell the body, *King John, v. 6; Julius Cæsar, iv. 3;* effects of, *Hamlet, i. 5;* in the ear, *Hamlet, iii. 2; iv. 7;* given to Regan, *King Lear, v. 3;* asked for, *Cymbeline, i. 5; v. 5.*

Poking-sticks, *A Winter's Tale, iv. 3 or 4.* Instruments to plait ruffles with.

Polacks, the sledded, *Hamlet, i. 1; iv. 4.*

Poland, winter in, *Comedy of Errors, iii. 2.*

Pole, the north, *Othello, ii. 1.*

Polemon, of Mede, *Antony and Cleopatra, iii. 6.*

Policy, in war, contempt for, *Troilus and Cressida, i. 3;* in ill opinion, *Troilus and Cressida, v. 4;* combined with honour, *Coriolanus, iii. 2;* a heretic, *Sonnet cxxiv;* plague of your, *Henry VIII., iii. 2;* is from the devil, *Timon of Athens, iii. 3.*

Politeness. See COURTESY.

Politician(s), management of, *Coriolanus, ii. 3;* a dead, *Hamlet, v. 1;* a scurvy, *King Lear, iv. 6.*

Polixenes, King of Bohemia, in *A Winter's Tale.* The jealousy of Leontes is aroused against him, and he would be murdered but for Camillo, who warns him and flees with him. He opposes the marriage of his son with the shepherdess, but gives consent when she is found to be the daughter of Leontes, King of Sicily. He first appears in *i. 2.*

Polonius, the lord chamberlain in *Hamlet*, first appears in *i. 2.* His advice to his son, *i. 3*, is said to be copied from John Lilly's romance of "Euphues: the Anatomy of Wit," published in 1580; his advice to his daughter, *i. 3;* his death, *iii. 4.* Polonius is officious, confident in his own wisdom and vain of it. "Hamlet's ugly sarcasms seem disproportioned to his offenses, which are the harmless folly of an old man, until we remember the annoyance and irritation one experiences when in deep feeling or perplexity, at the confident, self-satisfied, shallow judgment of some worldly-wise person who imagines his system of weights and measures to be infallible."

Polydore. See GUIDERIUS.

Pomanders, *A Winter's Tale, iv. 3* or *4.* Little perfumed balls of paste worn as amulets.

Pomegranate, *I. Henry IV., ii. 4.* Name of a room in an inn. See BUNCH OF GRAPES.

Pomewater (a kind of apple), *Love's Labour's Lost, iv. 2.*

Pomfret (Pontefract), in Yorkshire, scene of *Richard II., v. 5.* Richard was confined in the dungeon of the castle; *Richard III., ii. 4; iii. 2, 3.*

Pomp, what is, *III. Henry VI., v. 2;* loss of, *Henry VIII., ii. 3;* take physic, *King Lear, iii. 4;* the gate too narrow for pomp to enter, *All's Well that Ends Well, iv. 5.*

Pompeius, Cneius, Pompey the Great (106–48 B. C.), incorrectly mentioned as one of the nine worthies, *Love's Labour's Lost, v. 1;* wars of, *Henry V., iv. 1;* celebration of the victory over his faction, *Julius Cæsar, i. 1;* ingratitude toward, *i. 1;* at Pharsalia, *v. 1;* death of, *II. Henry VI., iv. 1.* He was killed as he was leaving a boat in which he was landing on the shore of Egypt, at the instance of the king's officers, who desired to propitiate Cæsar.

Pompeius, Sextus, Pompey the Younger, character in *Antony and Cleopatra*, introduced in *ii. 1.* His rebellion, *i. 3, 4; ii. 1;* his motives, *ii. 6.*

"The young Pompey, a frank but thoughtless soul, the image of political levity, opposed to the moderate Octavius, fights for the cause of freedom in company with pirates, foolishly brave, without friends. . . . This confidence rests on the predictions of hope, on the command of the sea, on the love of the people, on all the most deceitful things in the world."—GERVINUS.

Pompey, servant of Mrs. Overdone in *Measure for Measure*, introduced in *i. 2*, a circumlocutory rascal.

Pompey's Porch, *Julius Cæsar, i. 3.* At the theatre built by Pompey on the Campus Martius. Cæsar was slain at the foot of the statue of Pompey, which stood there, not in the capitol.

Pont, King of, *Antony and Cleopatra, iii. 6.*

Pontic Sea, the, *Othello, iii. 3.*

Ponton, Lord, *I. Henry VI., i. 4.*

Poor, the, pride of, *Twelfth Night, iii. 1;* sleep of, *Henry V., iv. 1;* sufferings of—fable of rich and, *Coriolanus, i. 1;* neglected, *As You Like It, ii. 1; Timon of Athens, iv. 2.* See also ADVERSITY, POVERTY.

Poor-John (dried and salted hake), *The Tempest, ii. 2; Romeo and Juliet, i. 1.*

Poor soul, the centre of my sinful earth, *Sonnet cxlvi.*

Pope, the (Innocent III.), his quarrel with John of England, *King John, iii. 1;* the reconciliation, *King John, v. 1, 2.*

Pope, the (Clement VII.), *Henry VIII., ii. 2; iii. 2.*

Popilius Lena, a senator in *Julius Cæsar*, introduced in *iii. 1.*

Popinjay (parrot), a, *I. Henry IV., i. 3.*

Poppy, the, *Othello, iii. 3.*

Populace, the, excitement of, *King John, iv. 2;* treatment of the kings by, *Richard II., v. 2;* fickleness of, *II. Henry IV., i. 3; Julius Cæsar, i. 1; iii. 2;* applause of, *Julius Cæsar, i. 2.* See PEOPLE, PLEBEIANS.

Popularity, *Richard II., i. 4; v. 2; I. Henry IV., iii. 2; iv. 3; II. Henry IV., i. 3; Henry V., iv., chorus; Julius Cæsar, i. 3; Merchant of Venice, iii. 2; Coriolanus, ii. 1, 3; ii. 2; Hamlet, iv. 3, 5; Timon of Athens, i. 1;* fickle, *Antony and Cleopatra, i. 4; II. Henry VI., iv. 8; III. Henry VI., ii. 6; iii. 1; iv. 8;* (familiarity with the people), *Henry V., i. 1.*

Pork, the eating of, *Merchant of Venice, i. 3; iii. 5.*

Porpentine (porcupine), *II. Henry VI., iii. 1; Troilus and Cressida, ii. 1;* the fretful, *Hamlet, i. 5;* an inn called the, *Comedy of Errors, iii. 1; v. 1.*

Porpoises, signs of storm, *Pericles, ii. 1.*

Porringer, a pinked, *Henry VIII., v. 4.* A cap shaped like a porringer.

Port (gate), *Antony and Cleopatra, i. 3, and elsewhere.*

Portage (port-holes), *Henry V., iii. 1.*

Portance (carrying on, progress), *Othello, i. 3.*

Portents, *Julius Cæsar, i. 3 ; ii. 2 ; Hamlet, i. 1 ; King John, iii. 4 ; Richard III., ii. 3 ; I. Henry IV., v. 1.* See also OMENS.

Porter, a, character in *Macbeth, ii. 3.* His speeches are generally attributed to some other hand, though Dowden thinks they show that of Shakspere. Schiller in his translation substitutes a pious morning hymn for the porter's speech. Coleridge is positive that the actors interpolated the character, and Shakspere, finding it take with the mob, added the words from " I'll devil-porter it no further." Quite a different view is taken of the part by Ulrici, who says : " But the ordinary and every-day portion of society having been introduced, it must be depicted in complete truth, and therefore also in the comic light which is thrown upon it from its disproportionateness. Even the part of the Porter in *Macbeth,* over whose drunken drowsiness and silly meditations the fearful destiny which is to affect him and his country so deeply sweeps by without a trace, possesses so solemn a seriousness and tends so greatly to heighten the tragic effect that it could on no account be left out."

Portia, the heroine of the *Merchant of Venice,* first appears in *i. 2.* She is, perhaps, in the variety and degree of her fine qualities, the noblest character among Shakspere's women. Though a child of fortune, she is full of ready sympathy for those who suffer; though impulsive and ardent, her high sense of honour will not permit her to give her lover the slightest hint as to the caskets in the choice that involves her whole happiness; though provided with a decision that will do her intellect the greatest honour in the courtroom, she does not bring it forward until she has done her utmost by womanly persuasion to bring the Jew to relent on considerations of mercy and humanity. She is witty, clear-sighted, generous, elastic in temperament, prompt and decided in action.

Portia, wife of Brutus, character in *Julius Cæsar,* first appears in *i. 2 ;* her death, *iv. 3.* Unwilling to be excluded from the counsels of her husband, Portia inflicted a wound upon herself to prove her courage and fortitude. When Brutus fled from Rome after Antony's success, she fell into despair and slew herself.

Portrait(s), description of a, *Merchant of Venice, iii. 2 ;* two contrasted, *Hamlet, iii. 4 ;* love of a, *Two Gentlemen of Verona, iv. 4*

Portugal, Bay of, *As You Like It, iv. 1.*

Possess (inform), *Merchant of Venice, i. 3, and elsewhere.*

Possession, *Much Ado about Nothing, iv. 1,* "What we have we prize not," etc.; disillusionment of, *Troilus and Cressida, i. 2,* "Women are angels," etc.; *Antony and Cleopatra, i. 4; Lucrece, l. 867;* have is have, *King John, i. 1.*

Possessions, that men glory in, *Sonnet xci.*

Post, *Comedy of Errors, i. 2.* Allusion to the practice of scoring accounts on posts.

Posthumus Leonatus, character in *Cymbeline,* Imogen's husband, introduced in the first scene, where he is described. His wager, *i. 4;* he orders the death of Imogen, *iii. 2;* his vision, *v. 4;* his bravery, *v. 5.*

"His jealousy is not heroic, like Othello's; it shows something of grossness unworthy of his truer self. In due time penitential sorrow does its work; his nobler nature reasserts itself."—DOWDEN.

Posy (motto), of a ring, *Hamlet, iii. 2.*

Potato, the, *Merry Wives of Windsor, v. 5.*

Potents (powers or forces), *King John, ii. 1 or 2.*

Pouncet-box, *I. Henry IV., i. 3.* A perforated box for carrying perfumes in.

Pourquoi (why), *Twelfth Night, i. 3.*

Poverty, desperate—my, consents, not my will, *Romeo and Juliet, v. 1;* is bold, *Timon of Athens, iii. 4;* enforced, and willing, *Timon of Athens, iv. 3;* appearance of, *King Lear, ii. 3;* sufferings of, *King Lear, iii. 4;* makes vices apparent, *King Lear, iv, 4;* makes tame, *King Lear, iv. 6.* See ADVERSITY and POOR, the.

Powder, food for, *I. Henry IV., iv. 2;* a skill-less soldier's, *Romeo and Juliet, iii. 3;* (to salt), *I. Henry IV., v. 4.*

Power, just, *The Tempest, v. 1;* abuse of, *Measure for Measure, ii. 4;* worn out before well put on, *Coriolanus, iii. 2;* of a soldier in time of peace, *Coriolanus, iv. 7;* corrupting influence of, *Macbeth, iv. 3;* cannot bear remonstrance, *King Lear, i. 1;* do courtesy to wrath, *King Lear, iii. 7;* unlimited, *Henry VIII., ii. 2.* See also AUTHORITY, GREATNESS.

Poysam, the Papist, *All's Well that Ends Well, i. 3.*

Practice, and preaching, *Merchant of Venice, i. 2; I. Henry VI., iii. 1; Hamlet, i. 3.*

Practice (strategy, trickery), *Measure for Measure, v. 1; King Lear, ii. 1; Othello, v. 2.*

Practisants (plotters), *I. Henry VI., iii. 2.*

Præmunire, *Henry VIII., iii. 2.* A writ against one who sets up another authority than the king's.

Prague, hermit of, *Twelfth Night, iv. 2.*

Praise, of a daughter, *The Tempest, iv. 1;* of Angelo, *Measure for Measure, i. 1;* ironical, *Measure for Measure, v. 1;* of self, *Much Ado about Nothing, v. 2; Troilus and Cressida, i. 3,* speech of Æneas; for the sake of, *Love's Labour's Lost, iv. 1;* a seller's, *Love's Labour's Lost, iv. 3;* envy roused by, *As You Like It, ii. 3; v. 1;* of what's lost, *All's Well that Ends Well, v. 3;* in poetry, generally feigned, *Twelfth Night, i. 5;* influence of, on women, *A Winter's Tale, i. 2,* "Cram us with," etc.; Falstaff's, of himself, *I. Henry IV., ii. 4;* for bravery, *Coriolanus, i. 9; ii. 2;* bought, *Timon of Athens, ii. 2;* daily, found harmful, *Timon of Athens, iv. 3;* of Posthumus, *Cymbeline, i. 1;* in verse, *Sonnet xvii.;* gross, *Sonnet lxxxii.;* cry amen to, like unlettered clerk, *Sonnet lxxxv.*

Prat, Mother, name applied to Falstaff in disguise, *Merry Wives of Windsor, iv. 2.*

Prayer(s), *The Tempest, i. 1;* assaults mercy, *The Tempest, v., epilogue;* for another, *Two Gentlemen of Verona, i. 1;* fault of being given to, *Merry Wives of Windsor, i. 4;* true, *Measure for Measure, ii. 2;* temptation where, cross, *Measure for Measure, ii. 2;* empty, *Measure for Measure, ii. 4;* death believed to be hastened by, *I. Henry VI., i. 1;* daily, *II. Henry VI., ii. 1,* "Let never day nor night," etc.; of Edward IV., *III. Henry VI., ii. 3;* of the king, *Henry V., iv. 1;* pretence of, *Richard III., iii. 7;* of Richmond, *Richard III., v. 3, 5;* twofold force of—words, without thoughts, *Hamlet, iii. 3;* for Othello, *ii. 1;* before death, *Othello, v. 2;* profit in loss of one's, *Antony and Cleopatra, ii. 1;* in a storm, *Pericles, iii. 1;* need of, *Romeo and Juliet, iv. 3;* the Lord's, see LORD'S PRAYER, THE.

Preaching, and practice. See PRACTICE.

Precaution, before building, *II. Henry IV., i. 3;* in time of feast, *Timon of Athens, iv. 3.*

Precedent (first draft), *King John, v. 2.*

Precept(s), and practice, offered in sorrow, *Much Ado about Nothing, v. 1.* See PRACTICE.

Precepts (warrants), *II. Henry IV., v. 1.*

Precipices. See CLIFFS.

Precision, of a hypocrite, *Measure for Measure, i. 4, 5.*

Predictions. See PROPHECY.

Preferment, goes by favour, *Othello, i. 1.*

Prejudice, *All's Well that Ends Well, v. 3; Hamlet, i. 4;* religious, *Merchant of Venice, iii. 1.*

Prejudice (injure), *I. Henry VI., iii. 3.*

Prenzie. See GUARDS.

Presages, ill, *Venus and Adonis, l. 457.* See also OMENS, PORTENTS, PRESENTIMENTS.

Present, the, should be used, *All's Well that Ends Well, v. 3,* "Let's take the instant," etc.; *Timon of Athens, v. 1,* "When the day serves," etc.; seems worst, *II. Henry IV., i. 3;* worth of what is done in, *Troilus and Cressida, iii. 3;* this ignorant, *Macbeth, i. 5;* sacrifice of the future to, *Antony and Cleopatra, i. 4.*

Presentiments, of the dying, *Richard II., ii. 1;* of evil, *Richard II., ii. 2; Richard III., ii. 3;* of untimely death, *Romeo and Juliet, i. 4, end; iii. 5;* in a haunting song, *Othello, iv. 3,* "My mother had a maid," etc.

Presents, to the rich, *Timon of Athens, i. 2.*

Prest (ready), *Merchant of Venice, i. 1.*

Prester John, length of his foot, *Much Ado about Nothing, ii. 1.* Prester John was a name applied to the Kings of Ethiopia or Abyssinia. It is said to be a corruption of *Belul Gian,* precious stone, the first word having been translated and then corrupted into *Presbyter,* and then *Prester.* The precious stone was in a legendary ring said to have been given to the Queen of Sheba by Solomon, and left by her to her descendants.

Presumption, in ascribing to the act of men the help of Heaven, *All's Well that Ends Well, ii. 1.*

Pretence (plot), the undivulged, *Macbeth, ii. 3.*

Prevent (anticipate, forestall), *Twelfth Night, iii. 1; I. Henry VI., iv. 1.*

Prevention (discovery), *Julius Cæsar, ii. 1.*

Priam, King of Troy, character in *Troilus and Cressida,* introduced in *ii. 1;* allusions to: *All's Well that Ends Well, i. 3; II. Henry IV., i. 1; III. Henry VI., ii. 5; Hamlet, ii. 2; Lucrece,* lines *1448, 1466, 1485, 1548.*

Priapus, *Pericles, iv. 6.*

Pribbles, and prabbles, *Merry Wives of Windsor, i. 1; v. 5.*

Prick-song, *Romeo and Juliet, ii. 4.* Written music.

Pride, of authority, *Measure for Measure, ii. 2;* fallen with fortunes, *As You Like It, i. 2;* universality of, *As You Like It, ii. 7;* without contempt or bitterness, *All's Well that Ends Well, i. 2;* must have a fall, *Richard II., v. 5;* loses men's hearts, *I. Henry*

Prisoner's base, allusions to the game of, *Two Gentlemen of Verona, i. 2; Cymbeline, v. 3.*

Probal (probable), *Othello, ii. 3.*

Process (summons), *Antony and Cleopatra, i. 1.*

Procession, coronation, *Henry VIII., iv. 1.*

Proclamation, *Measure for Measure, i. 2.*

Procrastination, cowardly, *Hamlet, iv. 4 or 1.* See DELAY.

Procrus, not Shafalus to, was so true. *Midsummer - Night's Dream, v. 1.* Alluding to the story of Cephalus and his wife Procris. She was told that he had been overheard to say when resting from the chase, "Sweet Aura (air), come and fan me! come, gentle Aura!" Supposing Aura to be a woman, she was aroused to jealousy, and crept through the bushes one day to surprise him at his resting-place. But he, hearing the rustling, and supposing a wild beast was about to spring upon him, discharged an arrow, by which Procris was mortally wounded.

Proculeius, a friend of Cæsar in *Antony and Cleopatra,* introduced in *v. 1,* where Cæsar sends him with a message to Cleopatra; his interview with her, *v. 2.*

Prodigality, *Timon of Athens, i. 1, 2.*

Prodigal son, the, the calf that was killed for, *Comedy of Errors, iv. 3;* chamber painted with the story of, *Merry Wives of Windsor, iv. 5;* alluded to, *1. Henry IV., iv. 2.*

Prodigies. See OMENS, PORTENTS.

Prodigious (prodigal), *Two Gentlemen of Verona, ii. 3.*

Proditor (traitor), *I. Henry VI., i. 3.*

Proface (*pro vi faccia,* may it do you good), *II. Henry IV., v. 3.*

Proffers, unaccepted, *All's Well that Ends Well, ii. 1.*

Profligacy, burns out, *Richard II., ii. 1.*

Progeny (progenitors), *Coriolanus, i. 8.*

Progne, *Titus Andronicus, v. 2.* Sister of Philomela and wife of Tereus. She was changed into a swallow. See TEREUS.

Prolixious (delaying), *Measure for Measure, ii. 4.*

Prologue, to a special nothing, *All's Well that Ends Well, ii. 1.*

Prologues or choruses are introduced at the beginning of each act in *Henry V.,* of *Acts i.* and *ii.* of *Romeo and Juliet,* and at the beginning of *Henry VIII.*

Promethean fire, the, *Love's Labour's Lost, iv. 3;* Promethean heat, *Othello, v. 2.* Prometheus stole fire from heaven for men, and was condemned to perpetual imprisonment on Mount Caucasus, where a vulture continually gnawed his vitals.

Prometheus, tied to Caucasus, *Titus Andronicus, ii. 1.*

Promise, and performance, *Timon of Athens, v. 1;* kept to the ear, *Macbeth, v. 7.*

Promises, *Timon of Athens, i. 2,* "His, so fly beyond his state," etc.; *Merchant of Venice, iv. 1,* "Liberal in offers;" like Adonis's gardens, *I. Henry VI., i. 6;* mighty, *Henry VIII., iv. 2;* of the king, *I. Henry IV., iv. 3.*

Promontory, a strong-based, *The Tempest, v. 1;* the earth a sterile, *Hamlet, ii. 2.*

Promotion, service for, *As You Like It, ii. 3;* many so arrive at second masters, upon their first lord's neck, *Timon of Athens, iv. 3.*

Promptness, *All's Well that Ends Well, v. 3,* "Let's take the instant," etc.; *Julius Cæsar, iv. 3,* "There is a tide," etc.; *Macbeth, i. 7,* "If 'twere done when 'tis done," etc.; anticipating time, *Troilus and Cressida, iv. 5;* we must do something, and in the heat, *King Lear, i. 1.* See also OPPORTUNITY.

Pronunciation, criticism on, *Love's Labour's Lost, v. 1.*

Proof, of men, the true, *Troilus and Cressida, i. 3;* the ocular, *Othello, iii. 3;* let, speak, *Cymbeline, iii. 1;* let the end try the man, *II. Henry IV., ii. 2.*

Proof, lapped in (covered with armour of proof), *Macbeth, i. 2.*

Proper-false (handsome and deceitful), *Twelfth Night, ii. 2.*

Propertied (taken possession of), *Twelfth Night, iv. 2;* (enaowed). *Antony and Cleopatra, v. 2.*

Property, in slaves, *Merchant of Venice, iv. 1.*

Prophecy, by magic art, *The Tempest, i. 2;* a, *King John, iv. 2;* gift of, at death, *Richard II., ii. 1;* of Merlin, *I. Henry IV., iii. 1;* the king was the moldwarp, and the conspirators a dragon, a lion, and a wolf, that should divide the realm among themselves; of Richard II., *II. Henry IV., iii. 1;* may be drawn from history, *II. Henry IV., iii. 1;* of the king's death, *II. Henry IV., iv. 4, ena;* of Henry V., *I. Henry VI., v. 1;* as to Henry VI., *I. Henry VI., iii. 1;* regarding Suffolk, *II. Henry VI., i. 4; iv. 1;* regarding Somerset, *II. Henry VI., i. 4; v. 2;* "The Castle" was the sign of an ale-house; by Margaret, *Richard III., i. 3; iv. 4; v. 1;* regarding the princess, *Richard III., i. 1;* regarding Richmond, *Richard III., iv. 2;* of Nicholas Hopkins, *Henry VIII., i. 2;* Wolsey's, of his death, *Henry VIII., iv. 2;* Cranmer's, concerning Elizabeth and James I., *Henry VIII., v. 5;* of Cassandra, *Troilus and Cressida, ii. 2;* of

Ulysses, *Troilus and Cressida, iv. 5;* of Hector's death, *Troilus and Cressida, v. 3;* to Cæsar, *Julius Cæsar, i. 2;* of the witches, *Macbeth, i. 3; iii. 1;* of the fool, *King Lear, iii. 2, end;* found by Posthumus, *Cymbeline, v. 4.*

Prophets, jesters oft prove, *King Lear, v. 3;* lean-looked, *Richard II., ii. 4.*

Propontic, the, *Othello, iii. 3.*

Proposing (conversing), *Much Ado about Nothing, iii. 1.*

Propriety, the proper self, *Twelfth Night, v. 1.*

Prorogue (prolong), *Pericles, v. 1.*

Proscription, by Antony, Octavius, and Lepidus, *Julius Cæsar, iv. 1.* It really took place, not in Rome, but on an island near Bologna.

Proserpina, *A Winter's Tale, iv. 3* or *4; Troilus and Cressida, ii. 1.*

Prosperity, the bond of love, *A Winter's Tale, iv. 3;* begins to mellow, *Richard III., iv. 4;* all men akin in, *Troilus and Cressida, i. 3;* dangerous, *Julius Cæsar, ii. 1,* "It is the bright day," etc.; friends in, *Hamlet, ii. 2,* "It is not very strange," etc.

Prospero, the rightful Duke of Milan, character in *The Tempest,* introduced in *i. 2.* He has acquired magic art by long study, which cost him his throne, for his brother Antonio has taken advantage of his inattention to outside affairs to usurp his throne, and send him and his little daughter to perish at sea. On the island where they are cast he makes use of his magic art to hold in subjection Caliban and the spirits of the air. Though a fine and noble character, and a most loving and tender father, Prospero repels us by his severity with Ariel; but this severity we excuse on further study of the airy spirit. See ARIEL.

"Prospero, the great enchanter, is altogether the opposite of the vulgar magician. With command over the elemental powers, which study has brought to him, he possesses moral grandeur and a command over himself, in spite of occasional fits of involuntary abstraction and of intellectual impatience; he looks down on life, and sees through it, yet will not refuse to take his part in it. . . . It has been suggested that Prospero, the great enchanter, is Shakspere himself, and that when he breaks his staff, drowns his book, and dismisses his airy spirits, going back to the duties of his dukedom, Shakspere was thinking of his own resigning of his powers of imaginative enchantment, his parting from the theatre, where his attendant spirits had played their parts, and his return to Stratford."—DOWDEN.

Protector, the Lord, Gloucester's (Richard III.'s) title after the death of Edward IV., as guardian of the young king.

Protestations, of innocence, *A Winter's Tale, iii. 2;* of love, *Richard III., iv. 4;* too many, *Hamlet, iii. 2.*

Proteus, *III. Henry VI., iii. 2.* He was a son of Neptune, and changed his shape at will.

Proteus, one of the *Two Gentlemen of Verona,* keener and brighter than his friend Valentine, whom he tries to supplant, but fickle and treacherous.

Proud, the, respect only the proud, *I. Henry IV., i. 3.*

Proverbs, on tapestry and in rings, *As You Like It, iii. 2.*

Proverbs and Proverbial Expressions, quoted or alluded to: A crafty knave needs no broker, *II. Henry VI., i. 2;* a finger in every pie, *Henry VIII., i. 1;* a fool's bolt is soon shot, *As You Like It, v. 4; Henry V., iii. 7;* a friend in the court is as good as a penny in the purse, *II. Henry IV., v. 1;* a good candle-holder proves a good gamester, *Romeo and Juliet, i. 4;* a little pot is soon hot, *Taming of the Shrew, iv. 1;* all men are not alike, *Much Ado about Nothing, iii. 5;* all's well that ends well, *All's Well that Ends Well, iv. 4; v. 1;* all that glisters is not gold, *Merchant of Venice, ii. 7;* a man must not choose a wife in Westminster, a servant in Paul's, or a horse in Smithfield, lest he choose a quean, a knave, or a jade, *II. Henry IV., i. 2;* see PAUL'S; an old cloak makes a new jerkin, *Merry Wives of Windsor, i. 3;* an old man is twice a child, *Hamlet, ii. 2;* an two men ride of a horse, one must ride behind, *Much Ado about Nothing, iii. 5;* a pair of shears went between us, *Measure for Measure, i. 2, 3;* a pox of the devil, *Henry V., iii. 7;* as mad as a March hare, *Two Noble Kinsmen, iii. 5;* a smoky house and a railing wife, *I. Henry IV., iii. 1;* a snake in the grass, *II. Henry VI., iii. 1;* as sound as a bell, *Much Ado about Nothing, iii. 2;* a staff is quickly found to beat a dog, *II. Henry VI., iii. 1;* as true as steel, *Troilus and Cressida, iii. 2;* at hand, quoth pick-purse, *I. Henry IV., ii. 1;* a wise man may live anywhere, *Richard II., i. 3;* a woman will not tell what she does not know, *I. Henry IV., ii. 3;* a world to see, *Much Ado about Nothing, iii. 5;* ay, tell me that and unyoke, *Hamlet, v. 1.* Bairns are blessings, *All's Well that Ends Well, i. 3;* be jogging while your boots are green, *Taming of the Shrew, iii. 2;* beggars mounted run their horses to death, *III. Henry VI., i. 4;* better a witty fool than a foolish wit, *Twelfth Night, i. 5;* better fed than taught, *All's Well that Ends Well, ii. 2;* birds of a feather, *III. Henry VI., iii. 3;* black men are pearls in beauteous ladies' eyes, *Two Gentlemen of Verona, v. 2;* blessing of your heart, you brew good ale, *Two Gentlemen of Verona, iii. 1;* blush like a black dog, *Titus Andronicus*, *v. 1;* bought and sold, *Comedy of Errors*, *iii. 1;* *King John*, *v. 4;* *Richard III.*, *v. 3;* Brag's a good dog, but Hold-fast is better, *Henry V.*, *ii. 3;* buttered the horse's hay, *King Lear*, *ii. 4.* Cake is dough, *Taming of the Shrew*, *i. 1;* *v. 1;* care killed a cat, *Much Ado about Nothing*, *v. 1;* carry coals to Cancer, *Troilus and Cressida*, *ii. 3;* come cut and long-tail, *Merry Wives of Windsor*, *iii. 4;* comparisons are odorous, *Much Ado about Nothing*, *iii. 5;* confess and be hanged, *Othello*, *iv. 1;* cry him and have him, *As You Like It*, *i. 3;* cry you mercy, I took you for a joint-stool, *King Lear*, *iii. 6;* cucullus non facit monachum (the cowl does not make the monk), *Measure for Measure*, *v. 1;* *Twelfth Night*, *i. 5;* *Henry VIII.*, *iii. 1.* Dance barefoot at the wedding, *Taming of the Shrew*, *ii. 1* (said of an elder unmarried sister); dead as a door-nail, *II. Henry IV.*, *v. 3;* *II. Henry VI.*, *iv. 10;* death will have his day, *Richard II.*, *iii. 2;* delays are dangerous, *I. Henry VI.*, *iii. 2;* diluculo surgere saluberrimum est (to rise early is most healthful), *Twelfth Night*, *ii. 3;* dogs must eat, *Coriolanus*, *i. 1;* dun's the mouse, *Romeo and Juliet*, *i. 4.* Empty vessels sound loudest, *Henry V.*, *iv. 4;* every dog has his day, *Hamlet*, *v. 1;* every man at forty is a fool or a physician, *Merry Wives of Windsor*, *iii. 4;* every man to his trade, *Romeo and Juliet*, *i. 2;* every why has a wherefore, *Comedy of Errors*, *ii. 2.* Familiarity breeds contempt, *Merry Wives of Windsor*, *i. 1;* fast bind, fast find, *Merchant of Venice*, *ii. 5;* feast-won, fast-lost, *Timon of Athens*, *ii. 2;* finis coronat opus (the end crowns the work), *All's Well that Ends Well*, *iv. 4;* *II. Henry VI.*, *v. 2;* *Troilus and Cressida*, *iv. 5;* fire that's closest kept burns most of all, *Two Gentlemen of Verona*, *i. 2;* fly pride, says the peacock, *Comedy of Errors*, *iv. 3;* friends may meet, but mountains never greet, *As You Like it*, *iii. 2.* Give the devil his due, *I. Henry IV.*, *i. 2;* *Henry V.*, *iii. 7;* God's a good man, *Much Ado about Nothing*, *iii. 5;* God sends a cursed cow short horns, *Much Ado about Nothing*, *ii. 1;* God sends a fool fortune, *As You Like It*, *ii. 7;* good hanging prevents bad marriage, *Twelfth Night*, *i. 5;* good liquor will make a cat talk, *The Tempest*, *ii. 2;* good wine needs no bush, *As You Like It*, *v. 4, epilogue;* to bed at noon, to supper, etc., *King Lear*, *iii. 6.* Hanging and wiving go by destiny, *Merchant of Venice*, *ii. 9;* happy man be his dole, *Taming of the Shrew*, *i. 1;* *A Winter's Tale*, *i. 2;* *I. Henry IV.*, *ii. 2;* happy the child whose father went to the devil, *III. Henry VI.*, *ii. 3;* have is have, however men do catch, *King John*, *i. 1;* Heaven's above all, *Richard II.*, *iii. 3;* *Othello*, *ii. 3;* he must needs go that the devil drives, *All's Well that Ends Well, i. 3;* he that dies pays all debts, *The Tempest, iii. 2;* he that eats with the devil needs a long spoon, *The Tempest, ii. 2 ; Comedy of Errors, iv. 3;* he that will have a cake out of the wheat must tarry the grinding, *Troilus and Cressida, i. 1;* honest as the skin between his eyebrows, *Much Ado about Nothing, iii. 5;* Honour's train is longer than his foreskirt, *Henry VIII., ii. 3;* hunger breaks stone walls, *Coriolanus, i. 1.* If that you will France win, Then with Scotland first begin, *Henry V., i. 2;* ill blows the wind that profits nobody, *II. Henry IV., v. 3; III. Henry VI., ii. 5;* ill-gotten goods never prosper, *III. Henry VI., ii. 2;* I'll make a shaft or a bolt, *Merry Wives of Windsor, iii. 4;* Ill-will never said well, *Henry V., iii. 7;* it is a foul bird that defiles its own nest, *As You Like It, iv. 1;* it is an ill cook that cannot lick his own fingers, *Romeo and Juliet, iv. 2;* it is a poor dog that is not worth the whistle, *King Lear, iv. 2;* it is easy stealing a shive from a cut loaf, *Titus Andronicus, ii. 1;* it's a dear collop that's cut from one's own flesh, *I. Henry VI., v. 4.* Jack shall have Jill, *Love's Labour's Lost, v. 2; Midsummer-Night's Dream, iii. 2;* John Drum's entertainment, *All's Well that Ends Well, iii. 6.* Know a hawk from a hand-saw, *Hamlet, ii. 2.* Laid on with a trowel, *As You Like It, i. 2;* lead apes in hell, *Much Ado about Nothing, ii. 1; Taming of the Shrew, ii. 1;* fits all, like a barber's chair, *All's Well that Ends Well, ii. 2;* losers have leave to talk, *Titus Andronicus, iii. 1;* lost teeth in the service, *As You Like It, i. 1.* Make hay while the sun shines, *III. Henry VI., iv. 8;* measure for measure, *Measure for Measure, v. 1;* meat was made for mouths, *Coriolanus, i. 1;* misfortunes come not singly, *Hamlet, iv. 5;* more water glides by the mill than the miller wots of, *Titus Andronicus, ii. 1.* Neither fish nor flesh, *I. Henry IV., iii. 3;* not a word to throw at a dog, *As You Like It, i. 3;* now she sharpens; well said, Whetstone, *Troilus and Cressida, v. 2.* Omittance is no quittance, *As You Like It, iii. 5;* one born to be hanged will never be drowned, *The Tempest, i. 1;* one fire drives out one fire, *Coriolanus, iv. 7;* one is no number, *Romeo and Juliet, i. 2;* one may see day at a little hole, *Love's Labour's Lost, v. 2;* one nail drives out another, *Coriolanus, iv. 7;* out of God's blessing into the warm sun, *King Lear, ii. 2.* Past cure, past care, *Love's Labour's Lost, v. 2;* patience perforce is medicine for a mad dog, *Romeo and Juliet, i. 5;* pitch and pay, *Henry V., ii. 3;* pitchers have ears, *Taming of the Shrew, iv. 4;* poor and proud, *Twelfth Night, iii. 1;* praise in departing, *The Tempest, iii. 3.* Rules the roast, *II. Henry VI., i. 1.*

Satis quod sufficit, *Love's Labour's Lost, v. 1;* seldom comes the better, *Richard III., ii. 3;* service is no heritage, *All's Well that Ends Well, i. 3;* si fortuna, etc. (if fortune torment me, hope will content me), *II. Henry IV., v. 5;* she has the mends in her own hands, *Troilus and Cressida, i. 1;* sink or swim, *I. Henry IV., i. 3;* sits the wind in that corner, *Much Ado about Nothing, ii. 3;* small herbs have grace, great weeds do grow apace, *Richard III., ii. 4;* sold for a song, *All's Well that Ends Well, iii. 2;* sow cockle, reap no corn, *Love's Labour's Lost, iv. 3;* speak by the card, *Hamlet, v. 1;* springes to catch woodcocks, *Hamlet, i. 3;* steal an egg from a cloister, *All's Well that Ends Well, iv. 3;* still swine eat all the draff, *Merry Wives of Windsor, iv. 2;* still waters run deep, *II. Henry VI., iii. 1;* strike while the iron is hot, *III. Henry VI., v. 1.* Take all, pay all, *Merry Wives of Windsor, ii. 2;* take eggs for money (bear insults), *A Winter's Tale, i. 2;* take mine ease in mine inn, *I. Henry IV., iii. 3;* tell the truth and shame the devil, *I. Henry IV., iii. 1;* the cat would eat fish but would not wet her feet, *Macbeth, i. 7;* the end crowns all, see Finis, etc.; the ewe that will not hear her lamb when it baes will never answer a calf when it bleats, *Much Ado about Nothing, iii. 3;* the fool thinks he is wise, but the wise man knows he is a fool, *As You Like It, v. 1;* the galled jade will wince, *Hamlet, iii. 2;* the grace of God is gear enough, *Merchant of Venice, ii. 2;* the hare's valour plucks dead lions by the beard, *King John, ii. 1;* the raven chides blackness, *Troilus and Cressida, ii. 3;* there is flattery in friendship, *Henry V., iii. 7;* the third pays for all, *Twelfth Night, v. 1;* the weakest goes to the wall, *Romeo and Juliet, i. 1;* the world on wheels, *Antony and Cleopatra, ii. 7;* three women and a goose make a market, *Love's Labour's Lost, iii. 1;* touch pitch and be defiled, *Much Ado about Nothing, iii. 3; I. Henry IV., ii. 4; II. Henry VI., ii. 1;* truth should be silent, *Antony and Cleopatra, ii. 2;* two may keep counsel when the third's away, *Titus Andronicus, iv. 2.* Walls hear without warnings, *Midsummer-Night's Dream, v. 1;* we burn daylight, *Romeo and Juliet, i. 4;* wedding and ill-wintering tame man and beast, *Taming of the Shrew, iv. 1;* when the age is in, the wit is out, *Much Ado about Nothing, iii. 5;* while the grass grows, oft starves the steed, *Hamlet, iii. 2;* woo in haste and wed at leisure, *Taming of the Shrew, iii. 2.*

Providence, work of. *All's Well that Ends Well, ii. 1;* we are in God's hand, *Henry V., iii. 6;* Heaven has an end in all, *Henry VIII., ii. 1;* there's a divinity that shapes our ends, *Hamlet, v. 2;*

denies us for our good, *Antony and Cleopatra, ii. 1;* a special, in the fall of a sparrow, *Hamlet, v. 2.* See HEAVEN.

Provincial, here (of this province), *Measure for Measure, v. 1.*

Provost, a, or jailer, character in *Measure for Measure,* introduced in *i. 3,* a merciful man who seeks to mitigate the severity of Angelo's justice.

Prudence, *Much Ado about Nothing, ii. 1,* "Let every eye negotiate for itself," etc.; *Henry V., ii. 3,* "Trust none," etc.; *Henry VIII., i. 1,* "Be advised," etc.; *Henry VIII., i. 2,* "Things done well," etc.; *Richard III., iii. 3,* "When clouds are seen," etc.; when about to build a house or a kingdom, *II. Henry IV., i. 3;* men do their broken weapons rather use than their bare hands, *Othello, i. 3.*

Psalm, the hundredth, *Merry Wives of Windsor, ii. 1.*

Psalmist, the, *II. Henry IV., iii. 2.*

Ptolemy, *Antony and Cleopatra, iii. 6.*

Publican, a fawning, *Merchant of Venice, i. 3.*

Publius, son of Marcus, in *Titus Andronicus,* introduced in *iv. 3.*

Publius Silicius, a senator and a friend of Cæsar's, character in *Julius Cæsar,* introduced in *ii. 2.*

Puck, or Robin Goodfellow, a fairy in the *Midsummer-Night's Dream,* introduced in *ii. 1.* He is a merry jester, a sort of clown among the other daintier fairies. A book of his "Mad Pranks and Merry Jests" is known to have been published in 1628, but it is supposed that an edition had appeared forty years earlier.

Pueritia (boyhood), *Love's Labour's Lost, v. 1.*

Pugging (thieving), *A Winter's Tale, iv. 2 or 3.*

Puke-stocking (puce, a dark colour), *I. Henry IV., ii. 4.*

Pulpiter, most gentle, *As You Like It, iii. 2.* Jupiter in some editions.

Punctuation, *Midsummer-Night's Dream, v. 1, prologue,* "Standing upon points."

Punishment, capital, argument on, *Measure for Measure, ii. 2.*

Punishments, mentioned. See BAFFLE, CROWN, HACK, PILLORY, RACK, STIGMATIC, STOCKS, STRAPPADO, WHEEL, WHIPPING, WISP.

Punning, *Merchant of Venice, iii. 5,* "How every fool can play upon the word;" *Twelfth Night, iii. 1.*

Punto (thrust), *Merry Wives of Windsor, ii. 3;* reverso (backhanded), *Romeo and Juliet, ii. 4.*

Purchase, fourteen-years, *Twelfth Night, iv. 1.* Twelve was the usual time.

Purchase (profit), *I. Henry IV., ii. 1.* Purchase was also a slang term for stolen goods.

Purgation (examination), *As You Like It, v. 4.*

Purgatory, *Hamlet, i. 5 ; Othello, iv. 3.*

Puritan(s), allusions to: Wear the surplice over the gown—meet Papists, *All's Well that Ends Well, i. 3;* Malvolio a kind of, *Twelfth Night, ii. 3;* sings psalms, *A Winter's Tale, iv. 2* or *3;* "Tribulation of Tower Hill," in *Henry VIII., v. 4,* is by some supposed to be an allusion to the Puritans. See LIMEHOUSE.

Purples, *Hamlet, iv. 7.* The early purple orchis.

Purpose, let not, be shaken with compunction, *Macbeth, i. 5;* the deed should go with the, *Macbeth, iv. 1;* slave to memory, *Hamlet, iii. 2,* speech of Player King; must weigh with the folly, *II. Henry IV., ii. 2.*

Pursuit, pleasure of, *Merchant of Venice, ii. 6; Troilus and Cressida, i. 2; Antony and Cleopatra, iv. 7; III. Henry VI., ii. 5.*

Push-pin, game of, *Love's Labour's Lost, iv. 3.* It was played by simply pushing pins across one another.

Putter-out of five for one, *The Tempest, iii. 3.* That is, of money, as was done by voyagers to distant countries. If they did not appear to claim the five hundred per cent., the borrower kept the principal.

Puttock (kite), *Cymbeline, i. 1.*

Pygmalion, *Measure for Measure, iii. 2.* Allusion to the ivory statue that he made, which was endowed with life by Venus.

Pyramids, the, *Sonnet cxxii ; Antony and Cleopatra, ii. 7; v. 2.*

Pyramus, a character in the play acted in the *Midsummer-Night's Dream* before the duke. The part is taken by Bottom. In the old story, Pyramus was the handsomest youth, and Thisbe the fairest maiden, in all Babylonia, where Semiramis reigned ; allusion to, *Titus Andronicus, ii. 3* or *4.*

Pyramus and Thisbe, the play acted before the duke in *Midsummer-Night's Dream, i. 2 ; iii. 1; v. 1.*

Pyrrhus, *Troilus and Cressida, iii. 3; Hamlet, ii. 2; Lucrece, lines 1449, 1467.* He killed Priam.

Pythagoras, doctrine of (transmigration of souls), *Merchant of Venice, iv. 1; As You Like It, iii. 2; Twelfth Night, iv. 2.*

Quails, fighting, *Antony and Cleopatra, ii. 3.*

Quaint (neat, ingenious), *Two Gentlemen of Verona, ii. 1; iii. 1; Taming of the Shrew, iv. 3, and elsewhere.*

Quare (wherefore), *Love's Labour's Lost, v. 1.*

Quarrel(s), no valour in a false, *Much Ado about Nothing, v. 1;* between Hermia and Helena—Lysander and Demetrius, *Midsummer-Night's Dream, iii. 2;* the seven causes of, *As You Like It, v. 4;* between Lafeu and Parolles, *All's Well that Ends Well, ii. 3,* "Do you hear," etc.; of Constance and Elinor, *King John, ii. 1;* should be left to Heaven, *Richard II., i. 2; Richard III., i. 4;* of Pistol and Nym, *Henry V., ii. 1;* of an Irishman and a Welshman, *Henry V., iii. 2;* of Pistol and Fluellen, *Henry V., v. 1;* of Bolingbroke and Norfolk, *Richard II., i. 1–3; II. Henry IV., iv. 1;* of Vernon and Basset, *I. Henry VI., iii. 4; iv. 1;* just, *II. Henry VI., iii. 2;* among sons and brothers, *III. Henry VI., i. 2;* of Gloucester, Elizabeth, and Margaret, *Richard III., i. 3;* seeking a, *Romeo and Juliet, iii. 1;* beware of entrance to, *Hamlet, i. 3;* a drunkard full of, *Othello, ii. 3;* between Antony and Cæsar, *Antony and Cleopatra, ii. 2;* between Plantagenet and Somerset, *I. Henry VI., ii. 4;* thrice is he armed that hath his quarrel just, *II. Henry VI., iii. 2.*

Quart d'ecu (about eightpence), *All's Well that Ends Well, iv. 3.*

Quat (pimple), *Othello, v. 1.*

Queen, Margaret asserts her right to be, *Richard III., i. 3;* Anne would not be a, *Henry VIII., ii. 3;* over passion, *King Lear, iv. 3;* in jest, *Richard III., iv. 4;* of Carthage, see Dido.

Queen of Night, thrice crowned, *As You Like It, iii. 2.* Diana, Luna, Hecate, a triune goddess.

Queen of Richard II. See Isabella.

Queen, Cymbeline's, character in the play, first appears in *scene i.* She is the step-mother of Imogen, whom she hates for rejecting her son Cloten. She is able, crafty, and unscrupulous, and has complete ascendancy over Cymbeline. She gets the supposed poison, *i. 5;* her ability, *ii. 1, end;* her death and confession, *v. 5.*

Quell (murder), *Macbeth, i. 7.*

Quern (hand-mill), *Midsummer-Night's Dream, ii. 1.*

Questionable (conversable), *Hamlet, i. 4.*

Questions, a lover's, *As You Like It, iii. 2.*

Quibbling. See Punning.

Quickly, Mistress, hostess of the Boar's Head tavern in Eastcheap, character in *I. Henry IV.,* introduced in *ii. 4;* in *II. Henry IV.,* introduced in *ii. 1;* and in *Henry V.,* in *ii. 1.* In the latter play she is represented as married to Pistol, who speaks of her death in *v. 1;* she is also a character in the *Merry Wives of Windsor,* first spoken of in *i. 2*, and introduced in *i. 4*. She is housekeeper and servant for Dr. Caius, and an agent for the suitors of Anne Page. The identity of the Mrs. Quickly of the comedy with the Mrs. Quickly of the historical plays has been questioned, but without much reason.

Quicksilver, fled like, *II. Henry IV., ii. 4.*

Quiddits (quibblings, equivocation), *Hamlet, v. 1.*

Qui est la ? Paysans, etc., *I. Henry VI., iii. 2.* Who is there ? Peasants, poor people of France.

Quietus (settlement, as of accounts), *Hamlet, iii. 1.*

Quill, in the, *II. Henry VI., i. 3.* Of uncertain meaning; either in the *quile,* meaning heap, or in the *coil,* that is, in the confusion of the crowd.

Quillets (quibbles), *Love's Labour's Lost, iv. 3; I. Henry VI., ii. 4; II. Henry VI., iii. 1.*

Quills, the porcupine's, *Hamlet, i. 5.*

Quince, Peter, a character in *Midsummer-Night's Dream,* introduced in *i. 2.* He is a carpenter. and takes the prologue in the play before the duke, and the character of Thisbe's father. He is the manager of the performance, and a poet as well, for Bottom says, "I will get Peter Quince to write a ballad of this dream." He makes some of the funniest blunders in the piece, and in the prologue "doth not stand upon points."

Quintain, *As You Like It, i. 2.* A wooden figure on which young men practised, in their training in the use of arms.

Quintus, son of Titus Andronicus in the play of that name, introduced in *i. 1* or *2;* falls into the grave of Bassianus, and is taken for his murderer, *ii. 3* or *4;* executed, *iii. 1.*

Quip modest, the. See DUELLING.

Quis (who), *Love's Labour's Lost, v. 1.*

Quit (avenge), *King Lear, iii. 7.*

Quod me alit, etc., *Pericles, ii. 2.* What nourishes, extinguishes me.

Quoint, Francis, mentioned in *Richard II., ii. 1,* as one of the companions of Bolingbroke.

Quoits, the game of, *II. Henry IV., ii. 4.*

Quoniam (wherefore), *Love's Labour's Lost, v. 2.*

Quotations, of Scripture, *Richard III., i. 3; Merchant of Venice, i. 3; iii. 2.*

Quotations, in the plays. See HORACE, LILLY, OVID, SENECA, SIDNEY, and other names of authors quoted from.

Quoted (noticed), *Hamlet, ii. 1.* Pronounced and sometimes written *cote.*

Quotidian (daily fever), of love, *As You Like It, iii. 2.*

R, the dog's name, *Romeo and Juliet, ii. 4.* Dogs were said to *arre* and bark.

Rabato (ruff), *Much Ado about Nothing, iii. 4.*

Rabble, the, *Hamlet, iv. 5* or *2; I. Henry IV., iv. 2.* See MOBS, MULTITUDE.

Rack, the, *Measure for Measure, iv. 1;* called an engine, *King Lear, i. 4; Henry VI., ii. 5;* of this tough world, *King Lear, v. 3.*

Rack (clouds), *Antony and Cleopatra, iv. 12* or *14; Hamlet, ii. 2.* The word in "leave not a rack behind," *The Tempest, iv. 1,* may have the same meaning, or may mean *wreck,* as in "rack and ruin."

Rage, tiger-footed, *Coriolanus, iii. 1;* deaf as the sea, hasty as fire, *Richard II., i. 1;* of the great, *Antony and Cleopatra, iv. 1;* labyrinth of fury, *Troilus and Cressida, ii. 3;* eyeless, *King Lear, iii. 1.*

Raggedness, looped and windowed, *King Lear, iii. 4.*

Ragged-robin, said to be the "cuckoo-flowers," *King Lear, iv. 4.*

Raging-wood (raging-mad), *I. Henry VI., iv. 7.*

Ragozine, a pirate mentioned in *Measure for Measure, iv. 3.*

Railing, *As You Like It, iv. 3; Twelfth Night, i. 5; Troilus and Cressida, i. 3; ii. 1; Hamlet, ii. 2; King Lear, ii. 2.*

Rain, the, it raineth every day, song, *Twelfth Night, v. 1;* invocation to, *King Lear, iii. 2.*

Rainbow, the, *The Tempest, iv. 1;* secondary, called watergalls, *Lucrece, l. 1588.* See IRIS.

Rally, a, in battle, *Cymbeline, v. 3.*

Rambures, a French lord in *Henry V.,* first appears in *iii. 7;* his death at Agincourt, *iv. 8.*

Ramston, Sir John (correctly Thomas), mentioned in *Richard II., ii. 1,* as one of the adherents of Bolingbroke. He was warden of the Tower when Richard was imprisoned there.

Rancour, will out, *II. Henry VI., i. 1.*

Rank, pride and distinctions of, *All's Well that Ends Well, ii. 3;* differences and indications of, *A Winter's Tale, iv. 3* or *4;* disgrace to, *I. Henry IV., iii. 2;* proper observance of, *Troilus and Cressida, i. 3;* one's own doing, *Julius Cæsar, i. 2;* disadvantage of, *Cymbeline, ii. 1.*

Rank (jog), *As You Like It, iii. 2.*

Ransom, for life, *Comedy of Errors, i. 1;* demand for a, *Henry V., iv. 3; v. 3, 5, 6;* the sepulchre of the world's, *Richard II., ii. 1.*

Rape of Lucrece, the. See LUCRECE.

Raps (enwraps), *Cymbeline, i. 6.*

Rapture (fit), *Coriolanus, ii. 1.*

Rareness. See POPULARITY.

Rarity, gives value, *Sonnet lii.*

Rascal (a lean deer), *I. Henry VI., iv. 2, and elsewhere.*

Rash, Master, a prisoner, *Measure for Measure, iv. 3.*

Rat(s), *Hamlet, iii. 4;* leave a doomed ship, *The Tempest, i. 2;* an Irish, *As You Like It, iii. 2.* Referring to the saying that rats were rhymed to death in Ireland. See TRANSMIGRATION.

Ratcliff, Sir Richard, character in *Richard III.,* first appears in *ii. 2,* an adherent and confidant of Richard. See CATESBY.

Raught (reached), *Love's Labour's Lost, iv. 2; Antony and Cleopatra, iv. 9.*

Raven(s), feathers of, used in witchcraft, *The Tempest, i. 2;* young, must be fed, *Merry Wives of Windsor, i. 3;* chides blackness, *Troilus and Cressida, ii. 3;* allusion to the notion that they desert their young on account of their ugliness, *Titus Andronicus, ii. 3;* foresee death, *Julius Cæsar, v. 1;* ominous, *Macbeth, i. 5; Titus Andronicus, ii. 3; Hamlet, iii. 2;* o'er the infected house, *Othello, iv. 1.* The ill-omened bird was thought to hang over houses where the plague was. This is also referred to in *Much Ado about Nothing, ii. 3.*

Ravenspurg, or Ravenspur, *Richard II.. ii. 1, end; ii. 2, 3; I. Henry IV., i. 3.* It was a port at the mouth of the Humber, gradually destroyed by the encroachments of the sea, until, by the middle of the sixteenth century, it had entirely disappeared.

Ravings, of madness, *King Lear, iii. 4; iv. 6.*

Razed (a word applied to the damage done by a boar), *Richard III., iii. 2.*

Razes (roots), *I. Henry IV., ii. 1.*

Readiness, *Henry V., iv. 3,* "All things are ready, if our minds be so."

Reading, how well he's read, to reason against, *Love's Labour's Lost, i. 1.*

Reapers, dance with nymphs. *The Tempest, iv. 1.*

Rearmice. See REREMICE.

Reason, nobler, *The Tempest, v. 1;* and rhyme. *Two Gentlemen of Verona, ii. 1;* Love's physician, *Merry Wives of Windsor. ii. 1:*

Sonnet cxlvii.; "dares her no," or "dares her on," *Measure for Measure, iv. 4.* The first reading would mean, bids her not to denounce me. The second would mean, my reason dares her to go on and do it, since she will not be believed. In madness, *Measure for Measure, v. 1;* keeps little company with love, *Midsummer-Night's Dream, iii. 1;* a grand-juryman. *Twelfth Night, iii. 1;* and respect, not for manhood and honour, *Troilus and Cressida, ii. 2;* the receipt of, *Macbeth, i. 7;* dethroned, *Hamlet, iii. 1;* what we are without, *Hamlet, iv. 4;* sent after the thing it loves, *Hamlet, iv. 5,* "Nature is fine in love," etc.; in madness, *King Lear, iv. 6;* office of, *Othello, i. 3.*

Reasons, a woman's, *Two Gentlemen of Verona, i. 2;* if, as plenty as blackberries, *I. Henry IV., ii. 4;* good, must give place to better, *Julius Cæsar, iv. 3;* strong, make strong actions, *King John, iii. 4;* larded with, *Hamlet, v. 4;* like two grains of wheat in two bushels of chaff, *Merchant of Venice, i. 1.*

Rebeck, name of a musician in *Romeo and Juliet, iv. 4.*

Rebel(s), evils invoked on, *Richard II., iii. 2;* suspicion of pardoned, *II. Henry IV., iv. 1;* called on to repent, *I. Henry VI., iii. 3;* worthy to be a, *Macbeth, i. 2.*

Rebellion, untread the way of, *King John, v. 4;* of Bolingbroke, *Richard II., ii. 1-3; iii. 3;* difficulty of managing, *I. Henry IV., iv. 1,* Worcester's speech; offer of pardon for, *I. Henry IV., iv. 3; v. 1;* colour to face the garment of, *I. Henry IV., v. 1;* never forgiven, *I. Henry IV., v. 2;* ever rebuked, *I. Henry IV., v. 5;* ill-luck of—effect of the word on troops—turned to religion, *II. Henry IV., i. 1;* reasons for, *II. Henry IV., iv. 1;* Jack Cade's, *II. Henry VI., iv. 2-6;* of workingmen, *Henry VIII., i. 2;* of the plebeians, *Coriolanus, i. 1;* general, *Coriolanus, iv. 6.*

Rebukes, improved, *Measure for Measure, iv. 6; Much Ado about Nothing, ii. 3;* sensitiveness to, *Cymbeline, iii. 5,* "Forbear sharp speeches," etc.

Recheat, *Much Ado about Nothing, i. 1.* A hunting term, meaning a call sounded on the horn to bring back the dogs from a wrong scent.

Recklessness, caused by the world's treatment, *Macbeth, iii. 1.*

Reckoning, fit for a tapster, *Love's Labour's Lost, i. 2;* a pity to get a living by, *Love's Labour's Lost, v. 2.*

Reconciliation, of enemies, *Richard II., i. 1; Richard III., ii. 1;* of kings, *A Winter's Tale, v. 2.*

Recreation, melancholy from want of, *Comedy of Errors, v. 1.*

Recruits, Falstaff's, *II. Henry IV., iii. 2.*

Recure (recover), *Richard III., iii. 7.*

Rede (teaching or counsel), recks not his own, *Hamlet, i. 3.*

Redemption, by Christ, *Measure for Measure, ii. 2.*

Redime te captum, etc., *Taming of the Shrew, i. 1.* Redeem thyself, captive, for as little as thou canst; quoted from Terence as in Lilly's "Latin Grammar."

Red-lattice phrases, *Merry Wives of Windsor, ii. 2.* Ale-houses had red lattices.

Reeds, eaves of, *The Tempest, v. 1.* Reeds were used for thatch.

Refelled (refuted), *Measure for Measure, v. 1.*

Refinement, affected, *Twelfth Night, ii. 5; Hamlet, v. 1.*

Reflection, *Henry V., iv. 1,* "I and my bosom must debate awhile."

Reform, in character, patching, *Twelfth Night, i. 5;* unexpected, *I. Henry IV., i. 2, end; Henry V., i. 1;* in the state, *II. Henry VI., ii. 2.*

Regan, one of the daughters of King Lear, introduced in the first scene. Her professions of filial love, *i. 1;* treatment of her father, *ii. 4;* she becomes a widow, *iv. 2;* betroths herself to Edmund, *iv. 5; v. 1;* is poisoned by her sister, *v. 3.* See GONERIL.

Regicide, *A Winter's Tale, i. 2; Richard II., v. 6; Macbeth, i. 7.*

Regiment (authority), *Antony and Cleopatra, iii. 6.*

Regreets (greetings), *Merchant of Venice, ii. 9; King John, iii. 1.*

Regret, uselessness of, *Macbeth, iii. 2,* "Things without remedy," etc.; *Othello, i. 3,* "When remedies are past," etc.; for the dead, *Antony and Cleopatra, i. 2.*

Reguerdon (reward), *I. Henry VI., iii. 1.*

Reignier (René), Duke of Lorraine and Anjou, and titular King of Naples, Sicily, and Jerusalem, father of Margaret, queen to Henry VI., character in *1. Henry VI.,* first appears in *i. 1.* Suffolk speaks of his titles and influence in *v. 5;* York taunts his daughter with his high-sounding titles and poverty in the third part, *i. 4,* and Richard in *ii. 2.* At the close of the third part he is said to have pawned Sicily and Jerusalem to ransom his daughter.

Relationship, *Macbeth, ii. 3,* "The near in blood," etc.; *Hamlet, i. 2,* "A little more than kin and less than kind." See BLOOD, KINSHIP.

Religion, every error in, approved, *Merchant of Venice, iii. 2;*

fickleness in, *Much Ado about Nothing*, *i. 1;* pretense of, *Richard III., iii. 7.* See HYPOCRISY, QUOTATION.

Remediate (remedial), *King Lear, iv. 4.*

Remedies, lie in ourselves, *All's Well that Ends Well, i. 1;* heroic, for the state, *Coriolanus, iii. 1;* things without remedy should be without regard, *Macbeth, iii 2.*

Remember (remind), *The Tempest, i. 2.*

Remembrance, burdened with heaviness that's gone, *The Tempest, v. 1;* of a widow, *II. Henry IV., ii. 3;* of the valiant dead, *Henry V., i. 2;* sworn, *Hamlet, i. 5;* of things precious, *Macbeth, iv. 3;* summoned, *Sonnet xxx.*

Remonstrance, *King Lear, i. 1; A Winter's Tale, ii. 2.*

Remorse, *Much Ado about Nothing, iv. 1; King John, iv. 2; Richard II., v. 5, end; Richard III., ii. 1; v. 3; Macbeth, iii. 2, 4; v. 1; Hamlet, i. 5; King Lear, i. 4,* "O most small fault," etc.; *Othello, iv. 6, 9; Antony and Cleopatra, iv. 6, 9; Cymbeline, v. 1; Lucrece, lines 708, 730; A Winter's Tale, iii. 2.*

Remorse (pity), *Measure for Measure, v. 1; II. Henry VI., iv. 1; Merchant of Venice iv. 1,* and elsewhere.

Remotion (remoteness), *Timon of Athens, iv. 3; King Lear, ii. 4.*

Remuneration, the Latin for three farthings, *Love's Labour's Lost, iii. 1.*

Render (describe), *As You Like It, iv. 3.*

René, King. See REIGNIER.

Reneag, or **renege** (deny, renounce), *King Lear, ii. 2; Antony and Cleopatra, i. 1.* A word akin to *renegade.*

Renown. See FAME, GLORY.

Renunciation, easy, *Lover's Complaint, l. 239.*

Repentance, he who is not satisfied by, *Two Gentlemen of Verona, v. 4;* toward heaven, *Measure for Measure, ii. 3;* of Oliver, *As You Like It, iv. 3;* of a usurper, *As You Like It, v. 4;* forbidden, *A Winter's Tale, iii. 2,* "But O thou tyrant," etc.; of a tyrant, *A Winter's Tale, iii. 2, end; v. 1;* proposed, *I. Henry IV., i. 2; iii. 3; v. 2, 5;* leisure for, *Richard III., iv. 4;* without restitution, *Hamlet, iii. 3;* before death, *Cymbeline, v. 4,* "My conscience," etc.; of Enobarbus, *Antony and Cleopatra, iv. 9;* to patch up this old body for heaven, *II. Henry IV., ii. 4;* if my wind were but long enough to say my prayers, I would repent, *Merry Wives of Windsor, iv. 5.*

Reply churlish, the. See DUELLING.

Reports, false, *II. Henry IV., induction, i. 1.*

Repose, times for, *Henry VIII., v. 1;* foster-nurse of Nature, *King Lear, iv. 4;* from travel, *Sonnet xxvii.*

Representative, character of a, *Troilus and Cressida, i. 3.*

Reprisals, *III. Henry VI., ii. 2,* "To whom do lions," etc.

Reproof (rebuttal), *I. Henry IV., i. 2;* valiant, the, see DUELLING; Hamlet's, of his mother, *Hamlet, iii. 4;* for fickleness, *King John, iii. 1;* ill-timed, *The Tempest, ii. 1.*

Repugn (resist), *I. Henry VI., iv. 1.*

Reputation, the bubble, *As You Like It, ii. 7;* value of, *Richard II., i. 1; Othello, iii. 1, 3;* the immortal part, *Othello, ii. 3;* mistaken, *Sonnet cxxi.* See also NAME.

Rere-mice (bats), *Midsummer-Night's Dream, ii. 2.* The first part of the compound is from the Anglo-Saxon *hreran,* to stir, to flutter. The word is, therefore, equivalent to *flitter-mouse.*

Reserve, effects of, *I. Henry IV., iii. 2.*

Resignation, to the will of Heaven, *Richard II., v. 2;* to apparent evils, *Henry V., iv. 1,* "There is some soul of goodness," etc.; to the inevitable, *Antony and Cleopatra, iii. 6;* to death, *Merchant of Venice, iv. 1.*

Resolution, in spite of one repulse, *The Tempest, iii. 3;* sudden, *Two Gentlemen of Verona, i. 3;* should not be quenched with hope, *Measure for Measure, iii. 1;* dauntless spirit of, *King John, v. 1;* the native hue of, sicklied o'er with the pale cast of thought, *Hamlet, iii. 1;* placed, *Antony and Cleopatra, v. 2.* See DETERMINATION, WILL.

Resolved (assured), *I. Henry VI., iii. 4.*

Respect, too much, upon the world, *Merchant of Venice, i. 1.*

Respect (circumspection), takes away valour, *Troilus and Cressida, ii. 2.*

Rest, to set up one's, *Comedy of Errors, iv. 3; All's Well that Ends Well, ii. 1, and elsewhere.* To resolve upon, to lay a wager upon.

Restraint, result of excess, *Measure for Measure, i. 3.*

Results, great, from insignificant causes, *All's Well that Ends Well, ii. 1.*

Resurrection, the, allusion to, *Much Ado about Nothing, v. 3,* song, "Till death be uttered."

Retire (a retreat), *I. Henry IV., ii. 3.*

Retirement, from towns, *Two Gentlemen of Verona, v. 4;* from court life, *As You Like It, ii. 1; iii. 2;* in old age, *I. Henry IV., v. 1; King Lear, i. 1.*

Retort (reject), *Measure for Measure, v. 1.*

Retort courteous, the. See DUELLING.

Retreat, of Hotspur's soldiers, *II. Henry IV., i. 1;* a, *Coriolanus, i. 4.*

Retribution, certainty of, on earth, *Macbeth, i. 7; Richard III., ii. 1; iv. 4; v. 4; Timon of Athens, v. 5.*

Retrospection, *Sonnet xxx.*

Revel(s), a, *Hamlet, i. 4; Timon of Athens, ii. 2.*

Revenge, schemes of, *Merry Wives of Windsor, i. 3; ii. 1:* spirit of, overcome by kindness, *As You Like It, iv. 3;* of the Percys, *I. Henry IV., i. 3;* Clifford's, *III. Henry VI., i. 3, 4; ii. 3:* Warwick's, *III. Henry VI., ii. 3;* on one that loves, *Richard III., i. 2;* deaf to reason, *Troilus and Cressida, ii. 2;* Tamora in the guise of, *Titus Andronicus, v. 1;* against country, *Coriolanus, iv. 5;* Cæsar's spirit, ranging for, *Julius Cæsar, iii. 1;* threats of, *King Lear, ii. 4, last part;* taken during prayer, incomplete, *Hamlet, iii. 3;* should have no bounds, *Hamlet, iv. 7;* vows of, *Hamlet, iv. 5; Macbeth, iv. 3; Othello, iii. 3, end; v. 2;* suggestion of, *Cymbeline, i. 6;* the humility of Christians, *Merchant of Venice, iii. 1.*

Revenges, of Time, *Twelfth Night, v. 1.*

Revenue, farming the, *Richard II., i. 4.*

Reverbs (reverberates), *King Lear, i. 1.*

Reverence, angel of the world, *Cymbeline, iv. 2.*

Reverses. See ADVERSITY, FORTUNE, MISFORTUNE.

Revolt (desert), *II. Henry VI., iv. 2.*

Revolts, against Duncan, *Macbeth, ii. 2;* minutely, *Macbeth, v. 1;* of the plebs, see PLEBEIANS. See also REBELLION.

Revolution, spirit of, *Antony and Cleopatra, i. 3;* how it must be dealt with, *King John, v. 2.*

Reward, too slow for merit, *Macbeth, i. 4.*

Reynaldo, servant of Polonius, appears in *ii. 1* of *Hamlet.*

Rhesus, *III. Henry VI., iv. 2.* Ulysses and Diomedes broke into his tent and stole his white steeds, because of a prophecy that Troy could never be taken if once they drank from the Xanthus.

Rhetoric, sweet smoke of, *Love's Labour's Lost, iii. 1.*

Rhinoceros, the armed, *Macbeth, iii. 4.*

Rhodope, *I. Henry VI., i. 5* or *6.* A celebrated courtesan, erroneously said to have built the smallest and finest of the pyramids at Memphis.

Rhyme, and reason, *Two Gentlemen of Verona, ii. 1; Love's Labour's Lost, i. 1;* neither, nor reason, *Comedy of Errors, ii. 2;*

one, like a butter-woman's jog (rank) to market, *As You Like It, iii.
2;* love in, *Sonnets xxxii., xxxviii.*

Rhymes, a lover's, *Midsummer-Night's Dream, i. 1; As You
Like It, iii. 2; iv. 3.*

Rhyming, taught by love, *Love's Labour's Lost, iv. 3.*

Rhyming planet, born under a, *Much Ado about Nothing,
v. 2.*

Rhys-ap-Thomas. See RICE-AP-THOMAS.

Rialto, the, *Merchant of Venice, i. 3; iii. 1.* The *Ponte di Rialto,* or bridge of the Rialto, over the Grand Canal at Venice, was
used as an exchange.

Ribaudred, or ribaldred (ribald), *Antony and Cleopatra, iii. 8
or 10.*

Rice-ap-Thomas (or Rhys), *Richard III., iv. 5.* He brought
re-enforcements for Richmond to Bosworth Field.

Rich, and poor, the, fable concerning, *Coriolanus, i. 1.*

Richard, Kings II. and III., dramas of. See KING RICHARD II.
and KING RICHARD III.

Richard, Duke of York, son of Edward IV., character in *Richard III.,* first appears in *ii. 4.* See EDWARD V. and PRINCES IN THE
TOWER.

Richard I. (*Cœur de Lion*), King of England from 1189 to 1199,
King John, i. 1; ii. 1.

Richard II., eighth king of the house of Plantagenet, born
1366, died 1400. He was the son of Edward the Black Prince, and
succeeded his grandfather, Edward III., in 1377, at the age of eleven.
He is introduced in the first scene of the play that bears his name,
where two nobles bring their quarrel before him, and where is presented "the germ of all the after-events in his insincerity, partiality,
arbitrariness, and favouritism, and in the proud, tempestuous temperament of his barons." In *iv. 1,* he resigns the crown and is sent
to the Tower; in *v. 2,* he is killed by Exton. In person Richard is
represented as very handsome, having a fair, delicate, and feminine
style of beauty; in character he was weak, with an overweening confidence in his divine right and the respect of his subjects for it. He
is given to indirect methods and dissimulation, is easily depressed
and easily excited with hope and confidence. At the same time the
reader's sympathy is aroused by his amiability and by his misfortunes. But in his weakness he had spent his revenues foolishly, and
consequently had resorted to extortionate taxes, and even confiscation. Allusions to him in other plays: his unkingly conduct, *I.*

Henry IV., iii. 2; prophecy by him, *II. Henry IV., iii. 1;* penitence for his dethronement and murder, *Henry V., iv. 1.*

Richard III. (1450–1485), character in the second and third parts of *Henry VI.,* under the names of Richard Plantagenet and Duke of Gloucester. In *II. Henry VI.* he is introduced in *v. 1,* and in *III. Henry VI.* in *i. 1.* His courage, *i. 4;* his purpose to gain the crown, *iii. 2; iv. 1;* his deformity, *iii. 2.* In *v. 5* he stabs the prince, and offers to kill Margaret; and in *v. 6* stabs King Henry. The play that bears his name begins with a soliloquy, in which he declares his designs; his name presented to the citizens and the crown offered to him, *iii. 7.* He enters crowned in *iv. 2,* and orders the murder of the princes; is reproached by their mother and denounced by his, *iv. 4;* his courage at Bosworth, *v. 4;* his death, *v. 5.*

"There is something sublime and terrible in so great and fierce a human energy as that of Richard concentrated within one withered and distorted body. This is the evil offspring and flower of the long and cruel civil wars—this distorted creature, a hater and scorner of man, an absolute cynic, loveless and alone, disregarding all human bonds and human affections, yet full of intellect, of fire, of power." —DOWDEN.

Riches. See GOLD, MONEY, WEALTH.

Richmond, Margaret, Countess of, *Richard III., i. 3.* She was the mother of Henry VII. Stanley was her third husband.

Richmond, Henry Tudor, Earl of (1456–1509), afterward Henry VII., character in *III. Henry VI.,* introduced in *iv. 6,* where the king, whose half-brother he was, utters a prophecy concerning him, and in the same scene it is resolved to send him to Brittany. He appears again in *Richard III.,* as the head of the Lancastrian party. In *iv. 3* he is called a Breton, from his residence in Brittany. He is spoken of in *iv. 4* as being in Wales, first appears in *v. 2,* and is made king in *v. 5.* He is represented in the play as pious and conscientious. By his marriage with the daughter of Edward IV., he united the claims of the houses of York and Lancaster.

Riddance, from a knave, *Much Ado about Nothing, iii. 3.*

Riddles, Dull's, *Love's Labour's Lost, iv. 2;* one proposed to suitors, *Pericles, i., prologue;* book of, *Merry Wives of Windsor, i. 1.*

Ridicule, one must seem senseless of, *As You Like It, ii. 7;* indifference to, *Much Ado about Nothing, ii. 3;* of the Greek generals, *Troilus and Cressida, i. 3.*

Right, to do a great, do a little wrong, *Merchant of Venice, iv. 1;* o'ercoming might, *II. Henry IV., v. 4;* warring with right, *Troilus and Cressida, iii. 2.*

Rigol (circle), *II. Henry IV.*, *iv. 4; Lucrece, l. 1745.*

Rim (entrails), *Henry V.*, *iv. 4.*

Rinaldo, steward to the Countess of Rousillon in *All's Well that Ends Well*, introduced in *i. 3.*

Ring(s), exchange of, *Two Gentlemen of Verona, ii. 2;* refused, *Two Gentlemen of Verona, iv. 4;* Shylock's turquoise, *Merchant of Venice, iii. 1;* Portia's, *Merchant of Venice, iii. 2; iv. 1, 2; v. 1;* with death's-heads in, *Love's Labour's Lost, v. 2;* proverbial phrases on, *Merchant of Venice, v. 1; As You Like It, iii. 2; Hamlet, iii. 2*, "The posy of a ring;" an old, *All's Well that Ends Well, iii. 2, 7; iv. 2; v. 3;* exchange of, at marriage, *Twelfth Night, v. 1;* thumb, *I. Henry IV., ii. 4;* engagement, *Richard III., i. 2;* the king's, an emblem of his authority, *Henry VIII., v. 1, 3;* one shining by its own light, *Titus Andronicus, ii. 3* or *4;* of Posthumus, *Cymbeline, i. 1; ii. 4; v. 5.*

Ringlets, the green, sour, *The Tempest, v. 1.* A fungous growth that was supposed to be made by dancing fairies.

Ringwood, *Merry Wives of Windsor, ii. 1.* A common name for a dog.

Riot, a, *Merry Wives of Windsor, i. 1.*

Risk, of everything on one cast, *I. Henry IV., iv. 1.*

Rivage (bank, shore), *Henry V., iii., chorus.*

Rivality (equality), *Antony and Cleopatra, iii. 5.*

Rivalry, necessary, of Antony and Cæsar, *Antony and Cleopatra, v. 1.*

Rivals, in love, quarrels of, *Two Gentlemen of Verona, ii. 4.*

Rivals (associates), *Hamlet, i. 1.*

Rive (to fire), *I. Henry VI., iv. 2.*

Rivers, flowery banks of, *The Tempest, iv. 1;* drown their shores, *Richard II., iii. 2.*

Rivers, Anthony Woodville, Earl, character in *III. Henry VI.*, introduced in *iv. 4*, and in *Richard III.*, introduced in *i. 3.* He was a son of the Woodville, lieutenant of the Tower, in *I. Henry VI.*, and brother of Elizabeth, Lady Grey, who became the wife of Edward IV. His marriage with a rich heiress, daughter of Lord Scales, is spoken of in *iv. 1* of the former play, where Gloucester upbraids Edward IV. with having given her to his wife's brother rather than to one of his own. He was seized by Richard's orders and beheaded at Pontefract (1483), *Richard III., iii. 3;* his ghost appears to Richard, *v. 3.* Lord Rivers translated from the French the second book printed in England by Caxton, "Dictes and Sayeings of the Philosophers." He made other translations, and also " Divers Balades ayenst the Seven Dedely Synnes."

Rivo, *1. Henry IV., ii. 4.* A Bacchanalian exclamation, meaning unknown.

Roan. See ROUEN.

Roaring, an extempore part, *Midsummer-Night's Dream, i. 2 ;* of lions, *The Tempest, ii. 1.*

Roast, rules the, *II. Henry VI., i. 1.*

Robbery, if unknown to the robbed, *Othello, iii. 3 ;* of reputation, *Othello, iii. 3 ;* in behalf of charity, *Troilus and Cressida, v. 3*

Robin, Falstaff's page, *Merry Wives of Windsor, i. 3.*

Robin Goodfellow. See PUCK.

Robin Hood. See HOOD.

Robin Redbreast (ruddock), allusion to the notion that he covers the dead, *Cymbeline, iv. 2.*

Rochester, scene of a part of *I. Henry IV.* It is twenty-eight miles southeast of London.

Rod, the, more mocked than feared, *Measure for Measure, i. 4.*

Roderigo, a Venetian gentleman, character in *Othello,* introduced in *i. 1.* He is in love with Desdemona, and is made a dupe by Iago. His encounter with Cassio, *v. 1.*

"Without any fixed principle, but not without the moral notions and sympathies with honour which his rank and connections had hung upon him, is already well fitted and predisposed for the purpose; for every want of character and strength of passion, like wind loudest in an empty house, constitute his character."—COLERIDGE.

Rogero, a gentleman at the palace, *A Winter's Tale, v. 2.*

Rolands, *I. Henry VI., i. 2.* Roland was one of Charlemagne's twelve peers.

Romage (rummage, overturning), *Hamlet, i. 1.*

Roman(s), degenerate, *Julius Cæsar, i. 3 ;* promises of, *Julius Cæsar, ii. 1 ;* such a, *Julius Cæsar, iv. 3 ;* the noblest, *Julius Cæsar, v. 5 ;* the injurious, *Cymbeline, iii. 1.*

Roman fool, play the (Cato of Utica?), *Macbeth, v. 5.*

Romano, Giulio, a painter of the sixteenth century, spoken of as a sculptor in *A Winter's Tale. v. 2.*

Roman thought, a, hath struck him, *Antony and Cleopatra, i. 2.*

Rome, scene of parts of *Titus Andronicus, Antony and Cleopatra, Coriolanus, Julius Cæsar,* and *Cymbeline ;* her knowledge of her neighbours, *Coriolanus, i. 2;* attacked, *Coriolanus, iv. 6;* dissensions in, *i. 1; iii. 1–3; iv. 2, 3;* gratitude of, *Coriolanus, iii. 1.* "Now the good gods," etc.; ingratitude of—a wilderness of tigers, *Titus Andronicus, iii. 1;* degenerate, *Julius Cæsar, i. 2;* loved more, *Julius Cæsar, iii. 2.*

Rome (papal), curse of, *King John, iii. 1;* dictation of, *King John, v. 2;* tricks of, *Henry VIII., ii. 4, end.*

Romeo, hero of *Romeo and Juliet,* first appears in *i. 1.* He is in love with Rosaline, Capulet's niece; goes to Capulet's feast, *i. 5;* in Capulet's garden, *ii. 2;* marries Juliet, *ii. 6;* slays Tybalt, and is banished, *iii. 1;* in Mantua, *v. 1;* slays Paris and dies, *v. 3.* See ROSALINE.

"The wise Friar Laurence perceived that 'affliction was enamoured' of the susceptible qualities of this deeply agitated and violent nature, and that he was 'wedded to calamity.' . . . Reserved, disdainful of advice, melancholy, laconic, vague and subtle in his scanty words, he shuns the light, he is an interpreter of dreams, his disposition is foreboding, and his nature pregnant with fate."— GERVINUS.

Romeo and Juliet was first published in 1597, but the version then printed is supposed to have been rewritten from an earlier one, dating as far back as 1591. The story is very old. Some of the chief incidents appeared in a Greek romance by Xenophon of Ephesus. It was first told in Italian by Luigi da Porto, of Vincenza, who died in 1529. His novel was published six years after his death. It was told again by Bandello, in 1554, and from him translated into French by Boisteau. William Paynter translated the French version into English for his "Palace of Pleasure," 1567. But the story had previously appeared in English verse by Arthur Brooke, 1562. Shakspere no doubt used both Paynter and Brooke in his play, but it bears a closer resemblance to Brooke's poem, which has considerable merit, than to the other. But Brooke speaks in his preface of having seen the story on the stage not long before; so that there was an English or perhaps Latin play to which Shakspere and he may both have been indebted. The time is early in the fourteenth century; at least the occurrence on which it is founded is referred to the year 1303, and the events of the play occupy but a few days.

"The enmity of the two families is the hinge on which everything turns; very appropriately, therefore, the representation begins with it. The spectator must have seen its outbreaks himself in order to know what an insuperable obstacle it is to the union of the lovers. The animosity of the masters has rather rude representatives; we see how far the matter must have gone when those foolish fellows cannot meet without forthwith falling into a quarrel. . . . The reconciliation of the heads of the families over the dead bodies of their children, the only drop of balm left for the torn heart, is not possible except through their being informed as to the course of events. The unhappiness of the lovers is thus not wholly in vain; sprung out of the hatred with which the piece begins, it turns, in the cycle of events, back toward its source, and stops it up forever."—SCHLEGEL.

Ronyon (Fr. rognon, a mangy person), *Macbeth, i. 3.* Rump-fed; the rumps were given to the cooks.

Rook, the, ominous, *Macbeth, iii. 4.*

Rooked (lodged), *III. Henry VI., v. 6.*

Room, description of a, *Cymbeline, ii. 4.*

Rope-ladder, *Two Gentlemen of Verona, ii. 4; iii. 1.*

Rope-tricks, *Taming of the Shrew, i. 2.* Conjectured to be a blunder for rhetoric.

Rosalind, the heroine of *As You Like It,* first appears in the second scene.

"She is fresh as the morning, sweet as the dew-awakened blossoms, and light as the breeze that plays among them. She is as witty, as voluble, as sprightly as Beatrice, but in a style altogether distinct. In both the wit is equally unconscious; but in Beatrice it plays about us like the lightning, dazzling, but also alarming; while the wit of Rosalind bubbles up and sparkles like the living fountain, refreshing all around. Her volubility is like the bird's song: it is the outpouring of a heart filled to overflowing with life, love, and joy, and all sweet and affectionate impulses."—MRS. JAMESON.

Rosaline, the wittiest of the ladies attending on the princess in *Love's Labour's Lost,* beloved by Berowne or Biron, first appears in *ii. 1.* She is, perhaps, an earlier sketch of Beatrice.

Rosaline, the first fancy of Romeo, spoken of by him and his friends in the earlier part of the play.

"This" [Romeo's love to Rosalind] "has been to many a stumbling-block, and Garrick rejected it in the alteration of the play. To me it appears indispensable; it is like the overture to the musical sequence of moments which all unfold themselves out of that first when Romeo beholds Juliet. Lyrically taken, though not in respect of the action (and its whole charm surely rests on the tender enthusiasm which it breathes), the piece would be imperfect if it did not contain within itself the rise of his passion. But ought we to see him at first in a state of indifference? How is his first appearance exalted through this, that, already removed from the circumstances of cold reality, he walks out the consecrated ground of fancy! The tender solicitude of his parents, his restless pinings, his determined melancholy, his fanatical inclination for loneliness, everything in him announces the chosen one and the victim of love. His youth is like a thunderous day in spring, when sultry air surrounds the loveliest, most voluptuous flowers. Shall his quick change of mind deprive him of sympathy? or do we not argue from the instantaneous vanquishment of his first inclination, which in the beginning appeared so strong, the omnipotence of the new impression?"—SCHLEGEL.

Roscius, *III. Henry VI.*, *v. 6*; *Hamlet*, *ii. 2.* A Roman comic actor, died 62 B. C.

Rose(s), a, in the ear, *King John*, *i. 1.* Allusion to the fashion of wearing a flower or a knot of ribbon in the ear or the hair near it; by any other name, *Romeo and Juliet*, *ii. 2;* against the blown, *Antony and Cleopatra*, *iii. 11* or *13;* odours of, *Sonnet liv.;* red and white, *Sonnet xcix.;* at Christmas, *Love's Labour's Lost*, *i. 1;* of the fair state, *Hamlet*, *iii. 1.*

Rosemary, *A Winter's Tale*, *iv. 3* or *4; Romeo and Juliet*, *ii. 4; iv. 5; Hamlet*, *iv. 5; Pericles*, *iv. 6.* It was thought to strengthen the memory, and was therefore a token of remembrance; was used at weddings and funerals, and to garnish dishes at feasts.

Rosencrantz, a courtier in *Hamlet*, introduced in *ii. 2.* He and Guildenstern were schoolfellows of Hamlet, *iii. 4.* He calls them "adders fanged," and tells Rosencrantz in *iv. 2* that he is a sponge, soaking up the king's favour, rewards, and authorities. They carry the orders concerning Hamlet to England, *v. 2*, and are themselves sacrificed. It is not expressly told whether the two courtiers knew the nature of the order they carried; but Hamlet's answer to Horatio, *v. 2*, "They did make love to this employment," implies that they did, or that he thinks they did.

"Though directly they" [Rosencrantz and Guildenstern] "take no part in the action, they are nevertheless willing, for the sake of their personal aggrandizement and influence, to become the guilty instruments of another criminal's design. This subserviency, however, is but another and baser form of thinking and acting only for self, and it is therefore appropriately punished, not by the might of a foreign and hostile volition, but by the capricious sport of trifling contingencies."—ULRICI.

Roses, the, of York and Lancaster, *I. Henry VI.*, *ii. 4; iv. 1; II. Henry VI.*, *i. 1;* losses in wars of, *III. Henry VI.*, *v. 7;* battles of the Wars of, see BATTLES.

Ross, Lord William, a character in *Richard II.*, introduced in *ii. 3*, a partisan of Bolingbroke, who made him lord treasurer after his accession.

Ross, a thane of Scotland, character in *Macbeth*, introduced in *i. 3.* The title properly belonged to Macbeth, to whom it came by the death of his father, as that of Thane of Glamis is said in the play to have done.

Roted (learned by rote), *Coriolanus, iii. 2.*

Rother (a horned beast), *Timon of Athens, iv. 3.*

Rotherham, Thomas, Archbishop of York, character in *Richard III.*, first appears in *ii. 4.* He was kept in prison for a time by Richard.

Rottenness, in Denmark, *Hamlet, i. 4.*

Rouen (then pronounced and sometimes spelled Roan), scene of a part of *Henry V.;* taken by the French and lost again, *I. Henry VI., iii. 2.* It is in Normandy, sixty-seven miles northwest of Paris.

Rougemont, Castle. See EXETER.

Roundel (a dance), *Midsummer-Night's Dream, ii. 3.*

Rounder (circle), *King John, ii. 1.*

Rounding (telling a secret about in confidence), *A Winter's Tale, i. 2.*

Rouse, a cup in which to drink a health, *Hamlet, i. 4; Othello, ii. 3.*

Rousillon, an ancient province of southern France, scene of a part of *All's Well that Ends Well.*

Rousillon, Count of. See BERTRAM.

Rousillon, Countess of, a character in *All's Well that Ends Well,* appearing first in *i. 1,* mother of the young count. Just, clear-sighted, and affectionate, she does not allow her love for her son to blind her to his errors, nor do her pride of rank and dignity of station make her undervalue the merits of the lowlier Helena.

"But the whole charm and beauty of the play, the quality which raises it to the rank of its fellows, by making it lovable as well as admirable, we find only in the 'sweet, serene, sky-like' sanctity and attraction of adorable old age, made more than ever near and dear to us in the incomparable figure of the old Countess of Rousillon."—SWINBURNE.

Roussi, a French noble, mentioned. *Henry V., iii. 5; iv. 8.*

Rout, description of a, *Cymbeline, v. 3.*

Rowland, a gentleman mentioned in *Measure for Measure, iv. 5.*

Rowland, Child, *King Lear, iii. 4.* A fragment of an old ballad, a part only of which has been recovered.

Rowland de Boys, Sir, father of Oliver and Orlando in *As You Like It,* mentioned in *i. 1,* and other places in the play.

Royalty. See CROWNS, KINGS, PRINCES.

Roynish (scurvy), *As You Like It, ii. 2.*

Rub, there's the, *Hamlet, iii. 1.*

Ruddock (redbreast), the, covers the dead, *Cymbeline, iv. 2.*

Rudeness, a sauce to wit, *Julius Cæsar, i. 2.*

Rudesby (rude fellow), *Twelfth Night, iv. 1; Taming of the Shrew, iii, 2.*

Rue, *A Winter's Tale, iv. 3* or *4;* sour herb of grace, *Richard II., iii. 4; Hamlet, iv. 5.*

Ruff (the turned-over top of the boot), *All's Well that Ends Well, iii. 2.*

Ruffle (make disturbance), *Titus Andronicus, i. 1* or *2.*

Rugby, a servant of Dr. Caius in the *Merry Wives of Windsor,* first appears in *i. 4.* His worst fault, according to Mrs. Quickly, is that he is " given to prayer."

Rulers, virtues of, *Measure for Measure, iii. 2.*

Rules, of living, *All's Well that Ends Well, i. 1,* " Love all," etc.

Rumour, a pipe, *II. Henry IV., induction;* doubles numbers *II. Henry IV., iii. 1;* in cruel times, *Macbeth, iv. 2.*

Rumour, "the presenter" in *II. Henry IV.,* delivers the induction, painted full of tongues, a common character in the masque of that day.

Rural sports. See SPORTS.

Rush, Tib's, *All's Well that Ends Well, ii. 2.* Rush ring, sometimes used in rustic betrothals.

Rushes, lay you down on, *I. Henry IV., iii. 1.* It was the custom to strew floors with rushes.

Russia, a night in, *Measure for Measure, ii. 1;* Emperor of, Hermione his daughter, *A Winter's Tale, iii. 2.*

Rust, better to be eaten with, than to be scoured to nothing with perpetual motion, *II. Henry IV., i. 2.*

Rutland, call him, *Richard II., v. 2.* The Dukes Aumerle, Surrey, and Exeter were deprived of their dukedoms, but allowed to retain the earldoms of Rutland, Kent, and Huntingdon.

Rutland, Edmund Plantagenet, Earl of, third son of the Duke of York, a character in *III. Henry VI.,* introduced in *i. 3,* where he is slain in cold blood by Clifford, after the battle of Wakefield. He was seventeen years of age. His murder is spoken of in *Richard III., i. 2, 3,* and *iv. 4.*

Saba, *Henry VIII., v. 4.* Queen of Sheba.

Sabell, *Hamlet, iii. 2.* A yellowish colour; but some editions have *sables.*

Sack, the virtues of, *II. Henry IV. iv. 3.* The name was applied to several kinds of wine. Falstaff's is thought to have been sherry.

Sackerson, *Merry Wives of Windsor, i. 1.* An educated bear exhibited in London in Shakspere's time.

Sacrament, death without the, *Hamlet, i. 5;* taking the, *King John, v. 2; Richard II., i. 1; iv. 1; v. 2; All's Well that Ends Well, iv. 3.*

Sacrifices, at Delphos, *A Winter's Tale, iii. 1;* to appease the dead, *Titus Andronicus, i. 1* or *2;* spotted livers in the, *Troilus and Cressida, v. 3.*

Sad (serious), *Two Gentlemen of Verona, i. 3; A Winter's Tale, iv. 3* or *4, and elsewhere.*

Sadness, an unaccountable, *Merchant of Venice, i. 1; Richard II., ii. 2;* unlimited, *Much Ado about Nothing, i. 3.*

Safety, he that steeps his, in true blood, *King John, iii. 4.*

Saffron, *All's Well that Ends Well, iv. 5; A Winter's Tale, iv. 2.* Used to colour pastry with; also a fashionable colour in clothing.

Sagittary, the, *Troilus and Cressida, v. 5;* a sign in Venice, *Othello, i. 1.* The sagittary was an archer centaur who fought for the Trojans.

Sailors, characters in *Twelfth Night, Hamlet,* and *Othello.*

Sain (said), *Love's Labour's Lost, iii. 1.*

Saint(s), baiting a hook with, *Measure for Measure, ii. 2;* the great may jest with, *Measure for Measure, ii. 2;* to vex a, *Taming of the Shrew, iii. 2;* seeming a, and playing the devil, *Richard III., i. 3;* have hands that pilgrims' hands do touch, *Romeo and Juliet, i. 5;* a damned, *Romeo and Juliet, iii. 2.*

Saint Albans, scene of a part of *II. Henry VI.;* battle of (May 22, 1455), *II. Henry VI., v. 2, 3; III. Henry VI., i. 1; Richard III., i. 3.* The last reference is to the second battle, which took place February 17, 1461. The Yorkists were defeated by Queen Margaret's forces. Saint Albans is in Hertfordshire, twenty miles northwest of London.

Saint Albans, Mayor of, character in *II. Henry VI.,* introduced in *ii. 1.* The town was not incorporated until 1552, and therefore had no mayor at this time.

Saint Bennet's Church, in Illyria, *Twelfth Night, v. 1.* There was a Saint Bennet's church in London.

Saint Colmes' Inch (Saint Colomb's Island), *Macbeth, i. 2.* Sweno was made to pay heavily, according to the "Chronicle," for the privilege of burying his men at Colmes' Inch, now Inchcomb, a small island in the Firth of Forth.

Saint Edmund's Bury, scene of a part of *King John.*

Saint George, our ancient word of courage, *Richard III., v. 3.*

Saint Paul's Cathedral, *Richard III., iii. 6.* It was the custom to post bulletins there for the public to read.

Salad-days, my, when I was green in judgment, *Antony and Cleopatra, i. 5.*

Salamander, that, applied to Bardolph, *I. Henry IV., iii. 3.*

Salanio, or Solanio, character in the *Merchant of Venice*, introduced in the first scene, a friend of Antonio and Bassanio.

Salarino, a character in the *Merchant of Venice*, introduced in the first scene, a friend of Antonio and Bassanio.

Salerio, a friend of Bassanio in the *Merchant of Venice*, appears as a messenger in *iii. 2.*

Salic law, the, explained, *Henry V., i. 2.*

Salisbury, scene of *v. 1*, in *Richard III.* It is seventy-eight miles west-southwest of London.

Salisbury, William Longsword, Earl of, character in *King John*, introduced in the first scene. His abhorrence of John's treachery to Arthur caused him to go over to the side of France, *iv. 2;* but he returned after the accession of Henry III. He was a son of Henry II. and the fair Rosamund Clifford.

Salisbury, John Montacute, Earl of, a character in *Richard II.*, first appears in *ii. 4.* He was beheaded (*v. 6*) in consequence of his adherence to Richard. The earl in *Henry V.* was his son.

Salisbury, Thomas Montacute, Earl of, character in *Henry V.* and *I. Henry VI.*, appearing first in *iv. 3* of the former play. He was restored to his father's title, forfeited for adherence to Richard II., after about ten years, and was one of the ablest captains under Henry V. in France, where he was killed, as in the play, before Orleans, *I. Henry VI., i. 4.* He was "as full of valour as of kindness, princely in both." He had no son, and the title went to Richard Nevill, the Salisbury of the next play, who married his only daughter Alice.

Salisbury, Richard Nevill, Earl of, son-in-law of the preceding, character in *II. Henry VI.* He was at first a partisan of the king, but deserted to the Yorkists, fought at Saint Alban's, Bloreheath, Northampton, and Wakefield. At the last-named battle he was wounded and taken, and soon afterward beheaded. Warwick, "the king-maker," was his son, and succeeded to his father's title, though he is known in history and literature by the title that he received through his wife.

Sallet (a close-fitting head-piece), *II. Henry VI., iv. 10.*

Salt-butter rogue, a, *Merry Wives of Windsor, ii. 2.* One not rich enough to eat freshly made butter.

Saltiers (satyrs), *A Winter's Tale, iv. 3.*

Saltpetre, villainous, *I. Henry IV., i. 3.*

Salutations, *Coriolanus, ii. 1; Henry V., iv. 1; Othello, ii. 1;* quiet, *Midsummer-Night's Dream, v. 1;* to Octavia, *Antony and Cleopatra, iii. 6.*

Salvation, *All's Well that Ends Well, iv. 3,* "Sir, for a quart d'ecu he will sell the fee-simple of his salvation."

Samingo (San Domingo), *II. Henry IV., v. 3.*

Samphire, a gatherer of, *King Lear, iv. 6.*

Sampson, a servant of Capulet, character in *Romeo and Juliet,* appears in *i. 1.*

Samson, *Love's Labour's Lost, i. 2; I. Henry VI., i. 2; Henry VIII., v. 3.*

Sanctuary, the privilege of, *Comedy of Errors, v. 1; Richard III., ii. 4; iii. 1;* shall we desire to raze (to put the holy to base uses), *Measure for Measure, ii. 2, last part;* no place should be, for murder, *Hamlet, iv. 7 or 4.*

Sandal Castle, two miles from Wakefield, scene of *III. Henry VI., i. 2-4.* It was built about 1320; during the civil war it was besieged by the parliamentary army, and afterward destroyed by order of Parliament, and but little now remains of the ruins.

Sanded (sandy-coloured), *Midsummer-Night's Dream, iv. 1.*

Sands (Sandys), William, Lord, character in *Henry VIII.,* introduced in *i. 3.*

Sans (without, a French word in common use in Shakspere's time), *As You Like It, ii. 7, and elsewhere.*

Sarcasm, *Much Ado about Nothing, ii. 1.*

Sardis, scene of, *Julius Cæsar, iv. 2.* It is forty-five miles east of Smyrna, in Asia Minor.

Sarum Plain, *King Lear, ii. 2.* Sarum is the local name for Salisbury.

Satan, slanderous as, *Merry Wives of Windsor, v. 5.* See DEVIL.

Satiety. See SURFEIT, EXCESS.

Satire, keen and critical, *Midsummer-Night's Dream, v. 1;* wit larded with malice, *Troilus and Cressida, v. 1;* liberty for, *As You Like It, ii. 7; Love's Labour's Lost, v. 2.*

Satisfaction, *Merchant of Venice, iv. 1,* " He is well paid that is well satisfied."

Satisfy (quench), *Measure for Measure, iii. 1.*

Satis quod sufficit, *Love's Labour's Lost, v. 1.* Enough is as good as a feast.

Saturn, *Much Ado about Nothing, i. 3; II. Henry IV., ii. 4; Titus Andronicus, ii. 3; Cymbeline, ii. 5; Sonnet xcviii.*

Saturninus, a character in *Titus Andronicus,* son of the late emperor, and afterward emperor, introduced in the first scene, where he urges his hereditary claim to the throne. He is made emperor at the instance of Titus, and marries Tamora, queen of the Goths; kills Titus (*v. 3*), who has just slain Tamora; and is himself killed by Lucius, who becomes his successor.

Satyr(s), *A Winter's Tale, iv. 4;* Hyperion to a, *Hamlet, i. 2.* They were goat-like deities of the woods and fields.

Savages, life of, *Cymbeline, iii. 3; Twelfth Night, iv. 1.*

Saviolo, Vincentio. See DUELLING.

Saviour. See CHRIST.

Savoy, the, *II. Henry VI., iv. 7.* A palace of the Duke of Lancaster, destroyed in Wat Tyler's rebellion in 1381. It was on the bank of the Thames.

Saws, full of wise, *As You Like It, ii. 7.*

Say (a kind of woollen cloth), *II. Henry VI., iv. 7.*

Say (and Sele), James Fiennes, Lord, character in *II. Henry VI.,* introduced in *iv. 4.* In *iv. 2* Cade's men resolve to have his head, and in *iv. 7* he is taken. His head was set on London Bridge.

Say that thou didst forsake me for some fault, *Sonnet lxxxix.*

Scales, Thomas, Lord, character in *II. Henry VI.,* appears in *iv. 5,* spoken of in *I. Henry VI., i. 1;* his daughter, *III. Henry VI., iv. 1.* He was put to death by the Yorkists in 1460. His only daughter and heiress married Earl Rivers.

Scaling (weighing), *Coriolanus, ii. 3.*

Scall (scald-head), *Merry Wives of Windsor, iii. 1.*

Scambling, *Henry V., i. 1; v. 2.* Mondays and Saturdays in Lent were called scambling days. No regular meals were served, and members of the household scambled or served themselves as best they could.

Scamels, *The Tempest, ii. 2.* The meaning is uncertain: the sea-gull, the young of the limpet or scam, and the kestrel or stannyel, have been suggested.

Scandal, *Julius Cæsar, i. 2; Sonnet cxii.*

Scantling (portion), *Troilus and Cressida. i. 3.*

Scape-goat, Lepidus to be made a, *Julius Cæsar, iv. 1.*

Scarce had the sun dried up the dewy morn. *Passionate Pilgrim, vi.*

Scarecrow, of the law, a, *Measure for Measure, u. 1:* Talbot exhibited as a, *I. Henry VI., i. 4;* called a crow-keeper, *Romeo and Juliet, i. 4.*

Scarlet, and John, *Merry Wives of Windsor, i. 1.* Robin Hood's men.

Scarre, *All's Well that Ends Well, iv. 2; Cymbeline, v. 5.* So in some editions. The meaning is uncertain, but seems to be occasion or opportunity.

Scars, he jests at, that never knew a wound, *Romeo and Juliet, ii. 2;* shown by a candidate, *Coriolanus, ii. 2.*

Scarus, character in *Antony and Cleopatra,* introduced in *iii. 10,* friend of Antony.

Schoolboy, the whining, *As You Like It, ii. 7;* stupidity of the, *Much Ado about Nothing, ii. 1.*

School-days, friendship of, *Midsummer-Night's Dream, iii. 2.*

Schoolmasters, Miranda's, *The Tempest, i. 2;* pretended, *Taming of the Shrew, i. 1, 2.* See HOLOFERNES, EVANS, and PINCH.

Sciatica, *Measure for Measure, i. 2; Timon of Athens, iv. 1.*

Scogan, Henry, said in *II. Henry IV., iii. 2,* to have had his head broken by Falstaff. He wrote a ballad to the princes, sons of Henry IV.

Scone, a place near Perth, where the Scottish kings were crowned, *Macbeth, ii. 4,* and the last line of the play.

Scorn, in love, *Two Gentlemen of Verona, iii. 1;* in her eyes, *Much Ado about Nothing, iii. 1;* the slow finger of, *Othello, iv. 2;* of love, *Venus and Adonis, l. 252;* of the people, *Coriolanus, iii. 1; II. Henry IV., iv. 1;* the argument of one's own, *Much Ado about Nothing, ii. 3;* and derision never come in tears, *Midsummer-Night's Dream, iii. 2.*

Scotland, scene of the greater part of *Macbeth.* It is thought that a play on a Scotch subject was desired to be represented before James I. Its misery under Macbeth, *iv. 3;* its barrenness, *Comedy of Errors, iii. 2.*

Scots, invasions of England by, and king of, taken, *Henry V., i. 2.*

Scottish lord, a, described. *Merchant of Venice, i. 2.*

Scrimer (escrimeur, fencer), *Hamlet, iv. 7 or 4.*

Scripture, the devil can cite, *Merchant of Venice, i. 3;* odd ends from, *Richard III., i. 3.* See BIBLE.

Scrofula, cure of, by the king, *Macbeth, iv. 3.* See KING'S EVIL.

Scroop, or Scrope, Sir Stephen, a character in *Richard II.,* introduced in *iii. 2.* He was a loyal friend to Richard, but was afterward taken into favour by Henry IV. His son is the Lord Scroop who is a character in *Henry V.*

Scroop, Richard, Archbishop of York, character in both parts of *Henry IV.* In *i. 3* of the first part, he is spoken of as disaffected toward the king on account of the death of his brother, the Earl of Wiltshire. He was not, however, a brother of the earl, who was a Scroop of Masham, brother of Lord Scroop of *Richard II.,* and uncle of the one of *Henry V.* Many historians are said to have made the error into which Shakspere has fallen. The archbishop joins Northumberland's party in opposition to the king. In the second part he appears first in *i. 3,* where the conspirators meet at his palace. In *iv. 1* and *2,* they receive an embassy from the king and disperse their army. But the king's party did not keep its faith, and the archbishop was condemned with scarcely a form of trial and executed in 1405. This was the first instance of capital punishment inflicted on a bishop. He requested the executioner to despatch him with five strokes of the sword, in memory of the five wounds of the Saviour. He was regarded as a martyr, and pilgrimages were made to his tomb.

Scroop, Henry, Lord, of Masham, character in *Henry V.* His connection with a conspiracy to murder the king is spoken of in the prologue to *act ii.* He is exposed and ordered to execution in *ii. 2,* where the king reproaches him for his treachery toward a monarch whose intimate friendship he had enjoyed, and whose counsels he had shared. The king had sent him on an embassy to France, and he was said to have been corrupted while there by the offer of an enormous bribe. He was beheaded in 1415.

Scroyles (scrubs), *King John, ii. 1 or 2.*

Scruple, some craven, *Hamlet, iv. 4 or 1;* a Trojan slave for every, of Helen's weight, *Troilus and Cressida, iv. 1.*

Sculls, scaled (schools of fishes), *Troilus and Cressida, v. 5.*

Sculpture, *Cymbeline, ii. 4; A Winter's Tale, v. 2, 3.*

Scylla and Charybdis, *Merchant of Venice, iii. 5.*

Scythian, the barbarous, *King Lear, i. 1.*

Sea, the, storms on, *The Tempest, i. 1; II. Henry IV., iii. 1;* grew civil, *Midsummer-Night's Dream, ii. 2;* allusion to the notion that those buried in, could not rest for one hundred years, *Midsum-*

mer-Night's Dream, iii. 2; obeys the moon, *A Winter's Tale, i. 2; I. Henry IV., i. 2;* treasures of, *Henry V., i. 2;* backed with, *III. Henry VI., iv. 1;* the bottom of, *Richard III., i. 4;* what fool hath added water to, *Titus Andronicus, iii. 1;* in storm, *King Lear, iii. 7; Othello, ii. 1;* dangers of, *Pericles, ii., prologue;* watery kingdom, *Merchant of Venice, ii. 6;* a thief, *Timon of Athens, iv. 3.*

Sea-captains, characters in *The Tempest,* introduced in *i. 2,* and in *Twelfth Night,* introduced in *i. 2.*

Sea-change, suffered a, *The Tempest, i. 2, song.*

Seacoal, George, mentioned in *Much Ado about Nothing, iii. 3.*

Seacoal-fire, a, *II. Henry IV., ii. 1.* So called because the coal was brought across the sea.

Seal, the great, *Henry VIII., iii. 2.*

Sea-maid, music of, See under MAIDENHOOD.

Seamanship, *The Tempest, i. 1; Twelfth Night, v. 1,* " A bawbling vessel was he captain of," etc.

Sea-monster, the, *King Lear, i. 4.* Probably the hippopotamus, which stood for ingratitude.

Sear, *Hamlet, ii. 2.* The part of a gun acted on by the trigger; to be tickled of the sear, is to be easily moved.

Seas, the multitudinous, *Macbeth, ii. 2.*

Season, the right, makes perfect, *Merchant of Venice, v. 1;* roses and snow out of, *Love's Labour's Lost, i. 1;* the appropriate, *Antony and Cleopatra, ii. 2,* " Every time serves for the matter that is then born in it."

Seasons, inappropriate weather of, due to fairies, *Midsummer-Night's Dream, ii. 1;* supposed to allude to the peculiar weather of 1594; unnatural, are omens of ill, *II. Henry IV.. iv. 4.*

Sebastian, brother of the King of Naples, in *The Tempest,* appears in the first scene. He is a base character, aggravating his brother's grief at the loss of his son with reproaches and mockery, and plotting with Antonio to take the king's life in order that he himself may secure the throne.

Sebastian, name assumed by Julia in the *Two Gentlemen of Verona, iv. 4.*

Sebastian, brother of Viola in *Twelfth Night,* first appears in *ii. 1,* a simple, manly, straightforward character.

Secrecy, *All's Well that Ends Well, iv. 3,* "I am the grave of it;" no lady closer for, *I. Henry IV., ii. 3;* let your secrecy moult no feather, *Hamlet, ii. 2;* give it an understanding but no tongue, *Hamlet. i. 2.*

Secretaries, of Wolsey in *Henry VIII.*, were Dr. Richard Pace (*q. v.*) and William Burbank.

Secret(s), deep and dangerous, *I. Henry IV.*, *i. 3;* trusting a woman with, *I. Henry IV.*, *ii. 3; Julius Cæsar, ii. 1;* trusting the air with, *Titus Andronicus, iv. 2;* key of a, *Hamlet, i. 3;* hints about a, *Hamlet, i. 5, end;* revealing, *Hamlet, iii. 4;* rip the heart to find a, *Cymbeline, iii. 5;* two may keep, *Romeo and Juliet, ii. 4.*

Sect, a creature to begin a, with success, *A Winter's Tale, v. 1;* love a, *Othello, i. 3.*

Sectary, Cranmer called a, *Henry VIII., v. 3;* an astronomical (astrologer), *King Lear, i. 2.*

Security, for debt, Falstaff on, *II. Henry IV., i. 2;* obstacle to, *Macbeth, iii. 4;* mortals' enemy, *Macbeth, iii. 5;* for Scotland, *Macbeth, iii. 6;* our advantages lull us to false, *King Lear, iv. 1,* "Our means secure us;" make assurance doubly sure, *Macbeth, iv. 1;* fast find, fast bind, *Merchant of Venice, ii. 5.*

Sedges, *Two Gentlemen of Verona, ii. 7; Much Ado about Nothing, ii. 1; Taming of the Shrew, induction, 2.*

Sedition. See INSURRECTION, REBELLION.

Seel (to close up the eyes, as in the training of a hawk), *II. Henry IV., iii. 1; Macbeth, iii. 1; Othello, i. 3; iii. 3.*

Seely, Sir Bennet, mentioned in *Richard II., v. 6,* as having been beheaded. This character is variously called Sir Bennet or Benedict Seely, Sir John Scheveley, and Sir John Shelley.

Seemers (hypocrites), revelation of, *Measure for Measure, i. 4, end.*

Seeming, faults from, *Measure for Measure, iii. 2;* appearance of humane, *Othello, ii. 1;* I know not seems, *Hamlet, i. 2;* deceptive, *Much Ado about Nothing, iv. 1.*

Seen (versed), in music, *Taming of the Shrew, i. 2.*

Seen, to have, much, *As You Like It, iv. 1.*

Segregation (scattering), *Othello, ii. 1.*

Seized (possessed), *Hamlet, i. 1.*

Seleucus, Cleopatra's treasurer, introduced in *v. 2* of *Antony and Cleopatra,* where he declares her inventory false, and is reproached by her for his ingratitude.

Self, to see one's, as others see, *As You Like It, i. 2,* speech of Celia; my other, *Richard III., ii. 2; Troilus and Cressida, iii. 2;* swear by thy gracious, *Romeo and Juliet, ii. 2;* faults of one's, *Lucrece, l. 633.*

Semblable (like, likeness), *Timon of Athens, iv. 3 ; Hamlet, v. 2.*

Semiramis, *Taming of the Shrew, induction, 2 ; Titus Androni-cus, ii. 1.* A traditionary Queen of Assyria about 2000 B. C.

Semper idem (always the same), for absque, etc. (without this there is nothing), scraps of Latin that Pistol has picked up from mottoes, *II. Henry IV., v. 5.*

Sempronius, a kinsman of *Titus Andronicus,* addressed in *iv. 3.*

Sempronius, one of the lords, flatterers of Timon of Athens, introduced in *iii. 3,* refuses a loan to Timon on the pretence of anger at not having been applied to first.

Senators, characters in *Julius Cæsar, Timon of Athens, Titus Andronicus, Cymbeline,* and *Othello.*

Seneca, quotations from, *Titus Andronicus, ii. 1 ; iv. 1 ;* cannot be too heavy, *Hamlet, ii. 2.*

Senoys (Sienese), the, *All's Well that Ends Well, i. 2.*

Sensation, a theory of, *Lucrece, l. 442.*

Sense, common, *All's Well that Ends Well, ii. 1.*

Senseless, exceeding good, *Twelfth Night, iii. 4.*

Senses, of the king, have but human conditions, *Henry V., iv. 1 ;* other senses imperfect from the eyes' anguish, *King Lear, iv. 6 ;* untuned, *King Lear, iv. 7.*

Sentence, a, like a glove, *Twelfth Night, iii. 1.*

Sentences, drunk out of his five, *Merry Wives of Windsor, i. 1.*

Separation. See PARTING.

Sepulchre, the Holy, *Richard II., ii. 1.*

Sequent (follower), *Love's Labour's Lost, iv. 2.*

Serenade, Lysander's, *Midsummer-Night's Dream, i. 1.*

Serenity, of temper, *Hamlet, iii. 2.*

Sergeant, a soldier in *Macbeth, i. 2.* The title was applied to an officer of higher rank formerly than now. The sergeant ranked next to the esquire.

Sergeant-at-arms, a, character in *Henry VIII., i. 1.*

Sermons, in stones, *As You Like It, ii. 1.*

Serpent(s), look like the flower, but be the, *Macbeth, i. 5 ;* allusion to the belief that the bite of one could be cured by its blood, *Richard II., i. 1,* "I am disgraced," etc. ; allusion to the absence of, from Ireland, *Richard II., ii. 1,* "Now for our Irish wars," etc. ; lest pity prove a, *Richard II., v. 3,* allusion to the fable of the farmer and the viper ; of old Nile, *Antony and Cleopatra, i. 5 ;* the worm of Nilus, *Antony and Cleopatra, v. 2 ;* bred of mud by the sun, *Antony and Cleopatra, ii. 7.*

Serpigo (a skin disease), *Measure for Measure, iii. 1; Troilus and Cressida, ii. 3.*

Servant(s), true, *A Winter's Tale, i. 2,* "Why he that wears," etc.; treatment of a, *Comedy of Errors, iv. 4;* faithlessness of, *Henry VIII., ii. 1;* addressed by the master's name (Varro), *Timon of Athens, ii. 2;* faithful, *Timon of Athens, iv. 2;* kept feed, *Macbeth, iii. 4;* sworn (alluding to the custom of servants taking an oath of fidelity), *Cymbeline, ii. 4;* a good, does only just commands, *Cymbeline, v. 1;* an unprofitable, *Merchant of Venice, ii. 5.*

Service, of the antique world, *As You Like It, ii. 3;* zealous, of the king, *Henry VIII., iii. 2;* folly of faithful, *Othello, i. 1;* to the state, *Othello, v. 2.*

Servilius, a servant of *Timon of Athens,* introduced in *ii. 2.*

Sessa (cease), *Taming of the Shrew, induction, 1; King Lear, iii. 6.*

Setebos, the name of a god spoken of by Caliban as the god of his mother Sycorax, *The Tempest, i. 2; v. 1.* In Richard Eden's "History of Travayle," London, 1577, Setebos is given as the name of a god worshipped by the Patagonians.

Seven ages of man, the, *As You Like It, ii. 7.*

Several (a field enclosed, not common), *Love's Labour's Lost, ii. 1.*

Severn River, the, affrighted, *I. Henry IV., i. 3;* the sandy-bottomed, *I. Henry IV., iii. 1.*

Sewer (one who placed dishes on the table), *Macbeth, i. 7.*

Sexton, a, character in *Much Ado about Nothing, iv. 2.*

Seymour, Richard de St. Maur, Lord, spoken of in *Richard II., ii. 3,* as being at Berkeley Castle with the Duke of York.

Seyton, name of an officer attending Macbeth in *v. 3, 5.*

Shadow, a recruit in *II. Henry IV.,* appears in *iii. 2.*

Shadows, those that kiss, *Merchant of Venice, ii. 9;* of the king, *I. Henry IV., v. 4;* to fill the muster-roll, *II. Henry IV., iii. 2;* have struck more terrors than the substance of ten thousand soldiers, *Richard III., v. 3.*

Shafalus, true to Procrus, *Midsummer-Night's Dream, v. 1.* See PROCRIS.

Shaft, one sent after another, *Merchant of Venice, i. 1;* the rich golden (Cupid's), *Twelfth Night, i. 1;* or a bolt, see PROVERBS.

Shall, his popular shall, *Coriolanus, iii. 1.*

Shall I compare thee to a summer day? *Sonnet xviii.*

Shallow, Robert, a country justice in *II. Henry IV.,* introduced in *iii. 2,* and in the *Merry Wives of Windsor,* introduced in the first

scene. He is a fool, a braggart, and a liar, boasting of sins in his
youth which he never committed. The character is supposed to be
a caricature of Sir Thomas Lucy, who caused Shakspere to be arrested for stealing deer. See LUCY.

Shallowness, *All's Well that Ends Well, ii. 3,* "I did think
thee," etc., and "Do not plunge," etc.; Hastings accused of, *II. Henry IV., iv. 2.*

Shame, death the fairest cover for, *Much Ado about Nothing,
iv. 1;* hath spoiled the world, *King John, iii. 4;* marked by Nature
to do a deed of, *King John, iv. 2;* not to be borne, even at the
king's command, *Richard II., i. 1;* serves thy life and attends thy
death, *Richard III., iv. 4;* ashamed to sit upon his brow, *Romeo and
Juliet, iii. 2;* where is thy blush, *Hamlet, iii. 4;* a sovereign, *King
Lear, iv. 3;* imagines itself detected, *Lucrece, l. 1342.*

Shards (wings), of the beetle, *Macbeth, iii. 2; Antony and Cleopatra, iii. 2; Cymbeline, iii. 3;* (fragments of pottery), *Hamlet, v. 1.*

Sharked (gathered or snapped), *Hamlet, i. 1.* To shark is to
live by shifts.

Shaving, of the head before execution, *Measure for Measure,
iv. 2.* Prisoners often desired to receive the tonsure of the monks
before death.

Shaw, Dr. Ralph, *Richard III., iii. 5.* He and Friar Penker
are sent for by Gloucester to meet him at Baynard's Castle. Sir
Thomas More says they were "both doctors in divinity, both great
preachers, both of more learning than virtue, of more fame than
learning, and of more learning than truth." Dr. Shaw was a brother
of the lord mayor, Sir Edmund Shaw.

She, the unexpressive, *As You Like It, iii. 2.*

Shealed (shelled), *King Lear, i. 4.*

Shearman (tailor), *II. Henry VI., iv. 2.*

Shears, a pair of—proverbial saying, *Measure for Measure, i. 2.*

Sheba, Queen of. See SABA.

Sheep, love kills, *Love's Labour's Lost, iv. 3;* the harmless, *III.
Henry VI., v. 5.*

Sheep-biter (thief), *Twelfth Night, ii. 5.*

Sheep-shearing, feast at, *A Winter's Tale, iv. 3, 4.*

Shent (scolded), *Merry Wives of Windsor, i. 4; Twelfth Night,
iv. 2; Troilus and Cressida, ii. 3; Coriolanus, v. 2; Hamlet, iii. 2.*

Shepherd, the unfolding star calls up the, *Measure for Measure, iv. 2;* life of a, *As You Like It, iii. 2; III. Henry VI., ii. 5;*
philosophy of a, *As You Like It, iii. 2;* dead, *As You Like It, iii. 5.*

The dead shepherd is Marlowe, and the saw is quoted from his "Hero and Leander," published in 1598.

Shepherd, an old, is a character in *A Winter's Tale*, introduced in *iii. 3*, the reputed father of Perdita.

Shepherd, an old, a character in *I. Henry VI.*, father of Joan of Arc, introduced in *v. 4*, where he is denied by his daughter.

Shepherd to his love, the (by Christopher Marlowe), *Passionate Pilgrim, xx.*

Shepherdesses. See MOPSA and DORCAS.

Sheriff, of Northamptonshire, character in *King John.* Sir Simon de Pateshull.

Sheriff, a, character in *I. Henry IV.*

Sheriff of York, mentioned in *II. Henry IV.* Sir Thomas Rokeby.

Sheriff, a, character in *II. Henry VI.*

Sheriff, of Wiltshire, character in *Richard III.*, first appears in *v. 1.* Henry Long, of Wraxall.

Sheriff's post, *Twelfth Night, i. 5.* Set up at the sheriff's door for placing notices on.

Sherris, effects of, *II. Henry IV., iv. 3.*

Ship(s), scene on a, *The Tempest, i. 1;* carcass of a, *The Tempest, i. 2;* cannot perish, having thee on board, *Two Gentlemen of Verona, i. 1;* movement of, *Henry V., iii., chorus,* "Behold the threaden sails," etc.; the state like a, in danger, *III. Henry VI., v. 4;* Grecian, *Troilus and Cressida, prologue.*

Shipwreck, *The Tempest, i. 2; ii. 1; Comedy of Errors, i. 1; Twelfth Night, i. 2; A Winter's Tale, iii. 3; Merchant of Venice, iii. 2.*

Shirley, Sir Hugh, the Shirley mentioned in *I. Henry IV., v. 4,* as having worn one of the coats of the king at Shrewsbury, and having been slain.

Shirt, a, and a half, in a whole company, *I. Henry IV., iv. 2;* of Nessus, *Antony and Cleopatra, iv. 10.*

Shive (slice), *Titus Andronicus, ii. 1.*

Shoe-maker, the, should meddle with his yard and the tailor with his last, *Romeo and Juliet, i. 2.*

Shoe-tie, a traveller and prisoner, spoken of in *Measure for Measure, iv. 3.* This was a name commonly applied to a traveller.

Shog (jog), *Henry V., ii. 1, 3.*

Shore, Jane, *Richard III., i. 1; iii. 4, 5.* Mistress of Edward IV., and afterward of Hastings.

Shortcake, Alice, *Merry Wives of Windsor, i. 1.*

Shot, to pay, *Two Gentlemen of Verona, ii. 5.*

Shoughs (a shaggy kind of dogs), *Macbeth, iii. 1.*

Shoulder-shotten (having a dislocated shoulder), *Taming of the Shrew, ii. 3.*

Shovel-boards, *Merry Wives of Windsor, i. 1.* The broad shillings of Edward VI. were used in playing the game of shuffle-board, and were familiarly called by the name of the play. The game was also called shove-groat, and is alluded to in *II. Henry IV., ii. 4.*

Show, the outward, seldom jumpeth with the heart, *Richard III., iii. 1.*

Show, a street, *Coriolanus, ii. 1.*

Shrewd (shrewish), *Taming of the Shrew, i. 1, 2, and elsewhere.*

Shrewsbury, scene of part of *I. Henry IV.;* rebel forces at, *I. Henry IV., iii. 2;* battle of, *I. Henry IV., v. 3–5;* eve of the battle, *iv. 4;* offer of pardon before it, *v. 1;* reports of the battle, *II. Henry IV., i. 1;* Northumberland's failure to be at, *II. Henry IV., ii. 3.* It is one hundred and forty miles northwest of London. The battle was fought July 23, 1403.

Shrewsbury clock, fought a long hour by, *I. Henry IV., v. 4.*

Shrewsbury, Earl of. See TALBOT.

Shrieve (sheriff), *All's Well that Ends Well, iv. 3.*

Shrift, a short, *Richard III., iii. 4;* riddling confession makes riddling shrift, *Romeo and Juliet, ii. 3.*

Shroud (protection), *Antony and Cleopatra, iii. 11* or *13; III. Henry VI., iv. 3.*

Shrove-Tuesday, fit as a pancake for, *All's Well that Ends Well, ii. 2.* The English peasantry call the day "pancake Tuesday."

Shylock, the Jew in the *Merchant of Venice,* introduced in *i. 3.* His impassioned appeal in the first scene of the third act, "Hath not a Jew eyes," etc., is the only place where Shakspere seems to intend arousing the least sympathy for the usurer. In all other scenes his meanness and avarice are dwelt upon almost to the exclusion of his justifiable resentment at the insults to his race. He hates Antonio more for spoiling his business than for reviling his religion; and he would gladly see his only child dead before him if he might regain his ducats. There seems to be no reason to believe that Shakspere intended any rebuke to the Jew-hating spirit of his time.

"Hebler does not hesitate to call Shylock a comic personage, whose fate, proportionately, is no harder. rather milder, than that which finally befalls other comic characters, Falstaff, for example.

Gervinus is vexed that 'vulgarity and madness could go so far as to make a martyr out of this outcast of humanity.' A martyr he certainly is not, but we must allow extenuating circumstances in his favor. . . . But who made him a usurer ? . . . We know no other answer to this question but that the Christians have made Shylock what he is. We do not mean to say that Shakspere intended to hint at anything of the kind, although the temptation to draw such inferences lies nearer in this play than elsewhere in Shakspere. Whether the poet intended it or not, Shylock, in his hands, has become the representative of Judaism in its lowest degradation, and this degradation has undeniably been caused by centuries of political and social bondage."—KARL ELZE.

Sibyl, as old as, *Taming of the Shrew, i. 2;* work of a, *Othello, iii. 4.*

Sibylla (the sibyl), *Merchant of Venice, i. 2.*

Sibyls, the nine, of Rome, *I. Henry VI., i. 2.* There were not nine sibyls of Rome, but nine books offered to Tarquin by the sibyl. The number of all the sibyls is variously stated at from two to twelve, the last being the number given by the mediæval monks, who ascribed to each a prophecy of Christ.

Sicilia, scene of a part of *A Winter's Tale.*

Sicilian Lord, a, character in *A Winter's Tale.*

Sicily, King of. See REIGNIER.

Sicinius Velutus, a tribune of the people, character in *Coriolanus,* introduced in *i. 1;* Menenius on, *ii. 1.* He and Brutus are typical politicians, crafty, cowardly, dextrous, and vain of their authority.

Sick, the, Birone sentenced to visit and cheer them, *Love's Labour's Lost, v. 2.*

Sickness, untimely, *I. Henry IV., iv. 1;* thrown off, *Julius Cæsar, ii. 1, end;* leisure for, *I. Henry IV., iv. 1.*

Sic spectanda fides, *Pericles, ii. 2.* Thus faith is to be proved.

Sidney, Sir Philip (1554–1586), quotation from, *Merry Wives of Windsor, iii. 3,* "Have I caught my heavenly jewel," the first line of a song in "Arcadia." See under KING LEAR and HAMLET.

Siege (seat, rank), *Measure for Measure, iv. 2; Hamlet, iv. 7 or 4; Othello, i. 2.*

Siege, envious, of Neptune, *Richard II., ii. 1;* laugh, to scorn, *Macbeth, v. 5.*

Sieges, of Angiers, *King John, ii. 1;* end of the, of Harfleur, *Henry V., iii. 3;* of Orleans, *I. Henry VI., i. 2, 4–6; ii. 1, 2;* of Corioli, *Coriolanus, i. 4.*

Sieve, as water in a, *Much Ado about Nothing, v. 1; All's Well that Ends Well, i. 3;* a vehicle for witches, *Macbeth, i. 3.*

Sighs, cooling the air with, *The Tempest, i. 2;* to drive a boat, *Two Gentlemen of Verona, ii. 3;* of Imogen, *Cymbeline, iv. 2;* blood-drinking, *II. Henry VI., iii. 2;* blood-sucking, *III. Henry VI., iv. 4;* to shatter all his bulk, *Hamlet, ii. 1;* a spendthrift, *Hamlet, iv. 7* or *4.* The last alluding to the belief that sighing consumes the blood ; blows a man up like a bladder, *I. Henry IV., ii. 4;* a battery of sighs, *III. Henry VI., iii. 1.*

Sigh no more, song, *Much Ado about Nothing, ii. 3.*

Sight, annoyances to, *King John, iv. 1;* more impressive than hearing, *Lucrece, l. 1324.*

Sightless (invisible), *Macbeth, i. 5.*

Signs, of coming trouble, *Richard III., ii. 3;* in the clouds, *Antony and Cleopatra, iv. 12;* of the times, *Troilus and Cressida, i. 3.* See OMENS.

Silence, herald of joy, *Much Ado about Nothing, ii. 1;* in whom commendable—reputation for wisdom gained by, *Merchant of Venice, i. 1;* appeal of, *As You Like It, i. 3;* offending (flouts me), *Taming of the Shrew, ii. 1;* and speech, *All's Well that Ends Well, i. 1;* of innocence, *A Winter's Tale, ii. 2;* before a storm, *Hamlet, ii. 2;* not proof of want of love, *King Lear, i. 1;* intensifies feeling, *Venus and Adonis, l. 331;* be politic with, *I. Henry VI., ii. 5;* speech in dumbness, *A Winter's Tale, v. 2.*

Silence, a country justice in *II. Henry IV.,* first appears in *iii. 2.* He is a great admirer of Shallow, is very dull when sober, and very boisterous when drunk.

Silius, character in *Antony and Cleopatra,* introduced in *iii. 1.*

Silly-cheat (pocket-picking), *A Winter's Tale, iv. 2.*

Silly sooth (simple truth), *Twelfth Night, ii. 4.*

Silver, pale and common drudge, *Merchant of Venice, ii. 2.*

Silver, name of the spectre of a hound, *The Tempest, iv. 1;* a dog, *Taming of the Shrew, induction, 1.*

Silvia, a daring and witty girl in the *Two Gentlemen of Verona,* introduced in *ii. 4;* described by her father, *iii. 1.*

Silvius, a shepherd in *As You Like It,* in love with Phœbe, introduced in *ii. 4,* an importunate but humble and long-suffering lover, whom no repulses can drive away or incite to reprisals.

Similes, the most unsavoury, *I. Henry IV., i. 2;* currish, *Taming of the Shrew, v. 2.*

Simois, a river that flows from Mount Ida and joins the Scamander in the plain of Troy, *Lucrece, lines 1437, 1442.*

Simonides, King of Pentapolis, character in *Pericles,* introduced in *ii. 2,* father-in-law of the prince.

Simpcox, Saunder, an impostor in *II. Henry VI.,* introduced in *ii. 1,* who pretends to have received his sight by a miracle. His wife appears in the same scene.

Simple, Slender's servant in the *Merry Wives of Windsor,* introduced in the first scene.

Simpleness, and duty, *Midsummer-Night's Dream, v. 1.*

Simplicity, of the upright, *King Lear, i. 2, end;* how green you are and fresh, *King John, iii. 4.*

Simular (simulator, counterfeit), *King Lear, iii. 2.*

Sin(s), men of, *The Tempest, iii. 3;* some rise by, *Measure for Measure, ii. 1;* results of pardoning, *Measure for Measure, ii. 2;* most dangerous temptation to, *Measure for Measure, ii. 3;* compelled—charity in, *Measure for Measure, ii. 4;* comparison of—become a virtue—not accidental—a trade, *Measure for Measure, iii. 1;* remorse for, and fear of exposure—effect of one, *Measure for Measure, v. 4;* teach, the carriage of a saint, *Comedy of Errors, iii. 2;* cunning, can cover itself, *Much Ado about Nothing, iv. 1;* in chiding sin, *As You Like It, ii. 7;* allusion to the dogma of original, *A Winter's Tale, i. 2,* "The imposition hereditary ours;" gathering head, *II. Henry IV., iii. 1;* struck down like an ox, *I. Henry VI., iv. 2;* will pluck on sin, *Richard III., iv. 2;* mercy emboldens, *Timon of Athens, iii. 5;* resistance against, *Hamlet, iii. 4;* apprehensiveness of, *Hamlet, iv. 5* or *2;* plate, with gold, *King Lear, iv. 6;* one, provokes another, *Pericles, i. 1; Cymbeline, i. 7,* "The cloyed will," etc.; hidden in majesty, *Lucrece, l. 93;* with opportunity, *Lucrece, l. 878;* suffering for others', *Lucrece, l. 1478;* in the lovely, *Sonnets xciv.-xcvi.;* some, do bear their privilege, *King John, i. 1;* the oldest, committed the newest way, *II. Henry IV., iv. 4;* may be absolved in English, *Henry VIII., iii. 1.*

Since brass, nor stone, nor earth, nor boundless sea, *Sonnet lxv.*

Since I left you mine eye is in my mind, *Sonnet cxiii.*

Sincerity, in love, *Henry V., v. 2;* of Coriolanus, *Coriolanus, iii. 1,* "He would not flatter Neptune for his trident," etc.; folly of, *Othello, i. 1,* "But I will wear my heart upon my sleeve," etc.; in speech, *A Winter's Tale, i. 1.*

Sincklo, a name sometimes given to the first player in the induction to the *Taming of the Shrew*, and also to one of the huntsmen in *III. Henry VI*. It is thought to have been the name of an actor in Shakspere's company; but "Giles Senclowe is mentioned in the 'Paston Letters' as having been in Scotland with Queen Margaret."

Sinel (correctly, Finel or Finlay), Thane of Glamis, father of Macbeth, *Macbeth, i. 3.*

Singing, ridicule of Balthazar's, *Much Ado about Nothing, ii. 3;* Perdita's, *A Winter's Tale, iv. 3* or *4;* of Lady Mortimer, *I. Henry IV., iii. 1;* of the nightingale and wren, *Merchant of Venice, v. 1;* of Edmund, *King Lear, i. 2;* sing the savageness out of a bear, *Othello, iv. 1;* the singing-man of Windsor, *II. Henry IV., ii. 1.*

Sink-a-pace (cinque-pas), a dance whose measures are in fives, *Twelfth Night, i. 3.*

Sinners, at the gate of hell, *Macbeth, ii. 3.*

Sinning, more sinned against than, *King Lear, iii. 2.*

Sin of self-love possesseth all mine eye, *Sonnet lxii.*

Sinon, *III. Henry VI., iii. 2; Cymbeline, iii. 4;* in a painting, *Lucrece, lines 1521, 1529.* The Greek who, pretending to desert to the Trojans, persuaded them to admit the wooden horse.

Sir. This title was applied to curates, as Sir Nathaniel, Sir Hugh Evans, Sir Oliver Martext, Sir Topas, said to have properly belonged to such ecclesiastics as had taken the degree of bachelor of arts, or dominus.

Sirrah, generally used to an inferior, but Poins uses it to the prince in *I. Henry IV., i. 2.*

Sir-reverence (saving your reverence), *Comedy of Errors, iii. 2.*

Sisters, the weird. See WITCHES.

Sit (live, board), at ten pounds a week, *Merry Wives of Windsor, i. 3.*

Sith, sithence (since), *Measure for Measure, iv. 1; All's Well that Ends Well, i. 3; King Lear, i. 1, and elsewhere.*

Siward, Earl of Northumberland and general of the English forces that fight against Macbeth. He was the brother of Duncan's wife. His son Osberne is called in the play young Siward. They appear in *v. 4,* and young Siward is killed by Macbeth in *v. 7.* This famous earl was reported by tradition the descendant of a bear. He fought with Hardicanute and against Godwin on the side of the Confessor. It is said that when he came to die he said to his attendants: "Lift me up, that I may die standing like a soldier, and not grovelling like a cow. Put on my coat of mail; cover my head

with my helmet, put my buckler on my left arm, and my gilded axe
in my right hand, that I may expire in arms."

Sixpenny strikers, *1. Henry IV., ii. 1.* Bullies who would
knock a man down for sixpence.

Sizes (allowances of money), *King Lear, ii. 4.*

Skains-mates (companion scapegraces, originally brothers-in-
arms), *Romeo and Juliet, ii. 4.*

Skill, in contrast with ignorance, *Hamlet, v. 2.*

Skills (signifies), *Taming of the Shrew, iii. 2; Twelfth Night,*
v. 1; 11. Henry VI., iii. 1.

Skin, silver, laced with golden blood, *Macbeth, ii. 3.*

Skin-coat, your, *King John, ii. 1.* See HIDE.

Skogan. See SCOGAN.

Skull(s), *Romeo and Juliet, iv. 1; v. 3;* moralizing on a, *Hamlet, v. 1.*

Slab (glutinous), *Macbeth, iv. 1.*

Slander, will stain any name, *Comedy of Errors, ii. 1;* is forever housed when it gets possession—avoid occasion for, *Comedy of
Errors, iii. 1;* power of, *Much Ado about Nothing, iii. 1;* on Hero,
Much Ado about Nothing, iii. 2, 3; v. 1, 4; changed to remorse,
Much Ado about Nothing, iv. 1; on Diana, *All's Well that Ends
Well, v. 3;* none in an allowed fool, *Twelfth Night, i. 5;* venomed
spear of, *Richard II., i. 1;* poisoned shot of, *Hamlet, iv. 1 or iii. 5;*
damned nature of, *Othello, iii. 3,* "If thou dost slander," etc.; to
get office, *Othello, iv. 2;* sly, *Cymbeline, i. 6;* sharpness of, *Cymbeline, iii. 4;* mark of, *Sonnet lxx.;* the sting of, *A Winter's Tale, ii.
3;* a coiner of, *Troilus and Cressida, i. 3.* See also CALUMNY.

Slanderers, imprecation on, *Othello, iv. 2,* "A halter pardon
him," etc.; condemn themselves, *Sonnet cxxi.;* base newsmongers,
I. Henry IV., iii. 2.

Slang. See RED-LATTICE PHRASES.

Slave(s), that pays, *Henry V., ii. 1;* bred a dog, *Timon of
Athens, iv. 3;* mechanics, *Antony and Cleopatra, v. 2;* trusted with
a muzzle and enfranchised with a clog, *Much Ado about Nothing,
i. 3;* Shylock on the state of a, *Merchant of Venice, iv. 1.*

Sleave of care, the, *Macbeth, ii. 2.* Sleave is silk thread.

Sleep, seldom visits sorrow, *The Tempest, ii. 1;* life rounded
with a, *The Tempest, iv. 1;* an after-dinner, *Measure for Measure,
iii. 1;* of the traveller, *Measure for Measure, iv. 2;* shuts sorrow's
eye, *Midsummer-Night's Dream, iii. 2;* the image of death—trick
played upon Sly in, *Taming of the Shrew, induction, 1;* see also
LORD; to the great and the lowly, *II. Henry IV., iii. 1;* dwell upon

thine eyes, *Romeo and Juliet*, *ii. 2 ;* of the young, *Romeo and Juliet,*
ii. 3 ; Troilus and Cressida, *iv. 2 ;* untroubled, *Julius Cæsar*, *ii. 1 ;*
murdered, *Macbeth*, *ii. 2 ;* season of all natures, *Macbeth*, *iii. 4 ;*
secrets uttered in, *Macbeth*, *v. 1 ; Othello*, *iii. 3 ;* of the weary, *Cym-*
beline, *iii. 6 ;* life and death in, *Lucrece*, *l. 402 ;* the ape of death,
Cymbeline, *ii. 2.*

Sleeve, a pledge of love, *Troilus and Cressida*, *iv. 4 ; v. 2–4.*

Sleeve-hand (cuff), *A Winter's Tale*, *iv. 3* or *4.*

Sleided (unwrought) silk, *Pericles*, *iv., prologue.*

Slender, Abraham, an awkward country fellow in the *Merry*
Wives of Windsor, and a suitor to Anne Page, introduced in the
first scene.

"Slender and Sir Andrew Aguecheek are fools troubled with an
uneasy consciousness of their folly, which in the latter produces a
most edifying meekness and docility, and in the former awkward-
ness, obstinacy, and confusion."—MACAULAY.

Slenderness, hyperboles on, *I. Henry IV.*, *ii. 4 ;* "Away, you
starveling," etc.; "My own knee," etc., *II. Henry IV.*, *iii. 2, 4.* See
LEANNESS.

'Slid (by God's lid), *Merry Wives of Windsor*, *iii. 4.*

'Slight (by his light), *Twelfth Night*, *ii. 5,* and elsewhere.

Slighted (pitched), *Merry Wives of Windsor*, *iii. 5.*

Slip (a false coin), *Romeo and Juliet*, *ii. 4 ;* quibble on the word,
Troilus and Cressida, *ii. 3,* "If I could have remembered a gilt
counterfeit, thou wouldst not have slipped out of my contempla-
tion."

Slops (large boulstered trousers), *Much Ado about Nothing*, *iii.*
2 ; Romeo and Juliet, *ii. 4 ; Henry IV.*, *i. 2.*

Sloth, betrays to loss, *I. Henry IV.*, *iv. 3 ;* sleep of, *Cymbeline*,
iii. 6.

Slovenliness, punishment of, by fairies, *Merry Wives of Wind-*
sor, *v. 5.*

Slubber (slight), *Merchant of Venice*, *ii. 8.*

Slubber (soil), *Othello*, *i. 3.*

Sly, Christopher, a tinker, chief character in the *induction* to the
Taming of the Shrew. A lord who finds him dead-drunk has him
carried to his house and waited on when he awakes as if he were the
proprietor of the place.

"Sly is of the family of Sancho Panza, gross and materialistic in
his tastes and habits, but withal so good-humoured and self-con-
tented, that we would fain leave him unvexed by higher ideas or

aspirations; all the pains taken to delude him into the notion that he is a lord will not make him essentially other than 'Old Sly's son, of Burton Heath,' who has run up so long a score with the fat ale-wife of Wincot."—DOWDEN.

Small-pox, allusion to marks of, *Love's Labour's Lost, v. 2,* " Face full of O's."

Smalus, *A Winter's Tale, v. 1.* Apparently a prince of Libya.

Smatch (smack, tincture), *Julius Cæsar, v. 5 ; II. Henry IV., i. 2.*

Smell(s), an ancient and fish-like, *The Tempest, ii. 2 ;* villainous, *Merry Wives of Windsor, iii. 5.*

Smile, Jane, mentioned in *As You Like It, ii. 4.*

Smiles, the craft of, *Richard II., i. 4 ;* of Cassius, *Julius Cæsar, i. 2 ;* of Imogen, *Cymbeline, iv. 2 ;* when time shall serve, *Henry V., ii. 1 ;* and tears, *King Lear, iv. 3 ;* king of, *I. Henry IV., i. 3.*

Smiling, with millions of mischief in the heart, *Julius Cæsar, iv. 1 ;* one's cheek into years, *Love's Labour's Lost, v. 2 ;* smile and murder while they smile, *III. Henry VI., iii. 2 ;* and be a villain, *Hamlet, i. 5 ;* as the wind sits, *King Lear, i. 4.*

Smith, the weaver, a follower of Jack Cade in *II. Henry VI.*

Smithfield, now a part of London, scene of *II. Henry IV., iv. 7.*

Smoked (discovered or suspected), *All's Well that Ends Well, iii. 6 ; iv. 1.*

Smulkin, a fiend, *King Lear, iii. 4.* See MAHU.

Snail, the, *Comedy of Errors, ii. 2 ; As You Like It, iv. 1 ; King Lear, i. 5 ; Venus and Adonis, l. 1033.*

Snake, the, *Midsummer-Night's Dream, ii. 2 ; As You Like It, iv. 3 ;* scotched the, *Macbeth, iii. 2 ;* warmed the, *III. Henry VI., iii. 1.* See ADDER and SERPENT.

Snare, taken in his own, *Twelfth Night, v. 1,* " That thine own trip shall be thine overthrow."

Snare, one of the sheriff's officers in *II. Henry IV., ii. 1.*

Sneak-cup, a, *I. Henry IV., iii. 3.* One who baulks his glass.

Sneap (rebuke, snub), *II. Henry IV., ii. 1.*

Sneaping (pinching, nipping), *Love's Labour's Lost, i. 1; A Winter's Tale, i. 2.*

Sneck up (perhaps from " his neck up," that is, be hanged), *Twelfth Night, ii. 3.*

Snout, Tom, a tinker, character in *Midsummer-Night's Dream,* introduced in *i. 2.* He is cast for the part of Pyramus's father, but appears in the play as the wall.

Snow, a mockery king of, *Richard II., iv. 1;* consecrated, on Dian's lap, *Timon of Athens, iv. 3;* of Taurus, *Midsummer-Night's Dream, v. 2;* a little, tumbled about, becomes a mountain, *King John, iii. 4;* in harvest, *Richard III., i. 4.*

Snuff, took it in, *I. Henry IV., i. 3.* Snuff was made of aromatic substance before tobacco was used for it. Here there is a quibble on the cant use of the phrase.

Snug, a joiner, character in *Midsummer-Night's Dream,* introduced in *i. 2.* In the play before the duke he takes the part of the lion, and explains who he is, that the ladies may not be frightened —"a very gentle beast and of a good conscience."

So am I as the rich, *Sonnet lii.*

So are you to my thoughts as food to life, *Sonnet lxxv.*

Society, no comfort to one not sociable, *Cymbeline, iv. 2.*

Softly-sprighted man, a, *Merry Wives of Windsor, i. 4.*

So is it not with me as with that muse, *Sonnet xxi.*

Sol, the glorious planet, like a king, *Troilus and Cressida, i. 3.*

Solanio. See SALANIO.

Soldier(s), of Pharaoh, *Much Ado about Nothing, iii. 3;* bas for, to love, *Love's Labour's Lost, i. 2;* full of strange oaths, *As You Like It, ii. 7;* jests at a cowardly, *All's Well that Ends Well, i. 1,* "Under Mars," etc.; honour of a, *All's Well that Ends Well, ii. 1;* would have been a, but for those vile guns, *I. Henry IV., i. 3;* Hotspur and his comrades, *I. Henry IV., iv. 1;* Falstaff's, *I. Henry IV., iv. 2;* a braggart, *Henry V., iii. 6;* speaks like a, *Coriolanus, iii. 3;* not appreciated in peace, *Coriolanus, iv. 7;* dreams of a, *Romeo and Juliet, i. 4;* a better, *Julius Cæsar, iv. 3;* a daring, *Macbeth, iii. 1;* death of a, *Macbeth, v. 7; King John, v. 5; III. Henry VI., ii. 3;* your sister is the better, *King Lear, iv. 5;* little blessed with soft phrase—adventures of a, *Othello, i. 3;* one fit to stand by Cæsar—life of, *Othello, ii. 3;* endurance of a, *Antony and Cleopatra, i. 4;* should brook wrongs as little as gods, *Timon of Athens, iii. 5;* a brave, *I. Henry VI., iii. 2;* unapt to weep, *I. Henry VI., v. 3;* a true, hath no self-love, *II. Henry VI., v. 2.*

Soldiers, introduced on the stage in *All's Well that Ends Well, King John, Henry V., I. Henry VI., III. Henry VI., Richard III., Coriolanus, Titus Andronicus, King Lear, Antony and Cleopatra, Cymbeline, Macbeth.*

Soldiership, theoretical, *Othello, i. 1.*

Soliloquies, *Hamlet, i. 2; ii. 2; iii. 1; iv. 4; King Lear, i. 2; ii. 3; iii. 7; iv. 1; v. 2; Othello. i. 3; iii. 3; v. 2; Macbeth, i. 5, 7;*

ii. 1, 3; iii. 1; Richard III., i. 1, 2; Troilus and Cressida, ii. 3; v. 10; Romeo and Juliet, ii. 3, 5; iii. 2; iv. 3; v. 1; Timon of Athens, iv. 1, 3; Julius Cæsar, iii. 1; Cymbeline, ii. 2, 5; iii. 2, 3, 6; iv. 1, 2; v. 1; Pericles, i. 1, 2.

Solinus, Duke of Ephesus, character in the *Comedy of Errors,* introduced in *i. 1.*

Solitude, *Two Gentlemen of Verona, v. 4.*

Solomon, *Love's Labour's Lost, i. 2; iv. 3.*

Solon (about 638–559 B. C.), laws of, on a father's rights, *Midsummer-Night's Dream, i. 1.*

Solon's happiness, *Titus Andronicus, i. 1 or 2.* "No man can be pronounced happy till he is dead."

Solyman, Sultan (about 1495–1566), *Merchant of Venice, ii. 1.*

Some glory in their birth, some in their skill, *Sonnet xci.*

Somerset, John Beaufort, third Earl of, afterward first Duke, character in *I. Henry VI.* In *ii. 4* he calls for allegiance to the red rose of Lancaster. The Somerset of the second part is his brother. His daughter, Margaret Beaufort, became Countess of Richmond and mother of Henry VII.

Somerset, Edmund Beaufort, fourth Earl of, afterward second Duke, character in *II. Henry VI.* He was for some time chief of the king's party, and was accused by the Duke of York of various offences against the country, was arrested and imprisoned, but was afterward restored to office. He held the offices of Regent of France and Constable of England. He was slain at St. Alban's—*II. Henry VI., v. 2*—and is said in the first scene of the third part to have fallen by the hand of Richard, afterward King Richard III. His son, Henry, who succeeded him, was taken prisoner at Hexham and beheaded by the Yorkists. His second son, Edmund, became the fourth duke, and is the Somerset of the third part.

Somerset, Edmund Beaufort, fourth Duke of, character in *III. Henry VI.*, introduced in *iv. 1.* He commanded a force at Barnet, *v. 2*, and at Tewksbury, *v. 4*, where he was taken prisoner, *v. 5.* He was beheaded two days later, the last of the male line of the Beauforts. He was a son of the Beaufort of the second part.

Somerville, Sir John, character in *III. Henry VI.*, introduced in *v. 1*, a partisan of York.

Some say thy fault is youth, *Sonnet xcvi.*

Somnambulism, *Macbeth, v. 1.*

Son(s), the king envies Northumberland his, *I. Henry IV., i. 1;* his grief over his own, *Richard II., v. 3; I. Henry IV., i. 1; iii. 2;*

iv. 4, 5; devoted to their country, *Coriolanus, i. 3;* dead in honour, *Titus Andronicus, iii. 1.*

Song(s), old, *Twelfth Night, ii. 4; Pericles, i., chorus; Othello, iv. 3;* soothing, *I. Henry IV., iii. 1;* an exquisite, *Othello, ii. 3;* popular, *A Winter's Tale, iv. 3.* See also MUSIC and SINGING.

Songs: Come unto these yellow sands: *The Tempest, i. 2;* Full fadom five, *The Tempest, i. 2;* While you here do snoring lie, *The Tempest, ii. 1;* Where the bee sucks, *The Tempest, v. 1;* The master, the swabber, *The Tempest, ii. 2;* Farewell, master, *The Tempest, ii. 2;* Flout 'em and scout 'em, *The Tempest, iii. 2;* Honour, riches, marriage blessing, *The Tempest, iv. 1;* Who is Silvia? *Two Gentlemen of Verona, iv. 2;* To shallow rivers (by Marlowe), *Merry Wives of Windsor, iii. 1;* Whenas I sat in Babylon, *Merry Wives of Windsor, iii. 1;* Fortune, my foe (old song, alluded to), *Merry Wives of Windsor, iii. 3;* Fie on sinful fantasy, *Merry Wives of Windsor, v. 5;* Take, oh, take those lips away (authorship uncertain), *Measure for Measure, iv. 1;* Sigh no more, *Much Ado about Nothing, ii. 3;* The god of love, *Much Ado about Nothing. v. 2;* Pardon, goddess of the night, *Much Ado about Nothing, v. 3;* On a day, alack the day, *Love's Labour's Lost, iv. 3;* When daisies pied and violets blue, *Love's Labour's Lost, v. 2;* When icicles hang by the wall, *Love's Labour's Lost, v. 2;* You spotted snakes, *Midsummer-Night's Dream, ii. 2;* The ousel cock, so black of hue, *Midsummer-Night's Dream, iii. 1;* Now, until the break of day, *Midsummer-Night's Dream, v. 1;* If we shadows have offended, *Midsummer-Night's Dream, v. 1;* Tell me, where is fancy bred? *Merchant of Venice, iii. 2;* Under the greenwood tree, *As You Like It, ii. 5;* Blow, blow, thou winter wind, *As You Like It, ii. 7;* O sweet Oliver (fragment of an old ballad), *As You Like It, iii. 1;* What shall he have that killed the deer? *As You Like It, iv. 2;* It was a lover and his lass, *As You Like It, v. 3;* Then is there mirth in heaven, *As You Like It, v. 4;* Wedding is great Juno's crown, *As You Like It, v. 4;* Fire, fire, cast on water—Jack, boy! ho! boy!—Where is the life that late I led—It was the friar of orders gray, *Taming of the Shrew, iv. 1;* Was this fair face the cause, *All's Well that Ends Well, i. 3;* O mistress mine, where are you roaming? *Twelfth Night, ii. 3* (not by Shakspere); snatches of old popular, *Twelfth Night, ii. 3;* Hold thy peace—Three merry men—There dwelt a man in Babylon—O, the twelfth day of December—Farewell, dear heart—His eyes do show—Shall I bid him go? (the last three are from Corydon's Farewell to Phyllis)—Come away, come away, Death, *Twelfth Night,* *ii. 4;* Hey, Robin, *Twelfth Night, iv. 2* (not by Shakspere); I am gone, sir, *Twelfth Night, iv. 2;* When that I was a little, tiny boy, *Twelfth Night, v. 1* (not by Shakspere); When daffodils begin to peer, *A Winter's Tale, iv. 2* or *3;* But shall I go mourn, *A Winter's Tale, iv. 2* or *3;* Jog on, jog on, *A Winter's Tale, iv. 2* or *3;* Lawn as white as driven snow, *A Winter's Tale, iv. 3* or *4;* Get you hence, *A Winter's Tale, iv. 3* or *4;* Will you buy any tape? *A Winter's Tale, iv. 3* or *4;* Do nothing but eat, *II. Henry IV., v. 3;* Be merry, be merry, *II. Henry IV., v. 3;* A cup of wine, *II. Henry IV., v. 3;* Fill the cup, *II. Henry IV., v. 3;* Do me right, *II. Henry IV., v. 3;* Auld Robin Hood, *II. Henry IV., v. 3;* Orpheus with his lute, *Henry VIII., iii. 1;* Love, love, nothing but love, *Troilus and Cressida, iii. 1;* An old hare hoar, *Romeo and Juliet, ii. 4;* When griping grief, *Romeo and Juliet, iv. 5* (by Richard Edwards); of the witches, *Macbeth, iii. 5,* the song, "Come away," from Middleton's "Witch" is used; To-morrow is St. Valentine's day, *Hamlet, iv. 5* or *2;* They bore him barefaced on the bier, *Hamlet, iv. 5* or *2;* And will he not come again, *Hamlet, iv. 5* or *2;* For bonny sweet Robin, *Hamlet, iv., 5* or *2;* How should I your true love, *Hamlet, iv. 5* or *2;* In youth when I did love, *Hamlet, v. 2* (from a ballad attributed to Lord Vaux); Fools had ne'er less wit in a year, *King Lear, i. 1;* He that has, and a little, tiny wit, *King Lear, iii. 2;* Let the canakin clink, *Othello, ii. 3;* King Stephen was, *Othello, ii. 3;* The poor fool sat, *Othello, iv. 3;* Come, thou monarch of the vine, *Antony and Cleopatra, ii. 7;* Hark, hark, the lark, *Cymbeline, ii. 3;* Fear no more the heat, *Cymbeline, iv. 2.* Have I caught my heavenly jewel? (by Sir Philip Sidney), *Merry Wives of Windsor, iii. 3.*

Songs and Sonnets, Book of, *Merry Wives of Windsor, i. 1.* A popular book of the time, by the Earl of Surrey and others.

Sonnets, the, one hundred and fifty-four in number, were first published in 1609, in a small quarto, including also the *Lover's Complaint,* by Thomas Thorpe, who probably pirated them. They were alluded to in 1598 by Meres as "sugred sonnets" circulated among Shakspere's private friends. Two of them were published in the *Passionate Pilgrim (q. v.).* The time of writing may have extended over several years, and probably did. They are dedicated to W. H., but to whom these initials belonged is still a mystery. William Herbert, Earl of Pembroke, has been named, the first folio having been dedicated to him and his brother. Some have supposed the initials to be those of the Earl of Southampton *(q. v.)* reversed. The first one hundred and twenty-six are addressed to a man much

younger than the writer and deeply beloved by him. The remaining ones, excepting the last two, are addressed to a woman, dark-
complexioned, and not at all fair, or, it would seem, virtuous either,
who has been trifling with the writer and the friend to whom the
former sonnets are addressed. It is generally supposed that they
are the record of actual experiences of the poet, though it is possible
that they are dramatic and ideal. On this point Mr. Halliwell-
Phillips says:

"The words of Meres" ["his sugared sonnets among his private
friends"] "and the insignificant results of Jaggard's efforts" [to
make a collection of Shakspere's poems, in which he was able to include only two of the sonnets], "lead to the inference that these
strange poems were an assemblage of separate contributions made
by their writer to the albums of his friends, no two of the latter
being favoured with identical compositions. There was no tradition
adverse to a belief in their fragmentary character in the generation
immediately following the author's death, as may be gathered from
the arrangement found in Benson's edition of 1640; and this con-
cludes the little real evidence on the subject that has descended to
us. It was reserved for the students of the present century, who
have ascertained so much respecting Shakspere that was unsuspected
by his own friends and contemporaries, to discover that his inner-
most earnest thoughts, his mental conflicts, and so on, are revealed
in what would then be the most powerful lyrics yet given to the
world. But the victim of spiritual emotions that involve crimina-
tory reflections, does not usually protrude them voluntarily on the
consideration of society; and, if the personal theory be accepted, we
must concede the possibility of our national dramatist gratuitously
confessing his sins and revealing those of others, proclaiming his
disgrace and avowing his repentance, in poetical circulars distributed
by the delinquent himself among his most intimate friends. There
are no external testimonies of any description in favor of a personal
application of the sonnets, while there are abundant difficulties arising from the reception of such a theory. Among the latter is one
deserving of special notice, for its investigation will tend to remove
the displeasing interpretation all but universally given of two of the
poems—those in which reference is supposed to be made to a bitter
feeling of personal degradation allowed by Shakspere to result from
his connection with the stage. Is it conceivable that a man who
encouraged a sentiment of this nature, one which must have been
accompanied with a distaste and contempt for his profession, would
have remained an actor years and years after any real necessity for
such a course had expired? . . . When, in addition to this volun-
tary long continuance on the boards, we bear in mind the vivid interest in the stage, and in the purity of the acted drama, which is
exhibited in the well-known dialogue in *Hamlet*, and that the poet's
last wishes included affectionate recollections of three of his fellow-
players, it is difficult to believe that he could have nourished a real
antipathy to his lower vocation. It is, on the contrary, to be in-

ferred that, however greatly he may have deplored the unfortunate estimation in which the stage was held by the immense majority of his countrymen. he himself entertained a love for it that was too sincere to be repressed by contemporary disdain."

Sonnets to Sundry Notes of Music, title of the latter part of the *Passionate Pilgrim.*

So now I have confessed that he is thine, *Sonnet cxxxiv.*

Sonties (saints or sanctities), *Merchant of Venice, ii. 2.*

So oft have I invoked thee for my muse, *Sonnet lxxviii.*

Soon at night (very soon), *Measure for Measure, i. 5 ; Comedy of Errors, i. 2.*

Soothsayer, a, character in *Julius Cæsar,* appears in *i. 2,* where he warns Cæsar to beware the Ides of March, and in later scenes.

Soothsayer, a, character in *Antony and Cleopatra,* introduced in *i. 2;* prophesies to Antony, *ii. 3.*

Soothsayer, a, character in *Cymbeline,* introduced in *iv. 2,* where he speaks once only, and foretells success to the Romans ; he appears again as a prisoner in *v. 5,* where he interprets an oracle for Cymbeline.

Sophistry, in self-justification, *Julius Cæsar, ii. 1.*

Sophy (Shah), the, *Merchant of Venice, ii. 1; Twelfth Night, ii. 5; iii. 4.*

Soporifics, *Othello, iii. 3,* "Not poppy nor mandragora," etc.

Sorcerers, Ephesus full of. *Comedy of Errors, i. 2.*

Sorcery, *The Tempest, iii. 2,* see Magic; *II. Henry VI., i. 4.*

Sorrow, patience under, *Much Ado about Nothing, v. 1;* here I and, sit, *King John, iii. 1;* canker, *King John, iii. 4;* of the queen, *Richard II., iii. 4;* of the king, *Richard II., iv. 1;* for the dead king, *II. Henry IV., v. 2;* breaks seasons, *Richard III., i. 4;* for the dead, *Richard III., iv. 4;* a golden, *Henry VIII., ii. 3;* concealed, *Titus Andronicus, ii. 4* or *5 ;* more in, than anger, *Hamlet, i. 2;* each must bear his own, *Hamlet, iii. 2,* "Why let the stricken," etc. ; a rarity most beloved, *King Lear, iv. 3 ;* heavenly, *Othello, v. 2 ;* odd tricks of, *Antony and Cleopatra, iv. 2 ;* doubled by sight of unattainable relief, *Lucrece, l. 1114.* See Grief, Pain, Mourning.

Sorrows, come not singly, *Hamlet, iv. 5* or *2, 7 ; Pericles, i. 4.*

Sort (set), *Richard II., iv. 1; Richard III., v. 3.*

Sort and suit (rank and following), men of, *Measure for Measure, iv. 4.*

So shall I live supposing thou art true, *Sonnet xciii.*

Sossius, *Antony and Cleopatra, iii. 1.*

Sot (fool), *Merry Wives of Windsor, iii. 1; Twelfth Night, i. 5.*

Soto, *Taming of the Shrew, induction, 1.* A character in "Woman Pleased," by Beaumont and Fletcher.

Soul(s), give up the body rather than the, *Measure for Measure, ii. 4;* an evil, producing holy witness, *Merchant of Venice, i. 3;* the clothes the, *All's Well that Ends Well, ii. 5;* disputes with sense, *Twelfth Night, iv. 3;* the brain the dwelling of the, *King John, v. 7;* burden of a guilty, *Richard II., i. 3;* future of the, *Richard II., iii. 1;* sold to the devil, *I. Henry IV., i. 2;* grows with the body, *Hamlet, i. 3;* invulnerable, *Hamlet, i. 4;* prophetic, *Hamlet, i. 5;* in bliss, thou art a, *King Lear, iv. 7;* spotted, *Lucrece, l. 719;* in a dishonoured body, *Lucrece, l. 1169;* a true, *Sonnet cxxv.;* its fading mansion, *Sonnet cxlvi.;* all, were forfeit once, *Measure for Measure, ii. 2;* punishment of departed, *Measure for Measure, iii. 1,* " Ay, but to die," etc.; *Othello, v. 2,* "Blow me about in winds," etc.; harmony in immortal, *Merchant of Venice, v. 1;* if, fly in the air, and be not fixed, *Richard III., iv. 4.* See TRANSMIGRATION OF SOULS.

Sound and fury, life full of, *Macbeth, v. 5.*

Sources : Few of the plots of the plays were invented by Shakspere, possibly none, though there are some for which no originals have been found. Many of the stories are very old, and had appeared in several versions and languages; many were already familiar to English audiences of that day. They were, for the most part, bald narrations of incidents, dull plays, or simple ballads. Under the name of each play will be found mention of the principal source or sources drawn upon. Below is given an alphabetical list of them under the names of authors, or, in cases where the author's name is not known of the novel, play, or story :

ARIOSTO. The story of Ariodanto and Genevra, from his " Orlando Furioso," which was known in an English translation by Sir John Harington (1591), resembles that of Hero in *Much Ado about Nothing.* The " Search for the Island of Lampedusa," from the same work, has a description of a storm at sea, which has been likened to that in *The Tempest.*

" BARLAAM AND JOSEPHAT," is a middle-age Greek romance of about A. D. 800, in which appeared the story of the caskets (*Merchant of Venice*) for the first time, so far as is known.

BALE, BISHOP. "The Pageant of Kynge John," by Bishop Bale, was written about 1550. See below "Troublesome Raigne of King John."

BANDELLO. *Twelfth Night* is supposed to be founded mediately or immediately on his novel "Nicuola," the original of "Apollonius and Silla." See RICH. His story of "S. Timbreo di Cardona" has some features and names in common with *Much Ado about Nothing.* See also BELLEFOREST, BROOKE, PAINTER, and DA PORTO.

BARCKLEY, SIR RICHARD. His "Felicity of Man" (1598) has an "Account of Timon."

BELLEFOREST published "Histoires Tragiques," translations, in which was the "Hystorie of Hamblet," from Bandello.

BOCCACCIO. The story of the wager in *Cymbeline* is found in that of "Bernabo da Genova," and *All's Well that Ends Well* is drawn from his story of "Giglietta di Nerbona."

BROOKE, or BROKE, ARTHUR, is the supposed author of the poem "Romeus and Juliet," after Bandello.

CAXTON, "Recuyell of the Historyes of Troye" (circa, 1476), was consulted, perhaps, for *Troilus and Cressida.*

CHAUCER, GEOFFREY. His "Troylus and Cryseyde" may have been referred to by Shakspere in writing his drama.

CHETTLE. See WOLSEY, below.

CINTHIO, GIRALDI. His "Hecatommithi" has a story of a Moorish captain that seems to be a version of the one on which *Othello* is founded. See WHETSTONE.

DA PORTO LUIGI, published in 1535 an Italian novel telling the story of *Romeo and Juliet* for the first time, so far as is known, and the story was retold by Bandello in 1554.

"FAMOUS VICTORIES OF HENRY V., THE, CONTAINING THE HONOURABLE BATTELL OF AGINCOURT," a play written between 1580 and 1588, furnished the outlines of the two parts of *Henry IV.* and *Henry V.*

FIORENTINO, GIOVANNI, or S. GIOVANNI, of Florence. The incident of the buck-basket in the *Merry Wives of Windsor* is in his "Il Pecorone," as well as the circumstance of taking the husband into confidence. "Il Pecorone" also has the story of the bond used in the *Merchant of Venice.*

FOX, JOHN. His "Book of Martyrs" (1563) contains a passage that was probably before the writer of the first scene of the fifth act of *Henry VIII.*

GEOFFREY OF MONMOUTH, who wrote in the twelfth century, told the story of Lear and his three daughters.

"GERNUTUS, THE JEW," is the name of an old ballad giving the story of the bond that is used in the *Merchant of Venice.*

"GESTA ROMANORUM" is an old collection of stories in which the story of the caskets used in the *Merchant of Venice* and the history of *King Lear* are related.

"GL' INGANNATI" ("The Deceived."), an Italian play by an unknown author, strongly resembles *Twelfth Night*.

GOULART'S "Admirable and Memorable Histories" contains stories resembling those of the *Comedy of Errors* and *Measure for Measure*. It also gives the story of a trick played on an artisan by Philip the Good, Duke of Burgundy, evidently the original of the plot of the *induction* to the *Taming of the Shrew*.

GOWER, JOHN: Apollonius of Tyre, from his "Confessio Amantis," forms the basis of *Pericles*, in which Gower is introduced as the chorus. There was a version of the story in Laurence Twyne's "Patterne of Painefull Adventures" (1576).

GREENE, ROBERT. His "Pandosto: The Triumph of Time" (1588), afterward called "The History of Dorastus and Fawnia," furnished the material for *A Winter's Tale*. He is also the supposed author of the old play "Taming of a Shrew." In one of his works he refers to Shakspere as "an upstart crow beautified with our feathers—in his own conceit the only shake-scene in the country."

HALL, EDWARD, an early historian whose chronicles were probably consulted. He wrote of the "Union of the two noble and illustrate families of Lancastre and York" (1548).

HARINGTON. See ARIOSTO, above.

HIGGINS, JOHN, author of "How Queen Cordila in despair slew herself, the year before Christ 800," printed in "The Mirror for Magistrates" (1587), and perhaps referred to for *King Lear*.

HOLINSHED, RAPHAEL, wrote "Chronicles of Englande, Scotlande, and Irelande" (1577), which were largely drawn upon by Shakspere in the English historical plays, and in *Cymbeline*, *Macbeth*, and *King Lear*.

LODGE, THOMAS, a dramatist and novelist, was the author of "Rosalynde: Euphues' Golden Legacie" (1592), which furnished the plot of *As You Like It*.

LUCIAN, a Greek satirical writer, tells the story of *Timon of Athens*, and was one of Shakspere's authorities.

LYDGATE, "Historye, Sege, and Dystruccion of Troye" (1513).

MONSTRELET, ENGUERRAND DE, a French chronicler, 1390–1453: his account of the negotiations of Charles, King of Navarre, with the King of France for the Duchy of Nemours, may have furnished a hint for *Love's Labour's Lost*.

MONTAIGNE, MICHEL. The ideal commonwealth of Gonzalo in *The Tempest* is from Montaigne, whose works were translated into English by Florio in 1603. A copy of this translation, containing Shakspere's autograph, now in the British Museum, is the only book that is known to have been owned by him.

MONTEMAYOR : his "Diana" contains the story of the "Shepherdess Felismena," from which some part of the plot of *Two Gentlemen of Verona* is supposed to have been drawn. The resemblance is not close.

NORTH, SIR THOMAS, translated Plutarch's "Lives" from a French version into English (1579), and his works undoubtedly furnished Shakspere with materials for *Coriolanus, Timon of Athens, Julius Cæsar,* and *Antony and Cleopatra.* "The Life of Theseus" and "The Life of Pericles" also served in the *Midsummer-Night's Dream* and in *Pericles.*

"NORTHERN LORD," the, a ballad, has the story of the pound of flesh, resembling that in the *Merchant of Venice.*

OVID. Prospero's speech to the fairies in *The Tempest, v. 1,* is imitated from Medea's in Ovid, and many expressions in it are found in an old translation by Golding (1565–'87).

PAINTER, WILLIAM. His "Palace of Pleasure" (1566–'67) has the story of "Rhomeo and Julietta," from Bandello, "Giletta of Narbona," translated from Boccaccio, original of *All's Well that Ends Well,* and "The Life of Timon."

PLAUTUS. His "Menœchmi" was translated by W. W. (William Warner?), 1595, and resembles the *Comedy of Errors.*

PLUTARCH. See NORTH.

RICH, BARNABY, told the story of "Apollonius and Silla," on which *Twelfth Night* is based, in a collection called "Farewell to the Militarie Profession" (1581).

SAXO GRAMMATICUS, author of a "Historia Danica," in which the story of *Hamlet* appeared, wrote about the end of the twelfth century. See BELLEFOREST.

"SHREWD AND CURST WIFE LAPPED IN MOREL'S SKIN, THE," is an old poem, slightly resembling *The Taming of the Shrew.*

SIDNEY, SIR PHILIP. His "Arcadia" (1590) has a story, "The Paphalgonian Unkind King," resembling that of Gloster and his sons in *King Lear.*

"TAMING OF A SHREW, THE," is an old play of unknown authorship, on which *The Taming of the Shrew* was founded.

"TROUBLESOME RAIGNE OF KING JOHN, THE," a play by an unknown author, intervened between Bishop Bale's drama and that of Shakspere, which is thoroughly remodelled from it.

"TRUE CHRONICLE HISTORY, THE, OF KING LEIR AND HIS THREE DAUGHTERS," is an old play, written about 1593.

TWYNE, LAURENCE. See above, under GOWER.

"WAKING MAN'S DREAM, THE," is in a fragment of an old book of stories conjectured to be a collection by Richard Edwards, published in 1570. In it is a version of the story of "Philip, the Good Duke of Burgundy," already referred to under Goulart as the original of the plot of the *induction* to the *Taming of the Shrew*.

WHETSTONE, GEORGE. His "Promos and Cassandra" (1578) resembles *Measure for Measure*. It was founded on a story by Giraldi Cinthio, and was first written by Whetstone in a play.

WOLSEY, CARDINAL, a drama by Henry Chettle and others (about 1601), probably furnished some suggestions for *King Henry VIII*.

"YORK AND LANCASTER, FIRST PART OF THE CONTENTION BETWEEN THE TWO FAMOUS HOUSES OF, WITH THE DEATH OF THE GOOD DUKE HUMPHREY," etc., and the "True Tragedie of Richard, Duke of Yorke," and the "Death of Good King Henrie the Sixt," are the old plays on which the second and third parts of *Henry VI.* are founded. It is uncertain whether they were written by Shakspere himself, but it is highly improbable that they were, and doubtful whether the old plays came from the same hand.

Souse (to attack violently), *King John, v. 2.*

South, the foggy, *As You Like It, iii. 5;* *Cymbeline, ii. 3;* the sweet, *Twelfth Night, i. 1;* the dew-dropping, *Romeo and Juliet, 1. 4;* the spongy, *Cymbeline, iv. 2.*

Southam, *III. Henry VI., v. 1.*

Southampton, a seaport of Hampshire, scene of a part of *Henry V.*

Southampton, Henry Wriothesly, third Earl of, to whom the *Venus and Adonis* and *Lucrece* were dedicated, was a favourite of Queen Elizabeth until his marriage. He took part in the rebellion of Essex, was condemned for high treason, and kept in the Tower till the queen's death. He died in 1524. Some suppose that the *Sonnets* are also dedicated to him, his initials being simply reversed. For this, see SONNETS.

South Sea, of discovery, a, *As You Like It, iii. 2.*

Southwark, now a part of London, scene of *II. Henry VI., iv. 8.*

Southwell, John, or Thomas, a priest in *II. Henry VI.*, introduced in *i. 4.* He was priest and canon of St. Stephen's in Westminster. He died in the Tower before the time for his execution.

Sowl (pull), *Coriolanus, iv. 5.*

Sowter (cobbler), name of a hound, *Twelfth Night, ii. 5.*

Spain, *Comedy of Errors, iii. 2; Love's Labour's Lost, i. 1.*

Span-counter, *II. Henry VI., iv. 2.* A game in which the second player won by throwing his counter or coin within a span of that of the first.

Spaniel, love like a, *Two Gentlemen of Verona, iv. 2;* to play the, *Midsummer-Night's Dream, ii. 2; Henry VIII., v. 2; Antony and Cleopatra, iv. 10.*

Sparrow, Philip, *King John, i. 1.* The sparrow was called Philip because its note was thought to sound like the name; care of Providence for the, *As You Like It, ii. 3; Hamlet, v. 2.*

Spavins, *Taming of the Shrew, iii. 2; Henry VIII., i. 3.*

Speaking, to the purpose, *A Winter's Tale, i. 2,* "I have spoke;" Perdita's, *iv. 3* or *4;* is for beggars, *Troilus and Cressida, iii. 3.*

Spectacles, a pair of, *Troilus and Cressida, iv. 4.*

Speculation (vision), no, in those eyes, *Macbeth, iii. 4;* turns not to itself till it hath travelled, *Troilus and Cressida, iii. 3.*

Sped (finished), *Taming of the Shrew, v. 2, end.*

Speech, free, *Taming of the Shrew, iv. 3;* too much, *All's Well that Ends Well, i. 1;* a warlike, *King John, ii. 1* or *2;* daggers in, *Hamlet, iii. 2;* by the card, *Hamlet, v. 1;* rude in, *Othello, i. 3;* wild, *Troilus and Cressida, i. 3;* 'tis a kind of good deed to say well, and yet words are no deeds, *Henry VIII., iii. 2;* one excellently well penned, *Twelfth Night, i. 5;* sweet, *A Winter's Tale;* Hotspur's, imitated by the valiant, *II. Henry IV., ii. 3.*

Speed (success), *A Winter's Tale, iii. 2.*

Speed, the keen-witted servant of Valentine in the *Two Gentlemen of Verona*, introduced in *i. 1.*

Spells, *I. Henry VI., v. 4; Merry Wives of Windsor, iv. 2; Antony and Cleopatra, iv. 10.* See CHARMS.

Spendthrift. See EXTRAVAGANCE.

Spenser, *Passionate Pilgrim, viii.*

Sper (bar), *Troilus and Cressida, prologue.*

Spet (old past of spit), *Merchant of Venice, i. 3.*

Sphere, to be in too high a, *Antony and Cleopatra, ii. 7.*

Spheres, discord in the, *As You Like It, ii. 7;* music from the, *Twelfth Night, iii. 1;* spherical predominance, *King Lear, i. 2.* See ASTROLOGY.

Spider(s), the painter plays the, *Merchant of Venice, iii. 2;* **in** the cup, *A Winter's Tale, ii. 1;* a bottled, *Richard III., i. 3; iv. 4;* supposed to suck up venom, *Richard II., iii. 2;* -like, *Henry VIII., i. 1;* a brain more busy than the, *II. Henry VI., iii. 1.*

Spinster, a, on a wife's duty—reasons for being a, *Comedy of Errors, ii. 1.*

Spirits (courage, disposition), for anything not dishonourable, *Measure for Measure. iii. 1;* coy and wild, *Much Ado about Nothing, iii. 1;* undaunted, in a dying breast, *I. Henry VI., iii. 2;* wanton, *Troilus and Cressida, iv. 5;* high, before death, *Romeo and Juliet, v. 3;* I see there's mettle in thee, *Othello, iv. 2.*

Spirits (souls), finely touched to fine issues, *Measure for Measure, i. 1;* the delighted, see DELIGHTED; a thousand in one breast, *Richard II., iv. 1;* cannot be kept in bondage, *Julius Cæsar, ii. 1;* that gallant, hath aspired the clouds, *Romeo and Juliet, iii. 1.*

Spirits (of the air), in a cloven pine, *The Tempest, i. 2;* from the vasty deep, *I. Henry IV., iii. 1;* from under earth, *I. Henry VI., v. 3; II. Henry VI., i. 2; ii. 1;* of peace, *Henry VIII., iv. 2;* that tend on mortal thoughts, *Macbeth, i. 5;* the *Martii,* or spirits of revenge, the authors of murders; black and white, red and gray, *Macbeth, iv. 1;* the extravagant and erring, *Hamlet, i. 1.*

Spirits (ghosts), damned spirits all, *Midsummer-Night's Dream, iii. 2;* may walk again, *A Winter's Tale, iii. 3; II. Henry VI., i. 4;* no blood in, *Julius Cæsar, ii. 1;* will speak, *Hamlet, i. 1;* at death, *Sonnet lxxiv.* See GHOSTS.

Spleen, the, connected with laughter, *Measure for Measure, ii. 2; Love's Labour's Lost, v. 2; Taming of the Shrew, induction, 1; Twelfth Night, iii. 2.*

Spleen (passion), *Midsummer-Night's Dream, i. 1;* of a weasel, *I. Henry IV., ii. 3;* of all the fiends, *Coriolanus, iv. 1;* the venom of, *Julius Cæsar, iv. 3,*

Spleen (impetuosity), *I. Henry VI., iv. 6; Richard III., v. 3.*

Spoils, offered, *Coriolanus, i. 9;* despised, *Coriolanus, ii. 2;* not distributed, *iii. 3;* heavy, *v. 5.*

Sponge (drunkard), *Merchant of Venice, i. 2;* a king's favourite, *Hamlet, iv. 2* or *v. 6.*

Spoon(s), a long, to eat with the devil, *The Tempest, ii. 2; Comedy of Errors, iv. 3;* you'd spare your, *Henry VIII., v. 2.* The last refers to the christening-spoons given by the sponsors, sometimes called apostle-spoons, because they bore each an image of one of the apostles.

Sport, that pleases best, *Love's Labour's Lost, v. 2,* "Nay, my good lord," etc.; o'erthrown by sport, *Love's Labour's Lost, v. 2;* for ladies, *As You Like It, i. 2;* rural, *A Winter's Tale, iv. 3, 4;* very reverend, *Love's Labour's Lost, iv. 2;* painful, *The Tempest, iii. 1.*

Spot(s), of blood, *Macbeth, v. 1;* of anger, *Julius Cæsar, i. 2.*

Sprag (alert), *Merry Wives of Windsor, iv. 1.*

Sprighted (haunted), *Cymbeline, ii. 3.*

Spring, *Love's Labour's Lost, v. 2, song; Romeo and Juliet, i. 2; Sonnet xcviii.; Passionate Pilgrim, xxi.;* song of, *Love's Labour's Lost, v. 2;* flowers of, *A Winter's Tale, iv. 3.*

Spurs (the long roots of trees), *Cymbeline, iv. 2; The Tempest, v. 1.*

Spy, accusation of being a, *The Tempest, i. 2;* commissioning a, *Hamlet, ii. 1.*

Squander (scatter), *Merchant of Venice, i. 3;* squandering glances of the fool, *As You Like It, ii. 7.*

Square (quarrel), *Antony and Cleopatra, iii. 11* or *13, and elsewhere.*

Square, of sense, the, *King Lear, i. 1.* Obscure; perhaps the four quarters or complete domain of sensation.

Squares, the brave, of war, *Antony and Cleopatra, iii. 9.*

Squash (an unripe peas-cod), *Twelfth Night, i. 5; A Winter's Tale, i. 2; Midsummer-Night's Dream, iii. 1.*

Squier (square), *A Winter's Tale, v. 2; I. Henry IV., ii. 2.*

Squirrel, the joiner, *Romeo and Juliet, i. 4;* hoard of the, *Midsummer-Night's Dream, iv. 1.*

Staff, a, is soon found to beat a dog, *II. Henry VI., iii. 1.*

Stafford, the Lord of, *I. Henry IV.* Edmund, fifth Earl of Stafford.

Stafford, Sir Humphrey, and William his brother, characters in *II. Henry VI.,* introduced in *iv. 2.* They are slain in *iv. 3,* in Cade's rebellion. Cade calls them silken-coated slaves.

Stafford, Lord, character in *III. Henry VI.,* addressed by the king in *iv. 1.* He was Sir Humphrey Stafford, of Southwyck, a cousin of the two preceding, a Yorkist, and in the play is ordered with Pembroke to levy men, and prepare for war; but he afterward deserted Pembroke, for which offence he was attainted and beheaded in 1469.

Stafford, Humphrey, Henry, and Edward. See BUCKINGHAM.

Stage, the world a, *Merchant of Venice, i. 1; As You Like It, ii. 7; Sonnet xv.* See ACTORS.

Staggers, the, *Taming of the Shrew, iii. 2; All's Well that Ends Well, ii. 3; Cymbeline, iv. 5.*

Stains, on those that should be pure, *Lucrece, l. 1009;* of blood, *Macbeth, v. 1.*

Stale (decoy), *The Tempest, iv. 1;* (stalking-horse, butt), *Titus Andronicus, i. 1* or *2.*

Staleness, of the world, *Hamlet, i. 2.*

Stalking, like a strange soul upon the Stygian banks, *Troilus and Cressida, iii. 2.*

Stalking-horse, *As You Like It, v. 4.* A real or artificial horse from behind which a fowler shot his game.

Standard(s), *The Tempest, iii. 2;* advance your, *Richard III., v. 3.*

Stands upon (is incumbent), *Richard III., iv. 2; Hamlet, v. 2; Antony and Cleopatra, ii. 1.*

Stanley, Sir John, character in *II. Henry VI.,* introduced in *ii. 4.* The Duchess of Gloucester was banished to the Isle of Man and put into his care. The Stanleys in *III. Henry VI.* and *Richard III.* were his brothers.

Stanley, Sir William, brother of the preceding, character in *III. Henry VI.,* introduced in *iv. 5,* where he assists Edward IV. to escape from Middleham Castle, to which he had been sent by Warwick. In *Richard III., iv. 5,* he is named as one of those who have joined Richmond. The re-enforcements he brought to the field of Bosworth turned the battle against Richard; and Richmond, when he became Henry VII., made him lord chamberlain and one of his counsellors. He, however, was implicated in the rebellion of Perkin Warbeck, and was condemned, after a form of trial, and beheaded in the year 1495.

Stanley, Thomas, Lord, character in *Richard III.,* where he is also called Derby, though he was not made Earl of Derby until after the battle of Bosworth. He married the Countess of Richmond, and was therefore stepfather of Henry VII. He was present when Hastings was seized, and narrowly escaped death. He was sent to the Tower, but released through Richard, who suspected his loyalty, and kept his son George as a hostage for his good faith while he sent him to levy soldiers. He raised the men, but did not bring them on the field until the last moment, when his brother William's forces turned the victory to the side of Richmond.

Stanley, George, son of the preceding, is spoken of in *Richard III., iv. 5,* as being kept as surety for his father's good faith, " If I

revolt, off goes young George's head." He afterward became Lord Strange.

Stannyel, the, checks (the kestrel flies at), *Twelfth Night, ii. 5.*

Stanzo (old form of stanza), *As You Like It, ii. 5.*

Star-chamber matter, a, *Merry Wives of Windsor, i. 1.* The old court of star-chamber had jurisdiction in cases of riots.

Starchy. See STRACHY.

Starling, a, taught to speak, *I. Henry IV., i. 3.*

Star(s), shine no brighter for astronomers, *Love's Labour's Lost, i. 1;* harmony of the, *Merchant of Venice, v. 1;* a bright particular, *All's Well that Ends Well, i. 1;* two, not in one sphere, *I. Henry IV., v. 4;* cinders of the element, *II. Henry IV., iv. 3;* Diana's waiting-women, *Troilus and Cressida, v. 2;* cut him out in little, *Romeo and Juliet, iii. 2;* the northern, *Julius Cæsar, iii. 1;* a shooting, *Venus and Adonis, l. 815;* influence of, see ASTROLOGY.

Starve-lackey, the rapier and dagger man, a prisoner mentioned in *Measure for Measure, iv. 3.*

Starveling, Robert, a tailor, character in the *Midsummer-Night's Dream,* introduced in *i. 2.* He is cast for the part of Thisby's mother in the play of the artisans, but, as she has nothing to say, he acts the part of moonshine.

State, diseases of the, *II. Henry IV., iv. 1;* considerations of, in marriage, *Hamlet, i. 3.*

States, the married calm of, *Troilus and Cressida, i. 3;* when mighty, characterless are grated to dusty nothing, *iii. 2.*

Station, effect of high, on the wise and on the foolish, *Measure for Measure, ii. 4;* dignified by deeds, *All's Well that Ends Well, ii. 3,* " From lowest place," etc. ; being in too high a, *Antony and Cleopatra, ii. 7.*

Station (attitude), *Hamlet, iii. 4.*

Statist (statesman), *Cymbeline, ii. 4; Hamlet, v. 2.*

Statue, unveiling of a. *A Winter's Tale, v. 3.*

Stature, of Hermia and Helena, *Midsummer-Night's Dream, iii. 2;* of Rosalind, *As You Like It, i. 3.*

Statute-caps, *Love's Labour's Lost, v. 2.* Caps prescribed by law for persons below a certain rank.

Stealing, by line and level, *The Tempest, iv. 1;* the way to, *Merry Wives of Windsor, i. 3;* the wise call it conveying, *Merry Wives of Windsor, i. 3;* one's self, *Macbeth, ii. 3.*

Steel, true as, *Troilus and Cressida, iii. 3; Romeo and Juliet, i. 4;* when steel grows soft, *Coriolanus, i. 9.*

Stelled (starry), *King Lear, iii. 7.*

Stelled (steeled, engraved), *Lucrece, l. 1444; Sonnet xxiv.*

Stephano, a drunken butler in *The Tempest*, introduced in *ii. 2.* The plot that he lays with Caliban and Trinculo, to take the island and make himself king, is a travesty of the plot of Antonio and Sebastian.

Stephano, a servant of Portia in the *Merchant of Venice*, appears in *v. 1.*

Stepmothers, *Cymbeline, i. 1; Midsummer-Night's Dream, i. 1.*

Sterility, invoked, *King Lear, i. 4;* charm against, *Julius Cæsar, i. 2.*

Steward, in *Timon of Athens*, in some versions Flavius, *q. v.*

Stewardship, of talents, *Measure for Measure, i. 1,* " Thyself and thy belongings," etc.

Stickler (one who separates combatants, an arbitrator), *Troilus and Cressida, v. 9.*

Stigmatic (one marked, as by being branded for crime ; also applied to a deformed person), *II. Henry VI., v. 1; III. Henry VI., ii. 2.*

Stillitory (distillery), *Venus and Adonis, l. 443.*

Stoccata (a sword-thrust), *Romeo and Juliet, iii. 1.*

Stock-fish (dried cod), *I. Henry IV., ii. 4, and elsewhere.*

Stocks, punishment in the, *Two Gentlemen of Verona, iv. 4; All's Well that Ends Well, iv. 3; King Lear, ii. 2, 4; Coriolanus, v. 3; Richard II., v. 5; Comedy of Errors, iii. 1; Merry Wives of Windsor, iv. 5;* " Bilboes," a kind of stocks used at sea, a bar of iron to link together mutinous sailors, are spoken of in *Hamlet, v. 2.* The name comes from Bilboa, a place in Spain where steel instruments were made.

Stomach (variously used for appetite, pride, ambition, courage, anger), *Two Gentlemen of Verona, i. 2; Taming of the Shrew, v. 2; I. Henry IV., ii. 3; Henry VIII., iv. 2.*

Stomaching (holding grudges), *Antony and Cleopatra, ii. 2.*

Stone-bow (cross-bow for shooting stones), *Twelfth Night, ii. 5.*

Stones (the enamelled), *Two Gentlemen of Verona, ii. 7;* precious, *Lover's Complaint, l. 210;* from slings, *Henry V. iv. 7;* base, made precious, *Richard III., v. 3.*

Stony-Stratford, a market-town of Berkshire, *Richard III., ii. 4.*

Storm(s), raised by magic, *The Tempest, i. 1, 2; v. 1;* at sea, *Comedy of Errors, i. 1; A Winter's Tale, iii. 3;* stillness before a.

Hamlet, ii. 2; Othello, ii. 1; Pericles, iii., prologue, 1; on the heath, *King Lear, ii. 4, end; iii. 1, 2;* betokened by a red morn, *Venus and Adonis, l. 453.* See TEMPESTS.

Stover (fodder), *The Tempest, iv. 1.*

Strachy, lady of the, *Twelfth Night, ii. 5.* An obscure allusion, conjectured by some to refer to a story of a lady of the house of Strozzi; by others that "it was a hint to the audience to expect subsequent allusion to the Starchy affair"—that is, exorcisms attempted by Puritan ministers in the case of a family named Starchy, and that these allusions were in the scene where the clown, as Sir Topas, attempts to cast out the supposed devil from Malvolio *(iv. 2).* Dyce defines it as the judge's or lawyer's widow.

Strain, of noble, *Much Ado about Nothing, ii. 1; Julius Cæsar, v. 1;* of man, bred out into baboon and monkey, *Timon of Athens, i. 1;* a degenerate, *Troilus and Cressida, ii. 2.*

Strange, passing, *Othello, i. 3;* more, than fiction, *Twelfth Night, iii. 4.*

Strangers, I do desire we may be better, *As You Like It, iii. 2.*

Strappado, *I. Henry IV., ii. 4.* A kind of torture, produced by drawing a man up by his arms, which were tied behind, and letting him fall with a jerk.

Stratagems. See PLOTS.

Strato, a servant of Brutus in *Julius Cæsar,* appears in *v. 5.*

Straw, a wisp of, *III. Henry VI., ii. 2.* Scolds and wantons were often crowned with a wisp of straw when punished.

Strawberries, grow under the nettle, *Henry V., i. 1;* in the bishop's garden, *Richard III., iii. 4.*

Stream, music of a, *Two Gentlemen of Verona, ii. 7.*

Strength. See GIANT, HERCULES.

Stricter (more restricted), *Cymbeline, v. 4.*

Strife, among peoples of one faith, *I. Henry VI., v. 1.*

Strikers (borrowers, thieves), *I. Henry IV., ii. 1.*

Striving, to do better than well, *King John, iv. 2; King Lear, i. 4.*

Strokes, bad, with good words. *Julius Cæsar, v. 1.*

Stuart kings, the, *Macbeth, iv. 1.* See APPARITIONS.

Student-life, Shallow's, *II. Henry IV., iii. 2.*

Study, aim and fruitlessness of, *Love's Labour's Lost, i. 1; iv. 3;* most profitable when congenial, *Taming of the Shrew, i. 1.*

Stuff, such, as dreams are made of, *The Tempest, iv. 1;* as madmen tongue and brain not, *Cymbeline, v. 4.*

Styga, per, etc., *Titus Andronicus, ii. 1.* "I am dragged through the Styx, through the ghosts."—SENECA.

Style, aggravate his (add to his titles), *Merry Wives of Windsor, ii. 2;* a boisterous and cruel, *As you Like It, iv. 3;* a tedious, *I. Henry VI., v. 1.*

Styx, to hover on the shore of, *Titus Andronicus, i. 1 or 2;* like a stray soul upon the banks of, *Troilus and Cressida, iii. 2; v. 4.*

Submission, of a son, *II. Henry IV., v. 2; Richard III., ii. 2;* a French word, *I. Henry VI., v. 1.* See OBEDIENCE.

Subordinates, danger of too great fame to, *Antony and Cleopatra, iii. 1.*

Subordination, necessity of, *Troilus and Cressida, i. 3.*

Subscribed (signed away), *King Lear, i. 2.*

Subscription (submission), *King Lear, iii. 2.*

Subtle (smooth), *Coriolanus, v. 2.*

Subtleties, *The Tempest, v. 1.* Metaphor from an old name for fancy viands.

Subtractors (detractors), *Twelfth Night, i. 3.*

Suburbs, *Measure for Measure, i. 2.* Such people "lived mostly in the suburbs of London in Shakspere's day."—WHITE. Dwell I but in the suburbs of your good pleasure? *Julius Cæsar, ii. 1.*

Success, bad, of things ill-got, *III. Henry VI., ii. 2.*

Success (succession), *A Winter's Tale, i. 2.*

Sufferance, the badge of, *Merchant of Venice, i. 3;* of a dying beetle, *Measure for Measure, iii. 1;* ease comes of, *II. Henry IV., v. 4;* lingering, *Measure for Measure, ii. 4.*

Suffering, fellowship in, *King Lear, iii. 6, end;* unmerited, *Richard II., v. 1; King Lear, v. 2.*

Suffolk, Michael de la Pole, third Earl of. His death and that of the Duke of York, at Agincourt, are pathetically described in *Henry V., iv. 6.* He is again mentioned in *iv. 8.* The Suffolk of *I. Henry VI.* was his brother and successor in the earldom.

Suffolk, William de la Pole, fourth Earl of, afterward Duke, character in *I. Henry VI.,* introduced in *ii. 4,* and in *II. Henry VI.,* introduced in the first scene. He held high command in France under the regent Bedford, and was sent to negotiate the marriage of the king with Margaret of Anjou. According to the play, they were deeply attached to each other. Holinshed says the queen "entirely loved the duke." There is a prophecy concerning him in *II. Henry VI., i. 4,* alluded to again in *iv. 1.* He was unpopular with the people for having given up Anjou and Maine, and was accused of the murder of his rival, Humphrey of Gloucester. He was condemned on a charge of treachery, and banished by the king, *II. Henry VI., iii. 2.* On his way from the country he was seized and put to death by pirates, *iv. 1.*

Suffolk, Charles Brandon, Duke of, character in *Henry VIII.,* introduced in *i. 2.* He was the son of Sir William Brandon, who fell on Bosworth Field. He was called the handsomest man of his day, and was a great favourite with the king, with whom he was brought up. He married, for his third wife, Henry's sister, Mary Tudor, widow of Louis XII. of France. The unequal marriage gave occasion for the lines:

> " Cloth of frieze be not too bold,
> Though thou art matched with cloth of gold;
> Cloth of gold do not despise,
> Though thou art matched with cloth of frieze."

Suggest, suggestion (tempt, temptation), *The Tempest, ii. 1; All's Well that Ends Well, iii. 5; I. Henry IV., iv. 3; Lucrece, l. 37; Sonnet cxliv; Macbeth, i. 3,* and elsewhere.

Suicide, *The Tempest, iii. 3; Romeo and Juliet, v. 3;* cowardly, *Romeo and Juliet, iii. 3; Julius Cæsar, i. 3; v. 1;* shortens the time of fearing death, *Julius Cæsar, iii. 1;* the Almighty's canon 'gainst, *Hamlet, i. 2;* soliloquy on, *Hamlet, iii. 1;* burial of a, *Hamlet, v. 1;* Gloucester's intended, *King Lear, iv. 6; v. 2;* Roderigo's contemplated, *Othello, i. 3;* of Othello, *v. 2;* of Antony, *Antony and Cleopatra, iv. 12* or *14;* is it sin? *Antony and Cleopatra. iv., end;* of Cleopatra, *Antony and Cleopatra, v. 2;* prohibition against, *Cymbeline, iii. 4.*

Suitors, discussion of, *Merchant of Venice, i. 2; Taming of the Shrew, ii. 1;* poor, have strong breaths, *Coriolanus, i. 1.* See LOVERS, LOVE-MAKING.

Sullenness, *Much Ado about Nothing, i. 3.*

Summer, brevity of, *Sonnet xviii;* St. Martin's, *I. Henry VI., i. 2;* short summers have a forward spring, *Richard III., iii. 1.*

Sun, the, adoration of, *All's Well that Ends Well, i. 3,* "Thus Indian-like," etc.; that orbed continent, *Twelfth Night, v. 1;* looks on all alike, *A Winter's Tale, iv. 3* or *4;* plays the alchemist, *King John, iii. 1;* wandering knight—imitate the, *I. Henry IV., i. 2;* in March, nourishes agues, *I. Henry IV., iv. 1;* his fiery car, *Richard III., v. 3;* as certain as it is fire, *Coriolanus, v. 4;* Juliet is the, *Romeo and Juliet, ii. 2;* if Cæsar can hide it with a blanket, *Julius Cæsar, iii. 1;* too much in the, *Hamlet, i. 2;* perhaps an allusion to the meaning of the expression as homeless and friendless; influence of eclipses of, *King Lear, i. 2;* burn the great sphere, *Antony and Cleopatra, iv. 12* or *14;* weary, *Venus and Adonis, l. 178;* his daily course, *Sonnet vii;* the shadowed livery of the burnished, *Merchant of Venice, ii. 1;* men shut their doors against a setting, *Timon of Athens, i. 2;* the sun's a thief, and with his great attraction robs the vast sea, *Timon of Athens, iv. 3.*

Sun(s), our half-faced, *II. Henry VI., iv. 1.* The device of Edward IV.; three, *III. Henry VI., ii. 1.* An historical incident.

Sunday(s), sigh away, *Much Ado about Nothing, i. 1;* marriage on, *Taming of the Shrew, ii. 1.* Sunday was a favourite day for the ceremony.

Sunflower (marigold), the, *A Winter's Tale, iv. 3* or *4.*

Sunrise, *Love's Labour's Lost, iv. 3; Richard II., ii. 3; I. Henry IV., v. 1; Romeo and Juliet, i. 1; ii. 3; iii. 5; Venus and Adonis, l. 860; Sonnet xxxiii.*

Sunset, *King John, v. 4; Richard II., ii. 4; Richard III., v. 3; Julius Cæsar, v. 3.*

Superfluity, disadvantage of, *Merchant of Venice, i. 2;* to gild refined gold, to paint the lily, *King John, iv. 2.*

Superfluous (too rich), *King Lear, iv. 1.*

Supernatural, the, discredited, *All's Well that Ends Well, ii. 3;* belief in, *Julius Cæsar, i. 3; Macbeth, iii. 4,* "Can such things be," etc. See also OMENS and SUPERSTITIONS.

Superstitions, regarding fairies, *Merry Wives of Windsor, iv. 4; v. 5;* odd numbers, *Merry Wives of Windsor, v. 1;* the jewel in the toad's head, *As You Like It, ii. 1;* that a man rescued from drowning would do his rescuer some injury, *Twelfth Night, ii. 1,* "If you will not murder me," etc.; Pandulph shows how they may be turned to account, *King John, iii. 4,* "How green you are," etc.; concerning eclipses, *Macbeth, ii. 3; Hamlet, i. 1; King Lear, i. 2;* that the murdered bleed at the presence of the murderer, *Richard III., i. 2;* that blood will have blood, *Macbeth, iii. 4;* concerning the dead on shipboard, *Pericles, iii. 1.* See also OMENS, GHOSTS, DREAMS, MAGIC, and WITCHCRAFT. Coleridge says, "Superstition of one sort or another is natural to victorious generals," and Shakspere attributes superstitious fears to Macbeth and Cæsar.

Supplication, *Measure for Measure, ii. 2; Two Gentlemen of Verona, iii. 1.*

Sur-addition (surname), *Cymbeline, i. 1.*

Surfeit, the father of fast, *Measure for Measure, i. 3;* of honey.

I. Henry IV., iii. 2; of good things, *Merchant of Venice, i. 2.* See Excess.

Surge, the murmuring, *King Lear, iv. 6.*

Surgeons and surgery, allusions to: *Midsummer - Night's Dream, v. 1; Merchant of Venice, iv. 1; Twelfth Night, v. 1; 1. Henry IV., v. 1; Henry V., iv. 1; Troilus and Cressida, v. 1; Macbeth, iv. 3; King Lear, iv. 6; Othello, ii. 3.*

Surplice, of humility, *All's Well that Ends Well, i. 3.* Alluding to the controversy about wearing the surplice.

Surprise. See Astonishment.

Surreined (overworked), *Henry V., iii. 5.*

Surrender, summons to, *King John, ii. 1* or *2; Henry V., iii. 3.*

Surrey, Thomas Holland, Duke of, character in *Richard II.,* introduced in *i. 3.* His father was the king's half-brother, a son of Joan, "the fair maid of Kent," by her first husband, Sir Thomas Holland. He acted as marshal at the meeting of Mowbray and Bolingbroke, *i. 3,* in place of Mowbray, who was hereditary earl-marshal. At the accession of Henry IV. he was deprived of his title, Duke of Surrey, which he was the first to bear, and which has never been revived, but kept his former title, Earl of Kent. He afterward joined in the conspiracy against Henry, was taken and executed, and his head set on London Bridge.

Surrey, Thomas Fitz-Alan, Earl of, enters in *II. Henry IV., iii. 1,* but does not speak.

Surrey, Thomas Howard, Earl of, character in *Richard III.,* introduced in *v. 3.* He was the son of the Duke of Norfolk in this play, and is the Duke of Norfolk in *Henry VIII.* After the battle of Bosworth he was attainted, imprisoned, and deprived of his title; but he was released after three years, and restored to the title of Earl of Surrey. He commanded the English forces at Flodden Field in 1513, and for that service was restored to his father's rank and title as Duke of Norfolk. See Norfolk.

Surrey, Thomas Howard, Earl of, character in *Henry VIII.,* introduced in *iii. 2.* He was a son of the preceding. He also served at Flodden, and was afterward Lord Admiral of England and Lord Lieutenant of Ireland. The latter post he charges Wolsey in *iii. 3* with having obtained for him to get him away from the country, so that he could not aid Buckingham, who was his father-in-law. His son was the famous Earl of Surrey, scholar and poet, who was executed by order of Henry VIII. Norfolk, the character in this play, was destined for the same fate, but escaped by the death of the king the day before the one fixed for his execution.

Surveyor, of the Duke of Buckingham in *Henry VIII.*, was Charles Knevet or Knivet, cousin of the duke. He testifies against his master in *i. 2.*

Suspicion, *Merchant of Venice, i. 3; A Winter's Tale, i. 2; iv. 1 or 2;* ever on a traitor, *I. Henry IV., v. 2;* ready tongue of, *II. Henry IV., i. 1;* ground for, *II. Henry VI., iii. 2;* haunts the guilty, *III. Henry VI., v. 6;* want of, in innocence, *King Lear, i. 2, end;* poison, *Othello, iii. 3;* against Macbeth, *iii. 6;* ornament of beauty (suspect), *Sonnet lxx;* aroused, *Hamlet, iii. 2.*

Sutton-Co'fil (Coldfield), *I. Henry IV., iv. 2.* A town about twenty-four miles north of Coventry.

Swallow, the. *A Winter's Tale, iv. 3; Timon of Athens, iii. 6;* ominous, *Antony and Cleopatra, iv. 12.*

Swan(s), dying song of the, *Merchant of Venice, iii. 2; King John, v. 7; Othello, v. 2; Lucrece, l. 1611;* thy, a crow, *Romeo and Juliet, i. 2;* let the priest be the death-divining swan, *The Phœnix and the Turtle.*

Swans, Juno's (for peacocks), *As You Like It. i. 2.*

Swarths (swaths), *Twelfth Night, ii. 3.*

Swashers, three, *Henry V., iii. 2.*

Swashing (swaggering), *As You Like It, i. 3.*

Swearing, like a lady—like a comfit-maker's wife, *I. Henry IV., iii. 1, near the end;* by a gentleman, *Cymbeline, ii. 1;* why should I think you can be mine, and true, though you in swearing shake the throned gods? *Antony and Cleopatra, i. 3.* See OATHS.

Sweet Cytherea sitting by a brook, *Passionate Pilgrim, iv.*

Sweet love, renew thy force, *Sonnet lvi.*

Sweet marjoram, *King Lear, iv. 6.*

Sweetness, in speech, *Julius Cæsar, v. 1.*

Sweet rose, fair flower, *Passionate Pilgrim, x.*

Sweets, sour in digestion, *Richard II., i. 3;* to the sweet, *Hamlet, v. 1;* grown common, *Sonnet cii.*

Sweno, King of Norway, brought an army to Fife, and, with the aid of Cawdor, vanquished the Scots at Culros, but was afterward beaten by Macbeth, *Macbeth, i. 2.*

Swiftness, like the arrow, *Midsummer-Night's Dream, iii. 2;* of hope, *Richard III., v. 2.*

Swimmers, as two spent, *Macbeth, i. 2.*

Swimming, Ferdinand's, *The Tempest, ii. 1;* by **Cæsar** and Cassius, *Julius Cæsar, i. 2.*

Swinge (whip), *Taming of the Shrew, v. 2, and elsewhere.*

Swinge-bucklers (carousers), *II. Henry IV., iii. 2.*

Swinstead Abbey, *King John, v. 3, 6, 7.* Swinstead, or Swines-head, is in Lincolnshire, seven miles from Boston, and was itself once a port, the sea flowing up to its market-place, which was a harbour. John did not die there, as in the play, but at Newark Castle, in Nottinghamshire. The story of his death is thus told by Roger of Wendover: "While Louis was continuing the siege of Dover for a length of time, and without success, John, with a large force, had been committing terrible ravages in the counties of Suffolk and Norfolk. At last he took his way through the town of Lynn, where he was received with joy by the inhabitants, and received large presents from them. He then took his march toward the north, but in crossing the river Wellester, he lost all his carts, wagons, and baggage-horses, together with his money, costly vessels, and everything which he had a particular regard for; for the land opened in the middle of the water and caused whirlpools, which sucked in everything, as well as men and horses, so that no one escaped to tell the king of the misfortune. He himself narrowly escaped with his army, and passed the following night at a convent called Swineshead, where, as was thought, he felt such anguish of mind about his property which was swallowed up by the waters, that he was seized with a violent fever and became ill; his sickness was increased by his pernicious gluttony, for that night he surfeited himself with peaches and drinking new cider, which greatly increased and aggravated the fever in him. He however left that place at early dawn, although in pain, and proceeded to the castle of Lafort [Sleaford] to take up his quarters, and at this place he was in such pain, that on the following day it was with difficulty that he reached Newark on horseback; there his disease gained ground, and he confessed himself and received the eucharist from the Abbot of Croxton. . . . Being then asked by the abbot where he would wish to be buried in case he should die, he answered, 'To God and St. Wolstan I commend my body and soul.' After this, on the night next after St. Luke the Evangelist's day [October 19, 1216] he departed this life, having reigned eighteen years and a half; his body was dressed in royal robes and carried to Worcester, and was there honourably buried in the cathedral church by the bishop of that place." Nothing now remains of the original abbey, which was founded in 1154. It was demolished in 1610, and the materials were built into a stone mansion, known also as Swines-head Abbey.

Switzers, *Hamlet, iv. 5* or *2.* Mercenary soldiers, the king's guards. The Swiss served various countries as mercenaries.

Sword(s), a charmed, *The Tempest, i. 2;* to open the world with, *Merry Wives of Windsor, ii. 2;* study the word and the, *Merry Wives of Windsor, iii. 1;* wooed with the, *Midsummer-Night's Dream, i. 1;* sworn by, *A Winter's Tale, ii. 3; Hamlet, i. 5;* hidden with crowns, *Henry V., ii., chorus;* of a lath, *II. Henry VI., iv. 2;* carve a passage with—voice in the, *Macbeth, v. 7;* tender-mindedness does not become a, *King Lear, v. 3;* of heaven, *Measure for Measure, iii. 2;* eat, *Much Ado about Nothing, iv. 1; Troilus and Cressida, ii. 3.*

Sword-and-buckler, prince, a, *I. Henry IV., i. 3.* The buckler was deemed a "clownish, dastardly weapon."

Sword-dance, allusion to, *All's Well that Ends Well, ii. 1; Antony and Cleopatra, iii. 2.* A dance in which skill was shown in the handling and striking together of swords.

Swordsmen, old, *Merry Wives of Windsor, ii. 3.*

Sycophants, *Timon of Athens, iii. 6; King Lear, ii. 2,* "Such smiling rogues as these," etc.

Sycorax, a witch, mother of Caliban in *The Tempest,* spoken of in *i. 2; v. 1.* She had had Ariel for her servant, and for disobedience shut him up in a cloven pine, from which Prospero released him after a dozen years.

"As long as I can remember the play of *The Tempest,* one passage in it has always set me upon wondering. It has puzzled me beyond measure. . . . It is where Prospero, relating the banishment of Sycorax from Argier, adds:

'For one thing that she did,
They would not take her life.'

. . . At length I think I have lighted upon a clue which may lead to show what was passing in the mind of Shakspere when he dropped this imperfect rumour. In the 'Accurate Description of Africa,' by John Ogilby, folio, 1670, page 230, I find written as follows: 'In the last place, we will briefly give an account of the Emperor Charles the Fifth, when he besieged this city [Algier]. This prince, in the year 1541, having embarqued upon the sea an army of 22,000 men aboard eighteen galleys and an hundred tall ships, not counting the barques and shallops, and other small boats, in which he had engaged the principal of the Spanish and Italian nobility with a good number of the Knights of Malta. . . . They next fell to battering the city by the force of cannon; which the assailants so weakened, that in that great extremity the defendants lost their courage and resolved to surrender. But as they were thus intending, there was a witch of the town, whom the history does not name, which went to seek out Assam Aga, that commanded within, and prayed him to make it good yet nine days longer, with assurance that within that time he should infallibly see Algier delivered from that siege, and the whole army of the enemy dispersed so that Christians should be as cheap as birds. In a word, the thing did happen in the manner as foretold; for, upon the 21st day of October, in the same year, there fell a continual rain upon the land, and so furious a storm at sea, that one might have seen ships hoisted into the clouds and in one instant again precipitated into the bottom of the water; insomuch that that same dreadful tempest was followed with the loss of fifteen galleys and above an hundred other vessels; which was the cause why the Emperor, seeing his army wasted by the bad weather, pursued by a famine, occasioned by wrack of his ships in which was the greater part of his victuals and ammunition, he was constrained to raise the siege, and set sail for Sicily, whither he retreated with the miserable reliques of his fleet. In the meantime, that witch being acknowledged the deliverer of Algier, was richly remunerated and the credit of her charms authorized. . . . And hereupon those of Algier, to palliate the shame and the reproaches that are thrown upon them for making use of a witch in the danger of this siege, do say that the loss of the forces of Charles V. was caused by a prayer of one of their Marabous, named Cidy Utica, which was at that time in great credit, not under the notion of a magician, but for a person of holy life. Afterwards, in remembrance of their success, they have erected unto him a small mosque without the Babason gate, where he is buried, and in which they keep sundry lamps burning in honour of him; nay, they sometimes repair thither to make their *sala*, for a testimony of greater veneration.' Can it be doubted for a moment, that the dramatist had come fresh from reading some *older narrative* of this deliverance of Algier by a witch, and transferred the merit of the deed to his Sycorax, exchanging only the 'rich remuneration,' which did not suit his purpose, to the simple pardon of her life? Ogilby wrote in 1670; but the authorities to which he refers for his account of Barbary are Johannes de Leo, or Africanus, Louis Marmol, Diego de Haedo, Johannes Gramaye, Braeves, Cel. Curio, and Diego de Torres, names totally unknown to me, and to which I beg leave to refer the curious reader for his fuller satisfaction."—CHARLES LAMB.

Sylla, *II. Henry VI., iv. 1.*

Sympathy, obligation of, *The Tempest, v. 1;* offered, *Merry Wives of Windsor, ii. 1, letter;* in sorrow, *Much Ado about Nothing, v. 1;* craving for, *Richard II., v. 1;* ignorant, *Lucrece, lines 1228, 1270;* with the wretched, *King Lear, iii. 4, 6; iv. 1;* in suffering. *Othello, iii. 3; Tempest, i. 2; v. 1.*

Syracuse, in Sicily, home of some of the characters in the *Comedy of Errors;* traffic between Ephesus and, *i. 1.*

Syracuse, Duke of, referred to in the *Comedy of Errors, i. 1.*

Syria, a plain in, scene of a part of *Antony and Cleopatra.*

Table (in chiromancy, the whole collection of lines on the palm), *Merchant of Venice, ii. 2.*

Tables (memorandum-tablets), *Two Gentlemen of Verona, ii. 7; Hamlet, i. 5; Troilus and Cressida, v. 5.*

Tabor, music of the, *The Tempest, iii. 2;* Ariel's, *The Tempest, iv. 1;* a fool's, *Twelfth Night, iii. 1; Much Ado about Nothing, ii. 3.*

Tabourines, *Antony and Cleopatra, iv. 8; Troilus and Cressida, iv. 5.*

Taciturnity, *Troilus and Cressida, iv. 2.*

Tailor, abuse of a, *Taming of the Shrew, iv. 3;* to turn, *I. Henry IV., iii. 1;* tailors were proverbially fond of music; made by a, *Cymbeline, iv. 1; King Lear, ii. 2;* an exclamation made on falling, *Midsummer-Night's Dream, ii. 1;* goose of a, *Macbeth, ii. 3;* the, with his last, *Romeo and Juliet, i. 2.*

Take all my loves, my love, yea, take them all, *Sonnet xl.*

Take, O take, song, *Measure for Measure, iv. 1* (of doubtful authorship).

Take thine old cloak, stanzas from the song, *Othello, ii. 3.* The song is to be found in Percy's "Reliques."

Takes the cattle, *Merry Wives of Windsor, iv. 4.* An animal stricken by the fairies with disease was said to be taken.

Taking (infected) airs, *King Lear, ii. 4;* (witchcraft), *King Lear, iii. 4.*

Talbot, John, Lord, afterward Earl of Shrewsbury, character in *I. Henry VI.* This famous general was taken prisoner by the French at the siege of Patay in 1429, alluded to in *i. 1,* where his bravery at the siege is described. He first appears in *i. 4,* having been exchanged for Lord Ponton de Saintrailles. His successes are enumerated in *iii. 4,* and he is there made Earl of Shrewsbury, before the king's coronation, which took place in 1431, though, as a matter of fact, he did not receive the title till 1442. He was afterward made Earl of Waterford and Wexford. In *ii. 3* the Countess of Auvergne alludes to the fact that his name was such a terror in France that "mothers stilled their babes" with it, and expresses surprise at the insignificance of the great general's appearance. He conducted the siege of Bordeaux and took the town, *iv. 2-5,* and was defeated and killed at Castillon, *iv. 7.* This occurred in 1453, long after the execution of Joan, though it is not so represented in the play. Talbot's death ended English hopes of dominion in France.

Talbot, young John, son of the Earl of Shrewsbury, character in *I. Henry VI.*, introduced in *iv. 5;* his bravery, *iv. 5–7;* his death, *iv. 7.*

Talbot, Sir Gilbert, mentioned in *Richard III., iv. 5,* as one of the adherents of Richmond, a grandson of the Earl of Shrewsbury in *Henry VI.*

Tale, thereby hangs a, *Merry Wives of Windsor, i. 4; As You Like It, ii. 7; Taming of the Shrew, iv. 1; Othello, iii. 1;* an ancient, new told, *King John, iv. 2;* an honest, speeds best plainly told, *Richard III., iv. 4;* a sad, befits winter, *A Winter's Tale, ii. 1;* life like an idiot's, *Macbeth, v. 5;* effect of a frightful, *Hamlet, i. 5;* a round, unvarnished, *Othello, i. 3;* of woe, *Richard II., v. 1;* a true, *Merchant of Venice, iii. 1.*

Tale, as thick as, *Macbeth, i. 3.* Tally—fast as one could count.

Talents, thankfulness for, *Love's Labour's Lost, iv. 2;* hidden, *Twelfth Night, i. 3,* "Wherefore are," etc.; only felt by communications, *Troilus and Cressida, iii. 3.*

Talents (talons), *Love's Labour's Lost, iv. 2.*

Talking. See SPEECH, WORDS.

Talker(s), caution to a great, *Merchant of Venice, i. 1;* are no doers, *Richard III., i. 3;* exhorted to brevity, *Troilus and Cressida, i. 5;* like a woman, *I. Henry IV., i. 3;* a voluble knave, *Othello, ii. 1;* without action, *Titus Andronicus, v. 2.*

Tall (brave, fine), *Twelfth Night, i. 3,* and elsewhere.

Tallow-keech, *I. Henry IV., ii. 4.* A round lump ready to be carried from the butcher to the chandler.

Taming of the Shrew, The, a comedy first printed in the folio of 1623. The date of writing has been variously conjectured, the dates assigned ranging from 1596 to 1606. There was an older play, "The Taming of a Shrew," by an unknown author, guessed to be Robert Greene, published in 1594, but probably on the stage for some time before. In this there was little of the part of Bianca and her suitors; but Shakspere is not credited with the writing of this part. It is supposed to be the work of an inferior hand, either a colabourer with him, or one who revamped the old play, and whose version was in turn revamped by Shakspere, whose hand appears in the *induction* and the scenes in which Petruchio, Katherina, and Grumio are the chief actors. The story of the *induction* is told in the "Arabian Nights." It is given as an anecdote of Philip the Good, Duke of Burgundy, in Goulart's "Admirable and Memorable Histories," and as "The Waking Man's Dreame" in a collection of comic stories by Richard Edwards, published in 1570. That part relating to Bianca is founded on Ariosto's "Gli Suppositi," translated by Gascoigne with the title "Supposes." The story of the shrew has some resemblance to that in an old poem, "The Curst Wife Lapped in Morel's Skin." The time of the comedy is the time of Shak-spere.

"That delicious episode, the *Induction*, presents us with a frag-ment of the rural life with which Shakspere himself must have been familiar in his native county. With such animated power is it writ-ten that we almost appear personally to witness the affray between Marian Hacket, the fat ale-wife of Wincot, and Christopher Sly; to see the nobleman, on his return from the chase, discovering the in-sensible drunkard; and to hear the strolling actors make the offer of professional services that was requited by the cordial welcome to the buttery. Wincot is a secluded hamlet near Stratford-on-Avon, and there is an old tradition that the ale-house frequented by Sly was often resorted to by Shakspere for the sake of diverting himself with a fool who belonged to a neighbouring mill. Stephen Sly, one of the tinker's friends or relatives, was a known character at Stratford-on-Avon, and is several times mentioned in the records of that town. This fact, taken in conjunction with the references to Wilmecote and Barton-on-the-Heath, definitely prove that the scene of the *Induction* was intended to be in the neighbourhood of Stratford-on-Avon, the water-mill tradition leading to the belief that Little Wilmecote, the part of the hamlet nearest to the poet's native town, is the Wincot alluded to in the comedy."—HALLIWELL–PHILLIPPS.

Taming school, a, *Taming of the Shrew, iv. 2.*

Tamora, Queen of the Goths, character in *Titus Andronicus,* first appears in *i. 1* or *2,* as a prisoner, where she pleads for her son, about to be sacrificed on the tomb of the sons of Titus. She is re-leased, courted by the emperor, and made empress. She asks the pardon of Titus and his sons, intending to take vengeance on them treacherously. Her revenge, *ii. 3; iv. 4;* disguises herself as Re-venge, *v. 2;* killed by Titus, *v. 3.*

Tamworth, a market-town on the border of Staffordshire and Warwickshire; plain near, scene of *v. 2* in *Richard III.*

Tanlings (tanned persons), *Cymbeline, iv. 4.*

Tanta est, *Henry VIII., iii. 1.* So great is thy integrity of mind, most serene queen.

Tantæne, etc., *II. Henry VI., ii. 1.* "Dwells such wrath in celestial souls?"—VIRGIL.

Tapestry, often called painted cloth, *As You Like It, iii. 2;* the story of Cleopatra in, *Cymbeline, ii. 4;* the siege of Troy, *Lu-crece, l. 1367.* Proverbial phrases were often wrought on it. Turk-ish, *Comedy of Errors, iv. 1;* Tyrian, *Taming of the Shrew, ii. 1.*

Tapster, jests on a, *I. Henry IV., ii. 4;* reckoning fit only for a, *Love's Labour's Lost, i. 2.*

Tardiness, a, in nature, *King Lear, i. 1.*

Target, the device of three suns upon that of Edward IV., *III. Henry VI., ii. 1.*

Tarpeian rock, the, *Coriolanus, iii. 1, 2.* A precipice near the Capitol, in Rome, from which traitors and other malefactors were thrown.

Tarquinius, Lucius, surnamed Superbus, King of Rome, died about 495 B. C., *Lucrece, argument and poem.*

Tarquinius, Sextus, *Lucrece, argument and poem.*

Tarquins, the, allusions to, *Titus Andronicus, iii. 1; iv. 1; Coriolanus, ii. 1, 2; v. 4; Julius Cæsar, ii. 1; Macbeth, ii. 1; Cymbeline, ii. 2.*

Tarre (set on), *King John, iv. 1;* and elsewhere.

Tartar (Tartarus), *Comedy of Errors, iv. 2; Twelfth Night, ii. 5; Henry V., ii. 2.*

Tartars (cruel and tawny), *Merry Wives of Windsor, iv. 5; Midsummer-Night's Dream, iii. 2; Merchant of Venice, iv. 1; All's Well that Ends Well, iv. 4; Romeo and Juliet, i. 4.*

Tassel-gentle, *Romeo and Juliet, ii. 2.* Properly tercel-gentle, as in *Troilus and Cressida, iii. 2.* The male goshawk, which is gentle and docile.

Taste, things sweet to, prove in digestion sour, *Richard II., i. 3.*

Taunts, *Antony and Cleopatra, i. 3.*

Taurus, born under, *Twelfth Night, i. 3.* See ASTROLOGY.

Taurus, character in *Antony and Cleopatra,* introduced in *iii. 8.* Cæsar's lieutenant-general.

Tavern-bills, *Cymbeline, v. 4,* " A heavy reckoning."

Tawdry lace (necklace, or cheap lace sold at the fair of St. Audrey or Ethelreda), *A Winter's Tale, iv. 3 or 4.* St. Audrey was said to have been addicted to the wearing of necklaces in her youth, and to have died of a swelling of the throat, as a judgment, she thought, for her vanity.

Tawny coats, *I. Henry VI., i. 3.* The color worn by servants of high dignitaries of the Church.

Taxation, excessive, *Richard II., ii. 1; Henry VIII., i. 2; Julius Cæsar, iv. 3; Titus Andronicus, iv. 1.* See TRIBUTE.

Taxation (satire), *As You Like It, i. 2.*

Teaching, difficulty of following one's own, *Merchant of Venice, i. 2; I. Henry VI., iii. 1; Hamlet, i. 3.*

Tear(s), decked the sea with. *The Tempest, i. 2;* like winter's drops, *The Tempest, v. 1;* Silvia's, *Two Gentlemen of Verona, ii. 3; iii. 1;* of joy, *Much Ado about Nothing, i. 1;* of the deer, *As You Like It, ii. 1;* if ever you have wiped a, *As You Like It, ii. 7;* to season praise, *All's Well that Ends Well, i. 1;* the rainbow in, *All's Well that Ends Well, i. 3;* drowned with, *Twelfth Night, ii. 1;* not prone to, *A Winter's Tale, ii. 1;* Arthur's, *King John, ii. 1;* like a proud river, *King John, iii. 1;* villainy is not without, *King John, iv. 3;* of a man, *King John, v. 2; Henry V., iv. 6; Henry VIII., iii. 2; v. 1; Lucrece, l. 1790;* will make foul weather—despised—dig graves with, etc., *Richard II., iii. 3;* a world of water, *I. Henry IV., iii. 1;* for babes, *III. Henry VI., ii. 1;* with every word, *III. Henry VI., v. 4;* millstones for, *Richard III., i. 3;* the watery morn, *Richard III., ii. 2;* like honey on a lily, *Titus Andronicus, iii. 1;* of joy, *Timon of Athens, i. 2; Romeo and Juliet, iii. 5;* a house of, *Romeo and Juliet, iv. 1;* prepare to shed, *Julius Cæsar, iii. 2;* I forbid my, *Hamlet, iv. 7* or *4, end;* women's weapons, *King Lear, ii. 4;* of Lear, *King Lear, iii. 7;* of Cordelia, *King Lear, iv. 3;* crocodile, *II. Henry VI., iii. 1; Othello, iv. 1;* where be the sacred vials, *Antony and Cleopatra, i. 3;* of Antony, *Antony and Cleopatra, iii. 2;* of despair, *Venus and Adonis, l. 956;* of sympathy, *Lucrece, lines 1136, 1270;* of men, *Lucrece, l. 1790;* of one forsaken, *Lover's Complaint, lines 40, 50;* witchcraft in, *Lover's Complaint, l. 288;* cause illusions, *Richard II., ii. 2; Titus and Andronicus, iii. 2.*

Tearsheet, Doll. See Doll Tearsheet.

Te Deum, sung, *Henry V., iv. 8; Henry VIII., iv. 1.*

Tediousness, in talk, *I. Henry IV., iii. 1,* "I cannot choose," etc.; *Measure for Measure, iii. 1;* as tedious as a king, *Much Ado about Nothing, iii. 5;* tedious and brief, *Midsummer-Night's Dream, v. 1.*

Teen (anxiety, sorrow), *The Tempest, i. 2; Love's Labour's Lost, iv. 3; Richard III., iv. 1; Romeo and Juliet, i. 3.*

Teeth, significance of being born with, *III. Henry VI., v. 6;* did it from his, *Antony and Cleopatra, iii. 4.* Only outwardly, not from the heart. A great man, I'll warrant; I know by the picking on's teeth, *Winter's Tale, iv. 3* or *4.*

Telamon (Ajax), *Antony and Cleopatra, iv. 11* or *13, 12* or *14.*

Tell me, where is fancy bred? song, *Merchant of Venice, iii. 2.*

Tellus (the earth), *Hamlet, iii. 2; Pericles, iv. 1.*

Temperance, *As You Like It, ii. 3;* ask God for, *Henry VIII,* *i. 1; Othello, ii. 3.*

Tempest, a, foretold, *I. Henry IV., v. 1;* a, *Julius Cæsar, i. 3;* Lear contending with the, *King Lear, iii. 1, 2;* ill-omened, *Henry VIII., i. 1; Macbeth, ii. 3.* See STORMS.

Tempest, The, is one of the latest of the plays in date of composition, the evidence going to show that it was written in 1610 or 1611, subsequently to all the others except *A Winter's Tale* and *Henry VIII.* De Quincey, Campbell, Malone, Maginn, and others believe it to be the very last. The source whence the story came has not been discovered; but the plot is said to resemble that of "The Beautiful Sidea," by Jacob Ayrer, of Nuremberg; and it is thought that both were taken from some old tale or play. The fanciful commonwealth described by Gonzalo, *ii. 1,* is borrowed from a translation, published in 1603, of Montaigne's "Essays."

"'The Tempest' is a specimen of the purely romantic drama, in which the interest is not historical, or dependent upon fidelity of portraiture, or the natural connection of events, but is a birth of the imagination, and rests only on the coaptation and union of the elements granted to, or assumed by, the poet. It is a species of drama which owes no allegiance to time or space, and in which, therefore, errors of chronology and geography—no mortal sins in any species —are venial faults, and count for nothing. It addresses itself entirely to the imaginative faculty."—COLERIDGE.

Temple Garden, London, scene of *I. Henry VI., ii. 4.*

Temple Hall, the, *I. Henry IV., iii. 3.*

Temple(s), the solemn, *The Tempest, iv. 1;* of the mind, *Cymbeline, ii. 1;* of the body, *Hamlet, i. 3;* in the forest, *As You Like It, iii. 3.*

Temporary (time-serving), *Measure for Measure, v. 1.*

Temporizer, a, *A Winter's Tale, i. 2,* "Or else a hovering," etc.; policy of being a, *Coriolanus, iv. 6.*

Temptation(s), *Measure for Measure, ii. 1, 2;* the struggle with, *Julius Cæsar, ii. 1,* "Between the acting." etc.; of evil spirits, *Macbeth, i. 3;* trifling with, *Othello, iv. 1; Troilus and Cressida, iv. 4; The Tempest, iv. 1; Twelfth Night, iii. 4.*

Temptations, of life, *A Winter's Tale, i. 2.*

Tenantius, father of Cymbeline, mentioned in *i. 1; v. 4.*

Ten Commandments, the, *II. Henry VI., i. 3.* A common expression for the finger-nails.

Tender-hested (tenderly behested or governed), *King Lear, ii. 4.*

Tenderness, in a man, *Coriolanus, v. 3; Cymbeline, i. 2.*

Tenedos, island of, *Troilus and Cressida, prologue.*

Tennis, the game of, *II. Henry IV., ii. 2 ; Henry V., i. 2,* "When we have matched our rackets," etc. ; the incident is told in the old chronicles ; *Pericles, ii. 1 ; Henry VIII., i. 3 : Hamlet, ii. 1 ; Much Ado about Nothing, ii. 3.*

Tent (probe), *Troilus and Cressida, ii. 2 ; Cymbeline, iii. 4 ; Hamlet, ii. 2 ; Coriolanus, iii. 2,* and elsewhere.

Tercel-gentle. See TASSEL-GENTLE.

Tereus, *Titus Andronicus, ii. 4* or *5 ; iv. 1 ; Cymbeline, ii. 2 ; Lucrece, l. 1134 ; Passionate Pilgrim, xxi.* He dishonoured his sister-in-law, Philomela, and cut out her tongue ; she wrote his crime in needlework, and was afterward changed into a nightingale.

Termagant, *Hamlet, iii. 2.* A supposed god of the Saracens, introduced into the miracle-plays, a noisy ranter.

Terminations (terms), *Much Ado about Nothing, ii. 1,* "If her breath were as terrible as her terminations, there were no living near her."

Terras Astræa reliquit, *Titus Andronicus, iv. 3.* Astræa, goddess of innocence, left the earth when it became filled with crime, and was placed among the stars, where she became the constellation Virgo.

Terror, *Macbeth, iii. 3 ; Hamlet, i. 2.* See FEAR.

Testament, one, like those of worldlings, *As You Like It, ii. 1 ;* of war, *Richard II., iii. 3 ;* of love, *Henry V., iv. 6 ;* of Lucrece, *Lucrece, l. 1183.* See WILLS.

Tester, testern, or testril, *Two Gentlemen of Verona, i. 1 ; Merry Wives of Windsor, i. 3 ; Twelfth Night, ii. 3.* An old French coin varying in value at different times from six to eighteen pence.

Tewksbury, battle of (May 14, 1471), *III. Henry VI., v. 4, 5 ; Richard III., i. 2–4 ; ii. 1 ; v. 3.*

Tewksbury mustard, *II. Henry IV., ii. 4.* Mustard ground and made into balls, "the best the world affords."

Thaisa, daughter of Simonides, in *Pericles,* introduced in *ii, 2 ;* marries Pericles, *ii. 5 ;* her supposed death, *iii. 1 ;* her restoration, *iii. 2 ;* goes to serve Diana, *iii. 4 ;* is restored to Pericles, *v. 3.*

Thaliard, a lord of Antioch, in *Pericles,* introduced in *i. 1 ;* a tool in the hands of Antiochus.

Thanes, noblemen. On the establishment of the feudal system, after the conquest, the title baron took the place of thane. It is applied to the Scottish lords in *Macbeth.*

Thanks, currish, *Two Gentlemen of Verona, iv. 3 ;* beggarly,

As You Like It, ii. 5; good turns shuffled off with, *Twelfth Night, iii. 3;* for hospitality, *A Winter's Tale, i. 1, 2;* the exchequer of the poor, *Richard II., ii. 3;* honourable meed to men of noble minds, *Titus Andronicus, i, 2;* too dear at a halfpenny, *Hamlet, ii. 2;* to God, *II. Henry VI., i. 1; ii. 1.* See GRATITUDE.

Tharborough (third borough, a constable), *Love's Labour's Lost. i. 1.*

Tharsus, in Cilicia, Asia Minor, scene of a part of *Pericles;* famine in, *i. 4.*

Thasos, now Thasso, an island in the Grecian Archipelago, *Julius Cæsar, v. 3.*

That God forbid that made me first your slave, *Sonnet lviii.*

That thou art blamed shall not be thy defect, *Sonnet lxx.*

That thou hast her, it is not all my grief, *Sonnet xlii.*

That time of year thou mayst in me behold, *Sonnet lxxiii.*

That you were once unkind befriends me now, *Sonnet cxx.*

Thaw, a man of continual dissolution and, *Merry Wives of Windsor, iii. 5;* duller than a great, *Much Ado about Nothing, ii. 1.*

Theatre(s), the Globe. See O, this wooden; imagination at the, *Henry V., i., chorus;* of the world, *As You Like It, ii. 7;* "This wide and universal," etc. See also STAGE.

The expense of spirit in a waste of shame, *Sonnet cxxix.*

The forward violet thus did I chide, *Sonnet xcix.*

The little love-god, lying once asleep, *Sonnet cliv.*

Then hate me when thou wilt, *Sonnet xc.*

Then let not winter's ragged hand deface, *Sonnet vi.*

Theology, allusions to doctrines of; the atonement, *Measure for Measure, ii. 2;* "Why all the souls that were," etc.; original sin, *A Winter's Tale, i. 2,* "The imposition hereditary ours."

The other two, slight air and purging fire, *Sonnet xlv.*

The poor fool sat sighing, song, *Othello, iv. 3.*

Thersites, a "deformed and scurrilous Grecian," character in *Troilus and Cressida,* first appearing in *ii. 1.*

"The character of *Thersites,* in particular, well deserves a more careful examination, as the Caliban of demagogic life; the admirable portrait of intellectual power deserted by all grace, all moral principle, all not momentary impulse—just wise enough to detect the weak head, and fool enough to provoke the armed fist of his betters; one whom malcontent Achilles can inveigle from malcontent Ajax, under the one condition that he shall be called on to do nothing but abuse and slander, and that he shall be allowed to abuse as much and as purulently as he likes, that is, as he can; in short, a mule, quarrelsome by the original discord of his nature—a slave by tenure of his own baseness—made to bray and be brayed at, to despise and be despicable."—COLERIDGE.

"From the rest, perhaps the character of Thersites deserves to be selected (how cold and school-boy a sketch in Homer!) as exhibiting an appropriate vein of sarcastic humour amid his cowardice, and a profoundness of truth in his mode of laying open the foibles of those about him, impossible to be excelled."—GODWIN.

Allusion to Thersites, *Cymbeline, iv. 2.*

Theseus, Duke of Athens, character in the *Midsummer-Night's Dream,* introduced in the first scene. The festivities are to grace his marriage with Hippolyta.

He "is Shakspere's early ideal of a heroic warrior and man of action. His life is one of splendid achievement and of joy; his love is a kind of happy victory, his marriage a triumph. From early morning, when his hounds, themselves heroic creatures, fill the valley with their 'musical confusion' until midnight, when the Athenian clowns end their 'very tragical mirth' with a Bergomask dance, Theseus displays his joyous energy and the graciousness of power."—DOWDEN.

Shakspere, as usual, does not attempt to follow the classic story of Theseus, or give a classic setting to the characters whose names he borrows. Allusion to the perjury of Theseus, his desertion of Ariadne, *Two Gentlemen of Verona, iv. 4.*

Thessaly, the boar of, *Antony and Cleopatra, iv, 11 or 13.* Killed by Meleager.

Thetis, mother of Achilles, *Troilus and Cressida, i. 3.*

They that have power to hurt and will do none, *Sonnet xciv.*

Thief, the Egyptian. See THYAMIS.

Thief (thieves), every man's apparel fits, *Measure for Measure, iv. 2;* called St. Nicholas's clerks, *I. Henry IV., ii. 1;* false to one another, *I. Henry IV., ii. 2;* doth fear each bush, *III. Henry VI., v. 6;* afraid to keep, *Troilus and Cressida, ii. 2;* the sun, moon, sea, earth, and all things are, *Timon of Athens, iv. 3,* "Nor on the beasts," etc.; which is the, *King Lear, iv. 6;* what simple, brags of his own attaint, *Comedy of Errors, iii. 2.*

Thievery, an honourable kind of, *Two Gentlemen of Verona, iv. 1;* he will steal an egg out of a cloister, *All's Well that Ends Well, iv. 3;* of injurious time, *Troilus and Cressida, iv. 4.*

Thin, too, *Henry VIII., v. 3.*

Thine eyes I love, and they, as pitying me, *Sonnet cxxxii.*

Things, ill-got, have bad success, *III. Henry VI.*, *ii. 2;* bad begun, *Macbeth, iii. 2.*

Thinking, makes good or bad, *Hamlet, ii. 2 ;* too much, makes dangerous, *Julius Cæsar, i. 2.*

Thisbe, character in the play acted before the duke in *v. 1* of the *Midsummer-Night's Dream.* The part is taken by Flute. Allusions to, *Merchant of Venice, v. 1 ; Romeo and Juliet, ii. 4.*

Thomas, a friar in *Measure for Measure*, introduced in *i. 4.*

Thorn-bush, in the moon, *Midsummer-Night's Dream, v. 1.*

Those hours that with gentle work did frame, *Sonnet v.*

Those lines that I before have writ do lie, *Sonnet cxv.*

Those lips that love's own hand did make, *Sonnet cxlv.*

Those parts of thee that the world's eye doth view, *Sonnet lxix.*

Those pretty wrongs that liberty commits, *Sonnet xli.*

Thou, use of (an assumption of superiority by the speaker), *Twelfth Night, iii. 2,* "If thou thoust him."

Thou art as tyrranous so as thou art, *Sonnet cxxxi.*

Thou blind fool, love, *Sonnet cxxxvii.*

Thought, the slave of life. *I. Henry IV., v. 4;* that keeps the roadway, *II. Henry IV., ii. 2 ;* sessions of sweet silent, *Sonnet xxx. ;* annihilates distance, *Sonnet xliv;* quickness of, *Henry V., i., chorus;* the quick forge and working house of, *Henry V., v., chorus.*

Thought(s), Heaven make you better than your, *Merry Wives of Windsor, iii. 3 ;* are no subjects, *Measure for Measure, v. 1;* a woman's, *As You Like It, iv. 1;* in solitude, *Richard II., v. 5;* like unbridled children, *Troilus and Cressida, iii. 2 ;* murder in, fantastical, *Macbeth, i. 3;* in repose, *Macbeth, ii. 1;* our worser, Heaven made, *Antony and Cleopatra, i. 2 ;* give no unproportioned, his act, *Hamlet, i. 3;* our, are ours; their ends, none of our own, *Hamlet, iii. 2 ;* exciting, *Henry VIII., iii. 2 ;* sky-aspiring and ambitious, *Richard II., i. 3;* to thick the blood, *Winter's Tale, i. 2 ;* whirled like a potter's wheel, *I. Henry VI., i. 4.*

Thrasonical (boastful), *Love's Labour's Lost, v. 1; As You Like It, v. 2.* Thraso was the name of a boastful, swaggering soldier in Terence's "Eunuchus."

Threats, *The Tempest, i. 2,* "If thou more murmurest," etc.; *As You Like It, v, 1; A Winter's Tale, iii. 2; I. Henry VI., ii. 4,* "I'll note you," etc.; *Hamlet. i. 4; v. 1; King Lear, i. 4; Othello, ii. 3,* "He that stirs next," etc.; *Antony and Cleopatra, ii. 5,* "Hence, horrible villain," etc.; *Richard III., i. 2; iv. 4; I. Henry VI., i. 2; III. Henry VI., ii. 1; Romeo and Juliet, v. 3.*

Three farthings, look where, goes, *King John, i. 1.* Allusion to a thin silver coin having the head of Elizabeth on one side and a rose on the other.

Three Pile, Master, a merchant mentioned in *Measure for Measure, iv. 3.*

Threnos, *The Phœnix and the Turtle.*

Thrift, French, the humour of the age, *Merry Wives of Windsor, i. 3;* called interest—is blessing, *Merchant of Venice, i. 3;* the funeral baked meats do coldly furnish forth the marriage tables, *Hamlet, i . 2.*

Throngs, foolishness of, *Measure for Measure, ii. 4.*

Thrummed hat, a, *Merry Wives of Windsor, iv. 2.* One made of weavers' thrums.

Thumb, biting the, an insult, *Romeo and Juliet, i. 1;* pricking of the, indicates the approach of something evil, *Macbeth, iv. 1.*

Thumb-ring, an alderman's, *I. Henry IV., ii. 4.*

Thunder, how great men would use, *Measure for Measure, ii. 2 ;* tears the cloudy cheeks of Heaven, *Richard II., iii. 3;* appeal to, *King Lear, iii. 2;* thunder-bearer, darter, or master (Jove), *Lear, ii. 4; Cymbeline, v. 4; Troilus and Cressida, ii. 3.* See STORM and TEMPEST.

Thunderbolt, if I had a, in mine eye, *As You Like It, i. 2.*

Thunder-stone, the, *Othello, v. 2; Cymbeline, iv. 2.*

Thunder-storms, *The Tempest, iii. 3; v. 1; Julius Cæsar, i. 3; Macbeth, i. 1.*

Thurio, character in the *Two Gentlemen of Verona,* introduced in *ii. 4,* "a foolish rival to Valentine," who falls an easy victim to the scheme of Proteus.

Thus can my love excuse the slow offence, *Sonnet li.*

Thus is his cheek the map of days outworn, *Sonnet lxviii.*

Thyamis, an Egyptian robber-chief, who killed, or attempted to kill, his mistress before he was slain by his enemies, spoken of by the duke in *Twelfth Night, v. 1.*

Thy bosom is endeared with all hearts, *Sonnet xxxi.*

Thy gift, thy tables, are written in my brain, *Sonnet cxxii.*

Thy glass will show thee how thy beauties wear, *Sonnet lxxvii.*

Thyreus, character in *Antony and Cleopatra,* introduced in *iii. 12,* a friend of Cæsar; his message and whipping, *iii. 11* or *13.*

Tib and Tom, *All's Well that Ends Well, ii. 2.* Jack and Jill.

Tiber, the troubled, *Julius Cæsar, i. 1;* swum by Cassius and Cæsar, *Julius Cæsar, i. 2.*

Tickle-apt (dangerous to touch), *Coriolanus, iii. 2.*

Tide, a, in the affairs of men, *Julius Cæsar, iv. 3;* death supposed to occur at turn of the, *Henry V., ii. 3.*

Tides, high (times to be observed), *King John, iii. 1;* governed by the moon, *I. Henry IV., i. 2;* three, without ebb, ominous, *II. Henry IV., iv. 4.*

Tiger, a, raging in a storm, *Troilus and Cressida, i. 3.*

Tiger, the, name of an inn, *Comedy of Errors, iii. 1.*

Tile, the next that falls, *All's Well thatEnds Well, iv. 3.* Allusion, perhaps, to the story of a woman who laughed at a prophecy that she should die before her companions, and was immediately killed by a falling tile.

Tilley-valley (fudge), *Twelfth Night, ii. 3; II. Henry IV., ii. 4.*

Tilth (land ready to sow), *Measure for Measure, iv. 1.*

Timandra, a mistress to Alcibiades, character in *Timon of Athens,* introduced in *iv. 3.*

Time, goes upright, *The Tempest, v. 1;* sweet benefit of, *Two Gentlemen of Verona, ii. 4;* nurse of all good, *Two Gentlemen of Verona, iii. 1;* master of men, *Comedy of Errors, ii. 1;* a bankrupt, *Comedy of Errors, iv. 2;* cormorant, *Love's Labour's Lost, i. 1;* haste of, decides, *Love's Labour's Lost, v. 2;* hath not so dried, *Much Ado about Nothing, iv. 1;* slowness of, *Midsummer-Night's Dream, i. 1;* travels in divers places, *As You Like It, iii. 2;* the old, *As You Like It, iv. 1;* use the present, *All's Well that Ends Well, v. 3; Richard III., iv. 1; Hamlet, iv. 7;* the whirligig of, *Twelfth Night, v. 1;* wasted, *Twelfth Night, iii. 1; Richard II., v. 5;* must have a stop, *1. Henry IV., v. 4;* hath a wallet wherein he puts alms for oblivion, *Troilus and Cressida, iii 3;* like a fashionable host, *Troilus and Cressida, iii. 3;* old common arbitrator—past and to come, *Troilus and Cressida, iv. 5;* eyes and ears for the, *Coriolanus, ii. 1;* and the hour, *Macbeth, i. 3;* the last syllable of, *Macbeth, v. 5;* the, out of joint, *Hamlet, i. 5;* modifies love, *Hamlet, iv. 7* or *4;* shall unfold what plaited cunning hides, *King Lear, i. 1;* men are as the, *King Lear, v. 3;* king of men, *Pericles, ii. 3;* waste not, *Venus and Adonis, l. 129;* ravages of, *Sonnets, v., ix., xii., xv., xvi., lx., lxiv., lxv., 2.;* defeated by verse, *Sonnet, xix.;*

wasted, *Sonnet, xxx.;* thievish progress of, *Sonnet, lxvii.;* changes of, *Sonnet, cxv.;* love not the fool of, *Sonnet, cxvi.;* defied, *Sonnet, cxxiii.;* misshapen, *Lucrece, l. 925;* office and glory of, *Lucrece, l. 936;* slow to watchers, *Lucrece, l. 1573.* See LIFE.

Time, as Chorus, enters and speaks in *A Winter's Tale, iv. 1,* explaining that sixteen years have passed since the last act, during which time Perdita has grown up as the shepherd's daughter and Florizel has become a man. This speech is judged not to be by Shakspere, and has been attributed to Chapman.

Timeless (untimely), *Richard III., i. 2, and elsewhere.*

Times, wild, *II. Henry IV., i. 1;* evil, *Macbeth, iv. 3.*

Time-serving, *King John, iii. 1; King Lear, ii. 4; Measure for Measure, v. 1; Twelfth Night, ii. 3.*

Timidity. See COWARDICE.

Timon, a noble of Athens, introduced in *i. 1,* where his generosity is exhibited and praised; his extravagance in liberality, *ii. 1, 2;* confidence in his friends, *ii. 2;* they fail him, *iii. 1–4;* his last banquet, *iii. 6;* he leaves Athens, *iv. 1;* in the cave, *iv. 3,* his death and epitaph, *v. 3, 4.* Excessive and immoderate in everything, Timon passes from his lavish liberality and belief in the virtue of all mankind to excessive distrust and hatred, forsakes the haunts of men, and hurls revilings and curses at all with little discrimination.

"But Timon can only rage and then die. His rage implies the elements of a possible nobleness in him; he cannot acclimatize himself, as Alcibiades can, to the harsh and polluted air of the world; yet the rage also proceeds from a weakness of nature."—DOWDEN.

"Insanity arising from pride is the key to the whole character; pride indulged manifesting itself indirectly in insane prodigality; pride mortified, directly in insane hatred."—MAGINN.

Allusion to "Critic Timon," *Love's Labour's Lost, iv. 3.*

Timon of Athens, a play first published in the folio of 1623, and supposed to have been written within the period from 1602 to 1608. The sources whence the material was drawn were Plutarch's "Life of Marcus Antonius," and Lucian's dialogue "Timon, or the Man-Hater," and perhaps an old play that has been found in manuscript, and is supposed to date from 1600 or earlier, though it is very doubtful whether Shakspere had ever seen it. The critics are generally agreed that a large portion of the play is from the hand of some other writer than Shakspere, who was either a co-labourer with him, wrote a play that Shakspere took up and altered, or filled out a partly finished and abandoned work of his. The parts not his are supposed to be the greater part of *i. 1* after Apemantus enters, and the remainder of the act; the passage in *ii. 2*, in which the fool appears; the greater part of *Act iii.*, though Mr. White attributes the latter part of the first scene to Shakspere; the latter part of the speech of the steward in *iv. 2;* the third scene in *Act v.*, and perhaps the second. The time of the drama is that of the Peloponnesian war, B. C. 431–404.

Tinct (tincture, the grand elixir of the alchemists), *All's Well that Ends Well, v. 3.*

Tinkers, song of, *A Winter's Tale, iv. 2 or 3.*

Tire (to feed ravenously), *III. Henry VI., i. 1; Cymbeline, iii. 4; Venus and Adonis, l. 56; Timon of Athens, iii. 6.*

Tired with all these, for restful death I cry, *Sonnet lxvi.*

Tires, different kinds of, *Merry Wives of Windsor, iii. 3.*

'Tis better to be vile than vile esteemed, *Sonnet cxxi.*

Titan (the sun), *I. Henry IV., ii. 4; Cymbeline, iii. 4; Romeo and Juliet, ii. 3; Venus and Adonis, l. 177.*

Titania, queen of the fairies, introduced in *ii. 1, Midsummer-Night's Dream*, the same character as Queen Mab. The name Titania is adopted from Ovid, who uses it for Diana. See FAIRIES.

Tithe-tilth, *Measure for Measure, iv. 1, end.*

Titinius, a friend of Brutus in *Julius Cæsar*, appears in *iv. 2;* dies on the sword of Cassius, *v. 3.*

Title(s), of the king, the, *I. Henry IV., iv. 2, end;* bought too dear, a, *I. Henry IV., v. 3; Titus Andronicus, i. 2; ii. 5; Troilus and Cressida, v. 11; Cymbeline, iii. 4; Romeo and Juliet, ii. 3; I. Henry VI., iv. 7;* like a giant's robe upon a dwarfish thief, *Macbeth, v. 2.*

Title-leaf, a brow like that of a tragedy, *II. Henry IV., i. 1.*

Titus, servant of one of the creditors of *Timon of Athens*, introduced in *iii. 4.*

Titus Andronicus, character in the play of that name, a noble Roman, and general of an army sent against the Goths. He first appears in *Act i., scene 1 or 2*, having returned with prisoners and the bodies of his slain sons, and recommends Saturninus as emperor; pleads for his sons and gives his hand for them, *iii. 1;* his ravings, *iii. 2; iv. 3;* his letters to the gods, *iv. 3, 4;* kills Tamora's sons, *v. 2;* kills Lavinia and Tamora, *v. 3;* is killed by Saturninus, *v. 3.*

Titus Andronicus, a tragedy supposed to have been printed as early as 1594, though no edition earlier than one of 1600 is known to be now in existence. It is known to have been very popular on the stage. Many critics held the opinion that it was not Shakspere's, basing the opinion mainly on the repulsive and inartistic brutality of the plot; some think that he may have been the author of some passages, or have touched up the whole play. Coleridge rejects it on the evidence of measure, though he thinks it not improbable that some passages were written by Shakspere. Others, again, believe the play to be mainly his own, and suppose it to be his first tragedy, written when his powers were undeveloped in that direction, and that he may possibly have had one or more co-labourers who introduced the Latin quotations. Its date is fixed between 1585 and 1590 by an allusion to it in Ben Jonson's " Bartholomew Fair." The incidents are taken from an old mediæval story.

" The incidents and revolutions of fortune are horrible in the highest degree; and in this respect the play as much surpasses Marlowe's well-known pieces of violence and rage as it is superior to them in tragic energy and moral earnestness. The most fearful crimes are rapidly accumulated with steadily advancing enormity. When we think we have reached the summit of these most unnatural cruelties and vices, the next scene suddenly opens to our view a still higher ascent. The characters are sketches done with the coarsest touches and darkest colouring. . . . That, nevertheless, this drama is rich in isolated beauties, profound thoughts, and striking peculiarities—Shaksperean imagery which like lightning flashes over and illuminates the whole piece, and that single scenes are even deeply affecting and highly poetical—is generally admitted and requires no proof."—ULRICI.

To, used as an augmentative of a verb, *Merry Wives of Windsor, iv. 4.* To pinch, to bepinch, or cover with pinches. Spenser and Milton use it with all prefixed.

Toad, the jewel in the head of the, *As You Like It, ii. 1.* This stone was supposed to possess medicinal virtue; changed eyes with the lark, *Romeo and Juliet, iii. 5;* used by witches, *Macbeth, iv. 1;* paddock, *Macbeth, i. 1;* called poisonous, *As You Like It, ii. 1; Richard III., i. 2, 3.*

Toasts and butter, *I. Henry IV., iv. 2.* Cockneys; called eaters of buttered toasts.

Tod, a (twenty-eight pounds of wool), *A Winter's Tale, iv. 2 or 3.*

Tokens, the Lord's, plague-spots so called, *Love's Labour's Lost, v. 2;* tokened pestilence, *Antony and Cleopatra, iii. 10;* death-tokens, *Troilus and Cressida, ii. 3.*

Toledo, archbishopric of, desired by Wolsey, *Henry VIII., ii. 1.* The richest see in Europe.

Toll, *All's Well that Ends Well, v. 3.* Pay toll for, set up to oe bought; the bee, tolling from every flower, *II. Henry IV., iv. 4.*

Tom, poor, or Tom o' Bedlam, *King Lear, i. 2; iii. 4.*

Tomb, if a man do not erect his own, *Much Ado about Nothing, v. 2;* fame registered on the, *Love's Labour's Lost, i. 1;* epitaphs on, *Much Ado about Nothing, iv. 1; v. 1; Henry V., i. 2.* See GRAVE.

To me, fair friend, you never can be old, *Sonnet civ.*

To-morrow creeps in this petty pace from day to day, *Macbeth, v. 5;* is St. Valentine's day, song, *Hamlet, iv. 5 or 2.*

Tomyris, Scythian, *I. Henry VI., ii. 3.*

Tongs and bones, for music, *Midsummer-Night's Dream, iv. 1.*

Tongue(s), drowned in sack, *The Tempest, iii. 2;* a man that cannot win a woman with, *Two Gentlemen of Verona, iii. 1;* far from the heart, *Measure for Measure, i. 5;* the slanderer's, *Measure for Measure, iii. 2;* losing the, a penalty, *Love's Labour's Lost, i. 1;* swiftness of, *Much Ado about Nothing, i. 1; iii. 2;* weights upon the, *As You Like It, i. 2;* an ungoverned, *All's Well that Ends Well, ii. 4,* "Many a man's tongue shakes out his master's undoing;" an officious, *All's Well that Ends Well, iv. 1;* stopping a woman's, *A Winter's Tale, ii. 3;* fellows of infinite, *Henry V., v. 2;* charm (silence) thy, *II. Henry VI., iv. 1;* engine of thoughts, *Titus Andronicus, iii. 1;* blisters on the, for falsehood, *A Winter's Tale, ii. 2; Timon of Athens, v. 1;* in trees, *As You Like It, ii. 1;* of dying men, enforce attention, *Richard II., ii. 1;* of the bringer of ill news, *II. Henry IV., i. 1;* speaking is for beggars, *Troilus and Cressida, iii. 3;* a swift, *Comedy of Errors, i. 1;* be not thy tongue thy own shame's orator, *Comedy of Errors, iii. 2.* See WORDS.

Tongues (languages), I would I had bestowed the time in the, *Twelfth Night, i. 3.*

Tool(s), *The Tempest, ii. 1,* "They take suggestion as a cat laps milk," etc.; Lepidus a, *Julius Cæsar, iv. 1.*

Toothache, the, *Much Ado about Nothing, iii. 2; v. 1.* It was supposed to be caused by a worm that gnawed a hole in the tooth; he that sleeps feels not, *Cymbeline v. 4.*

Topas, Sir, a curate, *Twelfth Night, iv. 2.*

Topless (supreme), *Troilus and Cressida, i. 3.*

Torches, virtues like, *Measure for Measure, i. 1.*

Torfin. See CAITHNESS.

Torments, by magic art, *The Tempest, iv. 1.*

Tortive (twisted), *Troilus and Cressida, i. 3.*

Tortoise, a, *Romeo and Juliet, v. 1;* Caliban a, *The Tempest, i. 2*

Tortures, of a tyrant, *A Winter's Tale, iii. 2;* described by Autolycus, *iv. 3* or *4, near end;* death by, *Cymbeline, iv. 4.*

Toryne, taken by Cæsar, *Antony and Cleopatra, iii. 7.*

To shallow rivers, song by Christopher Marlowe, *Merry Wives of Windsor, iii. 1.*

Touch, play the, *Richard III., iv. 2;* to test as by touchstone; of hearts, *Timon of Athens, iv. 3;* of the king, for disease, *Macbeth, iv. 3;* one touch of nature makes the whole world kin, *Troilus and Cressida, iii. 3.*

Touchstone, the clown in *As You Like It,* introduced in *i. 2.*

"Touchstone is the daintiest fool of the comedies, and when we compare him with the clowns of the 'Comedy of Errors' or the 'Two Gentlemen of Verona,' we perceive how Shakspere's humour has grown in refinement."—Dowden.

"He is a genuine old English clown in the Shaksperean form, a fool with the jingling cap and bells, one who is and wishes to be a fool; the same personification of caprice and ridicule, and with the same keen perception of the faults and failings of mankind, as Jaques; but a fool with his own knowledge and consent, and not merely passive but active also. He speaks, acts, and directs his whole life in accordance with the capricious folly and foolish capriciousness which he considers to be the principle of human existence."—Ulrici.

Tournament, a, *Pericles, ii. 2.*

Tours, *II. Henry VI., i. 1.*

Touse (to pull, tear), *Measure for Measure, v. 1.*

Toward (at hand, coming), *Romeo and Juliet, 1. 5; Timon of Athens, iii. 6; King Lear, iv. 6; Antony and Cleopatra, ii. 6.*

Tower Hill. See Limehouse.

Tower of London, the, scene of a part of *Richard III.* Julius Cæsar's ill-erected (for ill purposes), *Richard II., v. 1.* Tradition says that Cæsar built the original part of the tower. It is again spoken of in *Richard III., iii. 1.*

Tower (to soar, a term in falconry), *King John, v. 2; II. Henry VI., ii. 1; Macbeth, ii. 4.*

Towers, cloud-capped, *The Tempest, iv. 1,* air-braving, *I. Henry VI., iv. 2.*

Towton, in the West Riding of Yorkshire, battle of (March 29, 1461), *III. Henry VI., ii. 3–6.*

Toy (whim), *Romeo and Juliet, iv. 1; I. Henry VI., iv. 1.*

Toys (idle rumours), *King John, i. 1, and elsewhere.*

Tract (course), *Henry VIII., i. 1.*

Trade (road or way), *Henry VIII., v. 1.*

Tradition, respect for, thrown away, *Richard II., iii. 2.*

Tragedian, counterfeit the, *Richard III., iii. 5.*

Train, of a gown, worth of, *II. Henry VI., i. 3.*

Traitor(s), all, profess loyalty, *As You Like It, i. 3;* plot against a, *All's Well that Ends Well, iii. 6; iv. 1;* a place in the world for—we are our own, *All's Well that Ends Well, iv. 3;* treatment of one deemed a, *Richard II., iii. 1;* curse on, *Richard II., iii. 2;* treatment of, *Henry V., ii. 2;* to his country, a, *Coriolanus, v. 3; Macbeth, iv. 2;* a toad-spotted, *King Lear, v. 3;* a passing, *III. Henry VI., v. 1;* a giant, *Henry VIII., i. 2;* in a worse case than the betrayed, *Cymbeline, iii. 4.* See JUDAS.

Traject (ferry), *Merchant of Venice, iii. 4.*

Trammel (to tie), *Macbeth, i. 7.*

Trances, *Romeo and Juliet, iv. 1, 3; v. 3; Othello, iv. 1; Pericles, iii. 2.*

Tranio, a servant of Lucentio in the *Taming of the Shrew,* who assumes his master's name and carries out the part with great cleverness, introduced in *i. 1.*

Translation, of Bottom, *Midsummer-Night's Dream, iii. 1;* out of honesty into English, *Merry Wives of Windsor, i. 3.*

Transmigration, of souls, allusions to the doctrine of, *Merchant of Venice, iv. 1; As You Like It, iii. 2,* "since Pythagoras's time;" *Twelfth Night, iv. 2.*

Trappings, of woe, *Hamlet, i. 2.*

Traps, some Cupid kills with, *Much Ado about Nothing, iii. 1.*

Trash (to check, a hunting-word), *The Tempest, i. 2.*

Travel, advantages of, *Two Gentlemen of Verona, i. 1, 3;* melancholy induced by, *As You Like It, iv. 1;* need of, to persons of rank, *King John, i. 1;* company in, *Richard II., ii. 3;* all places that the eye of heaven visits are to the wise man ports and happy havens, *Richard II., i. 3.*

Traveller(s), lying, *The Tempest, iii. 3; Love's Labour's Lost, i. 1; All's Well that Ends Well, ii. 5;* must be content, *As You Like It, ii. 4;* marks of—sell their own lands to see other men's, *As You Like It, iv. 1;* satire on a—Faulconbridge, *Merchant of Venice, i. 2; Henry VIII., i. 3.*

Travers, a retainer of Northumberland in *II. Henry IV.,* introduced in *i. 1.*

Traverse, *Othello, i. 3, and elsewhere.* A fencing term, meaning, to take a posture of opposition.

Tray, Blanche and Sweetheart, *King Lear, iii. 6.*

Tray-trip (an old game, played with cards and dice), *Twelfth Night, ii. 5.*

Treachery, *Two Gentlemen of Verona, ii. 6; iii. 1;* of Parolles, *All's Well that Ends Well, iv. 1, 3;* composed and framed of, *Much Ado about Nothing, v. 1;* of the dauphin, *King John, v. 4;* see MELUN ; charge of, *I. Henry IV., iv. 3,* "Then to the point," etc.; of John of Lancaster, *II. Henry IV., iv. 2;* of Judas, *III. Henry VI., v. 7;* in friends, *Henry V., ii. 2;* of the conspirators, *Julius Cæsar, v. 1;* killed with one's own, *Hamlet, v. 2;* of Goneril and Regan, *King Lear, v. 1;* proposed to Pompey, *Antony and Cleopatra, ii. 7;* curses on supposed, *Cymbeline, iv. 2,* "To write and read," etc.; monstrous, *I. Henry VI., iv. 2.*

Treason, is not inherited, *As You Like It, i. 3;* accusations of, *Richard II., i. 1; v. 2;* never trusted, *I. Henry IV., v. 2;* pardoned rebels arrested for, *II. Henry IV., iv. 2;* and murder—aggravated, *Henry V., ii. 2;* accusations of, *King Lear, iii. 7;* arrest for, *King Lear, v. 3;* felt most by the traitor, *Cymbeline, iii. 4;* condemned to die for, but no traitor, *I. Henry VI., ii. 4.*

Treasure, hidden, is fretted by rust, *Venus and Adonis, l. 767;* of Enobarbus, *Antony and Cleopatra, iv. 6.*

Treaties, *King John, v. 2; Henry VIII., i. 1; Antony and Cleopatra, ii. 6.*

Trebonius, one of the conspirators in *Julius Cæsar,* first appears in *ii. 1.*

Tree(s), shall be books, *As You Like It, ii. 2;* a rotten, *As You Like It, ii. 3;* o'ercome with moss, and baleful misletoe, *Titus Andronicus, ii. 3;* that have outlived the eagle, *Timon of Athens, iv. 3.*

Trencher-friends, *Timon of Athens, iii. 6.*

Trencher-knight (parasite), *Love's Labour's Lost, v. 2.*

Trencher-man, a valiant. *Much Ado about Nothing, i. 1.*

Trent, the third river of England, to straighten the channel of, *I. Henry IV., iii. 1.*

Tressel, an attendant of Lady Anne in *Richard III., i. 2.*

Trial(s), *Merchant of Venice, iv. 1; Measure for Measure, v. 1; Othello, i. 3; Comedy of Errors, i. 1; v. 1;* of Hermione, *A Winter's Tale, iii. 2;* challenge to knightly, *Richard II., i. 1, 3;* by combat, *II. Henry VI., ii. 3; King Lear, v. 3;* of persistence, *Troilus and Cressida, i. 3;* of Queen Katherine, *Henry VIII., ii. 4;* trial-fire, *Merry Wives of Windsor, v. 5.*

Tribulation of Tower Hill, *Henry VIII., v. 4.* See LIME-HOUSE and PURITANS.

Tribunate, advised abolition of the, *Coriolanus, iii. 1.*

Tribunes, hardness of the, *Titus Andronicus, iii. 1;* granted to the people, *Coriolanus, i. 1;* abused, *Coriolanus, ii. 1;* fear of, *Coriolanus, iv. 6; v. 1.*

Tribute, to the King of Naples from the Duke of Milan, *The Tempest, i. 2;* demanded of Britain by the Romans, *Cymbeline, ii. 4;* paid, *Cymbeline, iii. 1; v. 5.*

Trick(s), fantastic, *Measure for Measure, ii. 2;* Falstaff's, *1. Henry IV., ii. 4;* of gentlemen, *All's Well that Ends Well, v. 3.*

Tricksy spirit, Ariel, *The Tempest, v. 1.*

Trifle (unsubstantial thing), *The Tempest, v. 1.*

Trifles, a snapper-up of unconsidered, *A Winter's Tale, iv. 2* or *3;* light as air, *Othello, iii. 3.*

Trifling, with serious things, *Cymbeline, iv. 2.*

Trigon, the fiery, *II. Henry IV., ii. 4.* A term in astrology. When the three superior planets met in one of the three signs of the zodiac, Aries, Leo, or Sagittarius, they formed a fiery trigon, or triangle.

Trinculo, a jester, character in *The Tempest,* introduced in *ii. 2.* He conspires with Caliban and Stephano to kill Prospero and make Stephano king.

Trip and go, a morris-dance, *Love's Labour's Lost, iv. 2.* "A proverbial expression for 'I dare not tarry.'"

Triple (third), *All's Well that Ends Well, i. 1; Antony and Cleopatra, i. 1.*

Triton, of the minnows, a, *Coriolanus, iii. 1.*

Triumph, a Roman, *Coriolanus, ii. 1;* Cæsar's, *Julius Cæsar, v. 1;* honour of gracing a, *Antony and Cleopatra, v. 2;* an ale-house guest, *Richard II., v. 1.*

Triumviry, of lovers, a, *Love's Labour's Lost, iv. 3.*

Troilus, son of Priam, King of Troy, introduced in the first scene of *Troilus and Cressida;* described, *i. 2; iv. 5;* his despair, *i. 1;* discovers Cressida's falseness, *v. 2;* fights with Diomedes, *v. 4.* Coleridge says of his character:

" This [Cressida's vehement passion and shameless inconstancy] Shakspere has contrasted with the profound affection represented in Troilus and alone worthy the name of love: affection, passionate indeed, swollen with the confluence of youthful instincts and youthful fancy, and glowing in the radiance of hope newly risen—in short, enlarged by the collective sympathies of nature, but still having a depth of calmer element in a will stronger than desire, more entire than choice, and which gives permanence to its own act by converting it into faith and duty. Hence, with excellent judgment, and with an excellence higher than mere judgment can give, at the close of the play, when Cressida has sunk into infamy below retrieval and beneath hope, the same will, which had been the substance and basis of his love, while the restless pleasures and passionate longings, like sea-waves, had tossed but on its surface—this same moral energy is represented as snatching him aloof from all neighbourhood with her dishonour, from all lingering fondness and languishing regrets, while it rushes with him into other and nobler duties, and deepens the channel which his heroic brother's death had left empty for its collected flood."

Allusions to Troïlus: and Cressid, *Merchant of Venice, v. 1; As You Like It, iv. 1;* Cressida to this, *Twelfth Night, iii. 1; Much Ado about Nothing, v. 1;* in a painting, *Lucrece, l. 1486.*

Troilus, name of a spaniel, *Taming of the Shrew, iv. 1.*

Troilus and Cressida was first published in a quarto edition in 1609, probably an unauthorized edition. In the folio of 1623 it is placed between the histories and the tragedies, and paged with neither of them, perhaps because the editors shared the perplexity of later critics, and were in doubt as to where it should be classed. It is usually placed with the tragedies. Critics have also been puzzled to assign the probable date or period at which the play was written; the most plausible opinion is that it was first written at an early period and afterward rewritten when the poet's powers were in their full maturity, 1606 or 1607. The sources from which Shakspere probably drew were Chaucer's "Troilus and Creseide;" the "History of the Destruction of Troye," translated from the French of Raoul le Fevre by Caxton; Chapman's translation of Homer, and perhaps Lydgate's "Troy Book." The time is that of the Trojan war. In characterization, in single passages of beauty and wisdom, and in the working up of the details, this play is classed among the author's best; but it is lacking in unity of interest and in apparent design; so much so that some critics, notably Schlegel, have held its design to be a sort of ridicule of hero-worship, an ironical presentment of the story of the siege of Troy, and Charles Lamb says: "Is it possible that Shakspere should never have read Homer, in Chapman's version, at least? If he had read it, could he mean to *travesty* it in the parts of those big boobies, Ajax and Achilles? Ulysses, Nestor, and Agamemnon are true to their parts in the 'Iliad;' they are gentlemen, at least. Thersites, though unamusing, is fairly deducible from it. Troilus and Cressida are a fine graft upon it. But those two big bulks—"

Trojan horse, allusion to the, *Pericles. i. 4.*

Trojan(s), as courtiers and soldiers, *Troilus and Cressida, i. 3;* Hector was but a, *Love's Labour's Lost, v. 2.* Play on the use of the word for highwaymen as in *I. Henry IV., ii. 1.*

Troll-my-dames, *A Winter's Tale, iv. 2 or 3.* A game also known as pigeon-holes.

Tropically (figuratively), *Hamlet, iii. 2.*

Tropics, plants and animals of the, in Arden, *As You Like It, iv. 3.*

Trouble. See AFFLICTION, SORROW.

Trowel, laid on with a, *As You Like It, i. 2.*

Troy, in Asia, scene of *Troilus and Cressida;* six gates of, *prologue;* high towers of, *iv. 5;* the queen compares the uncrowned king to the devastated site of Troy, *Richard II., v. 1;* the burning of, allusion to, *II. Henry IV., i. 1; Hamlet, ii. 2; Titus Androni-cus, iii. 1; v. 3; III. Henry VI., iii. 2;* paying tribute to the sea-monster, *Merchant of Venice, iii. 2;* the siege of, in a painting, *Lucrece, l. 1367;* song about, *All's Well that Ends Well, i. 3.*

Troy, the hope of (Hector), *III. Henry VI., ii. 1.*

Troy, the queen of, *Titus Andronicus, i. 1 or 2.* Hecuba, who put out the eyes of Polymnestor, King of Thrace, and killed his two children, in revenge for the death of her son, who was murdered by Polymnestor.

Troyes in Champagne, scene of *Henry V., v. 2,* "a royal palace."

True, 'tis, 'tis pity, *Hamlet, ii. 2.*

Trumpery, *The Tempest, iv. 1; A Winter's Tale, iv. 3.*

Trumpet(s), a visitor announced by the, *Merchant of Venice, v. 1;* sounding to battle, *Richard II., iii. 3; III. Henry VI., ii. 2; Troilus and Cressida, i. 3; iv. 5; Macbeth, v. 6; Antony and Cleo-patra, iv. 8.*

Trundle-tail (a curly-tailed dog), *King Lear, iii. 6.*

Trunk, a, used in a treacherous stratagem, *Cymbeline, i. 6.*

Trust, begetting falsehood, *The Tempest, i. 2;* give, to but few, *All's Well that Ends Well, i. 1; A Winter's Tale, i. 2,* "I have trusted thee," etc.; a simple gentleman, *A Winter's Tale, iv. 3 or 4,* speech of Autolycus; abuse of, *Richard II., i. 1; I. Henry IV., v. 5;* in innocence, *II. Henry VI., iv. 2;* no use for, *Antony and Cleopatra, v. 2.*

Truth, ill-spoken, *The Tempest, ii. 1;* is truth, *Measure for Measure, v. 1;* to seek, in books, *Love's Labour's Lost, i. 1;* stranger than fiction, *Twelfth Night, iii. 4,* "If this were played," etc.; **swear,**

out of England, *I. Henry IV., ii. 4;* tell, and shame the devil, *I. Henry IV., iii. 1;* thought flattery, *I. Henry IV., iv. 1; Antony and Cleopatra, i. 2;* a quiet breast, *Richard II., i. 3;* told by instruments of darkness, *Macbeth, i. 3;* delight in, *Macbeth, iv. 3;* to one's self, *Hamlet, i. 3;* determination to find, *Hamlet, ii. 2;* is a dog that must to kennel, *King Lear, i. 4;* should be silent, *Antony and Cleopatra, ii. 2;* with beauty, *Sonnet liv.;* needs no colour, *Sonnet ci.;* catches nothing but mere simplicity, *Troilus and Cressida, iv. 4;* shown in the face, *Pericles, v. 1;* loves open dealing, *Henry VIII., iii. 1.*

Tubal, a Jew and friend of Shylock in the *Merchant of Venice,* appears in *iii. 1,* where he alternately enrages Shylock with reports of his daughter's extravagance, and consoles him with the news of Antonio's misfortunes.

Tuck (sword, rapier), *Twelfth Night, iii. 4.*

Tuck, Friar, *Two Gentlemen of Verona, iv. 1.* The father confessor of Robin Hood.

Tuition, of God, *Much Ado about Nothing, i. 1.*

Tullius, Servius, *Lucrece. argument.*

Tully (Marcus Tullius Cicero), murder of, *II. Henry VI., iv. 1;* oratory of, *Titus Andronicus, iv. 1.*

Tunis, in Africa, king of, *The Tempest, ii. 1.*

Turf, Peter, *Taming of the Shrew, induction, 2.*

Turk(s), to turn, *Much Ado about Nothing, iii. 4; Hamlet, iii. 2;* nose of, *Macbeth, iv. 1;* a malignant and turbaned, *Othello, v. 2;* base Phrygian, *Merry Wives of Windsor, i. 3;* stubborn, *Merchant of Venice, iv. 1;* defiant, *As You Like It, iv. 3; Richard III., iii. 5;* tribute of, *II. Henry IV., iii. 2.* To turn Turk was to become a turn-coat.

Turkey, the, allusions to, *Twelfth Night, ii. 5; I. Henry IV., ii. 1; Henry V., v. 1.* The turkey was not known in England till the time of Henry VIII. (1509 to 1547).

Turlygod, poor, *King Lear, ii. 3.*

Turn, a friend forever gained by one shrewd, *Henry VIII., v. 2.*

Turnbull Street, or Turnmill Street (a disreputable neighbourhood in London), *II. Henry IV., iii. 2.*

Turn-coat, courtesy a, *Much Ado about Nothing, i. 1.*

Turquoise ring, the, *Merchant of Venice, iii. 1.* This stone was supposed to possess magical properties: to fade or brighten according to the wearer's health, and to keep the peace between husband and wife, were among them.

Turtles (turtle-doves), *A Winter's Tale, iv. 3* or *4; v. 3; Love's Labour's Lost, iv. 3; I. Henry VI., ii. 2.*

Tutelary spirits, good or evil angels, *II. Henry IV., i. 2; Julius Cæsar, iii. 2; Macbeth, iii. 1; Antony and Cleopatra, ii. 3.*

Tutor, to the Earl of Rutland in *III. Henry VI., i. 3.* He was a priest, Sir Robert Aspall.

Twelfth Night, or What You Will, a comedy known to have been acted in 1602. The story bears a similarity to that of several earlier plays and novels—two Italian dramas, "Gl' Inganni" ("The Cheats"), another entitled "Gl' Ingannati" ("The Deceived"), a Spanish play, the "Engaños" ("The Deceits"), "The Twins," by Bandello, and "The Historie of Apolonius and Silla," by Barnabe Rich, the last of which it closely resembles in the part of the four lovers, though Shakspere has omitted the coarseness of Rich's tale, added all distinctive touches to the principal characters, and introduced the humourous personages that surround them. The scene is laid in Illyria, according to Shakspere's habit of using the unimportant particulars of his originals, but the titles and characters are English, and of his own time. *Twelfth Night* is one of the brightest, wittiest, and at the same time sweetest, of the comedies.

"The perfection of English comedy, and the most fascinating drama in the language. . . . It was appreciated at an early period as one of the author's most popular creations. There is not only the testimony of Manningham—a student at the Middle Temple, who saw it performed, and wrote of it in his diary—in its favour, but Leonard Digges, in the verses describing this most attractive of Shakspere's acting dramas, expressly alludes to the estimation in which the part of Malvolio was held by the frequenters of the theatre."—HALLIWELL-PHILLIPPS.

Twiggen-bottle (one covered with basket-work), *Othello, i. 3.*

Twilight, morning, *III. Henry VI., ii. 5.*

Twilled (brims of banks), sometimes written lilied, *The Tempest iv. 1.*

Twink, with a, *The Tempest, iv. 1.*

Twins, the two Dromios and the two Antipholuses in the *Comedy of Errors;* Viola and Sebastian in *Twelfth Night.*

Twire (to sparkle, or gleam out at intervals), *Sonnet xxviii.*

Two Gentlemen of Verona, The, one of the earliest of the plays, is supposed to have been written about 1591, or perhaps still earlier. The story of Proteus and Julia resembles that of Don Felix and Felismena in "Diana," by George de Montemayor, which Shakspere may have read in a translation by Bartholomew Yonge, pub-

lished in 1598, but made some years earlier; or from a play on the
subject, "Felix and Philomena," 1584. The scenes are laid in Verona, Milan, and a forest on the outskirts of Mantua. Charles
Knight thus presents the varying opinions of critics on this play:
" Theobald tells us, ' This is one of Shakspere's worst plays.' Han-
mer thinks Shakspere ' only enlivened it with some speeches and
lines thrown in here and there.' Upton determines that, ' if any
proof can be drawn from manner and style, this play must be sent
packing, and seek a parent elsewhere.' Johnson, though singularly
favourable in his opinion of this play, says of it, ' There is a strange
mixture of knowledge and ignorance, of care and negligence.' Mrs.
Lenox, who, in the best slip-slop manner, does not hesitate to pass
judgment upon many of the greatest works of Shakspere, says, ' 'Tis
generally allowed that the plot, conduct, manners, and incidents of
this play are extremely deficient.' On the other hand, Pope gives
the style of this comedy the high praise of being ' natural and unaffected.' Coleridge, the best of critics on Shakspere, has no remark
on this play beyond calling it ' a sketch.' Hazlitt, in a more elaborate criticism, follows out the same idea. Paul Dupont considers
that this play possesses a powerful charm, which he attributes to the
brilliant and poetical colouring of its style. He thinks, and justly,
that a number of graceful comparisons, and of vivid and picturesque
images, here take the place of the bold and natural conceptions
which are the general characteristics of Shakspere's genius. In
these elegant generalizations, M. Dupont properly recognizes the
vagueness and indecision of the youthful poet. The remarks of A.
W. Schlegel on this comedy are acute, as usual: It ' paints the irresolution of love, and its infidelity toward friendship, in a pleasant but
in some degree superficial manner; we might almost say, with the
levity of mind which a passion suddenly entertained and as suddenly
given up presupposes.' "

"The piece treats of the essence and power of love, and especially
of its influence upon judgment and habit generally, and it is not
well to impute to it a more defined idea. The twofold nature of
love is here at the outset exhibited with that equal emphasis and
that perfect impartiality which struck Goethe so powerfully in Shakspere's writings."—GERVINUS.

Two loves I have, of comfort and despair, *Sonnet cxliv;*
Passionate Pilgrim, ii.

Tybalt, Juliet's cousin, introduced in *i. 1* of *Romeo and Juliet.*
Mercutio calls him "prince or king of cats" in *ii. 4* and *iii. 1*, Tybalt

ɔr Tybert being the name of the cat in "Reynard the Fox." He is fiery and quarrelsome, forces a quarrel with Romeo and his friends, slays Mercutio, and is himself slain by Romeo (*iii. 1*).

Tyburn, love's, *Love's Labour's Lost, iv. 3.* The gallows was sometimes triangular.

Type (a distinguishing mark), *III. Henry VI., i. 4.*

Typhon, roaring, *Troilus and Cressida, i. 3.*

Tyranny, in the place or the person, *Measure for Measure, i. 3;* in the use of power, *Measure for Measure, ii. 2;* accusation of, *A Winter's Tale, ii. 3;* innocence shall make, tremble—tortures of, *A Winter's Tale, iii. 2;* murderous, *II. Henry VI., iii. 3.*

Tyrant, name of an apparition of a hound, *The Tempest, iv. 1.*

Tyrant(s), must have foreign alliance, *III. Henry VI., iii. 3;* friends of, *Richard III., v. 2, 3;* defeated, *Julius Cæsar, i. 3; iii. 1;* wills of, made the scope of justice, *Timon of Athens, v. 5;* rule of a, *Coriolanus, ii. 1; Macbeth, iv. 3;* service to a, *Macbeth, v. 4;* death to a, *Macbeth, v. 7;* fears and unscrupulousness of, *Pericles, i. 2.*

Tyre, a city in ancient Phœnicia, scene of a part of *Pericles.*

Tyrrel, Sir James, character in *Richard III.*, first appears in *iv. 2;* murders the princes, *iv. 3.* He was beheaded in 1502 as a conspirator with the Earl of Suffolk, and was said to have confessed the murder before his death. Sir Thomas More writes that he was a "brave, handsome man, who deserved a better master, and would have merited the esteem of all men, had his virtues been as great as his valour."

Ubiquity, *Twelfth Night, v. 1,* "Nor can there be that deity in my nature of here and everywhere."

Ugliness, *Comedy of Errors, iv. 2,* "He is deformed," etc.; Richard on his own, *Richard III., i. 1, 2;* and beauty, *Cymbeline, i. 6;* suggestion of, *Venus and Adonis, l. 133.*

Ugly, let the, be unmarried, *Sonnet xi.*

Ulysses, general of the Greeks, character in *Troilus and Cressida,* introduced in *i. 3.*

"The speech of Ulysses in *iii. 3,* when taken by itself, is purely an exquisite specimen of didactic morality; but when combined with the explanation given by Ulysses, before the entrance of Achilles, of the nature of his design, it becomes an attribute of a real man, and starts into life. When we compare the plausible and seemingly affectionate manner in which Ulysses addresses himself to Achilles, with the key which he here furnishes to his meaning, and especially with the epithet 'derision,' we have a perfect elucidation of his character, and must allow that it is impossible to exhibit the crafty and smooth-tongued politician in a more exact or animated style. The advice given by Ulysses is in its nature sound and excellent, and in its form inoffensive and kind ; the name, therefore, of 'derision' which he gives to it marks to a wonderful degree the cold, self-centred subtlety of his character."—GODWIN.

Allusions to Ulysses, *III. Henry VI., iii. 2 ; iv. 2 ; Lucrece, l. 1394.*

Umfrevill, Sir John, mentioned in the first scene of *II. Henry IV.,* as sending news of the battle of Shrewsbury by Travers to Northumberland.

Unaccommodated (uncivilized, not having the conveniences of life), *King Lear, iii. 4.*

Unaccustomed (unseemly), *I. Henry VI., iii. 1.*

Unanel'd (without extreme unction), *Hamlet, i. 5.*

Unbarbed (unshaven), *Coriolanus, iii. 2.*

Unbated (without a button on the point), *Hamlet, iv. 7; v. 2.*

Unbolted (gross), *King Lear, ii. 2.*

Unbraided (undamaged), *A Winter's Tale, iv. 3 or 4.*

Uncape (to throw off the dogs, so as to begin the hunt), *Merry Wives of Windsor, iii. 3.*

Uncertainty, of the world, *King John, v. 7 ; King Lear, iv. 1.*

Uncharge (acquit, hold guiltless), *Hamlet, iv. 7.*

Unclew (undo), *Timon of Athens, i. 1.*

Unconfirmed (unsophisticated), *Much Ado about Nothing, iii. 3.*

Unction, extreme, death without, *Hamlet, i. 5.*

Unction, that flattering, *Hamlet, iii. 4;* a poisonous, *Hamlet, iv. 7.*

Underlings, the fault is not in our stars, but in ourselves if we are, *Julius Cæsar, i. 2.*

Under-skinker (under-tapster), *I. Henry IV., ii. 4.*

Understanding, likened to a tide, *The Tempest, v. 1;* give it an understanding, but no tongue, *Hamlet, i. 2.*

Under the greenwood tree, song, *As You Like It, ii. 5.*

Undertaker (agent, overseer), *Twelfth Night, iii. 4.*

Uneath (not easily), *II. Henry VI., ii. 4.*

Unexpressive (indescribable), she, the, *As You Like It, iii. 2.*

Ungained, men prize the, more than it is, *Troilus and Cressida, i. 2, end.*

Unguem (nail), *Love's Labour's Lost, v. 1.*

Unhappy (mischievous), *All's Well that Ends Well, iv. 5.*

Unhatched practice (unripe plot), *Othello, iii. 4.*

Unhoused (unmarried), *Othello, i. 2.*

Unhouselled (not absolved), *Hamlet, i. 5.*

Unicorns, *The Tempest, iii. 3; Julius Cæsar, ii. 1; Timon of Athens, iv. 3.* They were said to be taken by the hunter's first attracting their attention, and then running behind a tree, which the animal would charge against, and run its horn into, thus being held fast and powerless.

Union, an (a costly pearl), *Hamlet, v. 2.*

Universe, the, filled with murmur and darkness, *Henry V., iv.. chorus.*

Unkindness, love increased by, *Measure for Measure, iii. 1,* "This forenamed maid," etc.; the only deformity, *Twelfth Night, iii. 4; Julius Cæsar, iii. 2,* "The unkindest cut," etc.; sharp-toothed, *King Lear, ii. 4;* cannot taint my love, *Othello, iv. 2;* mortal to women, *Antony and Cleopatra, i. 2.*

Unmannerly, *Hamlet, iii. 2; King Lear, i. 1;* better be, than troublesome, *Merry Wives of Windsor, i. 1, end.* A common expression.

Unplausive (unapplauding), *Troilus and Cressida, iii. 3.*

Unquestionable spirit, an, *As You Like It, iii. 2.* A dislike to being questioned.

Unrespective (unthinking, inconsiderate), *Richard III., iv. 2.*

Unshunned (unshunnable), *Measure for Measure, iii. 2.*

Unsisting (unresisting), *Measure for Measure, iv. 2.*

Untended (unprobed, neglected), *King Lear, i. 4.*

Untraded oath, a (one not in common use), *Troilus and Cressida, iv. 5.*

Up-spring, the swaggering, a dance, *Hamlet, i. 4.*

Urchins, *The Tempest, i. 2; Merry Wives of Windsor, iv. 4.* Malignant fairies in the shape of hedgehogs.

Ursula, a gentlewoman attending on Hero in *Much Ado about Nothing,* introduced in *ii. 1.*

Urswick, Christopher, a priest in *Richard III.,* appears only in *iv. 5.* He was chaplain to the Countess of Richmond and to Henry VII., and did much to forward the union of York and Lancaster by the marriage of Henry and the Princess Elizabeth.

Usance (interest), *Merchant of Venice, i. 3.*

Use, breeds habit, *Two Gentlemen of Verona, v. 4;* can almost change nature, *Hamlet, iii. 4;* everything for, *Romeo and Juliet, ii. 3,* "Nought so vile," etc.; *Venus and Adonis, l. 165;* gold put to, *Venus and Adonis, l. 767.*

Usurer(s), complaint of being called a, *Merchant of Venice, iii.*

1; Coriolanus, i. 1; have fools for servants, *Timon of Athens, ii. 2;* the, hangs the cozener, *King Lear, iv. 6.*

Usuries, the worser of two, *Measure for Measure, iii. 2.*

Usurpation, *The Tempest, i. 2;* of a dukedom, *As You Like It, i. 1;* in the woods, *As You Like It, ii. 1;* must be boisterously defended, *King John, iii. 4;* of Henry, *I. Henry IV., iv. 3,* " Then to the point," etc.

Usurper(s), *The Tempest, i. 2; As You Like It, i. 1; King John, ii. 1;* favour of an, *Richard II., v. 1;* cares of an, *II. Henry IV., iv. 4;* may sway a while, *III. Henry VI., iii. 3; Macbeth, iii. 6; iv. 3; Hamlet, iii. 4.*

Usury. See INTEREST.

Utis, *II. Henry IV., ii. 4.* Huitas, from the French *huit,* eight; the space of eight days after a festival, or the eighth day, sometimes applied to the festival itself; hence, a merry-making, a frolic.

Utter (to sell), *Romeo and Juliet, v. 1.*

Utterance (uttermost), *Macbeth, iii. 1; Cymbeline, iii. 1.*

Vacancy, but for, the air would have gone to gaze on Cleopatra, *Antony and Cleopatra, ii. 2;* you bend your eye on, *Hamlet, iii. 4.*

Vail (to lower, let fall), *Measure for Measure, v. 1; Merchant of Venice, i. 1; I. Henry VI., v. 3;* his stomach (pride, courage), *II. Henry IV., i. 1.*

Vain-glory, 'tis not, for a man and his glass to confer, *Troilus and Cressida, iii. 3.*

Valdes, a pirate, mentioned in *Pericles, iv. 1* or *2.* Name of an admiral in the Spanish Armada.

Valentine, St., day of, *Midsummer-Night's Dream, iv. 1; Hamlet, iv. 5.*

Valentine, one of the two gentlemen of Verona. He is honest, fair-minded, faithful, and somewhat obtuse.

Valentine, a gentleman attending on the Duke in *Twelfth Night,* introduced in the first scene, plays an unimportant part.

Valentine, a kinsman of Titus in *Titus Andronicus,* addressed in *v. 2.* He does not speak.

Valeria, a noble Roman lady, friend of Virgilia, wife of Coriolanus, and a character in the drama, introduced in *i. 3.* In Plutarch she is said to be the mover of the embassy of women, *v. 3.*

Valerius, one of the outlaws by whom Silvia is taken, in the *Two Gentlemen of Verona, v. 3.*

Valerius Publius, *Lucrece, argument.*

Valiant, the, taste death but once, *Julius Cæsar, ii. 2;* the truly, *Timon of Athens, iii. 5.*

Validity (value), *All's Well that Ends Well, v. 3; Twelfth Night, i. 1; King Lear, i. 1; Romeo and Juliet, iii. 3.*

Valour, praised, *Much Ado about Nothing, i. 1;* decay of, *Much Ado about Nothing, iv. 1,* "Manhood is melted," etc.; cannot carry discretion, *Midsummer-Night's Dream, v. 1;* and fear together, *All's Well that Ends Well, i. 1,* "So is running," etc.; esteem of women for, *Twelfth Night, iii. 2,* "For Andrew," etc.; the better part of—should be rewarded, *I. Henry IV., v. 4;* in adversaries, *I. Henry IV., v. 5;* compared to Hector's, Agamemnon's, etc., *II. Henry IV., ii. 4;* no true, with self-love, *III. Henry VI., v. 2;* the chief virtue, *Coriolanus, ii. 2;* true, *Timon of Athens, iii. 5;* dependent on the cause, *King Lear, v. 1;* when it preys on reason, *Antony and Cleopatra, iii. 11* or *13;* that plucks dead lions by the beard, *King John, ii. 1;* careless, *Troilus and Cressida, v. 5;* after drinking, *The Tempest, iv. 1; II. Henry IV., iv. 3;* like a lion's, *III. Henry VI., ii. 1.*

Value, is not wholly in the estimate, *Troilus and Cressida, ii. 2.*

Vanity, Malvolio's, *Twelfth Night, ii. 3,* "The devil a," etc.; *ii. 5;* preys upon itself, *Richard II., ii. 1;* a sweep of, *Timon of Athens, i. 2;* the puppet, *King Lear, i. 2;* of the world, *Cymbeline, iii. 3;* Cloten's, *Cymbeline, iv. 1.*

Vanquished, taunts to the, *King John, v. 2.*

Vant-brace (armour for the forearm), *Troilus and Cressida, i. 3.*

Vapians, the, *Twelfth Night, ii. 3.* See Pigrogromitus.

Variety, of people, *Merchant of Venice, i. 1,* "Now, by two-headed Janus," etc.; infinite, *Antony and Cleopatra, ii. 2.*

Varnish, the, of a complete man, *Love's Labour's Lost, i. 2;* on fame, *Hamlet, iv. 7.*

Varrius, a character in *Measure for Measure,* introduced in *iv. 5,* where he does not speak.

Varrius, a character in *Antony and Cleopatra,* introduced in *ii. 1,* a friend of Pompey.

Varro, a servant of Brutus in *Julius Cæsar,* appears in *iv. 3.*

Vast (a waste), *The Tempest, i. 2; A Winter's Tale, i. 1.*

Vastidity (vastness), *Measure for Measure, iii. 1.*

Vaudemont, a French earl, killed at Agincourt, mentioned, *Henry V., iii. 5; iv. 8.*

Vaughan, Sir Thomas, character in *Richard III.,* appears in *iii. 3;* sent to execution, *iii. 3, 4;* his ghost, *v. 3.*

Vaunt (beginning, van), *Troilus and Cressida, prologue.*

Vaunt-couriers (heralds, precursors), *King Lear, iii. 2.*

Vaux, Sir William, character in *II. Henry VI.,* first appears in *iii. 2.* He forfeited all his property for adherence to Lancaster. His son is a character in *Henry VIII.*

Vaux, Sir Nicholas, character in *Henry VIII.,* introduced in *ii. 1,* a son of the Sir William Vaux in *II. Henry VI.* His father's forfeited lands were restored to him at the accession of Henry VII.

Vaward (vanward), *Midsummer-Night's Dream, iv. 1.*

Vein, of Ercles, *Midsummer-Night's Dream, i. 2;* of King Cambyses, *I. Henry IV., ii. 4;* the giving, *Richard III., iv. 2.*

Veins, mustering to the heart, *Lucrece, l. 442.* See Blood, circulation of the; checks and disasters grow in the veins of actions highest reared, *Troilus and Cressida, i. 3.*

Velutus, Sicinius. See Sicinius Velutus.

Velvet, gummed (stiffened with gum), *I. Henry IV., ii. 2.*

Velvet-guards, *I. Henry IV., iii. 1.* Trimmings of velvet, much affected by the wives of wealthy citizens; and here applied to the women themselves.

Vendetta, the, of Capulets and Montagues, *Romeo and Juliet.*

Veneys (venues, passes in fencing), *Merry Wives of Windsor, i. 1; Love's Labour's Lost, v. 1.*

Vengeance, mercy nobler than, *The Tempest, v. 1;* threatened, *Much Ado about Nothing, iv. 1;* of Leontes, *A Winter's Tale, ii. 3;* omens of, *King John, iii. 4;* oath of, *King John, iv. 3;* of Heaven, *Richard II., i. 2;* sworn, *Titus Andronicus, ii. 3;* for Cæsar's wounds, *Julius Cæsar, v. 1;* just, *Hamlet, i. 5;* Laertes's vows of, *Hamlet, iv. 4 or 2;* sure, *King Lear, iii. 7;* invoked, *Othello, iii. 3,* " Arise, black," etc.; *v. 2; Lucrece, lines 1690, 1821.*

Venice, Italy, the scene of a part of the *Merchant of Venice* and of *Othello.*

Venice, Duke of, a character in the *Merchant of Venice,* introduced in *iv. 1.*

Venice, Duke of, character in *Othello,* introduced in *i. 3.*

Venice, senators of, characters in the *Merchant of Venice.*

Venice, Cupid in, *Much Ado about Nothing, i. 1;* as the traveller speaks of, *Love's Labour's Lost, iv. 2;* law of, to protect its citizens, *Merchant of Venice, iv. 1;* death at, *Richard II., iv. 1;* women of, *Othello, iii. 3.*

Venison, thanks for, *Merry Wives of Windsor, i. 1;* see Shallow; to kill, *As You Like It, ii. 1.*

Vent (impetuosity, as of hounds when they scent the game), *Coriolanus, iv. 5.*

Ventages (small apertures), *Hamlet, iii. 2.*

Ventidius, one of the false friends in *Timon of Athens*, introduced in *i. 2.* He has been released from prison by Timon (*ii. 2, end*), but, having grown rich, he refuses a loan to his benefactor, *iii. 3.*

Ventidius, character in *Antony and Cleopatra*, introduced in *ii. 2.*

Ventricle of memory, the, *Love's Labour's Lost, iv. 2.* Alluding to the old division of the brain into three ventricles, in the hindermost of which was memory.

Ventures, at sea, anxiety for, *Merchant of Venice, i. 1; iii. 2.*

Venturing, *Venus and Adonis, l. 567.* See also DARING, OPPORTUNITY.

Venus, doves or pigeons of, *The Tempest, iv. 1; Midsummer-Night's Dream, i. 1; Merchant of Venice, ii. 6;* love's invisible soul, *Troilus and Cressida, iii. 1;* smiles not in a house of tears, *Romeo and Juliet, iv. 1.*

Venus (the planet), *Midsummer-Night's Dream, iii. 2; II. Henry IV., ii. 4; I. Henry VI., i. 2; Titus Andronicus, ii. 3.*

Venus and Adonis, a poem first printed in 1593, and therefore one of the earliest of Shakspere's works. In the dedication he calls it the first heir of his invention; whether he meant by that that it was first of all his writings, or earlier than any of his plays, or than any that were wholly original, is uncertain. The story as told by Shakspere differs materially from Ovid's version, and is said to resemble more one by Henry Constable, published in 1600 in a volume called "England's Helicon," but not known to have been written before this one. The subject of the poem is repellent, but it contains descriptive passages of great beauty. See under LUCRECE.

Venus with young Adonis, *Passionate Pilgrim, xi.*

Veracity, faith in, *Coriolanus, iv. 5.*

Verb, a noun and a, such abominable words as no Christian ear can endure to hear, *II. Henry VI., iv. 7.*

Verbosity, and argument, *Love's Labour's Lost, v. 1; Troilus and Cressida, v. 3;* of Gratiano, *Merchant of Venice, i. 1.* See WORDS.

Vere, Lord Aubrey, *III. Henry VI., iii. 3.*

Verges, a character in *Much Ado about Nothing*, introduced in *iii. 3,* a meek imitator and disciple of Dogberry.

Verily, a lady's, is as potent as a lord's, *A Winter's Tale, i. 2.*

Vernon, Sir Richard, character in *I. Henry IV.*, appears in *iv. 1*, and *v. 1* and *2*. He was a partisan of the Percys, and one of the leaders at Shrewsbury, for which he was condemned and executed, July 23, 1403. He and Worcester are ordered to death in *v. 5*.

Vernon, Sir Richard (?), character in *I. Henry VI.*, first appears in *ii. 4*, the scene where the red and white roses are plucked in a quarrel with Bassett, a Lancastrian. Vernon is an ardent adherent of York. The quarrel is continued in *iii. 4* and *iv. 1*.

Verona, Italy, scene of the greater part of *Romeo and Juliet,* and parts of the *Two Gentlemen of Verona*.

Versatility, of the king, *Henry V., i. 1.*

Verse. See POETRY.

Verses, on trees—lame, *As You Like It, iii. 2.*

Vesture of decay, this muddy, *Merchant of Venice, v. 1;* the essential, of creation, *Othello, ii. 1.*

Via (away), *Merry Wives of Windsor, ii. 2; Love's Labour's Lost, v. 2; Merchant of Venice, ii. 2,* and elsewhere.

Vials, the sacred (lachrymatory), *Antony and Cleopatra, i. 3.*

Vice(s), prevalence of, *Measure for Measure, ii. 1;* results of pardoning, *Measure for Measure, ii. 2;* apparelled like virtue, *Comedy of Errors, iii. 2;* virtue misapplied turns to, *Romeo and Juliet, ii. 3;* self-accusation of, *Macbeth. iv. 3;* repeated, *Pericles, i. 1;* assume the marks of virtues, *Merchant of Venice, iii. 2;* fitly bestowed, *All's Well that Ends Well, i. 1,* "One that goes," etc.; want not impudence, *A Winter's Tale, iii. 2;* an old man boasting of his youthful, *II. Henry IV., iii. 2;* of a young man, *Hamlet, ii. 1;* through tattered clothes, *King Lear, iv. 6;* gods make instruments of, *King Lear, v. 3;* with beauty, *Sonnet xcv;* result of perseverance in, *Antony and Cleopatra, iii. 11* or *13*.

Vice, the old, *Twelfth Night, iv. 2.* A character in the old "Moralities," who leaped on the devil's back and beat him with a sword of lath, but was carried away by him in the end. The moral is that, though sin may be merry with the devil, it must become his prey in the end. There are other allusions, as to that reverend vice, *I. Henry IV., ii. 4,* to vice's dagger in *II. Henry IV., iii. 2,* the formal vice in *Richard III., iii. 1,* and the vice of kings in *Hamlet, iii. 4,* a "king of shreds and patches." The vice wore motley.

Vice (fist, grasp), *II. Henry IV., ii. 1.*

Victory, when without loss, *Much Ado about Nothing, i. 1;* exultation and rejoicing in, *King John, v. 5; II. Henry IV., i. 1; III. Henry VI., v. 3; Richard III., i. 1; Antony and Cleopatra, iv. 8.*

Video et gaudeo (I see and rejoice), *Love's Labour's Lost, v. 1.*

Vidisne quis venit (Do you not see who comes?), *Love's Labour's Lost, v. 1.*

Vidomar, Viscount of Lymoges. See AUSTRIA, ARCHDUKE OF.

Vienna, the scene of *Measure for Measure.*

Vile, the, see vileness in goodness, *King Lear, iv. 2;* praise of, *Timon of Athens, i. 1.*

Viliago (coward), *II. Henry VI., iv. 8.*

"**Vilia miretur,**" etc., a quotation from Ovid placed at the beginning of *Venus and Adonis.* "The vulgar admire the vile; to me golden-haired Apollo presents a full Castalian draught."

Villain(s), when rich, have need of poor, *Much Ado about Nothing, iii. 3;* faces of, *Much Ado about Nothing, v. 1; King John, iv. 2;* (serf and rascal), *As You Like It, i. 1;* determined to prove a, *Richard III., i. 1;* smiling, damned—smile and be a, *Hamlet, i. 5;* glozing their villainy, *Othello, ii. 3,* "And what's he," etc.; a plain-dealing, *Much Ado about Nothing, i. 3;* a self-confessed, *King Lear, i. 2;* a, with a smiling cheek, *Merchant of Venice, i. 3.*

Villainy, out-villained, *All's Well that Ends Well, iv. 3;* easy to practise on innocence, *King Lear, i. 2, end;* make mocks with love, *Othello, v. 2;* clothed with old odd ends stolen from Holy Writ, *Richard III. i. 3;* instruction in, bettered, *Merchant of Venice, iii. 1.*

Vincentio, the Duke of Vienna, in *Measure for Measure,* enters in the first scene. He is a man of purity, justice, moderation, and mercifulness, even toward errors to which he is himself under no temptation—a contrast to Angelo—but given to masquerading and mystery, justifying the appellation Lucio gives him, "the fantastical duke of dark corners."

Vincentio, of Pisa, a character in the *Taming of the Shrew,* introduced in *iv. 5.*

Vine, the elm and the, *Comedy of Errors, ii. 2;* every man shall eat under his own (in the days of Elizabeth), *Henry VIII., v. 4.*

Vinegia (Venetia), etc., *Love's Labour's Lost, iv. 2.* "O Venice, he who praises thee not has not seen thee." From Baptista Spagnolus, of Mantua.

Vinewedst (mouldiest), *Troilus and Cressida, ii. 1.*

Vintner, a, a character in *I. Henry IV.,* appears in *ii. 4.*

Viola, heroine of *Twelfth Night,* introduced in the second scene. She has been shipwrecked, and dresses as a man to protect herself in the strange country where she is, enters the service of the duke, with whom she falls hopelessly in love, and is made the confidant of his affection for Olivia and his messenger to her. In the delicacy and refinement of her character, and her high breeding and gentleness, she somewhat resembles Perdita.

"Viola is like a heightened portrait of Julia of the 'Two Gentlemen of Verona,' enriched with lovely colour, and placed among more poetical surroundings. She has not the pretty sauciness of Rosalind in her disguise, but owns a heart as tender, sweet-natured, and sound-natured as even Rosalind's. The mirth of the play belongs to other actors than Viola; her occasional playfulness falls back into her deep tenderness and is lost in it."—Dowden.

Viol-de-gamboys (gamba), *Twelfth Night, i. 3.* A violoncello with six strings, held between the legs.

Violenta, an unimportant character in *All's Well that Ends Well,* appears in *iii. 5.*

Violets, *Twelfth Night, i. 1; A Winter's Tale, iv. 3* or *4; Midsummer-Night's Dream, ii. 2; Measure for Measure, ii. 2; Richard II., v. 2; Henry V., iv. 1;* to throw a perfume on, is wasteful, *King John, iv. 2; Hamlet, v. 1; Pericles, iv. 1; Sonnet xcix.* The violet was an emblem of the early dead.

Virago(es), *Much Ado about Nothing, ii. 1; Twelfth Night, iii. 4; Taming of the Shrew, i. 1; et seq.*

Virgilia, wife of Coriolanus, a character in the drama, introduced in *i. 3.* Her gentle, fond, sensitive disposition is strongly contrasted with the character of Volumnia, her husband's mother. Coriolanus calls her "My gracious silence."

Virginalling (playing the virginals), *A Winter's Tale, i. 2.*

Virginity, *All's Well that Ends Well, i. 1.*

Virginius, did he do well, *Titus Andronicus, v. 3.*

Virgins, knights of Diana, *All's Well that Ends Well, i. 3.*

Vir sapit, etc. (the man is wise who speaks little), *Love's Labour's Lost, iv. 2.*

Virtue, of necessity, *Two Gentlemen of Verona, iv. 1;* to be shown forth, *Measure for Measure, i. 1;* some fall by, *Measure for Measure, ii. 1;* a bait to vice, *Measure for Measure, ii. 2;* looks bleak, etc., *All's Well that Ends Well, i. 1;* in the lowly, *All's Well that Ends Well, ii. 3,* "From lowest place," etc.; none like necessity, *Richard II., i. 3;* inheritance of, *III. Henry VI., ii. 2;* only felt by reflection, *Troilus and Cressida, iii. 3;* perverted, *Romeo and Juliet, ii. 3;* from lack of means for vice, *Timon of Athens, iv. 3;* of Imogen, *Cymbeline, i. 4;* escapes not calumny, *Hamlet, i. 3;* better assumed than wholly wanting, *Hamlet, iii. 4;* and cunning (wisdom), *Pericles, iii. 2;* influence of, *Pericles, iv. 5, 6;* in a face, *Lucrece, l. 53.*

Virtue(s), are sanctified and holy traitors to their possessors, *As You Like It, ii. 3;* a world to hide them in, *Twelfth Night, i. 3;* with beauty, *I. Henry VI., v. 5;* written in water, *Henry VIII., iv. 2;* obscured by one defect, *Hamlet, i. 4;* assume a, if you have it not, *Hamlet, iii. 4;* lie in the interpretation of the time, *Coriolanus, iv. 7.*

Virtuous, Dost thou think there shall be no more cakes and ale, because thou art, *Twelfth Night, ii. 3.*

Vision, the baseless fabric of a, *The Tempest, iv. 1.*

Visions: Katherine's, *Henry VIII., iv. 2;* Posthumus's, *Cymbeline, v. 4.* See DREAMS.

Visor, William, of Woncot, *II. Henry IV., v. 1.*

Vizaments (advisements, or considerations), *Merry Wives of Windsor, i. 1.*

Vizor, a virtuous, over vice, *Richard III., ii. 2;* *Macbeth, iii. 2.*

Vocation, no sin for a man to labour in his, *I. Henry IV., i. 2.*

Voices, of age, *Comedy of Errors, v. 1,* "Not know my," etc.; too rude and bold, *Merchant of Venice, ii. 2;* well divulged in (this may mean well reputed by men's voices, or said to be learned in languages), *Twelfth Night, i. 5;* soft, gentle, and low, *King Lear, v. 3;* beauty of, *Venus and Adonis, l. 428;* of Marcius, *Coriolanus, i. 6;* a sweet, *Pericles, v. 1,* "Who starves the ears she feeds, and makes them hungry, the more she gives them speech."

Volquessen, *King John, ii. 1* or *2*. The ancient name of the province now called the Vexin, which lay on the border-land between France and Normandy. It had been ceded by King Henry I. of France to Duke Robert of Normandy; but the French again took possession of it during the childhood of William the Conqueror, who did not attempt to retake it until 1087. In the course of the struggle Mantes was burned, and there William received injuries by a fall from his horse, of which he died.

Volsces, preparations of, for war, *Coriolanus, iii. 1;* incursion of, *Coriolanus, iv. 5.* A people inhabiting the southern part of Latium, finally subdued by the Romans in the Samnite wars, 343 and 326 B. C.

Volscian Senators, characters in *Coriolanus.*

Voltimand, a courtier in *Hamlet*, introduced in *i. 2.*

Volumnia, mother of Coriolanus, introduced in *i. 3;* her pride in her son's valour, *i. 3;* she disapproves his haste, *iii. 2;* her an-

ger, *iv. 2;* her suit to her son, *v. 3;* worth a city-full, *v. 4.* She has
her son's haughty pride of class, hateful contempt for the people,
thirst for honour, and, one might say, martial courage. By her
suit to her son, *v. 3,* she is said to have "saved Rome and lost her
son;" but she did not know that she was saving Rome at such a
cost. Her speech to him, beginning "Speak to me, son," is taken
very literally from the translation of Plutarch.

"The haughty temper of Volumnia, her admiration of the valour
and high bearing of her son, and her proud but unselfish love for
him, are finely contrasted with the modest sweetness, the conjugal
tenderness, and the fond solicitude of his wife Virgilia. . . . But the
triumph of Volumnia's character, the full display of all her grandeur
of soul, her patriotism, her strong affections, and her sublime eloquence, are reserved for her last scene, in which she pleads for the
safety of Rome, and wins from her angry son that peace which all
the swords of Italy and her confederate arms could not have purchased."—MRS. JAMESON.

"The poet gradually wins us to an admiration of the hero by the
most skilful management. First, through his mother. What a
glorious picture of an antique matron, from whom her son equally
derived his pride and his heroism, is presented in the exquisite scene
[*i. 3*] where Volumnia and Virgilia talk of him they love according
to their several natures! Who but Shakspere could have seized
upon the spirit of a Roman woman of the highest courage and mental power, bursting out in words such as these" [beginning, "His
bloody brow!"]—KNIGHT.

Volumnius, a friend of Brutus and Cassius in *Julius Cæsar,*
first appears in *v. 3.*

Voluptuousness, in troubled times, *Antony and Cleopatra, i. 4.*

Votress, the imperial [Elizabeth], passed on, in maiden meditation, fancy-free, *Midsummer-Night's Dream, ii. 1.*

Vows, lovers', *Two Gentlemen of Verona, ii. 2;* unheedful, *Two
Gentlemen of Verona, ii. 6;* of men, *Measure for Measure, i. 5;*
broken, *Love's Labour's Lost, iv. 3; v. 2;* Hermia's, *Midsummer-
Night's Dream, i. 1;* true, *All's Well that Ends Well, iv. 2;* Hermione's, *A Winter's Tale, iii. 2;* obligation of wrongful, *King John,
iii. 1; I. Henry IV., i. 3; iii. 2;* binding nature of, *Henry V., iv.
7;* sinful, not to be kept, *III. Henry VI., v. 1;* broken, *Troilus and
Cressida, v. 2;* peevish, *Troilus and Cressida, v. 3;* careless, *Hamlet, i. 3;* false, *Antony and Cleopatra, i. 3;* men's, *Cymbeline, iii. 4.*

Vox, you must allow, *Twelfth Night, v. 1.* Allow one to
speak.

Vulcan, a rare carpenter, *Much Ado about Nothing, i. 1;* black
as, *Twelfth Night, v. 1;* as like as, and his wife, *Troilus and Cres-*

sida, i. 3; imagination as foul as his stithy, *Hamlet, iii. 2;* badge of, *Titus Andronicus, ii. 1.*

Vulture, the, *Merry Wives of Windsor, i. 3; II. Henry VI., iv. 3; Titus Andronicus, v. 2; King Lear, ii. 4.*

Waftage (passage by water), *Comedy of Errors, iv. 1; Troilus and Cressida, iii. 2.*

Wager(s), as to the most obedient wife, *Taming of the Shrew, v. 2;* as to Imogen, *Cymbeline, i. 5;* nothing can seem foul to those that win, *I. Henry IV., v. 1.*

Waggery, *Cymbeline, iii. 4,* " A waggish courage."

Waggon, spokes of Queen Mab's, *Romeo and Juliet, i. 4.*

Wagtail, name applied to an officious person, *King Lear, ii. 2.*

Waist, and wit, *Love's Labour's Lost, iv. 1;* I would my means were greater and my waist slenderer, *II. Henry IV., i. 2.*

Waist (that part of a ship between the forecastle and the quarter-deck), *Troilus and Cressida, ii. 2.*

Wakefield, a market-town in the West Riding of Yorkshire, battle of (December 30, 1460), *III. Henry VI., i. 3, 4; ii. 1.*

Wakes, *Love's Labour's Lost, v. 2;* a man that haunts, *A Winter's Tale, iv. 2* or *3.* Churches held wakes in honour of the saints to whom they were dedicated, on their anniversaries.

Wales, scene of parts of *Cymbeline.*

Wales, Anne, Princess of. See ANNE.

Wales, Princes of. See EDWARD, THE BLACK PRINCE, EDWARD, PRINCE OF WALES, EDWARD V., HENRY V.

Walking fire (will-o'-the-wisp), *King Lear, iii. 4.*

Wall, a character in the play of the artisans in the *Midsummer-Night's Dream,* taken by Snout, the tinker. " This man, with lime and rough cast, doth present Wall, that vile wall, which did those lovers sunder "—" the wittiest partition that ever I heard discourse."

Wall, the weakest goes to the, *Romeo and Juliet, i. 1;* a beauteous, doth oft close in pollution, *Twelfth Night, i. 2.*

Walloon, a base, thrust Talbot with a spear, *I. Henry VI., i. 1.* An inhabitant of that part of Flanders between the Scheldt and the Lys.

Wandering knight, the sun a, *I. Henry IV., i. 2.*

Wandering stars (planets), *Hamlet, v. 1.*

Wannion, with a (with a vengeance), *Pericles, ii. 1.*

Wantonness, accusation of, *Sonnets cxxxvii., cxlii.-cxliv., clii.*

Wappened (or wappered, over-worn), *Timon of Athens, iv. 3.*

War, better than strife at home, *All's Well that Ends Well, ii. 3, near the end;* threatened, *King John, i. 1; ii. 1; Henry V., ii. 4;* devastations of, *King John, ii. 1, 2; Hamlet, iv. 4;* declarations of, *King John, iii. 1; v. 2; Henry V., i. 2; Cymbeline, iii. 1;* civil, *King John, iv. 3; v. 2; Richard II., iii. 3; I. Henry IV., i. 1; ii. 4; III. Henry VI., ii. 5; Richard III., ii. 4; v. 5;* like the god of, *King John, v. 1;* old men, boys, and women armed for, *Richard II., iii. 2;* dreams of, *I. Henry IV., ii. 3;* just, *I. Henry IV., v. 2;* chances of, *II. Henry IV., i. 1;* caution in, *II. Henry IV., i. 3,* an archbishop in, *II. Henry IV., iv. 1, 2;* prophecy of civil, *II. Henry IV., iv. 2;* counsel for, *Henry V., i. 2;* preparations for, *Henry V., ii., chorus; ii. 4;* sleeping sword of, *Henry V., i. 2;* spirit suitable to, *Henry V., iii. 1;* license of, *Henry V., iii. 3;* the beadle and vengeance of God, *Henry V., iv. 1;* fame of, *Henry V., iv. 3;* a country after, *Henry V., v. 2;* its attendants, *I. Henry VI., iv. 2;* a son of hell, *II. Henry VI., v. 2;* or devotion, *III. Henry VI., ii. 1,* "Shall we go throw away," etc.; end of—hath smoothed his wrinkled front, *Richard III., i. 1;* closet, *Troilus and Cressida, i. 3;* counsel in, despised, *Troilus and Cressida, i. 3;* ruthlessness in, *Troilus and Cressida, v. 3;* exceeds peace, *Coriolanus, iv. 5;* prophecy of—the dogs of, *Julius Cæsar, iii. 1;* preparations for, *Julius Cæsar, iv. 2; Hamlet, i. 1, 2;* cruel, *Timon of Athens, iv. 3;* farewell to, *Othello, iii. 3;* longing for, *Cymbeline, iv. 4.*

War, the Trojan, *Troilus and Cressida.*

War-cries, havoc, *King John, ii. 1; Coriolanus, iii. 1;* God and Saint George, *Richard III., v. 3.*

Ward, I am now in, *All's Well that Ends Well, i. 1.* The heirs of great fortunes were wards of the king in England and in Normandy under feudal laws. Here the law is attributed to the rest of France. The father should be ward to the son, *King Lear, i. 2.*

Ward (place of defence), *A Winter's Tale, i. 2; Troilus and Cressida, i. 2; Merry Wives of Windsor, ii. 2.*

Warden pies, *A Winter's Tale, iv. 2* or *3.* Made of wardens, large pears.

Warder, the king's, *Richard II., i. 3; II. Henry IV., iv. 1.* Throwing down the warder was a sign for the combat to stop.

Ware, the bed of, *Twelfth Night, iii. 2.* This famous bed, which is twelve feet square, is of oak, and very elaborately carved. It bears the date 1463; but as it seems by the carving to be of a later period, the date may have been marked on it to confirm the story that it once belonged to Warwick, the king-maker. It was in an inn at Ware—the Saracen's Head—in 1864, when it was offered for sale at auction, at one hundred guineas; but as no one raised the price, 't was bought in. One story is, that it was made and presented to the royal family, in 1463, by one Jonas Fosbrooke, and that Edward IV., being much pleased with the curious carving, gave him a pension for life. There is also a tradition that, years afterward, the bed was used on occasions when the town was very full; but those who tried to sleep in it were kept awake by pinches, scratches, and other small persecutions, caused, it was supposed, by the spirit of Jonas Fosbrooke, who resented the use of his favourite work, designed for royalty, by common people in a public inn.

Warkworth, a market-town of Northumberland, scene of parts of *I.* and *II. Henry IV.*

Warnings, from heaven, *Julius Cæsar, i. 3;* disregarded, *Lucrece, l. 491.* See OMENS.

Warriors, precarious fame of, *Sonnet xxv.* See SOLDIERS.

Wars of the Roses, prophecy of, *Richard II., iv. 1;* origin of the use of the roses as emblems by the partisans of the two houses, *1. Henry VI., ii. 4.* A red rose was the badge of John of Gaunt, a white one of his brother, Edmund of Langley. For battles of the Wars of the Roses, see BARNET, BOSWORTH, MORTIMER'S CROSS, SAINT ALBANS, TEWKSBURY, TOWTON, and WAKEFIELD.

Wart, a recruit in *II. Henry IV.,* appears in *iii. 2.*

Warwick, Richard Beauchamp (1381–1439), Earl of (mistakenly called Neville in *iii. 1*), character in *II. Henry IV.,* introduced in *iii. 1,* in *Henry V.,* introduced in *i. 2,* and in *I. Henry VI.,* where he is present in the first scene, but does not speak. He fought against Glendower at Shrewsbury, and in the wars in France, and made a pilgrimage to Palestine. He was regent of France from 1437 to 1439, and was one of the ambassadors sent to treat of the marriage of Henry V., who, at his death, appointed him guardian and tutor for his infant son, afterward Henry VI. In the " Rous Roll " he is shown holding the infant prince in his arms. The great earl was noted for his charity as well as for his ability and bravery, and the Emperor Sigismund spoke of him as the "father of courtesy." His daughter Anne married Richard Neville, who is the Warwick of the next play. In *ii. 4* of *I. Henry VI.,* Warwick takes the white rose with Plantagenet, and prophesies that the quarrel then begun between the roses shall send "a thousand souls to death and deadly night."

Warwick, Richard Neville, Earl of, "the king-maker," character in the second and third parts of *Henry VI.*, introduced in the first scene of each. He received the title and estates through his wife, heiress of the Beauchamp family, and afterward, at the death of his father, became Earl of Salisbury. He was on the side of York at first, and was in the battles at St. Albans and Towton; but he was offended at the marriage of Edward to Lady Grey, when he was negotiating a marriage with Bona of Savoy, *II. Henry VI., iii. 3,* and an estrangement followed. Later he joined the forces of Queen Margaret, and was defeated and slain at Barnet (April 14, 1471), *III. Henry VI., v. 2.* Allusions to him as the king-maker, second part, end of *scene 2; act ii.*, third part, *ii. 4; iii. 3;* to his device of the bear and ragged staff, *II. Henry VI., v. 1;* his power, "a bug that feared us all," third part, *v. 2.* One of his daughters, Isabella, married the Duke of Clarence; the other, Anne, married Edward, son of Henry VI., and afterward Richard, Duke of Gloucester, and is a character in *Richard III.;* Clarence's dream of him, *Richard III., i. 4;* Clarence's desertion of him for Edward, *ii. 1.* Warwick was said to have killed his horses at Towton, because he would not fly; at Barnet, to have fought on foot, for the encouragement of his soldiers. The former is commemorated by the figure of a horse on the side of a hill in Tysoe, in the county of Warwick, called the Red Horse, from the colour of the soil, and on Palm-Sunday, the anniversary of Towton, the people of the place meet together and "scour the horse," as it is called—clear away the vegetation that has accumulated on the figure.

Warwickshire, scene of *III. Henry VI., iv. 2, 3.*

Washford (Wexford, in Ireland), *I. Henry VI., iv. 7.*

Was it the proud, full sail of his great verse, *Sonnet lxxxvi.*

Wassail-candle, a, *II. Henry IV., i. 2.* A large candle used at a merry-making.

Was this fair face the cause, song, *All's Well that Ends Well, i. 3.*

Wastefulness, to gild refined gold, to paint the lily, etc., *King John, iv. 2;* of Falstaff. See WAIST.

Wat, name for a hare, *Venus and Adonis, l. 697.*

Watch, directions to the, *Much Ado about Nothing, iii. 3.*

Watch, winding up the, of wit, *The Tempest, ii. 1.*

Watch, give me a, *Richard III., v. 3.* A watch-light, marked to show the passage of time.

Watchfulness, power of, *Troilus and Cressida, iii. 3.*

Water, smooth, *II. Henry VI., iii. 1;* that glideth by the mill, *Titus Andronicus, ii. 1;* as false as, *Othello, v. 2;* the, was caught, and not the fish, *A Winter's Tale, v. 2.*

Water-casting, allusions to the practice of, *Two Gentlemen of Verona, ii. 1; Twelfth Night, iii. 4; II. Henry IV., i. 2; Macbeth, v. 3; Merry Wives of Windsor, ii. 3.*

Water-fly, *Hamlet, v. 2; Troilus and Cressida, v. 1.* A busy, officious trifler.

Waterford, Ireland, Talbot, Earl of, *I. Henry VI., iv. 7.*

Water-galls, *Lucrece, l. 1588.* Secondary rainbows.

Waterton, Sir Robert, mentioned in *Richard II., ii. 1,* as one of the companions of Bolingbroke.

Waters, a boat for all, *Twelfth Night, iv. 2.* Ready for any port.

Water-work (water-colours), *II. Henry IV., ii. 1.*

Watery star (the moon), *A Winter's Tale, i. 2.*

Wax, love like an image of, *Two Gentlemen of Verona, ii. 4.*

Wax, a form of, *King John, v. 4.* Allusion to the superstition that an individual could be destroyed by melting before the fire a waxen image of him; alluded to also in *Two Gentlemen of Verona, ii. 4; Richard III., iii. 4;* sting of, *II. Henry VI., iv. 2;* a wide sea of, *Timon of Athens, i. 1.* The last is probably an allusion to the waxen tablets anciently used for writing, as one might say now, a wide sea of foolscap; uses of, in sealing, *Cymbeline, iii. 2.*

Waywardness, of age, *King Lear, i. 1.*

Weakness, *Troilus and Cressida, i. 1;* great results from, *All's Well that Ends Well, ii. 1;* physical, of a great man, *Julius Cæsar, i. 2.*

Wealsmen (legislators, commonwealth men), *Coriolanus, ii. 1.*

Wealth, a burden for death to unload, *Measure for Measure, iii. 1;* power of, *Merry Wives of Windsor, iii. 4;* confiscated, *Merchant of Venice, iv. 1;* misery brought by, *Timon of Athens, iv. 2;* and peace, imposthume of, *Hamlet, iv. 4* or *1;* desire for, *Lucrece, l. 141; King Lear, i. 4;* faults that are rich are fair, *Timon of Athens, i. 2.* See GOLD, MONEY.

Weapons, holy saws of sacred writ for, *II. Henry VI., i. 3.*

Weariness, in a prince, *II. Henry IV., ii. 2;* sleep of, *Cymbeline, iii. 6.*

Weary with toil, I haste me to my bed, *Sonnet xxvii.*

Weasel, spleen of the, *I. Henry IV., ii. 3;* quarrelous as the, *Cymbeline, iii. 4;* as a, sucks eggs, *As You Like It, ii. 5;* very like a, *Hamlet, iii. 2.*

Weather, unseasonable, due to strife among the fairies. See SEASONS.

Weather-cock, invisible as a, *Two Gentlemen of Verona, ii. 1.*

Weaver(s), psalm-singers, *I. Henry IV., ii. 4;* three souls out of one, *Twelfth Night, ii. 3.* Weavers were noted for psalm-singing; Goliath with a weaver's beam, *Merry Wives of Windsor, v. 1.*

Web-and-pin (cataract of the eye), *A Winter's Tale, i. 2; King Lear, iii. 4.*

Wedding journey, a, *Taming of the Shrew, iv. 1.*

Weeds, in spring, *II. Henry VI., iii. 1;* a crown of, *King Lear, iv. 4, 6;* the fattest soil is most subject to, *II. Henry IV., iv. 4;* grow apace, *Richard III., ii. 4; iii. 1.*

Weeds (garments), *Twelfth Night, v. 1; Coriolanus, ii. 3; King Lear, iv. 1, and elsewhere.*

Weeping. See TEARS.

Weet (wit, know), *Antony and Cleopatra, i. 1.*

Weird Sisters, the. See WITCHES, the.

Welcome, a landlady's, *Two Gentlemen of Verona, ii. 5;* at a feast, *Comedy of Errors, iii. 1;* must appear in other ways than words, *Merchant of Venice, v. 1;* a general, *Henry VIII. i. 4;* and farewell, *Troilus and Cressida, iii. 3;* to a returning soldier, *Coriolanus, ii. 1;* treacherous, *Macbeth, i. 5;* of a hostess, *Macbeth, i. 6;* expression of, *Macbeth, iii. 4; Pericles, ii. 3; Romeo and Juliet, ii. 6.*

Well-liking (fat), *Love's Labour's Lost, v. 2.*

Welsh, the, accent of, *Merry Wives of Windsor,* Sir Hugh Evans in *i. 1, 2,* etc., and Fluellen's in *Henry V.;* the devil understands, *I. Henry IV., iii. 1;* love for cheese of, *Merry Wives of Windsor, v. 5;* cruelties of, *I. Henry IV., i. 1;* language of the, *I Henry IV., iii. 1,* last part; service of, in France, *Henry V., iv. 7.*

Were't aught to me I bore the canopy, *Sonnet cxxv.*

Westminster, scene of a part of *Henry VIII.*

Westminster, palace at, scene of a part of *II. Henry IV.*

Westminster Abbey, scene of the opening of *I. Henry VI.*

Westminster, the Abbot of, a character in *Richard II.,* introduced in *iv. 1.* He was the leader of the conspiracy to kill Bolingbroke; in *v. 6* he is said to have died "with clog of conscience and sour melancholy." The name of this abbot is not certainly known, but William de Colchester is generally supposed to be the one; though, from the fact that the date of his death is uncertain, it may have been his successor, Richard Harounden.

Westminster Hall, scene of *iv. 1* in *Richard II.* It was re-built by Richard, who was deposed by the first Parliament that met there.

Westmoreland, Ralph Neville, Earl of, character in *Henry IV.,* both parts, and in *Henry V.* He was the first earl, made so by Richard II., in 1397. He was, however, on the side of Bolingbroke, who rewarded him for his services with several important appointments. In *II. Henry IV. iv. 1,* he meets the archbishop and Mowbray to persuade them to abandon their rebellion. Of his twenty-two children, his oldest son died, leaving a son Ralph, who is the Westmoreland of *III. Henry VI.*

Westmoreland, Ralph Neville, second earl of, character in *III. Henry VI.,* grandson of the preceding. He is an adherent of the house of Lancaster, and is introduced in the first scene.

Westward, hoe ! *Twelfth Night, iii. 1.* The cry of boatmen on the Thames.

Wezand (windpipe), *The Tempest, iii. 2.*

Whale, this — Falstaff, *Merry Wives of Windsor, ii. 1;* the belching, *Troilus and Cressida, v. 5;* like a, *Hamlet, iii. 2;* to virginity, *All's Well that Ends Well, iv. 3.* The monster that was to devour Andromeda was represented as a whale in some old prints.

Whale's bone (walrus-teeth), *Love's Labour's Lost, v. 2.*

What is your substance, whereof are you made, *Sonnet liii.*

What potions have I drunk of siren tears, *Sonnet cxix.*

What's in the brain that ink may character, *Sonnet cviii.*

Wheat, two grains of, in two bushels of chaff, *Merchant of Venice, i. 1;* he that will have a cake of the, must tarry the grinding, *Troilus and Cressida, i. 1.*

Wheel, turn in the (like a turnspit), *Comedy of Errors, iii. 2;* (the burden of a song?), *Hamlet, iv. 5* or *2;* when a great, runs down a hill, let go thy hold, *King Lear, ii. 4;* death by the, *Coriolanus, iii. 2,* a punishment not used in Rome; of fire, bound upon a, *King Lear, iv. 7.*

Whelked (twisted, convoluted), *King Lear, iv. 6.*

Whelks (pustules), *Henry V., iii. 6.*

When as I sat in Babylon, song, *Merry Wives of Windsor, iii. 1.* A metrical version of Psalm cxxxvii., mixed with a song by Marlowe.

When as thine eye hath chose the dame, *Passionate Pilgrim, xix.*

When daffodils begin to peer, song, *A Winter's Tale, iv. 2* or *3.*

When daisies pied and violets blue, song, *Love's Labour's Lost, v. 2.*

When forty winters shall besiege thy brow, *Sonnet ii.*

When griping grief, song by Richard Edwards, *Romeo and Juliet, iv. 5.*

When I consider every thing that grows, *Sonnet xv.*

When I do count the clock that tells the time, *Sonnet xii.*

When I have seen by Time's fell hand defaced, *Sonnet lxiv.*

When, in disgrace with fortune and men's eyes, *Sonnet xxix.*

When in the chronicle of wasted time, *Sonnet cvi.*

When most I wink, then do mine eyes best see, *Sonnet xliii.*

When my love swears that she is made of truth, *Sonnet cxxxviii; Passionate Pilgrim, i.*

When thou shalt be disposed to set me light, *Sonnet lxxxviii.*

When to the sessions of sweet silent thought, *Sonnet xxx.*

Whêr (whether), *II. Henry VI., iii. 3; Comedy of Errors, iv. 1.*

Where art thou, Muse, that thou forget'st so long, *Sonnet c.*

Where is the life that late I led? *Taming of the Shrew, iv. 1.* A line from an old ballad now lost.

Where, to find a better, thou losest here, *King Lear, i. 1.*

Where the bee sucks, song, *The Tempest, v. 1.*

Whetstone, well said, *Troilus and Cressida, v. 2;* of a sword, *Macbeth, iv. 3.*

Whiffler, a, *Henry V., v., chorus.* An officer who preceded a procession to clear the way, sometimes a piper.

Whiles (until), *Twelfth Night, iv. 3.*

Whiles you here do snoring lie, song, *The Tempest, ii. 1.*

Whilst I alone did call upon thy aid, *Sonnet lxxix.*

Whipping, punishment by, *Taming of the Shrew, i. 1; II. Henry IV., v. 4; II. Henry VI., ii. 1; Antony and Cleopatra, iii. 11; Hamlet, ii. 2; All's Well that Ends Well, ii. 2; King Lear i. 4;* the impression of keen whips, *Measure for Measure, ii. 4.*

Whirligig, of time, the, *Twelfth Night, v. 1.*

Whitehall, named, *Henry VIII., iv. 1.*

Whiteness, of new snow upon the raven's back, *Romeo and Juliet, iii. 2;* of doves-down, *A Winter's Tale, iv. 3.*

Whitmore, Walter, character in *II. Henry VI.,* introduced in *iv. 1,* one of the pirates that captured the Duke of Suffolk, and the one to whose share he fell. The name Walter was pronounced with the *l* silent; the duke says:

> "A cunning man did calculate my birth,
> And told me that by water I should die."

Whitsters (bleachers), *Merry Wives of Windsor, iii. 3.*

Whitsuntide, or Pentecost, *Two Gentlemen of Verona, iv. 4; Romeo and Juliet, i. 5; Comedy of Errors, iv. 1;* pastorals at, *A Winter's Tale, iv. 3 or 4;* morris-dance at, *Henry V., ii. 4.*

Whittle (pocket-knife), *Timon of Athens, v. 1.*

Whoever hath her wish, thou hast thy will, *Sonnet cxxxv.*

Who is it that says most ? *Sonnet lxxxiv.*

Who is Silvia ? song, *Two Gentlemen of Verona, iv. 2.*

Whoobub (hubbub), *A Winter's Tale, iv. 3 or 4.*

Whoop, do me no harm, *A Winter's Tale, iv. 3 or 4.* Refrain of an old ballad.

Who will believe my verse in time to come, *Sonnet xvii.*

Why, every, hath a wherefore, *Comedy of Errors, ii. 2.*

Why didst thou promise such a beauteous day, *Sonnet xxxiv.*

Why is my verse so barren of new pride, *Sonnet lxxvi.*

Why should this a desert be ? love-verses, *As You Like It, iii. 2.*

Wicked, the love of the, *Richard II., v. 1;* their own enemies, *All's Well that Ends Well, iv. 3;* swords of the, turned against themselves, *Richard III., v. 1.*

Wickedness, confession of, *Titus Andronicus, v. 1;* Heaven sees all, *Henry V., iv. 1; II. Henry VI., v. 2; Hamlet, iii. 3; Pericles, i. 1;* relative, *King Lear, ii. 4,* "Those wicked creatures," etc.; unpunished, *King Lear, iii. 7;* leavens the good, *Cymbeline, iii. 4;* downward course of, *Henry V., iii. 3.*

Widow(s), dower of a, *Measure for Measure, v. 1;* Heaven, the champion of, *Richard II., i. 2;* speedy marriage of a, *Hamlet, i. 2;* fear to leave a, *Sonnet ix.*

Widow, a, a character in the *Taming of the Shrew,* introduced in *v. 2,* who marries Hortensio.

Widow, a, of Florence, character in *All's Well that Ends Well,* the mother of Diana. See CAPILET.

Wife (wives), a jewel, *Two Gentlemen of Verona, ii. 4;* may be merry and honest, *Merry Wives of Windsor, iv. 2;* are sold by fate, *Merry Wives of Windsor, v. 5;* duties of, *Comedy of Errors, ii. 1; Taming of the Shrew, v. 2;* reproaches of a jealous, *Comedy of Errors, ii. 1, 2; v. 1;* like vines, *Comedy of Errors, ii. 1;* submission of a, *Merchant of Venice, iii. 2;* a light, *Merchant of Venice, v. 1;* always go wrong, *Love's Labour's Lost, iii. 1;* those who rule their lords, *Love's Labour's Lost, iv. 1;* property in a, *Taming of the Shrew, iii. 2,* "She is my goods," etc.; kill a, with kindness, *Taming of the Shrew, iv. 1;* a detested, is worse than war, *All's Well that Ends Well, ii. 3;* jealousy of, *As You Like It, iv. 1;* revolted, *A Winter's Tale, i. 2;* what motive stronger than the name of, *King John, iii. 1;* fears of a, *I. Henry IV., ii. 3;* like a beaten, *II. Henry IV., iv. 1;* Gloucester's, *I. Henry VI., i. 1;* a good, *Henry VIII., ii. 4; iii. 1;* taking a—avenging the theft of a, *Troilus and Cressida, ii. 2;* a quiet, *Coriolanus, ii. 1,* "My gracious silence;" if you had been the wife of Hercules, *Coriolanus, iv. 1;* secrets from a—prayer to be worthy of a noble, *Julius Cæsar, ii. 1;* love of, *Othello, i. 3;* unfaithfulness of, *Othello, iv. 3, end;* advantage in the death of a, *Antony and Cleopatra, i. 2;* one not to be controlled, *Antony and Cleopatra, ii. 2;* praise of a, *Lucrece, l. 15.* See also WOMEN.

Wilderness (wildness), *Measure for Measure, iii. 1.*

Wild fowl, there is not a more fearful, than your lion living, *Midsummer-Night's Dream, iii. 1;* the opinion of Pythagoras concerning, *Twelfth Night, iv. 2.*

Wild-goose chase, a, *Romeo and Juliet, ii. 4.* A kind of horse-race in which the second was obliged to follow the leader wherever he chose to go; or any chase as hopeless as the pursuit of a wild goose.

Wilfulness, schoolmasters to, *King Lear, ii. 4, end;* hydra-headed, *Henry V., i. 1.*

Will, arbitrary, *Two Gentlemen of Verona, i. 3;* a strong, in a feeble body, like, *II. Henry VI., v. 3;* power of the, *Othello, i. 3,* peech of Iago; happiness of following one's own, *Cymbeline, i. 6.*

Will, play on the name, *Sonnets cxxxv., cxxxvi., cxliii., cxliv.*

Will(s) (testaments), not such a sickly creature as to make a, *Merry Wives of Windsor, iii. 4;* of Portia's father, *Merchant of Venice, i. 2;* of worldlings, *As You Like It, ii. 1;* a wicked, a woman's, *King John, ii. 1;* bid a sick man make, *Romeo and Juliet, i. 1;* Cæsar's, *Julius Cæsar, iii. 2;* he is said to have left about fourteen dollars to each citizen, a sum equal in value to at least one hundred dollars now; a last, *Lucrece, l. 1183; Pericles, i. 1.*

William, a country fellow in *As You Like It*, introduced in *v. 1*, in love with Audrey, who is captivated by Touchstone.

Williams, character in *Henry V.*, a soldier in the army, first appears in *iv. 1*, where Henry in his incognito talks with him and exchanges gloves with him. The outcome of the episode is in *iv. 8.*

Will-o'-the-wisp, called a Jack, *The Tempest, iv. 1;* a fire-drake, *Henry VIII., v. 4;* a walking fire, *King Lear, iii. 4.*

Willoughby, Lord William de, an unimportant character in *Richard II.*, a partisan of Bolingbroke, introduced in *ii. 3.*

Willow, the, allusions to it as a symbol of disappointed love, *Merchant of Venice, v. 1; III. Henry VI., iii. 3; Hamlet, iv. 7; Othello, iv. 3; Much Ado about Nothing, ii. 1.*

Wiltshire, James Butler, Earl of, spoken of in *III. Henry VI., i. 1.* He was a Lancastrian, was wounded at St. Alban's, taken prisoner at Towton, and beheaded in 1460.

Wiltshire, William le Scrope, Earl of, has the realm in farm, *Richard II., ii. 1.* He was a favourite of the king, who created him earl in 1395. On the landing of Henry of Lancaster, in 1399, he was taken and beheaded without a trial.

Win, they laugh that, *Othello, iv. 1.*

Winchester, Henry Beaufort, Cardinal, and Bishop of (1370–1447), character in the first and second parts of *Henry VI.*, introduced in the first scene of each. He was a son of John of Gaunt and Catherine Swynford, and was therefore an uncle of Humphrey, Duke of Gloucester, the relationship referred to in *I. Henry VI., iii. 1.* He was the leader of the peace party, Gloucester of the war party; their hatred toward each other is expressed in *I. Henry VI., i. 1, 3.* The play follows tradition in imputing to Winchester a share in Gloucester's death and the consequent remorse and horrible end; but there is said to be no authentic evidence in favor of it. He is described by Holinshed as "haughty in stomach, high in countenance, and strong in malice and mischief." He was called Cardinal of England, though the Bishop of Durham was a cardinal at the same time, and Beaufort's title was Cardinal of St. Eusebius.

Winchester, Stephen Gardiner, Bishop of. See GARDINER.

Winchester goose, *I. Henry VI., i. 3; Troilus and Cressida, v. 11.* Name for a vile disease, or one afflicted with it. A disreputable part of the town was under the jurisdiction of the Bishop of Winchester.

Wincot (Wilnecastle), in Warwickshire, near Stratford, *Taming of the Shrew, induction, 2.*

Wind, something in the, *Comedy of Errors, iii. 2;* sits in that corner, *Much Ado about Nothing, ii. 3;* churlish, *As You Like It, ii. 1;* little fire grows great with little. *Taming of the Shrew, ii. 1;* ill, *II. Henry IV., v. 3; III. Henry VI., vi. 5;* that bows the pine, *Cymbeline, iv. 2;* allusions to the south or southwest wind as bringing wet weather and disease, *The Tempest, i. 2; I. Henry IV., v. 1; Coriolanus, i. 4; Troilus and Cressida, v. 1; Cymbeline, ii. 3.*

Windmill, living with cheese in a, *I. Henry IV., iii. 1;* in St. George's Fields, *II. Henry IV., iii. 2.*

Windows, the eyes, *Richard III., i. 2; v. 3; Cymbeline, ii. 2.*

Winds, the, at sea, *II. Henry IV., iii. 1;* sightless couriers, *Macbeth, i. 7;* Lear's appeal to, *King Lear, iii. 2.*

Windsor, twenty-three miles west of London, scene of the *Merry Wives of Windsor.* It has been conjectured that Elizabeth was at Windsor Castle when, according to the tradition, it was written for her, and that it was first acted there, the scene being laid at Windsor to give the play a local interest. Herne's oak, which is introduced in *v. 3–5,* stood in Windsor Little Park.

Windsor Castle, scene of *v. 6* in *Richard II.;* spoken of in the *Merry Wives of Windsor, v. 5.*

Wine, the temptation of, *Merchant of Venice, i. 2;* good, needs no bush, *As You Like It, epilogue;* effect of, *Timon of Athens. iv. 3.* "Nor on the beasts themselves," etc.; of life, is drawn, *Macbeth, ii. 3;* good wine, a good creature, if well used—invisible spirit of, *Othello, ii. 3,* Cassio's speech; the conquering, *Antony and Cleopatra, ii. 7;* unkindness buried in, *Julius Cæsar, iv. 3;* loquacity after taking, *Henry VIII., i. 4.* See DRUNKENNESS.

Winning, would put any man into courage, *Cymbeline, ii. 3.*

Winter, song of, *Love's Labour's Lost, v. 2;* age like a lusty, *As You Like It, ii. 3;* a sad tale for. *A Winter's Tale, ii. 1;* humourous as, *II. Henry IV., iv. 4;* of our discontent, *Richard III., i. 1;* not gone, if the wild geese fly that way, *King Lear, ii. 4;* tames man, woman, and beast, *Taming of the Shrew, iv. 1.*

Winter's Tale, A, was written late in 1610 or early in 1611. It is founded on a story by Robert Greene, first published in 1588 under the name of "Pandosto," and again in 1609, with the title, "The Historie of Dorastus and Fawnia." See SOURCES. The story was very popular, and passed through many editions. Shakspere followed it quite closely in most points, but in the story Hermione is actually dead, and the love of Leontes for Perdita, merely hinted at in the play, drives him to suicide in the story. The time of the play cannot be determined, or, rather, it has no time. Pagan and Christian usages and expressions are recklessly mingled. The queen is daughter of the Emperor of Russia, and her innocence is attested by the oracle at Delphos. The scene of action is first in Sicilia, afterward in Bohemia, then again in Sicilia. This play is regarded as one of the best in its treatment of character and motive, though its plot defies all the unities.

Wisdom, in self-disparagement, *Measure for Measure, ii. 4;* in imprisonment, *Measure for Measure, i. 3;* an appearance of, in silence, *Merchant of Venice, i. 1;* waiting on folly, *All's Well that Ends Well, i. 1;* too great a show of, *All's Well that Ends Well, ii. 3,* "I did think thee," etc.; cries in the streets, *I. Henry IV., i. 2;* gained in a wild life, *Henry V., i. 1;* of Ajax, *Troilus and Cressida, ii. 3;* in combat with fortune, *Antony and Cleopatra, iii. 2;* in combat with blood, *Much Ado about Nothing, ii. 3;* he's a fool that will not yield to, *Pericles, ii. 4.*

Wise, the, folly of, *As You Like It, ii. 7;* knows his folly, *As You Like It, v. 1;* all places home to, *Richard II., i. 3;* do not wail, *Richard II., iii. 2;* the young and, do ne'er live long, *Richard III., iii. 1.*

Wise-woman (witch), *Merry Wives of Windsor, iv. 5.*

Wish(es), thy own, wish I thee, *Love's Labour's Lost, ii. 1;* the best, *All's Well that Ends Well, i. 1;* father to the thought, *II. Henry IV., iv. 4.*

Wishers, were ever fools, *Antony and Cleopatra, iv. 13 or 15.*

Wisp of straw, allusion to a, as the badge of a scold, *III. Henry VI., ii. 2.*

Wit, winding the watch of, *The Tempest, ii. 1;* not to go unrewarded, *The Tempest, iv. 1;* love bought with, *Two Gentlemen of Verona, i. 1;* borrows and spends, *Two Gentlemen of Verona, ii. 4;* without will, *Two Gentlemen of Verona, ii. 6;* on ill employment, *Merry Wives of Windsor, v. 5;* what is, in the great, is profanation in the humble, *Measure for Measure, ii. 2;* given to men in place of hair, *Comedy of Errors, ii. 2;* a skirmish of, *Much Ado about Nothing, i. 1;* Beatrice's, *Much Ado about Nothing, ii. 1; iii. 1;* some remnants of, *Much Ado about Nothing, ii. 3;* the wit is out when age is in, *Much Ado about Nothing, iii. 5;* Benedick's, *Much Ado about Nothing, v. 1, 2;* a manly, *Much Ado about Nothing, v. 2;* a sharp, *Love's Labour's Lost, ii. 1;* peddling second-hand,

Love's Labour's Lost, v. 2; turned fool, *Love's Labour's Lost. v. 2,* the whetstone of, *As You Like It, i. 2;* with understanding, *As You Like It, iii. 3;* in women, *As You Like It, iv. 1;* has much to answer for, *As You Like It, v. 1;* with honour, *All's Well that Ends Well, i. 2;* harmed by beef, *Twelfth Night, i. 3;* those that think they have, *Twelfth Night, i. 5;* enough, to lie straight, *Twelfth Night, ii. 3;* to play the fool, *Twelfth Night, iii. 1;* the cause of, in other men, *II. Henry IV., i. 2;* and sherris, *II. Henry IV., iv. 3;* encounter of, *Richard III., i. 2;* lack of, *Troilus and Cressida, ii. 1; Hamlet, ii. 2;* brevity the soul of, *Hamlet, ii. 2;* a bitter sweeting, *Romeo and Juliet, ii. 4;* pared on both sides, *King Lear, i. 4;* more man than, *King Lear, ii. 4;* depends on time, *Othello, ii. 3;* waits on fear, *Venus and Adonis, l. 690.* See also Wits.

Wit, skull of a, *Hamlet, v. 1;* an unconscious, *As You Like It, ii. 4,* "I shall never be 'ware of my own wit till I break my shins against it."

Witchcraft, of Sycorax, (*q. v.*), *The Tempest, i. 2;* allusions to, *Merry Wives of Windsor, iv. 2; Comedy of Errors, i. 2; ii. 2; iii. 2; Twelfth Night, iii. 4; I. Henry VI., i. 5,* "Blood will I draw;" a witch was supposed to be rendered powerless by loss of blood; *I. Henry VI., v. 3,* "Monarch of the north;" Ziminar, a devil invoked by witches; other allusions to, *II. Henry VI., i. 2, 4; ii. 1-4;* accusation of, *Richard III., iii. 4;* charm against (God save her), *Henry VIII., v. 4;* incantations of, *Macbeth, iv. 1.* See also under Mahu. In *Macbeth, i. 3; iv. 1;* and *v. 3,* many popular notions about witches are alluded to—that they could sail any sea in a shell or a sieve; that they could assume the form of any animal; that they sold winds; that they are connected with the moon; that they untie the winds to fight against the churches, etc. The use of the supernatural in the plays of Shakspere was in accord with the belief, universal in his time, in witchcraft, ghosts, omens, and portents of all kinds. The law against witches, which had been repealed in the time of Edward VI., was re-enacted in the time of Elizabeth, because they had so terribly increased; and during the reign of James I. the crime of witchcraft was made punishable by death upon the first conviction, Coke and Bacon being members of the Parliament that passed the law. King James published a book on "Demonology," in 1603; but men of far higher intellect were firm believers in the power of witches. Sir Thomas Browne declares that those who doubt it are atheists. Bishop Jewell, in a sermon before the queen, drew an affecting picture of the wasting away of the victims of sorcery. The names of familiars of witches, that are used in the plays, Barbason, Mahu, Smulkin, and others, are found in the writings of Reginald Scott, who published a book on witchcraft, in 1584, and of other authors of the time.

Witch(es), Sycorax, *The Tempest;* of Brentford, the, *Merry Wives of Windsor, iv. 2;* beards of, *Merry Wives of Windsor, iv. 2;* Ephesus full of, *Comedy of Errors, i. 3;* Joan of Arc accused of being a, *I. Henry VI., i. 5;* the Duchess of Gloucester accused, *II. Henry VI., ii. 3;* Edward's wife a, *Richard III., iii. 4;* an Egyptian, *Othello, iii. 4;* images of wax made by. See under WAX.

Witches, the, or the Three Weird Sisters, characters in *Macbeth*, playing substantially the same part as in the old record. These sisters answered to the fates of mythology, and are by some supposed to be the Norns or fates of Scandinavian mythology, the first of whom had to do with the past, the second with the present, the third with the future. The word is spelled "weyward" in the folio. They appear first in *i. 1*, and are seen by Banquo and Macbeth in *i. 3*, where they make their prophecy, of which the two speak again in *ii. 1*, and Banquo in *iii. 1*. They appear again in *iii. 5* and in *iv. 1*, where they show him the apparitions and make another prophecy.

"They are wholly different from any representation of witches in contemporary writers, and yet presented a sufficient external resemblance to the creatures of vulgar prejudice to act immediately on the audience. Their character consists in the imaginative disconnected from the good."—COLERIDGE.

Witching-time, of night, *Hamlet, iii. 2.*

Withal, I could not (could not help), *Merchant of Venice, iii. 4.*

Withers, our, are unwrung, *Hamlet, iii. 2.*

Withold, Saint, footed thrice the wold, *King Lear, iii. 4.*

Witness(es), false, *Henry VIII., v. 1;* conscience a, *Cymbeline, ii. 2;* of murder, *Macbeth, ii. 2.*

Wits, of the home-keeping, are homely—love inhabits in the finest, *Two Gentlemen of Verona, i. 1;* the five, *Much Ado about Nothing, i. 1; Twelfth Night, iv. 2; King Lear, iii. 4; Romeo and Juliet, i. 4;* the intellectual faculties, corresponding to the five senses; fat, *I. Henry IV., i. 2;* lack of, is no matter in England, *Hamlet, v. 1.* See also WIT.

Wit-snapper, a, *Merchant of Venice, iii. 5.*

Wittenberg, school at, *Hamlet, i. 2.* The university dates from the year 1502, while the Danish history, from which the tale of Hamlet is drawn, was written at about the end of the twelfth century.

Wittol, quibble on, *Merry Wives of Windsor, ii. 2, end.*

Wizard(s), prophecy by, *II. Henry VI., i. 4; v. 2; Richard III., i. 1.*

Woe, faintly borne, *Richard II., i. 3;* to the land governed by a child, *Richard III., ii. 3;* for England, *Richard III., iii. 4;* if sour, delights in fellowship, *Romeo and Juliet, iii. 2;* trappings of, *Hamlet, i. 2;* a charm against death, *Cymbeline, v. 3;* fellowship in, *Lucrece, lines 790, 1111.* See GRIEF and SORROW.

Woes, comparison of, *Much Ado about Nothing, v. 1;* a tide of, *Richard II., ii. 2;* wise men ne'er wail their present, *Richard II., iii. 2;* lose knowledge of themselves, *King Lear, iv. 6.*

Wolf (wolves), thy currish spirit governed a, *Merchant of Venice, iv. 1;* Irish, *As You Like It, v. 2;* have done offices of pity, *A Winter's Tale, ii. 3;* to make a, *II. Henry IV., i. 2;* eat like, *Henry V., iii. 7;* in sheep's array, *I. Henry VI., i. 3;* English, *I. Henry VI., i. 6;* arouse the jades that drag the night, *II. Henry VI., iv. 1;* loves the lamb, *Coriolanus, ii. 1;* sentinels of murder, *Macbeth, ii. 1.*

Wolsey, Thomas, Archbishop of York and cardinal, character in *Henry VIII.*, introduced in the first scene, where he is spoken of as a " butcher's cur." His father was a wealthy butcher at Ipswich. His power, ambition, and ability are spoken of in *i. 1;* he is charged with oppressive taxation, *i. 2;* hated by the commons, *ii. 1;* his reasons for urging the divorce, *ii. 1, 2;* Katherine to him, *ii. 4;* his double-dealing discovered, the king's ironical praise, his fall, and soliloquy, *iii. 2;* Henry reading the inventory of his property, *iii. 2.* (A mistake like this is said to have been made by the Bishop of Durham, and used by Wolsey to ruin him.) His death and character, *iv. 2.* This, put into the mouths of Katherine and Griffith, is taken almost literally from Holinshed. His farewell to greatness in the celebrated soliloquy is by some critics attributed to Fletcher. Wolsey is one of the great characters of the historic plays—haughty, ambitious, tricky, revengeful, he assumes equal power with the king, intends to make himself pope, pursues the unfortunate Buckingham to death, and raises the question of illegality in the king's marriage in order to bring about a union with the sister of the French king, and thereby further his own ambitious plans. But the king makes his own choice of Katherine's successor, and Wolsey's scheme falls to the ground, followed by his own ruin. In his fall he is represented in the play as noble, dignified, and Christian-like.

Woman (women), reason of a, *Two Gentlemen of Verona, i. 2;*

IV., i. 1; secrets with, *I. Henry IV., ii. 3;* the son of a, and yet
with fewer words than a parrot, *I. Henry IV., ii. 4;* shrewd tempt-
ers, *I. Henry VI., i. 2;* beauty, virtue, and government in—the
queen unlike, *III. Henry VI., i. 4;* when men are ruled by, *Richard
III., i. 1;* won by flattery, *Richard III., iv. 1;* love eminence, *Henry VIII., ii. 3;* are angels when wooed, *Troilus and Cressida, i. 2,
end;* that they had men's privileges—constancy in, *Troilus and
Cressida, iii. 2;* light, *Troilus and Cressida, iv. 5;* are governed
by the eyes, *Troilus and Cressida, v. 2;* hearing praise of valour,
Coriolanus, i. 9; a deputation of, *Coriolanus, v. 3;* tears of, *Coriolanus, v. 6; Lucrece, l. 1137;* Roman custom for, *Julius Cæsar,
i. 2;* in keeping counsel—weak-hearted, *Julius Cæsar, ii. 4;* will
all turn monsters if, etc., *King Lear, iii. 1;* sarcasms on, *Othello,
ii. 1;* Venetian, *Othello, iii. 3;* tears of, *Othello, iv. 1;* unkindness
to, *Antony and Cleopatra, i. 2;* charms of a, *Antony and Cleopatra,
ii. 2;* criticism of one, by another, *Antony and Cleopatra, iii. 3;*
never strong, *Antony and Cleopatra, iii. 10* or *12;* fickleness of,
Sonnet xx.; waxen minds of, *Lucrece, l. 1240;* not responsible, *Lucrece, lines 1244, 1257;* to woo, *Passionate Pilgrim, xix.*

Woman (to frighten as a woman), *All's Well that Ends Well,
iii. 2.*

Womanhood, let it not be believed for, *Troilus and Cressida,
v. 2.*

Woman-tired (governed by a woman), *A Winter's Tale, ii. 3.*

Won, things, *Troilus and Cressida, i. 2, end.*

Wonder, at unnatural things, *Macbeth, iii. 4; The Tempest,
v. 1; Othello, ii. 1; Richard III., iii. 7;* attired in, *Much Ado
about Nothing, iv. 1;* rarest argument of, *All's Well that Ends Well,
ii. 1;* nine days', *As You Like It, iii. 2;* ten days', *III. Henry VI.,
iii. 2;* a sonnet beginning "Wonder of nature," *Henry V., iii. 7.*

Wondered (endowed with wonderful power), *The Tempest, iv. 1.*

Wood, or wode (wild, frantic), *Midsummer-Night's Dream, ii. 1;
Venus and Adonis, l. 740.*

Woodbine, *Much Ado about Nothing, iii. 1; Midsummer-
Night's Dream, ii. 2; iv. 1.*

Woodcock (a gullible or cowardly fellow), *Much Ado about
Nothing, v. 1; Taming of the Shrew, i. 2; Love's Labour's Lost, iv.
3; All's Well that Ends Well, iv. 1; Twelfth Night, iv. 2.*

Woods, life in tne, *As You Like It, ii. 1;* ruthless, *Titus An-
ronicus, ii. 1, 3;* Bolingbroke's felled, *Richard II., iii. 1.*

Woodville, Richard, Lieutenant or Constable of the Tower, afterward Earl Rivers, character in *I. Henry VI.*, appears in *i. 3.* He was said to be the handsomest man of his day in England. He married the widow of the Duke of Bedford, Jacqueline of Luxembourg, without waiting for the consent of his sovereign; for this offence he was fined a thousand pounds; but he was soon forgiven, and was made Baron Rivers in 1448. His daughter Elizabeth became the wife of Edward IV., and his son Anthony is the Earl Rivers of *Richard III.* After the marriage of his daughter, he became a zealous Yorkist, and being taken by the insurgents after the battle of Edgecote (July 26, 1469), he and his son, Sir John Woodville, were beheaded, without trial, at Coventry.

Woodville, Anthony. See RIVERS.

Wooing, by a figure, *Two Gentlemen of Verona, ii. 1;* an odd, *Taming of the Shrew, ii. 1;* in haste, *Taming of the Shrew, iii. 2;* in rhyme, *Love's Labour's Lost, v. 2;* a king's, *Henry V., v. 2;* an unique, *Richard III., i. 2;* love sweeter in, *Troilus and Cressida, i. 2, end;* idle, *Hamlet, i. 3;* a soldier's, *Othello, i. 3;* women were not made for, *Midsummer-Night's Dream, ii. 1* or *2;* wedding and repenting, *Much Ado about Nothing, ii. 1.*

Woolward, go, for penance, *Love's Labour's Lost, v. 2.* Go clothed in wool instead of linen, sometimes imposed as a penance.

Worcester, burial of John at, *King John, v. 7.* The stone coffin of John was found in the cathedral at Worcester, July 17, 1797.

Worcester, Thomas Percy, Earl of, character in *I. Henry IV.,* introduced in *i. 3.* He is Hotspur's uncle, and in rebellion against the king. His defection from Henry's predecessor is recounted in *Richard II., ii. 2.* He is calculating, false, and selfish, and will not report to Hotspur the king's offer of mercy, lest he himself should in the event of a reconciliation live constantly under suspicion. Westmoreland says of him, "This Worcester, malevolent to you in all aspects," *i. 1.* He was taken prisoner at Shrewsbury, and beheaded two days later.

Word(s), crammed into the ears, *The Tempest, ii. 1;* his, are bonds, *Two Gentlemen of Verona, ii. 7;* evil, double deeds, *Comedy of Errors, iii. 2;* ill, empoison liking, *Much Ado about Nothing, iii. 1;* high, to low matter, *Love's Labour's Lost, i. 1;* pronunciation of certain—longest of all, *Love's Labour's Lost, v. 1;* an army of good, *Merchant of Venice, iii. 5;* a man of (Parolles, which means words), *All's Well that Ends Well;* dallying with, *Twelfth Night, iii. 1;* bethumped with, *King John, ii. 2;* like a woman's, *I. Henry IV., i. 3;* of the dying, *Richard II., ii. 1;* windy attor-

Worthies, the Nine, *Love's Labour's Lost, v. 1; II. Henry IV., ii. 4.* They were : three heathens—Hector, Alexander, and Cæsar; three Jews—Joshua, David, and Judas Maccabæus; and three Christians—Arthur, Charlemagne, and Godfrey of Bouillon. Shakspere includes Pompey and Hercules.

Worts, quibble on, *Merry Wives of Windsor, i. 1.* A general name for vegetables of the cabbage kind.

Wound(s), one, to be healed by many, *King John, v. 2;* notion that they open in presence of the murderer, *Richard III., i. 2;* the custom of showing, when seeking an election, *Coriolanus, ii. 3;* he that never felt a, jests at scars, *Romeo and Juliet, ii. 2;* one not so deep as a well, nor so wide as a church-door, *Romeo and Juliet, iii. 1;* Cæsar's, *Julius Cæsar, iii. 1, 2;* a, *Venus and Adonis, l. 1052.*

Wreak (revenge), *Romeo and Juliet, iii. 5; Titus Andronicus, iv. 3, 4; Coriolanus, iv. 5.*

Wreck, of the Dauphin's forces, *King John, v. 3;* as rocks cheer them that fear their, *III. Henry VI., ii. 2;* as men thrown upon sand from a, *Henry V., iv. 1.*

Wren(s), the youngest of nine, *Twelfth Night, iii. 2.* The wren was said to lay nine eggs, and the last bird hatched was the smallest; and as Maria was very small, she was called the youngest wren of nine; may prey where eagles dare not perch, *Richard III., i. 3;* parental love of, *Macbeth, iv. 2.*

Wrest (an active power), *Troilus and Cressida, iii. 3.*

Wrestling, allusions to: on the hip, *Merchant of Venice, i. 3; Othello, ii. 1;* a wrestling-match, *As You Like It, i. 2.*

Wretchedness, *Comedy of Errors, v. 1,* "A needy, hollow-eyed," etc.; last resort of, *King Lear, iv. 6;* of hanging on princes' favours, *Henry VIII., iii. 2;* in poverty, *Romeo and Juliet, v. 1.*

Wrinkles, of age, *All's Well that Ends Well, ii. 4;* likened to kingly sepulchres, *III. Henry VI., v. 2;* let them come with mirth and laughter, *Merchant of Venice, i. 1.*

Writhled (wrinkled), *I. Henry VI., ii. 3.*

Writing, comes by nature, *Much Ado about Nothing, iii. 3;* let it be held treacherous, *Cymbeline, iv. 2;* a baseness to write fair, *Hamlet, v. 2;* in a martial hand, *Twelfth Night, ii. 3.*

Wroath (ill fortune), *Merchant of Venice, ii. 9.*

Wrong(s), it is dishonourable to remember, *Coriolanus, v. 3;* to Brutus and Cassius, *Julius Cæsar, iii. 2;* pocketing up of, *Henry V., iii. 2;* humanity must prey upon itself, *King Lear, iv. 2;* to do a great right, do a little wrong, *Merchant of Venice, iv. 1;* fears attend the steps of, *King John, iv. 2 ;* flattery a, *Richard II., iii. 2 ;* to wear wrongs like raiment, *Timon of Athens, iii. 2.*

Wrying (swerving), *Cymbeline, v. 1.*

Wye, the, a river in Herefordshire and Monmouthshire, repulse at, *I. Henry IV., iii. 1 ; Henry V., iv. 7.*

Xantippe, as curst and shrewd as Socrates's, or a worse, *Taming of the Shrew, i. 2.*

Yare, yarely (quick, speedy, active, skilfully), *The Tempest, i. 1 ; v. 1 ; Measure for Measure, iv. 2 ; Twelfth Night, iii. 4 ; Antony and Cleopatra, ii. 2 ; iii. 7,* and elsewhere.

Yaw, *Hamlet, v. 2.* A sailor's word, meaning not to obey the helm ; to move unsteadily.

Yclep'd (called, from clepe), *Love's Labour's Lost, i. 1 ; v. 2.*

Yead (Edward), *Merry Wives of Windsor, i. 1.*

Yearn (to grieve), *Henry V., ii. 3 ; iv. 3 ; Julius Cæsar, ii. 2 ; Richard II., v. 5 ; Merry Wives of Windsor, iii. 5.*

Years, smiles his cheek in, *Love's Labour's Lost, v. 2 ;* reviewed, *Henry V., i., chorus ;* the vale of, *Othello, iii. 3 ;* course of, *Sonnet civ ;* as if the, had found some months asleep, *II. Henry IV., iv. 4.*

Yellowness (colour of jealousy), *Merry Wives of Windsor, i. 3, end ; A Winter's Tale, ii. 3,* "No yellow in't," etc. ; *Cymbeline, ii. 5.*

Yeoman (subordinate), *II. Henry IV., ii. 1.*

Yeoman-service, *Hamlet, v. 2.*

Yeomen, of England, *Henry V., iii. 1.*

Yesterday(s), O, call back, *Richard II., iii. 2 ;* all our, have lighted fools, the way to dusty death, *Macbeth, v. 5.*

Yew, double-fatal, *Richard II., iii. 2.* So called because it was used for bows, and the leaves were poisonous ; allusion to the custom of placing sprigs of it in the shroud, *Twelfth Night, ii. 4, song ;* used by witches when slivered in the moon's eclipse, *Macbeth, iv. 1 ;* in churchyards, *Romeo and Juliet, v. 3.*

Yield (requite), *Macbeth, i. 6 ; Antony and Cleopatra, iv. 2.*

Yorick, the king's jester, skull of, *Hamlet, v. 1.*

York, a city, capital of Yorkshire, 172 miles north of London, scene of *II. Henry IV., i. 3,* and of *III. Henry VI., iv. 7 ;* mayor of, *III. Henry VI., iv. 2.*

York, Archbishop of, mentioned in *III. Henry VI., iv. 3.* George Neville, brother of Warwick. See ROTHERHAM and SCROOP.

York and Lancaster, Houses of. See WARS OF THE ROSES.

York, Duchess of, a character in *Richard II.*, introduced in *v. 2*, where the treason of her son Aumerle is discovered by her and the duke. In *v. 3* she pleads with the king for his pardon. The mother of Aumerle, the Duchess Isabel, daughter of Peter the Cruel, King of Castile and Leon, died four or five years earlier than the time of the play; and the Duchess at this time was his step-mother, Joan Holland, daughter of the Earl of Kent. But Shakspere evidently intends the character for Aumerle's own mother.

York, Cicely Neville, Duchess of, wife of Richard, Duke of York, and mother of two kings, Edward IV. and Richard III., was distinguished for her beauty, and was called in her youth the "Rose of Raby." She is a character in *Richard III.*, where her son instructs Buckingham to throw a slur on her character—which is said to have been spotless—in order to prove Edward illegitimate, and put aside the claim of his son to the throne. The duchess appears in *ii. 2*, where she lays her curse on her unnatural son, hoping it may weigh heavier on the field than all his armour—a saying recalled when he is wearied by his beaver and his lance on Bosworth Field.

York, Edmund of Langley, Duke of, a character in *Richard II.*, first appears in *ii. 1.* In *v. 2* and *3* he denounces Aumerle, his traitorous son. Coleridge says: "There is scarcely anything in Shakspere in its degree more admirably drawn than York's character; his religious loyalty struggling with a deep grief and indignation at the king's follies; his adherence to his word and faith, once given, in spite of all, even the most natural, feelings. You see in him the weakness of old age, and the overwhelmingness of circumstances, for a time, surmounting his sense of duty, the junction of both exhibited in his boldness in words and feebleness in immediate act; and then, again, his effort to retrieve himself in abstract loyalty, even at the heavy price of the loss of his son." In contrast with this view is that of Gervinus, who regards York as the type of political faint-heartedness and neutrality and of cowardly loyalty to the strong and powerful, his weakness carried into unnatural obduracy when he urges his son's death under the fear that suspicion may fall upon himself.

York, Edward Plantagenet, Duke of, character in *Henry V.*, first appears in *iv. 3*, where he asks permission to lead the van at Agincourt. He is the Aumerle of *Richard II.*, whose part in the conspiracy to take the life of King Henry IV. is discovered in *v. 2.* He was restored to his father's title in 1406, and fought valiantly at Agincourt. His death on the field is described in *Henry V., iv. 6.*

He left no children, and the title was given to his nephew, who is the Duke of York in the three parts of *Henry VI.*

York, Richard Plantagenet, Duke of (1410–1460), character in the three parts of *Henry VI.* He was a son of the Earl of Cambridge, who was executed for a plot against Henry V., *I. Henry VI., ii. 5.* The son was relieved from the effects of his father's attainder in 1425, and restored to his titles and inheritance, *iii. 1,* and was afterward successively Constable of England, Regent of France, *iv. 1,* and Lieutenant of Ireland. He first appears in *ii. 4* of the first part, in a quarrel with Somerset; and it was under cover of hostility to Somerset that he placed himself in opposition to the king. In *v. 3* of the first part he captures Joan of Arc. He is introduced in the first scenes of the other two parts. In the first scene of the second part, and again in *iii. 1,* he declares in soliloquy his ambitious designs. His pedigree is given, though not altogether correctly, in *ii 2,* and his title to the throne. In *v. 1* he defies the king. In the third part, first scene, Henry consents to make him heir to the throne that he has seized, if he will give it up to him (Henry) during his lifetime. He fell at the battle of Wakefield, and his head was set on the walls of York. In the play, third part, *i. 4,* he is taken prisoner, and stabbed by Clifford and afterward by Queen Margaret, who has put a paper crown on his head. Of his four sons, Edmund, Duke of Rutland, was killed by Clifford, *III. Henry VI., i. 3,* just before his father's death; George, Duke of Clarence, was murdered in the Tower; and Edward and Richard reigned as Edward IV. and Richard III. (*q. v.*).

"The principal figure of the two plays, Richard of York, is almost throughout delineated as if the nature of his more fearful son were prefigured in him. Far-fetched policy and the cunning and dissimulation of a prudent and determined man are blended in him—not in the same degree, but in the same apparent contradiction as in Richard—with firmness, with a hatred of flattery, with inability to cringe, and with bitter and genuine discontent."—GERVINUS.

York, Richard Plantagenet, Duke of, the younger of the two sons of King Edward IV., the two little princes who were imprisoned in the Tower and assassinated by order of their uncle, Richard III. Although the weight of evidence goes to show that the princes were actually murdered, as in the play, many entertained doubts of it, and supposed that one or both of them escaped. Hence the claim of Perkin Warbeck, in the reign of Henry VII., to be Prince Richard, gained credence, and made his imposture formidable.

York, sun of, *Richard III., i. 1.* Edward IV., whose cognizance

was a sun, from the three suns that were said to have appeared at the time of his victory at Mortimer's Cross.

York-place, name of, changed to Whitehall, *Henry VIII., iv. 1.*

Yorkshire, Gualtree Forest in, scene of *II. Henry IV., iv. 1-3.*

Young, so, and so villainous, *As You Like It, i. 1;* the wise die, *Richard III., iii. 1;* so, and so untender, *King Lear, i. 1;* so, and so unkind, *Venus and Adonis, l. 187.*

Your love and pity doth the impression fill, *Sonnet cxii.*

You spotted snakes, song. *Midsummer-Night's Dream, ii. 2.*

Youth, home-keeping, *Two Gentlemen of Verona, i. 1;* salt of, left, *Merry Wives of Windsor, ii. 3;* men moved by, *Measure for Measure, i. 3, near the end;* aims and ends of, *Measure for Measure, i. 4;* wants of, *Measure for Measure, iii. 1;* blaze of, *All's Well that Ends Well, v. 3;* a stuff will not endure, *Twelfth Night, ii. 3, song;* is easily amused, *II. Henry IV., v. 1;* advice for, *Hamlet, i. 3;* wild oats of, *Hamlet, ii. 1;* becomes its careless livery, *Hamlet, iv. 7;* salad-days of, *Antony and Cleopatra, i. 5;* one's, in his friends, *Sonnet xxii.;* cannot live with age, *Passionate Pilgrim, xii.;* aptness of, *Timon of Athens, i. 1;* truth of, not to be trusted, *Cymbeline, v. 5;* friendship of, *A Winter's Tale, i. 2;* melancholy in, *Merchant of Venice, i. 2;* uncurbed, *II. Henry IV., iv. 4.*

Zanies, *Love's Labour's Lost, v. 2;* wise men the, of fools, *Twelfth Night, i. 5.*

Zeal, repaid with ingratitude, *Twelfth Night, v. 1;* to set whole realms on fire, *Timon of Athens, iii. 3;* Wolsey's, for the king, *Henry VIII., iii. 2.*

Zed, unnecessary letter, *King Lear, ii. 2.*

Zenelophon (or Penelophon), the beggar of the ballad of King Cophetua, *Love's Labour's Lost, iv. 1.*

Zenith, the, depends upon a most auspicious star, *The Tempest, i. 2.*

Ziminar, a devil invoked by witches, called "Monarch of the north," *I. Henry VI., v. 3.*

Zodiac, the, in his glistering coach, *Titus Andronicus, ii. 1.*

Zodiacs (years), *Measure for Measure, i. 3.*